The Equilibrist

(The Complete Series)

Erasmus Cromwell-Smith

The Equilibrist (The Complete Series)
© Erasmus Cromwell-Smith II
©Erasmus Press

ISBN: 979-8-9873115-8-5
Publisher: Erasmus Press.
Editor: Elisa Arraiz Lucca
Cover Design and Interior Design: Alfredo Sainz Blanco.
Proofreading: María Elena Peña, D. Suster.
First Edition.
Printed in USA.

erasmuscromwellsmith.com

Books written by the author

In English,

As Erasmus Cromwell-Smith II:

- The Equilibrist series,
(Inspirational/Philosophical)
- The Happiness Triangle (Vol. 1)
- Geniality (Vol. 2)
- The Magic in Life (Vol. 3)
- Poetry in Equilibrium
- The Equilibrist (Trilogy)

(Young Adults)
-The Orloj of Prague (Vol. 1)
-The Orloj of Venice (Vol. 2)
-The Orloj of Paris (Vol. 3)
-The Orloj of London (Vol. 4)
-The Orloj of Boston (Vol. 5)
-Poetry in Balance

As Erasmus Cromwell-Smith II
The South Beach Conversational Method
(Educational)
-Spanish
-German
-French
-Italian
-Portuguese

The Nicolas Tosh Series,
(Sci-fi)
- Algorithm-323
- Algorithm-325
- Algorithm-326

As Nelson Hamel (*)
The Paradise Island Series,
(Action Thriller)
-Miami Beach, Dangerous Liaisons
The Rebel Hackers Series,
(Sci-fi)
-The Rebel Hackers of Point Breeze
-The Rebel Hackers of the Glacial Dawn
-Threshold of Embodiment

En Español,

Como Erasmus Cromwell-Smith II:

-La serie del Equilibrista,
(Inspiracional/Filosófico)
- El triángulo de la felicidad (Vol. 1)
- Genialidad (Vol. 2)
- La magia de la vida (Vol. 3)
- Poesía en equilibrio
- El Equilibrista (La serie completa)

(Jóvenes Adultos)
-El Orloj de Praga (Vol. 1)
-El Orloj de Venecia (Vol. 2)
-El Orloj de Paris (Vol. 3)
-El Orloj de Londres (Vol. 4)
-El Orloj de Boston (Vol. 5).
-Poesía en Balance

Como Erasmus Cromwell-Smith II
El Método Conversacional South Beach
(Educacional)
-Inglés
-Alemán
-Francés
-Italiano
-Portugués

La serie de Nicolás Tosh,
(Ciencia ficción)
- Algoritmo -323
- Algoritmo-325
- Algoritmo-326

Como Nelsón Hamel (*)
La serie de la isla paraíso
(Acción Suspenso)
-Miami Beach, Relaciones peligrosas
La Serie de los Hackers Rebeldes,
(Ciencia Ficción)
-Los Hackers Rebeldes de Point Breeze
-Los Hackers rebeldes del amanecer glacial
- Umbral de la encarnación

(*) in collaboration with Charles Sibley.
All titles are or will be available in audio book

For my Children,
"...Our Blue Unicorns in Life exist, only if we can see them..."

TABLE OF CONTENTS

Note by the Author   7

BOOK I: THE HAPPINESS TRIANGLE   11
Introduction   13
The Equilibrist   15
Chapter 1: Freedom and Equilibrium   17
Chapter 2: The Land of Dreams   31
Chapter 3: The Power of Resilience   45
Chapter 4: The Magic in Life   57
Chapter 5: Courage   69
Chapter 6: Anger and Life's Circles   83
Chapter 7: Hope   93
Chapter 8: To Be Inspired   105
Chapter 9: Letting Go of the Past   115
Chapter 10: Winning and Self-Reliance   125
Chapter 11: The Importance of Small Details in Life   141
Chapter 12: Falling in Love   153
Chapter 13: True Love and the Three-Legged Stool   169
Chapter 14: Facing a Loss   185
Chapter 15: Overcoming a Loss   195
Chapter 16: The Happiness Formula   209

BOOK II: GENIALITY   227
Chapter 1: Optimism   229
Chapter 2: Of Fate and Fairy Tales   247
Chapter 3: Life, Character and Virtue   281
Chapter 4: Snap Out of It   297
Chapter 5: Faith   317
Chapter 6: Life, Evolution and Change   331
Chapter 7: Life Wizards   351
Chapter 8: Life as a Journey   365
Chapter 9: Of Wealth, Fame and Love   381
Chapter 10: Of Family, True Friendship and Love   397
Chapter 11: Life as a Circus   415
Chapter 12: Clarity in Life   435
Chapter 13: Gratitude   455

Chapter 14: Doubt   475
Chapter 15: Duality   495
Chapter 16: Geniality   513

BOOK III: THE MAGIC OF LIFE   553
Chapter 1: Adversity   555
Chapter 2: Coherence   591
Chapter 3: Virtue   601
Chapter 4: Forgiveness   623
Chapter 5: Reciprocity   643
Chapter 6: Defiance & Curiosity   671
Chapter 7: Decisions   685
Chapter 8: Resilience   703
Chapter 9: Life, Beauty, and Art   727
Chapter 10: Serenity, Courage, and Wisdom   751
Chapter 11: The Fable of the Old Young Man & the Jester   781
Chapter 12: Restlessness and Curiosity   805
Chapter 13: Convergence   832
Chapter 14: Ánimo, Animus, Anima   859
Chapter 15: Life's Endless Virtuous Circles   881

Parting Words by the Author   917
Poems Index   919
Acknowledgement   923
About The Author   925

Note by the Author,

"The Story Behind the Creation of the First Volume of The Equilibrist Series"

Sometimes, timely gifts come in minute packages. I sincerely hope this holds true for *The Equilibrist* series. In particular, I feel compelled to share the story of how the first volume came to life, as it portrays the many shades of the human condition.

The art behind this book's creation transcends anecdotal tribulations, circumstances, or environment. While these elements are compelling and worth exploring, they remain a tale yet to be told. Instead, this story was shaped not by the where, what, or who, but by something far more profound and deeply personal.

This magical scribble became art because of how it unfolded—as if guided by something beyond rational thought, driven solely by my raw, unfiltered essence. *The Equilibrist* is deeply personal to me because, unintentionally, it allowed me to express myself through written words in a way I had always dreamed of. It is the book I had always wanted to write, the checkmark on my bucket list: "Write a meaningful book." Regardless of how it resonates with others, the journey of creating it was a once-in-a-lifetime experience. Its completion brought immense personal satisfaction as I realized that feelings, dreams, and wisdom had fused seamlessly with words, transforming into pure and simple art.

It all began with small poems and short essays that I would visualize in my mind—sometimes just a word or a phrase, and other times an entire idea. There was no pattern or deliberate effort; I couldn't always discern the stimuli behind these inspirations. It was simply my reaction to life as it unfolded before me, filtered through the magnifying lens of my beliefs and experiences. Over three years, these writings accumulated into a pile. As I revisited them, I realized they weren't random musings but rather a tapestry forming a full life cycle, addressing profound themes and subjects that reflected my perception of life's journey.

The more I examined the stack, the clearer it became that it was different from anything else I'd written. During the same period, I was also writing novels—stories with plots and characters created purely for entertainment. Those works were deliberate and controlled. I would tweak, revise, and polish them endlessly, shaping fiction to fit neatly into reality through what I called "perfection by attrition." These novels became well-packaged products, ready for consumption.

But the poems and essays were entirely different. They grew organically, beyond my control, emerging in moments of inspiration. Night after night, the stack stared back at me, challenging me to understand where this unique creative process was heading.

Then, one day, I simply knew it was complete. Don't ask me how— I just knew. The natural question followed: What is this? Is it just a collection of poems and essays? I thought of the "pictures in exhibition" syndrome, where viewers see only the art on the walls, left to speculate about the artist's intent. How much richer would the experience be if the artist's thoughts and emotions were part of the narrative? Whether or not we agreed with the artist, their perspective would be a guiding light, enhancing the experience.

With this in mind, I asked myself: What should I do with these writings? The answer didn't come immediately. Months passed. Then, one unforgettable day, as if driven by the hand of God, I began reminiscing about the magical people and places that had shaped me since childhood. That's when the dam broke, and I started writing my narrative in earnest.

From the start, there was no predetermined order, yet the story wove itself effortlessly through the stack of poems and essays. Each piece fit as if predestined, falling into place with surreal precision. It was an emotional journey. The narrative became a compilation of myself—woven with the symbols, moments, and companions that had shaped my life. It wasn't overtly autobiographical or literal but rather an artistic reflection of my journey, capturing significant moments with profound meaning.

For what began as a "little book," *The Equilibrist* grew into something deeply meaningful. I hope you enjoy the series as much as I did while creating it and as I continue to do every time I revisit it.

Finally, every word of *The Equilibrist* series was written with my family as my guiding light. They were my north star, offering inspiration and clarity. I know they will see through the art, walk alongside me through its pages, and share in the journey as both guides and companions.

Erasmus Cromwell-Smith.

Book I

THE HAPPINESS TRIANGLE

Introduction

My name is Erasmus Cromwell-Smith II. I am a scholar and a writer. This book is the story of my father. It is the account of his 2017 poetry class at a New England College.

Throughout the years of my tenure, I received several requests from his former students asking me to tell the story of that particular class. I must confess that it took several requests until I became curious enough to spare the time to read about the anecdotical experiences his students had that year.

They were right; the more I read, the more intrigued I became until finally I decided to do it to honor his legacy. However, from the beginning, it was a complicated task, as shortly after his passing, his precious archives were sadly lost in a fire, and even though my father wrote extensively throughout his life, for a reason I still do not wholly understand, he never made public any of his poetry.

Thus, his literary legacy is limited to several works of fiction published over the years, which did not help me with the task at hand. In the end, the best sources of information were the students themselves, as most still had vivid memories and even some of the class notes. Both allowed me to recreate all the subjects covered that year and more than enough of my father's own words.

But the most difficult of all tasks was to find the books, scribbles, scripts, manuscripts, and writings he used for that class. In the end, it took several trips to his hometown to unearth each one. Fortunately, I was able to retrieve them all, including precise narrations of my father's mentoring sessions found in copious and detailed diaries left by each of his three mentors. As you will see, it was a worthy effort that once completed allowed me to bring out his world of poetry for you all to enjoy forever. It is with great pride that I introduce to you my father, Erasmus Cromwell-Smith

The Equilibrist

The old brownstone building complex has housed the Royal Cambridge Scholastic Institute for over two centuries. This top-ranked New England educational institution exudes a distinctly British flavor, a fitting match for its rich traditions, rigorous discipline, and demanding curriculum. No one embodies the school's character better than Professor Erasmus Cromwell-Smith. His thunderous voice, carefully measured in cadence, is nearly perfect in diction and carries the weight and precision of a Southern English accent.

Everything about the sixty-two-year-old, never-married, childless professor seems worn and wrinkled: his tweed jacket with leather shoulder pads, his cashmere cardigan, his leather briefcase, his shoes, his glasses, and even his lined face and disheveled hair. Yet, despite his unkempt and mundane appearance, his students describe him as an "awesome teacher" or, in the words of a great American, an "insanely great" poet. When he steps into his poetry class, the typically taciturn and reserved Professor Cromwell-Smith transforms, as if awakening from a catatonic state. He becomes a whirlwind of charisma, knowledge, talent, and unending patience, captivating every student in the room.

What no one knows, except his doctor and himself, is that earlier in the week, Professor Cromwell-Smith was diagnosed with an aggressive and incurable form of brain cancer. Without a miracle, the illness will soon incapacitate him, preventing him from doing what he loves most—teaching. Not one to succumb to inaction or self-pity, the professor quickly makes two significant resolutions. First, he will treat each day as if it is his last. Second, he will share with his class a series of life-long secrets he has treasured for over fifty years.

In this way, the class of 2017 is uniquely fortunate. They will be the recipients of an invaluable gift from their great master professor, though it comes with the risk that their time together may be abruptly interrupted by his advancing illness.

A young woman with long golden curls is the first to arrive. She has eagerly awaited this class ever since she heard Professor Cromwell-Smith recite a poem by the Chilean Nobel Laureate, Pablo Neruda. Today, as the students trickle in, they sense something different. The professor enters the room at a faster pace than usual. His jaw is tight, and his quick, purposeful strides back and forth—a behavior uncharacteristic of him—signal that he is eager to begin, whether or not everyone is ready. The nagging buzz of the classroom is interrupted as he speaks, his opening words for the new year breaking through the noise with deliberate intensity.

Chapter 1

Freedom and Equilibrium

"In my class, the most crucial rule is punctuality—just be on time for everything. If the class starts at eight, show up a few minutes early so you're ready and fully prepared by eight," the professor states firmly, his voice resonating across the room.

"This year, our class will be a journey into the world of poetry, but with a twist," he continues, his tone softening as he reaches into his well-worn leather briefcase and pulls out a stack of crumpled papers.

"Through narration and reading, I will be taking you to the place where I was born and grew up."

He glances briefly at the class, then looks down at the papers in his hand.

"Here we go," he says, signaling the start of the journey.

—✦—

I was born in 1954 in the small town of Hay-on-Wye, Wales. Back then, my birthplace was still medieval—literally. This was evident not only in its architecture and traditions but also in the mindset of much of its population.

Many traditions were rigidly upheld, serving to protect the village's character and folklore from the winds of change sweeping across the kingdom. My unexpected birth took place while my parents were still living in post-war Britain, which, nearly a decade after World War II, still bore open wounds, painful scars, and suffered economically, especially in the countryside. Reconstruction and repair of Great Britain's infrastructure were still ongoing in some of the most heavily ravaged areas. Entire families had been decimated. It was common for at least one family member not to have returned from the war.

Many who did come home were severely wounded—physically and, even more often, emotionally. At that time, Britain felt like a nation divided into two worlds: one part moving forward, and the other still grappling with the aftermath of a devastating conflict.

My hometown, however, possessed a unique charm. Its hamlets and cottages, pubs and narrow streets, and hand-painted store signs—all in picturesque yet muted tones—made it unforgettable. The town is renowned for its countless antique book merchants. Each tiny shop is a treasure trove of aged books, some of immense value and importance, with a few being the only surviving copies. Others are exquisitely written and illustrated by hand. Every store has its share of mysteries and secrets, labyrinths of knowledge waiting to be explored.

Some of the shops are surprisingly spacious, with cavernous interiors. Ancient books surround you—stacked in piles, nestled in wooden cabinets, seemingly everywhere you turn. Certain books are off-limits, preserved in air-ventilated, locked containers, while others are accessible to curious hands. Inside these bookshops, the scent of old paper and leather mingles with layers of dust, creating an atmosphere both enchanting and timeless. Adding to the mystique are the shopkeepers—erudite, often eccentric, and occasionally enigmatic—many of whom are the proprietors themselves. I was raised among these bookshelves, driven by my insatiable curiosity and a willingness to learn from the knowledgeable shopkeepers.

Throughout my childhood, I gravitated toward the brightest and most tolerant of these antiquarians—those patient enough to endure the frequent visits of an inquisitive, persistent youngster eager to uncover their treasures.

Thanks to a scholarship to Oxford, I left town for good in my mid-teens. By then, I had explored countless mysteries and amassed a wealth of knowledge I had yet to share with anyone. But all of that comes much later…

It all begins right after my eighth birthday.

I first see him at Mrs. Coe's shop. He has an incredibly funny-looking handlebar moustache that curls at the ends, and he keeps twirling it as if it's second nature. His striking green eyes are enormous, brimming with curiosity, and his lips are pursed into what looks like a tiny, frozen kiss. Intrigued, I watch him from afar, studying his movements until he pays, waves goodbye, and tips his tam-o'-shanter to Mrs. Coe.

As he steps out, he glances over and squints at me. For reasons I can't quite grasp, I feel compelled to follow him. Keeping a safe distance—always about twenty steps behind—I trail him through eight winding streets until he enters a bookshop.

A couple of minutes later, I gather my and step inside too. Little do I know that this small act will draw me into a world that will steer my life toward an endless journey of discovery and the pursuit of knowledge.

"Come right in, come on, young lad. Don't be shy... You must be into books, right?" says the man I've been following.

"Right, sir," I reply.

"Well, well, well. You've come to the right place," he says, flashing an enormous smile while twirling his eccentric moustache.

From that day on, once a week after school, I would spend hours exploring what became my favorite place on Earth: The Morris-Rose and Sons antique bookshop (est. 1832). Over time, Justin Morris IV, the shop owner, not only offered me a quiet space to sit and read but also began engaging me in long conversations.

One day, he selects for me a leather-bound manuscript that immediately captures my imagination. That manuscript becomes a gateway to a world of wisdom and wonder, sparking a journey I could never have anticipated.

Yesterday, as I tried to enter quietly while he was busy with customers, my clumsiness betrayed me. The shop's old bicycle bell wound and unwound in agonizingly slow motion, announcing my arrival. Then, to make matters worse, I tripped—twice—over the same old book lying on the floor. So much for a discreet entrance.

Today, walking on pins and needles, I navigate carefully through the store to my little reading nook. My heart races as I catch sight of the gold-burnished pages of my beloved, gigantic "good old" book waiting for me in its familiar spot.

Sometime later, after all his customers leave, he approaches and sits beside me.

It's been another timeless two hours with my eccentric, self-appointed mentor—a fitting and fortunate role for a single child with an overactive imagination, a natural inclination toward the land of dreams, and an ever-growing love for books.

"Why are the pages and the letters so large?" I ask, curiosity piqued.

"Some claim that those were the only sizes of paper available at the time," he replies with a twinkle in his eye. "Others suggest that without proper lighting or reading glasses, writers had to enlarge their work just to see what they were doing."

I nod thoughtfully, returning my attention to the text. "Freedom lies within you," I read aloud, painstakingly translating the Old English with a dictionary in hand. My tone asks for validation, but it's pointless—I can't make sense of it. After countless days of trying, I remain stuck, unable to decipher the meaning of the giant, ancient book.

He notices my frustration and leans in with infinite patience, the hallmark of a true teacher. "In life, there are always opposing forces pulling and pushing us to extremes," he begins. "A flow, like the pendulum of a clock, swings us from one side to the other. Balance is to find freedom within life's pendulum—like moving with the rhythm of a metronome."

I sit perfectly still, staring at the hand-painted image on the oversized, yellowed page. His calm, watchful eyes en me to persist. "Erasmus," he says softly, "lift the book and look at the spine from the top."

Puzzled, I follow his instruction. There, wedged between the leather cover and the spine, is a folded piece of paper. I carefully pinch it between my fingers and pull it free.

"Go ahead, read it," he urges with a knowing smile.

"The Quibbler and the Street Juggler"

Standing by the corner

under the broken streetlamp,

on a dusky, foggy, and misty night,

the quibbler does what he always does—

he mumbles and grumbles, rambles and tumbles,

spilling thoughts and words about anyone and anything.

His big blue eyes dart in near darkness,

right and left, left and right.

And they seem, while filled with magnetic intensity,

as if about to pop out,

of his eye sockets!

As he stares,

trying to track the pirouettes of the lonely shadow,

he wonders aloud,

"What is it with this fellow?"

Down the street, unaware of being watched,

he juggles while sitting high above the cobblestones,

pedaling the single wheel in quick bursts.

while glued to the saddle,

his body twisting and contorting

into impossible angles, acrobatic circles,

defying gravity with every motion—

backwards, downwards, upwards, and sideways.

"He juggles while in balance,
his hands are tirelessly keeping multiple objects
floating in the air,
but never handling more than two at once,
despite the swings, twists, and turns.
he never loses focus nor concentration
and does it all with absolute confidence,
and resolute determination.

"Yeah, yeah, yeah, but why juggle?"
the quibbler rambles non-stop.
"And so, what?
Who cares about living a life on the edge,
filled with contortions and near misses
at every turn?

"Because that's what we do in life,"
reason whisper back.
"We juggle and strive to maintain balance,
and through practice and experience,
we aim to master both—
just as he does—
until they feel second nature."

Finally,
reason prevails, and the quibbler concedes,

"As the juggler does,
again and again,

we strive and struggle through the streets of life,

sometimes by defying the impossible

and the improbable.

That's what we do,

That's who we are—

we seek, we find, we conquer,

then hang on for dear life.

"To maintain balance and master the art of juggling,

requires a disciplined and relentless effort,

for they are both essential keys,

to a wholesome and well-grounded life."

*

As I finish reading, I vividly picture the acrobat's movements—I can feel his freedom, almost touch it. "So, in life, you must juggle to maintain balance," my mentor begins, his voice steady and deliberate. "But to do so, you'll need to learn and practice endlessly. Both will grant you the knowledge, experience, and self-confidence to execute the seemingly impossible without fear. Mind you, like the quibbler, you'll always be surrounded by ignorance and pessimism. The naysayers will always be there—until your results silence them. Above all, never forget that maintaining balance requires continuous hard work."

I hang on his every word, wishing he would continue, but that's his style: precise, in motion, brief, and always to the point.

"All right then," Mr. Morris says emphatically, already engrossed in selecting our next reading.

He flips through the enormous pages of the book until he finds what he's looking for. Carefully, he sets the open book in front of me. On the right side, I see a hand-painted image of a tightrope walker suspended high above a crowd of onlookers. Then my eyes catch the poem beneath it.

I glance over the lines briefly before starting to read them aloud.

"The Equilibrist"

Our lives resemble those

of circus equilibrists.

We walk through a thin and narrow,

yet solid wire—

our emotional life.

The wire serves as our support system,

crafted from thousands of filaments

tightly wound together.

Embedded within it lie, among others,

our feelings, faith, friends, and family.

Equilibrium is demanding and challenging,

requiring relentless focus, practice, and attention,

just as the wire does,

life swings,

up and down, right and left.

As the tightrope walker

glides each slipper forward,

gently caressing the wire,

his feat, like our lives,

becomes a delicate balancing act.

The more he, like us, hones his sense of balance,

the more wisdom and experience he acquires,

the more self-confident he becomes.

For a man on a wire

near perfection is essential

with each of his well-choreographed moves.

Without a solid emotional life supporting us,

like the wire of an equilibrist,

there can be no balance in life.

When we fall into excesses of effort (like work),

or excesses of discharge (like fun),

we lose our equilibrium

and tumble from the wire.

The safety nets below,

if we are fortunate to have them,

become our lifesavers.

When supported by the wire,

and if we attain sound self-confidence,

we can walk unaided

through the swings of life.

But the ultimate balance

is only attained by the Equilibrist,

with the harmonic pole—

which is <u>Love.</u>

*

"Are we all equilibrists, Mr. Morris?" I ask.

"No, but we all should strive to be," he replies.

"Besides avoiding falling from the tightrope into excesses, why should we?"

"Balance is one of the foundations of happiness," he explains.

"But as important as balance is, the true message beneath this writing is about inner freedom. Freedom is perilous, my boy. It begins within you, and its practice demands a kind of self-confidence that only experience, and knowledge can provide."

He pauses, letting the weight of his words settle before continuing.

"There's no truer expression of the power that inner freedom gives than the performance of an acrobat. An acrobat thrives on it and performs because he draws strength from that freedom within."

As he speaks, a profound realization dawns on me: I am the one who must be free inside.

"Freedom lies within me," I blurt out, nodding as a quiet, knowing smile forms on my lips.

The words hang in the air of the old bookshop, mingling with the faint smell of aged paper and leather. They linger over the rows of antique books that have fulfilled their mission brilliantly for me today.

And that's how it all begins—with four words. A young boy captivated by ancient books and a wise old man who becomes a guiding light. From that day forward and forevermore, I have called him The Equilibrist.

— ✦ —

As the professor closes his narration, a contemplative silence settles over the room. Then, a hand goes up in the second row.

"Yes, Meera"

Meera, a philosophy major known for her penchant for connecting poetry with existential themes, lowers her hand and speaks thoughtfully.

"Professor, in *The Quibbler and the Street Juggler*, the quibbler represents pessimism and ignorance while the juggler embodies mastery and balance. Do you think the quibbler could also symbolize a part of us—the internal voice of doubt—rather than just external negativity? And if so, how do we silence it while striving for equilibrium?"

"An excellent observation, Meera. The quibbler indeed mirrors not only external naysayers but also our inner critic. Silencing it isn't as simple as ignoring it; instead, we must learn to channel its energy. The quibbler's constant questioning, when reframed, can sharpen our focus and fuel our determination. Mastery and balance are achieved when we allow reason and perseverance to guide us, transforming doubt into strength."

Meera nods, visibly satisfied with the response, and begins jotting notes furiously.

A hand rises near the back. Liam, a physics student with a flair for connecting science and art, speaks with measured enthusiasm.

"Professor, in *The Equilibrist*, the metaphor of the tightrope walker emphasizes the importance of balance in life. But you also mentioned the 'stick of love' as the ultimate tool for equilibrium. Could you elaborate on how love functions in this metaphor? Is it a stabilizer, or does it create its own challenges for the equilibrist?"

"Ah, Liam, you've touched on one of the poem's most profound layers. The stick of love is indeed a stabilizer, but it's also a force that requires delicate handling. Love steadies us by giving purpose and meaning to our balancing act. Yet, like the equilibrist's pole, it demands effort, skill, and care to maintain. Mismanage it, and it can throw you off balance entirely. True love, however—be it romantic, familial, or platonic—guides the equilibrist, making the walk-through life's challenges more purposeful."

Liam nods appreciatively, his analytical mind visibly engaged with the poetic concept.

Finally, Elena, an aspiring writer and literature major, raises her hand. Her questions often focus on themes of freedom and creativity.

"Professor, in *The Equilibrist*, you mention that freedom begins within and is tied to balance and self-confidence. But in *The Quibbler and the Street Juggler*, freedom seems more linked to overcoming ignorance and external forces. How do these two poems reconcile their definitions of freedom? Are they two sides of the same coin, or is there a deeper distinction between inner and outer freedom?"

"Insightful as always, Elena. The two poems indeed approach freedom from different perspectives. *The Quibbler and the Street Juggler* emphasizes freedom as a triumph over external forces—ignorance, doubt, and societal expectations. Meanwhile, *The*

Equilibrist focuses on inner freedom, achieved through self-discipline, balance, and confidence. Yet, these are not opposing ideas; they are interdependent. Outer freedom is incomplete without inner liberation, and inner freedom loses its meaning without engaging the world. Together, they form a complete picture of what it means to truly be free."

Elena smiles, her creative mind visibly inspired.

Time has evaporated in the blink of an eye. The dismissal bell snaps both the class and the professor out of their shared trance, pulling everyone back to the present.

"And with that, we conclude today's journey. Reflect on these ideas as you go about your week. Remember, poetry isn't just words on a page; it's a lens through which we view and shape our lives. Class, we'll continue my life's journey next week," the professor announces, his voice tinged with both finality and promise. "See you all next time."

The class begins to file out, buzzing with thoughtful discussions as the weight of the professor's words lingers in the air.

Chapter 2

The Land of Dreams

Today, the young woman with long, curled, golden hair sits in the front row, eagerly awaiting his arrival.

Professor Cromwell-Smith has never witnessed such behavior. It is 7:50 AM—ten minutes ahead of schedule—and his students are already seated, quiet, and ready to begin. He senses that he has captured not only their attention but also their imagination.

With a broad, quizzical smile, he stands up and delivers the word that has become one of his signature phrases:

"Awesome! Good morning, everyone."

"Good morning, Professor Cromwell-Smith," the class replies in unison.

"Let's go on, then. This time, I'll introduce you to someone who has been very important to me since my childhood."

—✦—

Paris-educated, the kind and ebullient middle-aged lady had received the finest education at La Sorbonne. Shortly before the outbreak of World War II, she fell deeply in love with a French circus acrobat. To the great disappointment of her parents, it was love at first sight. Upon graduating, they married, and she followed him wherever the circus traveled. Their idyllic life, like an extended honeymoon, was tragically cut short when he was called to serve his country. Not long after his departure, he was killed in action, leaving her a war widow, alone in their tiny "circus off-season" residence in a small village near Cannes, in the south of France.

Eventually, she returned home to Wales and took over one of her family's businesses: the generations-old antique children's bookstore. This new chapter suited her well, as she had always harbored a deep love for reading. Despite having many suitors over the years, she never opened her heart again. Her only love became her books—until I came along.

Everything about Victoria Sutton-Raleigh is small: her voice, her hands, her feet, her store, and especially her books, which are, quite literally, small. I visit her every Tuesday, where she treats me to tea with milk and Scottish shortbread biscuits. Her tiny Sutton-Raleigh Book Store for the Young (est. 1893) is renowned throughout Great Britain and beyond as the finest source of antique children's books.

To me, Mrs. V., as I call her, feels like a grandmother. She loves to read to me, and when I'm at her shop, I feel my age—nothing is too complicated to understand or follow.

"Young Erasmus, what about dreams today?" she asks.

"Dreamy lad. That's what Mrs. Coe calls me every day," I reply.

"Well, that's a compliment, young fellow."

"That's not how it sounds, Mrs. V. I think she says it to mock me," I protest.

"No matter what others think, dreaming is seeing life through magical magnifying glasses. Dreamers are like wizards, Erasmus. Would you like to become one?"

"Oh yes, I would."

"Hop in, then. Let's go for a ride."

Mrs. V. settles into her burgundy Chesterfield chair, and I squeeze in beside her, ready to let her guide me into the boundless world of dreams.

"The Balloon Salesman"

The young man with the tam-o'-shanter
wanders around the park,
a cloud of balloons follows him wherever he goes,
and one by one, the small children
come and go away,
with their balloons softly tied to their little fingers.

"Balloons, balloons for sale!
I sell them for a bargain.
I've got Reds, Blues, and Yellows—
Round, Tear Drop, or Heart-Shaped.
Just pick one, and this may be your LUCKY DAY!"

A whisper of a voice comes from nowhere.
The balloon salesman turns sharply,
his flustered movement tangling the lines
and the balloons hovering above him.

The child stares at the salesman—
arms crossed, slightly tilted head—
and the pose of a quite amused
yet potentially serious customer.

"How can I help you, young fellow?"
"Why do you sell balloons?"

As he works to untangle himself,

he gazes kindly at his inquisitor.

"That's an excellent question, young man.

What I sell are dreams."

"Dreams?"

"Well, as people grow older,

they often lose the ability

or desire to dream.

So, it becomes easy to buy one from me."

"But I do not see any adults buying balloons."

"That's right, only children like you

seem to have an interest,

let alone pay,

to walk away with their dreams,

tied in a knot around their fingers,

floating above their heads wherever they go."

"Why do we dream?"

"To chase our truest wishes and desires."

Finally freeing the lines,

he gathers his balloons

into a neat cluster above him

and faces his diminutive interrogator,

whose wide stance hasn't shifted an inch.

"But very few kids ask

as many questions as you do.

So, tell you what, kid:

Today is your LUCKY DAY!

Your curiosity is about to open new doors for you.

I will take you for a ride

into the world of dreams and imagination."

Then, a giant balloon with the colors of a rainbow,

gently lifts them into the open skies

drifting slowly towards the endless horizon.

"When we dream, we float above reality."

"From a balloon, the fields look greener,

the trees lusher,

the buildings and the streets

appear neatly organized,

and the lakes and the rivers resemble

the blood vessels of nature.

Because as we hover,
everything moves slowly underneath,

allowing us to see and appreciate better

the finer details in life."

"As in a dream,

there's no direction in a balloon flight.

We journey without a destination,

which provides us with absolute freedom—

that's because we have no constraints

and feel unfiltered."

"When we dream,
we see the truth about ourselves,
and visualize, wish, and think about life and people,

the way we really feel about them."

"When we float from above,

we are also able to see

The Magnificence of Life,

The perfection of nature and

The Harmony and Vastness of the universe."

Slowly, the giant balloon descends back to reality.

Then, the balloon salesman ties a big one

with bright and shiny colors

to the child's middle finger,

and he walks away smiling,

his dreams floating above him.

"Balloons, balloons for sale!

I sell them cheap!

I've got Reds, Blues, and Yellows.
Just pick one, and this may *be your LUCKY DAY!*"

*

I keep rocking my head, smiling with my lips tightly sealed in a clownish fashion, as I imagine my dreams floating above me, tethered by tiny strings wrapped around my fingers, preventing them from drifting away.

"Mrs. V., I always live in a balloon," I admit, slightly puzzled by my own words.

"My dear, what a wonderful gift you have," she chuckles warmly.

"But why does the world of dreams belong only to children?"

"That's the challenge for every adult, isn't it?" she responds with a knowing smile.

"Do people simply stop dreaming as they grow old?" I ask.

"Yes, they do," she says gently. "They let reality take control, dulling their ability to feel and wish without filters."

"I guess a life without dreams is a life without color," I say, somewhat hesitantly.

"It's a dull, sour life," Mrs. V. nods in agreement. "One lived stuck on ground level."

"Does dreaming make you happy?"

"Of course it does, since inspiration and blissfulness are needed to dream—and both are among the most essential ingredients of happiness."

"Then, Mrs. V., when I dream, is my mind not in charge?"

"Spot on, my apprentice. When you dream, your brain is merely a silent witness, an archive of your life's files from which your dream factory selects everything it needs for its creations."

Mrs. V. stands, walks down the narrow aisle, and selects a book from a shelf behind her desk. As she returns, her smile lights up the room, her reading glasses perched precariously on the tip of her nose, seeming as though they might fall at any moment as she peers down to find the correct page.

As she approaches, the scent of old leather and ancient paper surrounds her, mingling with the steady ticking of the antique wall clock. In that moment, Mrs. V., my sorceress mentor, and this magical setting feel utterly enchanting.

"This," she says, holding up the book, "is a wonderful piece about a young boy like you."

"The Boy in the Picture"

The boy leans forward, his hands pressed into the soil,
his legs bent, his feet hovering off the ground
except for his tippy toes.
He is ready to bolt like a sprinter.

But his head tells a different story.
He gazes into the distance
his neck stretched forward, tilted slightly to one side.

Is it an intense stare?
Is he just observing attentively?
No. His body radiates tension,
while his head exudes calm,
one body, two tales.

He's peeking—that's what he is doing.
He doesn't want to be seen,
as he is watching something he is not supposed to,
something he has been told countless times not to.
Yet, he still goes and does it anyway.

So, what is he doing...?

He dreams.

He dreams despite the dazzling lights

spilling from the barn in the distance.

His neighbor, a peculiar hermit with a funny gait and voice,

builds homemade rockets and launches them high up into the sky.

The boy dreams about the magician farmer

that turns the impossible into reality.

He marvels at the man's stubbornness,

his relentless determination,

even as his rockets fail again and again.

The boy is in awe of his creativity

and boundless energy.

'That's what I want to be,' he reasons.

'I want to reach the stars, the planets.

I want to soar through space and the universe.'

'Through him, I've learned

that anything is possible,

even though at home I am told it's not,

even though I am forbidden to watch,

even if those around me

don't understand what it means to dream.'

The boy leans forward even more.

visualizing the life ahead of him.

He is already living in the future.

He knows what he wants.

He knows where he's going.

And his journey begins right there,

kneeling on a dirt field,

peeking at a forbidden rocket factory in a barn,

built by an unlikely farmer-rocketeer.

It begins with an improbable

and seemingly impossible dream—

from a boy in a picture.

*

"That's you, isn't it?" she asks, her voice soft yet certain. *"Yes, Mrs. V., that's definitely me,"* I reply, offering a shy smile. *"Erasmus,"* she says, leaning in closer, her tone now serious yet filled with warmth. *"Always remember this: nothing can stop you from dreaming. When you dream, you visualize how you want to shape your future. When you dream, there is no limit to what you can achieve."*

— ✦ —

As the professor's voice fades and the students sit in contemplative silence, a hand slowly rises in the second row.

Hannah, a soft-spoken philosophy major with a passion for exploring human emotions, leans slightly forward. Her auburn hair frames her face, which is often lit by curiosity.

"Yes, Hannah?"

"Professor, in *The Balloon Salesman*, the act of buying balloons seems symbolic of reclaiming the ability to dream. But the poem suggests that adults often lose this ability as they age. Why do you think this happens, and is it truly possible for adults to reconnect with the unfiltered imagination that children possess?"

"An astute observation, Hannah. Adults lose their connection to dreams for many reasons: societal expectations, the weight of responsibilities, or a growing cynicism about what is possible. Children, on the other hand, live in a state of wonder, unbound by these constraints. To reconnect with that unfiltered imagination, adults must consciously foster curiosity, embrace vulnerability, and allow themselves to be inspired by life's simple wonders—like the floating balloons in the poem. It's not easy, but it's far from impossible."

Hannah nods, her curiosity visibly sparked as she scribbles notes in her journal.

A hand rises from the back row.

Ethan, an engineering student with a talent for crafting intricate mechanical models, sits upright. His dark-rimmed glasses glint in the classroom light as he adjusts them, his face a mix of intrigue and enthusiasm.

"Professor, in *The Boy in the Picture*, the boy is inspired by the hermit's improbable rocket experiments despite being told not to dream by those around him. Do you think this reflects how society often stifles creativity? And how important is rebellion against such constraints in achieving innovation?"

"Ah, an excellent question, Ethan. Society often imposes limits on imagination, equating dreams with impracticality. Yet, as the boy demonstrates, rebellion against such constraints is vital for innovation. True creativity stems from a willingness to defy norms and push boundaries. The boy's awe for the hermit's persistence mirrors how breakthroughs often emerge from the unrelenting determination of dreamers who refuse to accept 'impossible' as an answer. His rebellion isn't destructive, but rather constructive—it's the foundation of his future aspirations."

Ethan smiles, clearly resonating with the connection between dreams and engineering marvels.

Another hand rises from the front row.

Sophia, a creative writing major known for her vivid storytelling and sharp wit, leans slightly forward. Her floral notebook lies open, filled with colorful annotations and half-finished poems.

"Professor, both *The Balloon Salesman* and *The Boy in the Picture* explore dreams, but from different perspectives: one emphasizes imagination and freedom, while the other highlights determination and resilience. Do you think these two aspects of dreaming— playfulness and persistence—are equally important in shaping our lives, or is one more critical than the other?"

"What a beautiful question, Sophia. Both playfulness and persistence are essential in shaping our lives, though they serve different purposes. Playfulness, as seen in *The Balloon Salesman*, allows us to imagine possibilities and view the world with fresh eyes. Persistence, as shown in *The Boy in the Picture*, enables us to turn those imagined possibilities into reality, even when faced with obstacles. One inspires, and the other drives action. Together, they form a perfect synergy—an interplay that fuels both dreams and their realization."

Sophia smiles, her creative mind visibly inspired by the professor's insights.

As the professor glances at the clock, he signals the end of the discussion.

"And with that, my dear students, we conclude today's session. Let these poems serve as reminders that dreaming is not a passive act—it's a way of shaping your future. See you all next week. Class dismissed," says the eminent professor, standing distractedly as he juggles memories of his past life.

The students begin to file out, their faces alight with thought and conversation.

"Too much of a coincidence?" The young woman with curly blonde hair asks herself as she leaves the classroom, perplexed.

Chapter 3

The Power of Resilience

As the wise professor rides his old bicycle through the autumn leaves, he wonders, given his condition, how much longer—or even how safely—it is for him to continue this balancing act every day.

I suppose you'll only stop after you hurt yourself, he reflects, predictably concluding in the only way he knows. *No way, that'll only ground me while I heal. Resilience!* That'll be today's subject, the absent-minded professor reasons as he steps into his class.

Then, facing his students, Cromwell-Smith pauses, momentarily flustered as a vivid memory of the moment he first learned about resilience floods back to him.

"Class, today I will cover a period in my life when I learned about willingness, determination, and how to never, ever give up. Let me take you back in time—just a couple of years later in the story."

Shortly after my 10th birthday, albeit reluctantly, I start playing rugby every day at school. However, I have a serious problem: I keep twisting my ankle whenever I step onto an uneven surface. Not only is it painful—each time my ankle swells up as if stung by a bee—but it's also deeply discouraging, as it sets me back in training with the team. Finally, I'm fitted with an orthopedic inner sole for my right foot, and like magic, the problem vanishes! Nevertheless, my ankle

gives me the perfect excuse to convince my parents to end my brief foray into the world of sports. Long live the world of books!

Justin Morris IV, the Equilibrist, was born into vast wealth, passed down through three generations. Unfortunately, most of it was squandered by the poor judgment and drinking habits of his father, Justin Morris III. What little remained still gave him three great blessings: first, the unique life experience of having traveled the world with his family. Young Morris IV spent several years living royally in India, followed by equally lavish stays in Melbourne, Cape Town, and Shanghai. Second, he received an exceptional education at Eton. Third, before the family's fortunes collapsed, the family-owned antique bookshop in Wales was entrusted to him. Justin quickly fell in love with the shop, as his passion for books became not only his solace but also his calling. His handlebar moustache became his trademark, marking him as a charmingly eccentric antiquarian. Divorced for many years, with grown children living their own lives, my presence in his life seems to fulfill some of the paternal instincts left yearning for his kids' gone-by childhood years.

"I feel like an understudy. So what? Nothing wrong with being a replacement," I tell myself, accepting my role in his life.

Today, Morris-Rose and Sons has been unusually busy, with visitors from London. Mr. M., as I sometimes call him, has displayed endless patience with the customers, culminating in my helping him load twenty books into their vehicle.

"There you have it—one month's worth of sales in just two hours," he says, grinning.

He's happy, I realize, even as I restrain the darker part of myself that wants to complain about the wait.

"Mr. Morris, it's been ten days, and the ankle hasn't buckled again. I don't know how I managed to keep practicing and playing, but I did," I say, conveniently leaving out my ultimate desertion from the world of exertion.

The store is quiet now, in the absence of customers, but my senses are heightened. I can hear the little sounds of the world of books: pages opening and closing, a book being pulled from or filed onto a shelf, drawers moving, doors squeaking—all blending into an endless, soft cacophony in the background of my thoughts and readings.

The Equilibrist is busy canvassing an entire shelf. High atop the wooden ladder, he finally pulls out a thin blue book. From my vantage point, the silhouette of the old man standing at the top of the ladder appears to glow, as rays of light seem to filter through his figure. He waves the book at me enthusiastically, an unforgettable moment—a delicate balancing act and a vivid display of his sheer passion for what he loves most.

"Dear boy," he says, climbing down carefully, "resilience is a virtue that will carry you through any hardship or obstacle. If you make it part of your core, weaving it into your essence and your nature, it'll never leave you. Here's something to that effect—why don't you read it for both of us?"

"The Gift of Life"

When you hear the whispers of sorrow,

counter them with dreams of tomorrow.

When you feel the trappings of failure,

fight it with the thrill

and excitement of being alive.

When you feel emptiness and solitude,

counter them with your faith

and the strength of your heart.

When you find yourself in the jaws of defeat,

push back with conviction and grit.

When you feel zapped and exhausted,

tumble it by recharging, recovering with zeal.

When you feel consumed by poisonous anger,

dissipate it with grace and the power of forgiveness.

When you feel trapped and without options

in life's endless labyrinths,

conquer it by turning around and around,

looking and searching,

but never, ever giving up,

until you find the way.

And when you have defied life in such ways,

remember always—

such feats, are always

what is expected of you,

what is required of you,

since you were given the 'gift of life' by God.

*

"So, every challenge, grievance, or pain—every obstacle or mountain to climb—has a counteraction to overcome it. You must never sit still, waiting for things to happen. Always react, even if that reaction is small or involves choosing no action at all. Remember, in the grand scheme of things, you are accountable, and you must be grateful for your life," advises the Equilibrist. *"But what drives resilience is our own inner fire. When we learn to recognize and harness this, it gives us indomitable strength."*

Mr. Morris quickly flips through the book until he reaches a page brimming with vibrant reds, yellows, and blues. He pauses, then begins to narrate, his voice filled with emotion and his cadence rich with passion.

"The Unwavering, Unflickering, Tiny Little Flame"

At the very deep ends of my heart,

in a place where emotions are raw,

where feelings are unedited,

at Love's Nest and launching pad,

where passions reign free,

with indomitable force,

lies this unwavering, unflickering,

tiny, little flame

that simply

won't go away,

won't quit, won't die.

just continues to burn and churn,
steadily and stubbornly,
with overwhelming heat and
unstoppable intensity,
no matter what, no matter when.

Its serene hues of blue and yellow
are stunningly beautiful,
its blinding reds and oranges
breathtaking and powerful.

Thus, I ask myself,
'What is life without our tiny little flame?
What are we without it?'
Well, we either live a life
in black and white or one in full technicolor,
with our inner fire endlessly burning within.

At the very deep ends of my heart,
filled with feelings, emotions, passions, and Love
lies this unwavering, unflickering
tiny, little flame
that simply,
won't go away.

No matter what, no matter when,
it simply won't quit,
it simply won't die,

it never wavers,

it never flickers,

it never ends.

*

As Mr. M. closes the thin blue book with deliberate care, his hands linger over its worn cover, as if reluctant to part with its words. He looks at me, his expression a mixture of wistfulness and determination.

"That's the thing about resilience, my boy," he says softly. "It's a gift you give yourself every time you choose to keep going."

For a moment, the room falls silent, save for the faint creak of the old wooden ladder as it sways under his touch. The soft rustle of pages and the distant ticking of the antique clock ground me in the reality of this space, yet my thoughts feel far away. I glance at the blue book, still glowing faintly in the warm light, its words echoing in my mind.

As Mr. Morris turns to shelve the book back in its place, I realize that this wasn't just another lesson. It was a glimpse into his essence—a man whose unwavering flame has guided him through life's challenges. And in this moment, I begin to see my own.

This is the first time I see Mr. Morris overcome with emotion. Watching him, I begin to value myself a little more. I realize there are strengths within me—hidden reserves of resilience—that I need to recognize, tap into, and cultivate to succeed in life.

— ✦ —

The soft hum of the auditorium's air conditioning punctuates the silence as Professor Cromwell-Smith's voice fades. He glances up, momentarily disoriented, as if disentangling himself from the vivid memory he has just shared. Around him, the students sit in rapt attention, their expressions a blend of reflection and anticipation. The golden sunlight filtering through the tall windows paints the room with a quiet warmth, casting long shadows across the rows of seats.

Professor Cromwell-Smith straightens his posture and clasps his hands lightly together, his tone shifting as he addresses the room.

"And that," he says, his voice carrying the weight of decades, "is one of the most profound lessons Mr. Morris ever taught me. Resilience, like that tiny flame, burns within us all. But it's up to us to tend it, to protect it, and to let it guide us through life's storms." He pauses, letting the gravity of his words settle over the room.

The students lean forward slightly, drawn into the quiet power of his presence, their pens poised to capture whatever wisdom might follow. "And now," he continues, his gaze sweeping over the class, "I'd like to hear your thoughts."

The moment hangs in the air, the transition from past to present complete, as the students prepare to engage in a dialogue inspired by the story. As the professor's final words fade, a hand rises from the second row, and the professor gestures toward the student.

The hand belongs to Amelia, a psychology student with a keen interest in understanding human responses to adversity. Her thoughtful eyes light up as she begins.

"Professor, in *The Gift of Life*, the repeated use of counteractions—dreams against sorrow, faith against solitude, forgiveness against anger—suggests a structured approach to resilience. Do you believe resilience is purely a learned skill, or could it be something inherent within us that only needs to be uncovered?"

"An excellent question, Amelia. Resilience, as the poem illustrates, relies on counteractions—deliberate choices we make in response to challenges. While some individuals seem naturally predisposed to resilience due to temperament or upbringing, it is fundamentally a skill that can be cultivated. The repeated acts of countering negativity with positivity, of refusing to succumb, gradually build an internal framework of resilience. Over time, this framework becomes part of who we are, a reflexive strength we draw upon in times of need."

Amelia nods, scribbling notes thoughtfully, as another hand rises near the back of the room.

"Yes, in the back."

The hand belongs to Liam, an engineering student who frequently relates abstract concepts to real-world applications. His voice carries a mix of curiosity and conviction as he speaks.

"Professor, in *The Unwavering, Unflickering, Tiny Little Flame*, the imagery of the flame as both delicate and indomitable seems paradoxical. How can something so small and vulnerable embody such immense strength? And what does that teach us about our own inner fire?"

"Ah, an insightful observation, Liam. The flame in the poem is indeed paradoxical—tiny, yet unyielding; delicate, yet enduring. This reflects the nature of our inner strength. Resilience is not about being impervious to harm but about continuing to burn, no matter the odds. The flame's beauty lies in its constancy, not its size. It teaches us that our inner fire need not be grand or dramatic to be powerful; it merely needs to persist. This persistence, quiet yet unstoppable, is what enables us to overcome life's greatest challenges."

Liam sits back, clearly contemplating the metaphor's depth, as another hand rises from the front row.

"Yes, go ahead."

The hand belongs to Sophia, a literature major who often draws connections between poetic themes and broader philosophical questions. Her voice is calm yet probing.

"Professor, both poems emphasize the importance of internal strength in overcoming obstacles. *The Gift of Life* offers practical steps, while *The Unwavering, Unflickering, Tiny Little Flame* focuses on the emotional and spiritual essence of resilience. Do you think one is more effective than the other in fostering resilience, or are both approaches equally necessary?"

"What a beautiful question, Sophia. Both playfulness and persistence are essential in shaping our lives, though they serve different purposes. *The Gift of Life* provides a roadmap, offering actionable steps to counter life's challenges. It appeals to our rational side, guiding us through difficult moments with clarity. On the other hand, *The Unwavering, Unflickering, Tiny Little Flame* appeals to our emotions and spirit, reminding us of the inner fire that fuels those actions. Together, they create a balanced approach to resilience: practical strategies grounded in emotional strength. One without the other might falter, but together, they are formidable."

Sophia smiles, visibly inspired by the answer. As the professor glances at the clock, he signals the end of the discussion.

"And with that, my dear students, we conclude today's session. Remember, resilience is both an art and a discipline, a harmony of action and spirit. Let these poems guide you in discovering and nurturing your own unwavering flame. See you next week. That'll be all for today. Next session will be... let's just call it magical, and leave it at that," says Professor Cromwell-Smith, wrapping up his lecture with a mysterious smile.

The students begin to file out, their expressions reflecting the deep resonance of the discussion as they carry the professor's words into their lives. This time, the class doesn't leave after the professor exits.

Later, he learns that the students stayed behind, quickly forming a social media team to create a forum and discussion group about his poetry class. Millennials effortlessly disrupt anything classic or traditional, he reflects in quiet amusement, shaking his head as he rides his bicycle home.

Chapter 4

The Magic in Life

Today is Tuesday, and Professor Cromwell-Smith is running late. After spending hours searching for his favorite children's book, only ten minutes remain for him to reach his classroom on time. Cycling is out of the question—he won't make it. Through the window, he spots a campus patrol car passing by. Without hesitation, he bolts from the house and starts running after it.

"Stop! Stop!" he shouts, waving his arms frantically.

The officer rolls down the window, looking mildly amused. "How can I help you, Professor?"

"I need a ride. Without your help, young man, I won't make it on time."

"Hop right in, Prof; this isn't unusual for you absent-minded geniuses," the officer quips with a grin.

"Uhm," mutters Cromwell-Smith, already lost in thought as he settles into the passenger seat.

The officer nods in resignation, as if to say some things never change, and drives him across campus.

The professor strides into the classroom with a few minutes to spare, clutching the precious book.

"Class," he begins, his eyes gleaming, "today I've brought a copy of a book that made such an impression on me as a child that I kept asking Mrs. V. to read it to me just one last time. The book is called *The Magic in Life*, and, as the title suggests, it's simply loaded with it. Let me take you there."

— ✦ —

With my parents and ten friends in town, I've just celebrated my 11th birthday at the theme park in Blackpool. I must confess that my fascination with wizards, sorcerers, and magic in general has been ignited by a couple of books I read at Mrs. V.'s store. Unfortunately, my enthusiasm was crushed when I visited the new magic shop on Main Street. Learning the silly tricks behind the illusions deflated all my fantasies. As had happened with Christmas, I came to a disappointing conclusion: there is no magic, and there is no Santa!

It's Tuesday afternoon, and Mrs. V. immediately notices my foul mood the moment I step into her shop.

"Calamitous, calamitous calamity!" she exclaims, her theatrical tone breaking through my gloom. "There is no room for grumpy spirits in this shop."

"There is no magic, Mrs. V.; it's all a farce. It doesn't exist," I sigh, utterly defeated.

"Wait a minute, disappointed sorcerer. What are you talking about? There is magic everywhere—within you and all around us. Have a seat, and I'll cast a literary incantation on you. I'll read something absolutely magical."

Mrs. V. pulls out a book filled with vivid blues and yellows, its cover adorned with a tiny bronze metal lock made of two swinging doors with a keyhole in the center. From her coin pouch, she produces the

smallest key I've ever seen. She unlocks the book, opens it carefully,
and sits next to me on her beloved Chesterfield chair.

With a knowing smile, she finds the passage she wants and begins
to read, her voice brimming with joy and enchantment. The air seems
to change, and once again, Mrs. V.'s magic starts to work.

"The Magic in Life"

What is it?

Is it just light filtering and flowing

through everything,

or colors and tones that paint it all?

Or the forces of nature—sometimes sleeping giants,

some others, roaring thunder?

And where is it?

Is it in the overwhelming scenery

of the high mountains?

In the translucent green of the tropical seas?

Or in the serene beauty of flowers?

Is it on the sun exploding in thousands of reds

as it sets on the horizon?

Or on the moon's glow, casting its spell

through the night sky

in endless shades of white?

Is it just to gaze at the innocent smile of a child,

or the little dog wagging his tail,

or the loving eyes of a mother?

Or is it the countless stories

of Grandma's wisdom?

Or is it simply the family sitting at the table,

laughing, arguing, and sharing after a meal?

Or is it just being here…?

And where does it lie?

Is it only in the simple things,

or does it lie in kindness?

Does it lie in passion, happiness, or equilibrium?

Is it in the exhilarating high of winning?

Or in the deflating low of losing?

Is it in the passionate enjoyment

of competitive sports,

or in the quiet solitude

of extraordinary individual efforts?

Is it in the majestic flight of an eagle,

the indestructible frame of an elephant,

the outer space sounds of a whale,

or the deadly jaws of a croc?

Is it in the endless beauty of a piece of art

or the dazzling fantasy of a great movie?

Is it in the guilty pleasure of a magnificent meal

or in the feast to the senses of a timeless tune?

Is it within the silence and peace

of contemplation and meditation,

or in the never-ending enrichment

of spirit and soul through faith?

Or is it in our ability to distort mundane reality?

Is it in the world of <u>dreams, fantasies and imagination</u>—

of those who dare to risk,

or in the world of creators, inventors, and tinkerers

that turn <u>them</u> into art, products, and crafts?

How about in the contagious ingenuity of hope,

the disarming innocence of unstoppable enthusiasm?

or passing moments of genuine happiness,

when the trumpets of Heaven play

our 'Echoes of Life',

or is it in the atonement of our faults and errors

through the power of forgiveness and humility?

Or is it simply in the smile of who wakes up each day,

happy and thankful to be alive?

Could it be in the all-embracing clash

between endless passion and flesh?

Or is it simply when you are truly in Love,

and your heart no longer belong to you?

Where is it, then,

this enchanted life God has given us?

What is it,

this magic spell that granting us

the privilege of being alive?

The answer is in all of the above—
and much, much more.

Because there is unending joy
every second, we are alive!

The answer lies within us, and it is self-evident,

<u>The Magic in life is everywhere,</u>
<u>in everything around us</u>!

And in order to capture it
You only have to <u>LOVE LIFE</u>!
as it has been given to you,
by God.

*

"Young Erasmus, there is magic after all, isn't there?" the old woman enquires, her eyes twinkling with warmth.

"Mrs. V., you are a true wizard, and your books are your magic wand," I reply, still in awe of her ability to transform my mood.

"If so, would you be my young sorcerer apprentice?"

"I already am!" I exclaim. "So, that's it, Mrs. V.? All I've got to do is love life?"

"I would add, son, love yourself, love others, and love life, and all of it will be magical—or rather, a magical miracle—for you."

I hesitate for a moment, then ask, "I was wondering, Mrs. V., what do you mean for me? And what do you represent in my life?"

She smiles, her expression soft and wise. "We all need those special people who bring out the best in us," she says.

"So, what are you?" I ask, half teasing. "My mentor, my guide, a self-appointed granny?"

She chuckles, then turns serious, leaning forward. "Here is what I am to you…"

She opens the book right in the middle, and a stunning mythical figure bursts to life from the pages—its colors so vivid they seem to leap out at me. I can't take my eyes off it. Then, with her voice full of meaning, she begins to read.

"The Blue Unicorn"

Wizard, Wizard!

Bring me a blue unicorn,

one that sprinkles Magic into life,

innocence and candor to the spirit,

light and color to the soul,

passion and love into one's heart,

and meaning and purpose to each and every day

we are alive.

And in a snap!—I am staring at my dream.

In awe and wonder, I contemplate my fantasy…

Let a spell be cast, Wizard!

Let me have a unicorn,

let it be blue as the clearest of all skies,

and let it be strong

as to conjure all the forces of the universe.

On my unicorn, I want to ride through life,

on an endless journey,

around and around,

and turning the ups and downs,

into a "merry-go-round"

of effortless and well-lived circles.

Wizard, Wizard!

Bring me a blue unicorn,

one of those that makes life

a magic carpet ride,

one that makes it all

worthwhile.

*

If there are moments in a child's life when their entire being is filled with total happiness, this is undoubtedly one of them. I hug Mrs. V. tightly, my imagination running wild with a thousand dreams of adventures with my blue unicorn. For the rest of my life, this moment has remained alive as one of those enduring fantasies—replaying in countless variations, over and over again. In a way, ever since that day, my blue unicorn has never left me.

"We all need one in life, Erasmus," Mrs. V. says gently.

"I don't need one; I've already got one," I reply confidently.

She smiles warmly and caresses my forehead, her fingers running through my hair. "Young man, you are fortunate then, as our blue unicorns in life only exist if we can see them."

———✦———

Today, the class has run over by thirty minutes, yet no one has noticed the bell. Professor Cromwell-Smith has been finished for almost a minute, standing silently as his students slowly emerge from a quasi-state of hypnosis, one by one.

Then, something unexpected happens. A few students start clapping. Gradually, the sound spreads until the entire class rises to their feet in unison, breaking into a thunderous applause for their flustered professor. For a moment, Cromwell-Smith is stunned, but then, a rare and humble smile creeps across his face, his own moment of magic unfolding before him.

The applause gradually fades, and a student from the middle row raises her hand.

"Yes, go ahead."

The student is Emily, a biology major fascinated by the interconnectedness of life. She adjusts her glasses as she begins, her voice steady but curious.

"Professor, in *The Magic in Life*, the poem seems to argue that magic is everywhere, from nature to human connection and even in our perception of life itself. Do you think this magic is something we discover, or is it something we create for ourselves through the way we choose to live?"

"An excellent question, Emily. The poem suggests that magic is both discovered and created. It exists inherently in the world around us—in the grandeur of nature, the joy of human connection, and the beauty of art and faith. However, it takes conscious effort to perceive it, to cultivate the mindset of loving life and appreciating its wonders. In that sense, the magic becomes co-created, a partnership between the world's gifts and our ability to recognize and embrace them."

Emily smiles, visibly satisfied, as she jots down notes. Another hand rises from the back.

"Yes, you there."

The hand belongs to Marcus, an engineering student intrigued by the relationship between imagination and innovation. His tone is thoughtful yet probing.

"Professor, *The Blue Unicorn* appears to represent an idealized vision of life—one of boundless imagination and purpose. But in reality, life isn't always so magical. How can we hold onto this sense of wonder without becoming disillusioned when reality doesn't meet our expectations?"

"Ah, Mr. Marcus, a deeply perceptive question. The blue unicorn, as the poem portrays it, is indeed a symbol of our aspirations, dreams, and the magic we hope to find in life. But its lesson is not about avoiding reality; it's about shaping our perception. Life will always have challenges and disappointments, yet the ability to see magic lies within us. The blue unicorn exists for those who dare to see it—not as a denial of reality, but as a way of finding meaning and beauty within it. It's about transforming the mundane into the extraordinary through perspective and imagination."

Marcus nods, his expression pensive as he absorbs the professor's words. Another hand goes up in the front row.

"Yes, go ahead."

This time it's Meghan, a literature major who often delves into the emotional depth of poetry. Her voice is calm but reflective.

"Professor, both *The Magic in Life* and *The Blue Unicorn* explore themes of finding beauty and wonder in life. But the first poem feels grounded in the tangible—nature, family, and faith—while the second leans into the fantastical and symbolic. Do you think we need both perspectives to fully appreciate life's magic?"

"An astute observation, Meghan. Both perspectives are essential, as they complement each other. *The Magic in Life* anchors us in the beauty of the present moment, in the tangible and the real. It reminds us to cherish what we have and find joy in the world as it is. *The Blue Unicorn*, on the other hand, represents the boundless potential of imagination and aspiration. It urges us to dream, to see beyond the ordinary, and to create a life filled with wonder. Together, these perspectives create a balance, helping us appreciate the magic in what is while inspiring us to envision what could be."

Meghan nods, a small smile playing on her lips as she reflects on the professor's insight.

The professor glances at the clock, his rare smile returning. "And with that, my dear students, we conclude today's session. Remember, the magic in life isn't just found—it's created. Let these poems remind you to seek, embrace, and nurture the magic within and around you. See you next time."

The students gather their belongings, their expressions alight with inspiration as the professor stands by the desk, watching them with quiet pride.

Chapter 5

Courage

Professor Cromwell-Smith stands beside his old bike, frowning at a flat tire while anxiously checking his watch. He seems flustered and out of sorts when an older man on a bicycle approaches. The man stops, observes the situation, and pulls a small canister from his seat pocket, handing it to the professor.

"Here, use this," the man says, giving brief instructions.

Professor Cromwell-Smith hesitates, fumbling clumsily with the tire as he tries to follow the directions. The older man, growing visibly frustrated, drops his own bike, pulls the professor aside, and takes over. With a few deft moves, he attaches the nozzle to the tire, releases the contents of the can, and promptly inflates it.

Within moments, the tire is repaired, and the two are back on their bikes, pedaling toward campus.

"Professor Lichstein, today you are my savior," Cromwell-Smith says, his attempt at friendliness coming across as somewhat unconvincingly.

"Cromwell, you really need to learn some of the basic things in life," Lichstein replies dryly. "You know, the kind of mundane stuff you need to survive."

The two professors approach the faculty building, dismount their bikes, and park them side by side. Walking together toward the entrance, Cromwell-Smith's mind already seems elsewhere.

As he strides down the hallways, he is even more absent-minded than usual. By the time he enters his classroom, however, he is fully focused and ready for the day's lesson.

He is on a roll. Earlier this morning, his class was so overcrowded that he had to ask several students to leave, explaining they couldn't remain standing in the aisles. He assured them he'd try to secure an auditorium for the following week.

Now, as the professor lets his worn leather briefcase drop heavily onto his desk, the animated chatter of the classroom fades. His deep, resonant voice fills the room.

"Let's move right along then," he begins, his eyes gleaming with enthusiasm. "Today, I'll introduce you to my hero—an exceptional man who has had a profound influence on my life."

— ✦ —

Nigel Newton-Paine is a war hero. At the end of World War II, he was one of the few British officers flying American planes. On one unforgettable mission, he saved the lives of his entire crew. He managed to bring home his Flying Fortress bomber with only one of four engines functioning, a chunk of the right wing missing, and the fuselage riddled with bullet holes. His co-pilot and gunner were gravely injured, the landing gear was partially destroyed, and yet he landed the plane safely.

Newton-Paine passed out the moment he turned off the remaining engine. When his crew finally removed him from the cockpit, they discovered he had been shot in the abdomen and pelvis. The injuries were so severe that it took months for him to recover, and he never flew again. Left with a pronounced limp from the hip damage caused by the high-velocity gunfire, he was nevertheless hailed as a hero. Paine Arts Books and Collectables (est. 1949) is one of the newer antique bookshops in Hay-on-Wye. After a brief stint with Her Majesty's intelligence service, Nigel decided to dedicate his life to reading and studying art and music. Becoming an independent entrepreneur allowed him to turn his passion into a career.

I visit Mr. N. every other week on Fridays, though I've never felt entirely comfortable with his eccentric and aloof demeanor. His presence intimidates me, and his cane, always hanging on the wall, inspires an irrational fear. For reasons I can't quite explain, my instinct is to keep my distance.

When I'm around him, I'm more of an observer than a participant. Conversations with him feel like exercises in contemplation—one-way streets where I listen and learn. Yet despite the discomfort, every visit broadens my horizons and deepens my understanding of the world.

Today, however, is different. I sit alone in the shop, feeling a deep sadness. My aunt, Catherine Cromwell, passed away earlier this morning after a long illness.

Mr. Newton-Paine approaches, his expression unusually gentle.

"Young man, I've heard the news and have a couple of things that may help you. But first, let me ask you this:

Can we see beauty when in pain?

Can we still hear the music in spite of tragedy?

Can we contemplate adversity with respect but without fear?

Can we stand in the middle of a storm and truly believe it will pass?

Without waiting for an answer, he selects an enormous, leather-bound volume and places it on his lecturing podium. Slowly, deliberately, his voice steady and resonant, he opens the book and begins to read to me.

"A Song in the Rain"

Today, I woke up

staring at a choice,

feeling inspired,

I recall how arduous

it has been

to arrive at such crossroads.

Is happiness a choice?

I've asked myself,

again and again,

again and again.

In the end, the answer lies

in the most unexpected of places:

a song in the rain.

The music notes feel wet,

awash by the relentless downpour.

And yet,

the music quietly irrupts

gently piercing through.

The song weaves through the rain,

its tune and melody

drowning out the rhythm,

deafening the sound

of raindrops.

I can hear the music everywhere,

as the sky drums like a waterfall.

And yet,

nothing can extinguish

the beauty and the power

of a song in the rain.

*

"But how can there be music in the rain?" I ask, my voice tinged with skepticism.

"If you can hear and feel music spreading in spite of the rain," he says, leaning forward with quiet intensity, "then not only can you overcome anything in life, but you can also find joy, even in the direst of circumstances."

"A song through the rain," I repeat slowly, letting the words settle in my mind. "I like it very much, Mr. N. Thank you."

As I rise to leave, he speaks again, his tone softer but still commanding my attention.

"Stay a bit longer, if you care to do so," he says. "I've got a little something here that'll make your auntie both timeless and unforgettable. Here it goes…"

He turns the page of the large book on his podium, clears his throat, and begins to read, his voice carrying an air of reverence that fills the room.

"Way, Way Up There"

Way, way up there
where one can almost touch the sky,
well beyond the horizon,
an endless rainbow arcs,
filled with extraordinary colors,
so bright, so radiant,
a feast for the eye,
beyond wonder.

It points to the sky,
towards the heavens,
and through it,
after being picked up by an angel,
engulfed in magic stardust
and celestial magic,
soaring at lightning speed,
your loving aunt,
leaving Earth,
embarks on her final journey.

And way, way up there,
where one can almost touch the stars,
Catherine now sits,
forever resting after a journey
she could not quite complete.

Way, way, up there,
where infinity lies,

just look at the night sky —

and gaze at the shining star.

See how it glows,

watch how it sparkles.

That's your auntie, your mate.

That's your new journey companion,

now illuminating your road ahead,

guiding you,

as you complete your own journey,

through planet Earth.

Way, way up there

where one is in Heaven,

where glittering rainbows end,

sits a new star,

watching over you,

your guardian forever.

*

Overcome by emotion, I wander through Mr. N.'s store, letting the beauty of his words and their calming effect take hold of me. As I meander, my eyes are drawn to the awards and articles displayed on the walls. Each one feels like a story waiting to be uncovered.

"'Ace pilot saves the lives of his crewmembers', reads one framed article, encased in polished mahogany and glass. Beside it hangs a medal, gleaming softly under the light.

I turn around, and there he is—the man with the pronounced swing of his hips, moving about the store like clockwork. He instinctively fixes, aligns, and puts book after book back in its rightful place. I cannot take my eyes off him. Something about his movements reminds me so much of my auntie. She, too, was gregarious, a natural-born busy bee. But the similarity that has me transfixed is far deeper. She suffered from a degenerative hip, and the way her body moved as she worked mirrors the exact rhythm of my librarian mentor.

"How does it feel to be a hero?" I ask hesitantly.

He stops for a moment, then begins walking toward me with another frame in his hands. This one holds a piece of wrinkled, yellowed paper, its handwriting barely discernible.

"Dear boy," he begins, his voice steady but reflective, "old fighters don't open up easily. We've buried our memories deep, and it hurts too much to unearth them. And yet…" He pauses, looking directly at me. "Mentoring you makes it almost effortless. There's nothing more disarming than the innocent eyes of a child—or a young man like you."

He gestures toward the stained paper in the frame. "See those marks? That's blood. It belonged to an airman who was on his deathbed. We were both convalescing at the airbase hospital. He heard about what I'd done and asked to see me. The nurses wheeled me to his bedside, and he gave me this. I don't know if he wrote it himself, even now. He only said one thing before he passed: 'Courage trumps any army and obliterates any fear.'"

For a moment, silence hangs heavy in the room. I study the paper but shake my head. "I can't read it, Mr. N."

He smiles faintly. "Let me oblige. I'll do my best not to get too emotional."

He clears his throat and begins to read.

"A Strong Group of Few"

Once upon a time

there was this strong group of few.

They came from faraway lands,

they had wills forged in steel,

their flag was etched into their spirits,

their country sculpted in their souls

and their loved ones carved deep in their hearts.

Their courage trumped any army,

obliterated every fear,

and their overwhelming, indomitable fury

could neither be contained,

nor halted.

When the time came to defend and conquer,

their brave hearts roared,

and the Earth trembled.

They fought for one another with honor,

to defend and protect their flag, country,

and loved ones.

Then, the devastating force of their valor

crushed it all,

leaving nothing in its wake.

Once upon a time

there was this strong group of few.

They came from faraway lands,

they had brave hearts

and they could not be conquered

for their flag was engraved on their spirits,

their country sculpted in their souls,

and their loved ones carved eternally in their hearts.

*

At night, as I walk back home, I can almost feel the violent vibration of the flight control handles and hear the deafening roar of the lone engine that kept Mr. N.'s plane aloft as he brought it back to base. The story lingers in my mind, painting vivid images of courage and determination that seem almost too extraordinary to be real.

My steps are slower than usual, weighed down by the magnitude of what I've just learned. Mr. Nigel's words echo in my thoughts, his stories and poems filling the quiet night air around me. The framed articles and medals, the yellowed paper marked with blood, and his unwavering courage—all of it lingers like a shadow that refuses to fade.

The streets are quiet, and the stars above shimmer faintly, their light guiding me home. With every step, I feel the lessons of the day settling within me, their truths taking root and ready to grow into something greater.

— ✦ —

This time, it is Professor Cromwell-Smith who emerges from the past, his eyes distant and unfocused. The entire class sits in silence, captivated, unwilling for the moment to end.

Gradually, his gaze shifts from the world of memory back to the present. The classroom feels still, yet charged with the weight of the story just told. His students sit motionless, their expressions a mix of awe and contemplation, as though they too have traveled through time and space to witness the courage and resilience he described.

He takes a breath, his voice softer now, as he breaks the stillness. "Courage, my dear students, is not just the absence of fear—it's the ability to act in spite of it. It is the unwavering determination to move forward, even when every step feels impossible."

His words hang in the air, their impact visible on the faces of the students. The hum of the classroom seems to shift, the energy in the room transforming as the weight of the story settles over them.

"And now," he continues, his tone more measured, "I'd like to hear your thoughts. What do you take away from these stories and poems of courage?"

The atmosphere is charged with anticipation as hands begin to rise, each student eager to explore the profound themes that have unfolded before them.

A hand rises from the front row.

"Yes, go ahead."

The hand belongs to Eleanor, a history major fascinated by war stories and the human condition. Her voice is steady but reflective as she begins.

"Professor, in *A Song in the Rain*, the poem explores the idea of finding beauty and joy in the midst of adversity. Do you believe this perspective is something we can all develop, or is it unique to those who have experienced extreme hardships, like Mr. Nigel?"

"An excellent question, Eleanor. While those who face extreme challenges often cultivate a deeper appreciation for resilience, this perspective is not exclusive to them. The ability to find beauty in adversity is a skill—one that can be nurtured by anyone willing to shift their mindset. It requires intentionality—choosing to focus on the song rather than the rain. With practice, this perspective becomes a natural response to life's difficulties, enabling us to see joy where others might only see despair."

Eleanor nods thoughtfully, her pen racing across her notebook.

Another hand rises from the middle row.

"Yes, you there."

The hand belongs to James, a physics student who often seeks practical applications for abstract ideas. His tone is curious and probing.

"Professor, in *Way, Way Up There*, the poem portrays the departed as stars guiding us forward. It's a beautiful metaphor, but how can we take this concept and apply it in our daily lives when we are struggling with loss?"

"Ah, James, a deeply insightful question. The metaphor of the star represents more than just remembrance; it embodies the enduring influence of those we've lost. To apply it, we must focus on the values, lessons, and love they left behind. By integrating these into our lives, we honor their memory and allow their presence to guide us. It's about turning grief into a source of strength, finding comfort in the light they've left for us to follow."

James sits back, his expression contemplative as he processes the answer.

A hand rises from the back row.

"Yes, in the back."

The hand belongs to Isabella, a literature major who frequently explores themes of emotion and spirituality. Her voice carries a quiet intensity.

"Professor, both *A Song in the Rain* and *A Strong Group of Few* emphasize resilience and courage, but they seem to approach these themes differently. One focuses on finding joy in adversity, while the other highlights collective strength and unity. Do you think one is more important than the other in fostering resilience?"

"What a perceptive observation, Isabella. Both approaches are equally important, but their application depends on the context. *A Song in the Rain* speaks to personal resilience—the inner strength to find beauty and joy even in isolation. *A Strong Group of Few*, on the other hand, emphasizes the power of unity, how shared courage and purpose can amplify individual strength. Together, they remind us that resilience is multifaceted: sometimes it's about standing alone, and other times it's about leaning on others."

Isabella nods, a faint smile crossing her lips as she reflects on the answer.

"That'll be all for today," he finally says, his voice subdued as he gazes into nothingness, still firmly rooted in a world of heroes and unbelievably brave men. Slowly, his focus returns, and he glances at the clock, offering a rare, humble smile.

"Let these poems remind you that courage takes many forms. Whether it's finding a song in the rain or drawing strength from unity, courage is what allows us to move forward. See you next week."

The class begins to disperse, their expressions alight with thought as they carry the lessons of courage into their lives.

Chapter 6

Anger and Life's Circles

Sometimes, he can't help it—Professor Cromwell-Smith is not a morning person. Feeling a bit old and anxious about his deteriorating health, he is grumpy this particular morning. As he nurses his tea at home, the sound of raindrops tapping against the window mirrors his restless thoughts. Yet, he remembers what he learned from Mrs. V. long ago and decides to shift his perspective. By the time he steps out the door, the morning's grumpiness has given way to quiet resolve.

Arriving at the college, he walks into the lecture hall with an energy that belies his earlier mood. His presence is magnetic, as always, and the room grows silent in anticipation. The resolute professor stands before his students, ready to share one of his favorite secrets.

"Class, sometimes our days do not start well, and yet it is entirely up to us to steer them in the right direction. I remember vividly a particular day when I was handed a valuable life lesson."

—◆—

"Mrs. V.!" the cabbie yelled at the poor old man crossing the street. The milkman shouted at a couple of kids who had accidentally broken a few of his precious bottles as they crashed their bikes into each other. The mailman shouted at a pregnant lady because she didn't come out fast enough to collect her letters. The bartender cursed while throwing the drunk man out of the pub. The Indian man at the newsstand damned our creator as a teenager spilled a soda on his

magazines. *The plumber called upon his co-worker's mother when he accidentally broke a pipe they were working on, and the policeman vented in frustration, chasing a youngster for loitering in the wrong place. My history teacher pleaded for heavenly assistance to grace me with wisdom and responsibility, and my mom chased me out of the house when I told her she had a brand-new white hair above her right earlobe.*

"Has everyone gone mad? What is going on?"

Mrs. V. is bemused, scratching her head, seemingly wondering what to do with me.

"Modicum, Modicum, Modicus!" she recites, seemingly casting a spell of caution, restraint, and moderation on me.

"My lost young soul, you need a strong remedy for the spirit. Sit down, and I'll get you to read an antidote for the poison that is afflicting you at present."

She walks straight to a pile of huge, heavy books with a blissful smile. She picks the one on top, brushes off the dust, and brings it to me. She places it on my lap, sits by my side, opens the book right in the middle, turns back two pages, then asks me to read...

"The Land of the Happy People"

Once upon a time,

in a land not far from Heaven,

there were quite a few happy people,

surrounded by many more angry ones.

And as there were more in numbers,

happiness was usually overcome by anger.

And this gave way to another awkward problem—

the happier the joyful became,

the angrier the other grew.

Sometimes, happiness it seemed,

was not contagious enough.

For many, anger appeared to be

the only emotion that could truly feel.

It all made up for

a perplexing, almost surreal world,

where the angry resented,

even despised,

the permanent and unshakeable

sunny disposition and happiness of the others.

Was this a happy place clouded by anger?

Or an angry land punctuated by joy?

Which truly held the power?

Happiness or anger?

Could an angry person find happiness,

even fleetingly?

Was there any hint of anger or pain within happiness?

Could anger and joy walk side by side?

Could there be joy

amongst adversity and tragedy?

Could there be light in darkness?

Did the angry know how to smile?

Did the joyful understand sorrow?

Did the angry grasp what happiness was?

Did the happy fathom the depth of rage?

Was there a secret formula for happiness?

Once upon a time,

in a land not so far from Heaven

there were quite a few happy people.

In the end, they prevailed

over the many other angry ones

and ended anger and sadness forevermore.

*

"Should I presume that you, Mrs. V., and I are part of the happy people, and my mom, my teacher, and all those other folks aren't?" I ask, my voice tinged with curiosity.

"For the moment, yes," she replies, her tone firm yet kind. "But be careful; those angry individuals are everywhere, like body snatchers that can grab you at any time. And be mindful of anger itself, for it doesn't need anyone else—it can take over all on its own, poisoning your ability to be happy."

She pauses, leaning forward slightly. "My flustered mentee, ask yourself—why today of all days? Why did you notice anger in all those people? Why not yesterday or the day before? After all, they've had the same personality every day of their lives. And here's another thought—was it really their anger you detected, or could it have been your own?"

Mrs. V. lets her words sink in, and when they do, I look back at her, wide-eyed and silent, struck with awe and wonder.

"You see how easy anger can catch you," she continues. "In this case, it seemed like the anger of others. But in truth, my dear boy, it all depends on your attitude and the kind of life lenses you choose to wear when contemplating and judging others. Now, here's something else I want you to read—something about the paths we follow in life..."

She reaches for another book, her fingers grazing the worn leather cover as she pulls it from the shelf, ready to share another lesson.

"The Spinning Wheel of Life"

The spinning wheel of life
goes around and around,
that's why everything we see through,
comes and goes around, full circle—
to the place where it started,
or where it ended.

Yes, in many ways, life is a circle—
or better said,
a series of never-ending elliptical bends and curves,
of a bigger, wider circle.

What seems new and unique to you,
it has indeed already happened—
millions of times before!

Because you see...

with each turn of the wheel,

what was, what is, and what will be

are one and the same—

as in every one of life's turns,

there's a beginning,

then life takes us for a spin,

and then inevitably,

there is an end to everything.

But rejoice—

since the wheel perpetually spins,

an end is also a new beginning.

and as nothing truly ceases,

life is, therefore,

a constant, circular, flowing loop!

Spinning and spinning,

around and around,

what is, is,

what was, will be,

what will be, has already been,

and will be again...

But above all,

let us rejoice now!

Especially of those we love,

and what we hold dear—

whatever that is,

as we never know,

when it might end.

But do not be distracted,

For there are moments in one's life

that start at the very end,

and others that end at the very beginning,

thus, it is sound and astute to remember—

that an opening always awaits us in life,

the start of a new beginning.

So, let us spin the wheel of life

around and around,

we'll go in circles,

where the beginning,

the end,

and the middle of everything

are one and the same,

just a different spin.

*

"Mrs. V., is my life a circle then?" I ask, trying to piece together her wisdom.

"Not exactly," she says, her tone thoughtful. "Think about your circles in life as the trajectory of the wake you leave behind as you live. So, my obfuscated mentee, everything does come around full circle in life. In the end, we either draw well-lived and rounded circles—or we don't. That's why you should strive to be happy, to live a gentle, blissful, and inspired life, always following the better instincts of your heart."

She pauses, giving me a kind, knowing smile. "But, young lad, those are subjects we'll visit sometime down the road of your tutelage."

— ✦ —

Back in the lecture hall, Professor Cromwell-Smith pauses, letting the story settle in the minds of his students. He scans the room, noticing a few hands hesitantly raised. With a nod, he invites them to speak.

Rebecca, a Philosophy major with a penchant for deep questions, speaks up. Known for her sharp intellect and colorful scarves, she asks, "Professor, do you believe that anger, as you describe it, is an inevitable part of human nature? Or can it truly be overcome?"

The professor nods thoughtfully. "Rebecca, that is a profound question. Anger, in many ways, is tied to our instincts—a response to perceived threats. However, while it's natural, it is not insurmountable. Overcoming anger involves awareness and the conscious choice to seek understanding instead of reacting. It's about changing your lenses—how you view the world and others."

Michael, a History student with an analytical mind and a passion for debate, follows. His distinct feature is his precise, almost lawyerly way of speaking. "You mentioned that anger can poison happiness. Could you elaborate on how one can identify and neutralize such anger before it takes over?"

"Michael," the professor replies, "anger often hides in plain sight, camouflaged as righteousness or hurt. To identify it, one must ask: 'What am I protecting? What am I afraid of?' Neutralizing anger requires reframing—shifting the focus from what has been lost or threatened to what can be gained through patience and compassion."

A quiet yet observant student, Jane, majoring in Literature, raises her hand. Her love for poetry is evident in the way she often quotes lines during discussions. She asks, "Professor, is there a connection between anger and creativity? Can anger ever be a source of inspiration for art?"

The professor's eyes light up. "Jane, absolutely. Anger, like any strong emotion, can fuel creativity. Many powerful works of art and literature are born from intense feelings, including anger. However, the key lies in transforming that raw emotion into something meaningful—using it as a catalyst rather than a destructive force."

Finally, Raj, a Psychology major with an infectious enthusiasm and a quick wit, chimes in. "Professor, do you think society as a whole is more angry than happy? And if so, how can we, as individuals, shift that balance?"

"Raj, it does seem that anger dominates in many aspects of society," the professor acknowledges. "But happiness has a quiet strength. As individuals, we shift the balance by choosing kindness, practicing empathy, and fostering gratitude. These acts ripple outward, creating circles of positivity that counteract negativity."

As the session winds down, the professor moves to conclude. "Class, remember that happiness and anger are not just emotions—they are choices. The circles we draw in our lives are shaped by the emotions we nurture and the attitudes we choose. Go out and draw your circles with care."

Professor Cromwell-Smith ends his class by drawing a circle in the air with two fingers joined together. The gesture is simple but profound, and it resonates deeply with his students. One by one, they spiritedly emulate their inspirational time traveler, drawing their own circles in the air. It is a quiet, almost magical moment—a shared connection as the mesmerized group of students expresses their unity and admiration for the professor and his class.

From that day forward, the circles in the air morph into a ritual, evolving into a meaningful gesture among many of them, used as both a parting and a greeting.

"I'll see you all next week so we can continue our journey into past moments of my life, with poetry as our inspirational telescope. Class dismissed," Professor Cromwell-Smith says, his voice imbued with warmth and reflection.

He lets his last words linger, a moment of calm before the class wraps up. One by one, seemingly countless circles are drawn in the air as students bid farewell to their beloved professor and the unforgettable stories he shares.

Chapter 7

Hope

Today, New England has awoken to a regional state of emergency, as the tail end of a hurricane brushed the coastline the night before. Many communities lie in devastation, and countless families are now homeless.

Professor Cromwell-Smith, soaking wet, pedals his bicycle through the light but steady rain, navigating mildly flooded campus streets left behind by the storm.

When he enters the main building, the wetness seems to have followed him inside. Floors are slick, umbrellas drip in the corners, and raincoats hang limply from hooks, all adding to the pervasive sense of dampness.

"Things are quite messy out there," the professor says earnestly as he steps into his classroom, shaking water droplets from his hat.

The students sit quietly, their faces reflective, many of them likely affected by the tragedy in one way or another.

"Today," he begins, his tone solemn yet steady, "in light of the tragedy afflicting our state, I, and I am sure some of you as well, will go back to a moment in time where hope was the last thing I gave up on." Today, New England has awoken to a regional state of emergency, as the tail end of a hurricane brushed the coastline the night before. Many communities lie in devastation, and countless families are now homeless.

Professor Cromwell-Smith, soaking wet, pedals his bicycle through the light but steady rain, navigating mildly flooded campus streets left behind by the storm.

When he enters the main building, the wetness seems to have followed him inside. Floors are slick, umbrellas drip in the corners, and raincoats hang limply from hooks, all adding to the pervasive sense of dampness.

"Things are quite messy out there," the professor says earnestly as he steps into his classroom, shaking water droplets from his hat.

The students sit quietly, their faces reflective, many of them likely affected by the tragedy in one way or another.

"Today," he begins, his tone solemn yet steady, "in light of the tragedy afflicting our state, I, and I am sure some of you as well, will go back to a moment in time when hope was the last thing I gave up on."

— ✦ —

Over the last six months, my parents have been helping me apply to every conceivable university in England, France, and Switzerland. But despite my stellar academic record, rejections have been flooding in one by one. My parents' initial confidence, which I had adopted as my own, has been dealt a setback and progressively eroded, blow by blow. Now, talk of technical school or apprenticeship has begun to emerge here and there during their nightly fights of blame.

Today is Tuesday, and I know exactly where I want to go—or rather, where I need to go. And no one is better in dire moments than Mr. M., the Equilibrist.

On this foggy, misty day, the Morris-Rose and Sons antique bookstore is swarming with people and vehicles. From a distance, I see a couple of TV trucks and camera operators loading their equipment. A dozen or so people exit the bookshop, some with mics, others with headsets. Then, within ten minutes, the street corner returns to normal, as empty as its daily usual self. That's when I make my grand entrance, which is anything but grand—just a facade, as I am, once again, not noticed at all.

Mr. M. is busy taking notes on the phone, his body language betraying his stress. I sit in my favorite corner and watch him grow progressively angrier until he hangs up, returning the handset to its cradle just short of slamming it. He huffs and puffs, slowly calming down. It takes a while for him to come to his senses, and finally, he notices my presence.

"Not a good day, Erasmus," he sighs.

I begin to stand up, but he gestures for me to stay.

"Sit, sit; I did not mean to drive you away. I always have time for you. Mentoring is a labor of love that never ceases."

I hesitate, uncertain of what to do.

"Erasmus, you are not here today just to read. Something is troubling you; your eyes are lost and clamoring for tutelage."

"Indeed," I reply.

"What's troubling you?"

"Every university is turning me down."

"That's surprising, given your academic record. Do not worry, my son; you've earned it, and eventually, several of those academic institutions will gladly welcome you. Keep in mind, you and your

parents are aiming high. You want to go to the best there is in higher education, which is quite a feat. Paraphrasing Machiavelli, 'There is very little space in the upper rooms of the palace,' especially when a scholarship is involved."

He paces the room, finally makes up his mind, and walks briskly to the far end of the main hall. On top of the table is an average-sized green and gold book. He picks it up, and by the time he reaches me, the book is already opened to the chosen page. He then sits next to me, speaking as he does.

"My tormented and gifted mentee, let me read you something exceptional about the profoundness of hope and why it is such a powerful source of strength."

"Hope"

When things couldn't be worse or more dire,
when all our strength and fortitude seem depleted,
Hope is what always pulls us through.

Hope is how we outlast adversity
and surmount every obstacle.

Hope is the life vest for our spirit and soul.

Hope is always our passport to freedom—
liberating us from the shackles of our mind
and the chains of hardship.

When there is Hope
we are not afraid of being afraid
and there is simply no fear of fear itself.

Hope is always our safe conduct
to the land of endurance and resilience.
Hope is always the seed of courage.

Hope is one of the most powerful tools
to survive and persevere through the game of life.

Hope is that calming and steady inner power
that bestows us with boundless confidence
and steely resolve.

When there is Hope, we are always ready to restart,
rebuild, recreate, restore, renew,
rekindle, repeat, rely, redo,
and remake it all—over and over again.

When we hope, we are never willing to give up.

Hope in oneself and others
cures blindness and deafness in our soul and spirit,
illuminating life with shining lights,
whispering tunes and melodies
on seemingly non-existent paths
and non-existent doors.

Hope is our secret elixir for a life with purpose.

Hope is the wellspring of willpower
from which we draw meaning for our existence.

By being true to ourselves,

while we hope, we remain authentic.

Hope makes us feel invincible
against the most devastating storms.
Hope allows us to face the eye of any tempest
without blinking.
Hope equips us with stealth armor
beneath soft, gentle silk.
Hope empowers us to rise again,
never staying down.

We hope when we stubbornly believe
we can create a future better.
Not only do we know what we hope for,
but also, the degree to which we can achieve it.

proves stronger than any circumstance,
any challenge we face,
or any place in life's journey we find ourselves in.

Hope resonates deeply within our core,
spreading effortlessly to others.

When we hope, we deliberately choose
a positive, resolute mindset.
That is why Hope endures
when we clear away emotional roadblocks
from its path.

Hope is far more powerful

when we hope not only for our own well-being,

but also for that of our loved ones.

When we hope, we stubbornly believe

there is always a solution,

and a way in or out of any situation.

When we hope against the tides

despite oppressions and wounds,

and when we hope with the conviction

that the sacred and spiritual

transcend the mundane,

hope morphs into an existential shield

against failure, quitting, or surrender,

Hope becomes an existential weapon

against pessimism or defeat.

Hope is a virtuous, elevated state of being

that exalts our human condition

and strengthens our character.

Hope's greatest virtue

is its capacity to make us resilient.

Hope's most potent fuel is courage.

Hope builds and defines us as 'life warriors,'

ready to overcome and endure.

Hope is the ultimate exercise in self-determination,

And when no other liberty remains,

Hope is the last freedom standing,

enabling us to choose,

regardless of anything or anyone,

a brighter future ahead.

*

"Erasmus, hope is your greatest source of strength and freedom."

"Mr. M., is this how I'll never give up on anything?" I ask.

"Well, impetuous apprentice, there are times in life when you'll have to let go. This time, though, is entirely different, as hope should be your natural attitude. When you go after something, do it passionately, but always be fueled by the strength and resolve that hope grants you. So, it is not that you never give up; it is that you never lose hope and, therefore, never give up."

"Well, well, young man, you've fixed my day. Each time the media descends upon our little town to regurgitate the same tired story about our countless antique bookshops, they have this nagging habit of wanting to interview me, of all people. I simply cannot abide the sheer ignorance of the journalists they send over here."

He speaks with a relaxed smile. As I leave, I no longer harbor any doubts that he is right. I will be accepted, eventually, into one of the few upper rooms of the palace.

As I step out of Morris-Rose and Sons, the misty air wraps around me, softening the edges of the world. The book Mr. M. read from lingers in my thoughts, its words imprinted on my mind.

The rain has subsided, leaving behind a fresh, earthy scent, and the cobblestones glisten faintly under the pale light of the streetlamps. I walk home with a newfound sense of determination, Mr. M.'s wisdom echoing in my ears. Hope, I remind myself, is the unwavering guide through the labyrinth of life.

With every step, I feel lighter, as though the weight of rejection has been replaced by an unshakable belief that better days lie ahead. By the time I reach my door, the fog in my mind has cleared, leaving behind the steady glow of hope.

— ❖ —

Professor Cromwell-Smith brings the class back by reminding everyone that there are always new beginnings in life—moments that test our core—while Hope always stands at the center of those crossroads as our safe conduct to a better life.

The room remains silent, his words resonating deeply with the students. Slowly, his focus returns, and he looks around the classroom. His gaze lingers on each face, their expressions a mix of contemplation and quiet resolve.

"And that," he says, his voice steady but filled with quiet conviction, "is how I came to understand that Hope is not just a feeling—it is a choice, an attitude, and a source of strength that can carry us through life's darkest moments. Even when everything seems lost, Hope is the last freedom standing."

A hand rises in the front row.

"Yes, go ahead."

The hand belongs to Akiko, a psychology major with a composed demeanor and quiet intensity. Her voice is calm but laced with curiosity as she asks, "Professor, why is Hope the last freedom standing?"

"An excellent question, Akiko," he replies. "Because even in the face of great tragedy and hardship, through the loss of everyone and everything, nothing and no one can deprive you of your ability to Hope."

A profound silence follows as the professor seems to look each student directly in the eye while panning across the room. His stare is calm and resolute, as though he were a man entirely possessed by Hope.

A hand rises from the middle row.

"Yes, go ahead."

The hand belongs to Jennifer, a literature major with a keen interest in the resilience of the human spirit. Her tone is calm but inquisitive as she begins.

"Professor, in the poem *Hope*, the idea of it being 'the seed of courage' and 'the last freedom standing' is powerful. Do you think Hope is something innate in everyone, or is it something we have to learn and cultivate over time?"

"An excellent question, Jennifer. Hope is a bit of both. It is innate in that we are born with an inherent capacity to imagine and desire better futures, which is the foundation of Hope. However, life's hardships often challenge that capacity, and it is through those challenges that we learn to nurture and cultivate Hope. It becomes a skill—a deliberate choice to persevere, to believe in possibilities even when they seem out of reach. Over time, the more we practice Hope, the stronger it becomes."

Jennifer nods, jotting down notes as another hand rises from the back.

"Yes, in the back."

The hand belongs to Lucas, an economics student with a logical mind that often searches for practical applications in abstract ideas. His voice is thoughtful but probing.

"Professor, in the poem, it says, 'Hope equips us with stealth armor beneath soft, gentle silk.' How can something as intangible as Hope provide real protection in the face of tangible hardships?"

"Ah, Lucas, an insightful observation. The 'stealth armor' represents the inner strength and resilience that Hope grants us. While it may not shield us from physical hardships, it protects our spirit and mind, allowing us to endure, adapt, and overcome. Hope gives us the mental and emotional fortitude to face challenges without breaking. It empowers us to see beyond immediate suffering and to envision and work toward better outcomes. In that sense, Hope is a very real and formidable kind of protection."

Lucas leans back, nodding as he reflects on the professor's words.

Another hand rises from the side.

"Yes, go ahead."

This time, it is Hillary, a literature major who often connects poetic themes to broader philosophical ideas. Her voice is soft but deeply reflective.

"Professor, the poem speaks of Hope as an 'existential shield' and a 'wellspring of willpower.' Do you think Hope alone is enough to drive us forward, or does it need to be paired with something else, like action or faith?"

"A deeply perceptive question, Hillary. Hope alone is a starting point, but it is not enough to drive us forward on its own. It must be paired with action—small steps, even in the face of fear or uncertainty. Faith can amplify Hope, providing a spiritual foundation that reinforces it. Together, Hope, action, and faith create a powerful triad that equips us to persevere and build a brighter future. Hope without action is merely wishful thinking, but Hope combined with effort is transformative."

Hillary smiles, clearly moved by the response.

Professor Cromwell-Smith glances at the clock, his expression softening into a rare, humble smile.

"Have a nice day, everyone," he says, his voice calm and resolute.

As the students leave, one by one, they glance back with expressions of gratitude and newfound understanding, their quiet smiles reflecting the weight of the lesson.

There is Hope, after all, he reflects as he walks toward his old rusty bike, his thoughts lingering on the power of Hope.

Chapter 8

To Be Inspired

Today, the faculty has been magnanimous with Professor Cromwell-Smith, granting his class the use of a mid-sized auditorium. It seats more than two hundred students.

"How's everyone today?" he asks.

The room, designed in an IMAX style, gives the impression that the professor is speaking to each student face to face.

The space is packed, and the crowd's hum, buzz, and murmur grow louder. He nods in acknowledgment of their energy. Their presence humbles him as well—poetry rarely draws such a large audience.

"Allow me today to take you back to a moment in time when I was consumed by fear," he begins.

— ❖ —

As my 18th birthday approaches, I am filled with doubts about my future. I am about to leave home and live away from my parents for the first time in my life. Being accepted by Oxford was thrilling, but the euphoria lasted only a few weeks. My parents drove me to the beautiful city and university, and the experience was exhilarating—I loved every minute of it. But just a few days later, the jitters returned, stronger than before.

As I walk into Mr. Newton-Paine's shop, I am searching for advice and support. Fear is tightening its grip on me as my departure date looms closer. Upon entering, I see my fearless mentor cheerfully waving off an old lady visiting from Liverpool.

"Good morning to you, my dear young man," he says.

"I need your counsel, Mr. Newton."

"You do look like you are in need of it, Erasmus. What is it? I am all yours."

"I'm lacking determination. I am anxious and afraid. What should I do? I want to do well at Oxford, but I am not certain that I'm ready for it."

Tilting his head forward, my humble hero looks at me through his glasses, perched precariously at the end of his nose. I can feel his mind working, deliberating over his response. He limps away, heading to a shelf brimming with scrolls, and carefully pulls one out. He unrolls the manuscript with deliberate care, smoothing its edges and placing it on his lecturing podium, holding the top and bottom ends to keep it open.

"All you need to find, young scholar, is inspiration, and the contents of this scroll will help you discover the wisdom to seek and treasure inspiration in life."

Then, he begins to read. His very first words enrapture me, pulling me into their spell, and I feel my fears begin to dissolve...

"An Inspired Life"

To be inspired is

to be continuously and blissfully happy,

to inhale deeply and feel really, really, good

as we sigh in joy to the sweet taste

of purely and simply being alive.

Living an inspired life is a gift,

a magic incantation

that transforms us into life sorcerers—

the kind that asks for nothing,

but dispense wizardry in spades.

Behind an inspired person,

there is always something or someone

that ignites the spark

and connects with us profoundly.

Around an inspired person,

a powerful halo of positive energy radiates—

a magnetic field that draws out our best talents,

and attracts endless virtuous circles.

When we are inspired,

we are dressed in a mantle of immutability.

A permanent twinkle in our smile.

Eyes brimming with the peace and calmness

of a life in full.

When we are inspired,

we contemplate life,

through a magical magnifying glass—

a rosy picture, even in the most trying of circumstances.

That is why,

to be inspired requires

a great deal of ingenuity.

When we are inspired,

our best attributes are on call.
"Ifs," "buts," or "cants" are not our vocabulary,
and limits, boundaries, or periscopes,
are replaced by open horizons,
ready for the countless moon shots ahead of us.

For an inspired person,
everything is possible—
an opportunity waiting to be tapped,
an unsculpted stone,
an uncrafted melody,
an unwritten verse,
or a masterpiece yet to be born.

To live an inspired life is
to be in a state of readiness
to capture life's best offerings,
and to squeeze every drop from the journey.

It is when life as a whole is fertile ground
for our dreams, fantasies, and imagination,
and with all our good antennas up,
we acquire a noble altered state—
hypersensitive to all worth pursuing.

When we are inspired,
there is no burden, drag, or heaviness,
and everything becomes light, bright, and inviting.
Everything feels effortless.

Will moves mountains,

inspiration recreates them.

That's why inspiration renders will ordinary,

supersedes passion and conviction,

and reduces self-confidence to a mere tool.

Sometimes, inspiration strikes like a thunderbolt.

For some, it's simply a state,

a condition of sublime desire,

Sometimes, to be inspired

is to be moved by heaven and driven by angels,

For some others, it's to be provoked by the soul

and sparkled by the spirit,

but inspiration is always tuned and honed

by our hearts.

When we are inspired, we:

invent,

create,

tinker,

build,

craft,

solve,

visualize,

foresee,

explore,

study,

pray,

love,

try and try again,

give back,

do,

make,

and live in full.

Inspiration is the stuff of wizards,

life wizards that hover through it.

To be inspired,

to live an inspired life

and to be an inspired person

is to be continuously and blissfully happy.

A kind of happiness

where we are permanently grateful to life.

A kind of happiness

where we continuously pay back.

A kind of inspired happiness

that never goes away.

*

"Erasmus, take stock of your life and recognize how fortunate you are. You've grown up surrounded by love. Right on your doorstep lies a world that aligns with your passions, one in which you've been immersed from an early age. And now, to top it all, this extraordinary new horizon at Oxford—one of the best academic institutions in the world—has opened for you. Don't stand in your own way. This is your moment to spread your wings and soar. Seize it. Take hold of what

life offers you by the horns, confronting whatever is unsettling you from within. Go after it with all your heart. At the same time, remain grateful and savor every moment, especially those things you achieve through your hard work," says Mr. N., his words brimming with encouragement.

He continues, "To be inspired is a state—a condition driven by grace and nobility, born from a sublime and overwhelming desire to live, create, and find joy. Inspiration brings all your greatest gifts into harmony, transforming them into a highly functional force that allows you to be your absolute best. Erasmus, pursue inspiration in your life, as it will bring you continuous happiness."

Later that night, as I stroll back home, I feel life coursing through me, every breath filling my lungs with renewed energy. Slowly, my stride and gait begin to shift, and the tension etched into my face starts to fade. By the time I step into my house, a thousand thoughts have clicked into place.

My mum notices immediately. For the first time in weeks, my face carries a broad smile, and my eyes reflect a steely, resolute determination.

—✤—

Professor Cromwell-Smith pauses for a moment, his gaze distant as though he still stands before Mr. Newton-Paine in that bookshop. Gradually, his focus returns, and he looks out over the large auditorium.

He takes in the sea of faces, their expressions ranging from curiosity to quiet contemplation. The room feels charged with a collective energy, their minds traveling alongside his story, each student discovering their own meaning within the lesson.

"And that," he says, his voice steady but infused with emotion, "is how I came to understand that inspiration isn't just something we seek—it's something we must cultivate. To live an inspired life is to live fully, to embrace the joy of creating and the privilege of simply being alive."

As the professor's thoughts drift back to the present, he surveys the room, his gaze resting briefly on each student. Their faces reflect a mix of contemplation and quiet wonder, the words of the poem clearly resonating within them.

A hand rises from the center of the room.

"Yes, go ahead."

The hand belongs to David, a philosophy student known for his deep and analytical approach to abstract concepts. His voice is thoughtful as he asks, "Professor, in the poem, it says, 'Inspiration renders will ordinary, supersedes passion and conviction, and reduces self-confidence to a mere tool.' How can inspiration surpass such powerful forces? Isn't self-confidence fundamental to success?"

"A fascinating observation, David," the professor replies. "Self-confidence is indeed essential, but it is finite—it draws from the reservoir of our personal experiences and achievements. Inspiration, on the other hand, transcends those limits. It connects us to something far greater than ourselves, fueling us with boundless creativity and energy. While self-confidence can help us climb a mountain, inspiration can lead us to envision entirely new landscapes and forge paths no one has ever taken before. It makes the impossible seem not only attainable but inevitable."

David nods, visibly pondering the distinction.

Another hand rises in the front row.

"Yes, go ahead."

This time, it is Lila, an arts major with a penchant for exploring the intersection of creativity and emotion. Her voice carries a quiet intensity as she asks, "Professor, the poem describes inspiration as being 'tuned and honed by our hearts.' Does this mean inspiration is purely emotional, or is there an intellectual component to it as well?"

"An excellent question, Lila," the professor responds.

"Inspiration is a harmony of both emotion and intellect. Emotion provides the spark—the passion and drive to create. But intellect shapes that spark into something tangible, something that can be shared and appreciated by others. Together, they create a cycle of discovery and expression that fuels an inspired life."

Lila smiles, her pencil moving rapidly as she jots down notes.

One more hand rises in the back.

"Yes, in the back."

The hand belongs to Robert, an engineering student who often ties abstract concepts to practical applications. His voice is direct yet curious as he asks, "Professor, you mentioned that inspiration can strike like a thunderbolt, but it can also be a state of being. How do we sustain inspiration in our everyday lives?"

"An insightful question, Robert," the professor says with a smile.

"Sustaining inspiration requires cultivating an environment that nurtures it. This means surrounding yourself with people, experiences, and activities that align with your passions and values. It also involves maintaining a sense of gratitude and curiosity—two powerful forces that keep our hearts and minds open to inspiration. While thunderbolts of inspiration are exhilarating, the quieter, more consistent kind is what allows us to live an inspired life day by day."

Robert nods, his expression thoughtful as the professor glances around the room, his gaze lingering on the faces of his students.

"And that's a wrap," declares Professor Cromwell-Smith, his voice warm and steady.

The large auditorium is filled with dreamy expressions. Most attendees appear to be elsewhere, journeying to faraway places within themselves. As the professor observes them leaving, he sighs with deep satisfaction.

He notes the involuntary, reflexive actions of the departing crowd—many, if not all, continue to take deep breaths, savoring each inhale as though they are tasting what it truly means to be inspired.

There is inspiration, after all, he reflects, as he gathers his belongings and heads toward the door, his own heart lighter with the knowledge that today's lesson has resonated deeply.

Chapter 9

Letting Go of the Past

Professor Cromwell-Smith awakens this morning with a blinding headache. It began the previous evening and persisted throughout the night. Yet, there is no time to waste.

"Treat each day as if it is your last," he reminds himself.

As he pedals steadily through the empty streets, the pain begins to ease, little by little, and clarity settles over him. Arriving at campus, he dismounts his bike with deliberate care, taking a moment to gather his thoughts. By the time he reaches the oversized auditorium, the growing hum of his students' chatter fills him with purpose.

He steps inside, places his worn leather briefcase on the desk, and surveys the room.

"Class," he begins, his tone steady yet reflective, "today, I'll take you to a moment in time when I learned to use the power of the present as a key tool for dealing with grudges."

The professor's gaze drifts for a moment, his eyes distant as though reaching across decades.

"Let me take you back," he continues, his voice softer now, "to a time when I returned home searching for answers and found myself seeking the wisdom of a very dear mentor."

— ❖ —

On my second visit home, I feel a strong urge to seek Mrs. V.'s words of love and wisdom. With great trepidation, I walk straight from the train station to her shop. The moment I step inside, suitcase in hand, she notices me and smiles warmly. Without hesitation, she takes rapid, short steps toward me and embraces me tightly against her chest. For the first time in weeks, I feel safe and protected. As I begin to relax in her arms, her sharp, inquisitive eyes already sense that something is wrong.

"My dear boy, what has brought you here before going home? What's troubling you?" she asks.

"Mrs. V., how can I deal with resentment?"

"Are you holding any grudges, young Oxford student?"

"Not me, but a couple of fellows do against me," I reply.

"Why?"

"Oxford traditions in one case. A girl in another."

"Well, you can't control what others feel or how they behave. Each person writes their own life pages, day by day, in indelible ink on a book that is entirely theirs. But I do have a little something that bluntly depicts the futility of not letting go—of being stuck in the past and unable to move forward."

She turns around, scanning a nearby shelf, and pulls out a thin grey and white book with gold-coated page edges. She flips it open to a specific section and places it in my hands, letting me read.

"The Past and the Future"

Conventional wisdom holds that,

when you do the wrong thing,

eventually, the past catches up with you

and holds you accountable.

But there is also

the unspoken truth:

when we fail to act in the present,

when we neglect to harness the power of now,

we are not just deferring action—

we are postponing life itself.

And the future will inevitably

catch up to us as well.

When it does,

we may not like what we see,

because it will not belong to us.

We did not build it.

We did not create it.

While we won't own it,

it will own us.

So, we must ask ourselves:

are we postponing life?

Do we keep pushing it forward?

The future is coming—

just around the corner—

and when it finally arrives,

we may find ourselves stuck with it.

But if we start building our future

one day at a time—now!—

we can take ownership of it.

Only then,

the future will truly be ours.

*

"Mrs. V., what is the difference between the past and the future catching up with you?" I ask.

"One catches up with you for things you did, the other for what you failed to do," she replies.

"Erasmus, you need to treasure and learn from your past, but never be a slave to it. Too many of us live 'ever after' consumed by things that no longer exist—things long gone but still lingering in the tortuous, masochistic, and narrow, very narrow corridors and labyrinths of our minds," Mrs. V. advises.

She continues animatedly, "You must live now! Do not skip a day. Do not push forward what you can do today—but do it free from the negative fantasies left behind in the past."

I ponder this for a moment, then ask, "But what if moving on is not enough to cure a grudge?"

"My young inquisitor," she says with a knowing smile, "I have right here the best antidote for wicked thoughts, a poisoned spirit, and an angry heart. Read this, my dear boy..."

She gestures to the open book in my hands, its gold-edged pages glinting in the light, inviting me to discover its wisdom.

*

"Reach Out"

Lend a hand.

Share a dream.

Join in Hope.

Pray for others.

Extend a favor.

Give a kiss.

Embrace each other.

Teach those in need

Learn from the wise.

Take nothing.

Always forgive.

Draw upon the strength of truth

Love with passion.

Remember your friends.

Practice the power of humility.

Shine on one another.

Wait with grace and patience.

Gift with sincerity.

Receive with gratitude.

Live alongside others.

Entrust your heart to someone else's.

Reach out—reach out to life.

*

"So, is it all about giving?" I ask.

"To cure a poisoned spirit and an angry heart stuck in the past, absolutely yes!" Mrs. V. replies with conviction. "My precious mentee, holding grudges keeps you trapped in endless loops of pain,

chained to the past. When you give, you must do so despite the behavior of others. That makes your deeds not only genuine but also liberates you. Your actions become independent, unconditioned by how others respond to you."

— ✦ —

As Professor Cromwell-Smith concludes his recollection, the classroom feels suspended in time. The faint scratching of pens and pencils ceases, and an attentive silence fills the space.

He closes his eyes for a moment, steadying his breath as he returns to the present. When he opens them, the professor surveys the room, observing the quiet intensity reflected in his students' expressions.

"Letting go of the past is not just an act of forgiveness," he says, his voice steady and deliberate, "but a profound way to reclaim your present and shape your future."

The weight of his words settles over the class, a moment of shared understanding binding teacher and students together.

Professor Cromwell-Smith surveys the room, his expression softening as he observes the thoughtful faces of his students.

"Remember this: when you reach out—when you give unconditionally—you not only heal others but also liberate yourself."

As the classroom settles into a reflective silence, Professor Cromwell-Smith surveys the attentive faces before him. He takes a moment to adjust his glasses and leans slightly forward, his tone inviting yet contemplative.

"I'd love to hear your thoughts or questions about today's poems. What resonated with you? What sparked curiosity?" he asks, his gaze moving across the room.

A hand rises from the second row.

"Yes, go ahead."

The hand belongs to Emma, a political science student known for his pragmatic approach to complex topics. His voice is calm yet probing as he asks, "Professor, in the poem *The Past and the Future*, it talks about 'postponing life.' How do we know if we are deferring something important versus simply waiting for the right time?"

"An excellent question, Emma," the professor replies. "The difference lies in intention. Deferring something important often stems from fear, procrastination, or indecision, while waiting for the right time is a deliberate act of patience. To know the difference, ask yourself: 'Am I taking steps, no matter how small, toward what I want? Or am I standing still, hoping the problem will resolve itself?' If it's the latter, you may be postponing life."

Emma nods, visibly considering the distinction.

Another hand rises from the back.

"Yes, in the back."

The hand belongs to Maya, a psychology major with a focus on emotional resilience. Her tone is thoughtful but deeply curious as she asks, "Professor, the poem *Reach Out* emphasizes giving as a cure for anger and grudges. But what if the act of giving feels hollow— what if it doesn't make us feel better?"

"An important point, Maya," the professor responds. "When giving feels hollow, it's often because we are focused on the reaction or recognition we hope to receive. Genuine giving must be unconditional—free from expectations. The act itself is what liberates us, not the response it garners. Sometimes, the liberation is subtle, growing over time as we continue to give with sincerity and humility."

Maya nods slowly, her brow furrowed in thought as she writes down his answer.

A hand rises in the front row.

"Yes, go ahead."

The hand belongs to Carlos, an economics student with a strong interest in the intersection of relationships and success. His voice is steady but introspective as he asks, "Professor, in *The Past and the Future*, it says, 'When we fail to act in the present, we are not just deferring action—we are postponing life itself.' How do we reconcile this with the idea that some actions take time to plan and execute?"

"An insightful question, Carlos," the professor replies.

"Planning is an essential part of meaningful action, but planning without execution is where the risk lies. Even small steps toward a goal ensure that you are living in the present while building the future. Life is not about rushing into action but about ensuring you are always moving forward, however slowly."

Carlos leans back, his expression contemplative as the professor's words resonate.

Professor Cromwell-Smith's class continues to grow, and today they have moved to an even larger auditorium, now designated as their permanent oversized classroom. As the students begin to leave, many notice their teacher looks unusually frail and tired, waving them off from behind his desk—a departure from his usual routine of standing and engaging with them as they depart. Several glance back at him, their expressions a mix of quiet gratitude and subtle worry, realizing he does not seem well.

Though he maintains his composure until the last student exits, he is clearly struggling. As the silence of the empty auditorium envelops him, offering a moment of solace after the day's lesson, he finally lets go, slumping forward onto his desk. The heavy thump of his head hitting the surface echoes briefly and is the last sound heard in the vast hall for quite some time.

Chapter 10

Winning and Self-Reliance

It has been two weeks since Professor Cromwell-Smith was rushed to the hospital, found unconscious by a diligent night security guard. His head now shaved, his ashen skin tone, and the dark shadows beneath his eyes confirm the rumors circulating among students and faculty.

As Professor Cromwell-Smith approaches the campus gates, the brisk morning air fills his lungs, clearing the lingering fatigue from his body. Each pedal stroke feels deliberate, a reminder of the resilience he's built over the years. When he finally reaches the faculty building, he dismounts, adjusts his scarf, and strides in, greeted by the warm applause of his students.

Yes, he thinks as he steps into a standing ovation. The secret is out.

The faces he sees cheering convey a mixture of support, respect, relief, and joy at seeing him back in action. Everyone knows you are sick, he silently chastises himself.

Standing before the packed auditorium, the professor takes a moment to absorb the energy of the crowd. "Thank you, thank you all... Please, have a seat," he says, his voice steady despite the faint trace of exhaustion. He waits as the students settle, their attentiveness fueling his resolve to deliver a lesson worth remembering.

Among the crowd, a young woman with curly blond hair hesitates before sitting in the back of the room. She feels ambivalent, caught in the pull of the professor's story—a rabbit hole she senses she's falling into, yet she cannot resist the intensity of its allure.

"Today," the professor begins, his tone soft yet deliberate, "I'll refer to a period in my life when I started competitive sports and faced the culture of winning and losing for the first time. Little did I know that these lessons would help me face the challenges I now confront. It starts like this…"

— ✦ —

"Will he still be open or not?" I ask myself repeatedly as I ride the late afternoon train back home.

An hour later, as we cross the border between England and Wales, I mumble aloud about the subject that's been consuming my thoughts for the past few days.

"Rowing or rugby, or neither?"

Those are my choices. Later, as I walk the empty streets of my hometown, I reason that, having been raised in the world of books, the adrenaline rush and the desire to compete are foreign to me. I desperately need the wisdom of my fearless war hero.

That is why the very first thing I'm doing upon arrival, on this short visit from Oxford, is heading straight to his place. A wave of immense relief washes over me when I turn the corner and see lights emanating from his shop—the only ones lit on both sides of the street. Knowing his habits so well over the years, I've guessed correctly that he'd still be open.

"Mr. Newton, it is so nice to see you," I say, smiling.

"Come on over, dear boy; let me give you a hug."

He stands up with some difficulty, and I notice it as he swings his way toward me.

"I fell a few weeks ago," he says, quickly preempting my question as he lifts a shiny wooden cane to show it. "Now that you see our physical attributes are fleeting, even for former gifted athletes like me, may I know what brings you here at this late hour? Surely, there is an important reason."

"Mr. N., I don't know if I've got what it takes to compete. At Oxford, competition is everywhere—it's unavoidable. But I don't have the fire in my belly for it. I don't see the point or the thrill of it at all, and it worries me that I may fail because of it."

Newton-Paine smiles broadly, immediately recognizing that there is a literary prescription for his mentee.

"Come on, help me," he says, gesturing for me to follow him.

I walk alongside him until we're standing in front of a locked two-by-two glass box containing an enormous book, which, through the security glass, looks ancient. Mr. N. punches in the code, and the door opens.

"Erasmus, please carefully slide the book out by pulling the small rug underneath it," he instructs, guiding me step by step.

I follow his lead, and once the book is out, he gently opens it, using the delicate cord of the bookmark to flip to the precise page he has in mind.

"My reluctant competitor," he says with a warm, knowing smile, "this old and precious book contains the kind of wisdom you seek. Let me read it to you..."

"Winning is not for the Faint of Heart"

The road to victory is a game of survival. It is war.

You visualize yourself as a gladiator in the arena,

a stealthy ninja warrior poised to strike in the shadows,

a bullfighter confronting the fury of the beast.

You see yourself choosing between winning and losing

as if they were life or death.

You win when you want it so badly

that it burns inside.

You win when you want it so much more

than your opponent does.

You win when your mindset declares that nothing,

except your values,

can deter you from achieving success.

You win when your sole purpose

is to defeat your opponents.

You win by capitalizing on your strengths

and exploiting your adversaries' weaknesses

or simply by flat-out outworking them.

You win when, deliberately and quietly,

you strive to capture each one

of your opponent's strengths and virtues.

You win when, in your opponent's eyes,

you are fierce and steadfast

in your game plan and execution,

and yet discreetly tweak and adapt

in a split second.

You win when, in preparation for a contest,

you approach every task with tunnel vision

and such steely resolve

that nothing or no one is able

to prevent you from completing it,

because 'the art of winning' can only be mastered

by 'paying every due' and 'burning every candle.'

Preparing to be ready to win is a long road

that must be travelled in its entirety.

You win when you are one step ahead

of your opponent

and still, ask yourself, can I do it better?

You win when unflappable,

you 'keep on' going back

time and again to knock on the same door

previously slammed in your face.

You win when a 'no' is nothing

but an invitation to try again,

You win when you are totally and utterly impervious

to the word 'rejection.'

You win when you know how to seek,

take advice, and learn from those

who know how to win.

You win when you take on the better side

of your ego and make it

your friend, your ally, and your weapon,

because as opposed to the shallowness

and narcissism of arrogance,

self-confidence derives

from knowledge and experience,

and is, therefore, unshakeable.

You win when through discipline and perseverance

you acquire the knowledge and experience

that provides you with the self-confidence needed

to master whatever, you want to be the best at.

You win when you can use your anger

as a source of strength,

when you morph your rage

into a burning and unstoppable desire

and when you draw from your 'well of will,'

the fire and the fury needed to win.

You only win when you've endured

countless losses, defeats, stumbles, fumbles, and setbacks—

the worse they've been,

the better prepared you are to triumph in the future.

But for a path to victory,

one must harness and tame one's very own demons.

One must "rein in" a unique cast of free-spirited characters that inhabit the kingdoms of our mind and spirit.

That's why, in order to win, we must

conquer our own mountains,

break down our own walls,

vanquish enemy armies,

annihilate pessimists,

ridicule skeptics,

render mute the excusers and naysayers,

exile the slouches.

Calm the fearful, making them our allies.

Turn the doubters into charlatans.

And we must do it all this

within the confines of ourselves,

as we do it when in battle.

Sometimes, winning demands following your instincts—

your gut, your better fibers,

your primal, atavistic, animalistic nature,

all shaken and stirred into

a cocktail of raw passion.

Sometimes, winning requires you

to follow your brain,

your rational thinking,

your battle plans, strategy, and logic.

Often, you require both!

Though, on any given Sunday,

in the game of winning,

passion generally beats brains!

You win when you share and savor

the spoils of victory.

You win when you live, appreciate, and value

the journey to victory.

You win when it brings out the best in you,

you win when it makes you stronger and better,

when you win, you celebrate life.

But above all,

you win when you are not fooled by it,

but to the contrary,

always keep it in its proper place,

as winning,

even though an essential component of life,

is only a 'game of life.'

It is not existential or sacred

but mundane and passing.

It is not love or friendship, neither truth nor faith,

nor virtue or values,

but only a 'will and grit' booster, a worthy test

of the intensity with which you live your life.

But winning is not for the faint of heart

as it requires courage and strength.

Winning is for those that challenge life with their hearts,

for whom living a life in full inexorably embraces

winning as an intrinsic part of the equation,

to squeeze out of life the sublime passion of victory.

*

"So, Mr. N., I don't necessarily win against an opponent?" I ask.

"That's right," he replies. "Human beings are not always the adversary. Life is filled with obstacles, challenges, difficulties, and even tragedies—some seemingly insurmountable—that only the attitude of a winner can defeat."

"Bottom line, you're telling me that I need to know how to win to be able to navigate life's perils," I say.

"Right on, right on, my boy. You need an indomitable desire and will to triumph. It is a key ingredient for withstanding and conquering whatever life throws at you, or whatever you set your sights on. But, my maturing apprentice, there is an additional gift in this 20th-century book that will imbue you with even greater wisdom—wisdom to become a doer, a maker, and a wholesome life warrior."

Mr. N. then carefully parts the book, adjusting its second marking cord to the precise page he has in mind. His expression grows resolute, his voice deep with conviction, as he begins to read with even greater intensity than before.

"Self-Reliance"

Self-reliance is the practice and embodiment
of self-assertiveness.

It is being accountable, first and foremost, to oneself.

It is the realization that I must rely on myself

before anyone or anything else.

Even though out of love, generosity, a moral imperative—

or a combination of these—I may put others

before or ahead of me in life's endeavors.

When it comes to dependence, though,

I depend primarily on myself.

before, I depend on others,

I shall never expect, count, or rely on others

to act in my place.

For what I am meant to do,

what only I can do,

what only I should do,

must be done by myself.

Also, I rely on myself and what I believe in,

irrespective of and above what others believe.

Because I rely on myself first,

I remain immune to the opinions

and influence of others.

I rely on myself despite societal norms.

I trust my instincts and gut feelings,

not to replace,

but to precede any external norm, rule, or law.

By relying on myself, I break free from

the chains of conformism, indoctrination,

or the loss of my individuality.

Self-reliance establishes my identity,

my character, my personality—

in other words, my true self.

It is the foundation of my independence

and the seed of my self-worth, self-respect, and dignity.

If I can govern myself,

without undue help or influence,

then I have gained all of the above.

I will rely on myself first if I think, feel, and act

with integrity, without impulsiveness,

and in alignment with my spiritual, moral, and family values.

I trust myself because I believe in my abilities,

and that belief fosters the self-confidence

to face life as my authentic self,

true to my identity

and equipped with all my capacities and talents.

*

"Young Erasmus don't expect or even desire that anything will be handed easily to you in life. Just hold on firmly to the belief that you must earn it."

"You mean that caring and having empathy for others is something I could decide to pour my heart into, but its foundations will originate only from my own self-reliance," I say, attempting to clarify.

"Spot on, my boy, spot on. Self-reliance and individualism are often confused with being selfish. In truth, self-reliant people, even as they depend on themselves first, can still be fully dedicated to helping others in need. Self-reliance—depending on oneself—is not incompatible at all with giving," Mr. N. concludes with a knowing smile.

I stare at the World War II pilot for a long time, absorbing the power and wisdom of what he has shared with me today.

The time at Oxford is not only intense, formative, and memorable— it also flies by. All too soon, I graduate with honors, and thereafter, I find myself on my way to America with two old suitcases and a head full of dreams.

I am heading to the "land of opportunity" to complete my post-graduate studies, seeking to earn a master's degree at Harvard.

— ✤ —

The professor's voice softens as his story draws to a close. "And so, the lessons I learned during those days of competition have stayed with me, teaching me to value resilience, self-reliance, and the will to win—not just over others but over life's obstacles." He pauses, letting the weight of his words settle over the room before transitioning back to the present.

Professor Cromwell-Smith's voice is weak and hoarse as he wraps up the class.

He closes his eyes briefly, drawing a deep, steadying breath before opening them again to meet the quiet intensity in his students' gazes.

"Now," he says, his voice calm but resolute, "let's hear your thoughts."

A hand rises in the middle row.

"Yes, go ahead."

The hand belongs to Alice, a business student known for her ambitious nature. Her voice is confident yet curious as she asks, "Professor, in the poem *Winning is not for the Faint of Heart*, it mentions 'harnessing and taming one's demons.' How do we identify these demons, and how do we start to tame them?"

"An excellent question, Alice," the professor replies. "Our demons are often our fears, insecurities, and unresolved conflicts. Identifying them requires introspection and honesty—asking yourself what holds you back or fills you with doubt. Taming them starts with acknowledging their presence, understanding their origins, and channeling that energy into productive action. It's not about eliminating them but using them as fuel to propel you forward."

Alice nods, visibly impressed by the depth of his answer.

Another hand rises from the front row.

"Yes, in the front."

The hand belongs to Mark, an engineering student with a keen interest in resilience. His tone is thoughtful but direct as he asks, "Professor, the poem *Self-Reliance* talks about independence from societal norms. How do we balance this with the need to work within systems and structures that often demand conformity?"

"An important point, Mark" the professor responds. "Self-reliance doesn't mean rejecting systems outright—it means approaching them with discernment. Align your actions with your values and use the system as a tool rather than letting it define you. By staying true to your principles, you can navigate within structures without losing your individuality."

Mark leans back, his expression contemplative as he considers the professor's response.

A hand rises in the back row.

"Yes, in the back."

The hand belongs to Brittany, a psychology student fascinated by motivation. Her voice is steady but introspective as she asks, "Professor, in *Winning is not for the Faint of Heart*, it says, 'Passion generally beats brains.' How do we cultivate the kind of passion that drives success?"

"An insightful question, Brittany," the professor replies.

"Passion stems from a genuine connection to what you do. It requires exploration and persistence—finding what excites you and committing to it wholeheartedly. Passion is contagious and self-reinforcing, growing stronger as you invest time and effort into your pursuits."

Brittany nods slowly, her brow furrowed in thought.

A hand rises from the middle of the auditorium.

"Yes, go ahead."

The hand belongs to Aaron, a philosophy student known for his introspective inquiries. His voice is calm but probing as he says, "But Professor, I do rely on others all the time."

"Of course you do, Aaron," the professor replies, his voice gentle but firm. "We all rely on others—it's part of being human and living in a connected world. But the foundation of that reliance must be your own self-reliance. When you rely on yourself first, your relationships and collaborations become stronger, because they are built on mutual respect and independence rather than dependency. Always ensure your strength comes from within, so when you lean on others, it is by choice, not necessity."

Aaron nods slowly, the professor's words resonating deeply with him.

He lets the words settle over the room, giving them weight, before waving the students off until the following week.

"Remember, learning doesn't stop when the class ends. Keep asking questions and stay curious! Have a nice day, everyone. See you next week."

The students begin to file out, their faces reflective, carrying the weight of the professor's words with them. A couple of his students linger behind, their concern for him unspoken but evident in their quiet gestures. They watch as he gathers his belongings, his movements slow but deliberate. Without a word, they fall into step beside him, offering their silent companionship as they walk with him to his bike.

As he mounts the old bicycle, wobbling slightly and struggling for balance, they exchange glances, each thinking the same unspoken thought: How long is he going to last?

Chapter 11

The Importance of Small Details in Life

Professor Cromwell-Smith is feeling much better today. His aggressive tumor is shrinking, a miracle made possible by a state-of-the-art treatment that once saved the life of a former U.S. President.

"Treat each day as if it is your last," he reminds himself once more, as he pedals toward campus. The vibrant hues of spring seem to mirror his improved health and renewed inspiration. The crisp morning air lifts his spirits as he dismounts his old, rusty bike, parking it alongside a dozen others. With a momentary pause, he straightens his scarf and gazes toward the classroom building, his thoughts brimming with the bittersweet chapter of his life he plans to share today.

Minutes later, he steps into the auditorium, greeted by a gentle murmur of voices. The students quiet as he takes his place at the front, their expectant faces fueling his resolve. "One of the great mysteries in life," he begins, his voice steady yet reflective, "is the unexpected bends in the road—some for the worse, but others for the better. For the latter, we should always be grateful, as they are unforeseen gifts. There was a moment in my life when a lightning bolt struck me, leading to an epiphany. From that moment forward, my life has never been the same."

— ✦ —

Not quite four months into my master's degree, I fly home for a week to join my parents on their 25th wedding anniversary. But once there, I can't wait to visit Mrs. V. There's so much I need to share with her. Within hours of my arrival, I rush to see my beloved mentor. After fifteen minutes of pure joy and an outpouring of affection from my ever-effusive cheerleader, I can't hold it in any longer and begin earnestly sharing everything with her.

"Mrs. V., ever since I saw her for the first time, all I can do is…" I falter, my words caught in a knot of emotion. The lump in my throat chokes me, overwhelmed by a torrent of feelings.

"How can you love someone you've never met?" I ask, half to myself and half to Mrs. V.

"Tell me about her. Tell me, dear boy," she says, her tone encouraging and curious.

"It happened on my second weekend at Harvard, just before a football game. Their baton twirler caught my attention as the marching band approached. She had incredible dexterity, an intense yet joyous energy, and the most beautiful pair of eyes I've ever seen. Her huge, infectious smile made me chuckle, and I wished the moment would never end. This incredible magnetism seized and engulfed me, and I've not been in control of my heart ever since."

"And what did you do about it?" Mrs. V. asks dreamily, her head tilting slightly.

"Nothing. I was frozen. I couldn't take my eyes off her, following her every move, even from a distance. They disbanded and packed their things away, but I stood there as if paralyzed."

"And then?"

"That was three months ago. Now, I know everything about her, and she even accidentally introduced herself in a brief encounter. But otherwise, I've done nothing. I don't know what to do. I'm paralyzed by fear," I admit, the frustration evident in my voice.

"Erasmus," Mrs. V. says, her voice steady yet kind, "there is no prescribed formula for love, much less for how, whom, or even when you love."

She paces back and forth, her hand on her chin, clearly deep in thought.

"In matters of love, wisdom can be our guiding light. It sprinkles our instincts, feelings, and passions like a love compass, answering countless crosswords of the heart," she says, her words resonating with profound understanding.

Then, she picks up a small book from one of her desk shelves, one she seems to keep close for moments like these.

"Here is one of them. Hopefully, it will steer you into action in the pursuit of your infatuation. Read here, please, my dear," she says, offering the book with a knowing smile.

"The Better Instincts of our Hearts"

There are things in life
that we can only be done from our hearts
and those, we never regret.

In fact, we'll do them
over and over again,
in exactly the same way.

These are the acts of life

we draw from the better instincts of our hearts,

governed by passion, convictions, and principles.

Self-interest or consequences pale in comparison

to our beliefs,

for that someone for whom

we are ready to take a bullet for.

One thing is certain:

such monumental steps

are not driven by our brains!

Otherwise, we would never summon

the courage and selflessness

to hurt ourselves or act against our own best interests—

unless driven by matters of the heart.

These acts of valor

Are where heroes are born,

the course of history changes,

lives are spared or saved,

and humanity shines and rises,

to its most luminous heights.

Many are born with great instincts of the mind,

and many with great instincts of the heart.

But one of life's paradoxes

is that we often follow the instincts

where we are weakest,

inevitably leading us

to unfulfilled and disheartened lives.

In matters of love,

brain and heart are oil and water—

they do not mix well.

For the brain cannot create, govern,

control, or sustain love,

nor can love do so for the mind.

When we follow

the better instincts of our brains

in matters of love,

there is no love,

but rather thoughts instead of feelings.

What likelihood there is,

is an arrangement where we settle

for comfort and emptiness.

Because inasmuch as

the better instincts of our minds

serve us well,

when logic, convenience,

and common sense are required,

when we look back at life,

we will always realize that

immense, absolute, and wholesome happiness

only comes to us

when we have followed

the better instincts of our hearts.

*

"In this short visit to Wales, young man, the message you are getting from this old lady who loves you dearly is to always follow your heart," Mrs. V. says with a warm smile.

"Okay, okay, I get it. But how do I go about it? What do I do, Mrs. V.?" I ask eagerly, leaning forward in anticipation.

"Well," she begins, her tone deliberate, *"perhaps you can start by understanding what being blissful is all about. If you do, I'm certain you'll be able to act on your feelings while possessing the precious knowledge of one of the most important hidden treasures in matters of love."*

Mrs. V. carefully pages through the same beautiful book before handing it to me, already opened to the right passage.

"Read over here, my lovelorn mentee..." she says with an encouraging look, her wisdom practically radiating.

"Life is Bliss"

(The Importance of Little Details in Life)

If you want to live a blissful life,
pay attention to the little details—
both in the receiving and giving ends.

But not the kind where 'the devil is in the ...'
as those are simple, hiding in plain sight,
usually expected:
rules, norms, or stipulations

that we either follow, ignore, break, or circumvent.

So, they are narrow in human nature
binary in their scope—
they either bite you or they don't.

No, to live a life in bliss, you must pay attention
to a different kind of little details,
those that are gestures of love,
those that come straight from the heart.

They are usually spontaneous and unexpected,
often hold very little or no material value,
but always provide immense bliss and joy,
the kind when it is hard to breathe
as emotions bundle up in a knot
in both the throats of the dispenser and the recipient.

These types of little details require genial creativity,
but that comes easily when propelled
by overwhelming empathy and caring for others.

When we receive little details,
they hold their biggest value,
when we are richer, in health,
and things are better, well, and sound,
yet we are still humble enough to pay attention,
to appreciate and value
how much we are loved by others.

When we give,

the little details in life have their greatest worth,

when we are poorer, in sickness

and things are at their worst,

not good or simply bad,

yet we still have the heart and the desire

to give to others whom we care about.

It is on those extremes,

valuing what we are offered when we don't need it,

or caring about giving the very little we have left,

when little details in life matter the most,

become unforgettable, never leave

and stay with us forever.

Life is bliss when caught by surprise,

overcome by emotion

we hide our faces behind the palms of our hands,

when we find that little note left in our pocket,

leave that flower on her pillow,

or in those tiny precious gestures that Mom, Dad,

Granny and Grandpa never forget,

those little things that never fail to be there,

that supportive hug or kiss,

that reassuring or uplifting smile,

that contagious laughter,

those calming, maybe loving,

perhaps tender and grateful eyes,

any or all those little things

that make us react in bliss:

"What a gesture; they love me."

Or whisper to ourselves:

"Oh my, I love him, her, them, you... with all my heart."

So, if you want to live life in bliss,

pay close attention to the little details in life—

those that come straight from the heart,

those that are spontaneous gestures of love,

those that are just little things,

those that we offer and receive with absolute joy,

those that we never forget for the rest of our lives.

*

"Erasmus, love grows out of little things; love is captured through small gestures," Mrs. V. says softly. "Love is preserved and made of teeny, tiny details that we give and take, to and from one another."

In that moment, I realize—for the first time in my life—what it truly feels like to be blissful.

She continues, "Focus on giving with all your heart, but be mindful of whom you are giving to, as what makes those little details resonate is their catalyst: empathy."

— ✦ —

The professor closes the book of memories, his voice softening as he returns to the present. "And so, my dear students," he says, his tone filled with warmth, "I learned that love often resides in the smallest gestures—the details we give and receive that transform ordinary moments into extraordinary ones." The professor scans the room, a twinkle of curiosity in his eye. "Now, my dear students, I would like to hear your thoughts. What resonates with you from today's session?"

A hand rises in the middle row.

"Yes, go ahead."

The hand belongs to Sarah, a literature student known for her insightful perspectives. Her voice is reflective as she asks, "Professor, in *The Better Instincts of our Hearts*, it talks about monumental steps driven by the heart. How do we balance following our hearts with the practical demands of life?"

The professor nods thoughtfully. "An excellent question, Sarah. Balancing the heart and practical demands requires discernment. When the heart speaks, it often reveals our deepest truths. Practicality, however, ensures we can act on those truths sustainably. The key is to let the heart guide your purpose while allowing practicality to shape your path. Together, they create a harmony that sustains both passion and stability."

Another hand rises from the back.

"Yes, in the back."

The hand belongs to Louis, an engineering student with a keen interest in human behavior. His tone is contemplative as he asks,

"Professor, in *Life is Bliss*, it says that small details have the greatest worth when times are hardest. Why do you think that is?"

"An important observation, Louis," the professor responds. "Small details, particularly those born of empathy and love, shine brightest in hardship because they remind us of our shared humanity. When life feels overwhelming, even the simplest gestures—an unexpected smile or a kind word—can ground us, rekindle hope, and restore a sense of connection. They are proof that even in our darkest moments, light can be found."

A third hand rises.

"Yes, go ahead."

The hand belongs to Lena, a sociology student with a focus on relationships. Her voice is steady but curious as she asks, "Professor, you spoke about being mindful of whom we give to. How do we discern who deserves those gestures?"

The professor tilts his head slightly, considering the question.

"Lena, discerning whom to give to is less about worthiness and more about alignment. Ask yourself: Is the gesture rooted in sincerity? Does it align with your empathy for that person? If the answer is yes, then the act of giving is always meaningful, regardless of how it is received."

Finally, a hand rises from the front row.

"Yes, go ahead."

The hand belongs to Jacob, a philosophy student. His tone is probing as he asks, "Professor, you mentioned that empathy is the catalyst for meaningful details. How can we cultivate greater empathy in our lives?"

The professor smiles. "An excellent question, Jacob. Empathy begins with listening—deeply and without judgment. It grows through understanding others' perspectives and practicing kindness, even when it's inconvenient. Empathy flourishes when we are willing to see the world through another's eyes and act with compassion. It is both a skill and a mindset, one that enriches our lives immeasurably."

Professor Cromwell-Smith flashes a huge smile as he wraps up his class. Noticing the curiosity and expectant looks all around, he responds with enthusiasm. "Yes, yes. The answer is yes. In our next class, we will dive deeper into this chapter of my life," he declares.

As the questions wind down, the professor glances at the clock, his expression softening into a reflective smile. "Thank you for your questions, my dear students. Remember, life's beauty often lies in the smallest of details. Pay attention to them, for they hold the power to transform your experiences and relationships. Have a wonderful day, and I look forward to seeing you next week."

The students begin to file out, their expressions thoughtful and inspired. Among them, the young woman with curly blond hair lingers, her gaze fixed on the professor as he gathers his belongings. She watches as he exits the room, her curiosity deepening with every passing session. What began as something vaguely familiar becomes inexorably real to her, resonating more and more with each story he shares.

Chapter 12

Falling in Love

It is early morning, and the heat is already oppressive. As Professor Cromwell-Smith pedals deliberately through the quiet streets, his slow cadence mirrors the introspection that fills his mind. The vibrant colors of summer, however, seem to contrast with the tempestuous emotions churning within him. Each rotation of the wheels brings memories closer to the surface—places of the heart long buried but never forgotten. The intensity unsettles him completely, as a torrent of unearthed feelings floods every inch of his living self. By the time he reaches campus, a thin sheen of sweat glistens on his forehead, though the calm mask he wears betrays none of the turmoil within.

Shortly after, he enters the auditorium, where a crowd eagerly awaits him, their faces filled with anticipation. Their murmurs subside as his presence ignites a familiar energy in the room. He steps forward, adjusts his scarf, and begins with a smile, "Isn't this insanely awesome?"

"Dear friends, bear with me today as we traverse this phase of my life together," Professor Cromwell-Smith says, his tone a blend of excitement and vulnerability. "Please forgive me if I become a tad emotional. These are feelings that I—or any of us—can't simply rationalize." He takes a deep breath, his gaze softening as it drifts into the past. "All right, here we go," he says, steadying himself as the room falls silent, and the memories begin to unfold.

—✦—

It's been three weeks since I wrote to Mrs. V., sharing the joy and bliss of having found the love of my life. I thanked her a million times in that letter.

—✦—

Dearest Mrs. V.,

I have joyful news, made possible by your guidance. I'm madly in love, and we're both utterly happy. I won her heart through a series of tiny, heartfelt gestures and little details that awed her. I did it all by following the better instincts of my heart.

You are not going to believe this: her name is... well, I call her Vicky—Vicky as in Victoria! Isn't it amazing? You both share the same name. Victoria Emerson-Lloyd is her full name, and we've been inseparable for the last eleven months.

Mrs. V., let me caution you that I am neither a poet nor a writer. Nevertheless, I enclose a few verses I wrote for her that I want to share with you. The first one captures exactly how I feel about her:

"Love's Rabbit Hole"

How do you know when Love is knocking
at your door?
How do you know when it has arrived?
its music, the music of angels,
is all out there waiting for you.

How do you know that whoever has reached you,
maybe that travel mate

you've been wishing for, all along?

And how do you decide if it's the right time,

right there and then,

to step out of your shell,

knocking down your protective shields?

You know it,

because when that someone unexpectedly

irrupts into your life's journey,

it simply takes your breath away.

You know it,

when you can finally catch your breath

all you inhale feels at that moment

like there is absolutely

nothing else you'd rather be doing,

and no one else in the world

you would like to be with—,

other than your rabbit.

You know it,

as the world around you disappears

and you willingly fall

through the most scintillatious rabbit hole

you'll ever find in your life.

You know it.

when out of the blue,

the object of your desire

can do no wrong,

and everything they say or do

is painted in perfection.

through benevolent magnifying glasses

made of boundless candor,

ingenuity, and romance.

You know it,

when from the get-go,

you feel light, free,

confident, and at ease.

Life transforms into a journey of two,

impregnated with magic,

happiness, passion, and joy.

You know it,

because you become possessed

with an unexplicable certainty—

you feel safe, protected, and never alone.

And you know it.

Because you see yourself

visualizing your life, your future,

your family, your children—

only with your other half.

You know it.

Because Love's rabbit hole

is one you'll never want to climb out of.

*

Dearest Mrs. V., Vicky is lively and bubbly. She's fun and foolish, and she loves to dress in blue. Quite fitting, indeed, as she is my brand-new unicorn—although one with a very short fuse and temper. She's a fiery one, but she can also be mellow and deeply compassionate. Her cause at the moment is helping the homeless, and she longs to serve those in need.

I also love to see her running wild toward whatever she's doing, her golden curls flying everywhere as she burns that seemingly endless energy of hers. I adore her, Mrs. V.... and yet, we couldn't be more different! She dreams of becoming a criminal psychologist, while I haven't the faintest idea what I want to do with my life.

That's why I wrote the following script for her. I wanted to memorialize our life together in its smallest, most vivid details and contrast them with the polar opposites we embody, all while showing how profoundly intimate and intertwined our relationship has become.

Mrs. V., it has been an extraordinary discovery for me that being so diametrically different creates a kind of "love tension." It's this tension, I've realized, that sparks endless passion between us. Hence the name of this scribble:

"The Secret Lies in Opposite Ends at Work Forever"

You like to dance, and I don't.
You are spontaneous and blunt, and I am not.

You are loud and noisy,

I am silence personified.

You are social and friendly,
I am neither by default.

You love certainty and predictability,
I thrive in improvisation,
never knowing what to expect.

You have a short fuse that erupts
then fades like a volcano,
while my flame burns steadily, slowly,
for a long time.

You like to sleep late,
I rise early, way before dawn.

You plan meticulously ahead,
I rush everything at the last minute.

You love constant organization,
I like everything organized—most of the time.

You make cleanliness and neatness
happen without fail,
I enjoy them immensely.

You remember certain things with perfect clarity,
I remember others just as vividly.

You read people with absolute precision,
I read some—well, not all that well.

You love a good wine and cheese,
I am still learning to appreciate both.

You are a great and lightning-fast cook,
I can barely boil water.

You don't care much for breakfast,
I believe it's the most important meal of the day.

You don't like ice cream or chocolates,
I love them beyond reason.

You are effusive in celebration,
I am quietly reserved.

You play instruments with ease,
I wouldn't know where to start.
You love specific kinds of music passionately,
I adore all kinds from all over the world.
You aren't physically affectionate or touchy-feely,
I am all that, all the time.

You can be ferociously jealous,
I see it as just another game people play.

You call everything by its name,
I lace my words with endearments.

You love routines and predictability,
I thrive on chaos and spontaneity.

You dislike being barefoot or naked,

I embrace both with ease.

You love to talk about anything and everything,

I only do when I am deeply passionate.

You love when I read to you,

and I do so with gusto.

You never understand movies

but stay wide awake through them.

I fall asleep but somehow explain them later.

You always nap while I drive,

I bring us to our destination,

talking to myself the entire trip.

You hate driving,

I could drive forever.

You get grumpy when bored,

I don't even know what boredom feels like.

You rarely enjoy what you order at restaurants,

I always feed you from my plate,

otherwise, you help yourself

to what I've ordered.

You are cautious and fearful,

I leap first and ask questions later.

You are full of laughter,

mine is hard to come by.

You love a good dress and wear it well,
I couldn't care less about my wardrobe.

We couldn't be more different about,
With whom, how, when, where,
and what we work at.
But we couldn't be more alike
in how hard we go at it!
You type like the wind, super-fast,
I stumble along.

I read super-fast,
And you don't.

You hate carrying things,
I love doing it for you.

You lose your bearings easily,
I'm your human compass.

You rely on maps,
I rely on instinct.

You don't know how to strike a bargain,
or negotiate a price,
I revel in the thrill of negotiation.

You believe some things are impossible,
I believe almost anything is possible—

and you trust me with that.

You like to sit down,
be waited on and enjoy a good meal.
I prefer the simplicity of self-service.

You like a good and loud fight,
I am the quiet peacemaker—
anti-noise and anti-fight.

You don't overlook anything you dislike,
notice every flaw
I consciously distort and rewrite reality.

You stumble and fumble all the time,
I'm not much better at that at all.

You love to browse but hardly shop,
I can't wait to get out.

You are hard to please
when you want something.
When I do it for you,
I am always dead-on with size, type, and style.

Your fears disappear with board games,
where you cheat all the time.
While I am naive, clumsy, and foolish
and your gullible victim every time.

Your fears go out of the window

when it comes to jumping queues,

I am always hesitant and embarrassed,

but obediently follow your lead.

You are a terrible cyclist,

I am a terrific one.

You are a great swimmer,

mediocre would be a superlative,

when I do that.

You like the coast without sand on your feet,

I was raised on the beach

and love it as it is, wild and dirty.

You like perfectly tranquil, glorious weather,

the tougher and rougher it is, the better for me.

I am overwhelmingly physical,

you are always successful in slowing me down.

You are claustrophobic,

I have motion sickness.

You are afraid of heights,

I prefer rooms with a view from floor to ceiling.

You don't mind sitting in the middle,

I always sit in the front, the aisle, or facing the crowd.

You love ballet and the opera,

I love a good philharmonic orchestra and library.

We both love museums, just different parts of them.

You like to sit and munch,
I can spend hours at a bookstore
or looking at historical pictures.

You curse and use loaded words,
I never do so.

It's very hard to move on or let go,
with me, it's just a flick of a switch away.

You love to run but no longer can,
for me, running is a way of life.

The things we agree on are easy to spot
and write endlessly about.
But it is on the things where we are not alike,
that healthy tension abounds.
That's why the secret lies on two opposite ends
working together forever.

*

I've written to her like I've never written to anyone before in my life. Perhaps this is it—this is what I love to do. To write, or maybe teach about it.

Mrs. V., before I leave you, there is something else. Are you ready? I want to propose. Yes! I do. I wish with all my heart that Victoria would be my wife and companion forever.

But I am lost in a sea of fear and doubt. The fact is, I feel like I am nobody. I have nothing in the way of material things to offer her; I am not even certain of what I want to do with my future. Please help me. I need your wisdom and tutelage.

I'll be waiting anxiously for your reply.

Yours truly,

Erasmus

P.S. Your eternally thankful, now enamored, but still "a lost soul" mentee. By the way, I call her Vicky, so I'll never confuse her with you!

— ✦ —

As Professor Cromwell-Smith finishes reading his heartfelt letter to Mrs. V., his voice carries the weight of his younger self's emotions. The auditorium remains hushed, the students transfixed by the raw vulnerability of his story. He closes his eyes briefly, as if bidding farewell to the vivid memories that have resurfaced, before slowly returning his focus to the present. When he opens his eyes, the warm glow of recollection remains, illuminating his expression. Wearing an expression of deep emotion, he gently brings his class back to the present, his eyes scanning the room and taking in the quiet intensity of his students' gazes.

The students sit in thoughtful silence, the weight of his words sinking in. Among them, a young woman with golden curls sits glued to her chair. A whirlwind of emotions surges through her, tightening the knot in her throat and making her heart race. She remains paralyzed, caught between angst and revelation. So, it is him, she realizes, as the professor's words resonate deeply.

"When true love knocks at life's door, seize the moment and let it in," the professor declares, his voice resonating with conviction. "From that point on, your heart will take over and activate your happiness factory." He pauses, looking around the room. "Now, my dear students, I'd love to hear your thoughts. What questions or reflections do you have about today's lesson?" His invitation lingers in the air, encouraging even the shyest students to engage.

A hand rises hesitantly in the third row.

"Yes, go ahead," the professor encourages.

The hand belongs to Lindsey, a literature major known for her analytical mind. Her voice is steady but curious as she asks, "Professor, in *Love's Rabbit Hole*, you describe love as taking one's breath away and falling willingly into a rabbit hole. But what happens when the initial euphoria fades? How do you sustain that love?"

"Ah, an excellent question, Lindsey," the professor replies.

"The rabbit hole is the beginning, the catalyst for love. But sustaining it requires effort, empathy, and, as you'll see in the next poem, attention to the small details that preserve and nurture love. Love evolves, and it's the little gestures—both given and received— that keep the magic alive."

Lindsey nods, jotting down notes as her curiosity deepens.

Another hand rises from the back of the auditorium.

"Yes, in the back," the professor acknowledges.

The hand belongs to Ryan, a philosophy major with a penchant for deep, existential questions.

"Professor, in *The Secret Lies in Opposite Ends at Work Forever*, you highlight contrasts in relationships. How do we navigate those differences without them creating conflict?"

"An insightful question, Ryan," the professor responds.

"Differences can either divide or strengthen a relationship, depending on how they are approached. The key is mutual respect and understanding. Celebrate those contrasts as complementary forces that create a dynamic balance. Learn to compromise without losing yourself, and always communicate with empathy."

Ryan leans back, his expression contemplative as the professor's words resonate.

A hand rises near the front.

"Yes, go ahead," the professor says.

The hand belongs to Phillip, a psychology major with a keen interest in human behavior. "Professor, you mentioned in *Life is Bliss* that little details matter most when things are at their worst. Could you elaborate on why this is so?"

The professor's face softens. "Phillip, it is precisely during life's most challenging moments that those small gestures of love and care become lifelines. They remind us of our humanity, our connections, and the support that surrounds us. A kind word, a reassuring touch, or even a simple smile can provide immense comfort and strength when we need it most."

Phillip nods, her pen moving quickly across her notebook.

Finally, Professor Cromwell-Smith glances at the clock, his expression softening into a reflective smile. "Thank you for your questions, my dear students. Remember, life's beauty often lies in the smallest of details. Pay attention to them, for they hold the power to transform your experiences and relationships. Have a wonderful day, and I look forward to seeing you next week."

The students begin to file out, their expressions thoughtful and inspired. Among them, the young woman with curly blond hair lingers, her gaze fixed on the professor as he gathers his belongings. She watches as he exits the room, her heart racing with emotions that grow stronger with every passing session.

As most students linger in the afterglow of the professor's storytelling, it almost seems as though countless little red hearts are floating in the air above their heads—a testament to the magic he's just shared.

Chapter 13

True Love and the Three-Legged Stool

He has been pedaling for more than an hour, aimlessly navigating the back roads of campus. Professor Cromwell-Smith left home an hour earlier than usual, taking time to reflect and take stock of his life. He knows he has pursued his passions and fulfilled his dreams. Teaching is exactly what he loves to do.

Yet, what his mentors never taught him was how to find love. Today's session, however, will delve into that brief yet transformative period in his life when he found it. He is eager to share what happened with his class.

Feeling ready, he heads toward the school's main building. Before long, he enters the auditorium to find a large crowd awaiting him.

"How's everyone today?" he asks, his voice bright with anticipation.

"Awesome!" the students respond in unison, their energy electric.

"Then let's jump right into it. Shall we?" he says, his smile widening as the room falls silent, eager for the story to unfold.

— ✦ —

Today, it finally happened. It arrived early in the morning, but I have not opened it yet. It has been sitting in my left pocket the entire day, feeling as though it might burn through at any moment. Anxiously, I pat the flattish bulk now and then, reassuring myself it hasn't evaporated, vanished, or been lost. This self-inflicted torment

lasts through the entire morning and an unbearably long afternoon.
Only at day's end do I finally sit down, take a deep breath, and open
Mrs. V.'s long-awaited response.

"Obsequium, obsequium, obsequious," I read aloud.

Once again, her usual opening remarks are enchanting, like a
precious and priceless gift.

— ✦ —

Dear Erasmus,

I write to you with a gigantic smile on my face. Oh, my dear boy,
how happy you've made me and how thoughtful of you to share some
of the things you've written for Victoria. They are a breath of fresh
air, transporting me into a world I once lived in—until my only love
was lost forever at the Battle of the Bulge.

I've copied a couple of wonderful writings for you, ones that will
provide much-needed wisdom at this magnificent crossroads in your
life. The first one is simply about love.

Do you know what love is?

Do you know how to love?

Do you know how to be loved?

"What is Love?"

What a bewildering feat,
A pair of souls
smitten with one another.
The whisperings and whistlings
of a pair of infatuated hearts,
in a world of their own.

The peace and ease

of two spirits entirely comfortable

with each other,

at all times,

while enjoying

the most sublime of connections,

in a place where innate beauty

lies in abundance.

A twosome

in a state of constant flux,

where everything begins

and endlessly continues

through a symphony of reactions

to one another's

expressions of Love.

And,

by wrapping themselves

around each other's fingers,

they surrender completely,

seemingly doing with each other

what they please.

Forever spoiled,

neither can ever accept anything less,

but exactly the same or more,

from their other half.

That is how Love becomes

a perpetual exercise of

placing oneself

in the other's shoes,

That is why,

Love is the ultimate empathy,

the binding of two hearts

possessed by one another,

always and forever.

*

The second one is about true Love. My boy, that's the real deal. Is this what you are feeling? What about her? Do you know that most people never experience true Love, and of the few that do, many let it slip away?

So, let me open the doors to the magical world of true Love for you...

"What is True Love?"

True Love is,

when your heart no longer belongs to you.

True Love is,

when your life's glass is full

only when with your loved one by your side.

True Love is,

when you feel that you can move mountains

or split oceans for one another.

True Love hears and sees no evil.

It is unconditional,

no matter the deed or mischief.

True Love is,

when your skin aches

without your other half's touch,

and nothing feels warmer

than being in each other's arms.

True Love is,

when passion is so overwhelming,

just a flick of a switch away.

True Love is,

when success, defeat, or failure fade away,

and neither pain nor joy holds sway.

It is to be everything for each other,

to give all and then even more.

True love is in the greetings

that make us jump in joy,

and in the long embraces and farewells

that leave us breathless

our throats knotted with emotion.

True Love patiently waits and hopes

expecting nothing in return.

True Love is in the benign and forgiving stare,

the smiles bursting with joy and laughter,

the echoes of happiness in our lives.

True Love is,

when your soul mate becomes

part of your very essence,

when each spirit is split between both,

and both souls surrender, fusing into one,

while becoming travel mates

in the topsy-turvy journey of life.

True Love is,

life's colors

shine and blossom in full,

the bells of heaven ring,

and life's orchestra plays at its finest symphony,

while everything we feel

soars to ecstasy's zenith.

True Love can't be measured.

True Love can't be controlled.

True Love is empowering.

True Love is one of life's greatest gifts—

precious but often overlooked.

True Love is hard to find.

Perhaps you never will…

instead, it will find you!

True Love is a miracle,

one of the great wonders

of being alive.

*

Dear Mentee, always remember, true love is not driven by success, nor does it disappear in failure. When it does arrive, it stays with you forever.

Finally, in this precious little book, The Magic in Life, there is another wonderfully written script by the same author. It is impregnated with timeless wisdom in matters of love. It is about a three-legged stool...

Let me share it with you.

"The Three-Legged Stool"

What makes a great couple?

First comes **Friendship,**
Its foundations are honesty, loyalty,
fidelity and commitment.

In them reside communication
and the sharing of everything.
It is trusting without limits,
giving without expecting anything in return.

it is knowing what the other thinks without words
and understanding desires with just a glance.

It is completing each other's sentences,
complementing each other's

weaknesses and differences.

It is when respect and admiration
become the driving force and the support columns.

It is where true intimacy lies,
and where the walls and boundaries of a twosome
are built like a fortress—
providing comfort, privacy, strength, and safe heaven
to one another.

When there is true intimacy,
our other half becomes the person
who you are comfortable with at all times,
the one you never tire of seeing, talking to, or sharing with.
It is the person that sometimes acts as our parent,
some others as a sibling,
many others a spouse,
and often simply as a friend.
It is the person that motivates you the most,
but also calls you out,
makes you stop,
change course or make amends.
True friendship thrives on a healthy level of tension.

And true friendship is where
for better or for worse,
in sickness or in health
and for richer or poorer lie.

Second, comes **Passion,**

It's when the flesh ignites without control,

when blood and desire are like a fireball,

and two bodies become insatiable—

unable to get enough of each other,

no matter how, no matter when no matter where.

It's when lust overwhelms mind and body.

It is when one look, one touch, one image

is all it takes for mutual arousal to erupt!

It is when fantasy and imagination

transform into reality in a flash of flesh.

It is when everything about the other

is sensual, carnal, and seductive—

all the time at any time.

Third comes **Love,**

True Love is when your heart

no longer belong to you.

True Love is when the bells of heaven ring,

and the trumpets of life

play heart-shaped musical notes at full throttle.

It is the delicate rose garden

requiring constant, tender care,

producing immense, but delicate, fragile beauty.

True Love is when your skin aches,

missing the other's touch.

It is to be endlessly in awe, hopelessly infatuated,

and carelessly wrapped around each other's fingers.

It is when nothing feels warmer

than being in each other's arms.

True Love is gallantry and courtship,

it is poetry and total surrender.

It is when the colors of life shine and blossom in full,

life's orchestra plays its finest,

and everything you feel

soars to the pinnacle of ecstasy.

Friendship, Passion, and Love

are the three legs of a stool—

a symbol of a wholesome couple,

a couple that will last and endure life's challenges,

a couple that will stay together forever.

*

Dear Erasmus, a s you can see, a couple has three very different dimensions. Each one requires hard work. Each is distinctively different but equally important, as all are the foundations of a continuously happy, solid, and, therefore, lasting union.

True love, dear Erasmus, once it finds you, don't ever let it go, as it may never come back or happen again for you. And if indeed it does find you, always remember those three legs of the stool—friendship, passion, and love. All must be present for your relationship to endure and remain happy.

So, there you have it. Is it love? Is it true love? Do you have and feel the friendship, passion, and love that constitute a lasting pair?

Be happy, my son. I wish you all the best.

Your ecstatic old mentor,

Mrs. V.

P.S. Erasmus, what were those little gestures that won her heart? Please tell me more about yourself and Vicky. Who is this enchantress that stole my beloved mentee's heart?

— ✦ —

Her words linger in my mind, echoing with their significance. This is Mrs. V.'s way—always opening the door to deep questions, knowing the answers will shape me profoundly.

— ✦ —

Professor Cromwell-Smith is overcome by emotion, and so is the student body surrounding him. For many, the lingering question is how and why his own three-legged stool broke. A couple of teardrops slowly trace their way down the professor's pained face as his tight lips tremble, caught in a twisted bundle of suppressed grief.

As he finishes reading Mrs. V.'s letter and the three poems, his voice carries the weight of his younger self's emotions. He places the papers down on the lectern, his hands lingering as if reluctant to let go of the memories they represent. The auditorium remains hushed, the students transfixed by the raw vulnerability of his story.

Wearing an expression of deep emotion, he closes his eyes briefly, inhaling deeply as though bidding farewell to the vivid recollections that have resurfaced. When he opens his eyes, the warmth of remembrance remains, illuminating his expression. His gaze sweeps across the room, meeting the quiet intensity of his students' gazes.

"True love, my dear friends," he begins, his voice steady but filled with emotion, "is a rare and precious gift. It requires patience, courage, and, above all, the willingness to nurture those three legs of the stool: friendship, passion, and love." A few students shift in their seats, their faces pensive, as the weight of his words settles over them.

As the professor concludes his reading, he pauses, his gaze sweeping across the room. His eyes reflect a mix of nostalgia and quiet resolve as he leans slightly forward on the lectern.

"I'd like to hear your thoughts or questions about today's lesson," he invites, his voice warm and encouraging.

A hand rises near the center of the auditorium.

"Yes, go ahead," he encourages.

The hand belongs to Jimmy, a sociology student known for his inquisitive nature. "Professor, in *What is True Love?* you describe it as unconditional and empowering. How do you reconcile this with the idea that love requires hard work, as in *The Three-Legged Stool?*"

"An excellent question, Jimmy," the professor replies, his tone thoughtful. "True love is indeed empowering, but its endurance depends on effort and intention. While love itself may ignite naturally, sustaining it requires the work of building and balancing those three legs—friendship, passion, and love. Without that effort, even the strongest love can falter."

Jimmy nods, scribbling notes as he processes the answer.

Another hand rises from the back of the auditorium.

"Yes, in the back," the professor acknowledges.

The hand belongs to Nina, a psychology major with a focus on relationships and behavior. "Professor, in *The Three-Legged Stool*, you emphasize the importance of passion. How does one maintain passion in a long-term relationship?"

"A great question, Nina," the professor says with a slight smile. "Passion evolves over time. In the beginning, it's often fueled by novelty and infatuation. But as a relationship deepens, passion must be intentionally nurtured through shared experiences, physical intimacy, and creative ways of expressing desire. The key is never taking each other for granted and continuing to explore what excites and connects you both."

Nina nods thoughtfully, jotting down his advice.

A hand rises near the front row.

"Yes, go ahead," the professor says, turning his attention to the student.

The hand belongs to Elizabeth, a sociology major with a keen interest in symbolism. "Professor, in *What is Love?* you describe love as 'the ultimate empathy.' How does this empathy influence the way we navigate conflicts in a relationship?"

The professor's expression softens. "Elizabeth, empathy allows us to see and feel the world from our partner's perspective. It transforms conflict into an opportunity for understanding and growth. When we approach disagreements with empathy, we're more likely to listen, validate, and find solutions that strengthen the relationship rather than weaken it."

Elizabeth smiles, her pen hovering as she absorbs his words.

As the questions wind down, Professor Cromwell-Smith glances at the clock, his expression softening into a reflective smile.

"Thank you for your questions, my dear students. Remember, love is not just a feeling—it's a choice, a commitment, and a journey. Pay attention to those three legs of the stool. Nurture them, and you'll build something lasting and beautiful. Have a wonderful day, and I look forward to seeing you next week."

The students begin to file out, their faces reflective and inspired. Among them, a young woman with long golden hair hesitates. Her gaze remains fixed on the professor as he gathers his belongings. She watches as he exits the room, her heart racing with emotions that grow stronger with every passing session.

The poems, the three mentors, Oxford and Harvard! How could I have missed it? she thinks. Now, there are no doubts. The name Victoria Emerson-Lloyd is the final confirmation.

Her heart races with anxious determination as she watches him move toward the door. She steps forward, her voice ready to speak, but Professor Cromwell-Smith turns to her and gently says, "Not today, my dear. Please pull me aside next time. Have a nice day," his tone kind yet distant, as he finishes packing his things.

At first, the young woman feels dejected by his reply. But as her eyes catch the raw, pained expression etched across his face, she falters. It's going to be too painful, she reflects, clutching her books close to her chest as she hurries out of the room. I won't be able to bring myself to attend his next class.

Meanwhile, Professor Cromwell-Smith exits the room, his steps slow but steady. The bittersweet smile of someone who has carried both the burden and blessing of true love crosses his face. A couple of teardrops trace their way down his cheeks as he feels the release of emotions long buried, finally letting some of it out.

Chapter 14

Facing a Loss

Professor Cromwell-Smith pedals aimlessly through the quiet back roads of campus, the familiar rhythm of his bike providing little solace for his churning thoughts. The progressive weight of loss lingers heavily as he grapples with what he has been trying so hard to avoid. It is not the beginning of his love story, nor the magical fairy tale that unfolded along the way, but its stunning and devastating end. Forty-some years later, he must face the raw pain of his loss once more. Yet, the catharsis of the previous session has brought him to the right place. He feels calm and at peace with the beautiful parts of his past that he so dearly treasures, even amid the sorrow.

Totally immersed in his thoughts, he barely notices the path beneath his wheels or that he has arrived at the faculty building. By the time he parks his old bike, the weight has shifted slightly, settling into a quiet resolution. Still lost in his reverie, he slowly paces the college halls. It is only when he walks into the classroom that he snaps back to reality, observing the murmurs of his students and the faint rustle of papers as they settle in. Their curious gazes anchor him, providing the spark he needs to begin.

"I am ready," he tells himself, quietly resolute. Taking a moment to ground himself, he clears his throat, his voice steady yet tinged with reverence.

"Hi everyone. Today, I want to share with you something deeply personal," he says, his tone calm but charged with emotion. "In life, we all must deal with losses. Some are harder than others. Today, I'll share mine with you through the prism of poetry. It all begins with a letter I wrote to Mrs. V."

— ✦ —

Dear Mrs. V.,

I write to you with a heavy heart and the sad news that Victoria and I are no longer together. One day, she simply disappeared from campus. No note, no goodbye. Her studies abandoned; her home phone disconnected.

I took a train ride to southern Illinois in search of answers, but the trip was in vain. All I found was a vacated house, and her neighbors were as surprised as I was. She is gone, Mrs. V., just like that. Puff! She vanished.

It's now been three months, and I'll be graduating soon. I am totally lost. It feels as though a part of me has been yanked away, leaving a deep, unfillable void.

Mrs. V., it hurts—deep, deep inside. But I haven't given up on myself yet. Enclosed is a little something I wrote just for you...

"Sorting out the Rest"
Of all the 'ifs' and 'buts' we face,

none is more powerful

than the ones coming from those

who impart life lessons

and living tutelage.

We may pretend

we don't listen to them,

when in fact

we hear it all.

Somewhere along the way,

hopefully sooner

rather than later,

those words of wisdom,

almost always

finally register.

As we sort everything else out,

it is those wisely spoken truths,

that often come to us at just the right time—

guiding us, perhaps preventing mistakes,

or even after the fact,

helping us know what to do,

maybe even how to mend,

for the next time around.

*

Dear Mrs. V., Though I've learned not to dwell on the past but rather to treasure it, I wrote the following to evoke Victoria's presence, transforming the longing and the void of her absence into a world of truly wonderful memories.
Here is something I've just written for her...

*

"If I Could Find You Out There"

If I could touch the stars
with my heart,
the night's darkness would turn into
reds of roses and reds of fire.

If I could reach the sky
with my dreams,
the colors and tones of daylight
would turn into
inspired whites and passionate blues.

If I could shape words
from life's most soul-stirring moments,
they would turn into
endless shades of wisdom.

If I could simply be art,
the kind that brings joy to the spirit,
it would bloom into
greens of plenitude and yellows of life.

If I could soar to the moon
and gaze back
at Planet Earth,
it would glow like a rainbow,
turning into
every color that ever was.

But if I could only find you,

somewhere…

out there in the universe,

my dreams and my passion,

my spirit and my soul,

my life and my heart,

and all of my world,

would all,

become you.

If I could only find you out there,

somewhere in the Universe.

*

Dear Mrs. V., I also wrote about how I visualize Victoria in the future. She dreams of becoming a doctor of the mind, helping criminals, and you know what? I truly believe she'll be masterful at it.

So, I wrote to the future her, imagining the woman she'll become, and it has helped me a great deal to process my feelings and hold on to hope.

Here's what I wrote…

"A Labor of Love"

What a daunting task it is

to navigate through the darkest corners

of the minds of others, but not your own—

those paths where the ground is shaky,

the foundations cracked,

the Earth shifting,

and some of the tracks of life are blurry,

devoid of light and barren of well-being or happiness.

But perhaps there is no tougher job

than confronting minds

that not only lack meaning and purpose in life

but are also potentially or inherently,

wicked, devious, reckless, or delusional—

or simply love themselves so much

that there is no room or care for anyone else.

What a tough job it is to do good,

to uplift and improve the mindset of others in need.

What an impossible task it seems

to do that for those in need of redemption,

those yearning for a second act in life,

those that very few support or believe in.

What a tough job.

What an impossible job.

What a wonderful labor of love.

That's what you'll do,

and that's what you will be leaving in your wake.

<u>That's what you would have done!</u>

*

What else can I do? Please, share your wisdom and guide me,

showing me a way out of this pain.

Your amateur and aspiring poet mentee,

Erasmus Cromwell-Smith.

— ✦ —

Professor Cromwell-Smith is overcome by emotion, and so is the student body surrounding him. For many, the lingering question is how he managed to transform such deep pain into heartfelt poetry. A couple of teardrops slowly trace their way down the professor's pained face as his tight lips tremble, caught in a twisted bundle of suppressed grief. As he finishes reading the letter and the three poems, his voice carries the weight of his younger self's emotions. He places the papers down on the lectern, his hands lingering as if reluctant to let go of the memories they represent. The auditorium remains hushed, the students transfixed by the raw vulnerability of his story.

Wearing an expression of deep emotion, he closes his eyes briefly, inhaling deeply as though bidding farewell to the vivid recollections that have resurfaced. When he opens his eyes, the warmth of remembrance remains, illuminating his expression. His gaze sweeps across the room, meeting the quiet intensity of his students' gazes.

"Loss, my dear friends," he begins, his voice steady but filled with emotion, "teaches us to cherish what we have, to embrace the beauty of moments, and to find meaning even in pain. Let us explore these lessons together."

As the professor concludes, he pauses, his gaze sweeping across the room. His eyes reflect a mix of nostalgia and quiet resolve as he leans slightly forward on the lectern.

"I'd like to hear your thoughts or questions about today's lesson," he invites, his voice warm and encouraging.

A hand rises near the center of the auditorium.

George, a sociology student known for his inquisitive nature, raises his hand. His sharp features and ever-curious demeanor make him a familiar presence in class discussions. "Professor, in *Sorting Out the Rest*, you describe wisdom as something that comes to us at the right time. How can we distinguish between true wisdom and advice that might not apply to our situation?"

The professor nods thoughtfully. "George, true wisdom often resonates deeply. It's not about immediate application but how it aligns with your values and the lessons you've already learned. Reflecting on advice and comparing it to your experiences helps separate genuine wisdom from what might not fit your journey."

George scribbles in his notebook, his eyes alight with interest.

A hand rises from the back.

Rose, a psychology major with a focus on relationships and behavior, raises her hand. Her calm voice carries a steady confidence as she asks, "Professor, in *If I Could Find You Out There*, you use vivid and cosmic imagery. Do you think longing for something we've lost can help us grow emotionally, or does it hold us back?"

The professor's expression softens. "That's an insightful question, Rose. Longing is a double-edged sword. It can inspire growth by connecting us to the beauty of what we've experienced, but it can also anchor us in the past if we're unwilling to move forward. Balance is key—honoring the past while embracing the present and future."

Rose nods slowly, clearly reflecting on his answer.

Another hand rises from the front row.

Jacqueline, a history major with a keen interest in symbolism, speaks next. Her tone is thoughtful as she asks, "Professor, in *A Labor of Love*, you write about the difficulty of helping others navigate dark places. How do you think this kind of work shapes the person offering help?"

The professor smiles gently. "Jacqueline, helping others in such profound ways often requires immense strength and compassion. It can deepen empathy and resilience but also tests one's limits. The process shapes not just the lives of those being helped but also the helper, often leaving them with a greater understanding of human nature and their own capacity for love and perseverance."

Jacqueline's eyes brighten as she notes his words, visibly moved by the connection he's drawn.

As the questions wind down, Professor Cromwell-Smith glances at the clock, his expression softening into a reflective smile.

"Thank you for your questions, my dear students. Remember, loss and longing are not just sources of pain—they're also opportunities for growth and deeper understanding. Have a wonderful day, and I look forward to seeing you next week."

The students begin to gather their belongings, their expressions pensive and inspired. As they file out, the professor's gaze searches the room, pausing briefly at the empty seat where the young woman with golden curls usually sits. A pang of unease tugs at him, though he quickly dismisses it, refocusing on the few students lingering behind.

After the session ends, the professor stays for a good hour, answering questions from the smaller group of students who lingered after the bulk of the class had left. A tall, linebacker-like young man waits until the others leave.

Noticing the professor's subtle glance, he speaks softly. "She didn't come today," he says, referring to the girl with the golden curls.

"Ah, all right," Professor Cromwell-Smith replies quietly, his voice subdued. With a subtle nod, he walks away toward his office, though an eerie feeling settles deep in his gut, one he can't seem to shake. He pauses briefly, takes a deep breath, and continues on his way, his mind heavy with unspoken thoughts.

Chapter 15

Overcoming a Loss

This morning, Professor Cromwell-Smith feels blissful. After so many years, he has allowed himself to fully embrace the good memories of his one experience of true Love. Leaving home, he whistles and mounts his bike with renewed energy.

Truth be told, I've never found anyone else, he mutters, as if justifying it to himself. Excuses, excuses, and more excuses. Look at you! No family, frozen in time, living in a glass house behind a walled garden, shielding yourself from the world! His frustration causes him to snap back at himself, and his bike wobbles slightly.

No, no, no, he thinks, quickly regaining control. Digging up the past unearthed all these beautiful memories. It's simple: she was and still is the Love of my life. Tears of sheer happiness well up in his eyes as he pedals on, lost in thought, quibbling internally.

You are far from perfect, Erasmus, a darker voice in his mind challenges. His shadow self doubles down, rattling and shaking his sunny disposition with the weight of past self-inflicted wounds.

But Professor Cromwell-Smith brushes it aside. Self-defeating wounds won't work on me today, he reasons calmly. I feel at peace, filled with wonderful memories about the true Love of my life. Shortly thereafter, he walks into the large auditorium to find it packed to capacity. People are even sitting in the aisles, eager to hear him speak.

This time, I'll wait until the class ends. He'll surely be available, thinks the young woman with the golden curls, her resolve firm.

"Good day, class. Let us continue with the journey," says the Professor, his voice warm and steady. "I must confess that very few people I've met match Mrs. V.'s positive outlook and inspired attitude in life. She simply believes that every day we are alive is precious and should not be wasted, regardless of the circumstances."

— ✦ —

Today, I am taking one of my last exams before graduation, so her letter couldn't have come at a more opportune time. It is a morale booster from my perennial and inveterate cheerleader. With much trepidation, I set aside a full hour to read the anticipated missive. Little do I know that it will turn out to be one of the best life lessons I've ever learned.

— ✦ —

Dear Erasmus,

My heart sank when I read your letter. How challenging it can be to lock in true Love. First, Love has to find you, then life circumstances and timing must align, but then there is us—our own fears and insecurities—and others standing in the way. And finally, there is life itself, with all its twists and turns, its ups and downs.

My broken-hearted boy, I believe very few truly appreciate how elusive, fragile, and ephemeral true Love can be. But life goes on. Even as you long for and treasure what you had, regrets start piling up, threatening to swallow the precious and scarce time you have left on Planet Earth.

You must stay awake, my pained young soul. There are still the wonders of life to be enjoyed out there! Here is something to that effect that I hope will catch you before regret seeps in...

Mrs. V.'s words seem to leap off the page, wrapping me in their wisdom and urging me forward. In a trance, I continue reading:

"There is a Life to be Lived Out There"

Is there anything—anything—

that we seek

but never reach?

Is there someone—yes, that someone—

that we wait for,

but never find?

Is there anyone—anyone—

that we don't need,

but never leaves?

Is there a place—*that place*—

that we miss,

but never visit?

Is there a moment

that we want back,

but is gone forever?

Is there something—yes, something—

that we need,

but never seek?

Are there many, many things

that we must learn,

but never do?

Are there a few words—*those words*—

that we could or should have said,

but never did?

Is there such a person

that brings us joy and happiness,

but we don't appreciate them?

Is there a moment in time

that we regret,

but it's too late?

Is there a friend or loved one

that gives us so much,

without asking for anything in return,

but we don't value enough?

Is there a time, a moment, a place

in which we must stop or pause,

but we don't?

Is there a secret—*that secret*—

that we must have known or shared,

but never did?

Is there a past—*that past*—

that eventually will catch up with us,

but we never made amends to prevent it?

Is there a wait—a long wait—

that we endured to no avail,

and quit without trying, ever again?

Are there family and friends—yes! family and friends—

to be loved and cherished,

but we fall short?

Is there that little something

that we should have given,

but didn't?

Is there that true Love—yes, that Love—

waiting for us,

but we never go for it?

Is there a God

to fear, believe, and get close to,

but we fail to do so?

Is there happiness

to be found and enjoyed everywhere,

but we don't find it?

Is there inspiration

in many little, simple,

essential things,

and yet we aren't able to notice them?

Is there compassion

to gracefully give others,

but we can't feel it ourselves?

Is there forgiveness

to be dispensed,

but we don't act upon it?

Is there hope

for a better life and circumstances,

but we abandon it?

Is there so much

to be provided,

but we fail to do so?

Is there a lot needed by others—

yes! needed by others—

but we fail to recognize it?

Is there a future not to be postponed?

Is there a world—*our world*—

to be seized, to be squeezed, to be lived,

with spirit and desire?

Is there a life,

without ifs or buts,

without negative, regretful, or lingering grudges?

A world to give, receive, and enjoy—

a life, our life,

the only one we've got,

the only one we will ever have.

Yes! There is.

There is a life and a world,

ready to be lived,

waiting for all of us,

and it's happening right now.

*

Get out there and live. Don't cut yourself any slack, as being in Love with someone who is no longer there does not prevent you from living in full. Young Erasmus, life is not to be lived from the sidelines.

The bottom line is that we all want to be happy, but it is up to each of us to crack the riddle of joyousness. Rest assured, the key to solving it is never to detach but to be absolutely immersed in your life.

My dear, the following writing is something I treasure deeply. I always keep it handy and often return to it. I hope you will as well...

"Life's True Success is Being Happy"

(Life is Not a Spectator Sport)

Life is not a spectator's sport.

If you want to be entertained, you will,

as life offers countless options

from a never-ending carousel.

But once the show ends,

the thrill and fun escape in a hurry,

for being a spectator makes it impossible

to capture and retain

the passion and purpose of what others did.

Feeling good never lasts long

for the bystander.

The emptiness of a life without meaning

sinks in when you're alone

at night with your own pillow.

You can celebrate and rejoice

in the victories and defeats of others all you want,

but it lasts only a fleeting moment.

In the end, you are still you,

and nothing has changed.

Life, on the contrary, is a participant's sport,

where you play with passion and purpose,

bringing happiness and meaning.

These endure only as long as

you continue to churn and pour your heart

into everything you do.

A life with passion and purpose

is one where you are the main participant.

It's a life where you rise and fall, win and lose,

love and are loved in return,

where you give far more
than you receive or take.

It's a life where you dare, stumble, endure,
and never stop trying or give up!
A life endlessly curious and always learning.

It's a life in which you are totally immersed—
a life with meaning, a life in full!

In such a life, happiness is not pursued; it ensues,
a natural result of deliberate involvement
in wholesome living.

Because, in the end, what you truly seek is existential success.
What you are really after is vital achievement.
But success and achievement
never belong to spectators or bystanders.
They belong to life's players—
those who dare to be involved.

Life's true and highest success
is happiness:
an unceasing engagement,
a life perennially creating virtuous circles
that never end.

*

Young Erasmus, life's clock is ticking. Your life's battery is wasting away. You don't want to wake up one morning and realize your life is over. But let me caution you: after a breakup, one must be especially wary of falling in Love right afterward, particularly when driven by wealth or success. Such things can easily fool your heart.

Passions of that kind are not genuine; they are mere infatuations impregnated with the emptiness of material things. Instead of the comforting security they promise, they will only bring sadness and solitude, especially when you're alone at night with your own pillow.

I don't know if there is enough time left at Harvard, but if there is, do me a favor—and this time, do it for me:

FIND YOURSELF A SWEET, DEVOTED, & LOVING GIRLFRIEND.

Now, dear boy, one last matter of importance. I know we'll be seeing you back home soon after your graduation. I mention this because Mr. Morris, Mr. Newton, and I have prepared a special joint meeting just for you. By unanimous consent, we've named it 'The Final Session.' It will formally bring to an end your tutelage under this eclectic trio. Take great care of yourself, especially now, when you are so vulnerable. Farewell, my boy.

Love you dearly,

Mrs. V.

— ✦ —

The young woman with the curly blond hair cries silently, her emotions overwhelming her, and then she quietly slips away, unable to finish the class.

I understand so much more now, she thinks, wiping her tears as she realizes she'll miss him again.

Meanwhile, Professor Cromwell-Smith scans the room with humble gratitude, his gaze meeting the eyes of his students as they return to the present.

As the professor finishes reading Mrs. V.'s letter and the accompanying poems, he places the letter gently on the lectern. For a moment, he stands silently, allowing the weight of the words to settle over the room. The students remain transfixed, their expressions mirroring the emotional resonance of the story they have just heard. Professor Cromwell-Smith scans the crowd, his eyes reflecting both sorrow and gratitude, and smiles faintly.

"I'm open to your questions," he says, his tone inviting yet thoughtful, signaling the beginning of the discussion.

A hand rises near the center of the auditorium.

"Yes, go ahead," he encourages.

The hand belongs to Mia, a philosophy student with a particular interest in existential themes. "Professor, in There is a Life to be Lived Out There, the poem repeatedly asks, 'Is there...?' before answering in the affirmative at the end. Why did the author choose this structure, and what does it teach us about overcoming loss?"

The professor nods, his expression contemplative. "Mia, the structure mirrors the progression of grief and reflection. The rhetorical questions create a rhythm of introspection, guiding the reader to confront missed opportunities and regrets. By ending on a resounding 'Yes!' the poem reminds us that even in the face of loss, life holds infinite possibilities for renewal and joy. It's a call to action, urging us not to let loss define or paralyze us."

Mia smiles, clearly moved, as she jots down notes.

Another hand rises from the back of the room.

"Yes, in the back," he acknowledges.

The hand belongs to Caleb, a creative writing major known for his nuanced analyses. "Professor, in Life's True Success is Being Happy, the poem differentiates between spectators and participants in life. How does this idea relate to the concept of happiness as 'ensuing' rather than being pursued?"

The professor's face lights up with a small smile. "Excellent observation, Caleb. The distinction is crucial. Spectators are passive—they observe life but do not engage fully. Participants, however, immerse themselves in the highs and lows of life, creating meaning through their involvement. Happiness ensues because it is a byproduct of this deliberate engagement. It's not something we chase but something that arises naturally when we live with purpose and passion."

Caleb nods, visibly inspired by the explanation.

A third hand rises near the front.

"Yes, go ahead," the professor says, his gaze steady.

The hand belongs to Cynthia, a literature major specializing in resilience and healing. "Professor, in There is a Life to be Lived Out There, the poem emphasizes noticing life's simple joys and opportunities. How do we cultivate that awareness, especially in the midst of grief?"

The professor's expression softens. "Cynthia, grief often narrows our focus, making it difficult to see beyond the pain. To cultivate awareness, we must intentionally seek moments of gratitude and connection. It's about retraining our minds to recognize beauty and possibility, even in the smallest things—a smile, a kind word, or a quiet moment of reflection. Poetry is a powerful tool for this because it captures the essence of life's simple yet profound truths."

Cynthia nods, her pen flying across her notebook.

A final hand rises hesitantly near the side.

"Yes, go ahead," the professor encourages with a warm nod.

The hand belongs to William, an English major captivated by the interplay of form and meaning in literature. "Professor, in Life's True Success is Being Happy, the poem suggests that happiness is tied to meaning and involvement. How do we maintain this engagement in the face of life's inevitable challenges?"

The professor pauses briefly, his gaze reflective. "William, life's challenges test our resolve, but they also deepen our sense of purpose. Engagement requires persistence—continuing to strive, give, and connect, even when it feels difficult. It's about finding meaning in the effort itself, embracing the process as much as the outcome. Challenges, when faced with resilience and intention, often lead to greater fulfillment."

William leans back in his chair, clearly moved by the professor's insight.

"Next class will be our final session," the professor announces with a bittersweet smile, "as it was back then for me as well." His eyes sweep the crowd, but he realizes the young woman is no longer there.

She was here earlier. Hopefully, he thinks, *I'll catch up with her in the next session.*

As the class disperses, a group of students gathers around him.

"You look a lot better, sir," one of them observes.

"Indeed, I do," he replies with a nod. "It's certainly an unexpected bend in the road. Not long ago, I was close to death. I only had a few weeks to live.

But now, here I am—healthy again. That's life, you see. How else would I have been able to share my story with you?"

The Professor walks on, leaving the students with a collective sense of nostalgia. Though they eagerly anticipate Cromwell-Smith's final session, they can't help but wish his class would never end.

Chapter 16

The Happiness Formula

Erasmus Cromwell-Smith cycles through the campus streets, the early summer morning heat clinging to him like a second skin. Beads of sweat gather on his brow, and his shirt clings uncomfortably to his back. Yet, despite the oppressive warmth, he feels prepared. He pedals steadily, his mind clear and focused, ready to deliver the final chapter of his journey.

Arriving at the faculty building, he dismounts his bike with purpose and strides briskly toward the entrance. As he wipes his face with a wrinkled handkerchief, a small smile creeps onto his lips. The familiar buzz of anticipation fills the air, a feeling he has come to treasure.

Stepping into the classroom, he is greeted by a crowd even larger than the one at his previous session. People are sitting shoulder to shoulder, some even lining the aisles, their faces alight with expectation. He pauses for a moment, taking it all in, before offering a warm greeting.

"Good morning, everyone," he says, his voice carrying easily over the quiet murmur of the room.

As the last few students settle into their seats, he steps forward and sighs deeply, his expression a mix of gratitude and solemnity. "Over the past few months, you've accompanied me on a journey of discovery and wisdom. Poetry has been our telescope, allowing us to gaze at the vast universe of life. Today, we conclude with what proved to be one of the most memorable moments of my life."

— ✦ —

After graduating from Harvard, I return home for a final visit before relocating to America. Upon arrival, I receive a beautifully hand-painted invitation from my three mentors, summoning me to a grand final session where they will share additional wisdom and formally conclude their tutelage. Two days later, at the appointed hour, I enter Mr. M.'s store to find my mentors relaxed and smiling, their eyes radiating warmth. They greet me with effusive enthusiasm, including bear hugs, making me feel as though I have three additional parents. Mr. M. then unfolds a large sheet of paper and affixes it to a blackboard, revealing a triangle.

"Dear mentee, we present to you... The Happiness Formula. It is a fitting conclusion to our mentorship. Along with the many other lessons you've received, I am certain it will help you live an inspired and blissful life," he announces.

My mentors, having returned to their usual strict and articulate demeanor, observe me intently as I examine the geometric figure.

— ✦ —

Professor Cromwell-Smith pauses his narration to activate his and the auditorium's projector. In seconds, the image of a triangle illuminates the screen for all to see. He then resumes his story...

— ✦ —

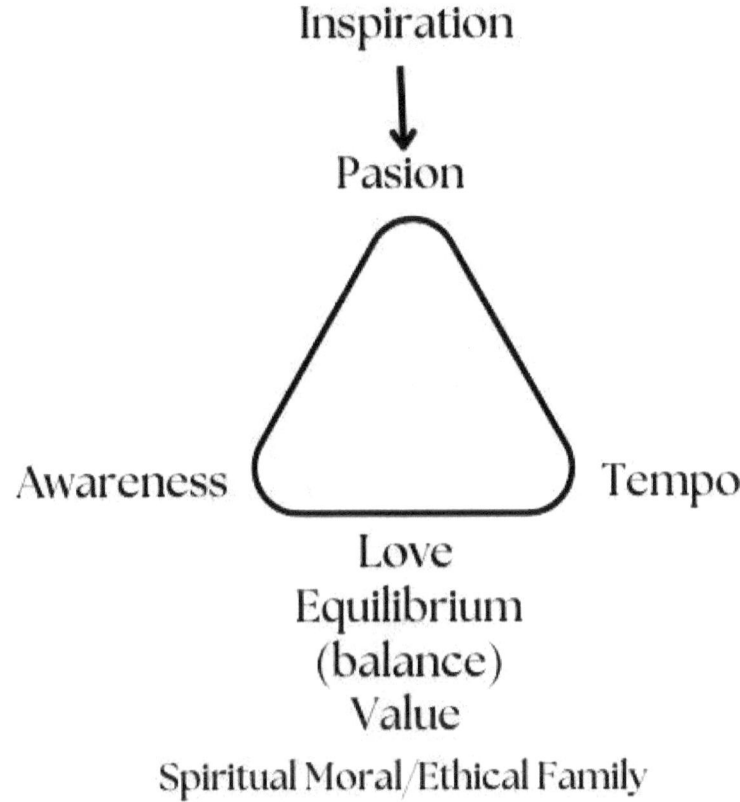

Inspiration
↓
Pasion

Awareness — Tempo

Love
Equilibrium
(balance)
Value
Spiritual Moral/Ethical Family

As I contemplate the figure in wonder, Mr. M. walks over and places his hands gently on my shoulder.

*"My eternally curious mentee, this figure reveals the three simultaneous attitudes to pursue in life for happiness to ensue. First, **Find your Passions** and live them fully. Second, **Maintain a Tempo** that aligns with your passions. And third, **Be Continuously Aware** and involved in your life—capture every moment and always be grateful for what you have. Below, you'll find the three essential building blocks that form the foundation of the Happiness Triangle.*

*"The first is **Love**, the key to unlocking your heart's treasures, powers, and strengths. The second is **Equilibrium** (balance), which is only possible through a stable emotional life acting as the support wire. The third is **Values**—family, moral, and spiritual principles— which form the root of the foundation. Together, these support the Happiness Triangle.*

"Finally, these three attitudes and foundational blocks are equally important. They are genuine sources of happiness, tightly connected and interdependent. This ecosystem of happiness is where inspiration is born and where it thrives. It propels us into a noble state of sublime desire and a highly functional condition that brings out the best in all of us.

"Always remember this, Erasmus: an inspired person is a wizard, a life wizard!" Mr. M. concludes gleefully.

"Young apprentice, the three of us have collaborated long and hard to create this final gift," Mr. N. adds, his tone solemn yet warm.

"It encompasses everything we have taught you. The triangle and this scribble outline a life path we all wish for you to follow."

He hands me the scribble and asks me to read it aloud. As I begin, I realize it contains the Happiness Formula in intricate detail, weaving together the lessons of my mentors into a cohesive and profound guide for life.

"The Happiness Formula"

Sometimes, we hope that simply by being alive,

happiness would be something we stumble upon

with utmost certainty.

But waiting for happiness to occur

by chance or luck

is the equivalent of expecting a reward without merit,

a prize without struggle or effort.

In other moments, <u>we wish</u>,

that happiness would be cast through a magic spell,

an incantation, a dream, or an illusion.

But there aren't too many sorcerers among us,

as 'life wizards' are very hard to find,

since the formula to morph dreams into happiness

is an exceptional virtue that very few possess.

Why is happiness so elusive,

unexpected, and ephemeral?

Can we ever find it, and if we do, would we recognize it?

If so, would we enjoy it?

Would we be appreciative of the privilege

and treasure it afterwards forever?

Some believe that

in order <u>to obtain happiness, it must be pursued</u>—

a deliberate pursuit to make it happen.

Others believe that <u>happiness ensues</u>,

as a 'consequence of' or is 'subsequent to,'

and therefore,

it is the outcome of the pertinent ways

we choose to live our lives.

Then there are those who claim

that happiness only manifests

in the face of tragedy and sorrow.

But pain, and suffering

rarely lead to ecstasy!

So, how do we find happiness?

Do we find it

through the intention and the desire to be happy?

Or do we discover it

along the paths and roads, we willfully take

towards the land of joy?

The answer lies in the Happiness Formula,

a synergy of three interconnected life attitudes

and three supporting pillars.

First,

find your **Passion**.

Passion is your life's engine.

Find what you love and do it,

recognize what you are passionate about

and stick to it, for it will greatly enhance the chances

that your strongest talents and abilities

will be put to good use,

and that you'll be performing,

in whatever your endeavor is,

to the best of your talents and abilities.

To do what you love is easy
and the amounts of effort, energy, determination,
discipline and persistence required
become irrelevant, without obstacles.

When you do what you love,
it brings you the greatest amount of
satisfaction, pride, and sense of accomplishment.

When you do what you are passionate about,
you'll never find ifs, buts, or excuses to get started,
nor would you talk yourself into inaction
or avoid your duties and responsibilities,
but to be a master at anything
takes time, growth, maturity, determination,
failure, innate talent, and passion!

Second,
productivity requires **Tempo**.
Tempo is the RPM of your life engine.
It is the pace at which you execute the delivery.
It is about how efficient you are.
Without rhythm and tempo,
you're quickly overwhelmed
and your life's engine slows down.
In today's world, an engine without the proper RPMs,
overheats and overloads in a heartbeat.
To multitask
and cope with the pace of modern life,

to be highly functional

and to be able to sustain a high tempo,

you'll need to constantly re-train yourself

so, you can perform at a tempo

commensurate with your goals.

And **Third**,

being alive requires **Awareness**.

<u>Capture your life through awareness.</u>

We cannot be bystanders in our own lives,

we must be totally involved,

we must be active participants,

capturing each moment

precisely as it is dealt to us.

We can't postpone our lives.

We can't afford to let our precious time

on planet Earth,

be just about day after day rolling

on top of each other

whilst we watch in a catatonic, zombie-like state.

We must be eternally grateful

for what we have and receive every day

and for our travel companions in life.

Passivity is out of the question,

action is an existential imperative!

Finally, life gives us minute signs,

tiny but crucially important messages

that contain clues

that without awareness, we may not be able to see,

as if we were walking blindly through it.

One thing is absolutely certain:

these light bulbs will be scattered

along our journey's path,

sometimes as symbols of life,

sometimes as calls to action

or simply as warning signs,

but all of them waiting for us

to be spotted and figured out as if they were puzzles

that, once solved, will light up our way,

enabling us to move forward in life,

with a fully lit road ahead of us.

But three **Supporting Blocks** are needed for happiness to thrive:

First,

you need **Love** to be happy.

Love is the foundation of happiness.

True Love is when

your heart does not belong to you.

Focus on giving out of your heart

and do it with passion.

Second,

you need **Equilibrium** between fun and work.

Set and keep your priorities in balance.

Balance only exists through

a solid emotional life underneath.

Equilibrium is born out of practice

and a healthy lifestyle.

And **Third**,

happiness thrives on solid **Values**.

Character and virtue are built from

spiritual, moral, and family values

through faith, truth, honesty

and unbreakable bonds of Love.

Out of his happiness ecosystem of three attitudes,

(Passion, Tempo, and Awareness)

and the three foundations supporting them,

(Love, Balance, and Values)

is where Inspiration is born,

where Inspiration thrives,

and propels us into

a noble condition of sublime desire

and a highly functional state

that brings out the best in all of us,

generating continuous happiness.

Inspiration may well be

the only source of continuous happiness.

Inspiration is the stuff of wizards,

life wizards!

*

As I finish, Mr. M. steps forward.

"Erasmus, here is a summary of the Happiness Formula," he says in a business-like tone, as though attempting to distance himself from his emotions. Then, he begins to read...

<u>Love, Equilibrium (Balance) and Values</u>
are the foundations of
<u>Awareness, Passion, and Tempo.</u>

When we truly love,
when we have a balanced lifestyle,
when we live according to our family,
moral/ethical, and spiritual values,
we have the keys to continuous happiness.

Then,

When we do what we love and do it with passion,
when we live with intensity, rhythm, and tempo,
when we capture, squeeze,
and 'live' every moment we are alive,
and when we focus on giving
and do it as well with passion,

WE ARE SIMPLY HAPPY!

Each of them is
a true and legitimate source of happiness.

— ✦ —

But the ultimate source of constant happiness

is a noble state of sublime desire,

a heightened level of hypersensitivity,

that brings the best out of all of us

and this is,

INSPIRATION!

This leads us to be inspired,

to be Inspired Persons, life wizards,

and to live

AN INSPIRED LIFE!

*

And that's it—my tutelage has ended. My three mentors gather around me, and in complete silence, each shakes my hand firmly, albeit briefly. Aside from a very effusive kiss on the cheek from Mrs. V., the moment is solemn and deeply meaningful.

As I leave my melancholic mentors, I am overwhelmed by an immense sense of pride and gratitude for each one of them.

"I am ready for life. World, here I go…!" I declare, my parting words carrying both resolve and excitement, as the trio waves from the doorstep of Mr. M.'s shop. I walk upon the cobblestones, heading home, ready to embrace whatever lies ahead.

— ✦ —

As Professor Cromwell-Smith concludes the reading of *The Happiness Formula* and its accompanying poems, the room is bathed in silence, the audience utterly captivated by the profound wisdom shared.

He pauses, his gaze sweeping across the students, allowing the weight of the lesson to settle in their minds. Finally, he steps back from the lectern, his expression inviting yet reflective.

"I'm open to questions," he says, his voice steady but warm.

A hand rises immediately from the middle of the auditorium.

"Yes, go ahead," he encourages.

The hand belongs to Caroline, a philosophy student known for her inquisitive nature.

"Professor, in The Happiness Formula, passion is described as the 'engine of life.' How can we discover what truly ignites that passion within us?"

"That's an excellent question, Caroline," the professor replies, his tone thoughtful.

"Finding your passion requires a willingness to explore and reflect. It's about noticing what brings you joy, energy, and fulfillment. Often, the activities that make you lose track of time or that challenge you in meaningful ways hold the key to your passions. Pay attention to those moments and let them guide you."

Caroline nods, jotting down notes with a contemplative expression.

Another hand rises from the back of the room.

"Yes, in the back," the professor acknowledges.

The hand belongs to Leonardo, a creative writing major with a flair for metaphor.

"Professor, tempo is emphasized as crucial for productivity in the poem. How do we find a balance between maintaining a high tempo and avoiding burnout?"

"Great question, Leo," the professor responds.

"Tempo isn't about constant speed; it's about finding a rhythm that aligns with your goals and abilities. It involves setting boundaries, prioritizing tasks, and making time for rest and reflection. When you understand your own limits and work within them, you can maintain a tempo that sustains rather than depletes you."

Leonardo smiles visibly inspired.

A third hand rises near the front. "Yes, go ahead," he says, turning to the student. The hand belongs to Peter, a psychology major captivated by discussions of self-awareness.

"Professor, in The Happiness Formula, awareness is described as essential for living fully. How do we cultivate such awareness in our daily lives?"

The professor's expression softens.

"Pete, cultivating awareness begins with being present. Mindfulness practices like meditation, journaling, or even a daily gratitude list can help. It's also about noticing the small details—the way light filters through a window or the warmth of a kind interaction. When you actively engage with the world around you, you deepen your awareness and enrich your experience of life."

Peter nods, his pen gliding quickly over her notebook.

One more hand rises hesitantly from the center of the auditorium.

"Yes, go ahead," the professor encourages with a slight smile.

The hand belongs to Daniel, an English major intrigued by the concept of inspiration.

"Professor, the poem describes inspiration as the ultimate source of happiness. How do we ensure that inspiration isn't fleeting but becomes a continuous force in our lives?"

"An insightful question, Daniel," the professor says.

"Inspiration flourishes when you remain curious and open to new experiences. It's about nurturing relationships, pursuing knowledge, and challenging yourself to grow. Gratitude also plays a role—acknowledging the beauty and meaning in your life creates fertile ground for sustained inspiration."

Daniel leans back, clearly moved by the response, his thoughts lingering on the professor's words.

As the questions wind down, The pedagogue glances at the clock, his expression softening into a bittersweet smile.

"Thank you for your thoughtful questions, my dear students. The formula we discussed today isn't just a guide; it's a way of life. Carry it with you as you navigate your own paths. Remember, happiness is not something to be found—it's something to be cultivated."

Professor Cromwell-Smith is elated but emotionally spent, as if he has just crossed the finish line of a long, arduous race where all the competitors were different shades of himself. He knows he is done—he has run out of words.

"Thank you all. This was…" He gestures with both hands like an orchestra conductor, inviting the audience to join him. They understand immediately, and together, they proclaim in unison:

"INSANELY AWESOME!"

With a big, broad smile, he bows his head in respect. He has nothing else to add—but life does. As the echo of their shared chant fades, the auditorium erupts in applause and cheers. That is when he sees her in the crowd—the young, curly, blond-haired girl raising her hand, jumping up and down, trying to catch his attention.

Interrupting the applause, the Professor raises his hand and calls out, "One moment, please!" Turning to her, he asks, "How can I help you, young lady?"

Abruptly, she begins speaking, her words rushing out as if there is no tomorrow.

"Professor Cromwell-Smith, I first came to one of your classes last year when you were reading a wonderful Pablo Neruda poem. I promised myself then that I would attend your entire course this year. It turned out to be one of the most transcendental decisions I've ever made. I didn't know then—none of us did—that you would veer off the curriculum and share your life with us through poetry. From the very first class, a picture began to emerge. Long before you even spoke of falling in Love, I knew," she says, her voice trembling with emotion.

"Professor, my mom has never stopped loving you. That's why I didn't have the strength to attend one of your last classes, as I assumed correctly that it would be about the breakup. My mother's parents simply did not want her to marry you; they wanted her to marry someone they had chosen since her childhood. That's how she came to marry my father and had three children, of whom I am the youngest.

"When my father passed last summer, after five years of agonizing illness, the three of us—her children—decided to find the man she has always adored, revered, and worshiped: you. God works in mysterious ways, Professor. It didn't take long to find you and, in my case, to get to know you and understand the man my mother considers her other half. Her only true Love in life." The knot in

Professor Cromwell-Smith's throat renders him momentarily speechless, unable even to breathe.

As he gathers his strength to respond, another unexpected bend in the road reveals itself.

The voice from the past comes from the very top of the stands: "Erasmus!"

His heart skips as he looks up. There she is, for the first time in over forty years. The familiar voice trembles, carrying a touch of hesitation and anguish. It is deeply emotional—primal even. It feels like both a lament and a plea coming straight from the longing heart of his other half, saturated with pure joy and an undeniable love that time never diminished.

"I am right here," she proclaims.

"I am right here, my Love," she affirms, as time stands still and true love, undeterred by decades of separation, graces them both once more.

Book II

GENIALITY

Chapter 1

Optimism

Royal Cambridge Scholastic Institute, 2018
(Erasmus and Victoria's Campus Home)

"Don't take too long, my love. I'm waiting for you," Victoria teases with a wink as she sends him off to class with a warm kiss and a hug. Professor Erasmus Cromwell-Smith is a new man. His once sad demeanor and worn-out, unkempt appearance, have vanished. Now, he wears the unmistakable look of love! The hand of a woman caring for him is evident, from his impeccable grooming to his perfectly pressed attire.

The morning sun glints off the polished frame of his bicycle as he cycles through the familiar streets, his demeanor a reflection of the inner transformation he has undergone. Arriving at the faculty building, he dismounts, his stride confident as he makes his way toward the auditorium. Stepping inside, he is met with the sight of an auditorium at full capacity, every seat taken and an air of eager anticipation filling the room.

Royal Cambridge Scholastic Institute, 2018
(University's Auditorium)

"Good morning. How's everyone?"

"Awesome, Professor Cromwell-Smith!" reply the highly motivated students, their enthusiasm mirroring the professor's own. His heart swells with joy as he smiles at the sea of attentive faces.

His students, clearly familiar with his favorite word, have already set the tone for an extraordinary session.

"I simply ask that you always be on time—no excuses," he announces, gazing intently at the crowd to underscore his point.

"Alright, let us begin then.

"The love of my life, Vicky, and I have reunited after forty years, thanks partly to one of my students in last year's class."

Cheers and applause erupt, momentarily interrupting the professor. Smiling, he waits patiently for the excitement to subside.

"The enabling student turned out to be Vicky's youngest daughter. Her participation in my class was fortuitous, as was her realization of who I was. Allow me to explain.

"Last year, at this time, I had been diagnosed with terminal brain cancer, which, thanks to a revolutionary treatment, is now in remission."

The entire class rises to their feet, clapping and cheering in joy. Cromwell-Smith responds with a humble smile and a slight nod. After a while, feeling slightly uncomfortable with the attention, he interrupts the crowd.

"Last year, assuming I didn't have much time left, I decided to change the class format into an evocative reminiscence of my life through the prism of poetry. Then, as the sessions progressed, Vicky's daughter realized who I was and decided to tell her mom that she had found me."

"Is the student your real daughter, Professor?" asks a student from the audience.

The professor pauses, placing a hand on his chin, his expression startled. "Let me explain, please," he says softly. Without directly answering the question at first, he continues.

"Years later, after her husband passed away, her children were compelled to find me."

"Class, throughout my years of solitude, even amidst the turmoil of unforeseen events, the ups and downs, and the anxieties of life, I never lost my optimism. That optimism is what we'll explore together this year.

"The story you're about to hear is one of the ultimate, inexorable triumph of optimism, despite the unexpected bends in life's road. We begin today with an overture of our academic journey. Please allow me to read to you an ode to the power of optimism."

"Optimism"
Optimism is a deliberate attitude
where we choose to contemplate life and its people,
through their best lights, colors, and mantels.

It is the predisposition to look, search, and find,
the better angle and perspective
on everything and everyone.
It is the natural inclination to visualize,
the best a person or circumstance has to offer.

It is that refreshing enthusiasm we bring
to every one of life's occurrences,
to any and each of its moments.

It is the unquenchable certainty,

that there always is

a shinier side and a brighter spot to be found.

It is that steadfast and indomitable self-confidence,

that there always is,

a better outcome possible,

in-store,

waiting for us.

Optimism is also,

that gentle, benign, and immutable belief,

that there is goodness on the other side of evil,

that there is strength in the face of weakness,

that there is virtue behind every flaw,

that there is an opportunity

when apparently there are none,

that there is incandescence in obscurity,

and luminescence in darkness.

Those blessed with optimism

live in another world, live an alternate life,

contemplating it all

with a permanent twinkle in their eyes.

Optimists are always

cheerful, self-motivated, fiercely determined,

and seemingly possessed with a secret elixir

that wipes away
pessimism, prejudice, negativism,
and grudges, from their lives.

Optimism always obliterates
'The loser before the start' syndrome.

With optimism, we see past, or right through,
everything and everyone.

Civilization has been built on optimism.
Progress is driven by optimism.
Every single human invention, creation,
or advancement,
has been born
of the candor, the innocence,
and the ingenuity of optimists.

No transcendental milestone
in humanity's journey
has ever been reached, or will be achieved,
without the unstoppable drive of optimism.
Authentic, legitimate, and genuine optimism
always marches forward—
undaunted, undeterred, and unyielding.

Optimism is utterly oblivious
to criticism, rejection, doubt, or skepticism.

Authentic optimism is also malleable—,

the more demanding the goals, obstacles, or challenges,

the bigger genuine optimism becomes.

Those bitten by the bug of optimism,

wear 'good blinders,' immune

to contrarians and naysayers.

In their own way

optimists intentionally distort reality

until the alternate vision

becomes the new reality.

Then, they enhance whatever is available,

through a perennially benevolent and candid vision,

of what, may, could, would, might,

and inexorably,

under such state and condition, will be.

*

As Professor Cromwell-Smith completes the reading of the scribble, optimism fills the air. His gaze is profound, and his smile serene as he pauses, allowing stillness to settle over the class. For a few seconds, absolute silence engulfs the auditorium, and the professor lets the message of optimism take root before continuing.

When he finishes, his smile lingers, and the weight of his words hangs in the air. A student raises a hand and asks, "Professor, how can we cultivate that kind of optimism in our daily lives?"

Another student follows, "What do you do when it feels like optimism is hard to hold onto?"

The professor nods thoughtfully before replying, "Great questions! To cultivate optimism, start by actively seeking the brighter side of situations, as I mentioned in the poem. Look for the best in people and circumstances, and remember that even in darkness, there is always potential for light.

"When optimism feels distant, remind yourself that it's a deliberate choice. Practice visualizing better outcomes. Optimism isn't blind; it's about holding onto that 'unquenchable certainty' that something good is always waiting to be discovered."

He pauses, his voice growing steadier. "Optimism is a deliberate attitude. If we're not born with it, or if it's not our natural inclination, we must learn it, teach ourselves to embrace it, and practice until it becomes second nature.

"The gift of life itself is the driving force of optimism. Always remember this: optimism is the key to opening many of life's doors— doors only an optimist can see. Optimism often holds the winning hand in the game of life.

His words resonate deeply, commanding the full attention of his class. Smiling and ready to wrap up the introductory session, he brings the discussion full circle.

"Today's session began a few months ago, just as we were finishing the final class of the 2017 academic year. We were about to leave when her daughter, Sarah, found me. Then, out of nowhere, the love of my life, Vicky, appeared unannounced, and called my name from the stands.

"This year's journey begins right at that unforgettable moment."

— ✦ —

Royal Cambridge Scholastic Institute, 2017
(University's Auditorium)
Last Class of the Previous Academic Year

The voice from the past comes from the very top of the stands.

"Erasmus!"

His heart skips as he looks up. There she is, for the first time in over forty years. The familiar voice trembles, carrying a touch of hesitation and anguish. It is deeply emotional—primal even. It feels like both a lament and a plea coming straight from the longing heart of his other half, saturated with pure joy and an undeniable love that time never diminished.

"I am right here," she proclaims.

"I am right here, my Love," she affirms, as time stands still and true love, undeterred by decades of separation, graces them both once more.

Victoria!" shouts Professor Cromwell-Smith, his lower lip trembling.

Then, suddenly, he takes off, running uncontrollably up the auditorium stairs.

"Victoria," he mumbles softly, this time with a broken voice overcome by emotion, as he climbs two steps at a time.

At first, Vicky is frozen in shock when she sees Erasmus running toward her, calling her name for the first time in four decades. Then, as if awakened from a daze, she begins running down the stairs. Moments later, Vicky crashes into him. With both his arms holding her tightly, Erasmus instantly becomes, once again, the safe and protective harbor she has longed for her entire life—a place where she never feels unprotected, sad, or alone.

In a moment of pure impulsiveness, they lose control in front of the entire class.

The auditorium falls completely silent as every single soul in attendance becomes transfixed by the sheer force of love manifesting before their eyes. It is as if the love story they had learned about during the previous academic year has come alive, unfolding like a movie before them.

Staring intensely at one another, Vicky and Erasmus are so close their noses almost touch. They pant, cry, and smile, overwhelmed by raw emotion. Unable to look away from one another, they are oblivious to the two hundred-plus students.

Erasmus tenderly takes Victoria's hand, and together, they exit the auditorium, walking deliberately.

Royal Cambridge Scholastic Institute, 2017
(Campus Forest)

Once outside, under the canopy of the moist campus forest, their restraint dissolves. They begin kissing one another's faces in quick, fervent bursts of indomitable passion. Time feels surreal and intensely charged for the reunited lovers.

Erasmus and Victoria have no time to spare—they succumb to the power of the present, savoring every second as if tomorrow may never come.

Boston, 2017
(Downtown, Riverside Walk)

Hours later, as they stroll through the city streets, Vicky and Erasmus exist in their own world. The past releases its grip, and calmness settles over them. Together, they find comfort in the present and begin to step into their future as one.

"Vicky, your daughter changed my life today," Erasmus says, his voice filled with gratitude. "It's not only that, by bringing you, she gave me the greatest gift a man still in love could ever receive, but she also paid a beautiful and inspiring homage to the devotion and selflessness you showed your dying husband. It's something I will never forget, and something I feel I must memorialize."

Vicky gently places two fingers over his lips and whispers, "Shhhh, my love. This moment is only ours and ours alone."

In a trance, Erasmus suddenly pulls his worn-out leather briefcase open and furiously begins to write on a crumpled piece of paper. Vicky knows better than to interrupt. Instead, she watches him in awe, just as she did all those years ago.

When he finishes, Erasmus looks up and begins to read the scribble to her, his voice heavy with passion and emotion, each word expressing how deeply he values what she did for her dying husband.

"Small Sacrifices"

Sometimes, life presents us
with seemingly impossible tasks
and insurmountable challenges, so demanding,
that we don't really know where to begin,

much less if we can respond or live up to them,

or even if we will be able

to hold on to the very end.

Sometimes, life presents us

with seemingly huge sacrifices,

which, more often than not,

come dressed in tragedy and pain.

Those moments test our entire self.

Every task expected of us

is tough, trying, unsavory, and even filthy

to execute and endure.

These calls of duty

present themselves to us

as tough sacrifices—

ones when every inch and instinct

of our ego and selfishness

reject and easily find excuses

to avoid or even start anything at all.

They include the people close to us,

who cannot take care of themselves,

or are handicapped, even terminally ill

and need assistance day in and day out—

for a while, for long, or the remainder

of their lives,

they are entirely in our hands.

Then there are those,
that are deprived of their freedom,
and depend and rely on our love, strength,
and support,
as we depend on theirs.

There are also those who are hungry or homeless,
or those in need of guidance, mentoring, tutoring,
coaching or life lessons,
but none have anything to offer us in the way
of material things.

These are some of those moments,
when life and God,
come calling to test us on
how good we are inside.

What is our worthiness
as human beings?
What is our heart really made of?
How ready are we to sacrifice and give much
without honestly expecting anything in return?

In reality, these are just small sacrifices—
and in a way, gifts—
that are asked and required of us
in return for all of those

that we receive and have received in the past.

Sometimes, life presents us

with seemingly huge sacrifices,

that are not what they seem.

They are opportunities

for us to pay forward,

the greatest gift of all,

one already given to us in kind:

The gift of life.

*

The gentle river breeze carries away Erasmus' beautiful words, and Victoria looks at him with teary eyes filled with immense gratitude. She tenderly caresses his face, as if reassuring herself that he's truly there.

"What's next for us?" Erasmus suddenly asks, his voice wavering as the painful memories of the past begin to creep in, threatening to take hold of his rational self.

Victoria notices his doubt and intervenes. "Life, Erasmus. That's what's ahead of us—life together, finally," she says softly. Taking his hand in hers, she squeezes tightly and looks straight into his eyes. With quiet but resolute certainty, she reassures him, "I will never leave you again, my love. Never."

The infatuated couple continues their walk along Main Street and then by the Charles River. The star-studded night serves as a celestial canopy over their private amphitheater. Vicky is in a trance of effortless happiness, while Erasmus, despite wanting to believe her with all his heart, remains full of doubts and fear.

— ✦ —

Royal Cambridge Scholastic Institute, 2018
(University's Auditorium)

The bell has been ringing for a while, snapping the class and the professor back to the present. A fitting conclusion awaits them.

"Class," begins Professor Cromwell-Smith, his voice steady and warm, "that magical day when Vicky and I reunited after such a long time is a testament to the unstoppable power of unconditional love and the inexorable triumph of optimism in life. For this reason, you must never let your optimism slip or wane.

"Remember, however, that optimism is a deliberate attitude. You choose to be an optimist because you want to be one. It's about training yourself to look for the brighter, better angle and the best outcome in life and people.

"In our next class, we'll return to my Harvard days in the 1970s and revisit how Victoria and I fell in love. I had written about the good news to one of my childhood mentors, Mrs. V., a beautiful, diminutive antiquarian from my hometown in Wales. She wrote back with priceless wisdom and precious advice about love but also complained that I hadn't told her how I won Vicky's heart.

"When we return, I'll share my reply to Mrs. V. as I tried to satisfy her queries. That said, I appreciate the enthusiasm in this room. If there's anything you're curious about or need further explanation on, please ask."

A hand rises confidently near the center of the auditorium.

"Yes, go ahead," he encourages.

The hand belongs to Dieter, a philosophy major, known for his thoughtful inquiries. His piercing green eyes shine with curiosity as he asks, "Professor, in *Optimism*, you describe it as a 'deliberate attitude.' How can we turn that into a consistent habit in our daily lives, especially when negativity surrounds us?"

"That's an excellent question, Dieter," the professor responds. "Optimism is a mindset that requires cultivation. Start small—focus on recognizing the brighter side of even mundane moments. Keep a gratitude journal to note positive events, no matter how insignificant they may seem. Over time, this practice becomes second nature, and you'll find yourself predisposed to seeking the good in life." He smiles before adding, "Optimism isn't about ignoring negativity but choosing to engage with life in a way that highlights its possibilities."

A second hand rises toward the back of the room.

"Yes, in the back," the professor acknowledges.

This hand belongs to Bill, a literature major from Boston with a love for storytelling and character analysis. His mop of dark brown hair bounces slightly as he leans forward. "Professor, in the poem, you state, 'There is goodness on the other side of evil.' How can we maintain that optimism when life feels overwhelming, and finding the brighter side seems impossible?"

The professor nods thoughtfully. "A poignant question, Bill. Optimism does not mean denial of difficulties—it's about resilience. When life feels overwhelming, pause and remind yourself of past challenges you've overcome. Reflecting on your inner strength and support system can help restore your faith in better outcomes. Optimism, as the poem conveys, is that 'steadfast belief' that light exists even in darkness—it's a deliberate choice to search for it."

Another hand rises near the front row.

"Yes, go ahead," says the professor with a welcoming smile.

The hand belongs to Leticia, a sociology major. Her strong and determined voice matches her personality as she asks, "Professor, in the poem, you state that 'civilization was built on optimism.' Could you elaborate on how this collective optimism connects to our individual actions?"

"An excellent question, Leticia," he replies, his tone reflective. "Humanity's greatest achievements—art, science, social justice—were all driven by individuals daring to believe in a better future. On a personal level, optimism fuels our ability to act boldly, take risks, and inspire change. When you approach challenges with optimism, you contribute to a collective spirit of progress, proving that individual hope can have far-reaching effects."

Leticia nods, jotting down notes with a look of satisfaction.

Another hand rises near the middle.

"Yes, please," he encourages, pointing toward the student.

The hand belongs to Jodie, a psychology major with a focus on emotional resilience. Her medium frame and blond hair frame deep blue eyes full of thought. "Professor, in *Optimism*, you say that 'optimists live in another world.' How can we help others find that world, especially those who have been deeply hurt or disillusioned?"

"That's a noble question, Jodie," the professor says with a gentle smile. "The best way to help others is by embodying optimism yourself. Lead by example—be the light they can follow. Share stories of resilience and success, offer a listening ear, and remind them of their strengths. Sometimes, simply being there for someone can reignite the spark they've lost. Optimism, after all, is contagious."

Jodie smiles, clearly moved by his response.

With the final question answered, a sense of closure settles over the room, signaling the end of the lively discussion. Professor Cromwell-Smith clasps his hands together and gazes out at his students with pride. "Thank you, my dear students, for your thoughtful questions and insights. Remember, optimism is both a choice and a practice. Nurture it, and it will nurture you in return."

The students begin gathering their belongings, their expressions pensive yet inspired. Several linger briefly, their gazes following the professor as he exits the auditorium, his mind already contemplating the next session.

"Remember, 'Those possessed with optimism live in another world.' Let's invite others into that world with us," the professor concludes warmly before wrapping up the class. "Thank you all for your thoughtful questions. Remember, optimism is a journey we embark on together. Let's support one another in finding the light, no matter how dim it may seem. That's all for today. See you next week."

As the professor leaves the auditorium, some students react to what they've just witnessed. "I wouldn't have missed this course for the world," gushes a second-timer. "He seems like a new man—happy and full of energy," agrees another. "There's only one way to describe it. True love found him," an enthusiastic young woman hypothesizes. "Again," finishes another, smiling knowingly.

And that is the last word as the students nod in agreement, each pondering their own journeys toward finding true love.

Chapter 2

Of Fate and Fairy Tales

Royal Cambridge Scholastic Institute, 2018
(Erasmus and Victoria's Campus Home)

"Dear, don't you ever leave my life," Victoria whispers, her fingers gently caressing Erasmus' forehead. The infatuated couple cuddle in bed at first, but as their desire overflows once more, their two bodies fuse into one; it seemingly lasts forever. They can't get enough of each other in their insatiable, passionate crusade.

Erasmus kisses her forehead as Victoria sleeps, contemplating her ethereal and tranquil beauty. He chuckles softly, marveling at his own fortune. Moments later, shortly before 6:00 AM, he quietly leaves the house.

The early morning air is cool, tinged with the faint scent of dew clinging to the grass. Today feels different, charged with an energy Erasmus can't quite name. Opting for an invigorating jog instead of his usual bike ride to campus, he finds himself striding along the hilly, tree-lined back roads of the university grounds. The rhythm of his steps matches the rising sun, becoming a melody of thought, carrying him through moments of longing, joy, and gratitude. As he approaches the faculty building, Erasmus feels the weight of the day ahead—a story to share, lessons to impart, and hearts to inspire.

After running for over an hour along the hilly, tree-lined back roads of campus, his thoughts drift back in time, revisiting long-dormant places of the heart. The sight of the faculty buildings on the horizon fills him with both anticipation and calm. Though Victoria is only a short distance away, a wave of longing strikes him unexpectedly, a testament to the depth of their bond. Soon, he will share their courtship and life together with his class—a thought that fills him with warmth.

A long run, a bracing shower, and a few moments of quiet reflection bring him fully into the present. Refreshed and composed, he makes his way to the auditorium, his steps purposeful and steady.

Royal Cambridge Scholastic Institute, 2018
(University's Auditorium)

"How's everyone today?" he asks, his voice bright.

"Insanely awesome!" the student body replies, their enthusiasm drawing a smile from the professor.

A pause follows, then an unexpected collective response erupts.

"Insanely awesome!" the students echo in unison.

"Awesome!" he replies with matching enthusiasm.

"Before we go back in time, as this is a love story, allow me to read you a fitting and profound overture to it," he announces, his voice earnest as he begins to read.

"Of Fate and Fairy Tales"

Where does a fairy tale begin?

How does it start?

How is it created?

Where can we find one?

And once we do, how do we turn it on?

When is it that our life's pages
shine and sparkle in all their splendor,
and our hearts suddenly fill
with magical dreams
and reciprocate love?

It is commonly said and acknowledged that fate is,
predictable, inexorable, ineludible,
inescapable, inevitable;
making us mere terrestrial beings
careening through the existential universe,
towards pre-planned destinations or outcomes.

Such a belief is not only false,
but it is crucially wrong,
as it derails our spirits under the conviction
that our lives occur in some sort
of pre-ordained fashion.

But fate is just a banal excuse,
dressed under a fake historical costume of legitimacy.
Its only purpose is to justify a non-deliberate life
lacking meaning and purpose.

The fact is, we create our own fairy tales.
The burden is on us, no one else.

We can make a fairy tale out of anything,

anyone, or anywhere.

Life is a never-ending fairy tale if we make it such.

There is extraordinaire, magnificence, splendorness,

felicitousness and awesomeness,

around every corner, right in front of us,

as well as inside each one of us,

ready to be uncovered and released,

as long as we are able to see life and its people

with a touch of candor, ingenuity, and good faith.

And yet, there is nothing accidental or fortuitous

about fairy tales.

Many of us think that someday

we are going to run into

a fairy godmother, a wizard, an enchantress,

or even a prince on a white horse,

or a goddess of virtue, beauty, and strength,

that will sweep us off our feet.

What we must realize, though,

is that we are each one of those characters already,

as they all reside inside our own spirits.

So, how do we turn a fairy tale on?

First and foremost, with an unquenchable desire,

to live, love, and dream.

Also,

we can by recognizing and appreciating

the inner beauty that resides in each human being,

no matter who they are.

And by understanding that,

no matter how dire they may seem,

every circumstance, every moment,

every challenge, obstacle, or hardship,

no matter how unsavory they may seem;

every failure, defeat, or rejection,

no matter how deflating they may appear;

they all have not only existential value

but also enchantment,

for us to discover, enjoy, and experience.

*

Professor Cromwell-Smith finishes his overture, blissful and ready to guide his class into a real fairytale.

"As I mentioned in our previous class, one of my greatest mentors back in Wales was an extraordinary antiquarian I fondly called Mrs. V. Spirited and cheerful, Victoria Sutton-Leigh was my biggest cheerleader and played an instrumental role in shaping my life as I grew up.

"When I wrote to her, sharing the news that I had fallen in love with Vicky, she replied with a question: what were those 'little gestures' that had won Victoria's heart? That is precisely where we will begin today—answering Mrs. V.'s question by journeying back to where Vicky and I fell in love: the sands of time.

"Today, we'll pick up the story at Mrs. V.'s antique bookstore in the heart of Wales, right after she receives my response to her inquiry. It begins like this ..."

— ✦ —

Hay-On-Wye, Wales, 1976
(Mrs. V.'s Antique Bookshop for the Young)

On a quiet Friday afternoon, Mrs. V. eagerly awaited my response. When the mailman arrived, she wasted no time, stepping outside to retrieve her correspondence with palpable anticipation.

Harvard, 1976
(Letter from Erasmus and Vicky to Mrs. V.)

"Mrs. V., you were right. I was so excited to tell you about winning her heart that I completely skipped over the story of how I did it. Please forgive me. But this time, I've left nothing out—not even Vicky—as both of us are narrating it to you," Erasmus writes, bringing a wide smile to Mrs. V.'s face. Her delight soon turns to surprise as she realizes the words that follow are from Vicky herself.

— ✦ —

Dear Mrs. V.,

Greetings from New England. I've heard so much about you—all of it wonderful. I want you to know that I love Erasmus with all my heart. True love has indeed found us, and I adore him. Mrs. V., you've done a marvelous job mentoring and shaping your endearing, precious boy. I sincerely hope to meet you in the near future.
Yours truly,

Vicky—the enchantress who stole your beloved mentee's heart.

— ✦ —

Mrs. V. is deeply touched by Erasmus and Vicky's introductory words. Yet, her heart is wracked with anticipation as she prepares to read the rest of the letter. Despite her excitement, she doesn't abandon her cherished routine. She walks over to her old Chesterfield armchair, where she had spent countless hours reading to young Erasmus. Once settled comfortably, she opens the letter and begins to read:

— ✦ —

Dearest Mrs. V.,

This is the story of how Vicky and I found our way to each other's hearts. At the start, it begins with little notes that I manage to drop here and there, continually surprising her while I often catch a glimpse of her reaction.

However, it doesn't begin smoothly. Her initial response is defensive, as though I've trespassed on her private space. Yet, she never tears the notes up, which tells me that her heart is listening—somehow.

The second setback comes as outright rejection. Her reactions grow cold and expressionless, as though she has erected a shield between her rational and emotional self. Little do I know, I'm about to learn an important life lesson: that defensiveness or aggression often stems from fear and insecurity.

— ✦ —

Note #1
(University Cafeteria)
"Your laughter makes me chuckle."

Vicky turns her head and scans the crowd, but she cannot identify the culprit. Frustrated, she folds the handwritten note left on top of her diary.

"This isn't funny, guys. I'm nobody's clown," she complains to her classmates in the cafeteria. Her statement is met with incredulous stares. Embarrassed, she stands and leaves.

At first, she dismisses the note, but curiosity prevails. She keeps stealing glances at the intrusive, unwelcome message. A casual peek becomes a lingering stare until her eyes finally settle on the words scribbled on the other side:

"Life in Bliss"

"If you want to live life in bliss,

pay attention to the little details,

those that come straight from the heart,

those that are spontaneous gestures of love,

those little things,

those that we offer and receive with absolute joy,

those that we never forget,

for the rest of our lives."

*

She carefully folds the note.

It's a keeper, she decides, a shiver running deep inside her. Her dormant heart stirs awake, and try as she might, she cannot ignore it.

— ❖ —

Note #2
(University Library)

Vicky bursts into uncontrollable laughter.

"He did it. He finally did it. Isn't that amazing? We should all be so proud of him," she proclaims to her classmates in the library. The announcement triggers cheers, high fives, and embraces as everyone celebrates the college quarterback's NFL draft selection.

"Victoria, you should run for student council as Miss Congeniality. It suits you better," teases a friend-rival classmate.

Victoria, however, isn't listening. Her focus is fixed on a small yellow note in her hands.

"Your heart is noble and amazingly beautiful. Your spirit is fierce and loyal. Your soul is pure and innocent. You are an awesome woman."

"Who's the Romeo writing these notes? I don't find it funny at all!" she exclaims, waving the folded note at a nonchalant crowd, careful not to reveal its contents.

Later, sitting alone, she wrestles with her curiosity but ultimately surrenders. She unfolds the note, unsure of what to expect but compelled to read.

"Life is Not a Spectator Sport"

Feeling good for long
never happens to the bystander.
There is no success or achievement
as a spectator in life,

but only fun and intensity

which are shallow and passing,

as the emptiness of a life without meaning

will settle in,

when you are alone at night

with your own pillow.

Life, to the contrary, is a participant's sport,

in which we are the main protagonists,

and in which happiness

is not pursued but ensues,

because of our deliberate involvement

in a wholesome life experience."

*

Who does he think he is? she wonders, cutting herself off mid-thought.

He's right, Victoria, whether you like it or not, he's right, she concedes silently.

The mystery of his identity grows alongside her racing heartbeat. She notices the artistry in his handwriting, marveling at the beauty of the calligraphy as her eyes linger on the impeccably written note.

— ❖ —

Note #3
(Ice Cream Parlor)
"How could anyone enjoy ice cream so much? I love to see the ecstasy on your face, chocolate plastered all over it. Happiness has a name and a face, and it is you, Victoria."

She finds the note while sitting alone, chuckling at the thought of her usual self, ice cream smeared from mouth to cheeks. She folds it carefully and joins her best friend, Gina. As the two prepare to leave the ice cream parlor, Victoria's heart skips a beat. She spots him sitting in a booth in the corner, facing the street. Hidden from his view, her pulse quickens.

"Hi," Victoria says softly, her voice warm and disarming.

Erasmus turns to face her, and she senses his surprise. As their eyes lock, an unspoken connection pulls them together with sudden, undeniable force. He remains silent, frozen by her presence.

"I meant to introduce myself days ago, but I haven't seen you around in a while," she says, trying to bridge the gap. Erasmus stiffens even more. Her gaze remains steady, and then she blurts out, "I saw you looking at me that day from the stands."

She refers to the first time Erasmus ever saw her, twirling her baton as part of the Harvard Band during a football game's opening ceremony.

Hearing her recollection, Erasmus feels a shiver ripple through him.

So, it was mutual, he realizes, but his voice betrays him, and he remains silent.

"I'm Victoria," she continues, flashing a radiant smile.

Erasmus hesitates, shyness paralyzing him. Yet, to his great relief, he somehow manages to respond.

"I'm Erasmus. It's nice to meet you," he blurts out with a sheepish, nervous smile, still motionless as if nailed to his seat.

Victoria stands before him, her wide eyes scanning every inch of the startled young man. Erasmus, in turn, gazes at her with shyness and admiration. The two remain frozen in time, their mutual attraction so intense and palpable that even Gina, their accidental witness, is left in awe, speechless. Though neither says much, they connect on the deepest level.

"See you around then," Victoria says casually, turning away in one fluid motion. The two Harvard freshman friends step out into the street.

"A Brit?" Victoria wonders aloud, catching her breath. "I love how proper English sounds coming from a man."

"Victoria, who are you kidding? The accent? Who are you trying to fool? I've never seen you introduce yourself to anyone in here. Quite the contrary—they chase you like flies," Gina teases, challenging her.

But Victoria isn't listening. Her mind replays every moment of the encounter: his gorgeous eyes, sculpted jawline, Hellenic nose, strong hands, masculine gestures, and deep voice.

He is gorgeous, she thinks, searching her mind for someone he reminds her of. Suddenly, she freezes, a chill running through her.

"I've got it. I've got it!" she exclaims. "He's a younger version of Elizabeth Taylor's husband—the Brit she married twice—Richard Burton. Yes, that's him!" Her heart races as she delights in the realization, swept up in a whirlwind of emotions.

Unable to resist her curiosity, Victoria peeks at the back of the note. Though she planned to read it later, the pull is irresistible. She unfolds it and begins to read, captivated by the words:

"Love's Rabbit Hole"

How do you know when love

is knocking at your door?

You know it because when that someone

unexpectedly erupts into your life's journey,

it simply takes your breath away.

*

Victoria's lower lip trembles as she realizes the intensity of her feelings. A faint smile tugs at her lips, and her incandescent eyes betray a mixture of awe and fear at the prospect of nascent love.

— ✦ —

Note #4
(University Grounds After a Round of Frisbee)
As Victoria gathers her books from the park bench to head to class, a small note catches her eye.

"Wearing shoes of a different color makes you look vulnerable and absent-minded—something you are not. But seeing your inner child is endearing. I love it!"

Tentatively, she glances down at her feet. Horror! How did it happen?

"Vic, I thought it was you making a fashion statement. You're losing it ... or perhaps it's a breeze coming all the way from across the Atlantic. Should we call it 'Brit love'?" Gina teases.

"So, you have nothing better to do than play Cupid?" Victoria fires back, scanning the grounds for Erasmus, but he's nowhere to be seen.

"He's not here, Vic. I already looked around," Gina replies. "By the way, I don't think the Brit is writing the notes. I thought back, and I can't recall seeing him around when you got the others—except the other day at the ice cream parlor."

It's true, Victoria thinks, disappointed. Hopeless, wishful thinking of mine. Her awakening heart pulls in two completely different directions, leaving her torn.

To her great relief, she remembers the writing on the back of the note awaits her. As she reads it, Victoria is swept into places of the heart she never wants to leave.

"Love's Rabbit Hole" (cont.)

You know it because
when you can finally catch your breath,
all you inhale feels like, at that moment,
there is absolutely nothing else
you would like to be doing,
nor is there anyone else in the world
with whom you would rather be,
than your rabbit.

*

She chuckles softly, letting out a wistful sigh.

My rabbit? she wonders, becoming more at ease with the sensation of love unfolding within her. But reality crashes back. I've got to find him first! she reminds herself, frustrated by the continued mystery of his identity.

— ✦ —

Note #5 and Gesture #1
(Student Dorms)

"Vic, you better come to the door," Gina calls as the two prepare to leave for class.

At the doorstep of their dorm, three balloons and a narrow rectangular gift box rest on the floor. Taped to one of the balloon strings is a large card with Victoria's name written in bold capital letters.

Victoria hastily opens the card.

"So, you never again confuse your shoes in the darkness as you leave early in the morning," it reads.

She looks down and realizes, to her dismay, that she's wearing one dark blue loafer and one black loafer—again. The horror!

Gina notices and bursts into loud laughter.

"How could he have known?" Victoria asks, startled.

"Obviously, you've done it before," Gina says mockingly.

Victoria opens the gift box and finds a sleek reading light inside.

"Who is this guy, Gina? I've got to find out," Victoria says, her curiosity and excitement growing.

Now wearing matching shoes, she steps out of the dorm with a smile, the gift already endearing itself to her. She loves the light and has even used it, but it's the note she craves most. It doesn't take long before she begins to read it. As expected, it doesn't disappoint.

*

"Love's Rabbit Hole" (cont.)

You know it,

when from the get-go,

you feel comfortable, confident,

and light on your feet,

and life becomes a journey of two.

Soon after,

you become possessed

with this inexplicable certainty

that you are safe, protected,

and never alone.

*

Who is he, and why doesn't he show up? Victoria wonders, the need-to-know burning through her entire being.

— ✦ —

Note #6 and Gesture #2
(Student Dorms)

"Vic, the phantom of the camp strikes again," Gina announces playfully.

At their doorstep lies another surprise, this time in a cardboard takeaway tray holding two coffees and a handful of fresh doughnuts. It's their favorite breakfast, and the aroma feels like heaven to the two freshmen.

Once again, the note doesn't disappoint.

"On Wednesdays, you are always running late because you work until late at the homeless center on Tuesdays. The next day, you often miss breakfast."

"How does he know?" Victoria asks, incredulous.

"Because he cares, Vic," Gina answers, her voice gentle.

This time, an utterly joyous Victoria reads the back of the note aloud to Gina:

"Our Better Instincts of the Heart"

In matters of love,

the brain and the heart are like oil and water;

they don't mix well together,

because the brain cannot

create, govern, control, or sustain love—

and vice versa.

*

As they finish reading, the two friends sit in silence in their dorm room, nodding in unspoken agreement, each lost in thought.

Victoria has fallen in love. The only problem is, she still doesn't know with whom.

—❖—

Note #7 and Gesture #3
(The Broken Baton)

On Friday, Erasmus travels overnight by train to New York City. He arrives at the store as it opens at 8:00 AM. By 8:30 AM, he's back at Penn Station, and by early afternoon, he's returned to Boston.

Meanwhile, Victoria is devastated. Her cheerleading baton had broken the previous day, leaving her distraught. Worst of all, after rehearsal, Harvard's marching band leader apologizes and informs her that she won't be able to march that day.

"Victoria, there's no point in you marching without your baton," he says sympathetically.

Dejected, Victoria trudges to her locker, dumps everything inside, and heads for the showers.

When she returns, wrapped in towels and still feeling hopeless, something catches her attention. A package rests on top of her locker. Her heart leaps as she recognizes the shape of the box. Involuntarily, she covers her face and gasps.

With trembling hands, she grabs the box and opens it, filled with an exhilarating premonition. Her breath catches as she takes in the contents, and soft tears spill down her cheeks as she's overcome by emotion.

Inside the box, a card reads:

"I tried to repair the broken one, but I couldn't, so I got you a new one. Victoria, our band is nothing without you."

Victoria picks up the broken baton from the box and laughs through her tears at the mangled Scotch tape holding it together. Then, holding her brand-new baton gleefully, she notices the back of the note. All her feelings bundle up inside her as she begins to read:

"What is True Love?"

True love is

when your skin aches

without your other half's touch,

when nothing is warmer than being

in each other's arms.

True love is

when your heart does not belong to you.

*

Right then and there, her instincts are sprinkled with love's magic stardust. She wants him. She needs him. Her heart is no longer hers.

Let it be him. Please, let it be him, she wishes fervently, torn between the Brit and the note writer, desperately hoping they are one and the same.

—◆—

Note #8 and Gesture #4
(The Round-Trip Trek)

Erasmus has been in the library for hours, spending half the time immersed in work and the other half daydreaming about Victoria. He keeps picturing her from earlier that day, leading the marching band with a radiant smile and her brand-new baton.

"Mr. Cromwell-Smith," a voice calls out.

"Yes?" he replies, snapping out of his reverie.

"Please follow me. We have an urgent long-distance call for you."

Erasmus quickly follows the middle-aged woman as she strides purposefully through Harvard's ancient corridors. At the university switchboard, she directs him to a telephone booth.

"Lift the handset, young man; your mother is on the line," the operator instructs.

His heart pounds as he picks up the receiver.

His mother's trembling voice comes through the line. "Son, your father has had a heart attack. We're all at the hospital with him. He's getting the best care possible, but he's been asking for you repeatedly. About an hour ago, he begged me to contact you and keep you informed. He loves you dearly, Erasmus."

"But— but how is he, Mum? Will he be okay?"

"Son, he's very ill and may not make it. I'll call again tomorrow morning with an update. If we could afford it, we'd fly you home right away, but... you know we simply can't."

"I know, Mum, I know. Thank you for calling. Please don't spend any more money. I love you. Tell Dad I love him very, very much."

Erasmus hangs up, anguish overtaking him. Lost in a whirlwind of emotions, he leaves the switchboard and begins walking. Along the Charles River, memories of his father flood his mind. He loses track of time, unaware of the distance he covers. By the time he returns to his dorm, it's nearly midnight. Somehow, he gets into bed and falls into a restless sleep, dreaming of his father all night.

At first, the persistent knock seems distant. Half-asleep, Erasmus stirs, remembering that his mother promised to call back. He hurries to the door, expecting to see the switchboard messenger.

But when he opens the door, no one is there. Confused, he glances down and spots an envelope on the floor, addressed to him. Feeling a sense of foreboding, he picks it up and opens it. Inside is a small note:

— ✦ —

Dear Erasmus,
Fly home and be with your father for as long as you need.

— ✦ —

For a moment, he doesn't understand. The simple words confuse him, but gratitude quickly replaces bewilderment—until reality hits.

I wish I could, but we can't afford it, he thinks bitterly.

Then he notices the envelope's unusual weight. He reaches inside and pulls out its contents.

His breath catches.

Oh my...

A round-trip airline ticket to London. The departure time is just four hours away. There's also a train ticket to his hometown upon arrival.

Thirty minutes later, Erasmus is sprinting across campus to meet the waiting cab. In his haste, he nearly collides with another student. Realizing it's his best friend, Matthew, he stops and throws his arms around him.

"Thank you, Matt. Thank you!" he shouts, overwhelmed with emotion.

But Matthew remains still.

"Erasmus, don't thank me. Thank her," Matthew says firmly. "She turned this campus upside down to raise that money."

"What are you talking about? Who is she?" Erasmus asks desperately.

"Never mind. I can't tell you. Just go home. Go see your dad," Matthew replies, resolute.

"But how did you guys even find out?" Erasmus asks, still bewildered.

"A faculty professor told us, so we could keep an eye on you. Now, man, just go. Get going!" Matthew insists, pushing him toward the cab.

As Erasmus begins to run again, he turns one last time, his hands raised in a final plea for answers.

"She's amazing. You're one lucky bastard," Matthew calls after him. "C'mon, go! Go home!"

Is it her? Erasmus wonders as the cab speeds away. Who else could it be? His mind races, and his heart dares to hope. It must be her...

Wales Regional Hospital, United Kingdom, 1976

"Mum!" Erasmus calls out as he strides into the hospital lobby.

His mother turns, and her sleepless face brightens with a broad smile, erasing her sadness, even if only for a moment. She runs toward him, overcome by emotion.

"My beautiful boy," she whispers as she wraps him in a warm embrace. For the first time in days, Erasmus feels safe and protected.

"How did you make it all the way here, son?" she asks, tears of joy streaming down her face.

"Someone who cares deeply, Mum. It was a gesture from a big, big heart," Erasmus says cryptically.

"But who?" she asks.

"That, I still need to find out when I get back."

Together, they tiptoe into his father's hospital room.

"Father," Erasmus says softly, leaning in to wake him.

His father squints almost imperceptibly, then his eyes flutter open, recognition dawning instantly. His gaze locks on Erasmus, his eyes widening before a faint smile appears.

"Son," he whispers.

Erasmus steps to his father's bedside and embraces him tightly, resting his head on his chest. He is overwhelmed by a swirl of emotions: fear, relief, and love.

Later that evening, Erasmus learns how close his father had come to passing away. But as the days pass, his father's condition improves faster than anyone expected. Soon, he is out of danger and hopefully on the path to a full recovery. Predictably, his father begins urging Erasmus to return to America.

Father and son spend countless hours together, reminicescing seemingly every memorable family aneccdote. When Erasmus finally says goodbye to his parents, he steps outside for the first time in a week and finds himself standing in the light of day. On the train back to London, guilt nags at him for failing to contact his antiquarian mentors back in his hometown.

Boston, MA, 1976
(Harvard University Dorms, Saturday 6 PM)

With his father on the mend, Erasmus arrives back in Boston a day before his 21st birthday—just in time for a short getaway planned to celebrate.

The plan is to take the train to the coast with a small group of friends, board the ferry for an overnight trip to Martha's Vineyard, and spend Sunday cycling along the island's beaches.

But Erasmus can't stop thinking about the woman whose generosity made it possible for him to visit his father. Who is she? The question gnaws at him. He is determined to find out and hopes to extract the truth from his friends over the weekend.

He clings to the hope that she might be the gorgeous baton twirler who's captivated his heart. Could she be the one?

She hardly knows me. How could she care? he wonders, trying to temper his hope with reason. That's what you are—a perennial dreamer. But then his thoughts circle back. Whoever she is, I've got to meet her and thank her. Whoever she is, her heart is pure gold.

His musings take another turn. Perhaps she found out it was me sending her the notes, poems, and baton! He smiles, his hope rekindled. But the smile fades just as quickly as doubt creeps back in.

Be honest, Erasmus. Your infatuation is teetering on the edge of a delusional cliff. He shakes his head, but the thoughts refuse to leave him.

How can you get anywhere with the beautiful baton twirler? You didn't even invite her to celebrate your birthday. He knows it's a feeble excuse, but he tries to convince himself that she wouldn't have been able to come anyway. Harvard's football team had a game earlier that day—four hundred miles away on the road.

He sighs, the thought of her lingering in his mind.

Harvard Marching Band Bus, 1976
(100 miles away from Boston, Saturday 8 PM)

"Vicky, you don't know what you're doing anymore," Gina says, her tone a mix of exasperation and concern.

"I know I'm being impulsive, Gina, but I'm happy. I'm just following my heart," Victoria replies, her voice resolute.

"And you have. Buying the Brit that ticket was awesome, but what's he done for you?" Gina presses.

"I don't know, and I don't care. I have this strange, uncontrollable desire to protect him," Victoria admits, her expression softening.

"You're still fixated on him being the phantom of the dorms, the note-writer! I told you, he's not—he couldn't be."

"Then who is he?" Victoria asks, her eyes narrowing.

"Let him surface, let him show himself, and then you'll know if he's your Prince Charming," Gina sighs, exasperated.

"The coach told me that whoever got me the baton had to go all the way to New York City overnight to get it," Victoria says defiantly, her determination growing.

"Yeah, that was quite the gesture, and I'd be head over heels for the guy, just like you are," Gina admits with a small smirk. But her sharp tongue isn't done. "The problem, Victoria, is that you're trying to fit a Brit square peg into a magnificent round hole. They don't fit."

Victoria's eyes well with tears, and Gina immediately softens. "I'm sorry. I just don't want to see you hurt."

Gina sighs and puts a comforting hand on Victoria's shoulder. "About your latest crazy idea, I'm coming on your weekend trip—if only to protect you from yourself."

Victoria smiles faintly, grateful for her friend's support.

Martha's Vineyard, 1976
(Sunday Morning)

By 7:00 AM, the small group of Harvard students gathers their things and leaves the cozy bed-and-breakfast. They hop on their bikes and head toward the picturesque city center. However, their visit is brief—most shops are still closed this early in the morning. All they really want is sand and water.

They zigzag across the island's beaches, splashing in the waves, racing along the shoreline, and soaking up the sun. By noon, they are crusty with sand, saltwater, island winds, and a hefty dose of spring sunshine.

At 12:15 PM, they arrive at a small seafood restaurant in the city center, where they have a lunch reservation. The group plans to cut the cake for the birthday boy during the meal.

The restaurant, a family-run spot, is packed with customers, buzzing with the lively chatter of weekend visitors. As the group gets seated, laughter erupts when Matthew and Greg recount their earlier stunt.

At a deserted beach on the island's southwest side, the two had stripped naked and raced from the sand dunes straight into the water.

"The two of you looked awful naked," Erasmus jokes, shaking his head. "After just a bit of sun, your pale skin looked more like lobster tails!"

The group bursts into laughter, their camaraderie filling the air as they enjoy the moment together.

— ❖ —

Gesture #5
(The Martha's Vineyard Magic Moment)
Suddenly, two hands cover his eyes from behind. The movement is slow, deliberate, caressing, and tender.

"Hi," she whispers in his ear, her voice soft and warm, sending a chill down his spine.

Erasmus feels a knot tighten in his throat, and before he knows it, his entire body is trembling. Then, the unexpected happens—he turns around, holding her face gently with both hands. For a moment that feels like an eternity, they cradle each other's faces in their palms, their eyes locked in an intense, unspoken connection.

The world around them fades into oblivion.

Erasmus leans in, drawing her face closer, and kisses her passionately. She reciprocates, her affection as fervent as his, and they lose themselves in the embrace.

"Hey, can you two lovebirds interrupt your wonderful love dream—or should I say open-ended kiss—so we can cut the cake and get out of here?" Gina quips, her voice cutting through the enchantment in typical fashion.

The group laughs as the brief ceremony follows. Afterward, Gina, who accompanied Victoria on the trip, returns to Boston with

Erasmus' friends, leaving the young couple alone on Martha's Vineyard.

Martha's Vineyard, 1976

Erasmus and Victoria spend the rest of the day strolling hand in hand around the island, their laughter and shared stories filling the air. They embrace often, kissing as if the world might end tomorrow.

On an empty, moonlit beach, their connection deepens. Together, they make love for the first time, their passion clumsy and unpracticed but tender and beautiful. It is uninhibited and harmonic, as if their hearts had always known each other.

But the night isn't done granting its magic. As they lie on the warm sands, still wrapped in each other's arms, Erasmus begins to whisper.

Victoria tilts her head, trying to understand. His dreamy eyes meet hers as his words begin to take shape. Slowly, they cascade into a rhythm of art and inspiration—a poetic offering just for her.

"My Radiant Goddess of the Night"

Here we are

under a star-studded sky,

in the silence of the night,

over the moist,

still warm sands

of an empty beach.

Here we are on this magic island,

where our story,

that of just the two of us,

has begun.

My Radiant Goddess of the Night,

where are you taking me?

Where are you taking us

with this nascent love of mine?

When I see you,

I sigh in joy,

with just your presence.

When you look at me,

my infatuated heart

makes me tremble.

Just one touch or a slight brush

from that warm, silky skin of yours

makes me moan all over

in ecstasy-filled desire.

And when you embrace me,

I feel this inexplicable plenitude,

a blissful certitude,

that I am at a safe harbor,

protected and no longer alone.

My radiant Goddess of the Night,

where are you taking us?

Where are you taking me

with this nascent love of mine?

*

Victoria shivers with intense joy, her body trembling as she listens.

Then, without hesitation, she leans in, pressing her lips to his in an endless kiss of gratitude and love.

Late at Night, on the Train Back to Boston, 1976

Leaning on each other, Erasmus and Victoria doze off as the train speeds toward Boston. The young couple radiates utter happiness, their enamored faces glittering with the glow of nascent love. They look completely at ease, lost in their newfound connection.

Suddenly, Victoria's voice, filled with playful urgency, teases Erasmus out of his delightful dream.

"Tell me it's you. It's got to be you. Tell me, tell me, please!" she cries, her plea flowing straight from her infatuated heart.

Erasmus knows perfectly well that she already knows the answer, but he gives in to her improvised charade with sweet enthusiasm.

He nods ever so slightly, flashing a small, mischievous smile.

"I knew it! I knew it!" Victoria exclaims, her words tumbling out between kisses as she jumps into his arms in a state of pure euphoria.

"And I presume that you were the guardian angel who made it possible for me to make it all the way to Wales?" Erasmus teases in return, his eyes sparkling.

"And brought you back as well. Don't you forget that!" Victoria replies with a playful grin.

Their laughter fills the train, spilling into the quiet night like wildfire, the echoes dancing between two incandescent hearts.

Boston Main Train Station, 1976

The train's arrival interrupts their never-ending kiss. Hand in hand, Erasmus and Victoria step off, their bond unmistakable. From that moment on, walking hand in hand becomes their custom.

Hopelessly inseparable, the couple moves in together within weeks. Their new chapter begins with a poetic overture, as Erasmus composes a verse for his love—one that Victoria later calls irresistible.

Standing in their newly rented studio for the first time, Erasmus reads the poem aloud to her, his voice steady with emotion.

"There is Something About You"

Ever since that day we met,

there is something about you

that makes life magical.

Don't ask me how,

but it is this irresistible

and wickedly beautiful spell you cast,

that simply makes us happy, whole, and safe.

There is something about you,

that paints the world in vivid colors

making every sunrise

a wondrousl beginning,

and every sunset

not only a glorious conclussion but also,

a promise of new beginnings.

There is something extraordinary about you

that always feels anew.

There is something extraordinary about you

that breathes live into love itself,

making love come alive,

and one twinkles, shivers, and sighs deeply

with a smile.

There is something about you,

that captivatess my heart,

and makes it forever yours.

*

"Welcome to the journey," Erasmus barely whispers as Victoria drowns him in hugs and kisses. Their embrace grows heated, and they hurriedly walk to their new bedroom. A world of endless love and passion awaits them.

Mrs. V.'s Antique Book Store for the Young
Hay-On-Wye, Wales, 1976

Back in Wales, Mrs. V. sits on her cherished Chesterfield armchair, gently rocking, her face beaming with pride for her beloved mentee.

Erasmus and Victoria's letter rests on her lap, its words a treasure. The tips of Mrs. V.'s dainty fingers trace the paper as if it were a rare artifact, her touch reverent and loving.

Her fingertips begin tapping gently on the words, almost as if sending a silent message to the young couple—a wish to help preserve and protect their true love forever.

— ✦ —

Royal Cambridge Scholastic Institute, 2018
(University Auditorium)

The professor stands motionless, staring at his class for what feels like an eternity, his eyes lost in the past. A deeply melancholic smile crosses his face as he slowly returns to the present. Scanning the room, he notices several teary faces, each one glistening with tears of happiness—like his own.

"There are moments in life," he begins, his voice steady but reflective, "where we are blessed with immense and wholesome joy. Most of these moments come unexpectedly, like bends in the road. But when one arrives, be ready. Seize it. Don't let it slip away or miss a beat. These rare opportunities are few and far between, and we never know how long they'll last—or if they'll ever come again."

He pauses, letting the weight of his words settle.

A hand rises hesitantly in the middle row. The professor nods toward Jimmy, a first-year philosophy major with thick-rimmed glasses and a lanky frame, his hands fidgeting nervously on the desk.

"What role does fate play in love, according to your experiences?" Jimmy asks, his voice tinged with shyness.

"Excellent question, Jimmy," the professor replies, his tone warm.

"Fate may set the stage, but our choices and actions are how our love stories are truly written. We must actively engage with our emotions and dreams to shape our destiny. Think of it as a blank canvas; fate might provide the frame, but we are the artists who bring it to life."

Another hand rises near the front. The professor gestures toward Lynn, a second-year literature student wearing denim overalls and her long curly light brown hair framing her curious face.

"How can we recognize the significance of small gestures in a relationship?" Lynn asks, her voice steady and thoughtful.

"Small gestures often hold the greatest meaning," the professor says, his expression thoughtful. "They are the threads that weave our fairy tales, showing us that love thrives in the details. Think of the notes I shared with Victoria—they were simple, but they carried the weight of my heart. Life holds extraordinary magnificence around every corner and within us, waiting to be discovered. Remember, we create our own fairy tales. And it often starts with the little things—notes, words, or even just a thoughtful smile."

A hush falls over the room as the professor concludes his response.

"Class, I'll see you next week. I'll be taking you back to a memorable day when Vicky and I met an exceptional lady who would become an important part of our lives."

"Class dismissed," announces Erasmus.

As students pack their belongings, their chatter fills the air.

"I want to fall in love like that," declares a dreamy-eyed brunette, her energy palpable despite never having cared for poetry before taking Professor Cromwell-Smith's class.

"Who wouldn't want someone to steal your heart away and take you into the land of the happy hearts?" muses a tall, red-haired girl, the captain of the volleyball team. Her voice is wistful, her eyes reflecting a longing for her own true-love fairy tale.

Chapter 3

Life, Character, and Virtue

Royal Cambridge Scholastic Institute, 2018
(Erasmus and Victoria's Campus Home)

"Come here, my irresistible Brit," Victoria whispers, her eyes fixed intensely on Erasmus. Slowly, she lifts the corner of the bed comforter, enticing him to squeeze in beside her. Hypnotized by her charm, Erasmus dutifully complies, wearing an expression of joyful obedience as though he has no choice in the matter.

"What am I going to do with you?" she teases, her voice light with affection.

"Anything you may desire, my lady," he replies, his voice already thick with longing.

Later, when Vicky opens her eyes, the first things she sees are Erasmus' warm smile and her favorite treat: a glass of freshly squeezed orange juice.

"You always manage to coax me out of my morning grumpiness," she grumbles playfully, though her contented smile betrays her.

"Erasmus, where are you taking your students today?" she asks asthey sit together for breakfast.

"Back to the day you and I met Mrs. Peabody," he says, his tone thoughtful.

With a dreamy look, Victoria seems to drift into the distance before absentmindedly blurting out, "Quite a day, dear. Quite a day. To me, she will always be Mrs. P."

"Good old Mrs. P., indeed," Erasmus replies with a soft chuckle.

As Erasmus finishes his coffee, he glances at the clock and sighs. Time to go. Rising from the table, he leans over and places a gentle kiss on Victoria's forehead. "I'll see you later, my love," he says softly before heading out the door.

The crisp morning air carries a faint scent of autumn leaves as Erasmus strides across campus, his steps purposeful yet unhurried. The familiar sight of the faculty buildings on the horizon pulls him from his reverie, centering his thoughts on the task ahead. He pauses briefly under a tree, taking a deep breath as if gathering the essence of the moment.

Royal Cambridge Scholastic Institute, 2018
(University Auditorium)

Professor Cromwell-Smith walks into a packed auditorium, his mind still lost in memories of the past. He has no recollection of how he got there. *My subconscious must have navigated me here,* he muses, unconvincingly trying to justify his absentmindedness.

"How's everyone today?" he asks with enthusiasm.

"Insanely awesome!" a host of spirited students reply in unison.

With a slight nod of gratitude, the professor smiles, eager to begin.

"From a very early age, I gravitated toward the world of books. My first true friends were three antiquarians from my hometown in Wales. Well, serendipity struck again. While living in Boston with my newfound love, Vicky, I encountered a similar connection—with New England and its antiquarians. The first was a sweet and unforgettable lady we met by accident, literally stumbling into her shop while on a long bike ride along the northern shore of Massachusetts. Today, we will revisit that memorable day by going back in time. It starts like this..."

— ✦ —

Harvard, 1976

Having fallen madly in love, Vicky and Erasmus have been living together for months. From the start, their comfort with each other has been effortless, and they've settled into routines that suit their personalities and preferences. During the week, alongside their academic responsibilities, they both work as tutors. On weekends, they make the most of their free time, often exploring Massachusetts by bike.

Their adventures typically begin with an early train ride to a random destination, bikes in tow. From there, they cycle through the state's charming coastal towns or scenic countryside, covering forty to fifty miles in a day. At night, they crash at one of the countless bed-and-breakfasts scattered across the region.

This particular weekend begins like many others. On Saturday morning, they board a train to Manchester-by-the-Sea, equipped with their bikes and a picnic basket. Their plan is to ride along the coastline, passing through Gloucester, Rockport, and Newbury, before ending their journey at Sand Point on Plum Island. They'll spend the night in a cozy inn and return to Boston on an early train Sunday morning.

As their escapade begins, Erasmus and Victoria pedal along quiet roads, their senses immersed in the sounds of chirping birds, the rhythmic crash of ocean waves, and the vibrant pastel hues of the New England countryside. The briny sea air invigorates them as they ride.

After soaking in the stunning views at Halibut Point and Cape Ann, the couple meanders into the quaint enclave of Lanesville.

Lanesville, Massachusetts, 1976

As Erasmus and Victoria pedal into the picturesque village, a postcard-perfect storefront catches their eye. The sign reads: 'Peabody & Co. Antique Books (est. 1890).' Erasmus is immediately transfixed. Victoria would later describe his reaction as if the entire world had disappeared, herself included, leaving only the store before him.

Upon entering Peabody & Co., the first thing anyone notices is the broadest, most inviting smile and a thunderous, contagious laugh—both belonging to Eleanor Peabody-Smith. Her frame, round in every way, moves with surprising agility and purpose. Mrs. P., as she's affectionately known, hails from a distinguished New England family with roots stretching back to the 18th century. She married her first love young, living an idyllic life until tragedy struck ten years into their childless marriage, when her husband was lost at sea during a heavy storm. After briefly practicing law—a profession she found unfulfilling—she discovered her true calling: running her beloved antique bookstore.

Erasmus stands in a trance, his mouth slightly ajar and his eyes wide with awe as he surveys the stacks of books around him. Mrs. Peabody approaches with a welcoming smile.

"And who do I have the pleasure of welcoming on this beautiful morning to my humble place of enlightenment?" she asks warmly.

Vicky, startled but delighted, struggles to contain her enthusiasm as the sheer magnitude of old books overwhelms her senses. The distinctive smell—old leather? Paper? Or a blend of both?—fills the air. She observes the apparent chaos of the store but senses an underlying order. This store is a reflection of its owner, she thinks. Everything in plain sight—both the books and the woman. You could probably find anything here in seconds.

Meanwhile, Mrs. P. eyes the young couple thoughtfully. A beautiful young couple interested in my antique books. What am I missing? she muses.

"All right then," Mrs. Peabody says, bringing them back to reality. "Make yourselves comfortable. May I offer you something to drink— perhaps a freshly brewed iced tea?"

Erasmus, still lost in thought, politely declines. All this ice Americans consume, he reflects, how do their throats not freeze?

"Howdy, I'm Erasmus," he finally says, his accent unmistakable.

"And I'm Victoria," adds Vicky.

"Well, well, I am Eleanor, Eleanor Peabody-Smith," Mrs. P. declares proudly. She gestures at Erasmus. "Brit?"

"I'm Welsh, ma'am."

"Whereabouts in Wales?"

"Hay-on-Wye," Erasmus replies.

"It figures," she says with a knowing smile. "Also known as 'Book Town,' the Mecca of antique bookstores. That explains it."

Erasmus smiles sheepishly at her compliment.

"And you, Victoria? Midwest?"

"Yes, Waterloo, Southwestern Illinois."

"A twosome of the New and Old World," Mrs. P. laughs, her eyes sparkling.

"Mrs. Peabody, he doesn't drink anything with ice," Victoria explains with a grin.

"How silly of me. I'll spare the ice—but only for him, right?" Mrs. P. says with a wink.

"Now, young man, what on earth could my modest book piles possibly offer a resident of the antiquarians' citadel in Wales?" she asks, handing them their drinks.

"He's in his element," Vicky explains, noting Erasmus' silence. "This is his passion."

Erasmus finally speaks, his voice warm and intimate. "You remind me of... back home."

"Is that so? Tell me about it," Mrs. P. prompts, her curiosity piqued.

Still absent-minded, Erasmus doesn't answer. Vicky fills the silence.

"He grew up surrounded by antique bookstores in his hometown. Some owners became his lifelong mentors. It all started when he was just eight years old. Mrs. V. is one of them—Victoria Sutton-Raleigh."

Mrs. Peabody's face lights up with recognition. "Sutton-Raleigh antique books for the children. The best of its kind. She's a war widow from a wealthy Welsh family, isn't she?"

Vicky turns to Erasmus for confirmation.

"Yes, she is," he replies, finally engaging.

"Well, I've dealt with her over the years. She's prompt, diligent, and dependable. I periodically receive orders for antique children's books from her," Mrs. Peabody says, her tone full of admiration.

Erasmus listens intently, his excitement growing. Then, abruptly shifting topics, he asks, "Mrs. Peabody, I recently finished reading Benjamin Franklin's autobiography and fell in love with his writings on character and virtue. Do you have anything on that subject?"

"As a matter of fact, I do, my son," she replies.

What follows is a spectacle. Mrs. Peabody moves through the cluttered store with surprising agility, climbing a feeble-looking ladder one moment and kneeling on the floor the next. Suddenly, she strides purposefully to a specific spot, retrieving an enormous book with both arms as if cradling a treasure. She places it on a large dining table buried under stacks of ancient volumes, clearing space to open it.

"This poem encapsulates the essence of Franklin's ideals on character and virtue," she says, her voice tinged with reverence.

"Though it feels timeless, it was written quite recently. Let me read it to both of you."

She pauses, allowing the young couple to absorb the moment, their faces turned toward her with eager anticipation.

Mrs. Peabody opens the book with care, releasing a cloud of dust and an intoxicating mix of old paper and leather into the air. Vicky, now fully initiated into the world of antique books, watches with wonder as the antiquarian begins to read.

"Life, Character, and Virtue"

One's character is our calling card to life,
as well as the legacy our wake leaves behind.

Our character defines
not who we think we are,
much less what we pretend to be,
but who we truly are deep, deep inside.

Our character is respected when
we exibit immutable honesty and unwavering frankness.

Our character inspires emulation when
we are uncompromisingly ethical,
approach everything with unquestionable rectitude
and indomitable integrity,
and uphold a spirit with purpose,
and a soul imbued with meaning.

Our character is revered when

it radiates boundless compassion,

selfless generosity,

and the humblest wisdom.

Our character is forged through
dependable and immanent self-discipline.

Our character flourishes through
unyielding perseverance, unrelenting grit,

unflinching resilience,
and the insatiable pursuit of insight,

knowledge, and spirituality.

Our character remains authentic only when
we consistently practice
inescapable forgiveness of oneself and others,
coupled with a readiness to rectify
and learn from our mistakes.

Our character is revealed by what
we are truly made of
when demanded by life and its challenges,
which may require abnegation, sacrifice,
or even relinquishment—
the ultimate test of the fiber and nature
of our hearts.
Our character perpetually renews itself
remaining crystalline through
unstained innocence, unpremeditated candor,

joyful spontaneity, and boundless ingenuity.

Our character builds a legacy through
everlasting and selfless deeds, empathetic
and mindful judgment,
unbreakable courage, unwavering effort,
unyielding resolve, relentless pace,
obsessive zeal, steadfast firmness,
unleashed talent, incomparable ability,
timely impulsiveness and unfettered ingeniousness.

Our character transcends when
we are 'ready to be' or 'forever are' in love
with life, everyone,
and our true love with sustained passion.

Being alive offers us countless paths that,
in the pursuit of moral excellence,
elevate our character to its zenith,
and create a state of unrepentant virtuosity.

*

When Mrs. Peabody finishes, Erasmus and Vicky hold one another's hands tightly as if sharing energy absorbed from the force and strength of the words they've just heard. They're both visibly shaken by the power of the old scribble. Soon, questions start to form, but their parallel thoughts are interrupted by their mind reader host.

"Character and virtue are not God-given gifts with which you are born. On the contrary, they require persistence and hard work to

build, grow, acquire, and preserve them," teaches Mrs. P her scholarly wisdom in full force.

"Always remember this: your virtues define your character, and your character defines your legacy," she concludes. "Thank you, Mrs. ... can we call you Mrs. P.?" Victoria asks.

Eleanor Theresa Peabody-Smith flashes her signature smile once more. "Of course, you may, dear."

"Then again, thank you, Mrs. P." The grateful young couple bid farewell before resuming their cycling trip along the New England coastline.

— ✦ —

Royal Cambridge Scholastic Institute, 2018
(University's Auditorium)

As Professor Cromwell-Smith concludes his engaging lecture on the importance of character and virtue, he takes a moment to let the weight of his words settle in the classroom. The atmosphere is charged with anticipation as the students reflect on the profound lessons shared. He brings his class back to the present with a broad smile, as if imitating Mrs. P. himself. He gestures to the students, inviting them to embark on a journey of deeper introspection.

"Class, Mrs. Peabody called upon us to realize the crucial importance of character and virtue. Over time, the memorable sessions we spent with her grew in importance and helped Vicky and I build character and strength," says the professor. He continues. "Always remember this: character sits at the confluence of what others think and what we think about ourselves deep down inside.

Virtue, besides being an essential component of a wholesome character, not only needs to be acquired and developed but is, at the same time, the essential life tools we depend on in order to overcome, sustain, outlast, and endure our existence."

The professor pauses, his gaze sweeping across the auditorium as though still hearing Mrs. Peabody's words reverberate in the depths of his mind. Slowly, he exhales, his expression warm yet reflective.

"Mrs. P. taught us that character is not a birthright—it is a lifelong pursuit, built through discipline, forged in adversity, and enriched by virtues. Her wisdom remains with me, just as I hope it will with you," he adds, his voice steady yet tinged with emotion.

The students sit in rapt silence, the weight of his words lingering in the charged atmosphere. With a slight smile, the professor gestures toward the raised hands in the audience. He realizes that in their attentive eyes lies a quiet trust, he resolves to continues to address them by their first names only—a small gesture to bridge the gap between teacher and learner, and to remind them they are equals in curiosity.

"Professor Cromwell-Smith, how do you think we can actively cultivate character in our daily lives?" asks Sarah, a pre-law student with striking confidence in her voice.

"That's an excellent question, Sarah," the professor replies with a nod. "The key lies in intentionality. Start by being aware of your values and aligning your actions with them. As Mrs. P. said, 'Virtue is acquired and developed.' Practice compassion, honesty, and self-discipline every day, even in small matters. Over time, these actions will shape your character like water shapes a stone."

"Professor, you mentioned that character is tested through adversity. What advice do you have for maintaining integrity during tough times?" inquires Michael, a thoughtful philosophy major seated in the second row.

"Adversity is the ultimate proving ground, Michael," Erasmus begins, his tone deliberate. "During such times, reflect on what truly matters to you—your core principles. When faced with a dilemma, ask yourself: 'Does this decision align with my values?' Remember, resilience and self-discipline are built through practice. Stay true to your principles, even when it's difficult, and you will emerge stronger."

"Professor, can virtues like compassion or humility really have an impact in today's competitive world?" asks Priya, a driven business major who exudes ambition.

"Absolutely, Priya," the professor responds without hesitation. "Compassion and humility are not signs of weakness—they are strengths. In fact, they are often the qualities that inspire trust and loyalty, both in personal and professional relationships. As Mrs. P. taught us, virtues are not just moral ideals; they are practical tools for creating meaningful connections and building a legacy."

"Professor, how do you reconcile the idea of character being 'forged through discipline' with the notion of spontaneity and joy in life?" asks Jonathan, a curious art history student with a penchant for abstract questions.

Erasmus chuckles softly before answering. "Great question, Jonathan. The two aren't mutually exclusive. Discipline provides the structure, the foundation upon which spontaneity and joy can flourish. Think of it like music—discipline is the rhythm, while spontaneity is the melody. Together, they create harmony."

With this, Professor Cromwell-Smith brings the class to a close.

"He's definitely a new man," observes a regular in the professor's classes.

"Absolutely! His enthusiasm and passion are through the roof," adds a tall brunette student.

"He's also giving us more of himself," one of the professor's most ardent followers chimes in.

"His current classes are almost twice the length of his earlier sessions." A veritable sea of students contemplates the lanky figure as he pedals away on his old rusty bike.

"It's all a matter of love. It's that simple. He's truly happy for the first time in many years," reflects the leader of the web-based forum about Cromwell-Smith's classes.

The professor ends the session with a warm smile and parting words that linger in the air: "Thank you for your thoughtful questions. Remember, as Mrs. P. teaches us, your character is your legacy. Build it with care, and let your virtues guide you through life's challenges and joys."

As students gather their belongings, a few linger near the stage, their faces reflecting the profound impact of the day's lesson.

"I'm so inspired by this session," Sarah says to her friend as they walk out.

"Me too. I'm going to start keeping a journal to reflect on my actions and values every day," Priya adds, her voice filled with determination.

The students' energy fills the room, carrying forward the wisdom of Mrs. Peabody and their professor. As Erasmus watches them leave, he feels a sense of profound fulfillment, knowing that the lessons shared today will resonate far beyond the auditorium's walls.

Chapter 4

Snap Out of It

Royal Cambridge Scholastic Institute, 2018
(Erasmus and Victoria's Campus Home)

"Time to wake up," Erasmus whispers tenderly. His voice is soft, filled with love. Victoria feels the warm breath on her skin, her lips curling into a smile even as her eyes remain closed. She reaches for him, wrapping her arms around his frame.

"Got you, my prince valiant!" she teases, pulling him closer until their bodies press tightly together. His warmth makes her tremble with delight. Her legs and arms curl around him, holding him as though she never wants to let go.

Victoria radiates pure happiness, while Erasmus beams his never-ending, contented smile. Their shared joy feels timeless, an unspoken acknowledgment of the love that sustains them in every moment.

Campus Backroads

Some days, they cycle. Others, like today, they walk. Victoria leans on Erasmus, her arm wrapped around his, her head resting on his shoulder. They stroll leisurely along the tree-lined streets of campus, their steps unhurried as they savor the crisp autumn morning.

The early signs of fall are all around them: a slightly chilly breeze, temperatures dipping into the low fifties, and a kaleidoscope of New England foliage in red, yellow, and brown. Leaves scatter at their feet, swirling with each gust of wind. But Erasmus' thoughts are already straying toward the story he will share with his students—a tale of lessons learned and transformations embraced.

As the couple huddle together against the breeze, the building for Erasmus' classroom comes into view.

"Vicky, do you remember when I was constantly obsessing over everything?" Erasmus asks, breaking the gentle silence.

"How could I forget? Sometimes, you were driving both of us crazy," Victoria replies, her voice tinged with humor.

"Do you remember what we did to fix it?" he presses.

Victoria pauses, a fond look in her eyes as she recalls the memory. Then, a grin spreads across her face. "That was a fortunate set of circumstances," she says.

"Indeed, they were, Vic. Indeed, they were," Erasmus agrees, his excitement growing.

"Mr. L.?" she recalls suddenly.

"That's right, Vic, Mr. L!" he exclaims with a spark of enthusiasm.

Erasmus kisses her goodbye. Victoria, playful as always, gives him a gentle push. The gesture sends him spinning into poetic overdrive.

"My love," she says, her tone warm and encouraging, "that memorable encounter turned out to be the perfect prescription for your occasional obsessive fits. What a wonderful gift you have for your class today. Be the best you can be, my love."

With those words ringing in his ears, Professor Cromwell-Smith feels a surge of inspiration, her words echoing in his mind. He walks into the building, an extra spring in his step. The true love of his life has just sent him off in a noble state of mind and spirit. By the time he steps through the doors of the lecture hall, he is ready to bring the past to life for his eager students.

Royal Cambridge Scholastic Institute, 2018
(University Auditorium)

The lively chatter of students pulls him fully into the present, their eager faces reminding him of the importance of sharing these timeless lessons. The packed auditorium buzzes with energy as Professor Cromwell-Smith enters, whistling a cheerful tune. He pauses briefly at the front, his eyes scanning the room with a thoughtful, almost pensive intensity.

"How's everyone this morning?" he asks, his voice jovial.

"Ready for you, professor!" the students reply, their enthusiasm palpable.

"More often than not, we are our own worst enemies," he begins, his tone both serious and engaging. "Somehow, we manage to get in our own way, sabotaging our paths and disrupting the roads we're meant to take."

The room grows quiet as the students lean in, captivated.

"Today, I'll share a story about a time when an eccentric antiquarian taught Victoria and me a great lesson about how to avoid self-defeating behaviors," he continues.

The professor adjusts his glasses, his expression reflective. "There was a time back in my Harvard days when I was driving everyone crazy," he says, a faint smile tugging at his lips.

"I would get fixated on something—an idea, a task, or even a passing thought. And once it caught my attention, I would immerse myself so completely that the world—and everyone in it—became secondary. Day after day, I found myself testing the patience of those around me."

He pauses, letting his words sink in.

"That is, until one unforgettable day changed everything. It started like this..."

— ❖ —

Harvard, 1976

Harvard and Yale's rivalry is timeless and relentless. Each year, the two institutions fiercely compete for supremacy, with no clear victor as the results swing back and forth. Among the many contests, football stands as the most ferocious battleground for their enduring competition.

New Haven, Connecticut, 1976

This weekend, Erasmus and Victoria travel to Yale University in New Haven, Connecticut, for the big game. Harvard is playing on Yale's turf this year. Erasmus sits in the stands, watching as Victoria, Harvard's baton twirler, leads the band with her usual infectious energy.

From his seat, Erasmus is captivated. No matter how radiant and charismatic Victoria typically is, today she seems to shine even brighter. Her exuberance is magnetic, her enthusiasm sparkling. Above all, she radiates sheer happiness, and Erasmus finds himself hopelessly smitten by the sweet elixir of true love.

After her duties with the band are complete, the lovebirds venture into town. A French movie at the Shubert Theatre on College Street catches their eye: Les Uns et Les Autres (The Ones and the Others), directed by Claude Lelouch with music by Michel Legrand.

Huddled together in the cozy theater, they are enchanted by the film—a mesmerizing tapestry of ballet, classical music, and jazz, allegorizing the lives of Rudolf Nureyev, Glenn Miller, and Herbert von Karajan. By the time the credits roll, both are spellbound by the vibrant essence of French culture, and the movie becomes one of their all-time favorites.

As they leave the theater, fate intervenes once more. Across the street, Victoria spots something that sparks her curiosity.

"Erasmus, look—a boulangerie & bistro! Why don't we grab a bite?" she suggests, her excitement bubbling.

Inside, the tiny eatery greets them with the aroma of freshly baked bread and pastries. They sit on small, cozy chairs, a modest table between them.

"In my hometown, we have a boulangerie like this," Victoria shares, her voice tinged with nostalgia. "I grew up with real French bread and pastries."

Confidently, she steps up to place their order.

"We'll have two warm croissants, crispy on the outside and flaky inside; strawberry jam or orange marmalade; French butter on the side; and two café-au-lait, please. Oh, and a pain au chocolat to share. Thank you."

Erasmus stares, amused by her spitfire ordering. The sequence feels so natural to her, yet it leaves no room for debate—or for ordering the courses in any traditional order.

"Is this some sort of ritual for you, Vic?" he teases.

Victoria just chuckles, her joy infectious. The croissants prove heavenly, melting in Erasmus' mouth, and he marvels at the display case filled with at least twenty types of freshly baked bread.

Their main course is a simple yet exquisite bouillabaisse soup. The rich, slow-to-savor dish sets a perfect pace as they chat and laugh, building their own little world.

Then Erasmus notices something outside the window: a series of belt-driven ascending trays carrying... books.

His expression shifts to one of obsession, and alarm bells go off in Victoria's mind.

Oh boy, what is it this time? she wonders, already bracing herself.

Victoria follows his gaze. "Dear, those are...?"

"Antique books, Victoria," Erasmus replies, his voice filled with wonder.

Waving to the waitress, he asks urgently, "Excuse me, where are those books going?"

She smiles knowingly. "That's the cargo elevator for Mr. Lafayette's store upstairs. It's a clever way to catch visitors' attention—hoping some will become actual clients."

"He sells antique books?" Victoria asks, intrigued.

"Yes. Lafayette Antique Books has been around for 150 years. It started in New York City, but Mr. Lafayette moved here a few years ago after selling the original store. He owns this building now and rented the ground floor to us for the bakery."

Before their soup is finished, Erasmus throws a ten-dollar bill on the table, grabs Victoria's hand, and leads her out of the eatery.

They find the stairs and climb to the top. The sign reads:

'Lafayette Antiquarians: The Finest Antique Books in Town (est. 1867).'

"Vic, if not for your craving for croissants, we'd never have found this place," Erasmus says, grinning as they enter. "This is no coincidence. Everything is Gallic today!"

The store is breathtaking—a massive, classical space with floor-to-ceiling bookshelves framed in mahogany and oak. The scent of gardenias and roses fills the air, creating an unexpectedly refined atmosphere.

"It feels like a private library in an English manor," Erasmus whispers, awestruck.

"I've never seen anything like this," Victoria admits. "It's like a book museum."

By the window sits a tall, imposing man under the glow of a brass floor lamp. He puffs on a classic curled pipe, utterly absorbed in the book before him.

"That's Édith Piaf," Erasmus murmurs as faint music drifts through the store. Her powerful voice stirs childhood memories of his Francophile mentor, Mrs. V. "She's one of the greatest French singers of all time."

The man finally notices the young couple and stands abruptly, startled. His towering height—easily 6'5"—becomes evident as he stiffens, masking his initial surprise with caution.

"Welcome. May I help you?" he asks, his baritone voice measured.

Erasmus replies, "We're in town for the football game."

"Harvard?" the man guesses, already skeptical.

Victoria senses his judgment. 'Bad luck. He hasn't had a client in hours, and we're about to bear the brunt of his frustration', she thinks.

Erasmus, oblivious, steps forward. "Perhaps you have something about freeing one's spirit from limitations and obstacles?" Erasmus asks, his gaze fixed intensely on Victoria, as if he is involuntarily presenting a self-assessment.

A flicker of surprise and disbelief crosses Lafayette's face, morphing his expression into a smirk.

"Excuse me!" Vicky interjects impulsively, caught up in the moment. Both men turn their attention to her, noting her tone of voice. "How about something that helps overcome obsessive behavior or how to break free from situations that tend to exacerbate it?" she blurts out, capturing Erasmus's intent but with a slightly accusatory undertone.

Both Vicky and Mr. Lafayette gaze at Erasmus, but he remains oblivious, still fixated on his request.

In the meantime, the eccentric antiquarian's demeanor shifts from skepticism to curiosity and interest.

"Kids, I'm not a counselor. I sell precious, ancient books," Lafayette states firmly, recognizing the dejected expressions on their faces, which affects him on a deeper level. "Alright, let's start from the beginning. Why would you expect an antique bookstore to offer

counseling?" he asks, his tone softened with a touch of affection. It serves as an icebreaker, at least for a fleeting moment.

"We're not seeking counseling per se. We just want to look at and perhaps read a few of your manuscripts," explains Erasmus, attempting to sound assertive.

"Then why didn't you just ask?" Mr. Lafayette responds brusquely, his grumpiness dissipating. "Is this something you typically do, visiting antique bookstores to read?" the now willing and intrigued antiquarian inquires.

A brief pause ensues, and Vicky once again steps in to rescue her absent-minded boyfriend. "He has done precisely that all his life."

"Is that so?" Lafayette remarks, acknowledging Erasmus as a fellow member of the exclusive club of antique book readers. "Why didn't you say so earlier?" the old man asks, curious about the young man's potential.

"Mr. Lafayette, I presume?" Vicky asks, redirecting the conversation toward the tall antiquarian.

"Piedmont Lafayette. And may I know who I have the pleasure of speaking with?" he asks, further easing up with the tone of a man with a purpose.

"Victoria and Erasmus, sir," she quickly replies, eager to make her next point.

The large man nods, wearing a curious expression.

"Erasmus hails from Hay-on-Wye in Wales," Vicky blurts out suddenly.

Mr. Lafayette appears surprised, chiding himself for jumping to conclusions. "And I suppose he has grown up surrounded by this kind of environment?" he predicts the rest of Vicky's explanation with a broad smile on his face.

"And the store owners have been his lifelong mentors," Vicky promptly adds.

With his Mediterranean appearance, slightly tanned skin, jet black hair, and deep green eyes, Lafayette exudes an air of sophistication.

Erasmus and Victoria quickly learn that he holds an arts and literature degree from Columbia University and has been married to a French ballet dancer for thirty years, raising two grown-up children together. In his youth, Lafayette showcased his natural athleticism in soccer and basketball, with aspirations of joining the NBA. However, a knee injury redirected his path, and he soon discovered a passion for the world of antique books, following in the footsteps of his family's tradition.

"Very well, young Victoria and Erasmus, what were you both inquiring about earlier?" he asks, striding away from them.

"He knows exactly what to look for. He's a very attentive listener, even if he seems not to be," Vicky reflects, relying on her instinctive judgment to gauge his reaction. Before long, Lafayette returns, carrying two exquisite ancient books. Despite their size, they seem almost pocket-sized in his impossibly long arms.

"Alright, let's see. Here I have the perfect remedy to dispel the confusion that obsession can bring. It may not be as old as most of

the books and scribbles in here, but its wisdom is timeless. Allow me to read it to you," Mr. Lafayette suggests.

"Snap"
(Snap Out of It)

There are moments in life that overwhelm us.

They seize us right in the gut,

and suddenly,

we crumble inside,

clueless about how to cope with the situation.

Sometimes, it's simply doubts creeping in,

anguish spreading throughout our spirit,

or cold, paralyzing fear.

Other times, the shell shock is more profound.

We might be in pain, grieving a loss.

But in modern life, though,

the prevailing catalysts are

pressure, and stress,

induced by an ever-increasing overload,

coupled with a frantic, neurotic pace.

But what about simply snapping out of it?

Snap!

Snap out of it!

Snap away from the moment—

freeze the picture around you,

freeze life's image.

Just **freeze** it!

Dettach yourself from your situation.

Think only of beautiful images,

and let them take you over.

Focus on what you have, not what you lack,

not what you have lost.

Dream about what you want,

visualizing it with all your heart.

Snap out of it!

Do it without fear, without doubts.

Remind yourself that **"quitting."**

does not exist in your vocabulary.

Snap away automatically,

right when the situation arises—

without delay,

halt these poisonous states

before they even start.

Now relax.

Let go.

Contemplate the image you've frozen

from the outside.

Then, as you decompress,

you'll uncover your coping mechanisms.

Did you focus on one thing and one thing only?

If so, then you snapped away

through a meditative state.

Or did you simply do it by being aware

of the situation, and separating from it?

Or did you do it by freezing the moment?

Freezing the image?

Freezing the picture?

Or did you do all of it?

In the end, how you did it matters only

as to the path to take next time.

What truly matters

is that now you know how to snap out—

how to snap away from the moment.

Now you know

how to conquer life's circumstances,

before they conquer you.

*

As Mr. L. finishes reading in the magnificent oak and mahogany store, Vicky stares intensely at Erasmus, looking for a reaction of understanding. She thinks that if he genuinely paid attention, this would help him.

"It's not about snapping out and losing control, but exactly the opposite. It's about snapping out to regain control of yourself and

the circumstances or situations in which you may find yourself," Mr. L. clarifies.

He astutely (and correctly) senses that the reading has significantly impacted Erasmus, who is fighting his own demons. He continues, this time more directly. "Erasmus, think of it as a safety mechanism, an emergency brake that halts you immediately, preventing anything from getting started. The idea is that you catch yourself before you're lost to whatever world you fall into, especially where you are always your worst enemy."

"Fine, I get it, I get it," snaps Erasmus, seemingly surrendering, "OK, Vicky, I'll do it. Promise. I will."

"Victoria, I have a second poem. It's about dreamy, uncluttered spirits," announces Mr. Lafayette, eager to continue. Mr. L. then starts to read a scribble that begins on the rooftops of London:

"The Chimney Sweep"

The chimney sweep sits on the rooftops
of the city's moonless night.

Stars by the millions gaze down at him,
a magnificent gathering in the universe,
through luminescent eyes,
radiating infinite shades of white,
in full display, just for him.

The sweep is done for the night.
His job thoroughly completed—
unclugging and freeing,

the chimneys, and spirits,

of the city dwellers.

Now, he waits for the spectacle to unfold.

As the large metropolis succumbs to slumber,

its gateways and launching pads cleared,

debris removed, and pathways open,

the city's people are primed to dream.

And so, it begins …

First, a few,

then an avalanche of dreams

soar unimpeded,

emerging from countless chimneys

into the night sky.

They streak across the heavens,

projectiles at lightning speed

racing towards the firmament of the universe,

taking dreamers' dreams,

far away into the limitless space,

in the direction, and watchful eyes,

of millions of stars gazing and waiting for them.

*

"We all need our chimney sweeps to free our spirits and dreams so they can soar to the deepest confines of the universe," says an inspired Mr. Lafayette.

From that moment on, a beautiful bond grows between Mr. L. and the young lovers. Though their meetings are infrequent, Victoria and Erasmus make a point to visit whenever the Harvard football team plays near New Haven. As Victoria had predicted, over time, the connection between Mr. L. and Erasmus becomes intrinsic to the latter's life—even after Victoria's vanishing act. Mr. Lafayette's wisdom serves as a guiding light through Erasmus's years of solitude, offering him perspective and strength when he needs it most.

As we left the antique bookstore that day, I carried not just books but life-changing lessons. Little did I know how often I would rely on them.

—◆—

Royal Cambridge Scholastic Institute, 2018
(University Auditorium)

Professor Cromwell-Smith looks out at his class, bringing them gently back to the present. Yet he notices that only a few faces show an eagerness to return.

"That memorable first encounter with Mr. Lafayette," he begins, "not only provided us with invaluable life tools but also delivered a crucial realization about our fallibility. Class, what happened to Vicky and me—the parting, that is—could just as easily happen to any of you.

"To prevent it, you must learn to extract yourself and disengage from situations that overwhelm you. By 'snapping out' of it, you allow yourself to pause and observe from the outside. This perspective helps clear the day, the circumstance, and the road ahead, unblocking and unsabotaging it—freeing it from the constraints of your own ego or emotional chaos."

"These poems remind us that whether we snap out of our struggles or unclog our spirits, the power to change our circumstances lies within us," The pedagogue reasons. He pauses, letting the weight of his words settle. As Professor Cromwell-Smith concludes his reflections, he steps forward and gestures toward the students. "Now, let's hear your thoughts. Who has questions about what we've explored today?"

Natasha, a thoughtful young woman with curly hair and wearing a cozy sweater, raises her hand. Her major is psychology, and she often brings a reflective depth to the class discussions.

"Professor," she begins, "in *Snap Out of It*, you mention the importance of overcoming negativity. How can we apply that to our everyday challenges?"

"Great question, Natasha!" the professor responds, his tone warm and encouraging. "The message in *Snap Out of It* is about recognizing when negativity takes hold and making a conscious decision to disrupt that cycle. It's a practice of self-awareness. By deliberately pausing and redirecting our focus toward gratitude or positivity, we regain control. This shift allows us to see challenges as opportunities for growth rather than obstacles."

Daniel, a tall, enthusiastic student with glasses and a graphic tee, raises his hand next. A literature major, Daniel is passionate about analyzing the symbolic nuances in poetry.

"In *The Chimney Sweep*, you describe the act of dreaming and freeing one's spirit. How can we hold on to that sense of hope in the face of life's challenges?" he asks.

"Excellent point, Daniel!" the professor exclaims. "The chimney sweep symbolizes the effort we must make to keep our spirits unclogged—free from doubt, fear, or negativity. Life's challenges can dim our hopes, but the key is to nurture our dreams. Treat them like fragile yet powerful entities. Protect them, and let them remind you of what is possible. When we focus on our aspirations, we can rise above life's weight and find clarity."

Lynn, an expressive and animated art history major wearing a colorful scarf, eagerly raises her hand. "Professor, both poems emphasize clarity and freedom of the mind and spirit. Is there a specific practice you'd recommend to cultivate that clarity?"

The professor nods appreciatively. "Lynn, cultivating clarity is about creating habits that center and ground us. Meditation, journaling, or even moments of quiet reflection can help us step back from the chaos and reconnect with ourselves. The goal is to regularly clear away the mental debris so we can think and act with purpose."

As he glances around the room, Professor Cromwell-Smith realizes his students crave more. Their eager expressions spur him to share a final piece of wisdom.

"For our dreams to soar unimpeded, we must make a deliberate effort to constantly cleanse our spirits," he says softly. His voice carries the weight of lived experience and heartfelt sincerity.

"Remember, it is through clarity and lightness that we rise."

He concludes with a warm smile. "Class, next week, we'll travel back to the moment Vicky and I met an extraordinary person who lived on the outskirts of Boston. A person who forever touched our lives."

As the session winds down, Professor Cromwell-Smith looks out at his students, their faces reflecting introspection and curiosity. With a warm smile, he closes the discussion. "Thank you for your thoughtful questions. Remember, these lessons aren't just poetry—they're tools for living. Class dismissed."

On his way out, the pedagoue notices his students' faces—some reflecting introspection, others brimming with the readiness to "snap out" of their own doubts. In their eyes, he sees the unmistakable spark; his students are getting ready to fly away as the dreams of dreamers often do.

Chapter 5

Faith

Royal Cambridge Scholastic Institute, 2018
(Erasmus and Victoria's Campus Home)

It is early morning, near dawn, when Erasmus suddenly awakens.

"What is it, dear?" Victoria asks, her voice laced with concern.

Erasmus is drenched in sweat, his eyes glossy and disoriented. Slowly, he comes to and recognizes that she's lying next to him. A wave of comfort spreads across his face.

"I was having a bad dream," he replies groggily, still half asleep.

"The same dream?" Vicky asks, her concern carefully masked.

"Yes," he answers, frustration creeping into his voice.

"Look at me!" she says defiantly, holding his face with both hands.

"I'm not going anywhere, my love. Erasmus, you've got to have faith."

He nods sheepishly, snapping out of it.

(Campus Backroads)

In the mild autumn weather, a giggling Victoria and Erasmus pedal lazily down the streets of Cambridge, weaving in playful zigzags as if nothing had happened.

"Faith, Erasmus. I never lost faith that I would find you somewhere down the road of life," she states with quiet assertiveness.

Her words linger in his mind, a steadying force as they pedal through the crisp morning air.

As the enamored couple approaches the main faculty building, Erasmus feels the weight of the day ahead settling on him. Struck by a sudden memory, his thoughts shift from playful moments with Victoria to the lessons he is about to impart.

"Do you remember when we both ran into Faith?" asks an inspired Erasmus.

"You mean Thomas Albert Faith?" Victoria replies, her face lighting up at the mere mention of their old friend.

Erasmus nods slightly, his grin mischievous.

"Of course I do," Victoria says. "Dear, your class better be prepared for it. What a magnificent idea! Just be yourself," she adds, giving him that little extra boost he has come to rely on.

Royal Cambridge Scholastic Institute, 2018
(University Auditorium)

The class is assembled and buzzing with energy as Professor Cromwell-Smith storms in, full of life.

"Hello, class!" he greets enthusiastically.

"Hello, Professor!" many voices reply in unison.

"Today, you'll meet a very special man who transformed the way Vicky and I viewed life. It was at a time when I desperately needed to grow—spiritually and emotionally. It begins like this…"

—✦—

Riverside Village, Boston Suburbs, 1976

Victoria and Erasmus have been rowing for hours on the Charles River, their rhythm slow and steady. The rowboat, uncomfortably narrow but thrillingly fast, glides gracefully across the water. The young couple's movements are synchronized to choreographic perfection.

Along the way, they stop twice. First, they dock at a seafood joint on the riverbank, hunger pressing them indoors. Still dressed in their rowing attire, they step in eagerly.

"Your hair looks so pretty with those colored ribbons," Erasmus says gallantly.

Victoria blushes slightly, smiling. "Can we switch places when we row again?" she asks, chuckling softly.

"Why?" Erasmus asks, puzzled.

"So I can be the one watching your gorgeous silhouette against the scenery on the way home," she teases, her voice brimming with affection.

Erasmus flashes a big smile in response.

"So, your first New England clam chowder was in Boston?" she quips, teasing him as Erasmus devours chunks of the famous dish.

"Yes," he replies, grinning mid-bite.

Their second stop is a riverside winter garden enclosed in glass. Its vibrant colors and peculiar location catch their attention.

Inside, the garden is even more stunning. The couple meanders along its labyrinthine paths, surrounded by lush greenery. As they turn a corner, they notice a man seated at a picnic table. An enormous book, its aged leather cover glinting with gold-burnished pages, is propped before him.

Erasmus halts, his gaze fixed.

"That's an ancient book," he murmurs to Vicky. "Why would someone have it here, in the open? It's so rare to see something like that."

The man, absorbed in his reading, doesn't notice them at first.

Erasmus approaches, hoping the crunch of his steps on the pebbled path will draw the man's attention. The burly reader, with light brown hair and a stocky build, glances up briefly, then stands abruptly. Cradling the book in his arms, he leaves in a hurry.

Erasmus and Victoria exchange a glance before following at a discreet distance. The man walks through the narrow streets of the village, finally entering a store.

"Let's wait and see what happens," Erasmus suggests.

A few minutes later, the man exits the store, casting a brief glance in their direction before marching away. The book is no longer in his possession.

Tentatively, the couple approaches the shop. A sign above the door reads: 'Faith Antique Books & Co. (est. 1907).' Further down the display window, a smaller sign catches their eye.

"Please inquire about a limited number of our books available to let," Erasmus reads aloud. "That explains it," he remarks, recalling the burly man and the book.

"Do you think it's just religious books in there?" Victoria asks as they step closer.

"It's possible, but faith isn't strictly a religious term," Erasmus replies.

He hesitates before opening the door. The familiar chime of a bell greets them, evoking memories of Erasmus's childhood in the antique bookshops of Hay-on-Wye. The scent and sound are comforting, though the store's interior is a surprise.

Stark and modern, the shop features chrome and glass elements. Ten long rows of bookshelves rise thirty feet to the ceiling, which is lined with glass panes.

"I've been in this area for thirty years, and this is a first for me," declares a high-pitched voice from behind them.

Startled, Victoria and Erasmus whirl around to face a bold, stocky man with a broad grin.

"Coming to visit us dressed as oarsmen, no less," he says with a chuckle.

The young couple laughs, their initial tension melting away.

"This is also a first for me," Erasmus replies confidently.

"How so?" the man asks, intrigued.

"A faith-focused antique bookstore," Erasmus explains.

The store owner, amused by their response, erupts into hearty laughter. Erasmus and Vicky discover that he is a Harvard Business School graduate who had previously worked as an investment banker on Wall Street. After spending over a decade in London, where he married his second wife, an antiquarian, he found his true passion in the world of antique books and left the finance industry behind.

"Faith is my name. Thomas Albert Faith. We carry books of all kinds, from all walks of life."

Introductions follow, and a conversation ensues, filled with warmth and curiosity.

"Mr. Faith," Erasmus ventures, "we were wondering if you could share some of your writings on a particular subject?"

"And what subject would that be?"

Vicky seizes the opportunity, her instincts sharp as ever.

"Faith," she says simply, staring intently at Mr. Faith.

A pause follows.

"Faith?" he repeats, confused.

"Yes, faith," she clarifies. "It's something he struggles with all the time. Would you happen to have an old, impactful writing that could offer some existential clarity?"

Mr. Faith smiles, amused. "Let me share something I've treasured all my adult life."

He strides confidently down the second hallway, climbing a tall ladder to retrieve a small blue book. Holding it aloft triumphantly, he descends and joins the young couple at a chrome and glass table. Seated with them, he begins to read in earnest.

"Faith"

Faith is a celestial force that we willfully invoke
to profess our credos with overwhelming intensity.

Faith morphs believing into an unstoppable inner strength
that becomes our spiritual engine
and dotes us with a continuum of goodness
and a giving soul.

Faith is awareness of the spirit
and mindfulness of the soul.

Faith is the indispensable source
of meaning in our lives.

It is mysterious, dealing with two rational,
unsolvable, and existential questions:
The conundrum of creation and the enigma of a higher calling.

Faith is the realization that even though
there are many questions about our universe's origin,
that we do not have an answer for:
- We have no proof how it was created?
- Neither do we know where are we going after life?
we still deliberately chose to believe wholeheartedly
and steadfastly in the existence of a Creator of it all.

Faith is our rudder and keel
steering us through
life's labyrinths of uncertainty.

Faith is unconditional love—
an immutable, unwavering, unflickering
and indomitable stubborn belief
that there is a reason and a higher purpose
for us being here,
dictated by our creator.

When we profess is hidden inside a cocoon,

Faith is nothing but an empty shell of falsehood.

Individualistic faith thrives behind walls of weakness,

erected to shy away from the world

through self-serving beliefs,

mere tunnel vision fantasies,

like mirages in the desert.

The world of darkness awaits us <u>when faith is blind</u>.

A life without a periscope

may lead us down perilous paths

leading to dire, unintended ruin.

<u>When we profess misguided faith</u>,

life quickly loses its compass and purpose.

Without direction–fake passions and beliefs

propel us forward,

into tumbling trajectories,

where, if our endeavors prove to be hazardous or hurtful,

Faith becomes a runaway train

that derails, crashes, and burns.

To the contrary,

<u>Faith is authentic</u> and enduring

when driven by virtue and belief

in The Creator.

<u>But we are not born in faith or virtue</u>

as both have to be acquired

and they grow in tandem,

feeding off one another.

Faith ages over time, like a fine wine,

out of our relentless pursuit,

through hard work and discipline,

of virtue, excellence, and an inalterable,

unassailable belief in the creator of all things.

When we have faith,

we see light in darkness,

offer love when there is hate,

we offer compassion

when there is pain and suffering,

we provide healing where there are wounds,

we show loyalty when there is betrayal,

we willingly reconcile when there is conflict,

we readily forgive when there is hurt,

we sacrifice and abnegate for those that need it most,

we rise to the occasion when the situation could not be worse,

we acquiesce and adjourn when the circumstances require it,

we are always austere and humble,

we are grateful and anonymous in our actions,

and our hearts are pure, crystalline,

joyful, and wholesome.

Above all, we trust our Creator teachings.

When we have faith, we acclaim life and humanity,

elevating our existence to a higher calling—

one where we acquire through creed and conversion,

a noble purpose of Spirit

and a God-driven meaning for the Soul.

*

As Mr. Faith finishes, the powerful words linger throughout the store.

"Young man," he says, his tone firm yet kind, "use faith as a source of inner strength. It'll teach you to believe and see through any obstacle life may present. Faith is also the best resource to neutralize and overcome doubt, indecisiveness, and fear. Erasmus, the more faith you profess, the more you will grow as a man."

— ✦ —

Royal Cambridge Scholastic Institute, 2018
(University Auditorium)

Reluctantly, Professor Cromwell-Smith brings his audience back into the lecture hall.

"Class," he begins, his voice steady and profound, "faith is the strongest, deepest, most indomitable, and unbreakable of all beliefs. It'll carry you through the deepest sorrows and pains, devastating losses, and seasons of weakness, through obliterating storms and shattering quakes. Faith enables you to forgive with grace and give without expecting rewards. Faith nurtures you with a benevolent heart, a driven spirit, and a calm soul.

"Faith is always pure and genuine as we walk alongside the creator."

The oration concluded, the professor opens the floor for questions.

The professor scans the room, his gaze landing on Lewis, a second-year history major who rarely speaks in class. Today, however, his hand is raised.

"Professor," Lewis begins, adjusting his baseball cap nervously, "Mr. Faith spoke about believing in something greater. How can we apply this concept to our goals and ambitions without losing sight of our authentic selves?"

"Excellent insight, Lewis!" Professor Cromwell-Smith replies, his tone encouraging.

"The lesson highlights that true faith empowers us to rise above our circumstances. When we believe in something greater than ourselves, we create a sense of purpose that guides our actions. Faith helps us align our ambitions with larger beliefs, ensuring that our journey is not only about achievement but also about staying true to our core values and fostering genuine connections."

The professor's response earns a thoughtful nod from Lewis, who seems reassured by the answer.

Next, Megyn, a philosophy student with a sharp intellect and an eye for detail, raises her hand. A notebook filled with meticulous notes rests open in front of her.

"Professor," she begins, her voice steady, "isn't faith a religious term?"

The professor smiles knowingly. "Megyn, religion is perhaps the most widely recognized method of practicing faith, but it is far from the only way. Faith manifests in many forms. We place faith in our partners, loved ones, humanity, our friends, and even in ourselves."

Megyn adjusts her glasses and presses further. "So, faith isn't exclusive to any particular religion?"

"Right, it isn't, Megyn" the professor affirms gently. "All religions practice faith, but it transcends any single belief system. Faith is the driving force behind them all. It lies within us, ready to illuminate our lives with a celestial halo—a light that radiates outward but originates from within."

"We may come from different backgrounds and corners of the earth, but ultimately, we all breathe the same air, walk under the same skies, and share the same capacity for faith."

The professor's words settle over the room, leaving a sense of quiet reflection. As the students begin to pack their belongings, a few linger, discussing the day's lesson in hushed tones.

"I'll see you all next week," Professor Cromwell-Smith concludes. As he leaves the auditorium, he is deeply moved by the faces of his students. Each one reflects an unmistakable expression of hope—a quiet testament to faith, the existential condition that binds them all. The professor notices a few students lingering, their quiet conversations reflecting the depth of the day's lesson.

Amara, a third-year political science major with a keen interest in ethics, turns to her classmate. "Faith as a guiding force—not just religiously but personally. That's something to think about," she murmurs thoughtfully.

Theo, a freshman in the arts program with a talent for sculpture, nods in agreement. "It's like having an anchor in chaos. I can see how that could apply to my work—faith in the creative process."

The professor observes these interactions as he steps into the crisp autumn air, rustling the leaves on the old oaks lining the campus paths. Each student's expression lingers in his mind—hopeful, introspective, and determined.

He is deeply moved by the realization that they leave not only with the lesson of the day but with an understanding of faith's transformative power—a foundation for living a meaningful, purpose-driven life.

Chapter 6

Life, Evolution, and Change

Royal Cambridge Scholastic Institute, 2018
(Erasmus and Victoria's Campus Home)

A sweet smell stirs her awake. At the foot of the bed sits a breakfast basket filled with French pastries.

How does he manage this time and time again? Vicky wonders, stretching languidly, still half-asleep. The soft tune of Jimmy Durante's *"Make Someone Happy,"* one of her favorite songs, plays faintly in the background. She inhales deeply and smiles, starting her day grinning from ear to ear—all thanks to her beloved Brit.

"Live each day as if it is your last," she recites dutifully, rising from bed. She wanders through the house in search of Erasmus. After her effusive giggles, exuberant hugs, and a series of playful kisses, they sit down to eat.

"It still amazes me that for years we frequented the same antiquarians in this city and yet never crossed paths," Victoria whispers, sipping her tea and delicately nibbling on her selection of patisserie.

"Even more puzzling is that knowing us both, Mr. Ringwald never put us in touch," Erasmus laments.

"Out of discretion, dear. Mr. Ringwald knew about my marriage and children. He probably realized how much it would hurt you to hear about that," Vicky says gently.

"Vic, was he right though? I'm not sure," Erasmus muses.

"He was, yes. For instance, did you ever specifically ask him about me or my whereabouts?"

"No, I didn't. It never occurred to me," Erasmus admits, reflecting.

"Well, neither did I. Perhaps a part of me didn't want to know," she explains softly. "My rational side knew I had a family and a husband, and they came first. I suppose I just didn't want to open that door."

"Our shared love for antique bookstores must have kept a faint link between us," Erasmus wonders aloud, searching for meaning in their lost years.

"Perhaps," Victoria murmurs, still unconvinced, handing him the car keys.

As they step outside, a blast of cold air envelops them, a stark reminder of the overnight snowstorm. The morning is white and frosty, with winter making its presence known in New England.

"Apropos, Vic," Erasmus begins, "today's class is about the memorable day we met Mr. Ringwald for the first time."

"That day is one I've cherished my entire life. Everything about it was so special," Victoria says, her eyes glittering with warmth at the memory.

"To my surprise, my irresistible Brit," she adds, "I'm coming with you today. How much time do we have?"

"Just under an hour before class begins," Erasmus replies, startled by her spontaneity.

"Perfect. I just need to make a quick stop at BU beforehand," Victoria says.

"Whatever my lady desires," Erasmus replies gallantly.

As they drive through the frozen landscape toward the university, Victoria applies makeup, a sight Erasmus loves to watch. Today, however, his focus remains mostly on the icy roads. Soon, he pulls into the driveway of Victoria's BU faculty building.

"I just need to sign a few forms and let them know I'll be back before lunch. Ten minutes tops," she says, stepping out of the car briskly.

"Careful on the ice, Vic!" Erasmus calls after her, but she's already out of sight.

Royal Cambridge Scholastic Institute, 2018
(University Auditorium)

Forty-five minutes later, the couple strolls into Erasmus's class. Victoria heads straight for a quiet spot among the students, but her presence does not go unnoticed. A faint murmur ripples through the auditorium, growing louder as students exchange curious glances.

The buzz subsides only when the professor clears his throat.

"Good morning, everyone," Erasmus greets with a broad smile.

"Good morning!" the students reply in unison, many still recalling the last time they saw Victoria—the day she and the professor reconnected.

"Well, as you've all noticed, we have a special guest with us this morning," he announces. "I was as surprised as you when I learned about her impromptu visit today."

Victoria blushes as heads continue to turn toward her.

"The fact is, when my other half heard about today's topic, she couldn't bear to miss it," Erasmus adds with pride. "And so, with all that being said, the story begins like this…"

— ✦ —

Harvard Theatre, 1976

Erasmus peeks nervously through the curtains, scanning the audience. His careful planning will all be for nothing if she's not here. 'Something must have happened,' he thinks, despair rising. 'Most of the audience is already seated. Where is she? he asks himself, panicking.'

"The event is about to begin. Everyone, please take a seat," a voice booms over the tannoy.

'It's still not too late to quit,' Erasmus thinks, doubt creeping in. He has never done anything like this in front of an audience before.

"Good morning, everyone. Welcome to the 10th Annual Harvard College Poetry Contest. Let me introduce you to the jury," announces the event host.

'Point of no return, mate. You can't back out now, Erasmus thinks, swallowing hard. In a few minutes, you'll be making a complete fool of yourself in front of everyone.'

He peeks through the curtains one last time—and freezes. There she is, sitting in the front row. While consumed by panic, he had completely missed her arrival.

Adrenaline surges through him, his despair instantly replaced with determination. He looks again, and this time, he chuckles softly. His confidence has returned. He is read

Victoria and Gina sit in the front row, attending a poetry contest for the first time. Victoria appears at ease but carries a faint sadness in her expression. Gina, meanwhile, looks surprised and a little out of place.

"Where's Erasmus?" Gina asks, glancing around.

"He couldn't make it," Victoria replies with a hint of melancholy.

"But he begged me not to miss it, so I could tell him all about it later tonight."

Though she tries to sound casual, Vicky feels a distinct void in his absence.

At that moment, Erasmus's spiraling thoughts are interrupted by the voice of the master of ceremonies.

"Our first contestant comes all the way from Wales, in the United Kingdom! His name is Erasmus Cromwell-Smith, and he will be reading a very special poem dedicated to his unsuspecting sweetheart in the audience. Mrs. Victoria Emerson-Lloyd—could you please stand?"

A stunned Victoria rises slowly, completely caught off guard. A knot of intense emotions forms in her throat. But as Erasmus steps onto the stage, his loving gaze locks onto hers, and a wave of calm washes over her. Her body relaxes, and a radiant grin spreads across her face.

Erasmus approaches the lectern, clears his throat, and begins to read. His loving, warm voice instantly captivates her.

*

"Whispering at Your Heart"

What is it that makes you so magnificent?

You are special because you are

unique and inimitable.

You are magical because everything you touch

with your magic wand

falls under a divine spell.

You are as beautiful as your heart is,

You are intense as your feelings are,

You are as driven and indomitable as your passions are,

You are as immutably firm as you are fiercely loyal,

crafted out of unwavering convictions

and unbreakable beliefs.

Your relentless discipline and perseverance

makes you tirelessly steady.

Hence, your consistency never falters

or ceases to be.

You are sincere, genuine, and honest;

irrespective of what others think or say,

you always follow your heart.

You are built of boundless strength,

courage, and integrity.

You are so valiant that time and again,

you always combat fear with unwavering resolve.

You are stunning in the morning
irresistible at sundown.

You are genuine and adorable,
filled with ingenuity and candor.

You are noble and dependable;
rain or shine, in wind or heavy seas,
you are always there.

You are virtuous and giving,
forever ready to forgive and help others.

You are humble,
quick to admit your faults and make amends,
and you wear this eternal halo,
bestowed by heaven's angels,
an impenetrable shield
protecting you from anything or anyone.
It is forged from unshakable faith,
a steadfast character,
and a fierce and relentless pursuit of excellence.

All of this and more is you,
Victoria.
I love you.
Forever yours,
Erasmus.

*

Harvard Theatre, 1976

As applause breaks out, the couple has eyes only for each other. Suddenly, it's as if the rest of the world fades away, leaving them alone in their own wonderful bubble.

"Thank you," Victoria mouths to Erasmus, her hands pressed against her heart.

He nods in acknowledgment, mirroring her gesture with his own hands.

For a brief moment that feels eternal in its intensity, they simply stare at each other, lost in infatuation.

The Streets of Downtown Boston, 1976

When Erasmus emerges from backstage and sits beside Victoria, the couple only wants to be alone. Together, they wander the streets of Boston without a destination in mind, their laughter echoing in the cool evening air.

As the clamorous sounds of the city attempt to pierce their bubble, Erasmus instinctively steers them toward the riverbank. They stroll down a quiet, dead-end street, when something catches his eye—a fleeting glimpse of a cart piled high with books, pulled by a shadowy figure.

Erasmus stops abruptly, his senses heightened. Spinning around, he fixes his gaze on the end of the street and is rewarded with the validation of his instincts.

"Are those what I think they are?" Victoria asks, following his penetrating gaze, though she already knows the answer.

"Indeed, they are, Vic. Let's go check them out," Erasmus replies.

Hand in hand, they walk briskly toward the book cart. Their path leads them to a small shop, and they halt in surprise. The cart they had seen earlier now rests at the store's entrance. In the window, two large round stickers read:

"Going Out FOR Business Sale."

Erasmus reads the sign above the shop aloud:

'Ringwald and Brothers Antiquarians (est. 1860).'

At that moment, a diminutive man, barely 5'2", emerges from the shop. He shuffles over to the cart, carrying an enormous stack of books inside with surprising ease. His eccentric appearance catches their attention—he wears a red plaid vest and sports disproportionately large arms, head, and shoes for his stature.

Percival Ringwald, a Boston native, married late in life. On their wedding night, he promised his antiquarian wife that they would visit every place he had traveled before they met. Decades later, he has kept that vow. When not exploring the world together, they immerse themselves in their shared passions: philosophy, poetry, and the antique bookstore.

Erasmus and Victoria watch in fascination as Mr. Ringwald unloads the books with the strength and efficiency of an ant. Once finished, he pulls the cart to the side, then abruptly turns to face the couple, hands on his hips.

"What are you two waiting for?" he asks, jolting them out of their daze.

Erasmus and Victoria tighten their grip on each other's hands, momentarily speechless.

"Erasmus and Victoria, right?" the man continues, a mischievous grin spreading across his face.

The couple exchanges incredulous looks.

"What did you expect?" Mr. Ringwald says with a chuckle. "The two of you have been making noise in our small community. Good noise, I might add—terrific noise, in fact."

Gesturing toward the door, he adds, "Well, come on in."

Inside, the store is breathtaking. Mahogany wall panels stretch from floor to ceiling, thirty feet high, forming a perfect rectangle. Thousands of books are impeccably arranged on shelves that climb all the way up.

"How are you going out of business with a place like this?" Erasmus asks, awestruck.

"Tell me, young man," Mr. Ringwald replies with a sly grin, "when have you ever seen a store bringing in stock while going out of business?"

Erasmus hesitates. "I guess... well, never, sir."

"Exactly. So, what does that tell you?"

"Is it just a marketing ploy?" Victoria ventures cautiously.

"Right on, Victoria. The key is in the word 'for' instead of 'of.'" He gestures toward the window, his grin widening.

"Sir, you know our names, but we don't know yours," Victoria says, nudging for an answer.

"You think you don't, but you do," Mr. Ringwald replies cryptically.

Victoria's mind races. 'The Riddler.' That's what I'll call him. Mr. R., that's it, she decides.

"OK, Mr. R., we get it," Erasmus says, picking up on Victoria's train of thought.

"So, I'm Mr. R. now, am I?" the antiquarian responds, clearly amused.

Victoria watches Erasmus pace around the shop, his hands clasped behind his back, scrutinizing every detail.

"Mr. R., what about change?" Erasmus asks, his tone pensive.

"What about it?" Mr. R. counters.

"Do you have anything on the subject?"

Victoria interjects, "Erasmus struggles with change. It doesn't come easily to him."

"What about evolution?" Mr. R. replies.

"Are you suggesting we read about evolution instead?" Erasmus asks, growing accustomed to the man's questioning style—and starting to enjoy it.

"Not instead of, but alongside. Change and evolution are practically joined at the hip, you know?" Mr. R. explains.

Without waiting for a response, he moves swiftly through the store, shuffling toward a portable hi-lo against one wall. Climbing halfway up, he pulls down a massive volume from a high shelf.

"This one," he announces upon his return, "explores change and evolution through the lens of philosophy. Let me read it to you."

*

"Life, Evolution, and Change Among Us"

Two of the most fundamental states in life
are measured by each stroke forward
on the hands of our life clock.

The corroboratory tick of the larger, faster hand
is that of the sound of change,
while the smaller, steadier hand,
validating its clicks are those of the sound of evolution.
If the minutes tick,
then the hours will inevitably click on.

Change engenders evolution,
not the other way around.
If change signifies the transition
from one condition to another,
then evolution is a series
of guided advancements born of change.

Change is doors opening;
evolution is tstepping through and staying within.

Change is the pursuit of something new, different,
perhaps even disruptive.
Evolution is the realization of such endeavor.

Change is the end of a paradigm,
evolution defines the new one.

Change demands willingness and desire;
evolution becomes self-evident.

Change can ignite second chances;
evolution is the second chance fulfilled.

Change is lasting and most effective
when accompanied by consciousness
and rewarded by evolution.

Change and dogma
are like oil and water.
Evolution acts as the filter that separates
and casts dogma aside.

Change is easily measurable—
it is seasonal and occurs in bursts.

Evolution, too, is quantifiable,
but it flows constantly,
cutting through every season.

When we change for others, our heart leads,
and evolution crowns our new and richer royal heart.

When something changes us,
the presence or absence of evolution
is the undeniable proof of whether change
was for better or worse.

Change flourishes when driven by mindfulness,

and evolution is the harvest.

Real change requires truthfulness;
and evolution is its validation.

Monsters could be born out of change,
when combined with material things
such as greed or power;
then, instead of evolution, we could regress,
doomed to a downward spiral.

Change could also be opportunistic
or it could be deliberate,
but its execution and validation
are governed by the same tool:
the steady hand of evolution.

When we change,
we willingly shift, transfer, or transform;
we break, deviate, mutate, or alter;
we switch courses or conditions,
depart from old beliefs,
or shift sequences and norms.

When we embrace change with open hearts,
we shed the weight of stagnant pasts.
It flows through us, a cleansing stream,
awakening courage, reigniting dreams.

But only through evolution
do these changes take root and thrive..

Change is not bound by time,
but by opportune circumstances,
and evolution is the reward for proper timing.

Change is virtuous when driven by moral truisms,
evolution is the embodiment of those virtues.
Change gains recognition when it is unpretentious,
its worth proven by the evolution that follows.

Because we fear it,
change demands courage and valor;
evolution is the medal of honor we earn.

To resist change is to wrestle with chaos,
a storm of fear and fractured will.
To embrace it is to waltz with harmony,
a symphony guided by purpose and skill.

Through the dance of change and evolution,
our lives are never static—
forever in motion,
renewing themselves in a constant state of flux.

When we embrace change,
we align ourselves with the laws of nature
and the essence of life itself,

welcoming a universal truth:

perennial transformation.

In this rhythm,

the sounds of change

and the winds of evolution

tick and click in perfect harmony,

moving inexorably forward,

never ceasing, never swaying away.

Click-tick...Tick-click...Tick-tick...Click-click...

*

Mr. Ringwald draws his reading to a close with a contemplative pause and a deep breath. "I believe it was Machiavelli who once said, 'If you want to see people at their worst, bring them changes" His voice softens, resonating with thought. "Our fear of change only serves as a roadblock on our existential paths, built on false perceptions of comfort, safety, and the familiar."

"When I began this journey as an antiquarian, I thought I was simply collecting books. But over the years, I've realized it's about much more—the stories behind them, the lives they touched, and the changes they inspired."

"That's fascinating, Mr. R. What drove you to pursue this path?"

"Ah, my dear boy, it was the thrill of discovery! Each book is a portal to another time, another world. Change, you see, is not something to fear—it's the very essence of life. Every page turned is a step forward."

"Change feels daunting sometimes. How do you embrace it without hesitation?"

"Embrace it? No, I dance with it! Life is a waltz, my boy. You must learn the steps. Yes, it can be challenging, but remember—every step forward is a chance to learn, to evolve."

"It's like when we met. I never anticipated how life would twist and turn, yet here we are."

"Exactly! Life is a series of beautiful twists. Don't resist them; let them guide you."

— ✦ —

Royal Cambridge Scholastic Institute, 2018
(University Auditorium)

Professor Cromwell-Smith's dreamy eyes refocus as he returns to the present, meeting the startled yet curious gazes of his students.

"Much of the art of a wholesome life resides in the power of change—by constantly renewing and reinventing oneself. Don't fear it. Embrace it," he declares, smiling with quiet satisfaction.

"Questions?" he prompts, looking around the room.

Tina, a third-year philosophy student known for her thoughtful reflections, raises her hand. "Professor, you mentioned that change drives evolution. How can we actively embrace change, especially when it feels uncomfortable?"

"An excellent question, Tina," Professor Cromwell-Smith responds warmly. "The process begins with a shift in mindset. As the poem suggests, change is a natural and essential part of life. To embrace it, we must view it not as a threat but as an opportunity for growth.

When we adapt to change with intention and openness, it paves the way for evolution, allowing us to grow into stronger, wiser versions of ourselves."

Johnny, a freshman in the arts program with a passion for sculpture, raises his hand next. "Professor, Mr. Ringwald spoke about the fear of change being a roadblock. How can we overcome that fear and evolve positively through our experiences?"

"Insightful question, Johnny!" the professor replies, his tone encouraging. "Fear of change often stems from the unknown. To overcome it, we must face it directly and reflect on past changes in our lives. Consider how those changes shaped and strengthened you. When you see experiences as lessons, you can approach future changes with confidence and a renewed sense of purpose."

The professor pauses, scanning the room for further questions. The silence is thoughtful, indicating his students are deeply engaged with the subject.

With that, Professor Cromwell-Smith smiles and brings the session to a close. "That will be all for today. See you next week."

As the professor scans the room, his gaze lands on Victoria. She is standing, tears glistening in her eyes, her face illuminated by a radiant smile. Slowly, she places both hands over her heart and mouths the words, "Thank you."

Erasmus tips his head ever so slightly in acknowledgment, placing both hands over his own heart. With lips miming the words, he responds, "I love you."

The student body, captivated by the tender exchange, watches in awe as the professor and his soul mate remain suspended in their private world, as if time itself has paused.

Hand in hand, Professor Cromwell-Smith and Victoria walk out of the auditorium. As they pass, Erasmus notices the twinkle in his students' eyes—a newfound openness to change and evolution.

Chapter 7

Life Wizards

Royal Cambridge Scholastic Institute, 2018
(Erasmus and Victoria's Campus Home)

Erasmus always wakes earlier than Victoria. In the pre-dawn darkness, he moves quietly around the house—something he rarely did when living alone. It's one of many habits they've reacquired from their time together as young lovers. In many ways, it feels as if they were never apart.

Today, Erasmus discovers life is even rosier than his idealist heart imagined. Entering his study, he switches on the brass floor lamp. The golden burnished letters of a familiar antique book immediately draw his attention. On the worn Chesterfield sofa lies a leather-bound volume he has searched for his entire life.

Carefully, he picks up the book, emotions soaring. The title reads *Life Wizards,* written in sweeping, flourished lettering.

"I've looked for you for so long," Erasmus whispers, overwhelmed. Opening the book, a small card slips out and falls to the floor. Recognizing Victoria's handwriting, he smiles.

Holding the book, he sits on the sofa and begins reading.

*You make me so happy, Erasmus. I don't know how I could have left you all those years ago. Please forgive me. I know you've wanted this book ever since you first read it with Mrs. V., your childhood *mentor. I've never forgotten the day you shared those wonderful passages with me, the day we found it at the Library of Congress.*

With all my love,

Yours forever,

Victoria.*

Teary-eyed, Erasmus looks up to see Victoria standing in the doorway.

"Oh, Vic, you shouldn't have," he stammers, rising to embrace her. "This must have cost you a fortune. How did you find it?"

"Do you remember where you first saw this book?" Victoria asks, her voice warm with nostalgia.

"The Library of Congress," Erasmus replies with excitement.

"Yes. That place was overwhelming in the best way. Rows of books, whispering stories from the past, just waiting for someone to uncover them," Victoria reminisces.

"Yes, the country's Athenaeum. It was there I first learned to appreciate the power of words," Erasmus says, his joy fading slightly as he notices the stern look in her eyes.

Victoria steps closer, her unshed tears glinting like reflections of vulnerability.

"I've carried this burden for so long. I thought leaving you was the only way to save myself," she whispers.

"Vic, you don't have to carry this alone anymore. We can face it together, just like we always did," Erasmus reassures her, gently taking her hands.

"I'm sorry," she says.

"For what?"

"I made a terrible mistake back then."

"You were forced to?"

"That's the sanitized version I tell my children," she admits with a trembling voice.

"What do you mean?"

"No one can be forced to marry, not where I'm from. The truth is, part of me was intimidated by your intellect and knowledge. I felt like I was falling behind, like I wasn't enough. I resented you for it, even though I loved you. It scared me."

Victoria's confession pours out, a torrent of words soaked in guilt. She speaks of her insecurities, her feelings of inadequacy, and how they fueled sarcastic remarks and small acts of rebellion.

"I started building a list of reasons why I couldn't stay with you, even as I knew deep down they were excuses. My mother's insistence on marrying someone else became my perfect escape. And I took it. I betrayed us, Erasmus. I betrayed my heart. Even now, I struggle with the guilt, feeling like I don't deserve you."

Erasmus listens silently, stunned yet unsurprised. He always sensed there was more to her departure. He blamed himself for not helping her overcome her insecurities.

"Vic," he says finally, "the past no longer exists. I've never stopped loving you. That's what matters most."

"But I've changed, Erasmus. I'm not the same person you met."

"Let me be the judge of that. If anything, hardship has helped you grow. Your capacity to love remains unchanged."

"Why did you wait for me so long?" she asks.

"Because neither of us found true love again," Erasmus replies.

"You never considered moving on?"

"You know me, Vic. I could never be with someone I didn't love. Love is a beautiful kind of emotional dependence, but once that bond is broken, it's like shattering delicate porcelain. It can't be put back together the same way. The best you can do is treasure what's lost."

"Why did our porcelain never break?"

"I suppose because the bond never broke. True love endures, sustained by the strength of its foundations," Erasmus reflects.

Victoria's tears slow as clarity dawns. "I realize now my insecurities held me back from embracing our love fully."

"And recognizing that is the first step toward healing. Love and forgiveness are intertwined. We learn from the past to forge a brighter future," Erasmus concludes.

"I want to embody that love and light, just as you do," Victoria says. To Erasmus' relief, her eyes are calm, unburdened at last.

Later, as he pedals to class with *Life Wizards* safely tucked away, Erasmus chooses to focus on the day ahead, leaving the last two enlightening hours with Victoria safely stored in his heart.

Royal Cambridge Scholastic Institute, 2018
(University Auditorium)

"Good morning, how's everyone today?" Erasmus calls out.

"Insanely awesome, professor!" the spirited class replies.

Smiling broadly, Professor Cromwell-Smith begins his lecture.

"Earlier this morning, Victoria presented me with an incredible gift," he says, pulling a book from his bag and holding it up for all to see.

"This is a copy of *Life Wizards*. I first had the privilege of reading it with Mrs. V, my mentor in Wales, during my formative years. After her passing, I searched tirelessly for this book but never succeeded in acquiring it. Today, I'll share the story of when this book unexpectedly crossed my path while it was on loan to the Library of Congress. It begins like this…"

— ✦ —

Library of Congress, Washington, D.C., 1976

Standing in the heart of the grand, ornate reading room, Erasmus and Victoria are awestruck by their surroundings. They exchange glances and burst into laughter, their voices echoing through the hallowed space, drawing disapproving looks from nearby readers.

"This place is incredible," Victoria whispers, her eyes scanning the cavernous room.

"The Great Library of Alexandria in ancient Egypt is often regarded as the largest and richest library in history," Erasmus explains quietly as they meander through the labyrinth of desks. "This, Vicky, is the Alexandria of our time."

The couple is in town for a football road game, but Erasmus has meticulously planned their D.C. itinerary to include a visit to this monumental repository of knowledge. For him, there's no better place to start his first visit to the capital than at the greatest library in the world.

Hand in hand, he eagerly leads Victoria to the antique books section. Most of it is restricted, so Erasmus contents himself with admiring the rare volumes from a respectful distance, marveling at their artistry, bindings, and gilded covers.

As they prepare to leave, they wander into the open antique books section. Erasmus's attention is drawn to a series of books by a German author beloved by Mr. M., one of his mentors. Then, something stops him in his tracks. His eyes widen, his breath catches, and his body stiffens.

Victoria notices instantly. "What is it?" she asks, recognizing the familiar look of obsession.

"Vic, that's the book I've told you so much about!" he whispers, barely able to contain his excitement.

"Which one?" she asks, following his gaze.

"Life Wizards!" Erasmus says, his voice trembling as he guides her to the shelf.

"How did it end up here?" he wonders aloud, his tone tinged with awe.

Later, as they sit together in a designated reading area, they discover the book is on loan from Mrs. V.'s Sutton-Raleigh's Antique Books for the Young store in Wales.

"My favorite poem in this book is Life is Bliss, but there's another one about the extraordinary individuals who inspire us profoundly," Erasmus says, flipping through the pages with reverence. He pauses, glancing at Victoria with a knowing smile before he begins to read.

"Life Wizards"

If you want to find where life wizards lie,

pay attention to those who have lived long

and still possess candid and innocent hearts.

Their spirits are genuine, playful, almost childlike.

Their souls remain gentle,

brimming with goodness and good faith.

Their intent is always noble and transparent,

untainted by even an iota of malice.

Their personalities

are made out of extraordinary attitudes—

spontaneity, ingenuity, inspiration,

and above of all, a boundless love for life and others.

Life wizards laugh in abundance,

Their joy echoing for all to hear.

They smile at everyone and everything,

whether silly, profound or simply for no reason at all.

They give to and dote upon others,

with boundless patience and tolerance.

Always ready to serve, help, assist,

educate or rescue,

they remain forever at the service of others.

They are humble yet wise,

at ease with not taking anything too seriously,

ever seeling the lighter side of life.

Fittingly, these whimsical,

scintillating individuals

carry no self-consciousness about their true selves.

Hence, our life's wizards are recognized and defined

not by themselves,

by others throughout their lives.

They are also steadfast and dependable,

the ones who we turn for solace,

the ones we lean on,

providing a safe harbor

in the direst of circumstances.

These life sorcerers inhabit a world

where every moment and every person

are precious and irreplaceable.

Their reactions are always measured,

always assuming good faith,

and giving the benefit of the doubt first.

Their benevolent

and perpetually sunny disposition

stems from the richness of their virtues

and the strength of their character

A flawless, self-regulating compass

allows them to exercise impeccable judgment

producing noble reactions regardless of circumstance.

These exceptional people
effortlessly elevate themselves above the mundane.

But above all, their attitude towards life
shows us that, no matter how long we have lived,
there are still those who somehow
manage to filter out the poisons of the spirit, heart, and soul,
that we encounter along the paths of life.

Although life wizards have their own trials to bear,
The weight of the world, the shadows of care.
Yet through darkness, they light the way,
Transforming struggles into the glow of a new day.

Life wizards are easy to identify,
but hard to truly value or live with for long,
as they inadvertently may make us feel inadequate.

That is precisely our challenge–
How to emulate and learn from these life sorcerers,
when their intense inner lights
may make ours seem opaque and dark.

So, pay attention to these champions of life
who know how to keep everything in balance
and who find everyone and everything priceless.

Seek out these exceptional fellow life companions—
life wizards–

who possess the magic formula

of how to live a happy life

while preserving candid and innocent hearts.

So radiant are these souls, with their guiding glow,

Leading us gently through life's ebb and flow.

Life wizards, though scattered, endure,

With hearts that hold wisdom steadfast and pure.

For such old souls,

rare as they are,

are not frequently found.

*

"Sometimes, dear, you feel like one of those to me," Vicky admits to Erasmus as they leave the majesty of the library behind them.

"I have a long way to go, Vicky. There are no shortcuts in life. To master anything, one must travel the entire road, pay all their dues, and burn every candle," says a content young Erasmus.

— ✦ —

Royal Cambridge Scholastic Institute, 2018
(University Auditorium)

As Professor Cromwell-Smith finishes reading and closes the book with care, he brings his class back, seemingly from a deep trance. He looks out at his students, their faces reflective and thoughtful.

"Now, I'd love to hear your thoughts and questions about the themes we discussed, especially regarding the nature of life wizards and personal growth," he states, his tone inviting.

Maya, blonde-haired young woman majoring in psychology, raises her hand. "Professor, you talked about life wizards having innocent hearts. How can we cultivate that kind of innocence as adults, especially when we face so many challenges?"

"Ah, Maya, that's a profound question," Erasmus replies with a warm smile. "To cultivate that innocence, embrace curiosity and wonder. Allow yourself to find joy in the mundane and approach life with an open heart. Remember, 'Their reactions are always measured, always assuming good faith.' It's about seeing the good in others and yourself."

Phillip, a young man with neatly styled hair pursuing a business degree, raises his hand next. "But what if we've made mistakes in our past? How can we still embody those qualities if we feel inadequate?"

"Phillip, the poem speaks to that challenge," Erasmus answers thoughtfully. "Acknowledge your past, but don't let it define you. True wizards recognize their flaws and grow from them. It's through these experiences that you shine even brighter."

Aisha, a petite girl pursuing a history major, she has flowing black hair and striking chestnut eyes, she speaks softly yet confidently. "I struggle with balancing my emotions. Sometimes, I feel like my insecurities hold me back. How can we break free from that?"

"Aisha, you're not alone in that struggle," the professor says gently.

"The poem highlights that life wizards 'never fail to elevate themselves effortlessly above the mundane.' Cultivate a mindset that embraces growth. Let your emotions guide you, but don't let them bind you. Recognize your value and the light you bring into the world."

James, a creative writing major, raises his hand. "Professor, you mentioned that life wizards love life and smile at everyone. How can we foster that attitude when we face negativity?"

"James, it's essential to guard your spirit," Erasmus replies. "The poem states, 'They are humble yet wise, at ease with not taking anything too seriously.' Surround yourself with positivity and practice gratitude. By choosing to smile despite adversity, you embody the essence of a life wizard. Transform your challenges into lessons and see them as opportunities for growth."

As the session winds down, Erasmus looks out at his students, their faces reflecting both introspection and inspiration. For a moment, he feels a profound connection to each of them, as if the light of life wizards is beginning to glow in their hearts.

"Class, life wizards even though they have their own life trials to endure, still manage to preserve the most innocent of hearts. They love life and smile at everyone. They have playful souls and don't take anything or anyone too seriously. They're the ones we seek for safe harbor in dire circumstances. For them, every moment and all people are precious and irreplaceable. They always have a sunny disposition and possess the secret to being continuously happy. As we navigate life, let's aspire to be those life wizards for ourselves and others. We have so much to learn from one another."

He pauses, letting the weight of his words settle.

As the students gather their belongings, he shares on final thought: "Let's try—try our utmost to spot those who have seemingly mastered life, for they have so much to teach us. Only when we get close to them, emulate them, embody them, will we become true wizards of life."

"Thank you all for your thoughtful questions," he concludes, nodding to the class before packing his papers away.

His students remain curiously silent despite class coming to an end. They share a collective thought: a life wizard already stands before them.

When they finally leave, they carry not just a lesson, but a vision of what they could become. And as Erasmus watches them go, he smiles, his heart full, knowing that the seeds of wisdom have been sown.

Chapter 8

Life as a Journey

Royal Cambridge Scholastic Institute, 2018
(Erasmus and Victoria's Campus Home)

The smooth rasp of Louis Armstrong's voice drifts softly from the bedroom radio as Victoria stirs awake.

Here we go again, she thinks, smiling faintly, well accustomed to Erasmus' musical morning rituals. She stretches languidly, then props herself against the headboard.

Her gaze instinctively sweeps the room, landing on him seated comfortably on his beloved Chesterfield, completely immersed in a book. As the morning light filters through the windows, her attention is drawn to the small antique table beside him. Two exquisite orchids—her favorite flowers—stand proudly, accompanied by a giant card and a small rectangular box. Her heart quickens.

"I love you, dear," she murmurs impulsively. Erasmus looks up, his loving smile lighting up the room.

"Morning, Vic," he replies, walking over to her. "I love you too."

He places the flowers on her bedside table and hands her the wax-sealed card and the crystal-encrusted fuchsia gift box.

Victoria eagerly opens the card and reads aloud, "Welcome back to the journey."

"Do you remember when I first welcomed you to join me on this journey?" he teases.

"Of course. At Boston's train station, after our first trip to Martha's Vineyard. The beginning of us," she recalls with a soft smile.

She tears open the gift box to reveal a delicate silver necklace with a diamond-encrusted baton pendant. A note inside reads: *'Since you already have a ring, I thought this would better symbolize our bond.'*

Overcome, Victoria wraps her arms around his neck, her emotions spilling over. Erasmus gently clasps the necklace around her neck and whispers, "Victoria, will you marry this old Brit?"

Tears streaming, she whispers back, "There's nothing else in the world I'd rather do."

Victoria reaches for a small box hidden in her bedside table. Handing it to Erasmus, she says, "This has been waiting for you. I always knew today would be the right moment."

Erasmus opens it to find a small charm inscribed with *'Life is a journey.'*

"Do you remember who gave us this?" Victoria asks.

"How could I forget? It was on our second visit to the Riddler," Erasmus replies, already lost in reminiscence.

Royal Cambridge Scholastic Institute, 2018
(In Transit)

The morning air is crisp as Erasmus steps outside, his satchel slung over his shoulder. Victoria stands at the doorway, watching him with a wistful smile.

"Don't forget your lecture notes," she calls, handing him a carefully prepared folder.

"Thank you, my love. I'll see you later," he replies, planting a quick kiss on her cheek before heading to the faculty building.

Pedaling his bike through the tranquil campus, Erasmus takes in the vibrant hues of autumn leaves scattered along the cobblestone paths. The rhythmic hum of his wheels on the pavement mirrors the steady pace of his thoughts. Each turn of the pedal brings him closer to the faculty building, and with it, the excitement of sharing today's story with his students.

Arriving at the faculty building, Erasmus secures his bike and takes a moment to adjust his tie. The familiar buzz of campus life surrounds him—students chatting, professors hurrying to their lectures, and the faint chime of the clocktower marking the hour.

He ascends the stone steps and pushes open the heavy wooden doors, greeted by the warm scent of polished oak and the faint murmur of conversation echoing through the halls. With purposeful strides, he navigates the corridors, exchanging polite nods with colleagues.

Royal Cambridge Scholastic Institute, 2018
(University Auditorium)

Professor Cromwell-Smith enters the lively auditorium with an air of enthusiasm.

"Alright, today I want to take you back to the second encounter Vicky and I had with the Riddler. You may recall our first visit to Mr. Ringwald and those insightful conversations about evolution and change. The second time we met him turned out to be just as memorable, if not more so."

— ✦ —

Boston Marathon, 1976
(Heartbreak Hill)

Victoria and Erasmus have been running for three hours. The race started smoothly, with gentle downhills and an energized crowd cheering them on. But as they ascend Heartbreak Hill, the relentless incline drains their stamina.

"How are you holding up, Vic?" Erasmus asks, his breath labored.

"Everything aches... my body's screaming at me to stop," she groans.

"Hold on a little longer—we're three-quarters of the way through."

"When does this hill end?"

"It doesn't," he says with a wry smile. "We just keep going."

They reach a hydration station, gulping down cups of water before pushing forward. Finally, they spot the finish line at the end of a long downtown straightaway. Hand in hand, they cross it together, just shy of their four-hour goal.

"Well done, Vic! You crushed it—nine minutes per mile!" Erasmus exclaims, beaming.

Victoria chuckles, devouring her second banana. I'm here for you, my love, to pull you out of your little bookish shell, she thinks fondly.

"Erasmus, let's visit the Riddler," she suggests casually, though it's part of a plan.

"On a Monday? Would he even be open?" Erasmus mutters, confused.

She smiles knowingly. "What day is it today?"

He stops short. "Oh... right. Marathon Monday."

Ringwald and Brothers Antiquarians, 1976
(Downtown Boston)

"Mr. Ringwald, how are you this morning?" Erasmus asks as they enter the store.

"How do you think? Half of downtown is shut down!" the Riddler grumbles, clearly irritated.

Victoria and Erasmus settle into a quiet corner, letting him vent.

His sharp tone softens as he notices their exhausted but cheerful demeanor.

"You two look like you've been through the wringer. Why are you here instead of nursing your aches at home?"

"It was my idea," Victoria admits. "We were in the area, and I couldn't resist stopping by."

The Riddler smirks, shaking his head. "You've just completed a 26.2-mile journey. That's no small feat. It mirrors life, you know—challenging, exhausting, but rewarding."

He shuffles to the back of the store, returning with a large, thin book

"This has been with me for years. Let me share something with you."

As he begins to read, his words echo through the store, captivating his audience.

"Life as a Journey"

We travel through life
from the moment we arrive on Planet Earth.

Wherever we are, whatever we do,

we are always moving forward,

always heading somewhere.

But it is in the journey where life truly resides—

not in the destination.

So instead of suffering,

or merely enduring the voyage,

we strive to enjoy it,

striving for the best life has to offer

at any given moment.

Life, in many ways, is a magnificent, vast,

yet treacherous ocean.

Our journey is the path we chart,

the wake we leave behind,

accompanied by fellow travelers

who join us along the way.

We are the vessels sailing through it all.

Among our fellow travelers,

Some are steadfast, others fleeting.

Some we choose; others we don't,

but the most loyal stay with us forever.

Our life's vessel is sturdy and resilient.

If we trust it, guide it, and nurture it,

our ship will weather rogue waves

and withsand even the fiercest storms.

Life's journeys unfold because we seek to travel,

traversing the seas of the Earth,

Knowing there are endless places to explore,

and countless people to meet.

As in life, on an ocean voyage,

We reach countless ports of call—

some picture-perfect, filled with trappings,

adorned with treasures,

and others with rocky shores

or perilous landings.

At times, sandy beaches welcome us,

while other destinations are harsh,

demanding significant sacrifices.

On occasion, the seas are calm,

a gentle breeze allowing smooth sailing.

On those precious days, the sun shines kindly,

And the rain is but a soft drizzle.

During such times, the symphony of the sea

conducts a magnificent concerto,

each note echoing

the inspiring music of life.

In those moments,

We seemingly float or walk on water,

riding the waves, kiting the wind,

skimming the surface or diving beneath.

These days, we rejoice,

celebrating the ocean's majesty,

Life's voyage becomes a joyful ride,

we wish would never end.

Yet, there are times we struggle to swim,

barely able to stay afloat.

The sea pulls us down

with its heaviest waves,

its fiercest currents.

On those days, the oceans weep,

crashing against the rocks in pain,

while the skies drum and lament

in opaque colors of sorrow.

In those moments,

it all feels soaked in sadness and nostalgia.

Yet, we resist, endure, and survive,

sailing on to face another day.

Sometimes, we are battered by storms,

only to realize after

that with preparation and vigilance,

we could have avoided the worst.

Life's grand travail can be rough and trying.

The ocean's forces may rise,

as though fury itself simmers beneath the surface.

When the oceans transform into monsters in an instant,
their waves become destroyers
of everything in their path.

In the stillness of dawn, the waters lie bare,
a mirrored expanse, untouched by despair.

Yet lurking beneath is the ocean's might,
a force to be reckoned with come the night.

Then the tempest arrives, with fury and roar,
Casting shadows that loom, shaking the shore.
Through the darkest storms, we learn to steer,
With trembling hands but hearts sincere.
Each wave that crashes, each gale that blows,
Leaves us wiser, as skies turn blue.

There are nights when the compass spins out of control,
And the stars hide their light, leaving shadows to console.
Each step is a battle, each wave a test,
Yet the journey demands our very best.

The sea air carries the salt of tears and strife,
As the winds howl truths that cut like a knife.
Waves crash, their spray cool against our face,
While the sun breaks through, offering a fleeting embrace.

Validating that when we fight and persevere,
we outlast the tempest.

There are no autopilots in life,

and so we must never take

the safe passage of our vessel for granted.

That's why, on a well-traveled journey,

We value the good days,

Accept the bad,

Knowing both will come sooner or later.

On the voyage of life, we experience

birth and love, death and hope,

triumph and defeat, faith and doubt,

wonder and awe, magic, and reality,

creation, destruction, and renewal.

We meet genius and mediocrity,

laziness, and tireless effort,

laughter and tears,

celebration and mourning,

fame and repudiation,

truth and falsehood, health and pain,

betrayal and forgiveness,

tragedy and renewal.

These experiences arrive on all kinds of days,

in all kinds of weather,

on all sorts of seas.

As the journey runs its course,

we will learn again and again

that only love, faith, courage,

experience, knowledge, and hope

can guide us through the rough patches.

Life's circle is, in truth, a journey—

we travel endlessly and without pause,

soaring above or struggling beneath,

through calm or high seas,

through rain or shine,

and across countless ports of call.

And we sail alongside travel companions

who join us along the way.

We journey relentlessly,

from beginning to end,

across the oceans of life,

with a restless spirit and a gypsy soul.

And as the sun sets, the sea becomes a mirror,

reflecting the truth we carry in our hearts:

The Journey is the Destination.

*

The Riddler's words resonate deeply as he reads aloud, their cadence imbued with wisdom and timeless truth. "Young Victoria and Erasmus, the ocean's force was so revered in Greek mythology that it was elevated to godly status. Like the ocean, life cannot be fought— it must be embraced. Harness its power and let it carry you forward."

As he finishes, the Riddler closes the book, his hands lingering on its worn cover as though reluctant to part with its wisdom. "Life's journey demands not just endurance but a willingness to see beauty in every twist and turn. Carry this lesson with you, and let it guide your way."

He hands them a small charm etched with the words, Life as a Journey. Victoria turns it over in her hands, tracing the engraving with a finger. "Thank you, Mr. Ringwald," they say in unison.

In an uncharacteristically impulsive gesture, Victoria kisses the Riddler on both cheeks. The old man stiffens momentarily but soon smiles.

As Erasmus and Victoria leave, they walk in quiet reflection, inspired by the profound wisdom of their journey thus far. The sea breeze carries the scent of salt, mingling with the distant hum of the city. Hand in hand, they walk in quiet reflection, inspired by the profound wisdom of their journey thus far.

— ✦ —

Royal Cambridge Scholastic Institute, 2018
(University Auditorium)

Professor Cromwell-Smith pauses after finishing his story, looking out at his class, he draws himself back to the present.

His gaze thoughtful, he reflects, "Let's take a moment to consider the ideas we've explored today. Life's journey, with its many twists and turns, offers countless lessons. These insights are not only deeply personal, but also universal. Each of you is navigating your own waters. Now, I'd like to hear your thoughts or questions about how we navigate this voyage and what it means to each of you."

Ethan, a tall, athletic man with bright, curious eyes and a major in marine biology, raises his hand. "Professor, you mentioned that life is like an ocean journey. How can we better navigate the storms that come our way?"

"Excellent question, Ethan," the professor replies thoughtfully.

"The poem reminds us, 'There are no autopilots in life.' It means we must actively steer our ship. When challenges arise, trust in your vessel—your abilities, knowledge, and the support of those around you. Prepare for the storms, but also embrace the calm days. Both are essential to your journey."

Sofia, a psychology major, with radiant eyes and flowing hair, raises her hand next. "Professor, you discussed the importance of fellow travelers in our lives. How do we choose the right people to journey with us?"

"That's a wonderful insight, Sofia. The poem reflects, 'Some we choose, others we don't.' Surround yourself with individuals who uplift and inspire you. Seek those who share your values and dreams—they will help you navigate tumultuous waters. Remember, genuine connections help us weather life's storms," he responds with enthusiasm.

Raj, a broad-shouldered young man majoring in engineering, with a pensive demeanor, speaks next. "How can we learn from the more painful experiences we go through?"

"A profound question, Raj. The poem emphasizes, 'We learn again and again that only love, faith, courage, experience, knowledge, and hope can see us through.' Painful experiences are powerful teachers. Reflect on each challenge's lessons and let them shape your resilience. Growth often comes through adversity," the professor replies.

Leila, a tall woman majoring in international relations, with striking green eyes, asks, "How do we maintain hope during rough patches when it feels like the waves are too much to handle?"

"Leila, maintaining hope during difficult times is vital. The poem reassures us, 'On the voyage of life, we experience triumph and defeat, faith and doubt.' In struggles, focus on your core values and lean on your support system. Hope is a guiding light—reminding us that, like the ocean, life is ever-changing. Calm waters will return," he answers, his voice tinged with emotion.

"Thank you all for your thoughtful questions. Our journeys may be challenging, but they are rich with experiences and lessons. Let's support one another as we navigate life's beautiful complexities."

Clearing his throat, he delivers his closing remarks.

"We are all on a never-ending, perilous, yet deeply rewarding voyage. Trust in your vessel—trust in yourself. Above all, remember: true fulfillment resides in the journey, not the destination. See you all next week."

As the professor watches his students leave, he imagines them as young sailors setting off on their own voyages, confident and eager to weather the waves ahead. A small, proud smile crosses his face.

Royal Cambridge Scholastic Institute, 2018
(Campus Steps)

As the sun dips below the horizon, a golden glow washes over the campus. Erasmus sits on the steps, lost in thought. The rustling leaves in the evening breeze echo the rhythm of his heart. He welcomes this quiet moment of reflection, letting the day's events unfold in his mind.

The transition from the lecture hall to the outdoors feels seamless, as if the walls dissolved into the vibrant hues of the sky. The physical environment mirrors his emotional journey; each step is a progression along the path of life.

Laughter and chatter fill the air as students filter out. Erasmus watches their interactions—enthusiastic hugs, whispered secrets, and joyful faces. Each exchange reminds him of the connections that form life's fabric.

He smiles as Victoria approaches the faculty building. *This is a pleasant surprise,* he muses, a premonition fulfilled.

As she draws closer, her presence warms the moment. Her eyes sparkle with curiosity and mischief, as they always do.

"What are you thinking about?" she asks, her voice a melody harmonizing with the tranquil evening.

"Life as a journey," he replies, his tone reflective. "How every moment, every interaction shapes us in ways we don't always see."

"Like this moment?" she teases, sitting beside him. "We're crafting our own story, one conversation at a time."

Their hands brush—a simple but profound connection. Erasmus feels a rush of gratitude for her presence, acknowledging how their intertwined paths enrich his life. He often finds poetry in these quiet moments, the unspoken verses flowing between them like a gentle breeze.

"Speaking of stories," Victoria begins, her eyes twinkling, "what about the Riddler's charm? It represents our past encounters and the essence of our journey forward."

"Exactly!" Erasmus exclaims, his enthusiasm mirrored in her expression. "It's a poetic integration of our experiences—a reminder that the journey itself is the treasure."

In that moment, they share a silent understanding. Their connection blossoms, rich with nuance and color.

"Every challenge—like that marathon—teaches us something invaluable. It's about balancing the highs and lows, the beauty and the struggle," Erasmus reflects.

"And in embracing both, we find fulfillment, don't we? Each step forward is a story waiting to unfold," Victoria replies, her gaze fixed on the horizon.

The stars begin to twinkle overhead as night falls, a reminder of the countless journeys still ahead. Erasmus takes a deep breath, feeling the weight of their shared experiences pressing gently against his chest.

"Let's make a pact," he proposes with quiet determination. "No matter where life takes us, we'll always cherish the journey together."

"Together," Victoria echoes softly, her voice resolute.

In their shared commitment, they find strength—a poignant reminder that the essence of their existence lies not in destinations but in the richness of their shared journey.

Chapter 9

Of Wealth, Fame, and Love

Royal Cambridge Scholastic Institute, 2018
(Erasmus and Victoria's Campus Home)

As the sun rises, its warm rays seep through the curtains, casting a golden glow across the room.

"Dear, ever since you proposed and gave me my precious baton engagement pendant, I've been putting off an important conversation," Victoria whispers in the quiet morning hours. They are both still in bed.

"More transcendental than our last talk? Or could it be?" Erasmus teases, caught by surprise.

"Well, in some ways it is, but this one is straightforward," she admits, her tone tinged with hesitation.

"My late husband left a substantial life insurance policy. I plan to use it to set up trust funds for the children. I also have savings and retirement accounts, and I'll eventually have Social Security. In short, I can take care of myself," she explains, now composed and businesslike.

Erasmus listens with kind eyes and a mischievous smile.

"Why are you looking at me like that?" she asks, uneasy at his reaction.

"Do you remember the first time you asked me that?" he replies, grinning.

"Of course I do, my love," she says, her voice softening.

"Vicky, you know how I feel about wealth and material things," Erasmus begins warmly. "But it's wonderful to see you care for your children's future."

"I just worry I'm neglecting our financial security," she admits.

"Once the trusts are set up, we'll rely on what we have after our teaching careers end and my brief stint as a criminal psychologist."

"Victoria, I was planning to do the same for your kids, even before you mentioned it," Erasmus says gently.

Victoria stares at him, incredulous.

"Erasmus Cromwell-Smith, don't joke about something this serious," she says firmly.

"I'm not joking," he assures her.

"How?" she asks, baffled. "You're the least materialistic person I've ever known."

"Exactly," he replies with a small smile.

"Life is expensive, but your intentions are noble," she says, not yet grasping his words' weight.

"Come with me, my lady," he says, taking her hand.

In their home office, Erasmus hands her three folders. She opens the first, and her jaw drops.

"I've published a few action thrillers and educational books. These are the royalties that have accumulated over the years," he reveals.

"You've been busy," she says, flipping through the pages, her voice filled with admiration.

"You're right—I don't care about wealth," he says.

"And you've always believed material wealth isn't freedom but chains," she recalls.

"Exactly," he agrees. *Victoria has always worried about making ends meet,* he thinks, watching her thoughtfully. *Now, her challenge is to trust in abundance.*

Her voice trembles. "This means more to me than I can express. It's like you see a future we can build together."

Softly, Erasmus affirms, "You deserve to feel secure, Vic. We're in this together."

"So, I've reconnected with my unmaterialistic monk, only to find he's unimaginably wealthy—but still the same monk," she teases.

"I had to keep my monk identity alive somehow," he jokes.

"We can do anything we want—travel the world, take a sabbatical, explore new places," he says excitedly.

"And the catch?" she asks knowingly.

"That we follow the same three principles I've lived by all my life," he says firmly.

"Austerity," she recalls.

"Exactly," Erasmus nods.

"Anonymity," she adds.

"Perfect."

"And freedom," she finishes with a proud smile.

"Do you remember when we first adopted those principles?" he asks playfully.

"Of course," she teases, the memory surfacing.

Their eyes meet, and an unspoken connection fills the room.

"So, we're thinking the same thing, aren't we?" she whispers.

"There's only one way to find out," he replies, his voice filled with temptation. Erasmus moves closer, caressing her cheek as their passion ignites.

Later, Erasmus realizes he's running late. For the first time, he feels the slight embarrassment of being five minutes late to his beloved lecture. But today, it doesn't matter. He's in love, swept up in joy and spontaneity, wholly immersed in the moment's bliss.

Royal Cambridge Scholastic Institute, 2018
(University Auditorium)

"Hello," Erasmus greets his audience, a sheepish smile betraying his uncharacteristic tardiness.

"Ahem," a ripple of collective throat-clearing moves through the student body, a playful acknowledgment of his delay.

"We understand, professor," a group of students stands, mockingly offering excuses on his behalf.

"Please accept my apologies. I'm not setting the best example today. But, despite this, I still expect punctuality from all of you," he says earnestly.

"We told you, professor, we understand," another group teases, causing a few chuckles to ripple through the room.

Puzzled and slightly flustered, Erasmus begins to respond when the next interruption catches him entirely off guard.

"A little bird told us," a chorus chimes in.

"What?" he asks, his confusion evident.

"A little bird arrived before you and told us you'd be late. She said you were taking us to a place today she wanted to relive and wouldn't miss for the world," announces a well-rehearsed group of four students, clearly enjoying themselves.

Scanning the room, Erasmus's eyes quickly land on her—standing amidst the crowd.

"I'm right here, love. Right here," Victoria says, her voice carrying a familiar warmth and a touch of mischief.

Caught entirely off guard, Erasmus freezes momentarily. His composure wavers as he struggles to balance his professional demeanor with the wave of emotions her presence evokes.

After a deep breath and an almost imperceptible sigh, he recovers, smiling warmly and winking at her in acknowledgment.

"Class," he begins, his voice steady once more, "today I'm taking you back more than forty years to a day when Vicky and I received a rather peculiar invitation. It sent us on an exhilarating journey of discovery and wisdom that lasted a lifetime."

He pauses, the room quiet in anticipation.

"It begins like this…"

— ❖ —

Harvard, 1976
(Victoria and Erasmus's Studio)

"Erasmus, are we going to accept this invitation or not?" Vicky asks, her tone edged with frustration.

"I'm not sure. What do you think?" he deflects.

"Stop dodging the question, and don't try to be a Riddler. There's only one in New England, and it's not you," she snaps, exasperated.

"Well, I'm thinking it over," Erasmus replies, a weak excuse.

"How much longer? That's the same answer every time," she retorts, her sarcasm sharp.

"I'll make up my mind soon," he promises unconvincingly.

"You'd better, or we'll miss it," she warns.

Erasmus reopens the card and reads aloud:

"Invitation: You are cordially invited to meet with a select group

of antiquarians across the country. A limited number of ancient

books will also be exhibited. Dinner and cocktails will be served."

'Why is he hesitating? This is exactly the kind of event that excites him,' Victoria wonders, growing impatient.

Impulsively, she grabs the card from his hand and rereads it aloud, her eyes lingering on the address at the bottom. Suddenly, the reason for his hesitation clicks into place.

"It's the address, isn't it? You're hesitating because it's at some rich man's house?"

Erasmus remains silent.

"Well, I'm going. Whether you come or not is up to you," she declares firmly, though she doesn't truly mean it.

Antique Book Exhibit Reception
(Boston Suburbs, 1976)

"Erasmus, we've been here for barely an hour, and you've already managed to alienate all three event hosts—some of the wealthiest men in New England. What's wrong with you?" Victoria asks, irritation clear in her voice.

"*Material wealth doesn't impress me. I have no respect for the arrogance of those who think it makes them superior,*" Erasmus replies flatly.

"*But they funded this event! Without them, it wouldn't have happened,*" she counters.

"*For that, I am grateful. I've expressed my appreciation sincerely to each of them,*" he concedes.

"*Where did this sudden disdain for wealth come from?*" she presses.

"*We Brits manage quite well, thank you—living among real people with meaningful lives,*" he responds defensively.

"*So, no wealthy man deserves your respect?*" Victoria asks sarcastically.

"*Oh, some do. But they're rare,*" he replies with conviction.

"*Give me an example,*" she challenges.

"*Andrew Carnegie,*" Erasmus states. "*Consider these points: the lasting impact of his institutions, the countless people who still benefit from his work, the age he started giving back to society, and how much of his wealth he donated during his life and after his death. That's the measure of a man.*"

"*But wasn't he ruthless in business?*" she asks.

"*It's not about how they make their wealth; it's about how they use it to better society,*" Erasmus explains.

"*Excuse me, may I interrupt?*" asks a tall, gaunt man in an oversized suit.

"We're having a private conversation," Erasmus says, slightly annoyed but intrigued by the man's Scottish accent.

"Terribly rude of me, I admit, but I couldn't help overhearing. Especially when you mentioned the Lilliputian giant from Dunfermline—Andrew Carnegie," the man remarks with a knowing smile.

Erasmus and Victoria are momentarily stunned.

"Who are you, sir?" Erasmus asks.

"Colin Carnegie," the man replies.

"Are you...?" Erasmus begins.

"Yes, I'm a distant relative," he confirms. "And, yes, I'm the antiquarian from Edinburgh, with locations in Glasgow and Inverness as well."

"I'm honored," Erasmus says, his tone softening.

"And you're from Hay-on-Wye, the famous Book Town?" Colin asks, eyes twinkling.

Erasmus nods, delighted.

"You've struck gold today," Colin announces. "I have a document related to your discussion—one that will deepen your understanding of Andrew Carnegie's philosophy. Would you like me to read it to you?"

"Yes, please," Erasmus replies eagerly.

Colin pulls an ancient scroll from his coat, its aged parchment crackling softly. As he begins to read, his voice resonates with wisdom, captivating Victoria and Erasmus and transporting them into the heart of another world.

"Of Wealth, Fame and Love"

In one way or another,

we all chase—

some of us relentlessly—

wealth, fame, and love,

often in this precise order of importance.

But these life illusions

don't always manifest

in such a prescribed pecking order.

The Truth is, we never know

who shows up first,

or if any of them

will ever present themselves at all.

And if they do,

we'll face one of life's most perplexing conundrums:

that what we are keenly after,

is not only elusive,

but usually comes

at the expense of something else.

— ✦ —

I once held wealth in trembling hands,

coins that shimmered, fleeting sands.

They slipped through fingers, left me bare,

a lesson carved in golden glare.

The clinking of gold in a velvet chest,

its polished sheen a fleeting jest.

Though its glow lit darkened halls,

it could not warm my spirit's calls.

— ✦ —

Fame once called with siren's song,

applause that echoed loud and long.

Yet in the quiet, I found dismay,

a hollow sound at the end of day.

The roar of crowds, their cheers so loud,

a fleeting thrill, a passing cloud.

The echoes faded, leaving me still,

longing for something deeper to fill.

— ✦ —

Love, elusive, I sought in vain,

through fleeting joy and hidden pain.

It was not in others, I came to see,

but in the freedom of being me.

Her touch was light as a morning breeze,

a whisper of warmth, a quiet reprieve.

In her gaze, I found a home,

where love could flourish, freely roam.

— ✦ —

As we chase wealth, frugality fades,

true worth, like shadows, slips away.

The smallest treasures, once so clear,
are lost in pursuits that cost so dear.

As we pursue reputation,
we risk losing anonymity,
letting the fiction of others' thoughts
shape the essence of who we are.

The roar of fame reshapes the self,
a fragile image perched on a shelf.
No longer guided by inner light,
we're swayed by the crowd, lost to sight.

— ✦ —

Love and freedom—two forces at play,
a delicate balance, not easy to stay.
Self and unity must intertwine,
for love to flourish and truly shine.

— ✦ —

We all chase wealth, fame, and love,
illusions below, aspirations above.
Yet as we circle back again,
the same questions haunt us now as then.
So here we stand, at the journey's end,
the same illusions still call and bend.
We must balance the triad we chase,
with virtues to anchor the endless race.

*

As the Scotsman finishes reading, he gazes warmly at the young couple, noticing the serene satisfaction reflected in their eyes.

"Mr. Carnegie, we'll be indebted to you for the rest of our lives," says Vicky, her voice imbued with gratitude and a sense of closure born from newfound wisdom.

"Austerity, anonymity, and freedom will guide me from now on," Erasmus declares solemnly, as if taking an oath. He silently resolves to maintain a lasting connection with the man from the Scottish Highlands.

With lighter hearts and playful spirits, the young couple bids farewell, feeling transformed by the encounter.

(Victoria and Erasmus' Studio)

"Why are you looking at me like that?" Victoria asks as they step into their cozy studio, her curiosity piqued.

"Vic, there's nothing more sensual to me than a confident woman in Katherine Hepburn flats," Erasmus begins, his tone teasing yet sincere. "A woman who moves with grace, radiating ease and comfort in every gesture, glance, and posture. It's the epitome of femininity."

"Why?" she asks, her intrigue deepening.

"I love it when a woman isn't concerned about her height—when something so trivial feels utterly irrelevant to her," he replies, his smile soft and affectionate.

"But am I short?" she asks, her pride faintly wounded and her doubt surfacing.

"Predictable reaction, right? My fault," he admits with a chuckle.

"No, Vicky, you're not short, and you know it. But that's precisely the point: height isn't the issue."

Her thoughts, however, have already wandered. The simple sensuality of the flats she wears now consumes her attention, ensnared by the poetic charm of Erasmus' words.

"So, my lady," Erasmus continues, his voice laced with humor, "what was your original question again?"

As she begins to answer, he takes her hand, leading them both into the sanctuary of their world—an endless realm of passion ignited by the magnetic tension between them. Their moments together are always illuminated by Victoria's lively spontaneity and her radiant presence, this time adorned with the timeless elegance of her Katherine Hepburn flats.

— ❖ —

Royal Cambridge Scholastic Institute, 2018
(University Auditorium)

Professor Cromwell-Smith brings his class back to the present with a broad smile, his gaze locking with Vicky's. She sits among the students, her hands pressed over her heart, a look of serene joy lighting her face.

"Let's open the floor for questions about the themes we've explored today, particularly the interplay between wealth, fame, and love," he invites, his tone warm and reflective.

Olivia, an undergraduate majoring in psychology, with long dark hair and empathetic brown eyes, raises her hand.

"Professor, how can we pursue our ambitions without losing sight of what truly matters, like love and relationships?"

"An insightful question, Olivia. As the poem suggests, '*what we are keenly after is not only elusive but usually comes at the expense of something else.*' Balance is key. Prioritize the relationships that ground you and remember that true fulfillment often lies in connection, not accumulation," the professor responds thoughtfully.

Daniel, a graduate student in economics, with an athletic build and a furrowed brow, speaks next.

"You mentioned the dangers of wealth and fame. How can we ensure that we don't let those illusions define us?"

"Great concern, Daniel. The poem warns that 'anonymity falsely becomes synonymous with failure.' It's vital to develop a strong sense of self, rooted in your values rather than external recognition. Fame and fortune should complement your identity, not define it," replies Cromwell-Smith.

Anjali, a literature major with almond-shaped eyes and straight black hair, raises her hand.

"In the poem, you discuss the risks of love and freedom. How can we preserve our individuality within a relationship?"

"Anjali, an excellent point. The poem reminds us that 'it takes great maturity and tolerance for both to coexist.' Communication is the cornerstone. Ensure that your individuality is celebrated rather than suppressed, and foster an environment where both love and freedom thrive together," he advises.

James, an undergraduate majoring in business raises his hand.

"Professor, do you think it's possible to achieve wealth while staying true to our values?"

"James, the poem illustrates that wealth, if pursued with integrity, can coexist with one's values. Seek avenues that align with your principles and contribute positively to society. Never let the chase for wealth override what you hold dear. Life presents us with three grand illusions—wealth, fame, and love—and mastering their balance is key," the professor replies with conviction.

Pausing for a moment, he addresses the class one final time.

"Thank you all for your thoughtful questions. Take this with you: What is austerity to wealth? What is anonymity to fame? And what is freedom to love?"

At that moment, Vicky's voice cuts in, filled with enthusiasm:

"I want you all to know your professor is still the same man he was when I first met him. He truly lives by the principles he teaches," she says, radiating conviction and pride.

The interruption startles some students, but no one minds. The professor places his hands over his heart, his expression tender.

"See you all next week," he says, content.

As Erasmus and Victoria leave the auditorium hand in hand, discussion groups linger behind, their voices alive with questions and insights. Many students observe the couple as they walk away, a quiet admiration filling the room. To them, the pair seem immune to life's three grand illusions, embodying the ideals they've just explored.

Chapter 10

Of Family, True Friendship, and Love

Royal Cambridge Scholastic Institute, 2019
(Erasmus and Victoria's Campus Home)

Victoria's three young adult children—Elizabeth-Victoria, 24, the eldest; Bartholomew, 22, the middle child; and Sarah, 19, the youngest—arrive unannounced, catching her mid-breakfast. Though surprised, she had anticipated their visit, having dropped hints for weeks.

The quiet of her morning gives way to the lively energy of their presence. The house fills with chatter, laughter, and the warmth of a family reunion. After the initial excitement fades, Victoria takes a steadying breath. She has something to share—something monumental.

"Erasmus asked me to marry him," she announces hesitantly, her voice steady but her eyes scanning their faces for a reaction.

"Congratulations, Mom!" they exclaim in unison, their voices a mixture of excitement and disbelief.

Victoria holds up the engagement baton, its unique design catching Bart's attention. He studies it, puzzled.

"Why a baton?" Bart finally asks.

"It's deeply symbolic for us," she explains, a knowing smile spreading across her face.

"Oh, the broken baton story!" Bart exclaims, remembering the tale they'd heard so many times growing up.

"Why didn't you tell us sooner, Mom?" Sarah asks, her tone soft but curious.

Victoria pauses before answering, her gaze dropping briefly to the table.

"I suppose I wanted to be sure it was real," she admits sheepishly.

Elizabeth, ever the composed eldest, leans in. "And? What did you say?"

"I said yes. With all my heart," Victoria replies, her voice carrying a mix of joy and vulnerability.

Bart leans forward, his tone gentle but firm. "Mom, can you stop feeling guilty now? We've all told you—this is what we want for you."

Victoria looks at her son, her eyes shimmering with emotion. "I know, Bart. I've carried that guilt for too long. But Erasmus makes me happy. I finally feel at peace."

"What made you say yes now?" Elizabeth presses gently.

Victoria's smile softens. "Because I realized that it's okay to choose happiness for myself. Erasmus values family as much as I do. He understands what's most important."

As the conversation deepens, the siblings surround her in a close circle of support.

"We're so happy for you, Mom," Sarah says, her grin wide and contagious.

"It's a big step," Bart interjects thoughtfully. "Are you sure about this?"

Victoria takes his hand, her voice calm and resolute. "I am. Erasmus and I have something special. It's time to embrace it fully."

"I guess we just want to see you happy," Bart admits, his voice thick with emotion.

"And I want the same for all of you," Victoria responds, her gaze sweeping over each of her children. "This isn't about losing anything—it's about adding to what we already have."

"Exactly!" Sarah exclaims, bouncing with excitement. "This is a new chapter for all of us!"

The three siblings pull their mother into a group hug, their collective warmth washing away any lingering doubts.

"What's next, Mom?" Elizabeth asks as they pull apart.

"We'll all live here," Victoria explains. "I've put our old home on the market and plan to move each of you in when you're ready."

"Wait, what?" Bart asks, surprised.

"And," Victoria adds, "I'm setting up trust funds for each of you using the proceeds from your father's life insurance policy."

"But what about you?" Sarah asks, concerned.

"I have enough saved—between my retirement plan and social security, I'll be fine. And Erasmus... well, he surprised me."

"How so?" Bart asks, raising an eyebrow.

Victoria hesitates, then smiles. "Let's just say, for someone who's always preached austerity, he's full of surprises."

"So, where is he?" Bart asks, glancing around. "We want to meet him."

Victoria laughs. "He's on his way to class, but he'll be back before noon."

As Erasmus steps outside, the brisk morning air clears his lingering doubts. He recalls Victoria's words about her children's enthusiasm to meet him, the thought warming him despite his usual nerves. Today feels monumental—yet another chapter in their shared journey.

Royal Cambridge Scholastic Institute, 2019
(Faculty Building)

As Erasmus parks his old, rusty bike, a mix of anxiety and excitement washes over him. Victoria had told him last night about her children's visit and their enthusiasm to meet him. Though they knew most of their mother's love story—her Harvard days and his own life before their reunion—meeting them now felt monumental. Erasmus' thoughts whirl. 'You silly old man, she's telling them about your proposal,' he realizes, a small smile breaking through his worry.

Stepping into the faculty building, the scent of polished wood and old books fills the air, grounding him in the comforting routine of academia.

He greets his students with renewed energy. "Good morning, everyone."

"Good morning, Professor," they reply in unison.

"Today, we're going to look back at a time when family came into our lives in unexpected and transformative ways." He pauses, his smile deepening.

"It begins like this…"

—✦—

Harvard, 1977

"Erasmus, my folks are traditional Midwestern Americans."

"That's okay; I'm looking forward to meeting them."

"I'm not sure the feeling will be mutual," she says abruptly.

Her remark startles Erasmus. "Why would you say that?" he asks, puzzled.

"I don't think it's anything negative about you. My parents don't even know about you," she replies, trying to explain.

"Exactly," he responds, but his words are met with a blank stare from Vicky.

"So, what is it then?" he presses, half-speaking to himself.

"They've always imagined I'd marry someone from my hometown, preferably from the same congregation. They simply can't envision anything else," Vicky admits.

"Then why did they let you come to Harvard?" he asks.

"They almost didn't. But I earned it academically, so in the end, they had to let me go," Vicky answers.

"See, maybe they're more open-minded than you think," he suggests optimistically.

She sighs, "I'm afraid not. They expect me to come back."

"But you're an adult, Victoria. Anyhow, what matters is what you want. What is it?" Erasmus asks, growing frustrated.

"All I want is to be with you," she says, and they share a heartfelt kiss.

"Wonderful! So, when do I meet them?" he asks naively.

"Someday in the future, but not now," she replies, letting the truth drop.

"What? Why?" Erasmus asks, confused.

"They don't know we're living together, and knowing you, I can't imagine you hiding it. With your British sense of propriety, you'd never leave anything unsaid or inaccurate."

"Then just introduce me as a classmate or however you like," he pleads, sensing her resistance.

"Not now, but maybe someday," she replies curtly.

"I think you're overthinking this, Victoria," he sighs, but to no avail.

When Vicky's parents arrive, they spend most of their visit urging her to complete her studies closer to home. Sadly, they leave town without ever meeting Erasmus.

Riverside Village, Boston Suburbs, 1977
(Mr. Faith's Antique Book Store)

"Victoria and Erasmus, Mr. Faith at your service. How can I help?" says a spirited Mr. Faith.

"Mr. Faith, we're hoping to learn more about dealing with family," Erasmus begins.

"What's the nature of the problem you're trying to address?"

"Victoria," Erasmus says, gently passing the question to her.

She hesitates at first but then gathers the courage to explain, though embarrassed, as she recounts the struggle with her parents.

Without a word, Mr. Faith leads them toward the back of the store.

"This building was a bank before I bought it two decades ago."

As they enter the vault, Erasmus is awestruck, his eyes widening.

The vault is filled with massive, ancient books, their covers radiating a timeless and priceless allure.

"Have a seat," Mr. Faith invites.

He carefully selects an enormous, ancient book and places it on the table, opening it to a marked page.

"You're approaching this from the wrong angle. You're reacting against their intervention, which is natural given their fear of losing you, Victoria."

"We're consenting adults. They have no right to dictate Vicky's life choices, much less who she loves or forms a family with," Erasmus protests.

Victoria's eyes widen—this is the first time he's mentioned the word "family" between them, a word she finds both comforting and daunting.

"Maybe you need to broaden your perspective," Mr. Faith suggests.

"How so?" Erasmus asks.

"It's not just about family," Mr. Faith replies enigmatically.

"What do you mean?" Erasmus presses.

"Those we hold dear include more than just family; they encompass true friends and everything tied to the heart. Once you understand

who belongs in your closest circles, the important questions become:What's our role? What are their expectations? What boundaries should we set—and respect?" Mr. Faith explains with wisdom.

Erasmus gazes at the eccentric antiquarian, filled with gratitude and curiosity.

"I must warn you, though—this isn't written like a poem or essay. It's more of a manifesto," Mr. Faith cautions.

The young couple listens intently, captivated by his words.

"It's written as a declaration of ideals," Mr. Faith says, "something akin to the Declaration of Independence."

"Like the Declaration of Independence?" Victoria asks, her naiveté shining through.

"Precisely, but focused on love, true friendship, and family. This ancient text outlines those relationships' duties, responsibilities, rights, and boundaries."

"Of Family, True Friendship, and Love"

In all matters of family, true friendship, and love,
reside those who are dearest to us,
alongside the bonds that hold us together.

The tight closeness and indivisible unity
of these three essential bonds
are among the most powerful sources of strength
and happiness in our lives.
But we must remain vigilant,
for once the closenessof these bonds is lost,

it is profoundly difficult—even trying—to recover.

This is why we defend and protect
our walls of intimacy.
Closeness and unity are not immanent;
they but must be earned
through daily work and sacrifices
we invest in family, true friendship, and love.

The power and strength of these bonds
originate from sticking together as a whole
irrespective of anything or anyone.

Happiness and joy stem from the intimacy and closeness
of living in full
along those we love and hold dear.

The warmth of a hug, arms entwined so tight,
A shield from the cold on the darkest night.
The clasp of a hand, firm yet kind,
A silent promise, "You're never left behind."
The laughter of children, a melody sweet,
Echoes through halls where love and kin meet.
A table of plenty, with hands held in grace,
Life's treasures are found in this sacred space.

Our actions, in matters of family,
true friendship, and love,
are guided by acts of conscience,

where we hold ourselves accountable first,

acting from within,

not because we are swayed or limited

by what those closest to us may do, say, or think.

Yet, the boundaries between what we must do

and what others expect of us

in matters of the heart, true friendship, and family

are often tenuous and delicate—

moving targets or even shifting sands.

I've walked through shadows, felt bonds grow thin,

Wondered if I'd ever feel whole again.

But in the silence, their voices called,

A love unbroken, where I thought it had stalled.

Once, I doubted the strength of these ties,

Felt the ache of absence,

heard only goodbyes.

Yet each trial taught me, through fire and strain,

That love rebuilds, like sun after rain.

This is true, unless we are willing and able

to set forth a declaration—

a manifesto that cloaks us

with the sacred mantle

of these precious existential bonds,

while simultaneously,

carving in stone, with clarity,

what we are truly pursuing.

It reads as follows:

Together,

We love with a boundless, endless grace,

Loyalty shining, time cannot erase.

In unity, we find strength to endure,

A bond unbroken, steadfast and pure..

We act with impeccable dignity.

We preserve the integrity of our honor.

We humbly pray.

We treasure every precious memory and moment.

We never surrender the power of hope.

We leave no business unfinished,

nor quit, abandon, jump ship,

run away, waver, or leave anyone behind.

And if we fail, we fall together—

but we always rise again.

Again, and again, and again.

Then,

As life's paths unfold into growth,

personal undertakings, and projects underway,

We nurture, prepare, support, uplift, motivate,

believe in, assist, guide, inspire,

and remain ever-present, available at any time,

whenever needed.

When circumstances call for swift action,

We confront, reason, admonish, claim,

challenge, refute, oppose,

prevent, redirect, listen deeply,

and when necessary, forbid outright.

And when our virtues, and values—

especially integrity and our capacity to give—

are tested to their limits,

we raise high the flag of truth.

In all we do,

we are endlessly patient, always ready to respond,

extend wisdom generously,

show compassion,

act with composure,

give what we can,

fulfill our promises,

and respect and value others.

When we falter or make mistakes,

we express remorse, make amends,

seek atonement,

and are always ready to forgive and be forgiven.

Etiquette, respect, and true decorum

are not only expected

but required. Thus,

We do not yell, curse, shout, or humiliate.

We never insult, demean,

seek revenge, judge, or criticize unjustly.

We strive to be a role model

by remaining humble,

pursuing frugality, modesty,

discretion, and balance.

Raising new generations is part of our duty.

Thus,

We provide, teach, hold accountable,

instill responsibility,

and invest in one another.

At our core, we cherish the simplest things,

The truths that honesty and kindness bring.

Sweet or bitter, we face what's real,

The strength of our bonds, the love we feel.

We laugh and enjoy,

smile, and have fun, rejoice, and share happiness.

Above all, we return, where we first began,

To family, friendship, and love's great plan.

In these bonds, life's true treasures lie,

A strength that endures as the years go by.

The heart of the matter, so simple, so clear,

Hold close those you cherish, keep them near.

For in love, true friendship, and family we find,

The anchors that steady both heart and mind.

<u>Together, we acclaim and celebrate</u>
<u>a life of Love, True Friendship, and Family.</u>

*

"Victoria and Erasmus, when it comes to love, true friendship, and family, we are like Dumas' three musketeers—'all for one, and one for all.' The list of everything we aspire to do and be is dense and comprehensive, yet it does not give us the right to govern those three sacred spheres. Victoria, you are a free, consenting adult, and only you can decide the course of your life," concludes the wise mentor, his voice calm but resolute.

"Thank you, Mr. Faith; we'll be indebted to you for the rest of our lives," Erasmus says sincerely, his gratitude evident as he takes Victoria's hand.

The shaken couple heads to the train station in silence, each lost in thought.

'My parents only want what's best for me,' she reasons, oddly defending them against her own heart, as the rhythmic clatter of the train tracks merges with the unspoken emotions between them.

— ✦ —

Royal Cambridge Scholastic Institute (2019)
(University Auditorium)

Professor Cromwell-Smith returns to the present, momentarily lost in thought. He takes a moment, letting the weight of Mr. Faith's words settle over him before drawing his gaze back to the present. The room before him feels alive with anticipation, the eager faces of his students reflecting the importance of the lessons they're about to explore.

"I'd like to open the floor for any questions about the themes we've explored, particularly regarding family, friendship, and love," he announces, his voice steady.

Patrick, a tall, athletic young man with short, sandy blonde hair and bright blue eyes, leans forward intently. Patrick is majoring in history with a focus on societal structures.

"Professor, how do we find the right balance between family obligations and our relationships?" he asks.

"Patrick, that's a vital question," Professor Cromwell-Smith begins.

"As the poem highlights, 'the power and strength of these bonds originate from sticking together as a whole.' Maintaining open communication with your family about your needs is essential while nurturing your relationships. Recognize that both can coexist and enrich your life."

Priya, a sociology student, passionate about interpersonal dynamics, raises her hand next.

"You mentioned that love and friendship are intertwined. How can we ensure our friendships support our family dynamics?" she asks thoughtfully.

"Excellent insight, Priya. The poem suggests that 'we are fiercely and endlessly loyal' to those we care about. True friends should uplift and support you through your family journeys, providing a safe space to express your thoughts and feelings. Seek friends who understand your familial responsibilities and respect your choices," the professor replies.

Marcus, a psychology major particularly interested in family therapy, raises his hand.

"Yes?"

"What if our family expectations clash with our desires? How do we navigate that tension?" he quizzes.

"That's a common struggle, Marcus," the professor reflects. "The poem reminds us that 'acts of conscience guide our actions in matters of family, true friendship, and love.' It's important to honor your feelings while considering your family's perspective. Find a way to communicate your desires and establish healthy boundaries. This approach can lead to mutual understanding and respect."

Jasmine, majoring in literature, intrigued by themes of human connection in poetry, stands up, "how can we cultivate deeper connections with our families without compromising our individuality?" she asks.

"Great question, Jasmine," he responds. "The poem emphasizes that 'we must be vigilant, for once the closeness of these bonds is lost, it is difficult to recover.' Nurturing your individuality while maintaining family connections requires open dialogue and honesty. Share your thoughts and passions with your family; allow them to see who you are as an individual while reinforcing the love that binds you together."

Professor Cromwell-Smith pauses, scanning the room. "Remember, family and friendship are intricate, but with love, understanding, and open communication, we can navigate the complexities of these relationships. Embrace the connections that enrich your lives, for they truly define our experiences," the professor concludes, though his own words unsettle him. A worried expression flashes across his face as old insecurities resurface. Rationally, he knows they're unfounded, yet his fears momentarily overwhelm him.

Suddenly, he feels an intense urge to see her. To the surprise of his class, the esteemed professor abruptly ends the session, barely managing a wave as he whispers, "See you all next week."

Just outside the auditorium, he nearly collides with her. "Vicky," he says, smiling in relief.

"You're certainly in a hurry today, dear," she replies with a smile.

But in an instant, she notices the fear lingering in Erasmus' eyes.

"I'm here, you old fool. I'm not going anywhere," Vicky says lovingly, her eyes brimming with tears yet full of resolve.

"Please, don't stop," he murmurs, beginning to relax.

"For as long as it takes, however many times it's needed, I'll always be here," she promises, comforting him again.

"Now, onto other matters—I need to talk to you about my kids," she announces. Erasmus' eyes widen slightly, but she quickly adds, "No need to panic, my love."

As the loving couple walks away, Erasmus feels his earlier doubts dissolve under the warmth of her presence. Her steady hand in his reinforces the truth he holds close: with her by his side, every challenge feels surmountable.

The auditorium remains packed with students, still reflecting on the profound subject covered by their eminent professor. Many begin to evaluate—some even reassess—their own families, friendships, and bonds, comparing them with what they've just learned.

Chapter 11

Life as a Circus

Royal Cambridge Scholastic Institute, 2019
(Erasmus and Victoria's Campus Backroads)

The night before, Victoria and Erasmus had enjoyed a lively evening, culminating in a splendid dinner at a family-owned New England seafood restaurant. It was a memorable night as the smitten couple finally experienced her children's full acceptance. Ultimately, what mattered most to her kids was seeing their mother with a spark in her eyes, relaxed, genuinely, and truly happy around Erasmus.

"Dear, you were wonderful last night," she exclaims joyfully as they pedal along the campus backroads.

"And may I add, they love you deeply, my lady," he replies spiritedly, zigzagging playfully on his old rusty bike through the early spring colors.

Victoria looks at him, feeling both proud and unburdened.

"Would you happen to remember when I first became enamored with the idea of being a mom?" she teases, subtly certain he won't remember.

"Well, the only time I recall you mentioning anything about it was at the circus," he replies promptly.

Victoria catches her breath, surprised and touched by his memory of such a meaningful moment.

"It was quite fortunate that we went to the circus that day," she says playfully.

"Lucky? It's more like well-planned. You had it all orchestrated," Erasmus responds, smiling, not falling for her feigned innocence.

Professor Cromwell is so lost in his thoughts that only the jolt of his bike hitting a bump near the faculty building brings him back to the present.

"The circus—that'll be today's topic," he says with sudden inspiration.

Victoria playfully nudges Erasmus with her shoulder as they pedal side by side.

"You know, I never thought I'd find myself with someone like you at this stage in my life."

"Someone as charming and amazing as me? Hard to believe, I know," Erasmus quips with a grin.

"Exactly! But honestly, I'm grateful for every twist in this circus," replies Victoria, laughing, as they arrive at the faculty parking lot.

After securing Victoria's bike on their car's rack and sending her off to her classes at Boston University with a warm kiss, Erasmus takes a moment to watch her drive away. His thoughts linger on the previous evening's laughter and the joy of being accepted by her children. With a contented smile, he adjusts his bag and heads toward the faculty building, his mind already weaving the day's lecture. The pedagogue walks to class with resolute steps, his mind swirling with images of traveling performers and circus tents.

Royal Cambridge Scholastic Institute, 2019
(University Auditorium)

As he enters the lively auditorium, a few students wave, their cheerful greetings echoing through the hall. Erasmus smiles, taking in the familiar energy of the room as he sets his notes on the podium.

"Good morning, class."

"Good morning, professor."

"Last week, I left rather abruptly due to a personal matter. Please accept my apologies," the professor says sincerely.

"Is everything all right at home, professor?" the class asks in unison, sounding genuinely concerned.

The professor looks at them, slightly taken aback, unsure of their intentions.

"What are you all up to?" he asks suspiciously.

Then he realizes—before they can start teasing him.

"Many of us witnessed the Shakespearean scene at the auditorium door last week, professor," one of the students explains with a grin.

A bit embarrassed, he cuts them off. "Enough roasting your professor this morning," he says, though his tone lacks conviction.

Seeing their expectant faces, he relents.

"All right, nothing unusual happened. Victoria simply wanted to greet me after class by surprise—and she did, and it was wonderful," he explains, flashing a reassuring smile.

'They truly care about my well-being,' he thinks, looking over the students with gratitude. Protocol quickly returns, and he regains his focus.

"Today, I'm going to take you back to a day when Victoria and I gained a wealth of wisdom after a visit to the circus. It begins like this…"

— ✦ —

New York City, 1977

Harvard had just played Princeton, and as usual, Vicky dazzled on the field with her baton maneuvers. As they left the stadium, she turned to Erasmus and said, "Take me to the store in New York City where you bought my baton."

A short train ride later, Erasmus scratches his head. Why would she want to go there? He wonders.

Soon, they're walking hand-in-hand through the streets of Manhattan, surrounded by the vibrant autumn colors of Central Park.

This must mean something to her, he thinks, sensing the moment's importance.

Entering the park through 69th Street and 5th Avenue, they walk across the grass with a carefree attitude. The young couple's exuberance is matched by the tightness of their handholding and the incessant free-spirited goofiness of their actions. They chase pigeons at the pond, smear ice cream on their faces at the fountain, spill popcorn on each other at Strawberry Fields, and release dozens of balloons into the sky just before Poet's Row.

"One day, maybe you'll be an iconic poet with a statue here," Vicky says suddenly, her eyes bright with hope as she gazes at the statues honoring great poets.

Inspired by her innocence and beauty, Erasmus replies, "Why not?"

And that's when the magic happens. He begins an improvised recitation, never taking his eyes off her.

"Let's call it..."

"One Verse at Poet's Row"

As the leaves fall

at Poet's Row,

I see your eyes sparkle

in the hues of the fall.

A gentle breeze whistles

as the spirit of the Big Apple

spreads to every corner

of the city's lungs.

The park is painted

in endless shades

of yellows, oranges,

and yes, hints of red, too—

seemingly all just for you,

my love.

Or perhaps is you, my muse—

Your dreams scintillating the park

with colors your spirit embraces.

Each word I weave, drawn from your light,

Guides my heart through the autumn night.

The leaves crunch softly beneath our feet,

The air, crisp and cool, carries autumn's sweet.

The hum of the city fades to a hush,

In this sacred place, time feels no rush.

But it is in this hallowed corner

that your smile shines brightest,

as your head full of dreams realizes

your heart has been swept away

by the spirit of the park

and by my very own,

while I recite this verse,

woven from precious fallen leaves

and my infatuated heart and soul.

*

Vicky extends her arms and pulls him close, holding him tightly. As she kisses him lovingly, her words are soft yet resolute, spoken from the depths of her devoted heart.

"My heart is completely and utterly yours, my love," she whispers, surrendering to his verse at Poet's Row. They talk endlessly, as if years had passed since their last meeting. By the time they exit the park at Columbus Circle, they are drenched in Central Park's bliss and the enchanting spirit of the Big Apple.

After a leisurely stroll through the bustling city streets, Erasmus is surprised when Vicky spends no more than five minutes inside the marching band instruments store.

"This place symbolizes your declaration of love to me. It was the turning point where your grand gesture won me over. When I learned that you'd traveled overnight to replace my broken baton, I felt an overwhelming desire to do anything for you, Erasmus. Even though I didn't know who had done it at the time, I prayed with all my heart that it was you," she says, her voice brimming with joy.

Victoria leans in and kisses him passionately, standing on one leg with the other bent up like a parting sweetheart from a wartime postcard.

"There's another reason I brought you here. Look at the address of the music store." She hands him a business card:

'The World of Marching Band Instruments'—the largest store of its kind, N.Y., NY (behind Madison Square Garden).

Then, she reveals a newspaper clipping:

'Ringling Brothers' performing at Madison Square Garden, New York, September through December 1977.

"I want you to take me to the circus," she pleads, her expression suddenly childlike.

Erasmus, unable to resist her enthusiasm, agrees with a warm smile. Together, they simply cross the street and proceed to have the time of their lives.

A few hours later, as they leave the arena, Erasmus takes the initiative.

"Let's catch the train and visit Mr. Lafayette in New Haven."

"Sure, but on one condition," she replies.

"You want to eat at the French bistro," he guesses, reading her mind.

"Bistro and boulangerie, dear," she clarifies, already savoring the thought of French pastries.

On the train, Vicky makes a heartfelt confession.

"Today at the circus, seeing all those children's happy faces, I felt, for the first time, an overwhelming desire to have children—to be a mother one day," she says with quiet conviction.

Erasmus pulls Victoria close, holding her against his chest, silently sharing her dream. But, out of shyness and uncertainty, he says nothing. His silence doesn't go unnoticed by Vicky, who fatefully misreads his kind heart.

New Haven, CT, 1977

Their host, Mr. Lafayette, beams as he sees them enter his shop. 'He may be three generations removed from France, but he's still 100 percent French to me,' Victoria thinks, noting his expressive gestures, impeccable posture, and distinguished attire.

"To what do I owe the immense pleasure of your august presence at my humble athenaeum today?" quizzes the towering antiquarian, his tone theatrical.

The young couple hesitates, momentarily unsure how to respond to his bombastic greeting.

"There's no game in town this weekend, right?" he asks, his grandiosity instantly deflating into casual familiarity.

"Harvard played at Princeton, so we took the train from New Jersey," Victoria explains.

"A fair journey just to visit your argumentative antiquarian," Mr. Lafayette declares with a knowing grin.

"We both wanted to see you. We went to the circus at Madison Square Garden earlier today," Victoria shares.

"And?" Mr. Lafayette asks, his tone suggesting he senses there's more to the visit.

"We were wondering if you have any old writings about the circus— or one in particular," Erasmus ventures.

Mr. Lafayette pauses, contemplating the question, a slow smile of certainty forming on his face.

"Yes, I do—and it's one of my favorites. I'll be right back," he replies, striding away with his impossibly long steps.

After what feels like an eternity, he returns, covered in dust but triumphant.

"Sorry, this one was buried deep, but it was worth the search. I have the perfect piece for you," he announces, seemingly oblivious to how long he was gone.

Mr. Lafayette then begins to read in earnest…

"Life as a Circus"

Life is like a circus,
that features the same cast of characters
springing to life from its pages.

We are surrounded by "ringmasters,"
those pulling the strings, building,
and driving "the machinery of civilization."

Then there are the "acrobats"—

the equilibrists and trapeze artists—

who defy gravity

performing jaw-dropping pirouettes

as part of their daily lives.

There are as well the "magicians" and "illusionists"

who make us believe,

in what seems unreal

through their ability to dream, visualize,

enhance or augment mundane reality,

and some of them actually dare

to trasnform those dreams

into true realities,

causing quantum leaps

for the advancement and evolution of society.

Then come the "jugglers,"

masters of dexterity and multitasking,

for whom balancing countless demands

is second nature,

not only to meet the challenges of a complex world

but, more importantly,

to be the ones who

assemble, operate,

and maintain

"the engines of civilization."

We also have the "lion and tiger tamers,"

who keep rule-breakers,

the wild and untamed, in check—

upholding social order and peace

by enforcing

of the laws of men.

Next come the "sword swallowers"

and "fire eaters,"

who defy danger and death

with every move.

As their feats don't allow

for a single false step or wrong move.

we usually hand them the controls

and put our lives in their hands

because we trust their skills

as well as their endless rehearsal and preparation,

to deliver us safely to our destination.

Then, there are the "cannonball men"

who thrive on excitement—

for them, the flights to nowhere,

are the high they need and seek—

for those fleeting seconds,

they are willing to take life to the limit,

and risk it all,

even though their trajectory

inevitably always ends,

in a crash-and-burn situation.

And of course, the "clowns and jesters,"

always after a practical joke or a roast,

whether through ridicule,

outrageousness or burlesque;

They are perennially chasing

The lighter side of things,

in pursuit of laughter and smiles,

which there are never enough in life.

Then come the "spectators and patrons,"

who witness and approve or disapprove

the show within a ring;

they are demanding and judgmental;

and as an intelligent herd,

they never miss a beat

and sometimes even alter,

the very acts of life in a circus.

The roar of the crowd, a cacophony of cheer,

As acrobats soar, suspended in air.

The scent of sawdust and caramel so sweet,

Blends with the rhythm of dancers' feet.

The magician conjures dreams from the air,

Illusions woven with delicate care.

The crowd gasps, then bursts into applause,

A fleeting moment that gives us pause.

Just as children never forget
their first time at the circus,
the greatest show on Earth,
appeals to the inner child in us all.
And this occurs because in a circus
we witness the show of life unfiltered—
without prejudice,
social rules, filters,
or the arrest of the mundane.

At times, I've felt like the juggler—
tasks piled high, my hands a blur.
Other times, the clown, hiding pain with a smile,
Yearning for truth beneath the guile.

The circus brings performers
displaying their finest talents,
boldly exposed,
executing dazzling acts—
rehearsed to perfection,
yet daring and improbable enough
that we cheer with childlike wonder.

As in life, circus performers
come from all walks of life.
They share one thing we all admire:
they do what they love,
following their passion.

Circus performers reach their heights

through relentless drive,

innate skill, and years of preparation.

We find circus performers,

on every corner of the streets of life—

not only as dazzling artists and elite athletes,

but as ordinary citizens,

tapping their full potential,

pursuing what they are good at.

Each of us holds within

a piece of these characters.

Perhaps part clown and full-blown illusionist,

or a bit of a trapeze artist with a juggler's flair.

Maybe a ringmaster with a clown's heart.

Whoever is the circus character that fits us best,

it is within thse characters

that some of our best talents reside.

On the circus characters,

we get to contemplate and appreciate

what happens?

When we tap our full potential.

Some are born to juggle, some to lead,

Others to sow the creative seed.

Our talents whisper, guiding the way,

Calling us forward, come what may.

Life, like the circus, demands each role,

A disciplined mind, a resilient soul.

For only with practice can we achieve,

The harmony we aspire to weave.

Life is a circus,

in as much as we allow our inner child

to rejoice and embrace its own characters—

without filters, fears, or prejudice.

By discovering which ones are ours,

we can soar

harnessing the best of our talents and passions,

like true circus performers do.

*

As Mr. Lafayette concludes his reading, he gazes with joy at Victoria and Erasmus. Their eyes, wide with wonder, and their captivated expressions reflect the power and depth of the poem they've just heard. But Mr. Lafayette isn't done yet.

"Most, if not all, of the characters in a circus exist within each of us. At the very least, we carry fragments of each one inside. But for some, we are truly destined to embody one of these performers. The challenge, then, is to ask ourselves: What are we? A ringmaster or an equilibrist? A trapeze artist or a juggler? A clown or a magician? Discovering this and mastering it holds the key to performing well in the circus of life," the wise antiquarian concludes.

Do we choose who we want to be in life?" Erasmus asks, his voice thoughtful.

"To some extent, yes. But to some extent, no. We're born with certain aptitudes that hint at what we might strive to master. You can't simply decide to be a trapeze artist in the circus; you become one if you possess a natural talent, a strong desire, and an unrelenting commitment to hone it. With those three elements in harmony, you can become a proficient trapeze artist," Mr. Lafayette explains, his tone deliberate and reflective.

"Why compare life to a circus?" Victoria asks, her curiosity piqued.

"To view life as a circus is an exercise in wisdom," Mr. Lafayette begins, his words weighted with meaning. "On one hand, life's circumstances mirror the roles these characters play when they perform for us. On the other hand, the extraordinary feats and orchestrated chaos of the three rings symbolize both hard-earned virtuosity and masterfully executed talent.

"To perfect one or more of the circus characters is to master life under similar conditions. After all, it cannot escape any of us that much of what we do in life—whether it's juggling responsibilities, balancing emotions, taming chaos, or pulling off acts of pure magic—echoes the roles of these performers. Life, like the circus, requires mastery, perseverance, and, above all, a willingness to embrace its unpredictable rhythm."

— ❖ —

Royal Cambridge Scholastic Institute, 2019
(University Auditorium)

As the memory fades, Professor Cromwell-Smith feels the significance of the lesson learned that day. He looks out at his class, the energy in the room grounding him in the present. With a faint smile, he begins, "Let's bring this back to today's topic—how life mirrors the circus. As we've seen, the circus is not just an entertaining spectacle but a profound metaphor for life. It reminds us that within each of us lies a performer, striving to master our roles. And just as every circus act requires practice, balance, and courage, so too does life. Now, let's explore how these themes resonate with you. The floor is open for any questions."

Isabella, a creative writing major, asks, "Professor, how can we recognize when we're playing roles that don't align with our true selves?"

"An excellent question, Isabella. The poem suggests that 'the greatest performers are those who embrace authenticity in their acts.' It's crucial to check in with yourself regularly. Reflect on your feelings and motivations—if a role feels unfulfilling or forced, it may be time to reassess and redefine that part of your life," replies Cromwell-Smith, his tone lively and encouraging.

"You talked about juggling different roles. How can we find balance without feeling overwhelmed?" asks Aaron, a second year engineering student.

"A great concern, Aaron. The poem implies that 'life's performance requires not just skill but also the wisdom to know when to step back.' Prioritization is key. Focus on what truly matters and learn to delegate or let go of less important roles. And remember, it's okay to take a break from the spotlight," replies the thoughtful pedagogue.

"In the poem, you mention the importance of embracing our inner child. How does that relate to our adult lives?" quizzes Chloe, a math major.

"That's a wonderful insight, Chloe," Professor Cromwell-Smith says, pausing thoughtfully. "Embracing your inner child allows for spontaneity and joy, qualities often lost in adulthood. The poem encourages us to 'reconnect with the playful spirit within,' reminding us that life shouldn't be solely about responsibilities. Moments of play and exploration are essential for a fulfilling life."

"What if we feel pressure to conform to societal expectations? How can we break free from that while still being part of a community?" asks Ethan, a philosophy student.

"An important question, Ethan. The poem states that 'true liberation comes from understanding and accepting your multifaceted self.' It's about staying true to your values while seeking a community that celebrates authenticity. Surround yourself with people who encourage you to shine, even when societal pressures suggest otherwise," replies the animated professor.

"Remember, life as a circus is a rich metaphor for our experiences. Embrace your roles, but always stay true to who you are at the core. Life is meant to be a beautiful performance, filled with joy and authenticity. Look within yourself and see if you can identify each circus character—an acrobat, a juggler, a clown. Then, ask yourself:

which one prevails within you? Which one are you inclined to master?" he concludes, embodying the spirit of a ringmaster.

"Thank you all for such an engaging class today. See you next week."

As the class files out, the esteemed professor lingers for a moment, seemingly lost in thought. He wonders which circus characters reside within him and which ones have guided his own life's performance.

Chapter 12

Clarity in Life

Royal Cambridge Scholastic Institute, 2019
(Erasmus and Victoria's Campus Home)

As Erasmus enters his cozy home studio in the pre-dawn darkness, a familiar thought resurfaces: *'She's oblivious to her deepest fears and disguises her inclination toward sorrow.'* Yet the sight of a steaming pot of tea and biscuits on the reading lamp table pulls him from his musings, making him feel unexpectedly cherished. Beside it lies a small note, which further brightens his mood: *"Love you, always have, always will."*

Lost in thought, Erasmus is drawn back to the present only by the sound of a soft voice in the background. Then, feeling her arms wrap gently around him, he greets her warmly.

"Dear lady of the night, what a delightful surprise to have you here so early."

"You seemed lost in thought," she whispers, her voice still heavy with sleep.

"You bring me immense joy, my dear. I wish we hadn't lost so much time apart," she says regretfully, her voice tinged with melancholy.

'Here we go,' thinks Erasmus, his perceptive nature sensing the direction of her words. He probes gently, "Why do you wish that?"

"Sometimes, I wish we could turn back time—to avoid our forty years apart," she confesses. He listens attentively, refraining from interrupting.

"I can't escape this continuous cycle of pain," she continues, her voice trembling. "Reliving our separation, David's illness and death, and the disruption of my career in criminal psychology—it all feels endless."

Her vulnerability pierces him, but he remains composed. "Dear, I have something crucial to share with you," she begins hesitantly. "It concerns a conversation I had with Gina back when my parents visited me in Boston."

"You mean the time you didn't introduce me to your parents?"

Erasmus recalls gently, his tone steady as he allows her to continue.

"This story has haunted me, replaying in my mind for years," Victoria admits, setting the stage for a deep revelation.

Harvard, 1977
(Gina's Dorm Room)

"Are you having second thoughts?" Gina inquires, breaking the silence.

Victoria hesitates before speaking. "Is being a teacher all he'll ever achieve?" she questions aloud, uncertainty coloring her words.

"Vicky, is your love conditional on success?" Gina challenges sharply, cutting through the hesitation.

"It seems so at times," Victoria replies, her voice wavering with self-doubt.

"You're just echoing what your mother has ingrained in you all your life," Gina points out bluntly. "But the real Victoria doesn't care about material wealth."

Victoria shifts uncomfortably as Gina's words hit home.

"No, Victoria," Gina continues with intensity, "your real worry is whether this absentminded intellectual Brit can provide the type of care you were taught to expect at home."

"I don't need anyone to take care of me!" Victoria retorts defensively.

"But you do," Gina presses. "You crave care, yet you also want control."

"What's wrong with that?" Victoria finally asks, her voice softening as she acknowledges her conflicting feelings.

"That won't work with Erasmus," Gina says matter-of-factly. "His independence and work ethic won't accommodate a relationship built on control. He loves you for being self-sufficient and industrious, not dependent."

Gina pauses for a moment, then continues, her tone gentler.

"Unless you address your deep-seated self-esteem issues with him, you'll always feel pressured to 'match up' to his world. The truth is, you're more afraid of feeling inadequate compared to him than actually being with him."

Victoria sits in silence, Gina's words unraveling her internal conflict.

"Erasmus has already seen and fallen for the true, confident, and genuine Victoria. Remember that—he loves you for who you are, not for what your parents or society expect you to be," Gina concludes, her voice firm yet encouraging.

Victoria looks away, her heart heavy yet a faint sense of clarity beginning to emerge.

Royal Cambridge Scholastic Institute, 2019
(Erasmus and Victoria's Campus Home)

"I should have listened to her advice, but I didn't, dear," Victoria admits, her voice heavy with regret.

"Vicky, regarding these persistent regrets, do you remember our session with Mrs. Peabody, where she shared that old manuscript about overcoming regrets?" Erasmus prompts, steering the conversation toward a teaching moment.

"Yes, I remember. Why do you ask?" she replies, her tone a mix of defensiveness and curiosity.

"Today in class, we'll revisit that lesson. I think it would be beneficial for you to join me," Erasmus suggests, his eyes soft with encouragement.

"With pleasure, dear," she agrees, though unease flickers behind her words.

"It will be quite fitting, my lady," he reassures her with a warm smile, feeling hopeful and relieved.

"Erasmus, the more I think about it, the clearer it becomes: our past doesn't have to dictate our future," she reflects, her voice tinged with determination.

"Absolutely! It's about recognizing those experiences and allowing them to guide us rather than hold us back," he responds with conviction.

The morning sun filters through the trees as Erasmus and Victoriadrive to his class in reflective silence, their hands clasped tightly on the center console—a quiet yet powerful symbol of their enduring love and mutual support. The hum of the car engine is the only sound between them, save for the occasional bird call through the open window. Neither speaks, but their silence is comfortable, each lost in thoughts of the journey that brought them here. Erasmus glances at her, his expression softening as he catches her pensive gaze turned toward the window.

"Ready, me lady? Shall we share what we've learned?" Erasmus muses aloud. Victoria nods, her grip on his hand tightening as the university's spires come into view, his thoughtful expression revealing the depth of his intent.

Royal Cambridge Scholastic Institute, 2019
(University Auditorium)

The familiar bustle of the campus greets them as they park. Erasmus adjusts the satchel over his shoulder, glancing at Victoria as she straightens her scarf against the cool morning breeze. The low hum of conversation and laughter drifts from students gathering in small groups outside the auditorium. As they approach the entrance, Victoria pauses, turning to Erasmus. "Thank you for bringing me today," she says softly. He smiles, placing a hand over hers.

"Always."

Together, they step inside, greeted by the echoing chatter of students settling into their seats.

"How is everyone today?" Erasmus greets his students with enthusiasm.

"Insanely awesome, professor!" the students respond in unison, their energy filling the room.

"As you may have noticed, Victoria has joined us today for a special reason. We're about to revisit one of our most memorable days," Erasmus announces, his tone setting the stage for an introspective and reflective lesson.

— ✦ —

Massachusetts Coast, 1977
(Sailing)

Erasmus, not typically a sailor, joins Victoria, a seasoned sailor from her childhood vacations on Lake Michigan, for a sailing adventure beginning in Newburyport. As they glide into the Atlantic along Salisbury Beach, Victoria patiently teaches Erasmus the basics of sailing, her expertise evident in every instruction.

As they grow more confident on the water, the natural beauty surrounding them begins to take over. Inspired, Erasmus launches into spontaneous poetry, his words an ode to the moment and their connection.

"The gentle breeze tousles those shiny curls of mine," he begins, his voice carried effortlessly by the wind. Victoria listens intently, visibly moved, her eyes reflecting the emotion of his impromptu verse. "What's that landmass over there?" Erasmus eventually asks, pointing toward the shoreline.

"That's Cape Ann," she explains, her tone proud and knowledgeable. "And just to the right, you can see Halibut Point."

"And where are we heading?" he inquires, curiosity sparking in his eyes.

"To a surprise location just to the right here in Ipswich Bay, known for its famous Ipswich clams," she reveals, her smile hinting at the mystery yet to unfold.

With a favorable wind at their backs, they continue along the coast, their laughter and conversation blending with the rhythmic sound of the waves. Eventually, they dock at a picturesque harbor, securing their boat and readying themselves for the next part of their adventure—an unwritten chapter eagerly awaiting their pen.

"Those Shinning Golden Curls of Mine"

The gentle breeze tussles freely,
those shiny curls of mine.

The vast ocean
shimmering liquid glass,
mirrors a magnificent canvas
stretching into eternity,
capturing those incandescent eyes
that achor my wandering soul,
to whom I forever belong.

With a cornucopia
of blues, silvers, and whites,
I am granted the privilege

of an endless palette,

to paint your radiant smile—

a smile that now owns me whole,

leaving no room to spare,

except for our two hearts,

tightly bundled together,

loving each other to infinity.

On one side of the horizon,

the sun rises

bringing soft, bright hues

to the new day,

along with an aura of ethereal beauty

surrounding your morning self—

a vision I contemplate in awe and wonder,

wishing it to be only mine.

Simultaneously,

on the other side of the horizon,

the sun sets

in vibrant tones,

same as your passions and fires,

to those I surrender eternally—

my heart now entirely yours,

no longer mine.

In the heart of the horizon,

our sails paint a story against the sky—

every stroke ablaze with the hues of our universe.

An extraordinary rainbow

arches across the heavens,

from end to end,

framing you at its center

in a timeless pose—

your radiant smile,

incandescent eyes,

and the gentle sea breeze

tousling freely

those gorgeous, shining golden curls of mine.

And as the sun bows to the horizon's edge,

its warm embrace whispers a quiet truth:

this moment, this love, is eternal—

a masterpiece etched in time.

*

Victoria sits motionless, her gaze fixed solely on him. Her lower lip quivers almost imperceptibly, and her eyes remain locked on his, reflecting absolute infatuation with his enchanting words. After a brief, spellbound silence, their conversation shifts back to more mundane topics.

"What's the name of that piece of land?" he asks, breaking the reverie.

"That's Cape Ann, and just to the right, you can see Halibut Point," she replies, her voice steady but still tinged with warmth.

"Is that our destination?" he probes, sensing the deliberate course she's charted.

"Actually, no. We're heading toward a small bay closer to us on the right called Ipswich Bay," she explains, gesturing toward the serene waters ahead.

"Why is it called that?" Erasmus asks, his curiosity piqued.

"You silly! Don't you know? It's famous for its Ipswich clams," she declares with delight, reveling in the rare opportunity to share something he doesn't already know.

"Is that our final destination?" he presses, intrigued.

"No, that's a surprise, dear," she responds with a teasing smile, her tone brimming with mystery.

With a gentle breeze at their backs, they glide effortlessly along the coast. Victoria expertly maneuvers the sail, guiding them closer to the picturesque harbor. As they near, Erasmus helps secure the sailboat to an empty wooden dock, tying it off with precision.

Lanesville, Massachusetts Coastline, 1977

After a leisurely stroll through the scenic surroundings, Erasmus realizes their location. They've arrived in Lanesville—the lair of their beloved antiquarian, Mrs. Peabody. The familiar sight of her charming storefront comes into view, and within moments, their effusive host greets them with open arms.

"Mrs. P.!" Erasmus exclaims, his face lighting up with joy.

"Well, this is a delightful surprise!" she responds cheerfully, enveloping both of them in a warm embrace.

Before they can exchange pleasantries, Mrs. Peabody fixes her gaze on Erasmus, her tone shifting to mock reproach. "Erasmus, back in

Wales, there's a melancholic fan of yours lamenting your absence," she scolds lightly.

"You haven't written to her in over a year," she continues, her expression softening despite her words.

"Mrs. V.?" Victoria asks, recognizing the name instantly.

"The one and only," Mrs. Peabody confirms, her stern expression momentarily returning before it dissolves into a fond smile.

Erasmus promises to write to his beloved mentor as soon as he returns home, his sincerity evident. Satisfied, Mrs. Peabody shifts her focus.

"Mrs. P., we need a remedy for the soul," he confesses earnestly.

"Ah, that's a transcendental matter requiring further clarification," she replies, her curiosity piqued.

"What is the affliction, if I may ask?" she inquires, her tone now serious.

"It's about regrets and sorrows. I'm constantly hung up on both," Erasmus admits, his voice carrying a trace of embarrassment.

"Mrs. P., make it a strong remedy, please. He really needs it," Victoria urges, her earnestness unmissable.

Mrs. Peabody is already in motion before Victoria finishes her plea. Despite the chaotic piles of books around her, she locates one within minutes—seemingly by intuition.

"This is one of my favorite readings," Mrs. Peabody begins, her voice softening. "Ever since I lost my husband to the sea during a fateful storm off the New England coast, these words have been my solace," she reveals, her eyes shimmering with unshed tears.

The revelation leaves Erasmus and Victoria momentarily stunned, unaware until now of her profound loss. With care, Mrs. Peabody places the book on her converted dining table. She begins to read aloud, her voice steady but rich with emotion, as if channeling her own journey of healing through the words on the page.

"Clarity in Life"

Craving an alternative reality of
"what ifs," "could haves" or "should haves"
is a futile search for a time machine—
an alternative reality or parallel dimension
that simply does not exist;
like grasping at shadows in a mirrored room—
each reflection leading nowhere but right back at us.

Lamenting past events, difficulties, or tragedies
in endless loops of pain
leaves us stuck, infinitely gasping for air.

Regrets and sorrows, fueled by insecurities,
fear, and guilt, act as magnifying glasses—
distorting and exaggerating true pain and real losses.

Regrets and sorrows lead us to places
where we find ourselves with those we neither like or love,
doing what we don't want,
longing for people and things we no longer have,
never had, or are simply not longer present.

Material wealth may liberate us from poverty,

but it cannot remedy fear, guilt, shortcomings,

false aspirations, or the emptiness of spirit and soul.

Riches are existentially hollow,

misleading us into a false sense of security,

often becoming a murky source

of future loneliness, regret, and sorrow.

We achieve clarity in life

when we have a clear purpose,

constantly focusing on our search for meaning.

We achieve clarity in life

when we are fully aware of our strengths and weaknesses,

relentlessly striving to build a wholesome set of virtues.

recognizing those we have already acquired ,

and actively putting them into practice.

We achieve clarity in life

when we conduct ourselves responsibly

while exercising judicious discipline.

We achieve clarity in life

when we seek, accept, defend, and protect the truth—

invariably and without compromise

We achieve clarity in life

when we are graced with redemption for our failings

through the power of faith and belief under the mantle of trust.

We achieve clarity in life

when we understand that we can continuously reinvent ourselves,

moving forward without breaking our core,

following our convictions with unwavering resolve

and treasuring true love,

using it as our source of happiness and inspiration.

Clarity in life inexorably leads to accomplishment

and self-confidence,

which, in turn, guide us to virtuous circles

where regrets and sorrows have no place

and no air to breathe.

Clarity in life expands our world, and broadens our horizons,

leaving no limits to the sky—

just the living universe and its endless firmament

drenched with stars whispering endless possibilities—

for us to experience, enjoy, and cherish.

*

Mrs. Peabody solemnly closes the book, her gaze lingering on Victoria and Erasmus. Her doting, pensive eyes carry the wisdom of her years. "Victoria and Erasmus, life is always in constant motion; lingering negatives are simply incompatible with the dynamics of being truly alive."

— ✦ —

Royal Cambridge Scholastic Institute, 2019
(University's Auditorium)

Professor Cromwell-Smith draws his class back into the discussion, building on Mrs. Peabody's poignant thoughts. The pedagogue pauses, his gaze lingering on the memory of Mrs. Peabody's voice echoing through her cozy shop. He closes his eyes briefly, drawing strength from the wisdom she shared so long ago. "That day stayed with me," he begins, his voice steady as he shifts his attention to the present. "Mrs. Peabody's words shaped how I approached regrets and clarity in life. They taught me that living fully means not letting the past define us." The room falls silent, the students hanging on his every word as he brings them into the heart of today's lesson. "Ever since that memorable ocassion, I have never again been trapped in those recurring painful thoughts."

Victoria turns toward him, her expression a mix of regret and realization. "Thank you," she says softly, her lips trembling with the weight of her acknowledgment.

Erasmus nods in acknowledgment, his solemn demeanor a silent signal—*enough, Vicky.*

Erasmus moves to the edge of the desk, leaning slightly as his gaze sweeps across the class. "Clarity," he says, his voice carrying a quiet authority, "is not about perfection. It's about seeing ourselves and our lives for what they truly are—and finding purpose amidst the chaos."

He pauses, allowing his words to settle. "Victoria and I revisited these lessons recently, and I believe they were worth sharing with you today. Clarity is a process, a continuous journey. Now, I'd like to hear your thoughts or questions about how we navigate this path."

"Professor, what about when the loss is irreplaceable?" asks Eleazar, a philosophy major.

"Eleazar," Erasmus begins thoughtfully, "in Korean culture, they define certain kinds of pain as unresolved sorrows. This philosophy, known as *Han,* acknowledges the existence of deep, enduring losses. Such sorrows are not hidden or avoided but confronted with acceptance. The pain doesn't vanish, but it no longer drives your life—it's placed where it belongs, allowing you to move forward," he explains sagely.

Another student, Leonard english literature major, raises his hand. "Professor, what should we do when regrets or sorrows start to take hold?"

Erasmus pauses briefly, his gaze steady. "Leonard , something I learned from my mother and have practiced since I was a teenager," he shares. "When you feel those emotions creeping in, first, breathe slowly and deeply. As you inhale, spell the word *LIFE* in your mind. Then, exhale and say *LIFE,* visualizing the word spreading throughout your being. Repeat this until the angst subsides. It works wonders," he assures them.

"How do we balance the need for clarity with the inevitable uncertainties of life?" asks Noah, a philosophy major.

"That's an essential question, Noah. The poem teaches that 'life is a constant dance between certainty and uncertainty.' Embrace the unknown as part of your journey. Clarity is vital, but so is adaptability. Recognize that uncertainty often leads to unexpected opportunities for growth," Erasmus replies, his tone encouraging.

As the final questions taper off, Erasmus offers a couple of closing reflections. "Clarity doesn't come from waiting for answers to fall into our laps. It comes from living, from questioning, and from accepting what is while striving for what can be. Carry that thought with you as you go forward."

He concludes, "Clarity in life isn't a destination; it's a continuous process of self-discovery and growth. It comes not only from reflection but from taking action. Embrace the journey and its lessons, recognize your strengths and limitations, and move forward with purpose."

"Thank you, everyone. That'll be all for today; see you next week," Erasmus finishes, his voice warm but resolute.

The students begin to gather their things, the hum of movement filling the room. As the professor and Victoria leave, they notice their students lingering, breathing deeply, their expressions marked by newfound calm. Victoria looks at Erasmus, her eyes shimmering with a newfound resolve. Together, they walk toward the door, passing students who pause to share their thanks or simply nod in quiet understanding.

"They seem at peace, dear. Perhaps now it's my turn to stop lamenting and regretting, as you did back then," Victoria says, her voice resolute.

"I'm sure you will, my lady. I'm sure you will," Erasmus replies cautiously, his heart full of hope.

Outside, the crisp air greets them as they step into the sunlight.

"Thank you for bringing me today," Victoria says softly.

Erasmus smiles, taking her hand. "It's always been you, my lady. Always."

They walk hand in hand through the campus park, their fingers interlocked in a gesture of enduring connection. Victoria's firm grip hints at an energy simmering within her.

"Dear, coming to class today has helped me bring clarity to my unresolved sorrows," she suddenly says as they sit on a bench in the park's serene setting.

"How so, my lady?" Erasmus asks, his voice gentle but probing.

"It's true; there are things I'll regret forever—pain that will never fade, and irreplaceable losses. But now I know I can place them in their proper context and continue to live fully," she reflects aloud. Erasmus listens attentively, delighting in her realization and resisting the urge to interrupt her flow.

"Today, remembering Mrs. Peabody has shown me that I've been addressing my unresolved sorrows constructively, even if inadvertently," Victoria continues, her voice steady with conviction. "Though I've regretted not following Gina's advice for years, I haven't repeated the mistake. Since the day we reunited, I've kept her wisdom in mind."

She turns to Erasmus, her eyes earnest. "The day I came to your class, I was consumed with nerves, unsure if you'd take me back. As I waited for Sarah to introduce me, I realized something: your desire to reconcile would come from strength, not weakness. It meant you had seen through the façade of my leaving and forgiven me. But the real challenge was whether I had forgiven myself."

Victoria's voice softens as she continues, "Taking me back didn't guarantee our future. Affinity and friendship might resume, but passion requires mutual desire. I knew that to rebuild our love, I had to confront my regrets and approach you with complete honesty."

She pauses, a small smile forming on her lips. "Erasmus, you've always loved self-sufficient, passionate women. I quickly realized that trying to control or manipulate you, even subtly, would never work. So, I left my old habits behind and resolved to let my heart guide me."

Erasmus stops walking, cups her face in his hands, and looks deeply into her eyes. "And you've succeeded, my lady. You're the same woman I fell in love with at Harvard—only stronger."

Overcome with emotion, he kisses her with gratitude and passion. Vicky wraps her arms around him, holding him as tightly as if to anchor him forever to her heart.

Chapter 13

Gratitude

Royal Cambridge Scholastic Institute, 2019
(Erasmus and Victoria's Campus Home)

The professor paces in his home studio, engrossed in a voluminous book. The pre-dawn darkness still blankets the room when Victoria surprises Erasmus. As is her custom, she approaches him from behind, wrapping her arms around him and letting her fingers trace gently beneath his robe and across his chest. She whispers in his ear, "I love you."

"Me too, my lady," he replies, setting the book down on her desk and clasping her hands over his chest as her touch continues to soothe him. "What a pleasure it is to see you at this early hour," he adds warmly.

"Well, yesterday, when you were staring at me in a way you'd never done before, I asked what it was you were looking at. You replied that you simply like to stare endlessly at my face. When I asked why again, you said that to explain it well enough, you were going to write me something about it," she recounts, framing her statement as an inviting lead-in.

"And my lady believes that I have somehow tackled and completed such a worthy yet challenging endeavor?" he asks, teasing her as he slowly turns around, though her cozy embrace makes it nearly impossible for him to focus.

"Knowing you, I'm certain you already did," she affirms with unwavering confidence.

Erasmus finds himself mesmerized by her every facial gesture and movement, his thoughts momentarily drifting as he loses himself in her presence once more.

"Erasmus, dear, come back to earth, please," she lovingly pleads, her voice coaxing him back to the moment.

A faint smile curves across Erasmus' lips. Without breaking their embrace, he reaches for a small scroll resting atop his desk, tied with a delicate string and an impossibly charming knot.

"Go ahead, open it. I planned to give it to you later this morning after you woke up, but I underestimated your ineffable curiosity."

Victoria unties the scroll with eager hands, her face lighting up with a radiant smile.

"Please read it to me, dear," she pleads softly, her tone filled with anticipation.

Erasmus adjusts his stance, his voice soft yet deliberate, and begins to read in earnest…

"Contemplating Your Face"

Over time, our faces become a reflection of our lives
and who we are truly inside.

As the masks of youth fade away,
the marks and scars reveal
the kind life we've lived
and the experiences we've endured.

Like a fingerprint etched on a well-weathered face,

every crevice, corner, ridge, or wrinkle—

each emanating from our unguarded rictuses

and spontaneous gestures—

echoes our deeds, victories, losses, defeats,

our pain and joy,

laid bare for all to see.

Like signage, they leave no place to hide.

Does our face look deeply angry?

What about mean-spirited? Perhaps artificial?

Or does it exude goodness, nobility,

a gentle spirit and an inspired soul?

Does it reflect shadows of darkness and solitude?

Or the bright hues of optimism and enthusiasm?

Does it vibe anguish or perhaps sadness?

Or does it resonate happiness?

Does it reveal depression and despair?

Or the vibrancy of cheerfulness and passion?

Whatever your honest answer is,

that is likely who you truly are.

Yet nothing in our face conveys more profoundly

about our nature and human condition

than our eyes.

Some eyes are downright scary,

portraying death in those who've encountered it,

for right or wrong reasons.

Others depict madness,

revealing glimpses

of the tumultuous, unsettled internal worlds

of the persons we face.

What about those that are simply empty—

and no one seems to be home?

An endless gallery unfolds across the human species:

the envious, the obsessed, the ambitious,

the vengeful, the sad, the angry,

the resentful, the greedy, and the hypocritical.

These stand in stark contrast to those eyes

that are gentle, benevolent, benign, giving, doting,

inspiring, healing, happy, joyful, patient,

grateful, forgiving, or simply twinkling—

even magical and outright awesome!

Then there is love.

Our eyes and faces transform under the mantle of love:

youth, freshness, rosiness, sparkle, and glow

cover us with a halo, projecting positive energy,

imbued with enchanting, contagious vitality.

In the soft twilight, your face becomes a map,

Each line and curve—a path we've traveled.

Echoes of laughter in the crinkle of your eyes,
And the warmth of years in your tender smile.

The look of love is a masterpiece,
where we see drawn on our loved ones
all that we share and treasure.

That's why when we contemplate the faces of our life partners,
we see well beyond what anyone else can,
as every move and angle reflects
a different moment of a life shared.

Each expression and gesture
reminds us of a different anecdote, circumstance,
or a life experience with them.

We place their laughter in eternal memories,
vividly remembering their smiles at countless occasions and places,
and we see their tears —of joy or sadness—
as those we shared or experienced as a couple.

We see in flashes drawn on their faces,
the movie of our life journey—
just like the first time we discovered
our love's maternal or paternal eyes at our children's births,
or their eyes of sadness at each of our departures,
followed by their bursts of joy and relief upon our safe returns,
and or their gestures of disgust at our transgressions
or disappointments,

or their immense happiness when their hearts are taken by surprise

by spontaneous gestures, heartfelt details,

or even a tiny single flower.

When we see that face that has journeyed with us for so long,

we notice every little wear and tear that is as much

a part of us as it is of them.

That's how we cannot help but contemplate—

unwittingly and to a degree unknowingly—

in awe and wonder, and the unique kind of beauty

crafted from the richness of a life story together,

filled with countless and unforgettable mementos.

That is the reason no one can appreciate, value, understand,

and read, see, and feel better

our life partner's eyes and faces than us—

simply because only we know

the life story and anecdotes behind them.

*

Her eyes are adrift in a sea of emotions as he finishes reading.

"You never cease to amaze me, my beloved Brit. Sometimes, you are simply enchanting and spellbinding. There's profound beauty and an addictive wizardry in your words, my love," she professes, her gaze brimming with immense gratitude.

Slowly, her expression shifts from enamored to teasing, her eyes alight with playful mischief. She moves closer, kisses him passionately, and takes his hand in hers.

Victoria draws him upstairs with deliberate intensity, and together, they lose themselves in their never-ending crusade of love.

(Victoria and Erasmus's Campus Home)

A couple of hours later, sunlight spills through the windows as Ella Fitzgerald and Louis Armstrong's *Our Love is Here to Stay* plays softly in the background. Sipping her morning coffee, Victoria gazes out the window, her heart buoyed by the music. In the distance, she spots Erasmus biking toward class, his figure gradually shrinking along the tree-lined road.

As the song transitions into Laura Pausini's *Amare Veramente* (True Loving), Victoria allows herself to drift into quiet reflection. *The well-hidden loneliness has vanished; the chronic melancholy is gone. Work is no longer an escape but a source of passion and pleasure. Oddly enough, I feel protected,* she muses.

She watches as Erasmus, now a tiny dot, disappears over the distant hill. A sudden jolt of fear courses through her—a visceral reaction to his sudden absence.

He's just gone over the hill, she tells herself, but unease lingers. Then Judy Garland's *Stormy Weather* begins to play, the ominous tune unsettling her further. *Maybe it's just my imagination,* she reasons. But the gut feeling persists.

Without hesitating, she unties her bathrobe, grabs her bike, and pedals furiously toward the hill.

The faint sound of a siren reaches her ears, making her heart race. As the wail grows louder, she cringes, dreading the confirmation that something has gone wrong. Moments later, an ambulance speeds past her, heading toward the hill.

Breathless, Victoria crests the hill and sees a campus security car and paramedics lowering a stretcher. An officer cradles Erasmus's head.

"Nooo!" she cries, leaping off her bike and rushing to his side. Dropping to her knees, she cradles his face, her hands trembling as tears stream down her cheeks.

"Ma'am, please step aside. Let us do our job," one of the paramedics orders.

But Victoria remains fixed, stroking Erasmus's face as she sobs. Just as the paramedics prepare to move her, Erasmus's eyes flutter open, and his gaze meets hers.

"Victoria," he murmurs, a faint smile gracing his lips.

Her sobs turn to laughter, her tears a mixture of relief and joy. "What happened, my lady?" he asks, bewildered.

"I thought I saw you fall, and something told me to come," she replies, still shaken.

"I was driving in the opposite direction when he hit a pothole, lost control, and veered toward my patrol car," the campus security guard explains. "I slammed on the brakes, but he landed on the hood, arms outstretched."

"Actually, that may have broken his fall and prevented a more serious injury," a paramedic adds.

Erasmus nods, beginning to piece it together. "I hit a pothole and lost my balance," he recalls.

After thorough checks and reassurances, Erasmus insists on going home with Victoria. Once the ambulance and patrol car leave, the couple stands alone atop the hill, the morning sun casting a warm glow over them.

"Dear, I'm so grateful nothing happened to you. When I saw you lying there, I thought I'd lost you," Victoria says, holding him tightly.

"This is one of those moments to show gratitude, don't you think?" she says, winking at him.

She places her hand on his chest and guides his hand to hers.

"Close your eyes," she whispers. "Being alive and having you are precious and irreplaceable gifts I must earn every day. Let us thank the Creator. Let us thank life," she professes with conviction.

Together, they recite in unison, their voices blending as one. When Erasmus opens his eyes, the first thing he sees is her steady, reassuring gaze.

"Of course, Victoria. How could I ever forget it?" he replies, a broad smile lighting up his face.

"You still have time," she says casually, though her intent is clear.

"For what?" he asks, his usual cluelessness returning.

"To make gratitude the subject of today's class," she responds with a playful grin.

"Do I?"

"You have an hour. Let's go back so you can shower," she teases with a wink, snaring him completely.

"What a wonderful idea, my lady. Let's pedal home," he says with a laugh.

The pair zigzags down the gentle slope, Erasmus on his old rusty bike and Victoria on her sleek, modern two-wheeler, their love as enduring as the rhythm of their wheels.

As the couple finishes their morning rituals, Victoria glances at the clock. "You'd better get going, dear, or you'll be late for class," she teases playfully. Erasmus nods, grabbing his leather satchel. "I suspect today's lesson might be more for me than the students," he says with a thoughtful smile, as they exchange a final kiss before parting. For the second time this morning, Victoria watches him bike away, the rhythmic creak of his rusty wheels fading into the distance. A small smile lingers on her lips as she murmurs, "Today will be extraordinary—I can feel it."

Royal Cambridge Scholastic Institute, 2019
(University's Auditorium)

As the pedagogue enters the auditorium, the familiar buzz of student chatter greets him. He pauses at the doorway, his eyes scanning the room as if soaking in the energy of the space. Adjusting his tie, he steps forward with a renewed sense of purpose. "Good morning, everyone. Let's make today's session one to remember," he announces, his voice carrying an infectious enthusiasm that immediately captures the room's attention.

"How's everyone today?" asks an inspired professor, his face alight with the lingering joy of a recent, passionate morning.

"Awesome, and you, professor?" replies the lively student body, their energy buzzing through the room.

"Today, I'll be revisiting a day I will remember forever, as I hope it will become for you as well. It begins like this..."

— ✦ —

New York City, Carnegie Hall, 1977

Invited by the Scottish antiquarian Colin Carnegie, who is on a short visit to the USA, Victoria and Erasmus travel overnight by train from Boston to New York City. After a day spent wandering the city's parks, museums, and public libraries, they attend a gala concert in their finest attire. It is their first time at Carnegie Hall, and the experience becomes unforgettable as rock virtuoso Rick Wakeman takes them on a "Journey to the Center of the Earth."

As they exit the iconic venue, Mr. Carnegie waits for them at the steps, his face radiating excitement.

"Victoria, Erasmus, what a pleasure it is to see you both here. I'm so happy you could make it! But tell me, how was it?" he gushes enthusiastically.

"Fantastic! I read all of Jules Verne's books as a child, but I never imagined I'd experience 'Journey to the Center of the Earth' as a rock concert, much less with a philharmonic orchestra in the background," exclaims an exuberant Erasmus.

"Mr. Carnegie, I assume this magnificent hall is also part of your relative's legacy?" Erasmus inquires.

"That's correct," he replies with pride. "Andrew Carnegie, my relative, built this grand hall as part of his philanthropic vision to elevate humanity through art and education."

"As you said, the magnificent deeds he left not only continue to exist and operate, but they have also become woven into the fabric of this country," Erasmus affirms, his voice filled with admiration.

"Well said, young man. His legacy has become like the air we breathe. At first, we're unaware we have it; we just use and enjoy it. It's the same with the man himself, Andrew Carnegie. His foundation, in real dollar terms—meaning adjusted for inflation—is the largest philanthropic organization ever created. Yet, that fact isn't widely known in this country," Mr. Carnegie explains enthusiastically.

"A true measure of the stature of the man himself," adds Erasmus.

"But as you've said, he's not appreciated enough," Victoria interjects.

"That's correct," acknowledges Mr. Carnegie with a somber nod.

"Why is that?" she asks, her exuberance tinged with a touch of naiveté.

"That, I'll leave for you to discover. It is a worthy endeavor, though. I sincerely hope that America recognizes and honors, commensurately, the great deeds of the man."

"Gratitude?" Victoria ventures thoughtfully.

"Indeed, young lady. His legacy has earned it in spades," states Mr. Carnegie with conviction. "On the subject of gratitude, let's have a seat. I've brought with me an ancient writing, so our encounter doesn't elapse without a measure of tutelage for you both," he remarks with a twinkle of mentorship in his eyes.

The trio finds a quiet pew inside Carnegie Hall, the grandeur of the space amplifying the weight of the moment. With deliberate care, Mr.

Carnegie retrieves a weathered manuscript from his satchel. Clearing his throat, the Scottish antiquarian begins to read in earnest...

"Gratitude"

The most profound forms of gratitude
are either celestial or existential in nature.

Enough has been professed and predicated to describe gratitude.
Yet, its essence does not lie in the question, "What is it?"
It resides in the how, why, and when.

We are truly grateful when we are selfless
in our gestures and expectations.

We express genuine gratitude in our actions
if we are keenly aware of its existential and imperative necessity—
to perennially reciprocate and give back to life and others,
and for the privilege of being alive.

For gratitude to be authentically conveyed,
for gratitude to resonate or be empathetic,
it must embody selflessness, humility, and respect—
the very essence of its how, why, and when.

Our mere existence is an inexplicable blessing;
for this, we thank our Creator
for ordaining us into this universe,
chosen over the trillions of other reproductive cells
that never make it into the journey of life.

Once we arrive, we have much to be thankful for—
each day we are alive, healthy, conscious,
surrounded by friends and family, and love.

In gratitude, we honor the loyalty
others demonstrate to us.
In gratitude, we cherish the faith
others maintain in us.

In gratitude, we acknowledge the worthiness
of each other's gestures.

In gratitude, we pay our respects to those who dote on us,
whether we deserve it or not.
In gratitude, we reciprocate with love the love we've received.
In gratitude, we reward the acts of kindness we are graced with.

In gratitude, we find greater joy in givng that in receiving.
In gratitude, we celebrate life's simple, candid moments.

Gratitude is most impactful when it comes
genuinely from the heart,
without the interference of ego or social rules.

In the quiet moments when hearts align,
I feel the weight of your hand in mine.
A bond unspoken, yet deeply known,
For this connection, I'm humbly shown.

True gratitude expects nothing in return.

It is spontaneous,

not dictated by anything or anyone

born soley of conscience.

Genuine gratitude is anonymous;

it is just an act of our conscience.

It uplifts those we are grateful for,

placing them at the forefront

while we remain quietly behind the scenes.

Genuine gratitude is never proportionate,

it is immeasurable and boundless,

expressed through acts of love, gestures, and sacrifices.

False gratitude, on the other hand,

is a narcissistic farce,

driven by self-interest and appearances,

devoid of sincerity or care for others.

Gratitude is a dependable source of inner peace,

happiness, and inspiration.

Its musical notes resonate with the better side of our humanity,

sparking of creativity and visualization

igniting one of life's noblest conditions—

to be perennially thankful

to the Creator for life and to others for their grace.

*

Colin Carnegie stares at them with a broad smile. "Now, let me share with you an exercise in gratitude—one that I hope you'll apply for the rest of your lives," states Mr. Carnegie.

— ✦ —

Royal Cambridge Scholastic Institute, 2019
(University's Auditorium)

Professor Cromwell-Smith brings his students back to the present, preparing to share what the Scottish antiquarian, Colin Carnegie, taught him and Victoria at Carnegie Hall so many years ago. It is the same practice Victoria had initiated earlier that morning after Erasmus's uneventful but frightening mishap.

The professor closes his eyes briefly, as if reliving the moment one last time. When he opens them, his gaze is steady and full of warmth.

"That night at Carnegie Hall wasn't just a lesson in gratitude; it was a turning point. It taught me that acknowledging life's blessings is not merely an act of reflection but a call to action," he says, his voice resonating with conviction. He pauses, letting the weight of his words settle over the room before continuing, "And now, let's bring that lesson into our own lives. Let me show you what Mr. Carnegie asked us to profess that night at Carnegie Hall," the professor states. "It's a timeless and invaluable lesson—one I hope you'll carry with you for the rest of your lives. Here's what I want you to do: please stand up," he instructs.

The entire student body rises, their curiosity evident in the hum of energy filling the room. The professor gestures for silence, and the buzz quickly subsides.

"This is what our beloved mentor taught us that day. Place one hand over your heart. Now, close your eyes and, within your mind, say: 'Being alive and healthy is a precious and irreplaceable gift that I must earn every day. Let us thank the Creator. Let us thank life."

The auditorium falls into profound stillness as hundreds of students perform the exercise. The atmosphere becomes charged with sincerity and introspection, the act of collective gratitude transforming the space.

After a moment, the professor continues, "Thank you all for your mindful participation today. Before we dive into questions, I want to leave you with this thought," Erasmus says, leaning forward slightly, his hands clasped on the lectern. "Gratitude is more than a fleeting emotion. It's a lens through which we view our lives—a compass that guides our actions. When you practice gratitude, you transform not just your perspective but the lives of those around you. Keep this in mind as we explore the themes of today's lesson," he concludes. "Now, let's open the floor for any questions about the themes we've explored, particularly the role of gratitude in our lives."

"Professor, how can we practice gratitude daily without it feeling like a chore?" asks Amira, a history major.

"That's an excellent question, Amira," the professor replies warmly. "The poem suggests that 'gratitude should be woven into the fabric of our daily lives.' Start small—keep a gratitude journal or share one thing you're grateful for at dinner each night. When gratitude becomes part of your routine, it feels less like a task and more like a natural and rewarding practice."

"In the poem, there's a line about gratitude illuminating our lives. How can we ensure that we're truly experiencing that illumination?" quizzes James, a psychology major.

"A great insight, James," Cromwell-Smith responds, his gaze thoughtful. "The poem conveys that 'we must be present to appreciate the light of gratitude.' Practice mindfulness—take time each day to pause and reflect on the good in your life. It's about training your mind to notice the positives amidst challenges, allowing gratitude to truly shine through."

"What if we're struggling to feel grateful due to difficult circumstances? How can we cultivate that feeling?" asks Sophie, a math major.

"Sophie, that's a valid and important concern," the professor answers gently. "The poem reminds us that 'even in our darkest moments, gratitude can be found.' It's essential to first acknowledge your feelings. Gratitude doesn't mean ignoring pain—it's about finding small glimmers of hope or joy, like a friend's support or a moment of beauty. Over time, these small acts of gratitude can help shift your perspective."

"How do we balance gratitude with the pursuit of our goals? Sometimes, it feels like we should be striving for more rather than just being grateful," inquires Liam, an engineering student

"That's a thought-provoking question, Liam," the professor replies. "The poem highlights that 'gratitude doesn't negate ambition; it enhances it.' Gratitude provides a foundation of contentment and perspective, allowing you to pursue your goals with a clear and motivated mind. It's not about settling; it's about appreciating what you have while striving for more."

"Thank you all for your thoughtful questions," the professor says, his voice filled with quiet conviction. "Remember, gratitude is a powerful force—it has the ability to transform your life and your relationships. Embrace it, and let it guide you toward a more fulfilling existence. See you all next week."

As the students file out, Erasmus lingers at the lectern, watching them thoughtfully. The quiet murmur of their voices fades as the room empties, leaving him in a moment of peaceful reflection.

As he leaves the auditorium, Professor Cromwell-Smith notices many students lingering, their hands over their hearts as they repeat the gratitude ritual. A smile spreads across his face as he observes the multitude of faces reflecting serenity and newfound clarity. The energy in the room is palpable, an unmistakable testament to the impact of shared gratitude.

Victoria appears at the door, her presence pulling him from his reverie. "Ready to go, dear?" she asks, her smile gentle yet knowing. Erasmus nods, joining her at the door. "Let's head home. Today feels like the kind of day to reflect—and to be grateful," he replies, taking her hand as they step into the crisp evening air.

Chapter 14

Doubt

Royal Cambridge Scholastic Institute, 2019
(Erasmus and Victoria's Campus Home)

Erasmus wakes up with a jolt. His first instinct is to check if she is still there, or if she had ever been by his side at all.

'Your deranged mind is driving you crazy,' he muses, gently caressing her forehead as she sleeps, her breathing steady and calm. *'You are poisoned by doubt and do not seem able or willing to escape it.'*

Quietly, Erasmus drags himself out of bed, his movements slow and heavy. He stumbles toward the kitchen to fix his morning tea, the comfort of routine guiding him. As he reaches the counter, he stops short—there, waiting for him, is a freshly prepared pot of tea, still warm. Next to it, a folded card catches his eye.

His hands tremble slightly as he picks it up and unfolds it to reveal a poem written in her delicate handwriting:

"Always There"

Today, my heart looked for you,
and I sighed in joy and relief,
for one more time, when I needed it,
my dream of you was still there.

Somehow, I'd expected it to vanish,

but that's just the other side of me—
the one that tries to keep me grounded,
not letting me go anywhere,
even when the winds of longing call.

Tonight, I went to bed early,
and your dream of me
remained precisely where you left it,
right there—
soft as the whisper of leaves
dancing in the evening wind,
cradled in the hush of the night.

Tomorrow, I'll be up before dawn,
and shortly after, at sunrise,
our dream will make itself present,
as it always does—
always there,
like the first light of day
spilling across the earth,
quiet and certain,
a promise fulfilled.

My heart, a quiet drum in the stillness,
Leaps at the sound of your tender call.
The rustling leaves seem to echo you,
As if the world conspires to keep us whole.

As sunlight filters through the trees,

Your dream lingers, a shadow of gold,

A warm breeze carrying your voice,

Whispering,

"I'm here; I'm right here, my love,

Always there!"

*

Erasmus smiles in joy as he rereads the poem. *"You old fool. What will it take to let go of your doubts and fears?"* he muses, his inner turmoil blending with the warmth of her words in a strange, almost pleasurable conflict.

"Did you like it?" she asks softly, standing at the kitchen door.

Erasmus turns around in slow motion, his face lighting up with a radiant smile. "I love it, my lady," he replies, closing the space between them to embrace her.

"I recently corresponded with good old Mrs. Peabody," she murmurs, her voice still heavy with sleep. "She was so kind to find it for me among her treasure chest of antique writings."

"You're amazing," he whispers, feeling her tremble in his arms.

"Not exactly, dear. I know exactly what you're going through. The same thing happened to me back then," she admits, her voice tinged with vulnerability.

"You mean doubts?" he asks, searching her eyes.

"Yeah. I was full of doubts and uncertainty, so I ran," she confesses, her guilt evident as she lowers her gaze.

"We've already gone through that, Vicky," he reassures her gently, brushing a strand of hair from her face. "But I do have a question lingering in my mind—something completely different," he adds, his tone shifting slightly.

"About what?" she asks, already sensing the gravity of his unspoken words.

"Before we get to that, I've got a little something here for you," Erasmus says, pulling a folded piece of paper from his robe pocket and handing it to her.

Her brow furrows as she takes it. "What is it?" she asks, unfolding the paper with curiosity.

"It's called *A Labor of Love*. I wrote it right after we first met," he explains. "It was written to the future you. It reflects how I envisioned what you would be, do, and achieve in your life as a criminal psychologist."

Victoria looks up at him, her expression a mix of astonishment and tenderness. She begins to read, her hands trembling slightly as the weight of his words envelops her.

"A Labor of Love"

What a daunting task it is
to navigate through the darkest corners
of the minds of others, but not your own—
those paths where the ground is shaky,
the foundations cracked,
the Earth shifting,
and some of the tracks of life are blurry,

devoid of light and barren of well-being or happiness.

But perhaps there is no tougher job
than confronting minds
that not only lack meaning and purpose in life
but are also potentially or inherently,
wicked, devious, reckless, or delusional—
or simply love themselves so much
that there is no room or care for anyone else.

What a tough job it is to do good,
to uplift and improve the mindset of others in need.
What an impossible task it seems
to do that for those in need of redemption,
those yearning for a second act in life,
those that very few support or believe in.

What a tough job.
What an impossible job.
What a wonderful labor of love.
That's what you'll do,
and that's what you will be leaving in your wake.
That's what you would have done!

*

As Victoria finishes reading, tears cascade down her face.

"This is beautiful," she blurts out, overcome by emotion and memories of the past. "I did exactly that for quite a while," she adds, tenderly caressing his face.

"Which brings me to my lingering question—why did you change careers?" asks Erasmus, sipping his morning tea.

"I was wondering when you were going to ask me about that," she replies with a slight, bittersweet smile.

"What happened, Victoria?" he presses gently.

Her gaze drops, and her voice softens. "A patient became obsessed with me. For more than a year, he harassed and threatened my late husband and me. It affected the whole family. Law enforcement intervened, and a judge slapped a restraining order on him. He was arrested several times, but all to no avail. His obsession and aggressiveness only escalated."

Victoria's voice falters, and Erasmus instinctively places his arm around her shoulder. Her head leans against his forearm as she remains motionless, fighting to regain her composure.
"It was a traumatic experience for all of us," she continues, her words heavy with pain. "In the end, I couldn't see patients anymore. The nightmares only stopped when I quit my practice altogether."

"How did you feel about your decision as time went on?" he asks softly.

"I didn't have a chance to reflect on it. My late husband got sick, and for the next five years, there was no time left for anything else," she laments.

"And now? Do you ever think about going back to it?" he persists, his curiosity sincere.

"No," she replies firmly, shaking her head. "I'm done with it. For me, it's now only about us," she says, leaning in to kiss him softly on the cheek.

Erasmus takes her hand. "What about you, dear? Why did you change colleges?" she asks, her tone shifting to match his earlier curiosity.

"Well, it had nothing to do with the colleges. I asked for a change because of you," he admits without hesitation.

"Me? Why?" she asks, incredulous.

"It was sort of a renewal. I needed to change my life. It was my own little way of moving on," he explains.

"Did you?" she probes.

"Yes, the new faculty did wonders for me," he acknowledges, "but no, I never moved on from us—that never materialized," he adds firmly.

"And you, my lady, never had any doubts?"

"When I left, I was consumed by them," she confesses, her eyes clouded with regret.

"I never did," he states with unwavering certainty.

"But why have them now?" she asks, her voice tinged with concern, trying to make sense of his lingering fears.

"That's what I can't figure out, especially their recurring nature," he replies with frustration.

"Perhaps what you're terrified of is me leaving again," she suggests thoughtfully. "A part of you might still hold fears and doubts about the same thing happening once more. But I bet it'll go away over time," she concludes, her psychologist's instincts surfacing.

Erasmus nods slowly. "It'll certainly go away at lightning speed if, every time I feel one of these panic attacks building, you stop me right in my tracks before it even gets going. And you do it so beautifully, with all of your expressions and little gestures of unconditional love," he affirms, his eyes filled with gratitude.

"Dear," Victoria says, her tone shifting to one of calm reassurance, "There are things inside all of us that are better left unexplained. Don't try to find an answer for everything." She hands him another slip of paper. "Please read this—it's another one of the scribbles Mrs. P. sent us."

Erasmus takes the note and unfolds it carefully, his heart swelling with anticipation as he begins to read.

"A Good Riddle"

A good riddle is hard to crack.
Inevitably, though, it always has a solution.
The same goes for a puzzle or a mystery.

But life is not always a riddle to be solved,
as its solutions don't come in the form of passwords.
More often than not,
they are created or simply altered along the way.

Thus, even though life's riddles are always there to be solved,
their solutions are not necessarily already present.

And if one must tread too carefully about what to ask for,

then some of life's riddles

are better left unresolved,

Like stars too far to reach.

They shimmer, untouched by answers,

Their light a quiet, endless speech.

*

"Thank you, my lady," he says thoughtfully. "Doubt—that'll be today's subject."

"Oh, Mrs. Poindexter, the librarian at Harvard," she replies instantly.

"You do remember!" he exclaims, affirming her response before continuing. "How could I forget? If only I had applied what we learned that day," he laments.

Erasmus paused, the dawn light casting a gentle glow around them. How many mornings had they shared like this, yet each felt uniquely significant? As memories swirled in his mind, he prepared to steer their conversation toward the day's pressing demands.

"You only have a slight problem, my dear," she warns playfully.

"And what would that be, my lady?" he asks, intrigued.

"Have you noticed what time it is?" she exclaims, her voice tinged with urgency. He glances at the wall clock; only fifteen minutes remain until class. Making it on time seems nearly impossible.

As Erasmus races out the door, the warmth of Victoria's support lingers in his mind, her words echoing softly: "Love you, my lunatic Brit." The familiar crunch of gravel underfoot and the morning sun peeking through the trees signal the start of another day filled with possibilities.

Royal Cambridge Scholastic Institute, 2019
(University's Auditorium)

Yet somehow, five minutes later, Victoria—still in her nightgown—drives the professor to class in his car. With only a minute to spare, he bolts out of the vehicle.

"Love you, my wicked lady," he shouts as he races away.

"Love you too, my lunatic Brit," she calls after him, her head poking out the window.

He dashes toward the faculty building, the familiar rustle of leaves filling the crisp air. As he sprints through the corridors, the distant laughter of students mingles with the scent of fresh coffee wafting from the campus café. The scene reminds him of countless mornings spent pondering life's questions, a comforting rhythm of his days.

Inside the auditorium, suspense builds as the seconds tick down. Would the professor be tardy again? Bets are placed. Those wagering he'll be late argue he's still in his honeymoon phase, while skeptics believe it's over, and punctuality will prevail.

10, 9, 8, 7, 6, 5, 4, 3...

As he enters the lecture hall, the students' chatter subsides, replaced by an expectant hush. Erasmus pauses for a moment, the weight of the morning's revelations merging with the lively energy of the room.

"Good morning, everyone," an out-of-breath professor proclaims as he bursts into the auditorium.

He surveys the audience, his gaze lingering for what feels like an eternity. As he paces to catch his breath, the silence thickens. Once he senses he has their full attention, he resumes speaking.

"Today's subject is doubt. Some of you doubted whether I'd make it to class on time. That's what we all do—grapple with doubt constantly. This morning, I'll take you back to the day when Victoria and I met a truly remarkable woman at a timeless Athenaeum, and she imparted a memorable lesson about this very subject.

"It begins like this…"

— ✦ —

Harvard's Widener Library, 1977

"Nowadays, this is the only way to get a hold of you two," Vicky's best friend, Gina, remarks with playful sarcasm.

"You've both turned into absolute love hermits," complains Erasmus's close friend, Matthew.

"We should all go out," Gina suggests, her tone bordering on impatience.

Distractedly, the infatuated young couple observes their friends' smiles and banter but says nothing in return.

"I guess that's it. We've lost them both," Matthew concludes with mock resignation.

"Of course, you haven't. Give us time," Victoria interrupts with a slight grin.

"Erasmus, what about your old mentors back in Wales? Have you forgotten about them too?" Matthew teases.

"Sort of. I did manage to write to one of them recently—Mrs. V— but only after a colleague of hers reminded me. I told her everything about Vicky," Erasmus responds, somewhat defensively.

"And?" Matthew presses, his curiosity piqued.

"She replied a while ago," Erasmus continues. "It was a wonderful letter, and she sent us several old writings with it. I particularly liked the one called The Three-Legged Stool," Victoria chimes in with enthusiasm.

"Now, Vic, explain something to me," Matthew begins, leaning in conspiratorially.

"And what would that be, Matt?" Victoria asks, raising an eyebrow.

"You went all out at Martha's Vineyard when you surprised Erasmus—covered his eyes, kissed him, and the rest is history. But Gina told us you didn't even know it was him!" Matthew chuckles, clearly enjoying the story.

A moment of silence follows as Victoria bites her lip, throwing Gina an accusatory glance.

"That's right, I didn't know. I just followed my heart, and I swear to you, I didn't enter the restaurant with any plan in mind. When I saw Erasmus, I completely lost control of myself," she blurts out, her voice thick with emotion.

"All those little gestures opened her heart, so that outburst was bound to happen," Gina observes clinically.

"Well, Prince Charming, you obviously won her over with the baton," Gina adds, her sarcasm softened by affection.

"And you, Victoria, captured his heart with the trip home," *Matthew declares.*

The love-struck pair exchanges knowing glances, their expressions revealing that everything just said is already etched deeply in their hearts.

"Hey, buddy, time to work," *Matthew announces, breaking the spell.*

"Vic, we have work to do. Let's go," *Gina nudges, ushering Victoria to another table.*

A couple of hours later, Erasmus and Victoria find themselves alone again in the cavernous library.

"Let's go check out the antique book section," *Erasmus suggests with a mischievous grin.*

Giggling and holding hands, they wander through the aisles, their attention more on each other than on the rules or the other patrons.

"May I help you?" *a stern, short, bespectacled woman asks, her tone clipped.*

"We're looking for antique books," *Erasmus replies.*

"Those need to be requested and read in a special section," *the librarian states, her patience waning.*

"Why a special section?" *Victoria asks, intrigued.*

"Video surveillance ensures they are handled with care," *the librarian explains curtly.* *"Now, what are you looking for?"*

"We're seeking ancient writings about doubt," *Erasmus responds.*

"Any particular period or author?" *she queries, her curiosity slightly piqued.*

"We'll leave that to you," Erasmus replies, a note of gallantry in his tone.

"May I ask the nature of your doubts?" the librarian inquires, clearly intrigued now.

"Of course! Mine is about what to do in life," Erasmus answers, glancing toward Vicky.

"Mine is whether I truly want to study criminal psychology," Vicky says, deliberately omitting her deeper, more personal doubts.

"Those are quite conventional at this stage of life. Why the interest in antique books?" the librarian probes further.

"I grew up surrounded by them in Wales," Erasmus explains simply.

"Ah, you're the boy from Hay-On-Wye, and you're the girl from Waterloo, Illinois," the librarian exclaims, her eyes lighting up.

"Yes, that's us," Erasmus confirms proudly, recognizing her connection to the New England antiquarian network.

"I didn't realize you were students at Harvard. I'm Felicia Poindexter," replies solicitiously the never married lifelong librarian.

"Erasmus Cromwell-Smith and Victoria Emerson-Lloyd. Nice to meet you," Victoria says warmly.

"Well, I know exactly what to get you. It's timeless and unforgettable," Mrs. Poindexter declares. "It will provide the wisdom you're seeking."

She disappears for only a moment, returning with a scroll in quick, deliberate steps.

"Perhaps it's presumptuous, but would you allow me to read it to you?" she asks, her voice filled with anticipation.

The young couple exchanges a glance, shrugging in unison, before Erasmus responds gallantly, "It would be an honor."

Mrs. Poindexter adjusts her glasses and begins to read in earnest...

"Doubt"

A doubt without trust, method, or purpose
sets us up for recurring anxiety and pain—
unfortunately, in vain,
as all of it will go to waste
when inexorably we fail.

In these types of vacillations,
when we doubt, we are hiding something.
Doubts become false shields and excuses
for the true roots and genesis of our behavior:
weakness of character,
lack of knowledge, shortcomings in ability or talent,
lack of preparation or planning,
among others.

These indecisiveness tendencies
seek to justify mediocrity and incompetence
through blame or suspicions of others,
when, in all likelihood, all that is wrong
lies solely within ourselves.

Such hesitations are like a deadly poison,

inevitably leading to inaction and paralyzing fear;

we become increasingly overwhelmed by

uncertainty, skepticism, apprehension,

and a nagging lack of confidence

that inexorably leads to errors in judgment.

This is why why these types of doubts

are the telltale signs of failure.

Doubt knocks at every door,

A guest we all must meet.

It shapes our path,

sharpens our mind,

A guide, both bitter and sweet.

The antidotes to doubt are trust, method, and purpose.

When we doubt and apply trust,

we dispel uncertaitnty

by granting the benefit of the doubt

to the person or situation.

We apply method when we are objectively uncertain;

the observation of facts can overrule

our inclination not to believe.

When we encounter uncertainty about beliefs or opinions,

we overcome it

by curing our incomplete knowledge or lack of evidence.

We apply purpose when we are on emotional overload,
under siege by avalanches of indecision.
We dissolve and break through them
If we discard the waste
and keep our endgame in sight.
And if we realize we don't have such,
then we eagerly develop one,
for purpose is the ultimate doubt breaker.

In the final analysis, a healthy dose of doubt
is essential to a wholesome life.
But our challenge is to embrace doubt,
always with trust, method, and purpose.

*

"Victoria and Erasmus, when you apply trust and good faith to doubt, you neutralize it. When you apply method through discipline and by verifying facts, you overwhelm it. When you confront doubt with purpose and determination, you crush it," declares a spirited Felicia Poindexter.

This serendipitous encounter marks the genesis of a lifelong bond between Erasmus and Mrs. Poindexter. In the years to come, all the way to her retirement, she will dedicate countless hours imparting her invaluable wisdom and guidance to him.

— ❖ —

Royal Cambridge Scholastic Institute, 2019
(University's Auditorium)

Returning to the present, Professor Cromwell-Smith smiles at the fond memory of the erudite librarian, his gaze sweeping over the eager faces before him. "That day at the Athenaeum taught me that doubt is not just a challenge—it's an invitation to grow," he remarks, seamlessly linking past wisdom to the lesson at hand, "Before we dive into your thoughts," the pedagogue continues, pacing thoughtfully, "remember this: doubt is not your enemy unless you let it linger. Confront it with trust, examine it with method, and dissolve it with purpose."

"Professor, why are doubts so pervasively nagging?" asks Barbra, a lierature major.

"Barbra, it is far too easy to sit idle, commiserating and doubting everything and everyone, while doing nothing. Doubts, without their three antidotes, are merely fake walls made of flimsy excuses. So always remember: when in doubt, apply trust, method, or purpose," he responds with precision.

"Professor, how can we effectively confront our relationship doubts without creating conflict?" asks Robert, a creative writing major.

"That's an essential question, Bobbie. The poem underscores that 'trust is one of the foundations that can weather the storms of doubt.' Open and honest communication is key. Extending a genuine benefit of the doubt to a person or situation can dissolve uncertainty instantly," replies the professor, his tone both firm and encouraging.

"What about purpose as the ultimate doubt breaker?" asks Lila, a sociology major.

"Lila, when you set a direction for your actions, choices, and existence—aligning them with something meaningful—this sense of purpose dispels any doubts you might face," the thoughtful pedagogue explains.

"See you all next week," he concludes, leaving the students to reflect. The august professor may have just gifted them a timeless formula for overcoming doubts and indecision.

As the class disperses, Erasmus lingers at the podium, observing the students' quiet introspection. A faint smile crosses his face, a testament to the power of shared wisdom.

Stepping outside the professor approaches his old, rusty bike, the inspired professor savors the magnificent spring day. Fittingly, he is in for a delightful surprise. At first, he barely recognizes his bike. A basket now adorns the front wheel cover, clipped to the handlebars. It is brimming with pastries, cheeses, fruits, and a red-and-white checkered mantle draped over the top. Curious, he lifts the mantle and finds a card nestled among the treats. Opening it, his heart swells with joy and infatuation as he reads the handwritten note:

"It is true that trust, method, and purpose do away with doubt. But what trumps it—banishing it for good—is true love."

The sound of a bicycle bell from outside draws his attention, instinctively, he raises his head, and his heart lifts as he glimpses, there she is, perched on her bike, holding her own picnic basket and five balloons swaying in the breeze.

"What are you waiting for?" Victoria teases before pedaling away with a mischievous laugh.

Erasmus quickly mounts his bike, chasing after her. That's when he notices the messages written on each balloon.

On the second largest balloon, he reads, "When in doubt, apply..." followed by "Trust," "Method," or "Purpose" on the smaller ones. Finally, his gaze falls on the largest balloon, a heart-shaped marvel. His eyes widen with surprise and joy as he reads the bold letters:

"And True Love Trumps Them All."

Chapter 15

Duality

Charles River, Boston, 2019

The nascent light of a new day filters through the Charles River's serene landscape, illuminating its natural beauty. Sun rays, painted with soft reddish and pale-yellow hues, linger as they gradually unveil the silent surroundings. The scattered fog patches dissolve lazily into the sky, making way for a crisp yet magnificent spring morning. Only the synchronized splashes of oars and the heavy breathing of two rowers break the tranquil silence as they maintain a steady, rhythmic pace across the quiet waters.

Erasmus and Victoria have been rowing for half an hour when they finally reach their familiar destination. At a secluded corner along the riverbank, they secure their boat. Following a well-practiced routine, they each retrieve their tightly bundled matching bodysuit warmers from their small backpacks and slip them on with ease.

Hand in hand, the enamored pair stroll a short distance to one of their favorite morning spots in town—a tiny French boulangerie with outdoor seating nestled at the river's edge. Its charming ambiance provides the perfect setting to savor Gallic treats in the crisp morning air.

"Dear, I would like to visit your hometown someday," Victoria says softly as they wait for their customary basket of French bread, pastries, and café au lait.

"My lady, nothing would give me greater pleasure," Erasmus replies, his thoughts already racing. Suddenly, his eyes brighten with inspiration, and a tender smile spreads across his face. "Tell you what, we'll go there this summer. We can travel by train across the old continent. I've always dreamed of exploring Europe with you." His gaze is intense yet affectionate as he lightly caresses her hand with his fingertips.

"I've only been to Europe a few times, mostly for conferences, so you'll have to show me everything—and take me everywhere—with lots of patience," she says, her voice brimming with excitement.
"It'll be my honor, my lady," he responds warmly, eager to fulfill her traveling dreams.

A distant rumble of thunder rolls through the air, hinting at a sudden shift in the idyllic weather. Erasmus instantly notices the change in Victoria's expression as clouded emotions flicker across her face. Through her eyes, he witnesses a rapid spectrum of feelings: at first, a nervous anger flashes; then confusion takes hold as her gaze darts about restlessly. But just as quickly, her focus returns to Erasmus. Caught in the act, her blue irises widen in surprise before softening with an unmistakable sparkle. Relief washes over her, and a radiant smile emerges. Erasmus gently tightens his grip on her hand, offering silent reassurance as he always does.

"There was a time when I couldn't control my fear of thunder," she admits, her voice thoughtful.

"With good reason, my lady. If lightning struck so close to you as a child, it's no wonder you developed this phobia," he says, playfully indulging her train of thought.

Victoria studies him, debating her response. Then, suddenly, she erupts into laughter.

"You are so utterly inept at faking anything, my adorable Brit," she exclaims, her voice full of amusement.

"My lady, why would I disrupt your cherished tale of childhood woe?" he teases, feigning innocence.

"Because you know I don't really mean to talk about it," she counters, her tone lighthearted.

"You mean that your struggle with bad weather stems from a telltale need for perfection. There was always something slightly wrong or incomplete in even the most extraordinary moments, wasn't there?" he observes bluntly now that she has opened the door.

"Yes, it was like that. If a day wasn't perfect, it felt ruined, and I missed out on so many moments I could have enjoyed," she reflects aloud, her words flowing like an impromptu monologue.

"But look at you now, my lady. You've come so far. Your instincts remain the same, but you've learned to rationalize them and move beyond their grip. It's remarkable," Erasmus says, his voice filled with pride.

"Having you by my side makes it so much easier, dear," she says, her gratitude evident.

"Do you remember how we found the solution to such an affliction?" Victoria asks suddenly.

"How could I forget? Mrs. Poindexter—good old Mrs. Poindexter—graced us with a timeless treasure about the dangers of seeing the world through extremes," he replies, his memory vivid.

"That was a memorable day at the Harvard library. Her lesson on duality was unforgettable," she agrees, her eyes widening at the recollection.

As often happens with deeply connected couples, the realization hits them simultaneously. They look at each other, sharing a knowing smile.

"Fittingly, I'll make duality the subject of today's class," Erasmus declares with a thoughtful expression as they finish their breakfast.

As they leave the cozy boulangerie, the morning air carries a renewed sense of purpose. The distant hum of the city intertwined with the rhythmic sound of their bikes' wheels spinning. Victoria's occasional laughter blends with Erasmus's playful remarks, their connection evident in every shared glance.

An hour later, as Victoria drives him to class, the pair reflects on the diminutive yet formidable librarian who had patiently mentored them on countless occasions throughout their youth. By the time they reach the campus driveway, the energy between them feels palpable, an invisible force propelling them forward.

As they approach the university buildings, Vicky pulls he car to a gentle stop near the auditorium steps. She leans across the console, her eyes sparkling with mischief, then proceeds to work her usual magic on him.

"Remember, dear, you're the magician today, in possession of a precious gift for your students. Go and be your best so they can be dotted with all its priceless dimensions. Let your students leave feeling spellbound," she whispers, her voice laced with encouragement with a warm and tender kiss. Her words fire him up, lifting his spirits into an inspired state. Erasmus steps out, grinning as he wavs back at her. With poetic strides and careless whistling, he marches to class as if walking on clouds. The brisk walk to the auditorium reinvigorates him, the morning's conversation lingering in his mind like a melody he cannot shake.

Royal Cambridge Scholastic Institute, 2019
(University's Auditorium)

"How's everyone today?" asks a spirited professor, his energy infectious.

"Insanely awesome, professor!" replies an enthusiastic student body, their excitement filling the room.

"Class, sometimes in life, we view people, the world, and life as choices between opposites. We trap ourselves in a mindset that sees only two options and obsesses over taking one or the other. In doing so, we limit our ability to consider alternative perspectives and lock ourselves into a narrow way of thinking," he begins, his voice charged with passion.

"Duality is a concept that haunted both Victoria and me throughout our childhood and teen years. We often felt torn, forced to choose between extremes, until an endearing librarian mentor provided us with a timeless life lesson—one that, forty years later, continues to guide us," the professor explains, his gaze sweeping across the captivated audience.

"Let me take you back in time," he continues, his tone shifting to one of storytelling. "The story begins like this…"

— ✦ —

Erasmus and Victoria's Studio, Boston, 1977

Young Erasmus heads out for an early morning run while Victoria sleeps a bit longer. When she finally wakes, her gaze falls on a glass of fresh orange juice on the bedside table. Next, her eyes land on a bouquet of sparkling red roses in full bloom, accompanied by a card. Her heart skips a beat as she reads the note:

"May life continue to give us the magic of true love forever. My beloved lady, you are cordially invited to an afternoon in the park with me. It'll be a picnic for two. I'll fetch you at exactly noon at the library."

She chuckles, her heart swelling with delight at her Brit wizard's romantic gesture. The day seems destined to be perfect. But her initial joy quickly unravels as her obsession with perfection takes hold, casting a shadow over her mood.

The morning does not go well for Victoria Emerson-Lloyd. The moment she steps outside, a light rain and lingering fog greet her, accompanied by distant thunder. Her spirits sink further.

"Why does bad weather have to ruin the picnic Erasmus prepared for us?" she frets, her frustration mounting.

Harvard's Widener Library, 1977

Arriving at the majestic library just before noon, Victoria sits with her former roommate, Gina, stewing over the spoiled morning. Distracted and annoyed, she fails to greet their mentor, the ever-watchful Mrs. Poindexter.

"What is it with young Victoria? Each time she's upset, her good manners vanish," observes the sharp librarian as she catches snippets of Vicky's loud complaints.

Oblivious to her surroundings, Victoria vents to Gina, detailing her morning misfortunes. Gina, growing restless, attempts to steer the conversation elsewhere. Sensing her friend's ambivalence about Erasmus, Gina decides to confront her.

"Victoria, why would you try to force Erasmus to move to your hometown if he wants to marry you? Why sabotage true love?" Gina asks incredulously.

"Because that's the only way it'll work out between us," Victoria retorts stubbornly.

"You've yet to give me a valid reason for forcing him," Gina counters.

Vicky falls silent, frustration bubbling under the surface. Gina, however, presses on.

"Let's face it—you have no real reason. It's not even convenient for you to go back home. Your future is here," Gina declares.

"But my family is all there," Vicky argues, her tone lacking conviction.

"You moved here to escape them, Vicky. Who are you fooling? Yourself?" Gina snaps back.

Victoria's eyes dart around the library, a mixture of confusion and guilt clouding her expression.

"Guilt-driven love doesn't work," Gina continues, her tone unwavering. "To expect this particular Brit to bend to your wishes through guilt is a recipe for disaster. And transactional love? 'If you come, we marry; if you don't, we won't'? That won't work with him either. You'll ruin what you have."

Vicky's thoughts spiral as Gina's words sink in. 'Maybe she's right; he'll never agree,' she thinks, a pang of realization hitting her.

As the clock strikes noon, Erasmus appears, walking briskly toward the pair.

"Ladies, it's a pleasure to see you both," he says warmly, bowing slightly as if from another era. He's blissfully unaware of the tension he's just walked into.

Noticing their forced smiles, Erasmus's brow furrows.

"What's going on here?" he asks, puzzled.

"I'll tell you, young man, better than your spoiled girl here ever could," interjects Mrs. Poindexter, her stern demeanor unmistakable as she approaches.

The trio turns toward her, startled.

"Mrs. Poindexter, how are you?" Erasmus greets her with a wide smile, extending his hand.

"Not so well, young man, as I've just listened to one of the most banal and superficial conversations I've heard in years," she retorts, her sharp gaze landing squarely on Victoria.

"That was private!" Gina protests, attempting to defend her friend.

"No, it wasn't. You broke the library's rules by speaking so loudly that everyone here overheard you—not just me," Mrs. Poindexter replies curtly.

Victoria and Gina sit silently, their faces red with embarrassment. Erasmus winks at Mrs. Poindexter, signaling his approval for her to continue.

"This pattern must repeat itself often. With your permission, I'd like to read you something—a perfect antidote to what's afflicting our immature young lady today," the librarian proposes, her tone softening slightly.

"It would be an honor, Mrs. Poindexter," Erasmus says gallantly. The girls nod sheepishly in agreement.

With determined steps, the diminutive librarian disappears into the stacks. They watch as she climbs a small ladder, her movements precise, retrieving a large yet thin book. Moments later, she returns, her eyes alight with purpose.

"Perhaps it's presumptuous of me, but may I read this to you myself?" she asks, her gaze resting on Erasmus and Victoria.

"It would be an honor," Erasmus repeats, his tone respectful.
With that, Mrs. Poindexter sits down before them, opens the book, and begins to read...

"Duality"

Here is the problem with duality.

At first sight, it seems to be something it is not—

a state of deliberate indecisiveness

An ignorant vacillation between choices,

Or even a willful duplicity.

Duality, however, is quite contrary

to what it appears to be,

at least as far as this verse goes.

We stumble into duality in life when

either we crave not one

but the totality of choices ahead of us,

or when we view everything and everyone

as a two-sided proposition of "either/or."

In truth, there is an "and."

It whispers in the choices we lust after,

The polar opposites we cling to,

While life's truth lies beyond,

Just out of reach eluding our grasp.

Not enough has been said about the first kind of duality—

the capricious art of wanting it both ways in life,

of wanting it all, simultaneously and at any cost,

no matter what, where, who, when, why, or how.

This often leaves no room for anything or anyone else.

Such voraciousness, in most cases, becomes a problem —

not only because we seldom enjoy either choice,

but also because malignant, greedy duality

is nothing but a pernicious existential waste of existence—

a futile exercise, an empty pursuit

in instant and constant gratification.

In that relentless chase,

the joy of the present is utterly forsaken.

Which is not only banal and empty,

but above all, devoid of any meaning and purpose.

Hence, we are not "living" nor "alive"

when we practice it or pursue it.

On the other hand, when duality is polarizing,

we see the universe, the world, life, and its people

as a battleground of opposing extremes—

antagonizing sides and irreconcilable differences all of the time.

Everything around us becomes

black or white,

good or evil,

exhilarating or angsty,

fulfilling or empty,

happy or depressive,

crowded or lonely,

entertaining or boring,

truthful or false,

faithful or treasonous,

real or fake.

Everyone we interact with becomes either

superior or lesser,

affluent or deprived,

healthy or unwell,

successful or a failure,

entitled or a parasite,

solvent or a social ballast,

with us or against us,

able or handicapped,

free or condemned,

innocent or scarlet letter bearers,

socially adequate or psychopaths.

Our emotional and rational lives are either

controlled or chaotic,

effusive or filled with resentment,

exuberant or frustrated,

on a high or a low,

abstinent or viced,

carnivorous or vegan,

nice or nasty,

generous or greedy and selfish.

But life's true light and lasting beauty

lie not on <u>opposite sides</u> but right down the middle,

the space in-between extremes where virtues converge
and harmony blooms.

Located in the area of confluence
where we ponder and tinker with all of our existential levers.
Instead of a world of pairs or duos,
of either "a" or "b" choices,
we discover a third alternative—
made entirely from both ends.

This is where and how life finds balance,
and why it is in the middle
where most, if not all, our existential virtues can be found—
namely temperance, uniqueness, out-of-the-norm prudence,
sound judgment, patience, endurance, tolerance,
forgiveness, creativity, artistry, a good-heart,
open-mindedness, clarity, cautiousness,
meditative states,
repentance, generosity, gratitude, moderation,
hope, inspiration, frugality, faith, change,
evolution, our conscience, our spirit, and our soul.

Duality by nature is incomplete and unfulfilling,
depriving us of all available choices,
pushing us into extremes,
locking us in absolute, rigid positions.
Duality can be dangerous,
casting opposites or extreme sides against each other,

creating potential or real conflicts and clashes

between the parties, based on the simple and diminutive desire

for one side to prevail over the other at any cost.

Duality blinds our hearts, spirits, and souls,

robbing us of the ability to experience life

and enjoy the universe, the world, nature, and others—

simply because we miss the third choice,

that of contemplating life halfway through extremes,

right down the middle.

*

As Mrs. Poindexter finishes the reading, Erasmus, Victoria, and Gina sit in stunned silence, their luminous eyes reflecting the profound impact of her words. It is as though a gigantic dark veil has been lifted from their minds.

"Thank you, Mrs. Poindexter," Victoria babbles sheepishly, instinctively taking the lead while the other two remain silent, their thoughts swirling.

Mrs. Poindexter regards Victoria with a sharp but kind gaze.

"Victoria, you wake up to a wonderful gesture from your infatuated Brit—beautiful flowers, a heartfelt card, freshly squeezed juice, and an invitation for a romantic picnic crafted just for the two of you. Do you know how many people wish they had someone to do even half of that for them? And yet, you manage to get yourself obfuscated over the weather. What's wrong with you? Life is too short, my dear. Take all the good and block out the bad stuff. Rarely, if ever, is life

perfect—whether convenient or not," she admonishes with a knowing tone.

Victoria nods fervently, her cheeks flushed with a mix of embarrassment and gratitude. "This is a lesson I will never forget, Mrs. Poindexter.

For the first time, I see it all so clearly. I promise you, from now on, I will do my utmost to get a grip on myself, to stay out of my own way, so I can enjoy the best life has to offer—no matter how flawed or incomplete it may be," she declares earnestly.

Mrs. Poindexter offers a small, satisfied smile before hurrying back to her duties, her stride purposeful, her expression one of certitude. It is clear to her that all three youngsters have absorbed the essence of her message.

Moments later, Victoria, Gina, and Erasmus step out of the library, their arms linked as if fortified by a newfound strength. The powerful lesson they've just received reverberates within them, gifting each a new lens through which to view life—a lens that makes space for joy, imperfections, and the beauty of the present moment.

— ✦ —

Royal Cambridge Scholastic Institute, 2019
(University's Auditorium)

"As the vivid memories of Harvard begin to fade, The Professor's gaze shifts to the present-day faces before him. The auditorium's familiar warmth and the expectant expressions of his students anchor him back to reality. 'And so, forty years later, her wisdom remains just as profound,' he says, his tone reflective yet vibrant."

"Class, as you reflect on the subject of duality and its perils, focus on the only place where virtue can be found in life—the middle ground, not the extremes," Professor Cromwell-Smith states in conclusion.

Erasmus pauses, letting the weight of the lesson settle in the room.

"Before we delve into your thoughts and questions, I'd like you to take a moment. Reflect on the instances where you've felt trapped between opposites. Consider how finding that middle ground could have shifted the narrative. Sometimes, the answers we seek don't lie at the ends of the spectrum but in the untamed space between."

"Professor, in our previous class, we covered the subject of doubt. How are duality and doubt related?" asks Elena, a political science major.

"That's an excellent question, Elena. They are actually closely linked. Doubt surges out of our inability to decide between extremes or absolutes and our incapacity to see the middle ground, thus escaping duality," clarifies the professor as the entire student body nods in realization.

"How can we cultivate a mindset that embraces duality rather than fearing it?" asks Mathew, a a philosophy major.

"That's an important inquiry, Mathew. The poem encourages us to 'view duality as a source of strength.' Start by reframing your perspective. Instead of seeing duality as a conflict, recognize it as an opportunity for growth and learning. Embrace your complexities and allow them to inform your decisions," the professor replies thoughtfully.

"Professor Cromwell, doesn't society have to evolve first before many of us as individuals can seek and embrace the middle ground?" asks William an engineer major.

"Wonderful question, Bill. Our civilization certainly has to reach a higher level in our social behavior and belief system to evolve out of the duality-driven environment we are currently in. This type of evolution is not only needed but is our next level up; it is being pointed out to us even from the world of science. For example, the next frontier in information technology is quantum computing. Currently—and not coincidentally, as in real life—the computer world is based on the binary system of 1s and 0s. Quantum computing, however, is based on a third state—a kind of trinary system (qubits)—that involves both choices, 1 and 0, at the same time, exponentially multiplying the processing power of a computer," he explains with animated precision.

Professor Cromwell-Smith pauses, scanning the room. His gaze lingers as if searching for confirmation that his message has landed. Without exception, the students sit in silence, their expressions contemplative, each seemingly absorbed in their own reflections. Through the prism of duality, they begin to see themselves, hopefully realizing the perils and narrowness of living under its shackles.

As the students file out, Erasmus lingers at the podium, watching their animated conversations. He notices a few students pausing near the door, their brows furrowed in thought, perhaps reflecting on their own encounters with duality. Smiling to himself, he gathers his notes and steps into the hallway, the echoes of their youthful curiosity still buzzing in the air. Outside, Victoria is waiting, her bike leaning casually against a lamppost. She waves, her presence as grounding as it is exhilarating. Together, they pedal into the golden afternoon, their shared rhythm a testament to life's perfect balance

Chapter 16

Geniality

Royal Cambridge Scholastic Institute, 2019
(Erasmus and Victoria's Campus Home)

In the early morning hours, both Victoria and Erasmus are fully awake. Her voice, at first, comes across as a loving whisper. Yet her solemn words quickly pierce their joyful coziness.

"Here we are, forty years later, and in many ways, nothing has changed in us as a couple. We love each other as we did then. But as individuals, we have changed. My doubts have now become guilt, and yours have morphed into fear. We've also had quite different life experiences," says a pensive Victoria as they lay in bed at dawn. In her mind, she also wrestles with lingering feelings of inadequacy, aware that her past choices loom large over their present.

"As I ponder love's intricate dance, each step is a memory, a fleeting chance. Through joy and sorrow, we find our way, like dawn's embrace at the break of day," apropos she adds, quoting Erasmus' poetry.

Looking into Victoria's eyes, Erasmus recognizes the spark that first drew him to her. Yet, the years had sculpted them both, carving paths that led to this moment—a testament to their resilience and growth.

Erasmus pauses, the dawn light casting a warm glow around them. How many mornings had they shared like this, yet each felt uniquely significant? As the memories dance in his mind, he prepares to shift their conversation to the day's looming challenges.

As today is the last class of the academic year, Erasmus's mind is elsewhere.

"Dear, where in the universe are you?" she asks.

Erasmus gazes at her with deep eyes and a wide smile. "My lady, love isn't perfect. There are always things missing, not working, or unattainable, but we focus on and enjoy what we do have," said Erasmus, turning philosophical.

'That's it! He just stopped me right in my tracks, and again, he wasn't even paying attention,' she reasons, feeling caught at the beginning of an act.

But this morning, for some reason, she just wants to poke holes in their idyllic perfection. The morning light filters softly through the curtains, casting a gentle glow on their intertwined forms, amplifying the moment's intimacy.

"How is it that you lived a monastic life for forty years?" she suddenly asks skeptically.

"This isolation was a conscious choice, a way to escape the complexities of relationships that often felt overwhelming," he replies. Then, with sudden realization, he asks uneasily, "Where are you going with this?"

"I just want to know," she replies capriciously.

"Why?" he asks defensively.

"Perhaps because it is so hard to comprehend," she says, sounding hollow but trying to justify herself.

"That's it: a lack of understanding?" he asks, unconvinced.

"A bit of jealousy as well," she finally acknowledges.

"Now, we are talking," he says, lauding the truth.

"That's what you wanted, right? To hear that I am jealous," she says, acting hurt.

"Not really," he replies dismissively.

"Of course not. Big Erasmus, sitting high up on Mount Olympus, does not believe or feel it. How do you define jealousy? Yes, I remember now—those are just games people play," she says, chastising him.

"Okay, Victoria, I realize that this big scene has a purpose. What do you want to know?" he asks, trying to nail down the subject.

"No girls for forty years?" she asks, her expression that of a teenager playing with fire.

"I never claimed to be monogamous. No true love for four decades is what I said," he clarifies.

"Oh, so there were girls," she shoots back in surprise, now with her hand scalded by the fire.

"A few," he replies cryptically.

"How many?" she presses, a knot forming in her throat.

"I did not keep count," he answers, trying to avoid the subject.

"What, two, three, ten, twenty?" she insists.

"Victoria, look at yourself! What are you doing? This is a futile and masochistic exercise, chasing water under the bridge," he states, trying to dodge the subject.

"Never close to something serious?" she persists relentlessly.

"Once," he replies.

"Who?" she asks, still hunting for the truth.

"My first book editor," he answers matter-of-factly.

"What happened?" she asks, needing to know more.

"I realized it was only success-driven love," he explains.

"Translate, please," she pleads in ignorance.

"This particular editor paid no attention to me when I was starting as a writer, but afterward, she was infatuated with my success more than with me. Without it, she wouldn't have been there, and I concluded there was no future with her," he reveals.

"Isn't that normal behavior?" she asks. Then, she immediately realizes she has just made a crucial mistake with him.

"Not for me, Victoria," he replies without an iota of amusement in his voice.

Silence finally descends upon them as if the eruption has run its course. But she knows better. 'He is not done,' she reasons accurately. "My lady, you just blurted out the other reason why you left— success—or lack thereof... fears..." he says in realization.

Victoria's eyes cloud up instantly, and she feels unmistakably guilty.

"This is simply your way of getting it out in the open," he says, holding her hands with a soft grip. Kissing them alternately, he finishes, "She was eight years my junior and very attractive. After dating her for over three years, I still had reservations about her. Then, one good night, she asked if I would ever pop the question."

"Did you?"

"I remember that I replied with a question," Erasmus affirms.

Victoria listens on pins and needles.

"Would you have been interested in me if you didn't know about my success?" he recalls.

"She was bluntly honest. 'No,' she said, and that was the end of it."

"Ironically, on the issue of parity between a couple, to me, the only way the matter of success is overcome by love is when success isn't known, hasn't yet arrived, or starts right at the onset of the relationship," he continues.

"So, the fact that when we got back together, I didn't know you had become so successful as a writer was huge for you," she affirms, intrigued.

"You have no idea how huge, Victoria," he sternly confirms.

She feels relieved but foolish at the same time. 'I don't even remember how Erasmus' fabric is cut and tailored either,' she reasons, scolding herself while quickly realizing the need to reacquaint herself with it. The sooner, the better.

"Dear, you know about the adjustments I made when we reunited. But what did you do yourself?" Vicky finally turns the tables.

Erasmus stares at her with the kind of calmness she has always loved about him—a calmness that makes her feel safe and protected.

"My lady, what has driven our love isn't guilt, wealth, or lack thereof. What you have done since we were reunited has been driven not so much by words but by facts and feelings," he says with profound clarity.

"Facts?" she asks, her brow furrowing in curiosity.

"What I mean by facts are actions expressed through boundless small gestures and teeny-tiny details we've shared from the beginning," he replies, his eyes brimming with warmth.

"My fearless, unmaterialistic Brit," she declares, pulling him into a proud embrace.

"Dear, what's the subject of your class going to be today?" she quizzes, sensing the significance of his mood.

"Geniality," he replies, his tone rattled but composed.

The single word lands like a heavyweight between them. Her face tightens with pain, but her eyes reflect understanding.

"Is this your last class of the year?" she asks rhetorically.

"Yes," he replies with quiet determination.

"I see," she says absently, her mind elsewhere.

"No worries, my lady. I am ready for it," he reassures her, his tone firm.

"In that case, go and kill that tiger, dear. I am sure you'll do a masterful job," she says, mustering as much strength as her anguished self allows.

A bit later, as Professor Cromwell-Smith leaves on his old, rusty bike, Victoria watches him pedal away through the window. Silent tears well in her eyes, and she lets them fall. She knows that in a short while, he'll be standing in front of his class, recounting the day she vanished from his life. At least it gives her comfort that earlier in the week, she was able to "fill in" the blanks for him about what she had done on that runaway day.

As Professor Cromwell-Smith pedals on, his bike sways slightly, a mirror to the ebb and flow of his thoughts. Today, his path points to the future, but his wake is filled with nostalgia.

'She is right. We are both scarred survivors of a long and winding road. But you know what? We made it, and here we are with plenty of life ahead of us,' he reasons, a flicker of hope lighting his contemplative eyes.

Royal Cambridge Scholastic Institute, 2019
(University's Auditorium)

"How's everyone today?" the spirited professor asks.

"Awesome!" is the collective response.

"Hmm," he blurts, not entirely satisfied, his right hand resting on his chin. The professor tries one more time.

"Okay, let's do that again," he urges them.

"Insanely awesome!" the student body responds in unison.

"Right on," he says, now satisfied.

With the auditorium's energy still rising, he commences their academic year's last journey.

"Today, we conclude our course with the subject of genius and geniality. In this last class, I'll take you to a remarkable day where two contrasting sides of life presented themselves—one like a comet that came and left in an instant and the other as a discovery of one of those treasures you hold onto for the rest of your life."

"It begins like this…

— ✦ —

Harvard, 1977
(Erasmus and Victoria's Studio)

Victoria has been staring at the letter she's not supposed to read for a long time...

In part, the letter states:

"Mrs. V., before I leave you, there is something else. Are you ready? ... I want to propose. Yes! I do, I want with all my heart for Victoria to be my wife and companion forever."

Vicky's reaction is utter fear. She wants to run and bolt out of the situation. For hours, Victoria sits paralyzed, losing touch with time. When she finally sees the hour, all hell breaks loose.

She has to hurry. Erasmus will be waiting for her at the train station in one hour for their trip to Cape Cod. But she's having a panic attack. 'Isn't this what you wanted since the day you met him?' she asks herself, unable to answer.

'A professor, that's all he'll ever be,' she quibbles against her crying heart with the same obsessive and flimsy excuse. 'He's way too smart for me as well,' she reasons, the growing hole in her heart knowing better than she does where she's heading—literally going off a cliff.

The phone rings, snapping her out of her dark cloud momentarily.

"Hi, Mom," she says with a trembling greeting while picking up the wall-mounted handset.

"Sweet daughter of mine, have you made up your mind?" her Mom asks, delicately applying pressure.

At that precise moment, Victoria finally succumbs to the self-inflicted pressure and excuses. She loses it! She alters the course of her life and sets herself on a path of self-destruction.

"Yes," Victoria replies sheepishly.

"And?" her mom quizzes in suspense.

"I just said it, yes," she fatefully says, not really knowing what she is doing.

"How wonderful! You have no idea how happy this makes all of us.

I'll tell everyone right away. When are you coming?" her Mom asks joyfully, in total relief.

"Today."

Victoria replies, seemingly sealing her fate.

"But don't you have classes?" her Mom asks, not meaning it.

"I'm quitting, Mom. I want to get it done and start a family," replies another Victoria—the rational one, surfacing from entombment and taking over the enamored side of her. Her mother doesn't argue; this is what she has been advocating all along. Victoria's Mom is ecstatic, as all she's ever known and was raised to be is a housewife, precisely what she wants for her daughter.

"I'm sure you know what you're doing, Victoria. We'll welcome you back with open arms, dear. I can't wait to see you. I'll go now and tell everyone. Bye," her mother says, hurrying to end the call and announce the "good news" to everyone.

Boston Main Train Station, 1977

Victoria walks through Boston's train station feeling miserable with all her things packed in two suitcases.

'You are betraying his and your own heart,' she reasons as a torrent of tears falls. When Victoria enters the main hall, she still has a choice. She can walk toward him and board the train to the Cape, or

she can walk to the Chicago-bound train and lose the love of her life—seemingly forever.

'Where is she?' thinks a nervous Erasmus, with less than ten minutes until departure. He wants to look for her in the main hall but is afraid he'll miss her at the agreed spot.

She stops and prays for divine guidance. 'If he finds me here, I won't be able to go home,' she cautions, as part of her wants to be spotted.

Five minutes are left until the train to the Cape departs. What to do? He can't miss the conference. He decides to check the main hall.

Victoria walks reluctantly and slowly toward the Chicago-bound train, and as she leaves the main hall, her heart jumps at the sight of him in the distance. She stops. Dejection. It's not him. She continues to walk, now with her head down, inexorably moving toward her prescribed and heartless future.

'Is that her?' he thinks for a moment. But the lady with two suitcases and her head down is heading in the opposite direction and is quickly swallowed up by the crowd.

'She is not here!' Erasmus panics as he scans the busy hall. Feeling dejected, he heads back and boards his train. Surely something came up. She'll be on a later train. I just hope nothing happened and she's safe, he reasons, trying to justify her absence.

The date is December 15, 1977, twenty-two months after they first met. It's a day neither of them will ever forget.

The Cape Cod Unexpected Bend in the Road

They walk into the room, and Erasmus is caught by surprise as the five occupants sitting at the round table all stand up with warm and welcoming smiles. There they are: Mrs. Peabody, Mrs. Poindexter, Mr. Faith, Mr. Lafayette, Mr. Ringwald, and Mr. Carnegie, who makes six. Erasmus immediately recognizes that there are eight chairs at the table.

"She couldn't make it to the station on time; you'll meet her tomorrow," he preempts them.

Erasmus shakes hands with each of his mentors, kissing the two ladies on both cheeks, the European way. Then he takes a seat where indicated.

"Young Erasmus, we've all discussed in advance what to do on this rare occasion of all of us having the opportunity to meet and sit with you. It is a real pity that Victoria is not here. But I'm sure you'll convey to her what we review here with you today," Mr. Carnegie solemnly states.

Erasmus nods unconvincingly at the suggestion.

"Young man, we want to talk to you about one subject that we all agree holds the key to your future," says Mrs. Peabody.

"Let us first share several anecdotal lessons with you, as they will lead us into the subject matter," says Mr. Lafayette.

"I'll start first if you all allow me," Mr. Lafayette announces—everyone in the room consents.

"Erasmus, the first anecdote is about illusions in life," Mr. Lafayette begins.

— ✦ —

The Case of the Magnificent Illusionist
(Mr. Lafayette)

"In my last year of high school," Mr. Lafayette begins, leaning forward with a spark of nostalgia, *"I was part of a soccer team that won the state championship for the third consecutive year. Just before graduation, my parents asked how I wanted to vacation before starting college. I expressed my desire to travel to Europe to watch my favorite professional soccer teams. So, as a graduation present, they sent me across the Atlantic with three of my closest teammates."* Erasmus envisions the excitement of those summer days, the thrill of the crowd echoing in his ears as Mr. Lafayette continues, painting vivid images of his European soccer adventures.

"During that summer, we traveled by train, cheering with the hooligans as Chelsea faced Manchester at Wembley. The atmosphere was electric as we chanted with thousands of passionate fans. We then watched Bayern take on Borussia in Munich, Saint Germain play Marseille in Paris, and Real Madrid go head-to-head with Barca in Barcelona. On our last weekend, we arrived in Italy to watch A.C. Milan play at home against Rome. We decided to spend Friday night in nearby Florence and then spend Saturday, the day before the match, wandering around the magnificent city."

He pauses, allowing Erasmus to visualize the artistry of Florence, the aroma of fresh Italian bread wafting through the streets.

"It all started the next day when we were admiring Michelangelo's David at the Galleria," Mr. Lafayette continues, gesturing as if to frame the statue. *"A young kid ran by, handing out*

flyers. He gave me one, and it immediately caught my attention. It was written in both Italian and English."

— ✦ —

"Come and experience the greatest illusionist on earth.
Don't miss it!
Teatro di la Buona Fortuna, 8:00 p.m."

— ✦ —

The excitement in Mr. Lafayette's voice is contagious, and Erasmus leans in closer.

"After reading it, I persuaded the others to join me for the show. At the theatre, we were in for a treat. The illusionist's specialty was making things disappear. One moment, he was center stage, and in a split second, he vanished, only to reappear in the back row. He did the same with his assistant, but only after cutting her in half. The audience gasped, a collective intake of breath, as the assistant reappeared unharmed. Then, he did it with members of the audience, who vanished from their seats and reappeared on the balcony. The grand finale defied the laws of gravity, logic, and common sense: an enormous elephant disappeared right before our eyes."

"Genius! I thought, shocked and in awe of what I'd just witnessed. Little did I know that the next day would deliver one of the greatest life lessons I've ever received."

As he describes the day of the big game, Mr. Lafayette's tone shifts.

"It started inconspicuously, with tens of thousands of tifosi cheering before the clash got underway. And who suddenly appeared at the center of the field? None other than the illusionist! The announcer

explained that on behalf of people experiencing homelessness—something he once was himself—the illusionist would kick a penalty shot and attempt to beat Milan's goalie. If he missed, the homeless charity would receive a hefty donation, but it would double if he scored. The entire stadium erupted in cheers for the popular artist."

Erasmus envisions the stadium, the vibrant colors of team jerseys, and the roar of the crowd echoing in his ears. But his expression shifts as Mr. Lafayette continues.

"My first observation was that he was ill-fitted, wearing the wrong shoes and oversized shorts. As he started to dribble the ball, he looked rather clumsy. I already knew the outcome by the time he ran towards the ball to take the penalty shot. However, I wasn't prepared for what happened. The illusionist planted his left foot just before reaching the ball while loading his shooting leg back. Then... a debacle. His loose soccer boot hit the ground first, burying itself in the turf. He tripped at sprinting speed, lurched forward in the air, and landed face-first at the startled goalie's feet."

The small conference room falls silent, the weight of the moment hanging in the air. "Needless to say, the illusionist suffered national embarrassment," Mr. Lafayette concludes. "The incident was covered ad nauseam by the Italian tabloid press. His popularity took a nosedive, and his amazing act shut down a few weeks later."

Erasmus ponders the lesson hidden within the illusionist's fall from grace. 'What does this teach us about genius?' he reflects, captivated by the unfolding dialogue.

"I'm sure you're asking yourself what this anecdote has to do with geniality. Please bear with us, as you will see—it goes to the heart of the matter," explains Mr. Lafayette, seamlessly transitioning into the next mentor's tale.

"Mrs. Peabody, the floor is all yours," states Mr. Lafayette, yielding the floor.

The Case of the Wise and Benevolent Attorney
(Mrs. Peabody)

"Thank you, Lafayette. Erasmus, I'll be talking about the hardships of others. In my younger years, after I graduated from law school, I clerked for a famous criminal attorney. One winter, during an ice storm, one of the partners of the law firm had a terrible automobile accident when a trailer truck lost its brakes and crashed into his car. He broke his back and was paralyzed from the neck down. Day after day, I accompanied my boss to visit his friend."

As she speaks, Erasmus feels a pang of empathy for the paralyzed attorney. The image of the once-thriving lawyer, now confined yet resilient, stirs something within him. He thinks of Vicky and their own trials—her growing ambivalence, apprehensions, and now her conspicuous absence. How has he perhaps overlooked her true needs, the significance of their shared experiences? Each moment, filled with pain or joy, contributed to their story—what is he missing? Mrs. Peabody's booming voice brings him back to the present.

"The amazing thing about these visits was that, besides the pleasantries, they were normal work encounters. My boss often told me that he and his disabled partner were focusing much better on the

cases, and their incremental productivity was benefiting their law practice," Mrs. Peabody continues, her eyes reflecting the warmth of her memories.

"However, an ugly situation occurred by year's end. The other partners of the firm, who had rarely visited him, attempted to deny the disabled partner's share of that year's profits, alleging that all he was doing in his condition was serving as an assistant to my boss. My boss and the paralyzed attorney promptly quit the firm and went on to form one of the most successful law firms in New England."

Her voice takes on a reverent tone. "Shortly before I left to join the world of antique books, I was privileged to witness the two of them practicing law together—they were almost unbeatable. But it took one last case for me to finally understand my boss's genius."

"What happened?" Erasmus asks, leaning in, his curiosity piqued.

"It happened like this: one of the most prominent businessmen in Boston was indicted for bribing public officials, fraud, and money laundering. He also filed for bankruptcy and was unable to hire attorneys. So, it became a pro bono proposition. Nevertheless, many prominent attorneys in the city paraded through the prison where he was being held to offer their help, but he kept rejecting them one by one. The press and the public began to question his gratitude, and the judge stated clearly that his patience was becoming exhausted—enter my boss."

Erasmus pictures the tension in the courtroom, the palpable anticipation in the air.

"We visited the disgraced businessman several times over the course of a couple of weeks. As we left from a visit, a reporter yelled a rhetorical question at us on one occasion. 'You guys are the first to have lasted more than two visits. Did you know that?'

"No comment," my boss replied with a small smile.

"A couple of days later, we were retained. I wondered why the prominent businessman engaged us, as at no point had the conversations indicated we would be hired as his lawyers. Eventually, although I was no longer working for him, my boss got him acquitted. Once out of prison, the man reinvented himself and became so successful that I have to assume my former boss was compensated handsomely. I do know that when my former boss ran unsuccessfully for Governor, the businessman financed his entire campaign," she concludes, her voice softening.

"Did you ever ask the businessman why he chose your boss?" asks Erasmus.

"Yes, I did, but I had already figured it out by then. We will cover that in detail at the end," wraps up Mrs. Peabody with a broad and loving smile.

"Mr. Faith," states Mrs. Peabody, yielding the floor to him.

The Case of the New York Cabbie
(Mr. Faith)

"Thank you. Dear Erasmus, my anecdote is about the average Joe, and it occurred while visiting New York City inside a yellow cab. At the time, I worked as an investment banker for one of the largest Wall Street firms and was stationed in London. I wasn't a happy camper

as my limo hadn't shown up when I exited the arrivals terminal at JFK. After fifteen minutes of waiting, I reluctantly boarded one of the dreaded banged-up, smelly, bouncy old New York taxi cabs."

"When, right at the beginning, the driver made his first daredevil maneuver, I prayed we would make it into the city in one piece. How wrong I was about the driver because of my countless prejudices and stereotypes."

"Let me turn on the AC with a bit of a wild forest aroma,' the driver stated with a heavy Middle Eastern accent. 'I will also handle the vehicle in my limo-driver mode, and you won't be bothered by the springy suspension when I drive steady," he said, flashing a big smile.

"Thank you," I responded, already somewhat relieved.

"You're American, but you don't live here,"the cabbie stated.

"How do you know…?"I started to ask, but he continued.

"And you haven't been here for a while. I picked it up by how you look at everything," the driver observed with pinpoint accuracy.

"Are you always this observant?" I asked, intrigued.

"It's my job,"the driver replied with a casual shrug, a hint of pride in his voice.

"Aren't you just supposed to drive?"I teased him.

I was acting defensively, rattled by how easily he was reading me.

"Like, how do you call it, an automaton, a robot? So, I am not human to you?" the taxi driver responded with contempt, clearly displeased by my remark. At that moment, I adopted my listening-only mode, becoming curious.

"Or maybe dumb, right?" he asked, his voice now a tad too loud.

"Not at all, sir. Please go on. I want to listen to what you say," I offered, hoping to defuse the tension.

"Over the course of driving a yellow cab in this city for over twenty-five years," he continued, his tone shifting to a passionate cadence, 'babies have been delivered in my cab, lives of wounded or injured New Yorkers have been saved, life-saving medicines have been safely delivered, crimes have been stopped, marriages have been engaged or broken, and others have been mended."

Erasmus listens intently, absorbing the richness of the driver's experiences.

"I've had psychopaths, predators, and molesters, as well as artists, directors, writers, politicians, and even a former president in my yellow cab. I've delivered crucial documents and executed all the silliest chores intrinsic to the life of this city—from carrying diapers to hand-delivering notes across town asking for forgiveness. I can read most men and many women. I can tell by people's accents where they come from. I see fakes, authentic and honest people, as well as crooks. I've driven for hours from bar to bar for others to celebrate. I've witnessed families reunite after decades apart. Marriages begin, end, or rekindle. I've witnessed loyalty, faithfulness, and the absence of both. I've patiently tolerated being preached by monks, mullahs, sheiks, imams, high clerics, rabbis, and priests. I've prayed with and for others. I've even given my car to a policeman chasing a bank robber—just like in the movies."

Erasmus feels a warmth spreading in his chest as he absorbs the depth of the driver's narrative. 'There's something extraordinary in every ordinary life,' he thinks, reflecting on the driver's words.

As Mr. Faith narrates the taxi driver anecdote, Erasmus begins to see the mentors not just as wise figures but as people who have faced their own struggles. Their vulnerabilities have given rise to a sense of camaraderie. He feels a flicker of hope. Perhaps he can forge his path, one filled with acceptance of his strengths and weaknesses.

"Mrs. Poindexter, I yield to you," says Mr. Faith.

The Case of Order in Chaos in the Middle East
(Mrs. Poindexter)

"Thank you, Mr. Faith," begins Mrs. Poindexter, her tone rich with anticipation. "Dear Erasmus, I'm going to tell you about a life experience I had on the subject of chaos and other unsavory things in life. It took place in Dubai, where I attended a world conference of librarians. Several colleagues suggested I visit the Old City Center, where I would find all kinds of artifacts and ornaments typical of the Persian Gulf. They also recommended visiting shops selling precious metals, especially gold."

"Well, the ride over there was hectic. The driver claimed to have lost his way, so it took forever. Finally, we arrived. After paying what the meter showed, I stepped out of the car. Suddenly, I was in a steam bath as a wave of hot air hit me. When I inhaled, the scorching air burned through my respiratory system. Surrounding me were copious amounts of bubbling, bearded men in robes and sandals. At that

moment, I realized I was utterly lost and had no clue where I was. The place began to overwhelm me."

"Instinctively, I walked toward the water, seeking a bit of sea breeze. Finally, I realized I was in the middle of a port—not one with gigantic boats, but quite the opposite. There were hundreds of small boats tied to one another. The activity was frantic. Goods, boxes, packages, and bags of all sizes were being loaded and unloaded in a chaotic fashion. All the men on the boats and around the dock were either moving something or going somewhere. They looked scruffy with their beards and sunburned skin. For some reason, I didn't understand at the time, the place caught my curiosity, and I started to see what was really going on around me."

"After a while, I recognized the boats taking goods out, likely going to Iran, then boats bringing in goods, probably Iranian products for the local market. Of all the small merchant boats, one in particular caught my attention. The tall man imparting orders was relentlessly directing others. It took me a while, but I figured out how he organized the goods by weight and type. I counted at least twenty dispatchers delivering various products to his small vessel."

'Choreography in chaos,' I reasoned. 'That's powdered milk. Those are medicines,' I thought as I witnessed the pandemonium. Boat after boat kept leaving while others arrived. The action was filthy, noisy, and chaotic but far more efficient and effective than what I'd observed at first sight."

"Why doesn't Dubai service Iran with big-scale logistics?" I later asked a UAE officer at the conference.

He responded, 'There's an international embargo on one side, and on the other, Iran has strict customs rules and taxes on imports.'

'Brilliant,' I thought, recognizing a constant drip of tailor-made shipments leaving every day and a channel for small Iranian exporters to send their goods and barter for sale here in Dubai."

"In the end, Erasmus, I learned in Dubai an important lesson directly relevant to the subject we are covering with you tonight," concludes Mrs. Poindexter.

"Mr. Ringwald, the honor is all yours," says Mrs. Poindexter, yielding the floor.

As Erasmus sits in the dimly lit room, surrounded by his mentors, he feels an undercurrent of emotion surging. Each story is not just an anecdote but a thread weaving a tapestry of human experience, shaping his understanding of genius in the most profound ways.

The Case of the Big German Boss
(Mr. Ringwald)

"Thank you, Mrs. Poindexter," begins Mr. Ringwald, affectionately known as the Riddler. "Dear young man, tonight I'll be speaking to you about knowing yourself. Years ago, before I entered the world of books, I worked for a multinational company based in Hamburg, Germany. The company was an American-owned enterprise. The U.S. owners employed me as an executive. However, the man in charge was a well-seasoned German who had worked for almost thirty years at IBM Germany.

To grow its market share, the company I oversaw bought another enterprise in the south of Germany, in Munich. The German boss and

I, representing the American owners, went to Bavaria to welcome our organization's new employees. Everyone was assembled in one big auditorium, where he and I made brief statements, followed by a Q&A session.

An employee stood up to ask a question of the big German boss from Hamburg. The live mic sat in the middle between the two of us. Seconds passed, and the big boss did not answer. I turned to him to see if something was wrong, but he just sat there, clueless. Suddenly, forgetting about the live mic, he turned to me and whispered, 'Mr. Ringwald, did you understand the question?'

"Yes, of course. Do you want me to translate it for you?" I replied in jest.

"Yes, please. No one can understand Bavarians in Germany but themselves," the big boss remarked, forgetting about the mic.
At that moment, the entire place burst into laughter.

"From then onwards, the evening joke became Bavarian after Bavarian asking me to translate their questions for the big boss. However, one employee in particular asked me a question I've never forgotten, and fittingly, it aligns with tonight's overall story.

A young intern stood up towards the end of the session and asked,
"Sir, how do you compete?"

"You mean us as a corporation?" I replied.

"No, you as an individual," the intern clarified.

"Well, let me think about it, as I've never been asked that before. How do I frame it?" I asked aloud.

"Alright, if you're competing against my strengths, my mindset is that I will crush you. If you're competing against my weaknesses, I will try to outwork and outlast you. If I still cannot beat you by then, I will join forces with you,' I replied to the intern in the spur of the moment."

Mr. Ringwald pauses, letting the weight of his words settle in the room.

"Later, as we left, the big boss needed to dig deeper. 'Herr Ringwald, how come you understood that kid and I didn't?' he asked.

"When I first learned German, I didn't understand many phrases, but I understood some words. So, I learned how to grasp the overall meaning of the messages. If you don't understand one hundred percent of what is being said to you, you block it out, and it all becomes unintelligible," I replied.

"So, at the meeting, I walked out with two fundamental lessons that have served me well throughout my life, and both are relevant to tonight's subject," concludes Mr. Ringwald with a wry smile.

"Mr. Carnegie, the floor is yours," says Mr. Ringwald, gracefully yielding to the Scottish antiquarian.

The Clarity of Genius
(Colin Carnegie)

"Erasmus, now I'm going to read to you an early 20th-century writing that will bring clarity to each and every story you've just heard. After I'm done, we will all comment and draw conclusions about the life lessons presented in these anecdotes," declares Mr. Carnegie, his voice resonating with anticipation.

The room quiets to a reverent stillness, the atmosphere charged with the weight of the preceding stories. Mr. Carnegie adjusts his glasses, retrieves an aged parchment from his satchel, and begins to read in earnest:

"Geniality"

If we are content to oversimplify what geniality is
and limit ourselves to terms like
cordial, affable, congenial, gracious,
sociable, cheerful, and kindly,
we rob it of its uniqueness and outstanding aspects.

Worst of all, we trivialize the genius in all of us,
an intrinsic part of our essence and sense of being.

Hence, the geniality we speak about in this scribble
is only that which emerges from genius.
Herein lies the challenge with genius:
we haven't yet figured out what it means to be one.

What does it mean to be genial, to act genially,
to possess genialness and geniality?
What is it to genialize ourselves, others,
and everything we touch?

When we ask, when we listen,
when we see beyond the surface,
we unlock the doors
to the infinite genius waiting to unfold.

Genius does not fear failure;

it embraces it as a teacher, a guide,

a partner in the dance of growth.

Each stumble sharpens our steps,

each fall shapes the resolve to rise anew.

The fact is, geniality resides inside each one of us—

ready and eager to be discovered, nurtured, developed,

harnessed, shared, and put into practice.

In a way, our geniality is like a genie in a bottle,

yet we often make it unnecessarily hard to become genial.

We think of geniality in terms of the most exceptional,

the unique,

and view the absence of geniality

as common or lesser.

We perceive people and things in binary terms—

Up or down. Geniuses do neither.

In fact, quite the contrary:

genialness levels the playing field.

Every day geniuses do not feel superior or inferior to others,

Such terms do not exist in their dictionary.

A genius is simply someone, anyone, everyone,

who has recognized, discovered, or found in themselves or others,

the best talents and abilities they were born with—

and has uncorked, liberated, and put them into practice.

Thus, a genius does not think in terms of being better

than others or others being less than him;

he is simply exceptionally good at what he does best, period.

Geniality can be found where we hold innate,

unlimited and notable talent.

We are genial when we tap into our maximum potential

and use our best strengths.

At such moments, we harness our superpowers

becoming masters of our genius potential.

But don't ever mistake it for simplicity—

genius only deals with hard stuff.

Nothing geniality tackles comes easy;

it just appears effortless from the outside,

in the hands of genial power, innate talent,

practiced skill and rehearsed abilitiy.

Ask yourself:

What am I truly, exceptionally good at?

What was I born and destined to be?

What am I passionate about and genuinely love to do?

Honestly, what is it?

Given my abilities, passions, and talents,

what can I do best in life?

If I don't know, let me make it my life's quest to find it out.

One thing is certain:

the genius in all of us does not reside

in those things we lack talent or desire for.

The main obstacle is that geniality can be intimidating;

instead of embracing and drawing near,

we shy away—

when, in reality,

we just do the opposite.

To elevate ourselves,

we must surround ourselves with people

who possess talents and abilities

we aren't as good at or don't have.

The absence of geniality occurs

when we embark in the futile and poisonous exercise

of comparing ourselves and envying the virtues

and strengths of others—

often against the backdrop

of our most glaring weaknesses and shortcomings.

Geniality is often confused

with extraordinary intellectual power,

transcendental mental superiority, or inventiveness.

Geniuses are perceived

as profoundly gifted individuals

with attributes so diverse and sophisticated

that we feel overwhelmed and inadequate in their presence.

The question we have to ask ourselves in those moments is:

Are we afraid?

Do we feel diminished and intimidated by extraordinary genius?

Or are we just afraid of ourselves?

It is always healthy to remind ourselves

that whatever someone else possesses,

we too have something equally valuable

in the universe of life.

We are all geniuses in one or a few things

where we shine and soar.

But we are all clumsy clowns in many others.

Hence, the genius within does not compare itself

to anything or anyone—

because such comparissons are pointless,

a zero-sum game.

Our humbling flaws

will always wait for us

on every corner of life's streets.

Our genius is not ours alone;

it thrives in the warmth of shared connections.

Like threads in a tapestry,

we weave a greater brilliance through unity, each thread

strengthening the whole

So, what are we waiting for?

Our genius eagerly awaits us.

Our genie in a bottle is ready to be uncorked and liberated.

Let us unleash the genius inside us all,

so we can perform at our maximum potential.

and fully embrace the heights of what we can be & achieve in life.

*

When Mr. Carnegie finishes reading, the mentors prepare for their closing reflections.

"Erasmus, I made a critical error in judgment by looking down on the taxi driver I met that day. I soon discovered the man was a genius in his own right, performing his role in life to the best of his ability. Was there any real difference between him and myself, the investment banker? Absolutely not. We were equals, each striving to do our best," Mr. Faith states, his tone carrying newfound conviction.

"Young man," Mrs. Peabody begins, her gaze steady and reassuring, "the brilliance of my former boss, the wise criminal attorney, lay in his ability to see people as they were, unchanged by

circumstance. Whether his partner became quadriplegic or his friend faced jail, he treated them with the same respect and dignity as before. It's no wonder they responded to him in kind."

"Erasmus," Mrs. Poindexter interjects, her voice strong and clear, "That day in Dubai, I faced oppressive heat, chaos, and noise in a foreign environment. Yet, by embracing the situation rather than rejecting it, I discovered the genius behind the seemingly disorderly activity. Always remember: nothing truly brilliant comes easily. Genius resides in tackling the difficult and the demanding."

"Dear apprentice," Mr. Ringwald says with a hint of humor softening his words, "the German boss in my anecdote failed because he avoided confronting the challenge of understanding his own people's accents, opting instead for the easy way out. On the other hand, when I told the intern about how I compete, I demonstrated self-awareness and an openness to learning. Genius doesn't stand alone—it thrives in collaboration and self-knowledge."

"Erasmus," Mr. Lafayette says with quiet authority, "the illusionist in my story was initially hailed as a genius, yet the moment he stumbled, that title was stripped away. This reveals two key truths. First, society's tendency to elevate and then dismiss others is fleeting and shallow. Second, while we may excel in a few areas, we're all clumsy in many others. True genius lies in embracing both aspects of ourselves."

Finally, Mr. Carnegie takes a deep breath, allowing the weight of the preceding reflections to settle. "Erasmus, while my colleagues' stories are poignant, they all connect back to the essence of the poem 'Geniality.'

This poem illuminates the core of what we've been discussing. It teaches that genius is not confined to intellect or extraordinary achievements. Instead, it resides in authenticity, humility, and the ability to recognize and nurture the unique gifts within ourselves and others.

Consider the illusionist from Mr. Lafayette's tale—praised for his skill yet discredited in an instant. This illustrates that genius isn't defined solely by success or public recognition. Instead, it's rooted in how we authentically engage with the world and embrace our vulnerabilities.

Mrs. Peabody's wise attorney exemplifies this principle, lifting others up while pursuing his path with integrity. Mr. Faith's cab driver reminds us that genius can manifest in the simplest yet profound ways, often found where we least expect it. Mrs. Poindexter's experience in Dubai underscores that brilliance often emerges from chaos, teaching us to seek clarity amidst disorder. Mr. Ringwald's lesson about competing highlights the importance of self-awareness, collaboration, and perseverance.

In essence, 'Geniality' compels us to move beyond superficial judgments, to honor the unique genius within each individual. It calls us to strip away comparisons, embrace our strengths, and transform our lives by recognizing the value in others.

So, Erasmus," Carnegie concludes, "as you continue your journey, remember that discovering your genius is as much about the *connections you forge as it is about your innate talents. Nurture them. Share them. And let them guide you toward an authentic and fulfilling life."*

Erasmus listens, his emotions surging as each story resonates deeply with his own struggles and aspirations. He can't help but smile, overwhelmed by the wisdom imparted to him.

The mentors gather around him, one by one offering embraces. Erasmus obliges, kissing both ladies on their cheeks in the European fashion.

"Thank you," he says, placing a hand over his heart.

"We're confident this encounter will help you unlock your potential. Rest well, Erasmus. We'll see you tomorrow at the breakout sessions," Mr. Carnegie says warmly.

Erasmus walks out, his mind racing with the invaluable lessons and insights he's just received. Pausing at the door, he turns back, waving in gratitude.

"This," he says with a smile, "was a magnificent gift."

Erasmus heads back to his room in his typical absentminded state, having gotten so engrossed in the mentor's session that he has lost track of time and reality. Erasmus finally sees his watch and realizes several hours have passed since he spoke to Gina.

Nerves quickly creep in as it dawns on him that he forgot about Vicky. Erasmus rushes to the room, and his heart sinks when he doesn't find her there.

He then tries his home number but gets no answer. Erasmus immediately calls Gina, but she takes almost half an hour to make it to the college switchboard. "Gina?" He asks, anxiety creeping into his voice. "Erasmus, she did it," Gina replies in a matter-of-fact, somber tone. "She did what?" he asks, dread pooling in his stomach.

"She's gone, Erasmus." Gina says, delivering the devastating blow.

Erasmus stumbles back onto the bed, his legs giving out under the weight of Gina's words. The phone receiver feels heavy in his hand, almost slipping from his grasp.

"Gone?" he whispers, his voice barely audible.

"Yes, Erasmus. She packed up her belongings and just… left town," Gina confirms, her tone tinged with a mixture of sadness and frustration. "I tried talking to her, but she wouldn't listen. She kept saying it was for the best."

"Did she say where she was going?" he asks, clinging to a thread of hope.

"No, she didn't. But if I had to guess, she's probably headed back home," Gina replies, the strain in her voice evident. "You know how she's been struggling with everything—the doubts, the pressure, her family's expectations."

"Specifically, what did she talk about?" insists Erasmus.

"Lately, she made a couple of statements here and there. She seemed afraid. When angry or down, she vented, but I never took it seriously," replies Gina, then she adds, "That perhaps she wasn't made to be a career woman. On other occasions, it was about you."

"What about me?" asks an anxious Erasmus.

"She said that she felt intellectually intimidated – whatever that means. However, the issue that obsessed her the most was financial security. She repeated more than once that maybe she ought to go back home and raise a family with a well-off hometown man that her family approved of," she recalls as the line remains silent for a while. Erasmus remains silent, his thoughts churning. The echoes of their last conversations flood his mind, along with the countless moments he'd missed the warning signs—the hesitations in her voice, the distant looks in her eyes.

"I should've known," he murmurs, the words more to himself than Gina. "I should've seen this coming."

"Erasmus, this isn't on you," Gina says, her tone firm yet kind. "She's been battling her own demons for a long time. You've done everything you could to support her."

A heavy silence settles between them, the weight of the moment pressing down on both.

He closes his eyes, leaning his head back against the wall, the ache in his chest growing sharper with every passing second.

"Thank you, Gina," he finally says, his voice quieter now, subdued.

"Call me if you need anything," she offers before the line goes dead.

The silence in the room feels oppressive, the echoes of Gina's words lingering. He glances at the stack of notes and papers on the desk, remnants of the mentor's session earlier that evening. Their words, their lessons, suddenly seem distant, drowned out by the turmoil in his heart.

"Thanks for being straightforward; now I know what to do. Take care, Gina," he says, placing the receiver down with trembling hands.

An overwhelming wave of feelings of sadness and growing anxiety quickly inundate him. He stands and walks to the window, staring out into the night. The cold Cape Cod air wraps around him as he opens the window, the crisp breeze bitting at his skin. He breaths deeply trying to steady himself. But, engulfed in a sea emotions, the clarity he desperately seeks slips through his grasp, leaving him floundering. Somewhere out there, she is leaving him behind. The thought claws at him, relentless and unyielding. For the first time in years, Erasmus feels utterly and completely lost. He simply does not have a clue what to do next...

— ✦ —

Royal Cambridge Scholastic Institute, 2019
(University's Auditorium)

As Professor Cromwell-Smith stands before his class, having just recounted the lessons from that pivotal day in Cape Cod, his mind drifts once more, albeit briefly, to 1977—a moment that shaped the man he is today. The pedagogue is exhausted but relieved. As he scans the audience, his gaze lands on Victoria. She stands, applauding intensely, tears streaming down her face. He nods in gratitude, his smile both reassured and proud. Her presence bolsters him, giving strength as he faces this painful yet transformative day. The entire auditorium rises to its feet, cheering for the weary, erudite poet.

Once the applause subsides, he resumes. "You see, life often presents us with pain and tragedy alongside beauty, wonder, and renewal. That memorable day had both: a comet that streaked through my universe only to vanish, and a profound encounter with six wise mentors who gifted me invaluable wisdom."

He pauses, letting the words settle, then continues. "I'd like to open the floor for questions, especially about the themes we've explored—geniality and tapping into your full potential in life."

Emily, a philosophy major, her bright smile radiating curiosity.

"Professor, you mentioned the taxi driver's perspective in New York. How can we learn to see the value in every experience, even in the mundane or chaotic?"

"Excellent question, Emily. The taxi driver's story demonstrates that every person brings unique contributions to the world. The poem teaches us that geniality lies in recognizing and valuing these contributions. By embracing the chaos of life, we uncover profound lessons and unexpected connections that can reveal and refine our talents. Often, our greatest growth comes from such moments," the professor replies thoughtfully.

Joseph, literature major, shifts nervously in his seat. When he finally speaks, his voice is soft yet earnest. "Professor, how do we find the courage to embrace our own genius when we often feel inadequate, like in the stories you shared?"

"Joseph," the professor begins with a reassuring tone, "acknowledging those feelings of inadequacy is the first step to unlocking your potential. The poem emphasizes that genius isn't about perfection but about recognizing and nurturing your passions and strengths. When we allow ourselves to be genuine and vulnerable, we open the door to self-discovery and create opportunities to connect with our true abilities."

Jennifer, a psychology major. Her brow furrows as she poses her question. "Professor, how do we maintain integrity and kindness in a world that often values success over character, as seen in the stories?"

"That's a crucial question, Jennifer," he responds warmly. "The anecdotes highlight that empathy and kindness are more enduring than mere achievements. The poem underscores this, reminding us that geniality is not just about intellect but about character. When we choose to uplift others, we embody true geniality. Success may fade, but how we treat others defines our legacy."

Maya, a creative writer major. Her expressive brown eyes spark with curiosity. "Professor, in the story about the illusionist, you mentioned how we often judge people by appearances. How can we shift our perspective to appreciate the genius in everyone, regardless of their circumstances?"

"That's a powerful question, Maya," he says with a nod. "The poem reminds us that we all have unique talents waiting to be discovered. The illusionist's story shows how judgment and failure can obscure the value we bring. To appreciate the genius in others, we must look beyond surface-level impressions and seek the depth of their journey. In doing so, we also learn to recognize the genius within ourselves."

"What about next year?" an eager student calls out.

"We'll continue with the same format," Erasmus replies. "But next time, we'll explore the forty years Victoria and I lived apart—an entirely different chapter."

Harper stands again, her eyes bright with enthusiasm. "Professor, your stories today struck a chord. They made me realize how interconnected our experiences are."

Erasmus smiles, touched by her words. "That's the essence of life, Harper—finding the threads that bind us together. Within those threads lies meaning, understanding, and growth."

The professor steps back, his expression growing solemn as he addresses the class one final time. "Always remember this: each of you carries a unique genius within. Your challenge is to discover it, cultivate it, and use it for the betterment of yourself and those around you. Genius isn't just extraordinary talent—it's the ability to fully embrace and deploy the best parts of who you are. Your genie in a bottle is your genius, waiting to be unleashed. What are you waiting for?"

Erasmus scans the audience once more, his eyes locking with Victoria's. She places her hands over her heart and mouths, "I love you." He mirrors her gesture immediately, his smile soft yet full of emotion.

"Thank you all for your thoughtful participation today," he says, bowing his head. With a playful movement, he mimics the hand gestures of an orchestra conductor and opens his arms wide. The entire auditorium responds as one:

"Insanely awesome!" they shout with exuberance, filling the space with energy and laughter—a fitting closure to a memorable class.

Book III

MAGIC IN LIFE

Chapter 1

Adversity

Royal Cambridge Scholastic Institute (2019)
(Erasmus and Victoria's Home)

The tick of the cuckoo clock is the only sound resonating through the still darkness of the early morning.

Professor Erasmus Cromwell-Smith has dozed off on his beloved Chesterfield sofa. Resting on his lap is the latest object of his insatiable curiosity: a 17th-century leather-bound book with gold-burnished pages exploring the subject of coherence. Nudged closely to his side, sleeping as soundly as him, is Victoria Emerson-Lloyd, the love of his life. Together, their faces form a portrait of plenitude—a radiant testament to the incomparable beauty of true love.

At the prescribed hour, the cheerful clucking of the cuckoo bird stirs them awake, announcing the arrival of a new day. As they stretch into one another, their shared smiles illuminate the room like the first rays of dawn.

This morning marks the beginning of a new academic year. The illustrious pedagogue is eager to embark on his first class.

"Dear, what will be the subject of your class today?" Victoria murmurs, still half-asleep.

"Adversity, my lady," Erasmus replies, his voice tinged with both seriousness and anticipation.

Not long after, Victoria kisses and waves him off as he pedals through the crisp autumn morning on his trusty, old rusty bike, the fallen leaves crunching under its wheels as he makes his way to class.

Royal Cambridge Scholastic Institute (2019)
(University Auditorium)

The auditorium is filled to capacity, buzzing with palpable energy. Students eagerly anticipate the return of Professor Cromwell-Smith, their excitement almost tangible.

The professor strides in with deliberate purpose, his expression bright and welcoming. Hand on his chin, he surveys the room, pausing momentarily as if connecting with each student individually.

A broad smile spreads across his face, eliciting a mix of chuckles and intense, focused stares from his audience.

"Welcome! How's everyone today?" he greets, his voice resonating through the hall.

"Awesome!" comes the collective reply, mirroring his signature phrase.

"I trust you all had a fun and enlightening summer," he says exuberantly.

Then, shifting his tone to one of firm authority, he continues, "A quick reminder—punctuality is a non-negotiable in this course. No excuses."

"As with the previous two years, we will follow the same format—one last time," he declares. "This year, we're delving into new subjects through narration, readings, and the lens of poetry. The first themes we'll explore are adversity and hardship," he announces, setting the stage for the year ahead.

"Are you ready for the journey?" he asks, receiving a sea of nodding heads in return.

"Adversity," he begins, pacing the floor with deliberate intensity.

"What happens when we face adversity? Have we been taught how to react, how to handle it, how to cope? Are we ever truly prepared?

And what about the aftermath? Suppose adversity strikes, and we overcome it—what then?" His questions linger in the air, inviting reflection.

Pausing for emphasis, he continues, "Today, we'll start right where we left off last year. On the night when the love of my life vanished. That day, adversity struck me unexpectedly, and I wasn't prepared to face it at all."

He stops, letting the weight of his words settle before delivering the opening line.

"It begins like this…"

— ✦ —

Cape Cod, Erasmus' Hotel Room (1977)
(Early Friday Night)

"She's gone, Erasmus," Gina's words reverberate through his mind, a relentless echo that refuses to fade. The weight of those three words settles heavily on his chest, each repetition carving deeper into his resolve.

Erasmus has only one idea in mind. He has to get back to Boston. He has to start looking for her.

Grabbing his coat, he hastily collects his belongings. The stack of notes and papers from the mentors remains untouched on the desk, their importance now eclipsed by the urgency of his mission. Within five minutes, Erasmus leaves the hotel room with luggage in hand. Right after checking out, he steps into the biting Cape Cod night. The cold wind lashes at his face, a stark reminder of the distance he must cover—not just in miles but across the fragile emotional landscape he now confronts.

As he rushes out, Erasmus runs headlong into "The Riddler," Mr. Ringwald, the antiquarian from downtown Boston.

"Erasmus, young man, what are you up to?" he asks, his gaze flicking to the small suitcase.

"Where are you going, luggage and all, at this hour of the night?" Mr. Ringwald presses, surprise evident in his tone.

Erasmus bows his head in courtesy but doesn't answer and rushes past the startled Riddler. As he walks away, guilt and gratitude war within him. He pauses momentarily, then turns and says, "Mr. R, I've got to go and see about a girl. Sorry."

"THE girl?" the Riddler calls after him.

"Yes, THE girl," Erasmus yells back, a faint smile tugging at his lips. Unexpectedly, Ringwald starts chasing him.

"Erasmus!"

"Yes?", Erasmus responds, slowing slightly.

"Take this and read it when appropriate," Ringwald says, out of breath as he catches up.

"Thank you, Mr. Ringwald," Erasmus replies, accepting the scroll with gratitude.

"For nothing, young man. I've got a gut feeling that you may need it," Ringwald predicts ominously.

"But you don't have to—" Erasmus begins to protest.

"C'mon, take it and use it. Now go. Go!" Ringwald insists.

With determined strides, Erasmus heads toward the train station, his mind racing with possibilities, regrets, and a single burning hope: finding Victoria.

Cape Cod Train Station, Mass. (1977)
(Friday Night)

Erasmus sits alone at the deserted Cape Cod train station. No more trains are scheduled for Boston, but he doesn't care; his nerves and angst have overtaken him completely. Hours later, still in the dark, a Good Samaritan gently shakes him awake.

"Are you going to Boston?"

"Yes."

"Then you better get moving; otherwise, you'll miss the train—it's about to leave."

Erasmus jolts upright and sprints, barely catching the train with no time to spare.

He's sound asleep again when the announcement awakens him.

"We're arriving at Boston's main station."

Erasmus heads straight home, where he methodically tears through the apartment, searching for a note, a clue—anything in writing. An hour later, he sits on the living room floor, staring blankly at the now lifeless surroundings.

'Nothing. Not a word,' Erasmus realizes, the thought stabbing deeply.

'She took everything. I don't even have a number or an address to reference,' he muses in turmoil, chastising himself for missing the signs. He spends an hour or more on the phone with directory assistance, all to no avail. The number is unlisted. Reality finally hits home mid-Saturday afternoon when he visits a professor who taught them both.

Professor Jenkins initially appears startled until Erasmus asks about Victoria's sudden disappearance.

"Oh, I know what you're referring to, young man. She wrote a letter to the admissions office notifying them she was dropping out. She also left a note thanking all of us, specifically her teachers, for everything we did for her. This kind of withdrawal from a highly functional, trouble-free student is rare, but in my experience, it's always due to extraordinary reasons and circumstances."

"Thanks, Professor Jenkins."

"I understand she's from out of state. What are you going to do now?"

"I've got to go and find out about my girl, sir. Thanks for your help, professor," Erasmus says, shaking his former teacher's hand with gratitude.

"Good luck, young man."

Saturday night proves unbearable. Erasmus spends it wide awake, haunted by her absence. By Sunday morning, a fiery determination replaces his despair. He knows he can't stay passive. He needs to act.

Harvard University Campus (1977)
(Sunday Morning, Erasmus and Victoria's Studio)

"Good morning, Gina," Erasmus greets her with forced civility.

"Seriously? What time is it?" Gina snaps groggily, immediately realizing her tone.

"Sorry, Erasmus. That was insensitive of me. How can I help?"

"Do you have her phone number or address?" he asks, desperation lacing his voice.

"No, I'm sorry. For some reason, Vicky never shared her family life or contact information with me," Gina replies, shaking her head apologetically.

"Ok, thanks anyway," Erasmus mutters, dejected.

The following week sees Erasmus in a quasi-catatonic state, hoping she'll somehow return. It isn't until the next weekend that he finally accepts the reality—she's not coming back.

Boston Main Train Station (1977)
(One Week Later, Saturday Morning)

'Eventually, I'll end up hating all train stations,' Erasmus reflects grimly as he boards a train bound for Chicago. *Halfway through the long journey, he discovers he's taken the wrong route. Instead of heading through New York to St. Louis—the correct path to*

Victoria's hometown of Waterloo, Illinois—he's traveling the long way around.

'Nothing I can do for now.'

Waterloo, Illinois Main Train Station (1977)
(Monday Morning)

'All it'll take is just to be in front of one another, and we will be reunited,' he reassures himself repeatedly.

The old, crumpled, yellowed pages of a station phone book finally come to his rescue. After hours of searching, Erasmus secures an address and phone number. However, dread creeps into his heart when his call meets an ominous recording: the line has been disconnected.

Fighting the sickly feeling in his stomach, he takes a taxi to her address. His heart pounds as he prays for the best while preparing for the worst.

"Young man, they moved out in the middle of the night," Victoria's neighbor announces bluntly. "We're in shock; we've been neighbors all our lives. Old Emerson and I grew up together. There must've been a compelling, private reason for them to vanish like bandits, hiding from everyone. Who knows—maybe their daughter got knocked up while at Harvard," the neighbor speculates, eyeing Erasmus with suspicion, as though he might be the culprit.

En Route by Train from St. Louis Back to Boston
(Via New York – 1977, Monday Afternoon)

Defeated, Erasmus boards the train home. He drifts in and out of restless dreams until a sudden memory strikes him: Mr. Ringwald's scroll. For a moment, panic grips him—did he leave it behind? But relief floods in as he retrieves it from his small suitcase.

Erasmus stares at the scroll, its purpose now clear. With reverence, he prepares to read it. First, he showers, shaves, and changes into a fresh set of clothes. Then, with a steaming cup of tea in hand, he finally sits down, ready to absorb its contents.

"Adversity"

Either by acts of men, nature, or humanity's creations,
fatefully, sooner or later,
weather systems will gather on the horizon,
events will unfold unexpectedly,
and inevitably, one way or another—
with or without warning—
adversity will strike
during our life's journey.

Adversity will affect us—
emotionally, spiritually, physically, materially—
often in any combination.

When we face hardship in life,
there is no choice.
We gather all our strengths, forces, and powers—
those we have and those we summon,
those distinct and those we reach for.

We confront adversity head-on,

without fear or hesitation,

with all our will and desire—

for ourselves or others—

to live and to overcome,

to prevail and rise back up,

to defeat and render adversity

completely annihilated and vanquished.

When we don't confront or face hardship head-on,

we become trapped—

lost in indecisiveness,

drawing circles within our minds,

wasting valuable time,

avoiding or delaying action.

These are moments—some lasting a lifetime—

where we find ourselves lamenting,

feeling sorry for ourselves or others,

procrastinating, commiserating,

while doing little to fight back.

When we behave in such ways,

our failure to act leads us nowhere,

except to an empty place,

where excuses sound hollow—

not only robbing us of our ability to live a life in full,

but also reflecting the attitude of a soldier

who runs away from the battle of life

without ever firing a single shot,

unwilling to face the enemy of adversity

with courage and conviction to defeat it,

or perhaps,

adapt to it.

Getting a grip on adversity is best

when we catch it early on.

When, out of foresight, anticipation,

preparation, and readiness,

we see it coming and are prepared for it,

we prevent it or stop it right in its tracks,

before it happens—right at its onset.

And yet, in many ways, adversity is also an opportunity,

sometimes for renewal and new beginnings,

other times, it marks the beginning

of the end of a bad spell.

How we react and cope with it

determines our success—

in overcoming and turning adversity

into something positive.

Hardship is formative and transformative,

rattling our core as a "comfort buster,"

testing our character, courage, and resilience.

If adversity is avoidable,

it is our existential duty

to do all within our power

to prevent it or stay out of its path.

But if it is inevitable,

we must adapt—

learning to live with it,

as our goal is to outlast and outwill it.

If hardship is irreversible,

we still seek to find and squeeze the most out of life,

wringing meaning from every second

we exist in the universe.

If it is mendable,

we fight like lions,

refusing to give up,

curing ourselves of it,

relentlessly to no end.

Yet, we must beware of "mirages in the desert,"

as hardships sometimes

are nothing but a figment of our imagination—

where we see obstacles and hurdles

where there are none.

We create them out of fear, insecurities,

pessimism, or depression.

Adversity is best faced with existential tools like

hope, conviction, optimism,

ingenuity, faith, and work ethic—

a busy mind and spirit,

all coupled with love.

Sometimes, we encounter the adversity of others

and don't know what to do.

Involuntarily, our perception of them

becomes contagious,

as if those afflicted with hardship

suffer from an infectious disease

we want to stay away from.

On other occasions, we act

as if those under hardship

have somehow suddenly changed—

fallen from their former selves.

We perceive them and behave as though,

because of their circumstances,

they are suddenly not worthy of us.

How wrong we are to conduct ourselves

in such ways.

Inevitably, we too will experience hardship

and may find ourselves

on the receiving end of such disdain—

of the same exact happenstance.

Thus, it is wise and existential
to treat the hardship of others
with the utmost respect,
a kind and giving heart.

Even if their battles are not ours,
it is wise to remind ourselves
that we are still soldiers of the same army,
fighting the same life war of existence.

Against unforeseen mishaps and vicissitudes,
hardship is greatly diminished when thought of
in comparative and relative terms.
No matter how difficult things seem,
they can always be worse.

Adversity is at its worst when it comes unannounced,
catches us unprepared,
and we are unguarded against it.

The best attitude against hardship
is to treat it as an enemy of war—
to whom we never surrender,
against whom we never quit.

On the contrary,

we fight and confront relentlessly,

until we defeat it and render it powerless.

But if we can't,

we adapt—

extracting what life still has to offer,

even within the circumstances,

because life never stops,

even as we overcome adversity.

Adversity must always be treated

as an existential opportunity—

a chance to awaken

from a life of comfort and complacency.

A chance to renew and reinvent ourselves.

But adversity becomes an opportunity

only if we choose to make it so.

*

As the words of the poem linger in the quiet of the train, young Erasmus leans back in his seat, staring at the passing countryside. The rhythmic clatter of the tracks beneath him seems to echo the steady resolve growing within his heart. The scroll's profound message has awakened something dormant, a quiet determination to face life head-on. His weary reflection in the window hints at the transformation taking place—a shift from sorrow to action. The train journey, though physically uneventful, has marked a pivotal turning point, setting him on a path that would ultimately shape the man he would become.

— ✦ —

Royal Cambridge Scholastic Institute (2019)
(University Auditorium)

The sudden ring of the bell jolts the professor and his class back to the present. Cromwell-Smith pauses, as if still transported back to that moment, "On that train ride back to Harvard," the professor continues, his voice steady but tinged with the wisdom of time and experience, "I made several pivotal decisions that helped me confront adversity and ultimately overcome how I felt. First, even though my wandering mind was consumed with turmoil, I kept the scroll with me, and as the Riddler had predicted, the moment arrived when I truly needed it. Secondly, despite not being in the mood, I resolved to open and read it. That decision turned out to be transformative, as its words illuminated a path forward—a path of decisiveness I chose to follow. Thirdly, by the time I returned to Boston, I had already resolved to move on with my life while preserving, without bitterness, all the wonderful memories of my time with Victoria. In this spirit, the very same day of my return, I wrote to Mrs. V. back in Wales, pouring out my feelings of longing and uncertainty. Her thoughtful reply gave me the encouragement, strength, and clarity I needed," the professor emphasizes, his gaze sweeping the attentive faces of his students.

"Not long after, I graduated from Harvard and made one final trip to my hometown of Hay-on-Wye in Wales before settling permanently in America. While there, I discovered that my childhood mentors had orchestrated a surprise mentoring session for me. It was during this gathering that they imparted the timeless happiness formula—an inspired recipe that became the final touch needed to straighten the course of my life for good. At the end of today's class, I will share a copy of this formula with each of you," he announces, a smile of quiet pride softening his features.

"Adversity is an intrinsic part of life," he continues, his tone now imbued with conviction. "It is often both the ultimate challenge to everything and everyone we hold dear and an opportunity to create something meaningful, perhaps even extraordinary, out of it. Adversity is a double-edged sword—hardship on one side, and on the other, a door that opens to renewal or a new beginning."

He pauses, stepping back from the desk to face his students. "Now, I open the floor for any questions or thoughts you might have on what we've discussed today."

Anna, a Literature and Philosophy major, with short curly brown hair and glasses that always seem to slide down her nose as she ponders deeply, raises her hand. "Professor, in the poem 'Adversity,' you speak of the moment when we don't confront hardship head-on, leading us into indecisiveness. I'm curious about the philosophical implications of this—do you think that avoiding adversity can be considered a failure of character, or is it more about human instinct for self-preservation? Is there a balance between retreat and confrontation in how we deal with personal challenges?"

"An excellent question, Anna," Professor Cromwell-Smith responds. "You're right to highlight the tension between instinctual retreat and the need for confrontation. From a philosophical standpoint, we can view avoidance as a natural response—human beings are wired for survival, and often our first instinct is to shield ourselves from harm. But, as the poem suggests, there's a line where this instinct crosses into passivity, and in those moments, we rob ourselves of growth. It's not about being reckless or overly confrontational; rather, it's about having the courage to face the challenge when it comes, even if that means starting small. I wouldn't define avoidance as a failure of character per se, but as a missed opportunity to engage with life's deeper lessons."

Carlos, a Psychology and Neuroscience major, tall with dark, neatly combed hair and a warm smile that contrasts with his usually serious demeanor, speaks next. "Professor, you spoke about the dual nature of adversity—how it presents both hardship and opportunity. From a psychological standpoint, how do we cultivate the resilience to see adversity not just as a threat but as an opportunity? Is it possible to actively reframe these experiences in a way that promotes psychological growth?"

"Carlos, you've hit the core of the challenge," Professor Cromwell-Smith responds. "In psychology, reframing is indeed a powerful tool—it's about shifting the lens through which we view an experience. Instead of seeing adversity purely as a threat, we can train our minds to view it as an opportunity for growth, learning, or even self-discovery. There's a fascinating process in cognitive psychology called cognitive restructuring, where we intentionally change negative or limiting thoughts into more constructive ones. Resilience isn't a fixed trait; it's a skill that can be cultivated with practice. This can start with acknowledging the adversity, processing it, and then asking, 'What can I learn from this? How can this moment make me stronger, more capable, or more understanding?' Over time, this mindset becomes automatic."

Jane, a History and Political Science major, with long black hair often tied into a neat ponytail, and a focused gaze that reveals her attention to detail, asks, "Professor, the poem seems to suggest that adversity is inevitable and, in some cases, irreversible. Do you think history shows us examples of how societies, as opposed to individuals, handle adversity? Are there historical moments where adversity has been 'irreversible,' and what can we learn from them?"

"That's a fascinating perspective, Jane," Professor Cromwell-Smith says. "You're absolutely right that history is rife with moments of collective adversity—whether that's war, political upheaval, or social injustice. Some of these events, like the fall of empires or the devastation of war, seem irreversible. Yet, what's striking is the resilience of societies that rebuild and transform in the aftermath. Take, for example, the recovery of Europe after World War II, or the Civil Rights Movement here in the United States. These moments of collective suffering and loss became the catalysts for significant change. The key lesson is that while some adversities may be irreversible, the ways in which we respond can reshape the future. It's a testament to the human capacity for reinvention, even when facing what seems like an insurmountable challenge."

David, an Economics and Sociology major, athletic build with a sharp jawline, often seen with a slight frown when analyzing social trends and patterns, asks, "Professor, the poem emphasizes confronting adversity with courage and will, and yet, it also speaks about avoiding unnecessary 'mirages in the desert'—things that aren't real obstacles. How do we distinguish between genuine adversity that requires confrontation and imaginary challenges that we create in our minds due to fear or insecurity? Is there a method to discern this distinction?"

"That's a very insightful question, David," Professor Cromwell-Smith responds. "The line between real adversity and self-created challenges can be incredibly thin. Often, our minds play tricks on us—fear, doubt, and insecurity can make challenges seem larger or more insurmountable than they truly are. One way to distinguish between the two is by questioning the source of the adversity. Is the challenge external—something truly outside our control—or is it rooted in our internal fears, anxieties, or projections? One method I recommend is the 'reality check'—take a step back and analyze the situation from an objective standpoint. Ask yourself: 'Is this something I can control? Is it based on facts, or is it influenced by my emotions and fears?' Real adversity demands action; imagined adversity often requires nothing more than a shift in perspective."

"That will be all for today. I'll see you all next week," Professor Cromwell-Smith concludes, his words lingering like echoes of wisdom. As the students rise and file out of the auditorium, he hands each of them a copy of the happiness formula, his gesture filled with quiet hope for their journeys ahead. As the last of his students exit the auditorium, their murmured conversations fading into the corridor beyond, Professor Cromwell-Smith lingers at the lectern, gazing out over the now-empty seats. The silence feels heavier, more contemplative, after the depth of their shared discussion. Gathering his notes and adjusting his glasses, he allows himself a rare moment of reflection. The echoes of the past and present intertwine, and he silently wonders which seeds of wisdom, if any, have found fertile ground among his students.

Straightening his posture, he walks toward the door, his mind already preparing for the next lecture—a chance to explore life's complexities further and, perhaps, to inspire a few more hearts.

The Happiness Formula

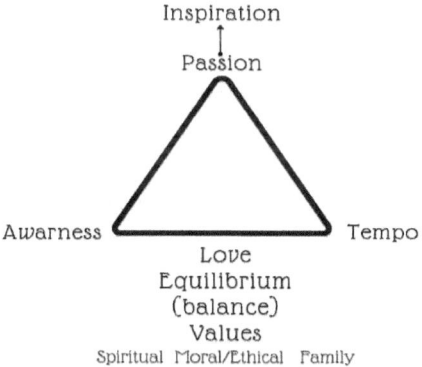

As the professor steps outside, he surveys the campus and feels a quiet satisfaction at the sight of students departing with expressions of gratitude and determination etched on their faces.

Walking toward his old rusty bike, his eyes land on a figure sitting on a bench in the distance. It's Victoria. Her shoulders quake as she cries inconsolably, her sobs audible even from afar. Gulping for breath between tears, she seems consumed by an overwhelming tide of emotion.

Without hesitation, Erasmus strides briskly toward her, his heart heavy with concern. Sitting down beside her, he doesn't say a word. Instead, he gently wraps his long arms around her, his embrace a mantle of love and protection. The world around them seems to fall away as he focuses solely on her.

'She needs to let it all out,' he thinks, his chest tightening with empathy as her pain seeps into the quiet space between them.

After a while, Victoria breaks the silence, her voice trembling.

"Erasmus, I sat through the whole class," she confesses, her words like a fragile offering. Her tear-streaked face turns toward him, her eyes searching his for understanding.

He is momentarily taken aback but quickly collects himself, nodding thoughtfully. After a pause, his voice comes soft and steady, a gentle anchor in the storm of her emotions.

"Alright, Victoria," he whispers, his tone inviting yet deliberate. "Why don't you go ahead and tell me what happened while I was looking for you?"

Her tears intensify momentarily as if his words have unlocked the floodgates. Engaging a voice fractured by emotion, she begins to recount the events of that fateful night. The memories spill out, raw and unfiltered, each word a fragment of the pain and guilt she has carried for so long.

Erasmus listens intently, his arms remaining firmly around her, offering silent reassurance as she lays bare the story that has haunted them both for decades.

— ✦ —

The Emerson-Lloyd Family Home, Waterloo, Illinois (1977)
(Victoria's Arrival from Harvard)

"Victoria, you can't force your entire family to uproot itself from one day to the next. This is our home. It's where we've lived all our lives, where you and your siblings were born, and where our lifelong friends are," her mother declares sternly, her voice brimming with finality.

Victoria, however, ignores her entirely.

"Mom, Dad, it's your choice: either we do it, or I'm on a train back to Boston today—this time for good," she asserts firmly, her tone unwavering.

Her father's face contorts in alarm. "Victoria Emerson-Lloyd, what sort of trouble are you in?" he demands.

"Love trouble, Dad. If he shows up here, I'm afraid I won't be able to resist him." Her voice cracks under the weight of her confession.

"Victoria, why don't you just tell us what's going on?" her mother presses, her distress palpable.

"The only thing happening here," Victoria cries, her tears falling freely, "is that I'm marrying the guy you want, not the one I love."

Her father freezes, visibly taken aback. "I'm lost! We don't want you to do that," he asserts, his eyes darting to his wife, who fixes her gaze on the floor to avoid his accusatory stare.

"Who is he?" her father urges, his tone softening.

"A British student," Victoria murmurs, her voice barely audible, "about to complete his master's degree."

Her father's bewilderment shifts to suspicion as he looks between his wife and daughter. "You two need to explain yourselves. What is this, then? An arranged marriage?" he asks, disgust edging into his voice.

"Victoria has made a sensible decision to raise a family with an experienced and well-to-do gentleman from the same region we're all from. The matter is settled, and there is nothing further to discuss," her mother declares, her tone firm and unyielding.

"You told me this was Victoria's decision! It sounds like you're coercing her to marry that man," he accuses, his piercing gaze landing squarely on his wife.

Victoria sits frozen, her mother's words slicing through her. Her emotional outburst has laid bare her true feelings, and all she wants now is to bolt to the train station and return to Erasmus. Across the room, her mother, visibly panicking, scrambles to regain control of the unraveling situation.

"Victoria," her mother interjects hurriedly, "let me speak to your father alone about this." Without waiting for consent, she ushers her perplexed husband into another room.

Victoria, caught in the turmoil, remains seated, her warring impulses raging within her. Moments later, her mother returns, a triumphant smile plastered on her face.

"Victoria, we have a property in Columbia, Illinois, just north of here. We can move there temporarily until you're married. It's also closer to your likely new university in St. Louis. Socially, being away for a few months won't impact us much," she announces cheerfully, her voice brimming with forced optimism.

Victoria shakes herself out of her trance, turning to Erasmus as she continues her tale. "Shortly after I got married, I moved and settled in Columbia, Illinois. That's where all my children were born. Not long after my return from Boston, I also enrolled at the University of Missouri in St. Louis, where I eventually completed my studies in criminal psychology. Years later, after I graduated, I started my teaching career, and then we moved to Boston. Still, to this day, I don't know how she persuaded my father to go along with it."

Her voice trails off, her gaze distant, as if still grappling with the memory of those fateful days.

— ✣ —

Royal Cambridge Scholastic Institute (2019)
(Campus Backroads)

The newly reunited couple strolls through the mushy grass path toward his home. Victoria's face shows visible relief, her shoulders slightly less tense than before. Erasmus, ever perceptive, senses that the real challenge now lies in her finding a way to forgive herself for the choices she made. With quiet determination, he tightens his embrace, a blanket of forgiveness wrapping around her as if to shield her from the storm within.

"I love you," he murmurs softly in her ear, his voice a steady anchor as she trembles, grappling with the uncertainty of her unfinished puzzle.

Victoria slows her steps and turns to gaze at him, her eyes brimming with gratitude and love. But in an instant, those eyes widen with surprise and awe. She notices the tiny scroll in his hand and immediately knows it is meant for her.

"Earlier this morning," Erasmus begins with a tender smile, "before I fell asleep on your shoulder, I wrote this little something for you, my lady."

He holds the scroll delicately, his fingers trembling slightly, and begins to read in earnest, his voice carrying the depth of his emotions…

"How is it that you make me feel so special?"

What are all those little things that you do?

What is it about the way you act?

What are those spellbinding words you say?

What is it about the magical verses you scribble?

All of it makes me feel so special,

my love.

Is it that you make me feel

whimsical,

happy,

loved,

adored, and revered to no end?

Or is it because, every single day, in the whirlwind of your devotion,

you remind me that I am for you the most important person in the

world, the very center of your universe?

This is the only way I can explain

how, while basking in joy,

I have no choice but to fee:

motivated,

inspired and

profoundly grateful.

That's how,

you bring out the best in me.

You draw from me all that I can give, simply because of who you are

and how you make me feel— so special, so unique, my love.

*

Victoria trembles, her breath hitching as the weight of his words envelops her. She sighs deeply, her emotions coursing through her like a tide of joy and release. Without hesitation, she leans in and kisses him passionately, a kiss that seems to transcend time itself. The moment stretches endlessly, an unforgettable union of love, forgiveness, and renewal that neither will ever forget.

Chapter 2

Coherence

Nantucket Island, New England, Mass. (2019)
(Sunday morning, dawn)

As the newly reunited couple sits on the sand with a wool blanket around them, the ocean, just a few steps away, reflects the calm of the air's gentle breeze. They sip their hot teas, warmed by knee-high wool socks—the perfect touch for a crisp 50° morning—while waiting for sunrise to break on the horizon.

A week has passed since their unfinished conversation, and day by day, the ghosts of the past have begun to subside. The joy of being together again gradually erodes lingering guilt and grudges, but Erasmus senses that Victoria is not yet free of the emotional scars she carries. He knows more revelations will surface as she confronts her pain.

"He was a psychiatrist," she suddenly blurts out.

"Who? …" Erasmus begins to ask, but she interrupts, continuing her monologue.

"And he was much older than me."

She pauses, momentarily lost in time. Erasmus clings to her every word, sensing the gravity of her dialogue, though he's unsure where it's heading.

'Maybe this explains her past behavior,' Erasmus reflects. 'No! Could it be?' His thoughts are interrupted as his heartbeat quickens.

"Twenty-eight years my senior," she finally says, her voice tinged with lament.

"Old enough to be my father but chosen to be my husband," she adds bitterly.

The revelation hits him like a thunderbolt. He looks at her, immersed in thought, as if questioning who Victoria really is.

"As I look back, I see now how he manipulated me, how he manipulated my mother, and in a way, my entire family to suit his needs," she continues.

"During the first few years, I fell under his perverse and coercive spell. He persuaded me, therapeutically speaking, that the most effective way to make a clean break from my feelings for you was to focus on every negative thing I could remember about you—and to repeat it over and over."

"Did it work?"

"In the beginning, yes. I created an alternate reality to justify my behavior. But over time, my true feelings resurfaced, and that was the end of that."

'Finally, the truth,' Erasmus thinks, feeling an onslaught of emotions.

"He exploited my vulnerability as his patient, using his intimate insight into my emotional state. He slowly steered me toward him, subtly coercing me with arguments about social convenience and material wealth."

As she speaks, the disjointed puzzle in Erasmus' mind begins to come together, piece by piece, offering clarity.

"Reluctantly, I convinced myself I could control him better than I could control you. His intellect and personality didn't intimidate me like yours did. I didn't feel inadequate around him as I often felt around you. I also believed his economic position was the safer path for me and the children I hoped to have."

Erasmus has a million questions but knows better than to interrupt the cascade of life-altering revelations.

"But, my love, my children and I later paid a heavy price for my poor judgment. I traded true love for a caretaker role," she laments.

"In the end, he was the only winner. By buying me, he pulled himself out of the lonely state of a divorced man who had never experienced a meaningful emotional connection," she asserts with sadness.

"I lived a miserable and unhappy life as a woman, longing for you all these years. Motherhood saved my sanity; my children filled my empty heart with joy. I poured myself into loving and raising them, giving them as normal a life as possible. Outwardly, I pretended everything was fine."

She pauses briefly, her tone darkening. "Before he became ill, he was already just an old man I cared for daily. Over time, my children saw through it. I began speaking openly about you and us—even in front of him. He despised it, reacting sarcastically, saying, 'What does it matter? I got you in the end.'"

Erasmus, now in a trance, reflects, *What Vic's daughter said last year in class about her mother marrying the man her family chose must have been Sarah parroting the family's official story*, he reasons.

"My children loved him like a distant relative," Victoria explains.

"There was no affection. I believe his children came only because of my persistence. He was never affectionate or close to them."

"How did you meet him?" Erasmus asks uneasily.

"He was my mother's psychiatrist. She insisted I see him when I turned eighteen, claiming I needed therapy for mood swings and bouts of depression," she recounts.

"After a month, he started asking me out for dinner. By the fifth month, he proposed to my parents. My mother immediately agreed, but my father was hesitant. Eventually, everyone ignored what I wanted."

She pauses again, the rising sun illuminating the vast ocean around them, creating a stunning backdrop to her revelations.

"Dear, after that scene, I left for Boston. Eventually, we met, and I didn't have contact with him again until I returned home three and a half years later," she continues.

"Poignantly, a long time later, when he was terminally ill, he confessed he'd been infatuated with my mother but knew she would never cheat on her husband."

"In a way, for him, having you was a twisted way of having your mother," Erasmus states aloud.

"Yes, and sadly, for her, it was the same—a twisted way of having him," she reveals.

Victoria pauses, the waves lapping at the shore echoing her turbulent emotions. "My doubts, anxieties, and insecurities drove me. My emotions were my undoing. This is simply the story of what happened."

Erasmus gazes at her for what seems like an eternity. Then, tenderly tightening his embrace under the cozy wool blanket, he whispers, "My lady, that beautiful sunrise is the announcement of a glorious new day. Don't you think it's time to move on?"

The soothing notes of Neil Diamond's "Hello" flow from their portable radio, signaling a renewed sense of life. They cuddle closer as the cool breeze picks up. Their teas, once warm, are now cold, a sharp contrast to their hearts, which glow with newfound warmth. Yet Erasmus notices lingering clouds in her eyes.

'More is to come,' he thinks, steady in his resolve. 'Whatever it is, I'll be ready.'

As he gently caresses Victoria's silky-smooth cheeks, the Platters' "Only You" begins to play. Standing together, their fingers entwine as they sway to the melody, their bodies impossibly close. Their satiated smiles exude peace, love, and joy, as the song's echoes envelop the nascent day.

Nantucket Island's Roads

Later that day, they pedal their way to the island's ferry, which will take them back to the mainland.

"What will be the subject of your class tomorrow, dear?" she asks curiously.

"Coherence."

"That is one anecdote I don't know about, right?"

"Right, it happened after I returned from Wales.

Royal Cambridge Scholastic Institute (2019)

(Next Day, University Backroads – on the way to the auditorium)

As he pedals steadily through the campus back roads, Professor Cromwell-Smith replays all the scenes Victoria described the day before, juxtaposing them with his own tribulations during that period of time.

Not long after, he walks into a packed auditorium, ready and eager to start.

"Good morning, everyone."

"Good morning, professor."

"At some point in time, hopefully sooner rather than later, we all must figure things out in life while looking for coherence. What do we want out of life? What does life mean to us? What is our purpose while we are here on our magnificent planet Earth? And one of the key existential tools that enable this examination is the glue that holds everything together so that things make sense in life. The glue is COHERENCE," affirms the eminent professor in his introductory remarks.

"When Victoria and I were living apart from each other, our lives were turned upside down. Today, I'll be taking you back to a day when I was handed an invaluable—lasting life lesson touching the subject of coherence."

"It begins like this …"

—✦—

Waldorf-Astoria Hotel, New York City (1977)

The coffee shop at the Waldorf-Astoria is packed with people from all over the world. Erasmus sips his customary and very British tea with milk while observing the potpourri of clothes, hats, faces, and bodily gestures.

"Erasmus, young man, what a pleasure it is to see you," exclaims the effusive Scottish antiquarian, Colin Carnegie, as he walks quickly toward him.

"Mr. Carnegie, it's so good to see you again."

"This time, it's just a short visit to the Big Apple," he says as he, quite fittingly, orders a hot tea with milk.

"Dear Erasmus, how have you been? Last time I saw you was at Cape Cod, at the New England Antiquarian Conference, where, as I understand it, you pulled a Houdini on all of us by vanishing in the middle of the night," quizzes and declares Mr. C., alluding to the famous escape artist.

"Mr. C., since I last saw you, I graduated from Harvard, went to Wales one last time, spent time with my family, and had a final and memorable session with my three mentors. Once back, I settled in Boston and accepted a teaching position at Brandeis University."

Carnegie stares at him in silence with a solemn smile.

"Extraordinary indeed. Congratulations, young man. But aren't you omitting something pertaining to your update?" states Mr. C., calling him out for deflecting the "escape stunt" aspect of his question.

Erasmus stares at Mr. C. with deeply saddened eyes.

"She is gone, Mr. C.!"

"She's obviously not here," states Carnegie while acknowledging within himself that, 'they were inseparable,' but there's firmness in his voice as if he's trying to get Erasmus to find courage.

"Unexpectedly, something quite transcendental must have happened, young man. This is the last thing I would've imagined. The two of you literally seemed like you were made for one another."

"My mentors back in Wales gifted me with a profound scribble named, 'the happiness formula.' It has been a great help to me in dealing with her absence, but I need your help on how to accept the loss."

"In moments like this, perhaps it's best to take a step back and contemplate things from a distance. I've got an idea. Come with me; let's take a stroll to my hallowed grounds while in New York," Mr. C announces as he signs the check.

They walk in pleasant weather, blended with the noisy background, through the streets of Manhattan. Erasmus pours out all his love, afflictions, and tribulations to the wise man from the Scottish Highlands. Time flies as they turn onto Fifth Avenue, and shortly thereafter, they enter the hall of the magnificent and timeless New York Public Library. As soon as they walk in, the plaque does not escape Erasmus. It's a dedication to the man who funded its construction and enabled its creation, Mr. C.'s distant relative, Andrew Carnegie.

'It figures, how fitting, right?' Erasmus mutters to himself.

'Where else would he have taken me other than here,' reflects Erasmus in admiration and with an almost imperceptible smile.

"Impressed?" asks Mr. C.

"Very much so, sir."

"Erasmus, always remember how many lasting good deeds this great Scottish American did and created with his wealth during his life."

"Always do, sir."

Mr. C. gets lost inside the library's magnificent Rose Room for a while until he finds exactly what he's looking for. Erasmus sees the energetic man walk back with an enormous, seemingly ancient leather-bound book.

"Erasmus, this is a timeless scribble about one of the most imperative, consequential, and existential tasks every one of us has to perform in life and one you're in desperate need of conducting as soon as possible," declares Mr. C. as he starts to read in earnest.

"Coherence"
(Figuring Things Out in Life)

Figuring things out in life
is to clearly define:
what we want out of life,
how we like to live,
who we chose to live with,
where are we heading,
what we believe in,

what we have a propensity for,

what we want to accomplish,

and what we intend to leave as our legacy.

Because, in the end,

we must seek and figure out

what life means to us.

Otherwise,

we wander through it

like lifeless souls

with empty spirits.

Figuring out life's meaning,

allows us to decipher and determine

our purpose and direction are in life.

Otherwise,

we bounce and drift aimlessly through life

like a rudderless vessel

or a craft without its compass.

Life's formula is different for each one of us.

The recipe of "How to Live"

is unique to every individual.

What makes sense for one, few, or many

may not make sense to others at all.

Thus, to avoid living someone else's life—

by copying their "sense-making"—

we must first figure out

what works for us,

then what works for others.

To figure things out in life,

we need coherence—

the glue that connects it all together.

Coherence is connecting in sensical harmony,

our existence with our aspirations and beliefs,

our actions with our dreams and goals,

our vocation, line of work, art or craft,

with our best talents and abilities,

our passions with mundane life,

our convictions and ideals

with what we practice in daily life,

our values and virtues with our faith,

our tempo with our life's clock,

our awareness of every second we have left on planet Earth,

our family, loved ones, fellow human beings

and the objects of our desire,

with the best side of our essence and nature.

To make sense of life

is to coherently connect

our life's meaning

with our life's purpose.

*

"Erasmus, coherence is the glue that creates sensical meaning and purpose in our lives; always remember, in order for us to resolve issues and figure things out, they have to make sense, and this is only possible through coherence."

Mr. Carnegie closes the leather-bound book with a decisive thud, its weight mirroring the gravity of his words. He places it gently on the table, his gaze locking with Erasmus's. "Now, young man, the rest is up to you," he says with a knowing smile, his voice tinged with a mix of encouragement and expectation. Erasmus nods slowly, the profound weight of the moment sinking in as he contemplates the wisdom just imparted.

The dim light of the Rose Room bathes them in an almost ethereal glow, as Erasmus watches Mr. Carnegie stride purposefully back into the labyrinth of bookshelves. Left alone with his thoughts, Erasmus lets the words linger, carving their place into his heart and mind.

— ❖ —

Royal Cambridge Scholastic Institute (2019)
(University Auditorium)

As his class comes back to the present, they find Professor Cromwell-Smith gazing intently at all of them.

The professor pauses, his eyes reflecting a depth of thought as he leans slightly against the lectern. "Mr. Carnegie's words stayed with me," he says, his voice softer now, almost reverent. "His insights on coherence became a compass, guiding me through some of my most challenging decisions." He straightens, his gaze sweeping across the room to meet the students' attentive faces. "Now, let us consider how we might apply such coherence in our own lives," he adds, drawing a contemplative silence over the class before continuing.

"So, what are you all waiting for?" he asks, his tone tinged with a hint of challenge.

Incredulous looks and surprised faces form and project themselves around the packed auditorium.

"Why don't you start figuring things out right away?" he presses, not letting the moment slip by.

"Now, I'd like to open the floor for questions." Professor Cromwell-Smith says, his tone inviting and warm. "Please feel free to ask anything related to the subjects we've covered today."

Charlotte, a fine arts major, known for her deep philosophical insights, raises her hand and is called upon.

"Professor, in the poem *Coherence*, the idea of connecting our aspirations with our beliefs and actions is emphasized. How do we reconcile the contradictions we sometimes experience between what we aspire to and what we practice daily? Can true coherence exist if our actions don't always align with our ideals?"

"An excellent question, Charlotte. The tension between our ideals and our actions is something many of us struggle with, and it's part of the human condition. In the poem, coherence is presented as the glue that holds all aspects of our life together. But it's important to recognize that coherence isn't about perfection; it's about striving for alignment. As we move through life, we must constantly reflect on our actions, learn from our mistakes, and adjust our behavior to better reflect our values. Coherence is an ongoing process, not a fixed state. It's the effort to make our lives and our actions as harmonious as possible with our beliefs, even if we fall short at times."

Benjamin, a journalism major, asks the next question.

"Professor, on a previous class, you spoke about the dual nature of adversity—how it presents both hardship and opportunity. From a psychological standpoint, how can we develop greater coherence in our lives when our emotional responses sometimes contradict our intellectual understanding of situations?"

"Benjamin, that's a fascinating question. The emotional and intellectual aspects of our lives don't always align, and this creates what we call cognitive dissonance. In psychology, one way to bring more coherence is through emotional regulation—learning to manage our emotional responses in a way that aligns with our intellectual understanding. It takes mindfulness, self-awareness, and practice. Over time, we can cultivate a sense of harmony by consciously working to bridge the gap between our emotions and rational thought, which is precisely what the poem refers to when it talks about connecting our actions, beliefs, and feelings."

Scarlett, a history major, is next.

"Professor, in *Coherence*, the idea of 'figuring things out in life' is central. You spoke about how coherence connects our existence with our aspirations and values. But sometimes, life presents us with challenges that shake our sense of coherence. How do we restore it when it feels like we've lost our way?"

"That's an insightful question, Scarlett. Life's challenges are often the tests that challenge our coherence—when we feel uncertain, adrift, or disconnected. The poem suggests that coherence is about harmonizing our inner and outer worlds, but when things become unbalanced, we need to return to our values and aspirations. It's about re-centering, reassessing where we've gone off-course, and realigning ourselves with our purpose. When we feel lost, it's often a sign that we've strayed from our core values, so restoring coherence is about taking a step back, reflecting, and making intentional choices to reconnect with what truly matters to us."

Sebastian, an Education major, speaks up next.

"Professor, the poem emphasizes the importance of coherence in making sense of life, but sometimes we're faced with contradictions that challenge that sense. How do we deal with situations where the alignment between our beliefs and actions seems impossible to reconcile? Is it a matter of making compromises, or do we need to revise our beliefs entirely?"

"Another very thoughtful question, Sebastian. In life, contradictions are inevitable—no matter how hard we try to maintain coherence, sometimes our circumstances or actions lead us into conflict with our ideals. The key is to approach this with humility and awareness. It's not about perfection, but about progress. If the alignment between our beliefs and actions feels impossible, we may need to reassess our priorities, reflect on whether our beliefs are still serving us, or whether a shift in perspective is needed. Making compromises can be part of the process, but only if those compromises don't undermine our core values. The goal is to navigate life with intention, and when necessary, to make adjustments that preserve our integrity."

"That will be all for today. I'll see you all next week," Professor Cromwell-Smith concludes, his words lingering like echoes of wisdom. He observes the expressions across the student body morphing into the curious looks of explorers about to embark on journeys into uncharted waters.

As the students rise and file out of the auditorium, he hands each of them a copy of the happiness formula, his gesture filled with quiet hope for their journeys ahead.

As the last of his students exit the auditorium, their murmured conversations fading into the corridor beyond, Professor Cromwell-Smith lingers at the lectern, gazing out over the now-empty seats. The silence feels heavier, more contemplative, after the depth of their shared discussion. Gathering his notes and adjusting his glasses, he allows himself a rare moment of reflection. The echoes of the past and present intertwine, and he silently wonders which seeds of wisdom, if any, have found fertile ground among his students.

Man's endless search for meaning and purpose in life. We all need to figure these two things out first, he reflects, recalling the poignant words of the eminent Holocaust survivor Viktor Frankl.

Straightening his posture, he walks toward the door, his mind already preparing for the next lecture—a chance to explore life's complexities further and, perhaps, to inspire a few more hearts.

Stepping out of the faculty building, his eyes fall on his trusted old bike, ready and waiting for the next journey.

Chapter 3

Virtue

Royal Cambridge Scholastic Institute (2019)
(Sunday Morning, Campus Backwoods)

Erasmus and Victoria meander through the trees, holding hands. His grip is resolute as he strives to make her feel safe and sheltered by his presence. But, above all, he wants her to sense that she is no longer alone.

'Last weekend's shared revelations at Nantucket Island were not her last,' he reminds himself as she leans closer to him while they stroll.

The river emerges into view through the foliage, and a fresh breeze whispers through the treetops. A small clearing reveals itself, and Victoria proclaims it an ideal spot to set up their picnic lunch.

Seated and laughing, the middle-aged couple reminisces about Erasmus' latest absentminded mishap. This one infuriated half the faculty as he introduced six of his colleagues attending one of his classes as his fellow professors visiting from Brandeis University— despite having left that venerable institution decades ago.

Right in the middle of her laughter, he notices something. Behind her broad, radiant smile, he discerns a pair of cloudy, solemn eyes.

'Deadly serious they are indeed,' he murmurs in anticipation.

Abruptly, they lock eyes, and she knows he has perfectly deciphered her mood.

'Here we go,' he realizes, bracing himself for her "previous life" dam-bursting exercise.

"Dear, there are still parts of my history that I want to share with you," she declares.

"I know, my lady. Do it at your own pace," he assures her gently, his tone receptive and steady.

"Well, I'm in a hurry, rushing because I feel open and comfortable sharing it with you right now. I also want to put it behind us," Victoria reasons aloud.

"As you wish, my lady. I'm all yours," he replies, smiling and kissing her softly on her lips.

"Well, let me take you back to a crucial moment when an old librarian imparted one of the most profound life lessons I have ever received. This lesson may very well be the reason we found each other again," she says, her words deliberate and weighty.

"It begins like this…

— ✤ —

For almost two decades after I got married, I had been living in Hamilton, Illinois, just across the river from St. Louis, Missouri. On this momentous day, I was supposed to drop off one of my daughters at her college before driving across town to teach a class at the university."

St. Louis, Missouri (1998)

(Mississippi River Bridge, crossing from Illinois to Missouri)

"Mom, I overheard the entire discussion," states Elizabeth, Victoria's 18-year-old daughter.

An eerie silence envelops mother and daughter as they drive through heavy rain across the Mississippi River into St. Louis' city center.

"Your father can be difficult at times, dear," Victoria replies softly. Victoria's oldest daughter is restless and conflicted. She yearns to speak her mind but respects her mother too much to unleash her full frustration.

"Petulant," Elizabeth blurts out impulsively.

Victoria flinches slightly, taken aback, yet she hesitates to respond with anything but love.

"He loves you all very much," Victoria tries to reassure her daughter again, her tone calm yet strained.

"How do you put up with him?" questions Elizabeth, her restraint breaking as her emotions spill over.

"Family always comes first, Elizabeth," Victoria pleads, but the hollowness of her words does not escape either of them.

"Mother, stop deflecting. Don't you think this is a conversation we need to have?" demands Elizabeth, her voice resolute and insistent.

Tension builds in the family van, the air thick with countless unspoken truths. Visibility is almost nonexistent, and the relentless rain reduces their progress to a slow crawl.

"You're absolutely right," Victoria admits after a pause. "Perhaps this is an excellent opportunity to do something I've wanted to do for a long time. You still have a couple of hours before your class begins; mine is three hours away. I'm taking you to a very special place where we can sit down and talk about anything you want."

St. Louis Public Library (1998)
(Downtown Area)

After so many years, the old habit persists. Every other week, Victoria visits one of the three librarians in the city. Over the years, they've all become close friends and, in a way, life mentors. Today, for the first time, she isn't visiting alone.

The head of the City of St. Louis' public library, Rebecca Samuels-Ortiz, is a 65-year-old dynamo of energy. With over three decades of experience at the library, she has practically adopted Victoria since they met about a decade ago. At a glance, Rebecca immediately senses Victoria's distress as she approaches, a young woman walking alongside her.

'Another clash with the mind doctor?' Rebecca muses. Then, the striking resemblance between Victoria and the young woman captures her attention.

The two women embrace warmly while young Elizabeth stands by, observing. She feels like she's stepping into a private world her mother has carefully guarded.

"Becca, this is my oldest, Elizabeth," says Victoria, pulling her daughter closer with one arm.

"Dear, Rebecca has been a close friend, mentor, counselor, and crying shoulder of mine for more than a decade," she adds, introducing Elizabeth to the effusive librarian.

Elizabeth and Rebecca exchange a hug. Rebecca, in the purest French tradition, kisses the surprised teenager on both cheeks.

"Your mom has told me so much about you," Rebecca declares warmly.

'Well, she hasn't told me a word about you,' Elizabeth thinks to herself, her skepticism rising.

'Besides, weren't we supposed to have a serious conversation about family matters?' she silently quibbles.

"Nice to meet you," Elizabeth says, outwardly polite but inwardly uneasy.

"The pleasure is mine," Rebecca responds with a welcoming smile.

Elizabeth nods back, her smile warmer than her growing discomfort allows.

Rebecca guides them across the library's main hall to a massive work and reading table. Seated at one corner, Rebecca and Elizabeth exchange subtle, inquisitive glances, as if sizing each other up.

"Victoria, for you to bring your precious daughter here is a remarkable step in the right direction," Rebecca states with conviction. "It's a step toward confronting reality, opening up, and making long-overdue decisions."

Elizabeth's frustration bubbles to the surface. "What are we doing here? I specifically asked Mom for a conversation about serious family matters," she blurts out.

Rebecca, unfazed, continues, her tone soothing yet firm. "But you brought Elizabeth here for a reason, didn't you?"

Victoria's tumultuous gaze mirrors her uncertainty, and Elizabeth is startled by Rebecca's insight. She turns to the older woman, her expression a mix of surprise and curiosity.

"Elizabeth, there are many significant things about your mom's life that you don't know. Some are painful, but many are wonderful," Rebecca begins gently. "You must be patient and allow her to open up at her own pace. Whatever she's ready to share, she will, in her own time. Bringing you here today was a transformative step for her—something she's long meant to do and worked hard to accomplish."

Elizabeth's anger softens as Rebecca's words resonate.

"Thank you for helping me understand," Victoria whispers, her eyes glistening with gratitude as she looks at Rebecca.

Mother and daughter embrace tightly, their bond deepened by the moment.

"Love you so much, Mom," Elizabeth says joyfully.

"Love you too, dear. Love you too," Victoria replies, her voice brimming with relief.

"Victoria, seize the moment. What you've been dreaming of for so long has finally happened," Rebecca declares.

Victoria's eyes widen in intensity, her exhaustion giving way to determination.

"Boston University has offered you a position—it's time for you to pursue your dreams and...find him," Rebecca says with finality.

"I'll be right back," she adds, stepping away to attend to some inquiring visitors.

'Boston? What's going on? Has my mother gone completely crazy?' Elizabeth wonders, her thoughts swirling in a storm of confusion and uncertainty.

"Find who, Mom?" Elizabeth asks, consumed by angst.

Victoria gently presses a finger to Elizabeth's lips.

"All in due time, dear."

Mrs. Samuels-Ortiz strides back with quick steps, a smile brightening her face.

"Elizabeth, be open and understanding with your mom. On this occasion, your best attributes must come to the forefront—tolerance, forgiveness, perseverance, and hope. They are all required of you now," Mrs. Samuels-Ortiz states as an overture.

The erudite librarian fixes her gaze on Victoria for what feels like an eternity. The moment has come to share what they've rehearsed so many times before. Finally, Victoria closes her eyes slowly and nods in consent. Mrs. Samuels-Ortiz then recounts to Elizabeth the story of her mother's love for Erasmus, their breakup, and the circumstances of her marriage to her father. Elizabeth sits motionless, her blank stare seeming to bore into a void as she absorbs and processes the revelations.

"Mom, why did you marry Dad if you didn't love him?" she asks insistently and continues without waiting for a reply. "The two of you are so different; you never agree on anything. Age-wise, he could be your father," Elizabeth admonishes.

Victoria's world spins as if it's careening out of control, her daughter's mature words slicing through her carefully maintained composure. But life begins to smile upon her for the good deeds she has done over the years and the amends she has sought to make in her pursuit of happiness.

"Mother, then there's all his philandering with patients. How long are you going to put up with it?"

Elizabeth's words are harsh, but Victoria finds great relief in the realization that her daughter is solidly on her side.

"Are you one of his conquests as well?" Elizabeth presses relentlessly. "And what's going on between Grandma and Dad? She adores him, but in a sick kind of way, Mom. If she weren't my grandmother, I would swear she has the hots for him," declares an even more outraged Elizabeth.

Victoria's emotional walls crumble, and she starts to sob intermittently, unsure of how to respond. Her face is soaked in tears as Elizabeth continues.

"Mom, we can do this another time," Elizabeth offers with concern, guilt, and understanding, gently caressing her mom's tear-streaked face.

"Aren't you mad at me?" Victoria asks.

"How could I be? I'm happy you truly do love someone because you don't love Dad."

"Elizabeth, perhaps the most important thing I should add to your perceptive observations is that what your father did professionally— acting as your mom's psychiatrist—was wrong. He exploited a

young, vulnerable woman and manipulated both your grandmother and your mom into a situation that nearly destroyed your mom's life," adds Mrs. Samuels-Ortiz.

Elizabeth remains composed, unshaken by the details that have haunted Victoria and Mrs. Samuels-Ortiz for so long. The reason is simple—she already knows much of it. What consumes her mind is one thing—her father's outrageous behavior.

"Mom, you never mentioned his philandering before," Elizabeth declares.

"Call me a fool or naïve, but perhaps it's because I don't love him, so I don't care. But it's mortifying that you, my child, are calling me out. We, as parents, fool ourselves endlessly, believing that our kids don't notice or understand the things we try to hide. How wrong we are. You see it all. You record everything. You even understand things, like this, better than we do. I've come to realize that every word, action, and display that affects our loved ones carries consequences, lying in wait in the future, inexorably catching up with us," Victoria capitulates in surrender.

"Victoria, it's clear that for some time now, your children have understood your situation. Elizabeth's words show they believe you've known all about the mind doctor's behavior and have intentionally looked the other way," intervenes Mrs. Samuels-Ortiz to expose the deeper truth.

Mother and daughter clasp hands, contemplating the erudite librarian before embracing each other tightly, as if holding on for dear life.

As they prepare to leave, Mrs. Samuels-Ortiz interjects with one final reminder.

"Just to remind you, Victoria, Boston University requires your reply right away. Do I have your authorization to give them an affirmative response?"

"Of course you do, Becca. Nothing and no one in the world will stop me from moving to Boston," Victoria asserts with conviction and finality, despite having no assurance of her husband's stance on the matter.

The old librarian beams with satisfaction, knowing her persistent efforts haven't been in vain. Victoria would never have confronted this issue on her own; she needed the steady push from her trusted friend.

As Mrs. Samuels-Ortiz waves them off, she watches the mother and daughter walk away, pride swelling in her heart. In this one encounter, she has fulfilled two long-standing missions—Victoria has finally shared her story with her children and taken the decisive step to move back to Boston in search of her true love.

— ✦ —

Royal Cambridge Scholastic Institute (2019)
(Picnic in the woods, by the riverside)

"Dear, Mrs. Samuels-Ortiz shared a wonderful ancient scribble with us that day. Its contents not only profoundly moved Elizabeth and me but also fortified my resolve, giving me the strength to make the decisions I eventually took to move closer to you. I would like you to share this with your class if you think it's appropriate," Victoria implores, pulling a small scroll from the picnic basket and offering it to him.

"What is it about?" Erasmus inquires while carefully unfolding it.

"Virtue," she replies with a quiet conviction.

Royal Cambridge Scholastic Institute (2019)
(Campus streets, the next day)

Professor Cromwell-Smith has been pedaling for almost an hour, weaving through the silent, empty campus roads. He's still absorbing everything he learned about Victoria's life, replaying the revelations and their impact on both of them. To his great relief, the previous night, Victoria slept soundly and woke up with a sunny disposition that warmed his heart.

With a lingering sense of fulfillment from their quiet morning together, Erasmus slowly makes his way to campus, the weight of their shared moments guiding him to class. His mind is alight with thoughts of the conversation ahead, eager yet reflective.

It's working, he muses with a soft smile, recognizing that she's steadily putting much of the emotional trauma behind her.

'Nothing compares to the companionship of love for overcoming pain and sorrow,' he reasons, his thoughts carrying him as he parks his old, rusty bike in the faculty parking lot.

Walking through the halls, the morning air feels especially invigorating. He's inspired in an extraordinary way. His admiration for Victoria swells—not just for how she has navigated her life following what he considers a monumental gaffe of existential proportions, but for the way she is now courageously reconstructing her future. She's confronting her past head-on, without glossing over any part of her personal history.

It's a rare and profound kind of bravery, and he treasures it deeply.

Royal Cambridge Scholastic Institute (2019)
(University's Auditorium)

As he enters the classroom, the familiar hum of students' voices brings him back to the present, grounding him in the purpose of the day. Erasmus glances over the eager faces, each student ready to engage with the new subject matter that awaits them.

"Good morning, everyone," he greets with a big, wide smile.

"Good morning, professor," the class roars back in unison.

"Today, we're going to be talking about virtue. I'll take you back to a pivotal moment when Victoria and her oldest daughter were given a timeless life lesson—one that helped them make crucial decisions that changed the course of their lives. These experiences, I believe, were instrumental in leading to our eventual reunion."

He pauses, letting the weight of his words settle over the room, before continuing, his voice calm and deliberate.

"It begins like this ..."

— ✦ —

St. Louis Public Library (1998)

Rebecca Samuels-Ortiz has been the head of the St. Louis Public Library for decades. The erudite librarian has served as Victoria's friend and life mentor for over a decade. On this momentous day, Victoria has brought her oldest daughter, 18-year-old Elizabeth, to meet Mrs. Samuels-Ortiz for the first time. It is a day to remember, as Victoria has made the monumental decision to move back to Boston with her family.

Mrs. Samuels-Ortiz, ever attuned to the gravity of the moment, retrieves a cherished manuscript. Her eyes sparkle with anticipation as she addresses the two women before her.

"Ladies, I have here a precious scribble—timeless wisdom that perfectly suits this occasion, especially as you prepare for such an eventful transition," she announces warmly, her tone a blend of solemnity and enthusiasm.

She carefully unfolds the manuscript and begins to read, her voice soft and resonant, espousing love and empathy with every word.

"Virtue"

Just by arriving on planet Earth,

just by being alive,

we are born in grace—

but we are not born in virtue.

Virtue must be acquired over time,

through hard work, dedication and perseverance.

Virtues are not obsequious.

On the contrary,

they must be:

learned and applied,

sought and sweated,

identified and pursued,

nurtured and harvested,

cultivated with discipline,

and developed with sacrifice.

We acquire knowledge

to gain insight, wisdom, and good judgment.

We build brave hearts and fortitude

to nurture courage, tenacity, and valor.

We practice compassion and benevolence

to learn empathy and mindfulness

which perennially results in loving mankind.

We exercise unwavering truthfulness

and unflinching integrity

to cement our honesty, honor, probity, and a good name.

We embrace serenity and silence

to pause, reflect

and become considerate, and thoughtful.

We live with order and neatness

to grow structured, methodical, and organized.

We pursue righteousness and rightfulness

to attain fairness, correctness, and impartiality.

We embody unfaltering hope, boundless generosity,

endless gratitude, and genuine humility

seeking to exceed and surpass

all we have received,

forming our legacy from it.

As our virtues grow,

they mature into a state of noble excellence.

As they evolve,

virtues become the genesis

and enablers of our beliefs and value systems.

Virtues are imperative tools of life,

without chasing and procuring them,

we are incomplete—

not fully functional, coherent, or guided.

Without virtues,

we march through life with blinders on,

unable to extract the fruits of joy

from a life lived in full.

Our virtues form the foundation of our values,

which, in turn,

become the pillars of our character.

Without a solid set of virtues,

our values are incomplete or flawed,

causing seismic faults in our character.

To be virtuous is to be equipped

with a precious set of attributes,

leading us to excellence.

It is to conduct ourselves

by extraordinary standards of nobility,

righteousness, sensibility, and rightfulness.

It is to live under the mantle of inspiration and joy,

guided by a virtuous existence—

a life in full.

*

Mrs. Samuels-Ortiz folds the manuscript gently, the faint rustle of the pages breaking the silence. She looks at Victoria and Elizabeth, her eyes filled with both hope and seriousness. "Victoria, this move marks a new chapter for you and your family. Carry these words with you as a guide, not just for yourself, but for your children as they forge their paths." She offers Elizabeth a warm, knowing smile.

The young woman nods thoughtfully, her mother reaching for her hand in a silent gesture of unity. The atmosphere is thick with unspoken emotions as Mrs. Samuels-Ortiz places the manuscript back in its protective sleeve. For a moment, no one speaks, the weight of the moment hanging gently in the room.

"I'll cherish these words, Rebecca," Victoria says at last, her voice steady but tinged with emotion. The three women share a brief embrace, one that seems to acknowledge the significance of the moment without the need for further explanation.

— ✦ —

Royal Cambridge Scholastic Institute (2019)
(University's Auditorium)

Professor Cromwell brings the class back to the present with an expression of absolute calm and tranquility. The pedagogue gazes across the room, his students silent and attentive. He lets the moment linger before speaking.

With Victoria's voice still resonating in his mind, the pedagogue feels a gentle pull towards the past. In his reflection, he finds himself transported back to that pivotal moment in St. Louis, where her history had intersected with her future.

"Class, virtuosity is only achieved by deliberate and disciplined effort over a prolonged period of time," he concludes, his words imbued with wisdom. His piercing gaze seems to connect with each of his elated students, leaving a profound impression.

"Now, I'd like to open the floor for questions," Professor Cromwell-Smith says, his tone inviting and warm. "Please feel free to ask anything related to the subjects we've covered today."

Amelia, a performing arts major, raises her hand and is called upon.

"Professor, in the poem *Virtue*, the idea of acquiring virtue through hard work and perseverance is emphasized. How do we reconcile the tension between the virtues we aspire to embody and the imperfections we experience in our daily lives? How do we navigate moments when our actions don't align with our aspirations?"

"Amelia, that's a profound question. The pursuit of virtue requires a continuous effort to align our ideals with our actions. Virtue is something we build over time, but as you've noted, there are moments when our actions don't reflect the virtues we strive for. This is the challenge of being human: we're constantly working to align who we are with who we want to be. In the poem, we see that virtue is not an innate trait but something we must actively cultivate through effort, discipline, and reflection. It's important to acknowledge that perfection isn't required—virtue is about striving, and in moments when our actions don't align with our aspirations, the key is to learn from those moments and keep pushing forward."

James, a Psychology major, asks the next question.

"Professor, in the context of virtue, how do we approach the emotional and cognitive challenges we face when trying to embody virtues such as compassion or courage? For instance, how do we remain compassionate when we feel emotionally drained, or how do we summon courage when fear seems overwhelming?"

"James, that's a great question. The challenge of embodying virtues, especially in the face of emotional or cognitive dissonance, is part of the human experience. In those moments, it's important to remember that virtue isn't about always feeling the right way—it's about taking action in alignment with our values, even when emotions are challenging. For instance, compassion isn't just about feeling empathy but about actively choosing to extend care, even when we're tired or overwhelmed. Similarly, courage isn't the absence of fear, but the willingness to act in spite of it. Over time, as we practice these virtues, they become more ingrained in our character. But, like all virtues, they require conscious effort and a willingness to continue cultivating them, even when it's difficult."

Daisy, a philosophy major, asks her question next.

"Professor, the poem suggests that virtues are the foundation of character, yet the process of developing them is a long and demanding one. How can we, as individuals, maintain motivation and resilience in the pursuit of virtue, especially when the results may not be immediately visible?"

"Daisy, that's an excellent point. The journey toward virtue is indeed long and sometimes grueling. It's easy to lose motivation when the results are not immediately apparent. One of the key ideas in the poem is that virtues don't just appear overnight—they are cultivated through consistent effort and practice. The best way to maintain motivation is to recognize that the process itself is a part of the reward. Virtue isn't just about the end result; it's about who we become along the way. Even small, incremental steps towards embodying virtue are valuable. It's also helpful to remind ourselves of the bigger picture—how living a virtuous life brings meaning, purpose, and coherence to our existence. In those moments of doubt, reflecting on our 'why'—the deeper purpose behind pursuing virtue—can reignite our resolve."

Henry, a creative writing major, speaks up next.

"Professor, the poem emphasizes that virtue is something we must actively pursue and cultivate over time. Given the current challenges and complexities of our world, how do we ensure that the virtues we develop are meaningful in the context of our modern lives? How can we navigate the often-overwhelming nature of modern existence while still prioritizing the cultivation of virtue?"

"Henry, that's a very relevant question. The modern world can be overwhelming, and it often seems like the pace of life makes it difficult to focus on the deeper aspects of our existence, such as cultivating virtue. However, it's precisely in such a world that the pursuit of virtue becomes even more essential. In the poem, we see that virtues are not just abstract ideals; they are the foundation of a meaningful and coherent life. Even in the chaos of modern existence, we can make choices that align with our values. The key is to remain intentional and mindful in our actions—whether it's taking time to reflect, practicing compassion, or maintaining integrity in our work and relationships. In a world filled with distractions, it's easy to lose sight of what truly matters. But by prioritizing the cultivation of virtue, we give ourselves the clarity and strength to navigate the complexities of life with purpose and meaning."

"That will be all for today. I'll see you all next week," Professor Cromwell-Smith concludes, his words lingering like echoes of wisdom. As the students rise and file out of the auditorium, he hands each of them a copy of the happiness formula, his gesture filled with quiet hope for their journeys ahead.

As the bell rings, the students slowly gather their belongings and file out of the auditorium, their faces marked with contemplation. Professor Cromwell-Smith gathers his notes, pausing briefly as he looks out at the now-empty hall. He allows himself a quiet smile, knowing that the words of *Virtue* will echo far beyond this classroom, shaping lives in ways that might only become evident in the years to come.

As the last of his students exit the auditorium, their murmured conversations fading into the corridor beyond, Professor Cromwell-Smith lingers at the lectern, gazing out over the now-empty seats. The silence feels heavier, more contemplative, after the depth of their shared discussion. Gathering his notes and adjusting his glasses, he allows himself a rare moment of reflection. The echoes of the past and present intertwine, and he silently wonders which seeds of wisdom, if any, have found fertile ground among his students.

Straightening his posture, he walks toward the door, his mind already preparing for the next lecture—a chance to explore life's complexities further and, perhaps, to inspire a few more hearts. The professor hurries out of the auditorium with a subtle knot in his stomach. As he departs, he notices the rapt expressions of many students, their faces etched with curiosity and a hunger for further understanding.

There's no path to virtuosity without a preceding stage of self-discovery, he reflects as he steps out of the faculty building, silently wishing that his students would undertake such an introspective journey.

As he approaches the parking lot, his eyes catch sight of Victoria waiting with their bikes. Relief washes over him, and he slows his pace, a broad smile spreading across his face as he takes in the sight of her.

"I'm right here, you old fool," she says playfully, her voice overflowing with affection and a deep understanding of him.

"I just rushed to make sure you were safe," he replies, attempting to justify his now-spent hurriedness.

"Time to go home, my demented Brit."

"Yes, my lady, your whims are my command," he responds with mock chivalry, his grin widening.

As the couple pedals away side by side, a group of students notices them and begins to comment.

"They look like a pair of teenagers, madly crazy in love," one observes, her voice tinged with admiration.

"They have to be," a tall young woman interjects thoughtfully. "After all, they're making up for so much lost time—a lifetime spent apart. What else would you expect?"

"My take," another student adds, "is that maybe we should try to be more like them all the time, not just when we're trying to make up for lost time."

Chapter 4

Forgiveness

Salisbury Beach, Massachusetts (2019)

Those seabirds sometimes replace the whistling sounds of the autumn wind. The air feels infused with the briny aroma of unspoiled marine life. The sands of the wide beach swallow their feet with every step they take. With his arm wrapped securely around her shoulders and hers snugly around his waist, they walk endlessly against the fading light, as if lost in their own intimate sunset.

Their weekend escapades feel second nature to them, an unbroken thread from their youthful days to their rekindled love. Erasmus senses the unspoken tension building within Victoria. Her eyes, though often warm and reflective, betray a lingering unease. Her hesitation is palpable, but her resolve quietly prevails.

"Dear, one more event happened right after my youngest child, Sarah, found you," Victoria begins, her voice tinged with gravity

"It was one of the most difficult moments I've ever faced with any of my children. But it needed to happen. I hadn't moved in with you yet. One morning, Sarah came into my bedroom and simply let out everything she had been holding inside," she says, her words weighed by the memory.

"It began like this ..."

—◆—

Victoria Emerson-Lloyd, Family Home (2017)
(Boston, Massachusetts)

"Mom, this may surprise you because I've always wholeheartedly supported your re-encounter with Professor Cromwell, but it wasn't like that initially. When the three of us decided to go and look for him, I was the only one who hesitated a little, but not for long. Later, when I finally met him as my teacher, the whole experience was amazing. The feelings that made me hesitate originally just disappeared," Sarah declares, her voice quivering slightly yet firm with conviction.

Victoria sits motionless, absorbing her daughter's words.

Sarah, usually so spirited and light-hearted, has never spoken with such solemnity.

"Mother, this may be a simplistic way of looking at things—after all, I am only a teenager—but your love life reminds me of a movie I adore," she ventures, laying the groundwork for her thoughts.

"As in The Vow, at some point in your life, you broke away from what you were supposed to be in life—another unhappily married career woman, raised in an environment where appearances and wealth trumped everything, and love was a rational decision of convenience. But at some point, you were brave and bold enough to leave home, abandon your prescribed career, and set out to pursue what you were meant to be. Life smiled at you, and true love found you. Unfortunately, when life-altering decisions came your way, you ran away and literally had an attack of complete denial. You seemed

to have forgotten all you had loved and enjoyed while on your own—being your true self under the mantle of true love. You erased the important little things: the endless gestures, the intensity, and the magnificence of a well-lived life. It all simply vanished. You replaced history with an alternate reality—a complete fiction of your imagination. Sadly, you returned to your old ways and, for a while, tried once more to be what your family and social environment expected of you—what you were 'supposed' to be all along. Of course, by doing so, you ran yourself off an emotional cliff, almost destroying your life until you snapped out of it and went back to your true love. You were so fortunate to find him again because, Mom, I'm a diehard fan of Professor Cromwell-Smith," Sarah concludes passionately, her words tumbling out like a torrent.

The stillness in the room is palpable, amplifying every breath and every movement. Victoria begins to cry softly, her arms crossed as she gently rocks herself.

"Enough," interrupts Elizabeth, Victoria's eldest daughter, entering the room and wrapping her arms protectively around her mother.

"No, dear. Let her be. She's right, you know," Victoria counters gently, pushing Elizabeth aside with care.

She approaches Sarah, who sits huddled on the sofa, her face buried in her hands. Kneeling in front of her, Victoria tenderly places her hands on Sarah's head, smoothing her hair with loving strokes.

"Look at me, dear," Victoria whispers, her voice firm yet overflowing with love. At first, Sarah peeks through her fingers *hesitantly, but her eyes widen in surprise as they meet her mother's gaze—brimming with acceptance and warmth.*

"What you've just released, vented, is essentially all true. You've seen through me in a way I would've never imagined. Dear, I work hard every single day to make amends for the bad choices I've made. I also promise to keep pushing forward until we can all leave the past behind us," Victoria says with conviction, her voice steady even as her eyes glisten with unshed tears.

Mother and daughter embrace tightly, their connection renewed as if an immense barrier has been shattered. In their union, the weight of guilt and misunderstanding begins to lift, leaving room for healing and hope.

— ✦ —

Salisbury Beach, Massachusetts (2019)

Night has set in, and a full moon shows the way for Erasmus and Victoria.

"My lady, your daughter was a bit too harsh on you. I can understand why she felt that way, and I don't excuse your actions, but she ignored your circumstances," states a solemn Erasmus.

"Dear, you know what? She wanted to hold me accountable and for me to take some responsibility instead of deflecting everything on her dad. And she was right in pointing that out to me because it gave me the courage and determination to share everything with you in the last few weeks," says Victoria with a relieved, big, broad smile.

"But the most beautiful thing coming out of that conversation with Sarah is that she adores you, my absentminded Brit."

Victoria celebrates by laughing and kissing Erasmus all over his face.

"My lady, let me suggest something to you. Tomorrow in class, I'll take everyone to a moment when I received a great life lesson about forgiveness. Please join me as I'm certain it'll be of great help to us, and hopefully, once and for all, we'll put closure to the open wounds about our broken past that still linger," pleads Erasmus.

"I'll bring Sarah along. I'm sure it'll also be helpful for her," Victoria enthusiastically declares.

The moment she hears the unmistakable, inseparable tune coming out of their battered radio, it triggers her feelings; she looks at him with inviting eyes.

"Aren't you going to ask me to dance?" she sweetly asks as the contagious slow dance rhythm of Aretha Franklin's "Giving Him Something He Can Feel" can be heard softly in the background as it makes its way through the star-studded sky and silver-lined blackness of the dormant ocean. Faraway in their own bubble of love, impossibly paused, they dance under the mantle of a radiant New England night.

Royal Cambridge Scholastic Institute (2019)
(Next Day, University Auditorium)

As Erasmus pedals through the quiet, misty streets of the campus, his mind shifts from the peaceful morning he shared with Victoria to the task ahead—teaching the concept of forgiveness. With each turn of the pedals, he is reminded of the lessons he himself has learned in the past few weeks and how they will guide today's class. The journey, though familiar, feels different today; it is not just the route he is taking to class but also the path he is walking emotionally.

Erasmus reaches the university auditorium, the familiar building now filled with the quiet hum of students settling in for class. His footsteps echo through the hall as he enters, his heart still stirred by his earlier conversation with Victoria. As he walks towards the lectern, he reflects on how much he has grown, and how today's lesson will hopefully guide his students toward the same healing he has found. He smiles briefly, nodding to a few familiar faces in the front row before he begins.

"How's everyone today?" asks the professor.

"Insanely awesome," is the collective response.

The class buzz sounds more like a murmur as everyone notices the presence of Victoria and her youngest daughter, Sarah, sitting on a couple of chairs provided by the professor.

"Forgiveness," Erasmus begins, his voice steady but filled with the depth of the experience he's shared, "is not merely a concept we learn about—it is a practice, an essential part of life that allows us to move forward." He pauses, letting the weight of the word settle in the room. "It is also one of the most challenging virtues we can cultivate, but it is the one that opens doors to healing and peace." His gaze sweeps the room, meeting the eyes of his students.

"Our willingness and ability to forgive are crucial elements of a happy and wholesome life," the professor declares.

"Holding grudges, resentment or ill feelings against others sends us in the opposite direction, disconnecting our gratefulness and indulgence for the privilege of being alive," he continues.

"Today, I'll be taking you back to a moment in my life when I learned the true meaning of forgiveness. A remarkable reunion with a very influential person in my life. That day, she provided me with the type of understanding I needed and a lifelong lesson about the existential virtue of forgiveness. It begins like this …"

— ✦ —

Boston (1979)

He doesn't know if it's a curse or a blessing that he has a few free summer weeks before the commencement of his teaching career. He prefers not to revisit any places he and Victoria frequented, nor is he inclined to meet with the antiquarians they had previously visited. To keep himself occupied, he starts to write—first a diary, then essays, short stories, and poems. Soon, he's toying with the idea of writing a novel. As the days pass, some of his emotional roadblocks begin to fade. That's how the idea of visiting one of his most trusted mentors takes shape and evolves until he finds himself on his way to see her.

Train Ride from Boston to Lanesville, Massachusetts (1979)

Leaving Boston's central station early, he's inundated with mixed emotions as the train carries him to Lanesville. The ride through the magnificent countryside stirs memories of Victoria—their bikes in tow, the picnic baskets, the overnight stays at bed-and-breakfasts, and particularly their visits with Mrs. Peabody, the ebullient antiquarian. His thoughts play like a movie, scene by scene, including every dialogue he and Victoria had shared with her. He recalls the last set of poems Mrs. Peabody sent to Victoria and how much they had both cherished them.

Lanesville, Massachusetts (1979)
(Mrs. Peabody's Antique Book Shop)

The quaint train station at Lanesville reinforces the feeling of nostalgia. After leaving the station, he pedals along the New England coast's shoreline road, looking forward to meeting his trusted mentor and friend. However, a little while later, he's disappointed—the shop seems empty as he steps inside the vast and chaotic space. After searching the store in vain, Erasmus sits, waits, and being his usual self, when not occupied with either mind or body, promptly falls soundly asleep!

He dreams of faraway places, traveling in search of Victoria, only to be turned away each time by cruel strangers who refuse to reveal her whereabouts. The intruding sound begins faintly, far off, and repeats every few seconds until it finally pulls him from his deep sleep. Slowly, he opens his eyes.

"It seems as if a full orchestra is needed to wake your highness up," an amused Mrs. Peabody announces.

Still groggy, Erasmus smiles warmly.

"I step out for a few minutes to get myself some breakfast, and voila, I find an intruder, a little bear, snoozing in my shop," she says in jest.

"Well, it's to be expected if Mama Bear leaves her shop unlocked when she's out of town; it shouldn't be a surprise, right?"

"The advantage of small-town living, young Erasmus, but you urbanites wouldn't understand that, right?" she teases, immediately realizing her mistake.

"Oops, I forgot you're a country boy as well," she adds, smiling along with him. But his sad eyes give away something deeper.

"Dearest young man, I know you're going through a hard time with what has happened between Victoria and you. I've corresponded with your steadfast advocate, Mrs. V, who is back in Wales. I've also consulted with a few of your small legion of antiquarian followers here in New England," she says, her tone softening.

"Mrs. P., I'm struggling to keep my head and heart free of anger or resentment. I only want to preserve the good memories, but sometimes it's hard," Erasmus confesses.

"I can completely understand and empathize. I, too, went through a breakup with my second husband under very similar circumstances," she replies, her eyes drifting back in time.

"Let me think, young man," she says, pacing back and forth until suddenly her eyes light up.

"I've got the perfect prescription to treat what ails you. Let me go and fetch it," she offers.

Mrs. Peabody's large frame and size sharply contrast with her surprising agility, which never ceases to amaze Erasmus.

'How can she kneel, climb, bend, and move with such ease and speed?' he marvels once again.

'She defies gravity,' Erasmus muses.

Soon, she's returning with an item in hand.

'Exactly as Victoria always said—within her chaos and piles of books, she knows exactly where everything is and finds it within seconds,' he notes.

"Erasmus, this is a timeless scribble. It's one that helped me get through the abandonment by my second husband. Let me read it to you."

As she begins to recite the poem, the words have an immediate soothing effect on Erasmus' restless spirit and melancholic heart.

"Forgiveness"

What is it to forgive?

Is it to erase from our memory those feelings—

fused anger and hurt,

lingering resentments,

or existential wounds,

caused by the acts of others or life vicissitudes?

Or is it to pardon transgressions

or betrayals by those we trust?

To absolve disloyalty from those we count on.

To excuse the consequential untruths

from those we blindly believe in.

Or is it to acquit the irreplaceable losses

caused by those we rely on?

To the offenses to our decency,

dignity, honor, and self-respect,

perpetuated by those we follow?

Or is it, perhaps to forgive ourselves first?

Yet the problem with forgiving our own acts,
is that we seek recognition and pardon from others first—
as though absolution from their words and gestures
could assuage the guilt we carry.

But guilt cannot be deceived
by fantasies or falsehoods.
The feeling of culpability dissolves
only when our conscience
allows it to,
when we genuinely accept responsibility.

Because
where forgiveness truly happens first, is within us,
and only through a genuine acceptance of responsibility
our feelings of guilt are first assuaged and then go away.

And this is how the stern watch
of our conscience is appeased,
opening the doors for us to be absolved.
Then and only then, what others think or say,
brings completeness
to forgiveness' virtuous circle,
one built out of authenticity and truthfulness.
Once inside this loop,
we can finally reach atonement.

When do we sincerely forgive?

Sometimes, we pretend to forgive, but we really don't,
denying its actuality.

Sometimes, we are simply unwilling to do so.

Both attitudes are poisonous to the spirit
and destructive to the soul,
because the longer they linger,
the more our true selves erode,
the more profound our sadness becomes,
and the more devastating the damage is
to our ability to live a life in full.

To truly forgive,
we must be genuinely willing and disposed
to have the courage to face the pain, the wound,
the offenses or their personas straight in the eye,
confronting them.

Then, whatever or whoever
is afflicting us,
we must let go,
foregoing at whatever pace our heart permits.

But, regardless of anything or anyone,
we must always seek finality and closure
to reach atonement.

What does it take to forgive?"

How do we know, in fact, we have forgiven?"

We recognize it because of our ability to forgive

is a requirement of our personal growth,

as well as for the enrichment and evolution

of our entire self.

Without the capacity to forgive,

our virtues and values have flaws,

and our meaning and purpose in life are clouded and murky,

preoccupied with overcoming the haze.

And without forgiveness,

we are plying through stuck in reverse,

lacking oxygen or inspiration

to breathe and infuse life into our spirit and soul.

Forgiveness is also a precondition

to experience the joy of living,

Without it, happiness is hampered,

limited and handicapped.

The genesis of the noble virtue of forgiveness

is the magical elixir of compassion and piety,

With compassion, we connect and empathize

with the pain and sorrow of

those in need of atonement.

With piety, we are illuminated and enlightened by grace

enabling us to devote ourselves,

with dutiful respect, sincerity, and veneration

to the atonement of ours and other's faults.

When we forgive,

we throw a spreading aura,

a mantle of goodness on everyone

and everything around us.

When we forgive,

our life renews itself

and our "existential time machine's" hands,

move forward in the right direction.

When we forgive,

right from our very own center of the earth,

a torrent of lava explodes into the sky,

freeing our core, our essence,

from life's emotional anchors,

ballasts and dead weights.

When we forgive,

we become worthier, thus more likely,

to be rewarded with forgiveness as well.

When we forgive,

we elevate ourselves to a state of

compassionate and pious grace,

where we can seek atonement for our spirit and soul.

*

As Mrs. Peabody concludes, her words resonate deeply, transcending the confines of her antique bookshop.

"Erasmus, forgiving is both empowering and liberating. You don't need to question how or why you feel as you do now because it is perfectly human to feel angry and dejected after what happened to you. What you need to focus on is taking ownership of the part and role you played and what you learned from it. You also mustn't stand still or allow yourself to get stuck in a quagmire; instead, you must keep moving forward. The trigger to do this is to forgive her and forgive yourself. That's how everything in life restarts and renews itself."

—✦—

Royal Cambridge Scholastic Institute (2019)
(University Auditorium)

Professor Cromwell-Smith returns his class to the present with a benevolent look in his eyes.

In the stillness of the classroom, Erasmus' thoughts drift to the past—the poignant moments he and Victoria shared as she faced her own emotional struggles. As he begins to speak, he recalls the lessons he learned from Mrs. Peabody and how her words on forgiveness helped him heal. His voice softens as he speaks, bridging the gap between the past and the present, tying his personal journey to the lesson he is about to share with his students.

"Forgiveness is one of the most powerful tools we can use to navigate life's undesirable outcomes. Without it, we risk carrying emotional anchors or roadblocks that hold us back."

"Questions, anyone?" Asks the professor with pensive tone.

Samantha is a philosophy major with a keen interest in ethical dilemmas, particularly around forgiveness and personal growth. She has shoulder-length blonde hair and often wears a thoughtful expression, reflecting on complex concepts during class. "Professor, the poem discusses the need to forgive not only others but also ourselves. How do we begin the process of self-forgiveness when our actions have caused harm to others, especially when those feelings of guilt persist despite our best efforts to move forward?"

"That's a very insightful question, Samantha. Self-forgiveness often starts with acknowledging the responsibility for our actions and feeling genuine remorse. However, it is essential to not get trapped in guilt, because it can paralyze us. True self-forgiveness involves accepting that we made mistakes, learning from them, and then allowing ourselves to move forward. The poem emphasizes that real forgiveness begins within, and that's where we need to focus first— on accepting our responsibility and letting go of the emotional weight that holds us back."

Jared is a psychology student known for his analytical mindset. With short brown hair and a tendency to take detailed notes, he is deeply engaged in understanding human behavior and emotions.

"Professor, the poem mentions that 'guilt cannot be deceived by fantasies or falsehoods.' How do we differentiate between genuine guilt and the guilt we impose on ourselves due to societal expectations or unrealistic self-judgment?"

"Jared, that's an excellent observation. Genuine guilt arises when we acknowledge that we've done something that conflicts with our values, whereas imposed guilt often stems from external pressures or distorted self-perceptions. The poem suggests that guilt dissolves when we take responsibility, but it doesn't mean we should carry it endlessly. Instead of suppressing or ignoring guilt, we need to confront it honestly and understand whether it's stemming from a true moral misstep or if it's been exacerbated by external expectations."

Rachel is an English literature major with a love for poetry and a passion for finding deeper meanings in texts. Her curly hair frames her face as she leans forward in her seat, eager to engage in the discussion. "Professor, in the poem, forgiveness is described as 'empowering and liberating.' Could you elaborate on how forgiveness serves as a tool for emotional freedom, particularly when we are forgiving someone who has wronged us deeply?"

"Rachel, that's a powerful question. Forgiveness, especially in cases where we've been deeply wronged, can feel like an emotional burden being lifted. The poem highlights that forgiveness frees us from emotional anchors and allows us to move forward. When we choose to forgive, we release the hold that anger, resentment, or bitterness may have over us. It doesn't mean we forget or condone the wrongs done to us, but by forgiving, we regain control of our emotions and start the process of healing."

Michael is a history student who enjoys reflecting on the past and its influence on present-day decisions. With glasses and a quiet demeanor, he is often the first to notice historical patterns in personal experiences. "Professor, the poem speaks about the importance of forgiveness in order to avoid emotional stagnation and the erosion of our true selves. In your opinion, how can societies or nations use forgiveness on a larger scale to heal from historical trauma and prevent societal divisions?"

"Michael, that's an insightful way to expand the conversation. Societies that carry the weight of historical trauma—such as war, injustice, or oppression—must recognize the value of collective forgiveness. The process involves not only acknowledging past wrongs but also creating opportunities for dialogue, healing, and reconciliation. Societal forgiveness isn't just about letting go of the past but also about fostering unity and progress. The poem's message can be applied to larger contexts, where forgiveness opens the door for societal healing and a better future."

As the class draws to a close, Erasmus feels the echoes of his own journey within the room. He gives his final remarks, offering the students a simple yet profound piece of advice. "Forgiveness," he says, "is the key to not only personal growth but also to living a life of peace and purpose. I encourage you all to reflect on your own capacity for forgiveness, both toward others and yourselves." With a final nod to his students, he watches them gather their belongings. He lingers for a moment, taking in the quiet, knowing that today's lesson may have planted seeds of healing in his students' lives, just as it did in his own.

"And that'll be all for today. It's a wrap. I'll see you all next week," declares the eminent professor as he concludes the session.

Victoria and Sarah smile proudly, their hands tightly clasped in a gesture of raw emotion and connection. As he approaches mother and daughter, they embrace in a spontaneous public display of family reconciliation.

The entire student body watches, rewarded with the poignant image of their beloved professor walking out, holding hands with each of his two ladies. To all present, it is a symbolic gesture—a living testament that, for him, forgiveness begins at home.

Chapter 5

Reciprocity

Charles River, Boston, Massachusetts (2019)

As dawn breaks on a cloudy day, Victoria and Erasmus walk, hands intertwined, along the misty river surrounded by fog patches. Nature gives off the smell and feel of a new day. Erasmus knows Victoria's pained past has all but run its course. Her troubled history is now out in the open, and the winds of a new life are blowing away her troubled past, allowing the two of them to address the wounds and scars from a distant perspective as they move forward. But he knows that there's still one more fuzzy cloud to visit – her life in Boston before they reunited.

'All in due time,' he tells himself.

As if she were reading his mind, Erasmus feels the tightening of her hand. A glance confirms the determined and stern look in her eyes – the same look that has preceded her recent outpourings about her life without him.

"Dear, right after that memorable encounter with Mrs. Samuels-Ortiz at the St. Louis Public Library, my husband was diagnosed with cancer. That tragic event turned our lives upside down, and everything else took the backstage," Victoria says.

"What happened with your plans to resettle in Boston?" asks Erasmus.

"That turned out to be one of the few good outcomes resulting from his illness, as I didn't have to create an excuse or try to force the inevitable. We just simply moved upon my decision that Boston was the right location to treat his illness," she replies.

"Did he interpret it that way?" asks Erasmus.

"Outwardly, yes, but I sense he knew my true reasons. As a matter of fact, after that meeting with Mrs. Samuels-Ortiz, I lost any fear of speaking up, voicing my desires in front of him. Little by little, I started to mention you in our family conversations. At first, he tried to stop it, but to no avail; he couldn't stop me from finally voicing my true feelings. You and I at home became fair game," she replies.

"But your actual move to Boston took a long time. I mean, decades had gone by the time you moved over here," he states.

"Thankfully, Rebecca Samuels-Ortiz took the initiative. She did what she thought was best for my future. She wrote and applied to several universities. I consented to her pursuing that initiative, not believing that it would ever pan out, but it did. At that point, there was no turning back. That's exactly what I needed – a slight push to break away from the chains of my thinking and upbringing," Victoria recounts.

"But wasn't it a bit of a quixotic quest? You had no idea where I was or if I'd started my own family," Erasmus says.

"That's true, but it felt as if I was getting closer to you. I knew it was all a fantasy, but it was one that I clung to for a long time. I never let go of it until I moved the family, at which point I was preoccupied," she elaborates.

"But once here, some more years rolled by," laments Erasmus.

"Yes, my love, that's sadly true. His illness took over, and everything else was held in abeyance. It would take five more years until he passed away for me to become alive again," she replies in angst.

Victoria's face turns deeply sad and inundated with anxiety. As she begins to cry inconsolably, Erasmus embraces her with a deep sense of his own guilt.

"I'm sorry, Victoria, we shouldn't have..." he says, ashamed.

"Shhhh, let me continue," she whispers, her satiated eyes exuding love for him as she places a couple of her fingers on his lips.

Like their joined life together, the river fog is slowly lifting, providing them with a clearer picture of their surroundings.

"Dear, after he passed away, I went through a very trying period of doubt. For the first time, I felt it was too late for us to resume. I believed there was no chance in heaven that you would want anything to do with me. I started to visualize you having a new life, married, and with kids. So, I did nothing," she concedes.

"How did you find out that your kids were searching for me?"

"That's another rabbit hole worth exploring," she announces with a spark in her voice.

"It all happened on an early morning surprise visit by my three kids," she says before earnestly starting to narrate.

— ✦ —

Emerson-Lloyd Family Home, Boston, Massachusetts (2017)
(Victoria's kids' family intervention)

"It seems like she's given up, guys," points out Elizabeth, her tone laced with concern.

"I agree. It's been three months, and she's sadder and more depressed than ever," notes Bart, his brow furrowed in thought.

"She's certainly not grieving Father," says Sarah, her voice steady but tinged with frustration.

"We all know that," retorts Bart, leaning back with a resigned sigh.

"After a lifetime of obsessing over it, it's like the dream has disappeared," states Elizabeth, her gaze distant.

"That may be true, but she's still in love with Erasmus," declares Sarah, her voice carrying a quiet certainty.

"If that's true, why has she given up and quit then?" asks Elizabeth, her words cutting through the tense atmosphere.

"Perhaps in her mind, too much time has passed them by, and the duration of our father's illness lasted for so long that she believes it's now too late," Bart reasons, his voice low and reflective.

— ✦ —

Charles River, Boston (2019)

While sitting by the riverside, Erasmus and Victoria huddle close under their trusted wool blanket. Their body language exudes a deep sense of immersion and intensity, as though the world around them has faded into irrelevance. Every word exchanged carries weight, reverberating in the quiet intimacy of the moment. Victoria speaks in a calm voice, a whisper tinged with absolute peace and contentment, her words flowing gently like the river beside them.

— ✦ —

Emerson-Lloyd Home, Boston (2017)

"So, what're we going to do about it?" probes Bart.

"Maybe we should do nothing. After all, it's her personal life," ventures Sarah.

"Isn't mom's personal life, at least in part, ours as well? Or do we want to see our mother all alone and miserable for the rest of her life?" challenges Elizabeth.

"She's dedicated her life to us. She's been impeccable and raised us with boundless love and affection. She cared for our father with absolute abnegation and devotion throughout his illness. It's now her time—her moment, and we must help Mom make it happen," asserts Bart with conviction.

"What about the memory of our father? Wouldn't we be betraying it?" an incredulous Sarah questions, her voice tinged with guilt.

"Get a hold of yourself. What memory? A man who hardly ever paid attention or professed love to us, his own kids. His sole interest and focus in life, besides his profession, were women, which, by the way, didn't include Mom. But it did include Grandma. Seemingly, she was one of the few female patients that got away, even though she initiated the poisonous relationship," argues Elizabeth with biting clarity.

"I agree. By now, we all know about his manipulative, controlling approach to engineering their marriage, and it was absolutely wrong. When a mind doctor exploits the emotional vulnerability of his patients, it's not only a violation of a doctor's oath but also deeply immoral," Bart declares emphatically.

"God forgive me for speaking the truth, but he was a malignant narcissist, one of the most dangerous human beings on our planet. People like him destroy lives, scorching the earth in their path and, in our mother's case, without a moment's hesitation. Now, we have a chance to get her life back—a life she lost in her youth. An existence wherein her heart, all her dreams, innocence, and zest for life reside," asserts Elizabeth, her voice brimming with resolve.

"Except for respect, which I'm uncertain he deserves, we don't owe him anything. We all, including Mom, were his victims, and yet dutifully and faithfully, we remained his family to the very end of his life. We owe him nothing more, nothing else," concludes Bart with finality.

Victoria's kids come together in an emotional embrace, shedding a few tears.

"Agreed. Now let's start looking for Erasmus Cromwell-Smith," Sarah declares, finally making up her mind.

— ✦ —

Charles River, Boston, Massachusetts (2019)

As the sun ascends, the fog gradually lifts, unveiling the river and its serene surroundings in their full splendor. Erasmus tenderly caresses Victoria's face, his touch both reassuring and affectionate.

Tears cascade down her cheeks, glistening in the early morning light. With a trembling voice yet an unwavering resolve, she begins to narrate in earnest...

— ✦ —

Emerson-Lloyd Family Home, Boston, Massachusetts (2017)

"Where do we begin? Maybe he's no longer in the area? What if he has a family, a wife, kids?" Elizabeth asks, her voice tinged with angst.

"We should still pursue our goal, resolve to find him, and bring closure to this situation," Bart concludes firmly.

"But we'll only tell her about his status if he's available, right?" Sarah asks, her youthful innocence shining through.

"Absolutely," Bart replies with conviction.

"Deal," Elizabeth affirms, her tone resolute.

— ✦ —

Charles River, Boston, Massachusetts (2019)

With the temperature rising, Victoria and Erasmus' blanket now serves as their floor mat. Like the awakening nature around them, their own veils of uncertainty are lifting. At last, they have achieved clarity and transparency after revisiting what had been left unresolved. After a brief pause, Victoria resumes her narration, her voice imbued with a cadence of joy and renewed purpose.

— ✦ —

Emerson-Lloyd Family Home, Boston, Massachusetts (2017)
(A Few Months Later, Victoria's Bedroom, Dawn)

Elizabeth, Bart, and Sarah tread cautiously into their mother's bedroom, as if walking on pins and needles. Bart, trailing behind, wrestles with a tangle of strings attached to a dozen colorful balloons, which pop and squeeze through the door in a chaotic display.

"Hey, guys," whispers Victoria as she awakens, her face lighting up with joy. The trio leans in to kiss her cheeks, their love radiating through the room. Her gaze sharpens as she notices the balloons, her curiosity piqued.

"Bart, those are truly beautiful. Come over here, please," she says, extending her arms to hug her son as he hands her the strings.

"Mother, today I'm a balloon salesman," Bart announces with a broad grin, casually dropping one of Erasmus' childhood poems in front of her.

The memory strikes Victoria like lightning. A wave of emotion washes over her, and she struggles to maintain her composure, forcing a smile. But her children catch the subtle tremor in her demeanor, the telltale sign of memories stirring within.

"Or maybe I'm the boy in the picture," teases Bart, alluding to another of Erasmus' cherished childhood poems.

Victoria's expression transforms as a surge of warmth and nostalgia overtakes her. Her mind races. 'They don't know. How could they know? How would they know?' A feeling churns in her gut, rising to the surface, betraying her outward calm.

"How do you..." she begins to ask, but her voice falters, caught in the storm of raw emotions. Tears glisten in her eyes as she gazes at her children, her hands trembling.

And then it happens—the words she has yearned to hear for decades pierce the air, cutting through the weight of time.

"Mom, I found him! ... I found your blue unicorn," Sarah announces, tears of joy streaming down her face.

Victoria's hands fly to her mouth, her entire body trembling. She struggles to speak, her voice barely a whisper. "You found him?" Her words are knotted, stuck in her throat, yearning for reassurance that this long-dreamt reality has come true.

"Where is he?" she blurts out suddenly, her voice cracking. In a frenzy, she leaps from the bed and embraces her children, her actions frantic and irrational, driven purely by instinct.

"Get dressed, Mom. I'll take you to him," Sarah says, her voice steady and resolute.

Victoria, dazed yet determined, rushes to her dressing room. She moves with a sense of frantic urgency, as if time itself is her enemy.

"Mom, you have to promise to do exactly what I say," Sarah insists, her tone commanding as Victoria searches for something to wear.

"All right," Victoria replies, her tone tinged with puzzlement as she hurriedly dresses.

"You can only reveal your presence when he's finished. Today is the final class of the academic year," Sarah instructs.

A brief silence follows as Victoria processes this revelation. "Is he a profess—wait a minute, is he your teacher?" she asks, her voice rising with incredulity.

"Yes, he is. Mom, do you promise...?" Sarah persists.

"Promise," Victoria replies, her excitement bubbling over. "Does he know I'm coming?" she hesitates, her nerves breaking through.

"No, Mom, it's a total surprise," Sarah reassures her.

"Hurry up then. We don't want to be late for his class. You don't want to make him wait any longer for you," Victoria exclaims, her eagerness evident.

As Victoria readies herself, an extraordinary sound fills the room— her singing. It's a melody her children haven't heard in years, the familiar humming of their mother from their childhood. Overwhelmed with emotion, the siblings hug each other tightly, tears of joy cascading down their faces.

"Guys, I think we finally have our mom back," Sarah says, her voice breaking, and her siblings nod in agreement.

On the way to the university, Victoria is consumed by a torrent of emotions—joy, anxiety, and anticipation. Her heart, dormant for so long, now races with life. But doubts linger. 'How is he? How does he look? Is he in a relationship? Would he want me back?'

"Mom, relax. Enjoy the moment," Sarah says soothingly. "I'm certain that the professor is still as much in love with you as you are with him. A crazy love, I should add, but true love after all. I've witnessed it firsthand, listening to how he's described the two of you,

class after class." Sarah's voice is steady and reassuring as she holds her mother's hand, squeezing it gently, offering unwavering support.

— ✦ —

Charles River, Boston, Massachusetts (2019)

Erasmus and Victoria are overcome with deep emotions as they reflect on the day they reunited after being apart for more than 40 years.

The middle-aged couple walks through the woods, heading home. Their hands are clasped tightly, her head gently resting on his shoulder. Both wear serene smiles, knowing that the burdens of the past have finally lifted, leaving their shared joy untarnished by lingering shadows.

"Dear, what's your class going to touch upon today?" asks Victoria, her voice soft as they step across their home's entrance into the outer hallway.

"Reciprocity," Erasmus replies with a thoughtful smile. "Which is what life offers you after a life of sacrifice, unyielding convictions, and unwavering loyalty. And, in the end, it paid you back in spades."

Royal Cambridge Scholastic Institute (2019)
(Campus Streets followed by Auditorium)

Erasmus zigzags on his old rusty bike as he pedals toward the faculty building. He takes a deep breath, his heart filled with warmth, still soaring from the joy of an unforgettable morning. Slowly but steadily, he approaches the parking lot, locks his bike, and strides purposefully toward his class.

'Her children's instincts weren't just right—they were uncannily precise, perfectly attuned to the moment and the circumstances,' he reflects, a broad smile spreading across his face as he navigates the bustling halls of the institution.

The distant rumble and murmurs of the class grow louder as he nears the auditorium, and he can feel their energy surging through the walls. Stepping into the lecture hall, the pedagogue shakes off the quite reverie f his earlier thoughts. The buzz of student chatter fills the room like a vibrant chorus, the excitement is palpable, with a purposeful stride and a puzzled look, he walks to the front, ready to lead the next intellectual journey. Then he spots the source of the commotion. Sarah, Bart, and Elizabeth sit proudly in the front row, their wide grins delivering an unmistakable message: *Erasmus, we're part of the team now.*

The professor nods ever so slightly, acknowledging their presence with a grateful smile.

"How's everyone today?" he asks, his voice momentarily thick with emotion.

"Insanely awesome!" comes the boisterous response from the students, amplified by his self-invited guests.

"Reciprocity," Erasmus announces as he regains his composure, his tone resonant and steady.

"While on a trip to the Far East, I learned that mutuality is an intrinsic and crucial part of life. Inevitably, as part of the circle of life, everything we give comes back to us, and everything we take is taken away from us as well."

He pauses, allowing the weight of his words to settle.

"It begins like this ..."

— ✦ —

Ginza District, Tokyo, Japan (1997)

Every summer for the past twenty years, I've traveled to Japan to deliver a seminar on Western poetry at Tokyo University. While in Japan, I've savored hiking the mountains around the capital on weekends. My favorite, by far, is the legendary Mount Fuji. I also delight in visiting the exquisite Kyoto Gardens, marveling at their serene beauty and intricate design.

On one particular trip, a Friday evening seminar ran late, causing me to wake up at noon on Saturday for the first time ever in Tokyo. Left with no clear plans, I found myself meandering through the bustling Ginza shopping district. Amid the dazzling neon lights and crowds, my attention was drawn to a low-rise building of about fifteen floors, showcasing the shape and logo of a renowned Japanese consumer electronics brand. Intrigued, I ventured inside, discovering that the entire structure was a demo center for the brand's latest innovations.

Floor by floor, I explored the futuristic showcase, marveling at gadgets yet to be released to the public. On one of the upper levels, I entered their high-fidelity sound room. From that moment, every visit to Tokyo included a ritual stop here, where I could immerse myself in hours of undisturbed tranquility.

The sound room was extraordinary—its purity so profound that the melodies seemed to emerge from a cocoon of absolute silence.

Listening to chamber music in this room was transcendent, as if I were seated in the front row of a concert hall with flawless acoustics. Vivaldi's Four Seasons, a perennial favorite of mine, played in harmony with a video showcasing the breathtaking beauty of Kyoto. The gardens and seasonal landscapes, rendered in vivid splendor, synchronized perfectly with the symphony's movements, each season vividly coming to life.

It was during one of these meditative sessions, completely enraptured by the interplay of Kyoto's imagery and Vivaldi's composition, that I met Atsushi Sanada. His presence was striking: a long, salt-and-pepper goatee framed his face, his bundled ponytail matched his serene demeanor, and his tiny round-rimmed glasses complemented his colorful wool turtleneck cardigan. Like me, he appeared completely transported, deeply engrossed in the music's exquisite sound.

"Do you feel the silence within the music?" he asked unexpectedly, his voice calm and his English flawless. His friendly gaze and unhurried manner drew me out of my reverie.

"Absolutely," I replied, already captivated by his insight. "That's why I make it a point to come here whenever I'm in Tokyo."

"Then you are fortunate," he continued, as if lost in his own thoughts. "To perceive such silence within sound is a rare gift."

He paused, his gaze contemplative, before speaking again. "Here is an ancient writing I've carried with me for years. It offers clarity for moments like this. It's a loose translation from Japanese." He handed me a tiny scroll, his manner reverent.

With a sense of trepidation and wonder, I unfolded the delicate scroll and began to read...

"Silence within the Music"

There is stillness in the air,
no sound within the music.

Fidelity proclaims perfection,
the notes exude glory.

Purity fills the air—
violins weep,
cellos cry,
trumpets sing,
and the piano chants
to the deepest ends of our hearts.

There is perfection in the room,
absolute serenity in harmony,
flawless stillness,
with room to spare,
to meditate and wonder,
to no end.

There is silence within the music,
there is silence as it plays,
there is silence in the air.

*

The wise man was no longer in the room when I finished reading. Anxious to return the scroll, I darted through the demo building, frantically searching for him. Arriving at street level, the swirling doors propelled me into the bustling rhythm of the Japanese metropolis. There he stood—calm and poised on the sidewalk, smiling at me.

"Atsushi," he introduced himself, extending his hand.

"Cromwell-Smith," I replied, clasping his hand firmly and returning the scroll with a slight bow of gratitude and respect.

"Care for a quick bite?" he asked.

"It would be my pleasure, Mr. Atsushi."

Before long, we stood in front of a series of vibrant window displays showcasing intricate "wax" replicas of various dishes. Each item bore a small sign with its name, description, and price—a masterpiece of Japanese efficiency. Within minutes, we were seated at a counter with our chosen meals and generous servings of sake.

"Thank you for sharing the poem with me," I said, my voice earnest.

"You're welcome. It was an instinctive reaction to your tranquil state of contemplation," Atsushi replied softly, his penetrating gaze offering a glimpse of wisdom beyond words.

"Mr. Cromwell, what brings you to Japan?" he inquired.

"Each year, I teach a seminar on Western poetry at Tokyo University."

His almond-shaped eyes narrowed briefly in curiosity, then widened as a warm smile spread across his face.

"*Serendipitous! You must visit my store,*" *he exclaimed, his enthusiasm palpable.*

"*What's your trade, Mr. Atsushi?*" *I asked, intrigued.*

"*Call me Atsushi, please,*" *he urged, his manner disarmingly relaxed.*

"*And how should I address you?*" *he queried.*

"*Erasmus,*" *I replied, making a conscious effort to shed my cultural stiffness.*

"*Well, Erasmus,*" *he said with a playful nod,* "*I deal in ancient writings and manuscripts, much like the one you read.*"

His revelation caught me off guard, igniting my curiosity. My eyes widened, betraying my excitement.

"*Serendipity indeed, Atsushi. Are you an antiquarian?*"

"*A Japanese version of one,*" *he replied with a modest smile.*

"*Then our stars are perfectly aligned,*" *I declared.*

"*And why is that, if I may ask?*" *he prodded.*

"*I was born and raised in Hay-on-Wye in Wales, famously known as 'book town,' surrounded by an abundance of antique bookstores. My proclivity for the world of books shaped my childhood and teenage years. I practically grew up inside those establishments, mentored by seasoned antiquarians who became lifelong influences.*"

Atsushi's lips tightened in a thoughtful smile as he nodded repeatedly, his satisfaction evident.

"*My humble shop has been in the family for four generations,*" *he shared, his words kindling my growing fascination.*

"Atsushi Sanada Shop of Antique Writings" (est. 1870)

Not long after, with plenty of green tea on hand, I find myself seated on a mat on the pristine wooden floor of the impeccable shop. My eyes wander in amazement at the sheer volume of scrolls meticulously displayed around me.

"Erasmus, what occupies your time when you're not visiting Japan?" Atsushi asks with a playful tone.

"I teach poetry and English literature at a New England college. I also write poems and fiction novels," I reply.

"Interesting. My initial impression of you was that your body language exuded serenity and meditation, but your restless eyes betrayed a sense of being lost and in pain. It felt as though you were searching for something—perhaps meaning or purpose—or mourning someone?" Atsushi observes with remarkable precision.

"Aren't we all?" I respond rhetorically, hoping to sidestep his probing insight.

"Indeed, we all are, Erasmus. But more specifically, are you?" he persists, cutting through my deflection with surgical precision.

"Yes," I admit after a moment. "A bit lost, searching for meaning and purpose, and, yes, mourning as well. I am in pursuit of my true self."

"One of the keys to living a fulfilling life is reciprocity. It's all in the balance of give and take," Atsushi begins, his voice steady and deliberate. "Too often, we focus on what we want or need to gain, ignoring what we have to offer, which is where true fulfillment

begins. *Your quest for identity must include a conscious effort to cultivate mutuality and a predisposition to generosity. Whatever you hope to receive from life or others, it will only come to you consistently once you learn to give first. This profound understanding is earned through life's experiences,"* he explains with a wisdom that feels both ancient and immediate.

"Atsushi, let me share an anecdote about reciprocity with you," he offers, his tone tinged with enthusiasm. *"Years ago, just before I opened my shop, I struggled to gather the resources needed. One of my uncles, a wealthy man, had the means to help me. I approached him for support, but his reaction was unexpected and disheartening. Instead of aiding me, he invested significantly more to establish an antique scroll shop of his own—directly in competition with me. To make matters worse, he sought my advice and help to launch his store."*

"What did you do?" I ask, my bewilderment evident.

"Of course, I helped him," Atsushi replies with a calm smile. *"I put forth my best efforts and my heart."*

"Did he compensate you for your efforts?" I probe further.

"I didn't want him to."

"But did he offer?"

"No, but that was irrelevant to me."

"Did he, at any point, support you in setting up your shop?"

"Not at all. On the contrary, he criticized me harshly, insisting I wasn't cut out to be my own boss. He even campaigned within the family, claiming my efforts were unnecessary because his shop was

already established. He thought if I failed, I would end up working for him."

"What happened next?" I ask, leaning in, captivated.

"I managed to open my shop. My uncle, lacking genuine passion for antiquities, eventually lost interest and moved on," Atsushi explains.

"And your family?" I inquire.

"Over time, they came to embrace my work and my store. Today, they fully support me, but it was a long journey. As for my uncle, his actions have left a lasting impression—not a favorable one—within the family."

"But why did you help him? I don't understand," I admit.

"You see, Erasmus, his actions defined him. They reflected who he truly was. My actions, on the other hand, reflect who I am. I didn't allow his choices to dictate my own. I compartmentalized his behavior and rose above the fray, responding with maturity and pouring my heart into helping him."

"But his selfishness was cruel," I argue.

"Be that as it may, once again, his actions defined him, not me."

"What reciprocity did he offer you in return for your generosity?"

"Nothing. And that, Erasmus, lies at the heart of reciprocity. True giving doesn't come with the expectation of something in return. It's not transactional. But let me share something that will illuminate this concept further."

Atsushi stands gracefully and moves toward a row of aged yellowish scrolls. He carefully selects one, studies it for a moment, and then returns with a look of quiet satisfaction.

"Let us share an exquisite example of ancient Japanese wisdom," he says, his voice imbued with tranquility as he begins to read, translating the words into English with seamless fluency.

"Reciprocity"

Nature blossoms as water drops.

All the world's colors light up around us

as the sun shines.

The entire universe high above glows,

as night falls.

Our entire self gets to live another day,

hence continues,

as we breathe.

Reality's images come to life for us to enjoy,

as we are able to see.

Our entire world exists as we think and comprehend—

consciousness, the genesis of human life.

The whole gamut of the worlds of physics and biology

can only be calculated, measured,

and understood through reciprocity.

At the heart of life's virtuous cycle

lies reciprocity.

If constant motion is the roar
of nature's engine at work,
reciprocity is the essential fuel
that powers it.

When we reciprocate with one another,
we appeal to the better angels within ourselves
and over humanity.

The true essence of receiving anything in life
lies in what we have given beforehand.

In truth, we have not truly given anything,
if nothing comes back.

Inexorably, sooner or later,
if we do good things and do them right,
if we perform good deeds,
life will respond in kind,
rewarding us in spades.

But if we don't, one way or another,
life will find its balance—
often in the most unexpected ways.

Everything and anything we have taken or received
without reciprocity in return
will be taken back, confiscated,

even yanked from us.

If we shoot arrows or throw stones,
we should expect them to rebound,
perhaps with greater force.

If we gift good deeds, books, and roses,
they will return to us in droves.

Mutuality is an immutable correlation—
greater than one,
never a one-way street.
Generosity and reciprocity are inseparable,
each intrinsic to the other.
Together, they create endless virtuous circles,
positive, upward spirals,
of endless giving and receiving.

To reciprocate is to express eternal gratitude
to humankind, life, and The Creator,
it is in essence, a way of paying,
for the privilege of being alive.

All of this comes,
with the lingering, handsome reward:
that everything we have contributed
to life itself and to others,
will, in due course, return to us
as blessings multiplied.

*

As Atsushi gently rolls the scroll closed, the shop falls into a contemplative stillness. He places the scroll back on its shelf with reverence, turning to Erasmus with a serene smile. "Erasmus, reciprocity is the essence of balance—not just in nature but within ourselves. If you nurture this principle, it will guide you toward harmony—always remember, in life, begin by asking yourself what you have to offer or contribute before you craft your wish list of desires."

Erasmus bows slightly in gratitude, his eyes drawn to the intricate calligraphy of the scrolls around him, each holding its own mysteries. Outside, the muted hum of Tokyo's bustling streets contrasts sharply with the tranquil haven of Atsushi's shop.

Breaking the silence, Atsushi gestures toward the teapot resting on a low wooden table. "Let us share tea before you go, Erasmus. Even a brief moment of communion can teach us more about giving and receiving."

The two sit on cushions, sipping the warm green tea in quiet reflection, the rich aroma mingling with the scent of aged paper and cedar. Erasmus, his heart full, feels the wisdom of reciprocity settle deep within him.

— ❖ —

Royal Cambridge Scholastic Institute (2019)
(University Auditorium)

Professor Cromwell-Smith prepares to shift from his personal reflections to the heart of today's lesson. He clears his throat, drawing his students' attention, back to the present. "The word 'reciprocity' should resonate consciously within each of you, from the moment you awaken to the moment you rest. What you give is precisely what you'll receive. Without giving, there's no reciprocal action to sustain the cycle in the long run!"

His voice echoes in the hushed room, the students sitting upright, their attention unwavering. "Let this principle guide you not just academically but in every facet of your existence," the professor concludes, his gaze meeting each pair of eyes in turn, ensuring the message lands firmly in their hearts.

With the story of his experiences shared, Erasmus looks around the room, his gaze inviting questions. The class is silent for a moment, before eager hands begin to rise.

Clara, a senior majoring in philosophy with a focus on ethics, speaks up with a deep sense of curiosity. "In the poem 'Reciprocity,' you mention that what we give is exactly what we'll receive. Could you elaborate on how reciprocity plays a role in personal growth, especially when we face life's most challenging moments?"

"An excellent question, Clara. Reciprocity, at its core, is about balance—what we put out into the world, emotionally, intellectually, or spiritually, inevitably comes back to us. During tough times, when we feel vulnerable or lost, embracing reciprocity can guide us toward healing. The more we give of ourselves—whether in love, forgiveness, or simply understanding—the more we open ourselves up to receiving the same in return. It's not about expectation, but about trust in the process of life and relationships. Growth comes when we learn to give without calculating, knowing that the universe operates on a balance that goes beyond us."

Mark, an English literature major with a particular interest in contemporary poetry, raises his hand with evident eagerness. "The poem 'Silence within the Music' speaks about the stillness found in sound. I was struck by how this theme resonates with the concept of inner peace. Could you explain how silence, or moments of stillness, contribute to a deeper understanding of reciprocity?"

"A thoughtful observation, Mark. Silence is often the space where true understanding begins. In both music and life, silence allows us to pause and reflect. In the poem, the silence within the music signifies a deeper connection, a moment of pure being. Similarly, in life, moments of stillness give us the opportunity to process, to listen, and to truly receive. Without these pauses, the flow of reciprocity becomes disrupted. By embracing silence, we make room for others to give to us, just as we offer ourselves in return. It's in those silent spaces that the most profound exchanges occur."

Olivia, a psychology major studying human behavior, raises her hand, her expression thoughtful. "The idea of forgiving oneself in 'Forgiveness' resonates deeply with me, especially the notion that forgiveness can't truly happen until we accept responsibility. How do you think this acceptance impacts our relationships with others, particularly when we've wronged them?"

"That's an insightful question, Olivia. Self-forgiveness is the foundation of all other forms of forgiveness. When we accept responsibility for our actions, we free ourselves from the shackles of guilt and defensiveness. This act of acknowledging our mistakes, without excuses or deflection, opens the door to healing. Only then can we approach others with sincerity and empathy, without being burdened by our own unresolved feelings. This process doesn't just heal the self, but it also enables more authentic relationships with others. When we forgive ourselves, we create the emotional space to truly forgive others and accept their forgiveness in return."

Alex, a political science major who often explores the intersection of personal values and social dynamics, speaks up with intensity. "In the poem 'Reciprocity,' there's a line that says, 'The true essence of receiving anything in life lies in what we have given beforehand.' Can you discuss how this principle applies to societal structures and our role in fostering mutual benefit in the broader community?"

"A very timely and significant question, Alex. This line speaks to the larger social fabric and how individual actions contribute to the collective well-being. In societal structures, reciprocity is often about giving to the community—whether through service, advocacy, or simply kindness—and in return, we create stronger, more resilient connections. It's easy to fall into the trap of taking more than we give, but true societal progress happens when we all recognize our responsibility to contribute to the greater good. By embracing this, we create systems that are not just transactional but transformational, where mutual benefit thrives and everyone has a stake in the well-being of others. Reciprocity, then, becomes the foundation of social harmony and progress.

The professor pauses, letting the weight of the statement settle over the room. Glancing at the clock, he gives a small nod and says, "That's it for today. See you all next week—class dismissed."

As the class comes to an end, the students slowly gather their belongings, still processing the weight of the pedagogue's words. A quiet reflection lingers in the air, marking the conclusion of another transformative session. Professor Cromwell-Smith exits, his students are left reflecting on whether there's more they could offer to their seasoned, insightful professor.

"My reward," he declares, seeming to read their collective thoughts, "is your enthusiasm and dedication to this class. Your reciprocation is evident in the self-satisfaction I derive each week we convene here," he says, his voice carrying an air of reassurance as he walks toward the exit.

The student body absorbs his words, their admiration deepened. They realize that their collective effort and his relentless dedication are part of an enduring exercise in reciprocity.

Out in the hall, Elizabeth, Bart, and Sarah await him. For a moment, the group remains motionless, unsure of how to proceed, until Sarah steps forward with a radiant smile and hugs Erasmus tightly.

Erasmus, visibly moved, extends his arms, wordlessly inviting Elizabeth and Bart to join. What follows is a spontaneous "pile-on" of hugs, laughter, and unrestrained affection. The hallway echoes with their shared warmth, a poignant display of love and gratitude that requires no words.

Chapter 6

Defiance and Curiosity

Royal Cambridge Scholastic Institute (2019)
(Victoria & Erasmus' Campus Home)

Time has lost meaning as the magic of Michel Legrand's music envelops their cozy campus home. Erasmus and Victoria sit tightly squeezed together on their beloved Chesterfield sofa, each holding a mug of hot tea. Their faces radiate bliss, their shared contentment so tangible it feels almost like something they can taste.

"If not for your children, perhaps we wouldn't be together right now," Erasmus reflects, his thoughts lingering on last week's surprise visit by the three of them to his class.

"They put their hearts and souls into trying to find you," Victoria responds softly.

Erasmus looks at her, puzzled, his mind assuming it was Sarah's solo effort that led to their reunion.

"In the beginning, they needed a little push," she reveals, a knowing smile forming on her lips. "They got it from the most unexpected place of all."

As the morning light peeks through their windows, Erasmus takes a moment to absorb the joy of their shared morning. With a contented sigh, he prepares himself for the class ahead, the warmth of his connection to Victoria fueling his steps toward the university auditorium.

Royal Cambridge Scholastic Institute (2019)
(Class Auditorium, Next Day)

Entering the bustling auditorium, the energy of the class contrasts with the quiet contemplation of the previous night. Erasmus, though grounded in the moment, feels a shift within him as he steps into the space where he has the chance to impart the wisdom he has gained from both his personal experiences and his life lessons.

"How's everyone today?" asks the spirited professor with a twinkle in his eyes.

"Insanely awesome!" is the collective response.

"Class, sometimes in life, we must rise to the occasion and defy the circumstances and odds we are presented with. There are moments when we must stand up to what seems inevitable, affirming that we're not yet ready to surrender."

A silence falls over the room as the professor intentionally pauses, allowing his words to resonate deeply in the imaginations of his students.

"Last night, Victoria shared an extraordinary anecdote with me about the incredible lengths her kids went to in their effort to find me. It carries two crucial life lessons about what to do when fate seems to be in charge," Cromwell-Smith declares, his voice full of intrigue and warmth.

"The story begins like this ..."

— ✦ —

St. Louis Public Library (2017)

The head librarian, Mrs. Rebecca Samuels-Ortiz, is in for the surprise of her life.

"Becca," comes a soft voice from behind her. She turns, and her jaw drops, her eyes reflecting total surprise.

"Elizabeth-Victoria?" she murmurs, confused, as she steps forward and embraces her effusively.

"Where's your mom?" she asks, noticing two youngsters with shy expressions standing a couple of steps behind. Samuels-Ortiz recognizes them immediately.

"You must be Sarah and Bart," she exclaims excitedly, approaching them with a broad smile.

"We came without her," replies Elizabeth.

Mrs. Samuels-Ortiz now looks baffled as she leads them to her office's conference table.

"There must be a very good reason for all of you to have made this trip all the way here—especially without her."

"Becca, you understand Mom in ways we don't. We need your insight and reaffirmation to ensure that what we're doing for her is the right course of action."

"And what exactly would that be?"

"We've decided to locate Erasmus," states Elizabeth firmly.

Samuels-Ortiz's eyes precipitously sparkle, and her soft words are filled with loving conviction.

"Nothing would make your mother happier than having a second chance at being with her true love."

"What about Erasmus, Mrs. Samuels-Ortiz? Perhaps his life has gone in a different direction, and maybe he even has a family. Why should we interfere? Isn't fate already set?" Sarah challenges their hopes, her expression concerned.

The old librarian pauses, immersed in deep thought as she contemplates her mentee's offspring.

"You may very well be right, Sarah, but there are moments in life when we must challenge fate's seeming inevitability. Please allow me to share an old writing that fits this occasion."

The trio nods their heads ever so slightly. Almost simultaneously, Victoria's faithful friend disappears into the labyrinthine shelves of her office in search of the scribble.

"This is a tradition that Erasmus brought from Wales, one your mother adopted for life," she explains as she returns with a thick leather-bound book with gold burnished pages. Opening it to a marked page, she begins reading earnestly.

"Defiance"

When it arises for legitimate and valid reasons,

defiance is a deliberate and positive attitude—

an existential tool that empowers us

to challenge and confront

any kind of hardship.

It is an indomitable force,

so potent that, regardless of

life's obstacles,

unbearable circumstances,

material or emotional shortcomings,

even profound pain and sorrow,

once unleashed,

it ensures that neither

our resilience,

our will,

nor our desire to live,

much less our fighting spirit,

can ever be bent or tamed.

When we resist

in defense of freedom, dignity, and justice,

when we stand for the sake of truth,

when we oppose

oppression, persecution, and tyranny,

when we antagonize

bigotry, hate, and discrimination,

when we remain steadfast

behind virtue, values, and principles—

defiance becomes intrinsic

to what drives and sustains us.

It becomes the very means

by which we withstand,

outlast,

and ultimately prevail.

Defiance is the purest expression,

the release valve within life's turmoil,

igniting the inner fires

that lie at our very core.

Those flames that can never be extinguished,

as they burn and churn,

fueling our deepest passions,

our most unshakeable convictions,

and our firmest beliefs.

Defiance is our fiercest, most primal display—

a sheer force of will and steely resolve

against anything or anyone,

no matter how difficult or unsavory,

that life hurls our way.

Defiance is the attitude

that defines us best,

as true-life warriors—

those who not only

refuse to be conquered by hardship

but who face it square in the eye,

attacking relentlessly,

treating it as an enemy in war,

fighting until it is

vanquished, obliterated, and defeated.

Defiance is an existential weapon

we always carry within us—

a force to bend and break

hardship's aim and pain.

In defiance, we turn the tables,

facing life's vicissitudes head-on.

It is how we drown and conquer our fears,

how we defeat

some of life's greatest impostors.

*

"That's what you are doing, kids. You're defying fate."

Elizabeth and Sarah, in rapture, begin to cry again. Bartholomeus sobs quietly while smiling. Their eyes reflect profound gratitude, but before they can respond, the old librarian continues.

"There's another attitude that applies perfectly to this situation. An attribute you must cultivate and exercise to energize your efforts until you succeed."

She turns to a different page in the leather-bound book, marked precisely for this moment. Fixing her gaze on them with intensity, the erudite librarian begins to read steadily, her voice carrying weight and emphasizing every word.

"Curiosity"

When we itch to explore,

when we crave adventure,

when we feel an inkling to discover,

when we cannot wait to incessantly

dig, search, find, check, investigate,

analyze, study, experiment, and validate.

When we are unafraid of change,

the unknown, the unseen,

anything or anyone new.

When we are

keen to break the mold,

swim against the stream,

oblivious to conventional wisdom,

improvising and adapting on the spur of the moment.

When we can contemplate life

with candid, innocent, and dreamy hearts.

When we are not intimidated by:

how high, how deep, how low,

how big, how small, how impactful,

how irrelevant, how celebrated,

how despised, how demanding,

how patient, how calm,

how passionate, how defeated,

how triumphant

we may be, go, or become.

Then, we are in possession

of the magical elixir of curiosity—

a whimsical, existential-inducing bug

that carries us on a riveting journey,

lifting us above mundane reality,

wrapped in the mantle of an endless pursuit,

to be awed, amazed, or simply blown away

by the acquisition of precious

knowledge and experience.

Curiosity takes us

to countless labyrinths, mystical places,

memorable people, and transcendental moments.

Curiosity engages us with restless spirits

and a soul soaked with "the light and energy of life."

As an agent of change and the pursuit of wisdom,

curiosity is one of the most valuable

existential tools we possess.

Through curiosity,

we constantly refine our life's purpose,

revisit, renew, and define our meaning.

With curiosity,

we remain goofy, loose, and foolish.

If we deploy and employ curiosity,

we are always ready for "change,"

readily embracing evolution as well.

*

Prevailing over their intense emotions, Victoria's children are now

smiling and visibly relaxed. Mrs. Samuels-Ortiz observes them with a satisfied expression, knowing she has fulfilled her mission with flying colors. As the group lingers in the comforting silence of shared understanding, the old librarian glances at the photograph on her desk—a younger Victoria holding a wide-eyed Elizabeth as a baby.

"Your mother," she says softly, "would be so proud of the strength you've shown today—your curiosity to uncover the truth and your defiant refusal to accept her apparent fate. Both of these attitudes are driving you. You're not only honoring her but also charting your own paths," she concludes with conviction.

The trio exchanges heartfelt goodbyes with the woman who has shaped so much of their mother's life. As they leave the library, the faint chime of the entrance bell seems to echo with promise—a sound that lingers in Rebecca's ears long after the door closes behind them.

— ✦ —

Royal Cambridge Scholastic Institute (2019)
(Class Auditorium)

As the professor's narration shifts back to the present, he pauses, seemingly lost in thought for a moment. "Mrs. Samuels-Ortiz's wisdom wasn't confined to the walls of her library," he says, his voice softer now. "It transcended generations, shaping not only Victoria's children but also every soul fortunate enough to cross her path. In her ability to wield defiance and curiosity as tools for transformation, she left a legacy that reminds us all to never accept the limits life imposes without question." The professor clears his throat, the weight of his reflection dissipating as he meets the eager gazes of his students.

"Class, curiosity is indispensable when we must or wish to decipher, analyze, or uncover decisions we're about to make or actions we're about to take, as we carefully weigh the consequences of our choices. On the other hand, defiance, when guided by just and rightful reasons, becomes a necessary stance to confront adversity, hardship, and especially the concept of fate," the pedagogue pauses, letting the weight of his words settle in the room. The quiet hum of anticipation fills the air. He smiles, a knowing glint in his eye, before offering the class a lesson in resilience: "Defiance and curiosity are not mere concepts," he says. "They are tools that allow us to challenge fate and the constraints of life itself."

A few hands are raised.

"Professor, haven't our studies shown us that fate is a completely false notion?" asks Kieth a History with long, jet-black hair pulled back in a ponytail.

"Spot on, Keith" the professor affirms with enthusiasm. "That is precisely the attitude we must take toward fate. The power of now— our ability to make decisions in the present—is what shapes our future. Fate is not some predetermined force; it is simply the consequence of the choices we make in the here and now. There is no fate," he affirms softly, the truth resonating in the quiet that follows. "Your actions shape your future—your curiosity and defiance are your most potent tools."

Ella, a philosophy major known for her insightful questions, asks with a thoughtful expression, "Professor, in 'Defiance,' you describe defiance as a force that can overcome adversity. How do you differentiate between healthy defiance that leads to growth and defiance that becomes destructive or self-destructive?"

"That's a very astute question, Ella," Erasmus responds, his eyes meeting hers with a look of respect. "Healthy defiance is rooted in a deep sense of purpose. It comes from a place of knowing what is right, standing up for personal values or the greater good. Destructive defiance, on the other hand, often arises from a place of resistance to growth or change. It's the refusal to see beyond one's immediate circumstances and can be driven by anger or fear. The key is self-awareness and a willingness to consider the consequences of one's actions."

Ella nods thoughtfully, her eyes still fixed on the professor as she considers the response.

Alexander, an engineering major with a penchant for asking probing questions, raises his hand with a contemplative look. "In 'Curiosity,' the poem speaks of the pursuit of knowledge and exploration. How do we maintain curiosity in a world that sometimes feels more rigid or set in its ways, especially in highly structured fields like mine?"

Erasmus nods, considering the perspective. "That's an interesting point, Alex. The world may feel rigid, but curiosity can still thrive in structured environments. It's about asking the right questions and looking for solutions in new and unexpected places. For engineers, curiosity is what drives innovation. The boundaries of what we know are constantly shifting because of the questions people continue to ask. Curiosity doesn't always mean breaking the mold, but sometimes simply seeing what's inside it, and seeing it from a different angle."

Alexander listens intently, nodding in agreement as he reflects on the professor's insight.

Lucia, a psychology major with a keen interest in human behavior, leans forward and asks, "In the poem 'Defiance,' there's a strong emphasis on fighting against hardship. But how do we reconcile this defiance with the psychological need to sometimes accept things as they are, especially when we can't control the outcome?"

Erasmus smiles, acknowledging the complexity of the question. "That's a very thoughtful inquiry, Lucy. I think defiance doesn't always have to mean fighting against everything. It can also be about not passively accepting what feels unjust or unnatural. It's about the ability to choose our response. Sometimes acceptance is the most defiant thing we can do, because it takes strength to surrender when needed, especially when we're faced with what we cannot change. True defiance is knowing when to stand up and when to step back, and having the strength to choose wisely."

Lucia nods in understanding, appreciating the depth of the response.

Victor, an international relations major with an affinity for literature, asks with a contemplative tone, "The idea of 'reciprocity' seems woven throughout both 'Defiance' and 'Curiosity.' How do you think these concepts relate to the way people interact globally, especially in terms of diplomatic relations and international cooperation?"

"That's an excellent connection, Victor," Erasmus responds, nodding thoughtfully. "Defiance and curiosity are not only personal tools but also vital elements in international relations. In diplomacy, defiance might look like standing firm on core values, even in the face of pressure, while curiosity is what drives us to understand the complexities of other cultures and the underlying reasons behind international conflicts. The ability to balance these two—holding firm when necessary, and remaining curious about others' perspectives—is essential for fostering cooperation and achieving peace in a globalized world."

Victor, deeply interested, takes a moment to digest the response before nodding in agreement.

With those final words, the class comes to a close, and the students, newly enlightened, gather their things in thoughtful silence.

"That will be all for today. Class dismissed."

As the professor leaves the room, the students wear expressions of profound thoughtfulness, as though they have been handed new, vital existential tools. With the intertwined magic of curiosity and defiance, they leave, ready to wield their newfound powers in the unfolding chapters of their lives.

Chapter 7

Decisions

Victoria and Erasmus' Home (2019)

There is a deluge outside. It's been raining for 24 hours. The middle-aged couple awoke at dawn. With hot teas and romantic tunes playing softly in the background, they remain bundled up in bed, indulging in a rare day of idleness. A passionate melody, Eros Ramazzotti's *Ma Che Bello Questo Amore* (How Beautiful Is This Love), fills the room, creating an ambiance of warmth and intimacy.

To Erasmus' delight, Victoria's feelings of guilt have almost completely dissolved. Over the past weeks, she has grown visibly more relaxed, her true self reemerging with each passing day. This transformation has brought forth her cheerful, carefree spirit, along with the enamored side of her that seems to draw her even closer, both emotionally and physically, to Erasmus.

"Dear, I have a secret to confess," Victoria announces with a mischievous undertone.

"OK, let me brace myself," Erasmus replies in mock apprehension.

"I preserved one of the writings Mrs. V. sent to us," she admits sheepishly.

"Which one?" he asks, his eyebrows rising in genuine surprise.

"The three-legged stool," she replies shyly.

"You preserved a priceless treasure, my lady. That scribble is invaluable," he remarks, his curiosity visibly piqued.

Erasmus stares at her with an intensity that seems to stretch into eternity, the music heightening the moment's depth. Victoria remains silent, Ornella Vanoni's *Dettagli* (Details) weaving its enchanting melody in the background.

Intrigued, Erasmus notices the familiar flicker in her eyes. "All right, my psychologist lady, where are you heading with this?" he asks, his tone probing yet tender.

"Nowhere," she replies evasively.

"Nowhere, as in, you have something to share but are hesitating to let it out?" he counters knowingly.

'*He always catches me before I even begin,*' Victoria reflects, startled by his instinctual ability to read her so easily.

"Dear, every time I read The Three-Legged Stool, I feel that our relationship back at Harvard had a true commitment of love and intense passion but lacked enough friendship or communication," she blurts out, her voice tinged with hesitation.

"Is that a justification or a fact, my lady?" he asks, his tone now stern as he absorbs her words.

"Intimacy was limited," she demurs, her voice wavering. Erasmus takes a long pause, his thoughts swirling as he reflects deeply. His gaze sharpens, and determination hardens his expression. Ornella Vanoni's *Nessuno al Mondo* (No One In The World Like You) plays, its emotive tones amplifying the tension.

"You mean to say that with just a glance, we could read each other's moods? Or that we knew what the other desired? Or how we could finish each other's sentences?" he begins, his voice growing more impassioned. "Or perhaps you're referring to the endless conversations—day after day, everywhere we went—about every facet of our lives? Or maybe it was the fact that during our time together, we were apart only for the briefest of moments? Is that the kind of lack of intimacy, friendship, and communication you're referring to?" Erasmus' words are laced with pointed sarcasm.

Victoria withdraws momentarily, grappling with his response and her own feelings. After a few moments of reflection, she regains her composure, meeting his gaze with renewed clarity and resolve. Laura Pausini and Gilberto Gil's *Seamisai* (If You Love, You Know) permeates the room with its enchanting melody.

"Did I create my own fantasy to justify my decisions and choices, dear?" Victoria asks, her voice barely audible over the music.

"I'm not sure. Please enlighten me," Erasmus replies, his tone tinged with annoyance.

"It seems that instead of gratefully accepting and enjoying what I have, the glass always appears half empty, and my focus is on what I believe I am missing," she declares, her words heavy with introspection.

"I don't think so," he finally articulates. "That's just a convenient excuse. Your real problem is that your perspective is negative even when your glass of life is full. When behaving like this, you always see your glass half empty while yearning to make your own fantasies real," he snaps, his words cutting through the warm atmosphere.

"Tell me about it," she pleads softly.

"Tell you about what?" he asks, puzzled.

"About our life together back then, at Harvard, from your perspective."

Erasmus pauses, his gaze turning inward as he searches through the recesses of his memory. His eyes lose focus, traveling back in time as Sandra Mihanovich's *Habla El Alma* (The Soul Speaks) fills the room, resonating deeply with their mood.

Lost in reminiscence, Erasmus recalls the places, the people, their laughter, the anecdotes, the readings, their shared rituals, plans, and the extraordinary dreams they wove together.

"Don't you remember any of it?" he finally asks.

"Of course I do, my love. I recall all of it vividly," she reassures him, her voice steady as her mind replays those cherished moments.

"But?" he probes, sensing there's more.

Victoria hesitates, her lips quivering as she wrestles with her thoughts. Charles Aznavour and Laura Pausini's *Parigi in Agosto* (Paris in August) drifts through the air, casting a contemplative spell over them.

"It's just that you've recorded and remembered our lives together in a way that I haven't. Either because I avoided it or because of my loss, I denied the extent to which I had it. You pointed out that I always see the glass half empty, and my perception, as a result, is limited. For me, without a doubt, it was the best period of my life. I regret that it went by so fast and was too short. But, if you hadn't helped me just now, I wouldn't have been able to remember our life together in the detail that you do. You've made my memories an immense treasure. You can literally recall every day, every minute, every moment. It's extraordinary. Now, I feel like I'm in a time machine, revisiting and reliving our life through your recollections in a way I didn't see before," she admits, her sincerity shining through.

"So, Vicky, you know the answer to your question better than I do. You know exactly what was missing in our three-legged stool."

"Nothing was missing," she speaks aloud, her voice firm with realization.

Erasmus knows better but chooses to remain silent.

Pablo Milanés' profoundly moving *Para Vivir* (In Order To Live) envelops them, pulling at their hearts.

"The only thing missing was me," she says, her epiphany dawning in her voice.

"You were there, alright, my lady, but only partly." Her newfound clarity inspires Erasmus, his admiration for her evident.

The rain has stopped, and daylight filters through the windows. Yellows, reds, and oranges replace the gray hues, bathing the room in warmth. Their embrace radiates a shared understanding, their tight hold a silent promise.

"If I may ask, my loving erudite, what will be the subject of your class this morning?" she inquires, her voice tender.

"Decisions," he says cryptically.

Victoria studies Erasmus intently, a quiet resolution forming in her heart.

"How fitting, dear. Well, I've decided I will never again look at life as a half-empty glass, always yearning for what I don't have. I promise to adopt the attitude of a half-full-glass kind of person," she declares with conviction.

"Fantastic, my lady," he replies, his delight unmistakable.

"All in the name of love, my dear," she murmurs, her voice sleepy but content.

Alejandro Sanz's *La Fuerza Del Corazón* (The Strength of the Heart) continues to play as the deeply enamored couple drifts into a world of dreams, wrapped securely in each other's arms.

Royal Cambridge Scholastic Institute (2019)
(Campus Streets)

'Remarkable,' With his heart still full from the morning, Erasmus pedals toward the faculty building, the brisk morning air, crisp and invigorating against his skin. *She's come full circle. She sought atonement by confronting her past head-on, and once she achieved it, she turned inward, focusing on her character and virtues*, muses.

The serenity of the morning with Victoria lingers in his mind, but he feels the weight of his responsibility as a teacher settle in once again. His thoughts shift, readying himself for another day in the classroom.

Royal Cambridge Scholastic Institute (2019)
(University Auditorium)

Professor Cromwell-Smith strides down the halls with a spring in his step, his heart swelling with pride for his other half.

As he enters the classroom, the pedagogue's mind shifts again, this time focusing on the students in front of him. He's aware, more than ever, of the delicate balance between the life he's shared with Victoria and the lessons he's about to impart. With a quiet breath, he readies himself to bridge the gap between the personal and the academic.

"Good morning to all of you," he greets his students warmly, his broad smile lighting up the room.

"Good morning, Professor Cromwell," the student body responds in perfect harmony, their voices filled with respect and enthusiasm.

"Decisions," he begins, his voice resonant and measured.

"So hard to take, so difficult to make. How many of us struggle daily, over long periods, or even our entire lives, wrestling with the choices we face?" he continues, his gaze sweeping across the room, ensuring every student feels the weight of his words.

"Today, I'll take you back in time to a moment when I was at a crossroads, grappling with a crucial decision. In my search for clarity, I turned to one of my most trusted mentors—an antiquarian steeped in the wisdom of New England."

He pauses, the room falling silent as his students lean in, captivated by the promise of his tale.

"It all begins like this …"

—✦—

By Train from Boston to New Haven, CT (1977)

I'm on my way to meet Mr. Lafayette, the antiquarian of gallant French ancestry. Victoria and I visited him every time Harvard played Yale University. He's always been a beacon of wisdom, helping me navigate the most challenging subjects or situations in my life.

When I arrive at his store in New Haven, he leaps from his trusted reading chair and hurries toward me with a bear hug and a kiss on each cheek—the French way—even though his Gallic ancestry is two or three generations removed.

"What a pleasure to see you here, Erasmus," he exclaims, his voice rich with warmth, tactfully avoiding the subject of Victoria's disappearance.

"The pleasure is mine, Mr. L.," I respond, slightly overwhelmed by his effusiveness.

"I know you're living in America now, but why don't you tell me exactly what you're up to?" he asks with genuine curiosity.

"A few months ago, I started teaching at Brandeis University. I love what I do, and I'm confident this is my calling in life. But when I'm alone, her absence still hurts. I came all the way here to see you because I need your guidance. Somehow, I need to find a way to let go and move on with my life," I plead, the pain in my voice unmistakable.

Mr. Lafayette studies me intently, his piercing gaze seeming to reach into the depths of my soul. For what feels like an eternity, he says nothing, his silence heavy with thought.

"Erasmus," he begins with measured clarity, "from what I've heard from your other mentors—my fellow antiquarians—and what I observe here today, it's clear that you must decide to move on. Not just acknowledge the need to let go, but consciously decide to put your breakup behind you. And once you've made that decision, implement it with unwavering resolve," he says emphatically, each word landing like a carefully placed stone.

He pauses for a moment, then adds, "I have a scribble that perfectly illustrates the predicament you find yourself in. Let me retrieve it."

With long, deliberate steps, Mr. Lafayette walks away, leaving me alone with my thoughts. He returns quickly, carrying an enormous leather-bound ancient book that looks as though it holds the wisdom of centuries.

"I will now read this to you," he declares, his voice imbued with the authority and passion of a true pedagogue.

"Decisions"

There are no worse decisions in life

than the ones we never make—

not to be confused with choosing to do nothing

or taking no action,

as those are still decisions we consciously make.

Why is it

that so many of us

are so utterly indecisive

about our lives and our futures?

Decisions to ponder, wander, and wonder.

Decisions we nail or blunder,

contest or tender,

waste or reap,

reach or press,

accept or reject,

rejoice or despise,

elevate or bury,

doubt or believe in,

pursue or avoid,

reverse or affirm,

lament or relish,

reluctantly take

or passionately embrace.

Decisions, decisions, decisions to make—

about which paths to follow,

the alternatives we choose,

or the course of action we take.

Being decisive is hard and difficult,

for it demands we conquer

our worst insecurities and fears.

Decisiveness is the consequence
of resoluteness and determination
to bring matters to a conclusion,
one way or another.

Being decisional is the result of readiness—
the readiness to form actionable options
and act upon them
by selecting
from the choices we face.

Decisions always reap guidance.
Through decisions, life's dynamics
unfold and take shape.

It is how everyone and everything,
for better or worse,
forward or backward,
moves and responds
within the circle of life.

In this context,
to decide is not a choice
but an existential imperative.

Without decision,
we fall into a catatonic void,
and life passes us by,
unclaimed and unfulfilled.

Decisions, decisions, decisions to make—

decisions that overwhelm us,

sucking the air out of our lungs,

yet persist, never disappearing.

To be alive requires decisionism.

It is essential to our existence.

There is no way around it.

When a choice presents itself,

when the moment arrives

to form an opinion,

choose a path,

or act—

make the decision,

move on,

and continue.

Decisions are immanent choices,

ones we must perpetually face

as long as we remain participants

in the circle of life.

*

"Mr. Lafayette's words hang heavy in the air, their truth undeniable. Erasmus sits in contemplative silence, the wisdom of the antiquarian's reading resonating deeply. As the train carries him back to Boston, his thoughts churn with newfound resolve, each mile marking a step closer to the decisions he knows he has to make."

— ✦ —

Royal Cambridge Scholastic Institute (2019)
(University Auditorium)

Professor Cromwell-Smith takes his class out of their deep concentration with a pointed reminder.

"Always remember, the worst decisions in life are those you never make. Indecision renders you a spectator, not a participant in life," emphasizes the eminent pedagogue, his words carrying the weight of conviction. The words of Mr. Lafayette still echo in the Professor's mind as he recalls his visit years ago. 'To decide is not a choice, but an existential imperative,' Lafayette had said. Now, back in the present, as the familiar faces of his students watch him attentively, Erasmus realizes that each moment is, in fact, a decision — one that shapes his own journey forward.

"Now, I'd like to open the floor for questions," Professor Cromwell-Smith says, his voice inviting and warm. "Please feel free to ask anything related to the subjects we've covered today."

Madison, a creative writing major, raises her hand and is called upon.

"Professor, in the poem *Decisions*, the emphasis is placed on the existential weight of the choices we face. How do we reconcile the tension between the necessity of making decisions and the overwhelming nature of those decisions, especially when the consequences are unclear or daunting? How do we avoid paralysis by analysis?"

"Madison, that's a thought-provoking question. The fear of making the wrong choice is something many people struggle with, and it often leads to a sort of 'analysis paralysis.' In the poem, we see that the real danger isn't in making a wrong decision—it's in failing to make a decision at all. Indecision itself is a decision, but it leads to stagnation. The key is to remember that no decision is ever completely without risk, and the uncertainty that comes with making choices is just part of the process. Instead of waiting for the 'perfect' moment to make a decision, we must trust ourselves to act, knowing that we can always adjust our course as we go. In a way, the act of deciding is what gives us clarity and direction."

Steven, a neuroscience major, asks the next question.

"Professor, in the poem, decisiveness is described as the result of overcoming insecurity and fear. From a psychological perspective, how can we develop a mindset that encourages decisiveness, especially when we feel overwhelmed or uncertain about the right choice?"

"Steven, that's an insightful question. One of the core challenges in decision-making is that it often requires us to confront our fears— fear of failure, fear of regret, or fear of making the wrong choice. In psychology, this is closely tied to self-efficacy, which is our belief in our ability to make effective choices and handle the consequences. To cultivate decisiveness, we need to build confidence in our ability to make decisions and trust in our capacity to adapt if things don't go as planned. This starts by setting small, low-risk decisions and building momentum. Over time, we learn that making decisions, even difficult ones, doesn't lead to catastrophe. Instead, it propels us forward, and that forward motion is often what helps us grow."

Lindsey, a literature major and a sharp focus in her eyes, speaks next.

"Professor, the poem describes life as a continuous process of decision-making, and yet, it also speaks of the overwhelming nature of those choices. How do we maintain a sense of purpose and coherence in our decisions when we're constantly confronted with so many paths to choose from?"

"Lindsey, that's an important observation. The poem speaks to the paradox of decision-making: while we are constantly making decisions, the sheer number of options can sometimes make us feel overwhelmed. The key to maintaining purpose and coherence is alignment—making decisions that reflect our values, goals, and sense of self. If we can stay connected to our core beliefs and what matters most to us, even the toughest choices become easier to navigate. It's about knowing what guides us and making decisions that align with that deeper purpose. Even when faced with many paths, when we act in accordance with our values, we create coherence and direction in our lives."

Leonard, a psychology major with an athletic build and a sharp jawline, speaks up next.

"Professor, the poem emphasizes the existential imperative of making decisions, yet it also highlights the toll that constant decision-making can take. How do we balance the need for action with the necessity of reflection and pause? How do we ensure that we're making decisions with intention rather than out of impulse or exhaustion?"

"Leonard, that's a nuanced question. The poem captures the urgency of decision-making, but it's also important to remember that decisions aren't just about speed—they're about intention. We can make decisions with purpose and clarity by creating space for reflection. While some decisions need to be made quickly, others benefit from taking a step back. This is where practices like mindfulness and self-reflection come into play. By pausing, reflecting, and gaining perspective, we can make decisions that are grounded in our true values, rather than reacting impulsively or from a place of exhaustion. Balance is key—decisiveness isn't about rushing through life; it's about making choices that align with who we truly are and what we want to achieve."

As the professor wraps the class, he observes the student body's contemplative expressions, their brows furrowed in thought. He surmises they are grappling with the decisions they have yet to confront and reflecting on the choices they've already made—or avoided—on their journey.

"That will be all for today. I'll see you all next week," Professor Cromwell-Smith concludes, his words lingering like echoes of wisdom. As the students rise and file out of the auditorium, he hands each of them a copy of the happiness formula, his gesture filled with quiet hope for their journeys ahead.

He watches them leave, each one likely pondering the choices they've yet to make, or the ones they've already committed to. His gaze lingers for a moment, feeling the weight of the day's lesson and the quiet satisfaction of a shared, unspoken understanding.

As the last of his students exit the auditorium, their murmured conversations fading into the corridor beyond, Professor Cromwell-Smith lingers at the lectern, gazing out over the now-empty seats. The silence feels heavier, more contemplative, after the depth of their shared discussion. Gathering his notes and adjusting his glasses, he allows himself a rare moment of reflection. The echoes of the past and present intertwine, and he silently wonders which seeds of wisdom, if any, have found fertile ground among his students.

Straightening his posture, he walks toward the door, his mind already preparing for the next lecture—a chance to explore life's complexities further and, perhaps, to inspire a few more hearts.

Chapter 8

Resilience

Martha's Vineyard, Massachusetts (2019)
(Gay Head Lighthouse)

Erasmus and Victoria have been pedaling around the island for hours. A gentle breeze makes their ride most enjoyable as they traverse the picturesque seaside landscape of blossoming flowers and manicured gardens. They dismount their bikes and walk toward the majestic cliffs known as "the Gay Head." Finding a comfortable spot, they sit down to enjoy the artisan sandwiches they've brought along.

"Erasmus, it's time," Victoria blurts out suddenly.

"Time?" he echoes, his tone incredulous.

"Yes, it's time for you to tell me about your personal life while we were apart," she says with a playful smile, her eyes sparkling with curiosity.

Erasmus, at first taken aback, pauses as he gazes at her, the surprise quickly melting away.

'Nothing wrong with being inquisitive; after all, she's been an open book with you,' he reasons. 'Besides, even if she hadn't been forthcoming, you'd still fill in the blanks. Isn't that right?' he questions himself, conceding fairness to her.

"Your orders are my command, my lady," he declares with a mock bow, signaling his readiness to comply.

The afternoon sun hovers high above the horizon, casting a golden glow over the cliffs as Erasmus begins to take Victoria on a journey through his past. His voice is calm but tinged with emotion as he shares a chapter of his life that had been shaped by both fulfillment and longing.

"Victoria, as you know, I started writing while we were at Harvard. It wasn't something I planned—it simply flowed onto paper, expressing the intensity of our love while we were together. Once I began scribbling, I found I couldn't stop."

He pauses briefly, looking out at the sea before continuing, his words carrying both pride and vulnerability.

"My first big project was a novel. It took an extraordinarily long time—especially at the start. I had no idea what I was doing. The process was filled with trials and errors, endless rewrites, and even the complete scrapping of entire manuscripts. Eventually, though, I managed to finish it."

Victoria listens intently, her gaze never wavering, as he continues.

"Soon after, albeit with great reluctance and low expectations, I took the finished manuscript to a publisher right here in town," Erasmus shares, his voice softening as he recalls the memory.

— ✦ —

Boston, Massachusetts (1989)
(Erudite Renaissance Press Offices)

"Your book is very poorly written, Mr. Cromwell," the female executive proclaims, her tone firm and unyielding.

Erasmus sits across from Rachel Thurman, the head editor at Erudite Renaissance Press and, without a doubt, one of the most strikingly beautiful women he's encountered since first meeting Victoria at Harvard. Her elegance and commanding presence are undeniable, yet her sharp critique cuts straight to the bone.

"This is not only my opinion but the consensus of several of our senior editors and proofreaders. They will not touch it as is," she states bluntly, her words leaving no room for ambiguity.

For most aspiring writers, this would mark the end of the road—a rejection delivered in no uncertain terms. Typically, such news would be conveyed in a written note or a brief phone call. But Rachel Thurman has chosen to deliver this verdict in person, motivated by an inexplicable fondness for the stubborn professor sitting before her. However, his unshakable self-confidence and immutable stubbornness push her buttons in ways she can't entirely ignore.

"And about your second submission," she continues, "poetry does not sell. Period. Don't waste your time." Her tone is final, her gaze challenging.

As she finishes her sentence, something unexpected happens. Erasmus smiles—a genuine, unbothered smile that catches her completely off guard.

'How ironic,' she muses, her irritation mounting. 'He's smiling after being told his work is unpublishable.'

"Professor Cromwell, I don't recall ever seeing an aspiring writer smile at me when rejected," she snaps, her frustration evident.

"Mrs. Thurman, perhaps you could join me for dinner, and we could discuss it further," he responds calmly, the suggestion leaving her momentarily speechless.

"What?" she exclaims, her voice rising in disbelief. "Mr. Cromwell, didn't I make myself perfectly clear?"

Her tone sharpens, but inwardly, she acknowledges his audacity.

'This guy is impervious to rejection,' she thinks, grudgingly admiring his indomitability.

It's then that his warm smile and gentle eyes manage to pierce through her defenses.

"You're serious?" she asks, her voice softening, a trace of teasing in her tone.

"It would indeed be a pleasure," he replies smoothly.

"When?" she asks, her resistance finally giving way to curiosity.

"Right now, as soon as you leave the office," he says, his tenacity never faltering.

For the first time, Rachel Thurman smiles back.

La Provence Bistro, Downtown Boston (1989)
(French Restaurant)

The dinner conversation begins with Erasmus sharing his memories of arriving in America, punctuated by shared laughter. "Everything seemed so modern and advanced other than the people's manners, language, and knowledge – all of which seemed to originate from a land of barbarians."

"I was also clumsy, odd, and would stumble into anything and everything," he adds with a wry smile.

After a few glasses of wine and savoring the finest gourmet cuisine, Rachel Thurman's tongue loosens, revealing her unchecked candor.

"I pride myself on dating the right type of man," she blurts out, her tone laced with arrogance.

"Rachel, let me be very frank with you," Erasmus interjects, choosing to ignore her self-important comment.

"Don't tell me! You're a superhero, and this disguise is your secret personality and persona?" she retorts, sarcasm dripping from her words.

"Perhaps I am; one never knows. But tell me something. If you like my book so much, what are you afraid of?" he counters, his question striking with unexpected precision.

Her smile vanishes as she studies him, intrigued by his boldness. Rachel senses the dynamic shift. The conversation is no longer light-hearted—it's becoming a battle of wits. There's a flicker of renewed interest in her eyes.

"Pardon my naïveté. I'm catching on. You're posturing, setting me up to negotiate my intellectual property rights. You're trying to manipulate, bargain, and extract a great deal for your publishing company," he presses further, unrelenting in his challenge.

Rachel opens her mouth to respond but pauses as his piercing eyes seem to unravel her intentions. She smiles mischievously, surrendering a couple of honest words.

"Business is business, Erasmus."

Ignoring her declaration, Erasmus remains silent. But her use of his first name catches his attention. He smiles, and she reads him just as well.

A distinct dissonance lingers between them, evident even on this first date. Rachel's priorities and Erasmus's values clash, their hearts beating to different rhythms.

Erudite Renaissance Press Offices (1991)

For several months, Erasmus's first book has held a prominent position on the bestseller list.

"Congratulations! Your first royalties' payment, Erasmus," Rachel exclaims, planting an impassioned kiss on his lips as she hands him the check.

Erasmus takes a cursory glance at the amount before slipping it into his pocket with little fanfare. Rachel's eyes widen dramatically.

'He couldn't care less,' she thinks in frustration.

"How does it feel to be a very wealthy university professor?" she probes, hoping to elicit some excitement.

"Exactly like it felt a minute ago. Nothing has changed. I never celebrate having nor making money, Rachel," he replies with casual indifference.

"Maybe now you can consider quitting that job of yours at the university and devote your time to writing full-time," she suggests, her exasperation seeping through her tone.

He doesn't bother to respond, leaving her simmering in silence.

Sniffles Highlands Trail, Telluride, Colorado (1991)
(Summer)

They've been hiking for hours, winding through dense forests and traversing open meadows. As they climb higher along a narrow mountain path, they're greeted by an explosion of wildflowers, sparkling streams, and, at 12,000 feet, an enchanting hidden valley.

At first, they hear a faint trickle, then the crescendo of a roaring waterfall, revealed like a secret behind a rocky turn. The idyllic scene seems untouched, perfect for a postcard.

Hungry and weary, they settle down to devour their artisan sandwiches and energy drinks. Their conversation is sparse, the silence between them untroubled.

"The view from my house is hard to match, but this stunning landscape might just do it," Rachel observes, her tone casual.

"But nothing is cozier than our condo overlooking the Charles River," she adds, her voice trailing off into a steady stream of admiration for her belongings, her rosy cheeks glowing in the crisp mountain air.

Erasmus listens, searching for a connection that feels increasingly elusive.

'What's hers is hers, but what's ours? Where's the heart in all of this?' he wonders silently.

Inca Trail, Cuzco, Peru (1991)
(Winter)

The day's hike has been grueling, a marathon of endurance through breathtaking scenery. At last, as they turn a sharp corner, Machu

Picchu unveils itself—a mystical city suspended in the clouds, its ancient walls basking in the afternoon sun.

"Rachel, we're on top of the world," Erasmus exclaims, drenched in sweat but exhilarated.

"Yep, another bucket list item checked off! I can't wait to tell everyone. I did it. I finally did it," Rachel declares, her enthusiasm laser-focused on the achievement.

Her self-congratulatory tone misses Erasmus's growing disenchantment.

'She's blind to the journey's wonder—the mountains, the history, the shared experience. Her triumph is about her circle, her conquest. Where's the empathy? The heart?' Erasmus reflects, his joy dimmed by the widening emotional chasm between them.

Hermitage Museum, St. Petersburg, Russia (1992)

In the heart of the Hermitage Museum, Erasmus is spellbound, absorbed in the museum's opulent treasures. For hours, he marvels at the intricate designs, the vivid colors, and the sheer artistry of Fabergé's masterpieces.

Rachel, meanwhile, shifts impatiently, stealing glances at her watch.

'How can anyone spend this much time on decorative trinkets? It's been three hours, and my checklist is far from done,' she fumes inwardly.

On a short break, Erasmus beams, his face lit with unrestrained excitement.

"Rachel, what an experience! The colors are mesmerizing. The integration of malachite, jade, lapis lazuli—it's extraordinary. And those imperial Easter eggs, they're incomparable," he gushes.

Rachel masks her irritation behind a tight grin, her patience worn thin.

"I hope you're ready to leave. Those eggs took up two hours," she mutters internally.

Erasmus, finally catching her lackluster expression, asks, "Bored, Rachel?"

"To death," she replies curtly, her words sharp enough to slice through his enthusiasm.

A few moments later, they leave the museum—one of the world's most extraordinary cultural treasures—abandoning its magnificence to pursue her checklist of sights around the city.

Erasmus walks in silence, the sting of her indifference a weight he cannot shake.

Cortina d'Ampezzo, Italy (1991)
(Winter)

"Where's Erasmus, Rachel?" Brigitte asks, glancing around the vibrant, snow-covered mountain restaurant filled with their lively group of friends.

"Skiing," Rachel replies casually, swirling her glass of wine, her cheeks flushed from the afternoon's indulgence.

"When do you two even see each other?" Mark, a colleague, prods curiously.

Rachel sighs and leans back in her chair. "Well, he's up before dawn, rushing to be the first on the slopes when they open. I don't even get out of bed until around eleven. Once I finally make it up the mountain, I track him down on his favorite runs. We ski together for a while and then stop for lunch."

"And after lunch?" Brigitte presses with a knowing look.

"Oh, he's relentless—he keeps going until the ski patrol chases him off the slopes," she adds with a bright smile, "But, during the pre-ski hours and all through the night, he's all mine."

Rachel waves at Erasmus, who emerges through the colorful crowd of skiers. His smile broadens as he spots her, his helmet and gear giving him the aura of a devoted ski enthusiast.

'They're like two dissonant clocks—hanging next to each other on the same wall yet ticking in completely different rhythms,' Brigitte muses silently, her observant eyes noting the gap in their connection.

Restaurant "Jules Verne," Eiffel Tower, Paris (1993)

"Erasmus, we've been together for four years. We've traveled the world. I've supported your teaching and writing careers, and we've become... comfortable with each other," Rachel begins, her tone a mixture of longing and frustration.

'Where is she going with this?' Erasmus wonders as he sips his wine, ever the picture of calm curiosity.

"It's been lovely, Rachel. You're right," he replies, uncertain of the storm brewing beneath her carefully measured words.

Rachel's patience snaps. She wants to yell at him, to demand attention, but knows it would only slide off his immutable exterior. She tries jealousy—it's never worked before, but she's desperate for a response.

"When are you going to ask me?" she blurts, the words flying out before she can stop them.

"Ask you about what?" Erasmus replies, his absent-minded professor demeanor showing no trace of awareness.

"To marry me, you silly fool," she half-shouts, her frustration bubbling to the surface.

Erasmus freezes, his sharp gaze narrowing as his lips press into a thin line. The charged silence makes Rachel's heart pound as she watches him, hoping for a declaration, fearing rejection.

"Rachel," he finally says, his voice calm but chilling, "let me bluntly ask you something. If I weren't a successful and wealthy writer, would you consider marrying me?"

The question lands like a thunderclap. Rachel's confidence falters, and she hesitates before responding. When she does, her honesty is like a blade.

"No, definitely not."

The weight of her words settles between them, an unspoken understanding sealing their fate. Whatever tenuous bond had kept them together evaporates in an instant.

Later that evening, they board their flight home. They chat casually, laugh about their trip, and even doze off against each other's shoulders, sharing a final semblance of intimacy.

When they land in Boston, they part ways at Logan Airport, kissing goodbye for the last time. They never speak or meet again.

'I really liked Rachel, and we had a wonderful time together,' Erasmus reflects days later. 'But she was never my type.'

— ✦ —

Martha's Vineyard, Mass., Gay Head Cliffs (2019)

Victoria's posture as she leans forward is one of a mesmerized listener brimming with questions.

"I get the picture, dear. I get it," she utters softly.

Still mulling over what to say, Erasmus hesitates, uncertain what to add next, but her quizzical expression compels him to continue.

"Victoria, I know exactly what's going through your mind. I understand that I owe you at least some level of transparency. While I won't delve into irrelevant details, I want to remain respectful to the women I became acquainted with during our years apart. I can tell you that several things were consistent in my life over the years, especially regarding female companionship. First, during our separation, I was seldom alone. Second, aside from my relationship with Rachel and another woman in Europe, all my associations were extremely discreet. Most of my companions were former—emphasis on former—students. Third, Rachel was not the first to propose marriage to me. This happened several times, but I was never inclined, much less willing, to accept. Fourth, the longest of these relationships lasted four years, while the shortest spanned six months. All these women, without exception, went on to marry happily and have children. Lastly, I won't disclose how many relationships there were, but Victoria, there were several," he states in a measured tone.

Victoria's face lights up with a mix of delight and clarity as she clings to his arm while they begin walking back to their bikes. Silence accompanies their journey toward the ferry terminal, but after a few minutes, Victoria halts abruptly, and Erasmus stops too.

"I'm proud of you, dear," she says, her voice trembling with emotion.

"I feel so fortunate to be loved this much by you. I'm the luckiest woman in the world. You longed for and waited for me all these years, hoping I would resurface."

Letting her bike fall to the ground, she steps forward to embrace him and kisses him passionately, her gratitude and affection pouring through her every gesture.

Together, they pedal through a kaleidoscope of colors as the sky transitions from the brightness of a clear day, with its crisp whites and yellows, into flaming hues of orange and incandescent red. By the time they near their destination, the night has enveloped the world in deep blues, a luminous full moon, and a canopy of star-speckled blackness, marking the end of their ride in serene splendor.

Train Ride from Hyannis Point to Boston (2019)

Victoria rests half-asleep on Erasmus's shoulder, the soothing rhythm of the train lulling her into a peaceful haze. Suddenly, she stirs and softly asks, "Sweetheart, what will be the subject of tomorrow's class?"

"Resilience, my lady," Erasmus replies, his mind already immersed in the preparation of his lecture.

As Erasmus pedals toward the faculty building, the weight of his conversation with Victoria lingers in his mind. He reflects on the power of resilience, which now shapes both his personal journey and the theme for the day's lecture.

Royal Cambridge Scholastic Institute (2019)
(University Auditorium – The Next Day)

He enters the auditorium, his thoughts still tangled with the idea of resilience that had come up in his earlier conversation. The students are already seated, awaiting his words, and as the door swings open, Erasmus is ready to guide them through another lesson that feels deeply personal today.

"How's everyone today?" Professor Cromwell-Smith greets his class warmly, his voice carrying a palpable energy.

"Insanely awesome!" the students respond in enthusiastic unison.

"Today, we'll be talking about resilience," he begins, pacing slowly across the stage. "Resilience is the ability to adapt and bounce back when life knocks you down. It's what allows us to face challenges, endure hardships, and emerge stronger. This is not just a survival skill—it's a virtue."

He pauses, his gaze sweeping the room to ensure he has their full attention.

"I'll take you back to a moment in my life when resilience became a defining element of my character. To overcome adversity, we must understand it, accept it, and then rise above it. The story begins like this …"

The professor's voice lowers, signaling the start of another journey into a deeply personal and meaningful life lesson.

— ✦ —

Rowing on the Charles River (1977)

Ever since Victoria and I first met Mr. Faith by chance while rowing along the Charles River, I've maintained the habit of visiting him at his shop on the outskirts of Boston every time I row.

Today, after docking and securing my rowboat, I stroll through the streets of the small village, my steps marked by trepidation and excitement at the thought of seeing my old friend and mentor, Thomas Albert Faith. His antique bookshop, adorned with his name, houses countless treasures of knowledge.

As I step into the sacrosanct place, Mr. Faith is busy dispatching a client, who exits right past me, arms laden with voluminous books clutched tightly against his chest. I hold the door ajar, and the diminutive customer barrels into his waiting limo driver on the sidewalk, who leaps to assist with the load.

"Erasmus, what a pleasure to see you. It's been a long time. Where have you been?" Mr. Faith calls out, moving toward me with his characteristic slow, deliberate steps. He wraps me in his signature bear hug, and, as always, the final squeeze knocks the wind right out of me.

"Mr. Faith, how have you been?" I squeak, struggling to catch my breath.

"Getting old, but otherwise fine," he replies warmly.

"Look at you, all grown up. You even look like a professor now," he adds, his broad smile lighting up the room.

"Mr. Faith, I thought about visiting you of all people because you're the best suited to help me," I announce sternly. "You see, I'm struggling with desire and perseverance. I love my work and devote myself entirely to it, but it feels hollow. Something's missing, and, worst of all, I recognize what it is. I indulge and get lost in thoughts and memories of my past," I confess.

Mr. Faith listens intently, pacing with deliberate steps as if weighing my words. Then, without a word, he strides to the far-right end of his impossibly tall, library-like athenaeum. From the first row, he selects a medium-sized leather-bound book and returns to me, his demeanor both solemn and reassuring.

"Erasmus, here I have the perfect prescription for your current affliction," he begins, his voice resonant with conviction. "It's a scribble I treasure deeply as it touches on the heart of what you're seeking. Your struggle is with resilience—a virtue you must cultivate to confront life's challenges and transcend them. I hope this writing will help you develop resilience as an existential tool moving forward."

With that, he opens the book to a page marked by a red cord. He quickly scans the old writing, and upon finding the precise paragraph, he begins to read in earnest, his voice imbued with the wisdom of ages.

*

"Resilience"

Resilience lies at the core
of the very essence of the human spirit.
It is a vital, virtuous existential condition,
composed of sheer character power,
and unyielding, awe-inspiring willfulness.

Resilience is the untamable drive,
burning fire,
unflinching defiance,
relentless resistance,
fearless courage,
stubborn perseverance,
unwavering belief,
and an unstoppable hunger—
the fuel required to live with the intensity,
passion, and endurance
needed to succeed at any endeavor.

The resilient person tries again,
never stops,
does not give in to exhaustion,
bounces back,
moves forward,
does not dwell on the past,
adapts in an instant,
perennially studies and learns,
and ignores rejection.

The resilient person uses fear as a strength

and does not comprehend the words:

boredom,

gossip,

lingering grudges,

or jealousy.

The resilient person endures hardship,

overcomes tragedy,

learns from criticism,

treats failure as an opportunity,

mistakes as lessons,

defeats as temporary,

uses "no's" as incentives,

and never, ever quits,

much less surrenders.

Resilience is that quasi-superhuman force

that allows us:

To embark on challenging and demanding quests,

with fortitude and self-confidence.

To endure right up to completion,

despite seemingly insurmountable

challenges, setbacks, and difficulties.

To dare life,

defying all odds,

with absolute conviction and self-belief—

that no matter who or what,

we will, in the end, succeed.

*

"As Mr. Faith's voice faded, Erasmus felt the words resonate deeply within him. The scribble had stirred something dormant—a flicker of determination, a spark to confront his inner struggles. As he left the bookshop and walked back to the river, the sound of oars slicing through the water mirrored the rhythmic beat of his renewed resolve."

— ✦ —

Royal Cambridge Scholastic Institute (2019)
(University Auditorium)

As Professor Cromwell-Smith moves from his personal story to the lecture, he feels the weight of the past experience shaping his words in the present, and as the pedagogue's message settles over the room, a profound silence ensues, broken only by the faint shuffle of papers and the occasional cough, while students exchange glances, their faces marked with a mix of awe and determination, clearly moved by the lesson on resilience that has struck a chord, leaving them inspired and introspective; Professor Cromwell brings the class back to the present with a few additional words of timeless wisdom.

"Resilience is intrinsic to the sacred, serving as a propelling force for those who defend truth, honor, honesty, family, and loved ones.

It is the same driving energy for individuals who, on principle, stand firm for an ideology, religious belief, ethnicity, nation, land, or social group. Resilience also applies to the more mundane pursuits of life—

when we passionately chase dreams, commit to ideas, or uphold duties to provide, respect, defend, and love.

Finally, resilience is indispensable for pragmatic endeavors, such as planning, building, delivering, complying, and ultimately finishing what we start," the erudite professor concludes, his words reverberating through the room.

With a final glance at his students, the pedagogue's voice takes on a more contemplative tone, as he prepares to bring the lecture to a close before opening the floor to questions. He pauses for a moment, allowing the weight of his words to settle in their minds.

Sarah, an English literature major known for her philosophical reflections, raises her hand, her face thoughtful.

"Professor, in 'Resilience,' the poem emphasizes unyielding persistence in the face of hardship. How do you reconcile this idea with the notion of knowing when to let go, especially when continued effort might only lead to further suffering?"

"That's an insightful question, Sarah," Erasmus responds with a thoughtful pause. "Resilience, in this sense, isn't about mindlessly pushing through every obstacle. It's about knowing when to press on and when to step back. True resilience involves awareness and discernment—it's recognizing when an obstacle is a lesson or an opportunity to grow, and when it's simply a signal that the best way forward is to let go and redirect one's efforts. It's not about stubbornly fighting every battle; it's about fighting the ones that matter and knowing when to conserve your strength for the right moment."

Sarah nods, contemplating the balance between persistence and knowing when to pivot, her eyes reflecting the weight of the professor's words.

Joshua, a psychology major with a focus on emotional resilience, leans forward, his curiosity piqued. "In the poem, resilience is described as a force that allows us to rise again after failure. But how do we distinguish between resilience and stubbornness? Can there be a fine line between the two?"

Erasmus offers a small smile, appreciating the depth of the question.

"There is indeed a fine line, Joshua. Stubbornness often comes from a place of ego—refusing to adapt or learn from failure. Resilience, on the other hand, is rooted in growth. It allows you to acknowledge failure, learn from it, and adjust your course. Stubbornness keeps you locked in the same pattern, while resilience empowers you to evolve. It's about choosing to stand back up, not because you have to, but because you have learned something important along the way."

Joshua seems satisfied with the response, his brow furrowed in thought as he considers the practical application of this idea in his own life.

Lynn, a biology major who has studied the neurological aspects of stress and resilience, asks, "Professor, resilience in 'Resilience' is presented as a kind of inner strength. From a scientific perspective, what role does the brain play in cultivating this strength, and how does it affect our ability to bounce back after emotional setbacks?"

"Great question, Lynn," Erasmus says, his tone appreciative. "From a biological standpoint, resilience is a function of both the brain and the body. The prefrontal cortex helps us regulate our emotions, make decisions, and adapt our behaviors in response to stress. The hippocampus, which is involved in memory and learning, also plays a key role in how we process setbacks and use them as tools for future growth. On a more emotional level, resilience is a learned behavior—it's the brain's ability to adapt to challenges, strengthen connections through experience, and build emotional fortitude. The brain, just like our hearts, is capable of incredible recovery, provided we give ourselves the tools and space to heal."

Lynn smiles, clearly fascinated by the intersection of neuroscience and the human experience of resilience.

Vincent, a history major with a particular interest in the psychology of leadership, poses his question with confidence. "Professor, 'Resilience' speaks of persistence, but how do you see this concept in the context of leadership? How does resilience manifest in leaders who face overwhelming odds?"

"That's an excellent connection, Vincent," Erasmus responds. "In leadership, resilience is not only about pushing through personal challenges but also about maintaining the strength to lead others through difficulty. A resilient leader demonstrates the ability to remain calm, adapt, and inspire action even when faced with failure or hardship. They don't shy away from challenges—they confront them head-on, not because it's easy, but because their responsibility is to guide others. A resilient leader embraces setbacks as opportunities for growth, not just for themselves but for their team.

They understand that every failure is a lesson, and every setback is a steppingstone to greater success."

Vincent nods, the gears in his mind turning as he considers how resilience might shape the future of his own leadership journey.

"That'll be all for today; see you next week," declares Professor Cromwell as he exits the auditorium.

"That'll be all for today; see you next week," declares Professor Cromwell as the bell rings, signaling the end of class. The students remain transfixed for a moment, their expressions a mixture of awe and determination, their eyes reflecting a collective resolve as they grasp the depth of resilience and its necessity for enduring and succeeding in life. Slowly, they begin to file out in silence, each carrying the message of resilience with them. Erasmus watches them leave from the doorway, knowing that today's lesson will resonate long after they've exited the room.

Chapter 9

Life, Beauty, and Art

Victoria's and Erasmus's Campus Home (2019)

"Erasmus, why is it so difficult for you to reveal your inner self?" Victoria asks in the quiet stillness of the early morning.

He remains contemplative, his eyes soft yet searching hers for a moment as though weighing her question carefully.

"I'm always an open book for you to read, my lady," he finally replies, though his puzzled expression and the flicker in his gaze betray him.

"Dear, why do I still have to pry things out of you? Perhaps you thought you could get away with only sharing your love affair with the publisher?" she teases, her smile widening as she reads the guilt in his eyes when he looks away.

His gaze sharpens, intensifying as he prepares to unveil something deeper, prefacing it with two cryptic words.

"Venice and Florence," he says, his voice distant, as if tethered to memories beyond their cozy home studio.

Her brows furrow in confusion, sensing he's about to open another door to his guarded soul. What she doesn't yet realize is that this door leads to a world she didn't know existed within him.

"I've been visiting both places every other year for forty years," he admits softly.

Victoria stiffens, startled by the revelation. They've shared more than two years back together, yet this is the first mention of Italy— Italy, of all places. She resists the urge to interrupt, choosing instead to wait as her curiosity swells.

"Vicky, at one time, both cities became a magnet for me," he continues, his words cryptic yet laced with meaning.

"Why?" she asks, her tone layered with skepticism and a touch of impatience. Her unspoken thoughts are clear: *What's all the fuss? Why the secrecy?*

"Antonella D'Agostino is an antiquarian living in Venice, Italy. She's about to turn 75, nearly a decade older than me. She's been married for 55 years to her childhood sweetheart, Luciano D'Agostino, a retired banker. Together, they have two children—a son who's an architect and a daughter who's a writer. Their children have given them twelve grandchildren and one great-grandchild," he narrates, his tone imbued with deep reverence and affection.

Victoria feels a rush of conflicting emotions as her imagination races. *He hasn't referred to her in professional terms,* she notes, her gut instinct flaring. A growing unease churns within her, as she senses where this might be heading.

But she couldn't be more wrong. Whatever scenario she's conjuring in her mind falls woefully short of the truth he's about to reveal.

"I met Antonella on my first trip to Italy while visiting her antique bookstore. I was 25 years old, and she was 35."

Victoria listens intently, trying to connect the dots but instinctively choosing to let Erasmus guide her through this labyrinth of revelations.

"She introduced me to the world of books authored during the Renaissance era. Through her, I became versed in deciphering the markings of ancient scribbles," he continues, his tone almost detached, as though trying to distance himself from the significance of the memory.

Victoria finds herself at a crossroads: let the story unfold naturally or press him for more details. Her curiosity, tinged with a streak of masochism, prevails. Placing her proverbial hand on the hot stove, she decides to prod further.

"Dear, what's the significance of this antiquarian in Italy?" Erasmus avoids her direct question, choosing instead to continue at his own measured pace.

"Antonella worked in tandem with Leonardo Conti, an antiquarian based in Florence. Throughout my life, I spent many summers shuttling back and forth between the two antiquarians and their cities. With their guidance, I became proficient in deciphering books written in the middle of the 15th Century onwards," he explains, his voice steady, yet Victoria senses an undercurrent of emotion.

Why is it that the story, as innocuous as it seems on the surface, still rings alarm bells? she wonders, grappling with the unease that churns in her gut.

Erasmus shifts his gaze, finally looking directly into her eyes. For the first time, she feels he's fully present, as though weighing his next words carefully.

"And?" she pushes, her tone laced with quiet insistence, implying that there's more beneath the surface.

"And what?" he counters, his tone feigning incredulity.

Victoria hesitates, momentarily pulling back, but her instincts override her caution.

"Did you?" she blurts out suddenly, her words cutting through the tension like a knife.

Erasmus holds her gaze, his expression unreadable as an eternity seems to pass. His eyes flicker with a faraway look, wandering through memories long buried.

"Is it important?" he asks, his voice betraying a subtle hesitation.

"It is to you. Obviously, you want me to know; otherwise, you wouldn't have raised the subject, at least not like this—emphasizing her personality more than her trade," Victoria counters, her tone sharp with irrefutable logic.

He remains silent, though she notices a fleeting sadness cross his eyes before it dissipates like a passing shadow.

"It was never meant to be something serious. She never contemplated leaving her husband. Neither did I want it to be more than an annual summer fling. It was always a discreet affair," he admits, the words spilling out with a noticeable sense of relief.

Victoria is entirely absorbed in the moment, her instincts whispering that something feels unresolved.

"When did it end?" she probes.

"Fifteen years ago," Erasmus replies, offering her a wave of relief.

"And yet, you chose to tell me this last, after disclosing all the other 'relevant' relationships in your past," she muses aloud, her tone laced with suspicion.

Victoria's words carry an unspoken accusation of something still unspoken, though Erasmus refrains from defending himself. Instead, he meets her glare with quiet resignation.

Why does this even matter anymore? It's all water under the bridge, her rational mind protests, but her emotions steer her in the opposite direction.

"Dear, how old are Antonella's children?" she asks, her voice sharper now.

Erasmus avoids her gaze.

"The oldest is … wait a minute, where are you heading with this?" he questions, his confusion evident.

"Erasmus, let me hazard a guess: both children are under forty, aren't they?" she counters, her rhetorical tone gaining momentum.

"What exactly are you implying, Victoria?" he asks, his discomfort deepening.

"Were Antonella and her husband unable to conceive children before you, the absent-minded love of my life, came into their lives?" she presses.

Erasmus falters.

"Yes, but how do you …?" he begins, only to trail off, his eyes widening as the weight of her implication sinks in.

"That wouldn't …" he stammers, his voice cracking.

"How do you know?" she persists, unwilling to let him evade the question.

Finally, he lowers his head, his body language heavy with surrender.

"I don't," he confesses.

Images of Antonella's vibrant, quintessentially Italian children flood his mind. Their happy and accomplished lives unfold in his memory, and he recalls his role as the beloved "uncle" from America—a relationship nurtured by Antonella herself.

"Victoria, you know what? Let it be. Whatever the truth may be, some things are better left as they are, even unsaid," he declares, his voice resolute, his gaze steady.

Victoria reacts instinctively. She moves toward him, placing her hands gently on his face, her eyes softening.

"I love you," she whispers, choosing to let the matter rest.

An important chapter of Erasmus's past has emerged, but its presence no longer looms. Together, they silently agree to move forward.

An hour later, as Erasmus readies for class, Victoria resumes their familiar routine.

"And what will be the subject of your class today, dear?" she asks, her voice calm and collected.

With a spirited energy, Erasmus heads for the door.

"Art and beauty," he replies over his shoulder.

Victoria waits, sensing there's more to come.

"It'll be about Florence and Venice, but strictly censored to the professional and poetic sides of it," he adds, turning to blow her a kiss before hopping onto his bike and pedaling off.

After a lingering kiss at the doorway of their campus home, Erasmus steps outside, feeling the warmth of the morning still wrapped around him. Victoria, standing at the doorstep, sends a playful kiss back, her hand lingering in the air as she watches him leave. As Erasmus rides to the university, the peaceful journey allows his mind to wander, shifting between memories of Italy, his conversation with Victoria, and the bustling energy of the campus he approaches, ready to engage his students. Now alone, Victoria reflects on Erasmus's Italian escapade, her thoughts a blend of curiosity and quiet acceptance.

— ✦ —

Royal Cambridge Scholastic Institute (2019)
(University Auditorium)

Entering the lecture hall, Erasmus feels the familiar weight of his role as professor settle upon him. The energy of the classroom, filled with eager faces, grounds him in the present. As he stands at the front, his heart steadies, and his mind shifts back to the intellectual landscape of art and beauty.

"Good morning, everyone," greets the venerable professor with a warm, resonant voice.

"Good morning, professor," replies the spirited student body in unison.

"Today, I'll take you back in time to revisit the Italian peninsula, where, in my early twenties, I met a couple of antiquarians who profoundly impacted my life. We'll recount a memorable occasion when they helped me better understand and appreciate my surroundings during that pivotal period," the sovereign professor begins, his tone imbued with anticipation.

"Inexorably, there was a time in the 15th century when all the roads for the world's antique books led to Italy—not just to Rome, but particularly to Venice and Florence. These cities, in their own right, were even more consequential than the ancient capital when considering the burgeoning market of printed books," Professor Cromwell-Smith elaborates, drawing his audience into the narrative.

"Prior to the 15th century, in 1440, the German-born Johannes Gutenberg invented the movable-type press, sparking a revolution in book printing. In the sixty years that followed, millions of books were published, heralding the birth of a European book trade and making the widespread dissemination of knowledge an irreversible phenomenon across all levels of society," he adds with fervor.

"In the mid-15th century, thanks to its immense wealth, the Italian peninsula became Europe's epicenter for publishing. This development was culturally fitting, as most books at the time were written in Latin or Greek—the languages of Rome and Athens. Venice and Florence emerged as dominant hubs for book production, fueling the Renaissance's intellectual and artistic flourishing. This abundance of books enriched minds like Leonardo da Vinci, who prized his library of magnificent volumes. These texts served as vital resources for his groundbreaking ideas, inventions, and, most notably, his unparalleled art," the professor continues, his passion for the subject unmistakable.

"This historical context sets the stage for the heart of today's lesson—art and beauty," he concludes, transitioning seamlessly into the story.

"It all begins in Florence, Italy, the heart of the Renaissance," Professor Cromwell-Smith continues, his voice steady and infused with admiration. "Florence was not only the creative hub for luminaries such as Leonardo da Vinci, Michelangelo, Galileo, Machiavelli, Dante, and Boccaccio but also a city that served as their intermittent home during this era of unparalleled enlightenment," he declares, his eyes scanning the room for engaged faces.

"This city wasn't just a geographical location; it was a crucible of ideas, a confluence of art, science, and literature that forever altered the trajectory of human history. Florence's spirit fostered an environment where intellects and visionaries thrived. They were drawn to its vibrant culture and patronage of the arts, a testament to the city's unmatched contribution to the Renaissance," he elaborates with unwavering conviction.

Without pausing for breath, the professor continues, fully immersed in the subject. "Here, genius wasn't an anomaly—it was a legacy. Florence didn't merely witness the Renaissance; it orchestrated it, birthing and nurturing minds that would shape our understanding of beauty, humanity, and the cosmos."

— ✦ —

Conti, Libri Antichi,
Antique Book Store, Florence, Italy (1979)

*The antique bookshop of Leonardo Conti is nestled within walking distance of the **Battistero di San Giovanni** and Florence's old city center. Il Signore Conti specializes in books from the Renaissance era, specifically between 1450 and 1500, when over two million books were printed across Europe, with the Italian Peninsula serving as the epicenter of this literary revolution. Conti is a renowned trader of books from this golden period, a reputation further amplified by his collaboration with another prestigious antiquarian, Antonella D'Agostino, who owns an antique bookshop in Venice.*

"Mr. Conti, Mrs. D'Agostino, the art and beauty of Italy are utterly overwhelming. It's almost impossible to process all the magnificence that surrounds me," I confess, struggling to contain my awe. "I wonder if you have any books written about art and beauty during the Renaissance era. If so, perhaps we could explore them together," I beseech the two antiquarians, my voice a mix of curiosity and yearning.

After a thoughtful exchange with Signora D'Agostino, Signore Conti is the one to act. Rising with purpose, he begins an intricate search among the mahogany shelves of his cavernous bookshop. The dim light of the shop accentuates the reverence with which he handles the volumes. Finally, from the very top of an imposing cabinet, he retrieves a brown leather-bound book. With a practiced hand, he clears the dust from its cover, revealing an aged but regal tome. By its weight and thickness, it's evident this book spans at least 500 pages, each made of cloth paper.

As he opens it, I'm immediately struck by the hand-painted drawings that adorn its pages. The vibrant colors, delicate lines, and intricate details seem to breathe life into the centuries-old artwork. The beautifully stylized fonts demand attention, while hand-written annotations grace the margins, providing a glimpse into the mind of the book's original owner.

Signore Conti carefully turns the pages, scanning them with an almost reverential focus. Finally, his eyes alight on the passage he seeks. His expression brightens with enthusiasm as he clears his throat. Then, with a voice propelled by passion and expertise, he begins to read aloud, transporting us all into the heart of the Renaissance.

"Life, Beauty, and Art"

Where does beauty reside? Where does it lie?

Where is it found?

Beauty begins within us—

inside all of us,

waiting to be discovered,

waiting to be tapped.

To see beauty in anything or anyone,

we must first recognize the beauty within ourselves.

Where else can beauty be found?

Understanding that it begins with us,

we come to realize and appreciate

that we are surrounded by it.

The beauty we possess

enables us to find it

in everyone and everything else.

However, attractiveness is not always apparent at first glance.

There is dirt and darkness

where diamonds are hidden,

mud and disease

where gold is unearthed,

seemingly buried beneath impenetrable rocks.

There is litter and chaos

where masterpieces are born,

debris and dust

where magnificent craftsmanship emerges,

slime and sulfur

where oil riches burst forth.

Incoherence and lack of meaning

mark the initial scribblings

of the finest works,

and pain, sweat, and tears

are the price of the noblest human achievements.

Where does beauty originate?

Sometimes, beauty is born of ugliness.

It is most deeply valued

when uncovered from the depths of what appears hideous.

Beauty is best appreciated

when it defies stereotypes

and challenges conventional wisdom.

Yet for many, beauty is conferred in abundance,

only to go unrecognized,

its existential worth overlooked,

its magnificence unrealized.

When beauty fails to ignite satisfaction,

the spirit and soul remain hollow and empty.

In all its dimensions, beauty—

whether in possessions or people—

requires a benevolent disposition to be admired.

As life's clock ticks, beauty changes and morphs.

But for those who truly know

how to feel and celebrate it,

beauty never fades, diminishes, or disappears.

Physical youth provides and masks beauty,

but through the years,

the richness of our spirit and soul—

or the lack thereof—

is etched into our faces.

Without the masks of youth,

we reveal who we truly are inside.

Life's truest beauty lies hidden,

ready to be uncovered,

if we make the effort to seek it.

The beauty of a life well-lived

ages with nobility and grace.

Beauty shines brightest

in those life travelers

who live free of limiting

dogmas, prejudices, or stereotypes;

those who find and cherish

pulchritude, attractiveness, and charm,

the liveliness and comeliness of existence,

grace, and anything pleasing to the senses.

True beauty resides in those

who celebrate life fully,

who truly love and are loved,

who give selflessly, expecting nothing in return.

It is found in those who actively participate in life,

who value the small gestures and details,

and who pour their hearts and souls

into everything they do.

They live with passion, inspiration, and happiness.

These are the ones who possess lasting beauty—
a beauty that transcends
place, circumstances, age, or material wealth.

Lasting beauty never fades.
It is one of life's most precious gifts—
one of the hardest to master.

It requires cultivation as an inherent virtue,
to appreciate, wear, and treasure it,
even when it seems absent.

But when does beauty become art?
Art is inherent in beauty,
just as beauty is inherent in art.
Art is born of beauty.
Art creates beauty.
Beauty must be perceived for art to exist,
as art transforms ordinary into sublime, exceptional,
and extraordinary into masterful.

Art alters perception,
not only making objects appealing,
but also evoking feelings with meaning and purpose.

Art creates an intimate, quasi-spiritual connection within us.
It speaks the language of the spirit,
mirroring the soul.

Art resonates with beauty,

infatuating the heart.

Beauty is always driven and born from art.

Like beauty, art exists in the eye of the beholder.

And if so, there are no limits—

no boundaries to what art can be.

A scribble, an essay, a craft—

everything beauty touches

transforms into art.

Art is a deliberate human creation,

inspired by talent, skill,

and the heart.

Even unintentionally,

art is shaped by method, technique,

and intuitive study

rooted in knowledge and intellect.

Art is grace and a blessing—

one cannot help but feel

the hand of the divine

behind its mastery.

At the crossroads of beauty and art

reside the most sublime connections

between the human spirit, soul, and creativity.

It is here that life's mastery lies,

where our unique talents are harvested,

where continuous inspiration and happiness are found.

When we master beauty and art,

we are truly alive.

Both require <u>vital engagement</u>—

a heightened sensory state,

intimately connected with creation.

We become champions of existence,

squeezing, feeling, and savoring

the best life has to offer.

*

"Erasmus, beauty and art are intricately entwined, forming a bond so profound that one cannot truly exist without the other," declares Antonella, her voice imbued with conviction.

"They are not merely complementary; when united, they become a force of nature," adds Leonardo Conti, his eyes glinting with passion.

"Together, they create contagious, continuous, and contiguous virtuous circles, serving as the very enablers for experiencing life at its fullest potential."

"As their words settled over him, Erasmus felt a profound connection to the interplay of beauty and art they described. The timeless wisdom shared in this Florentine shop would resonate with him for years, shaping not just his understanding of art but his very essence as a poet and educator."

— ✦ —

Royal Cambridge Scholastic Institute (2019)
(University Auditorium)

The weight of the past—of Venice, Florence, and the antiquarians he met there—lingers in his thoughts. Yet, as the present moment calls for his attention, Professor Cromwell-Smith returns to the lecture hall, ready to weave his past experiences into today's lesson on the profound relationship between life, beauty, and art.

Erasmus pauses, allowing the weight of history to sink in. The room is still, the air thick with anticipation. "Now that we understand the historical roots of beauty and art in the Renaissance," he begins, his voice commanding yet gentle, "let's explore how these ideals live on today. Ask me what you've always wondered about the relationship between life, beauty, and art."

Sophia, an art history major with a deep interest in Renaissance art and philosophy, asks thoughtfully: "Professor, in the poem 'Life, Beauty, and Art,' the idea that beauty can be born from ugliness is explored. How does this notion align with the Renaissance ideals of beauty, especially considering the period's emphasis on harmony and proportion in art?"

Professor Cromwell-Smith nods, appreciating the complexity of the question. "Ah, a brilliant observation, Sophia. The Renaissance ideal of beauty was indeed rooted in harmony and proportion, but what the poem suggests is that true beauty often emerges from struggle, from transformation. Think of the way Michelangelo's sculptures, like *David*, begin as rough blocks of marble—it's only through chiseling away, through a process of struggle, that beauty is revealed. In the Renaissance, artists believed in the idea of *arte povera*, that even in imperfection or the harshness of life, beauty could be discovered. The same can be said of human experience—beauty often comes through hardship, a concept that resonates with the poem's message that beauty is not just in the surface, but in the deeper, often hidden, parts of life."

Sophia nods thoughtfully, her mind processing the connection between art and life's struggles.

Liam, a philosophy major with a passion for aesthetics, raises his hand and asks: "Professor, the poem also suggests that beauty is most appreciated when it defies stereotypes. In a modern context, how can we apply this principle, especially in a society where beauty standards are often rigid and defined by external appearances?"

Professor Cromwell-Smith 's expression softens, appreciating the depth of the question. "Liam, that's a timely and profound question. In a world where social media and advertising often dictate what is considered beautiful, it's crucial to remember that true beauty defies those surface-level standards. It's not confined to the perfect figure or flawless skin. The poem reminds us that beauty is found in authenticity, in embracing the imperfections of both ourselves and the world around us. If we look at artists like Frida Kahlo or the works of writers like Virginia Woolf, we see that beauty arises from their unique voices and the depth of their experiences, not from conforming to established standards. To appreciate beauty in its full complexity, we must look beyond the surface and celebrate the richness that comes from individuality and resilience."

Liam considers the professor's response, a contemplative look settling on his face as he processes the connection between beauty and individuality.

Elena, an English major known for her reflective approach to literature, asks: "In the poem 'Life, Beauty, and Art,' it's suggested that art is born of beauty, and beauty is inherent in art. Could you expand on how this relationship works, particularly in the context of literary art?"

Professor Cromwell-Smith smiles, clearly intrigued by the question. "Elena, that's a wonderful inquiry. In literature, beauty is not always something you see with your eyes, but something you feel with your heart and mind. Art, particularly literary art, takes the raw material of life—often the mundane or painful—and transforms it into something that resonates with meaning and emotion. A well-crafted poem, a novel, or a story takes life's struggles, beauty, and imperfections and turns them into something that elevates our understanding. Think of a poet like Emily Dickinson, who turned ordinary scenes and emotions into works that transcend the everyday. Art is about transforming reality into something more profound, and beauty is that transformative force that connects the artist's vision to the audience's soul."

Elena's gaze deepens as she absorbs the idea that beauty in art is both transformative and deeply personal.

Amir, a sociology major with an interest in the intersection of culture and art, asks: "The poem mentions that beauty can be overlooked, its worth unrealized. In a society driven by consumerism, how can we help people recognize and appreciate the beauty around them?"

Professor Cromwell-Smith pauses, weighing the question carefully.

"Amir, you've touched on an important point. Consumerism often reduces beauty to something that can be bought, packaged, and sold—something we can possess rather than experience. To help people appreciate beauty, we must encourage them to engage with the world more mindfully, to seek beauty in the small, everyday moments—whether in nature, in relationships, or in the arts. It's about slowing down and truly seeing, feeling, and experiencing. We also need to foster spaces—both in society and in our education systems—where people can explore and create art that is not driven by commercial interests. When we value the process of creation over the end product, beauty becomes something that nourishes the soul, not just the pocketbook."

Amir nods thoughtfully, considering how cultural shifts might help reframe our relationship with beauty.

Ethan, a psychology major with an interest in how art affects the mind, asks: "Professor, the poem suggests that beauty is eternal for those who truly understand it. From a psychological perspective, why do you think beauty, in both art and life, has such a lasting impact on the human psyche?"

Professor Cromwell-Smith reflects for a moment before responding. "Ethan, beauty has a lasting impact because it connects us to something deeper than ourselves—it taps into the emotional and psychological core of who we are. When we encounter beauty, it evokes feelings of joy, awe, and meaning, often triggering a state of mindfulness. Psychologically, beauty can elevate our mood, reduce stress, and even inspire creativity. Art, in particular, acts as a mirror to our emotional lives, allowing us to process complex feelings and experiences. This is why beauty, whether in a painting, a poem, or a fleeting moment, can resonate with us throughout our lives—because it speaks to the fundamental human need for connection, expression, and understanding."

Ethan looks visibly moved, as if the conversation has unlocked a new perspective on beauty's psychological significance.

"I want each of you to conduct a simple but profound exercise. Identify everything and everyone you consider beautiful in your life, then distinguish those you regard as art," he instructs, his voice measured and deliberate.

"For our next session on a single sheet of paper, itemize beauty and art as they manifest in your world. Reflect deeply on how they interweave with your existence," he assigns, leaving the class immersed in their thoughts.

The room buzzes softly as students exchange contemplative glances, their pens hovering over notebooks as they begin to list the people, places, and objects that bring beauty and meaning to their lives. Some faces lit up with inspiration, while others grew pensive, delving into their memories. It is clear the professor's challenge has stricken a chord, sparking a deeper awareness of the art and beauty in their everyday existence.

Professor Cromwell-Smith steps back from the podium, a sense of fulfillment washing over him as he surveys his students. Their faces are marked by introspection, each seemingly lost within their own interpretations of beauty and art, weaving intricate connections between the lesson and the world around them. With a final nod, he turns and exits the lecture hall, leaving the students seated in quiet reflection. As he walks away, his mind shifts toward the solace of his home and the ongoing journey of understanding beauty in life and art.

Chapter 10

Serenity, Courage, and Wisdom

Boston's Riverside (2019)

The downpour has transformed into a merciless deluge. A northwestern surge has pushed the river to breach its banks, submerging Boston's streets. Massive streams of water carve new paths, while drivers cautiously inch forward, unaware of the worsening storm aimed directly at them. Visibility is near zero, rain pelting down in unrelenting sheets.

Elizabeth Victoria Emerson-Lloyd feels a strange motion under her vehicle—something sinister and powerful. Water begins to seep through the seams of her car doors, creeping into the cabin. Panic sets in as she grabs her tote bag and tries to open the door, but the force of the water outside holds it firmly shut. Instinctively, she rolls down her window—counter-intuitive yet lifesaving. As water surges to her ankles, her engine sputters and dies.

Acting on adrenaline, Elizabeth moves swiftly, twisting her body and pulling herself out of the window with athletic ease. But outside, the torrent is even fiercer. Water rises to her waist, rushing with alarming force. Clinging to her car door handle, she struggles to keep herself steady. Courage begins to wane as her precarious situation grows dire.

"Help!" she cries, her voice barely audible over the roar of the flood.

Those nearby are equally helpless, stranded by the raging currents. Then, as if by divine intervention, a pair of strong hands grip her firmly under her arms, lifting her effortlessly out of the water.

She's hoisted above the chaos. With swift, determined strides, her savior carries her towards the safety of a raised pickup truck parked on a hill overlooking the river, far from the danger zone.

"Relax, you're safe with me," a deep, calming voice reassures her, his breath warm against her ear.

Once inside the truck, Elizabeth sits near the heater, placing her bare feet against the blistering vent, her soaked clothes clinging to her skin. She avoids looking directly at her rescuer, afraid her eyes might betray the overwhelming emotions surging through her. She feels her pulse quicken—a mixture of gratitude and something more profound.

Her savior is striking—6'2" with jet-black hair, piercing blue eyes, and an air of confidence that radiates from his every movement. He admires her agility, recalling the remarkable sight of her pulling herself through the car window.

"I've got a pair of dry socks in my gym bag," he says, reaching for it. As he turns back, his hand grazes her forearm and leg, an unintentional touch that sends shivers coursing through her. She jolts slightly, and their eyes meet—locking, holding, and speaking volumes in silence.

Time seems to freeze as their gaze deepens. His hand finds hers, resting lightly on her knee, a gesture of both reassurance and undeniable connection.

"Jordan," he introduces himself, his voice soft but steady.

"Elizabeth Victoria," she replies, her words tinged with awe and disbelief.

"I don't want any socks right now," she teases, her voice playful yet trembling with the intensity of the moment.

"Wild woman, you're going to wear a warm pair of socks before you catch a cold," Jordan insists, his tone firm yet caring. With assertive yet gentle movements, he slides the socks onto her feet. Elizabeth feels a wave of heat—his touch electrifying her senses.

Her skin's warmth ignites an unfamiliar, intense sensation within him. Their words flow freely as they share their lives, passions, and dreams. The storm outside becomes irrelevant, a mere backdrop to the growing intimacy within the truck's cabin. Smoke curls in the air, mingling with the warmth of their voices and laughter.

By the time the night begins to wane, they've unraveled layers of each other's souls. Both outdoor enthusiasts, they bond over shared adventures, realizing the storm has forged a connection as natural and inevitable as the rivers they both cherish.

Their shared adventures evolve into a symphony of discovery and passion. Together, they conquer towering peaks, climbing Mount Wilson and Mount Sneffels in the majestic San Juan Mountains near Telluride, Colorado. The ascents are both grueling and exhilarating, cementing their bond as they revel in the breathtaking vistas that unfold with each step. These peaks become a shared sanctuary, but it is Jordan's turn to introduce Elizabeth to the skies.

Skydiving and kite surfing become thrilling new chapters in their lives, with Elizabeth embracing the adrenaline rush with unrestrained enthusiasm. Jordan, in turn, teaches her the art of gliding, a pursuit that quickly becomes their favorite shared activity. Soaring silently through the clouds, they revel in the unspoken connection and sense of freedom these flights bring.

Elizabeth, ever the linguist and polyglot, adds another layer to their relationship, teaching Jordan Spanish, Mandarin, and German. Lessons often blur the line between learning and play, their sessions punctuated by laughter, flirtation, and deepening intimacy. The fiery, seductive tension first ignited on that stormy night never fades; it only intensifies, infusing their lives and passions with an energy that fuels their every endeavor.

Over time, Elizabeth learns of Jordan's most cherished and solitary hobby—piloting hot air balloons. The mystery of his reluctance to share this pursuit with her intrigues her. Determined, she begins a playful but persistent campaign to join him. She teases and persuades, but Jordan resists, his reasons veiled behind an enigmatic smile.

Eventually, her persistence wears him down. On a crisp, clear morning, Jordan finally invites her to join him for a flight. They arrive at a secluded launch site, the vibrant balloon standing tall against the endless blue sky. As they prepare for takeoff, both harbor secrets—closely guarded surprises waiting to unfurl.

The morning is electric, charged with anticipation. As the balloon gently ascends, the world falls away, leaving only the whisper of the wind and the boundless horizon. Each is aware that the other has something to reveal, but neither speaks yet, savoring the beauty of the moment.

Elizabeth's heart races, not from the height, but from the weight of her secret. She glances at Jordan, his eyes fixed on the horizon, a subtle smile playing on his lips. Little does she know, his heart mirrors hers, thundering with the anticipation of his own surprise.

Above the world, amidst the serene expanse of the sky, their surprises unfold. What begins as a simple flight becomes a turning point, an indelible memory that reshapes their lives forever. It starts like this …

— ✦ —

Santa Fe, New Mexico (2019)
(Annual Hot Air Balloon Festival)

The scene is nothing short of magical. The sky, alive with vibrant hues, is a sprawling canvas painted by hundreds of hot air balloons, each uniquely shaped and radiating color. The annual Santa Fe Balloon Festival has transformed the heavens into a mesmerizing kaleidoscope, drawing aeronauts and dreamers from across the globe.

Among them, piloting his elegant balloon with practiced ease, is Jordan Augustus Morse, a brilliant aeronautic engineer. Nestled at his side, holding tightly to his arm, is Elizabeth Victoria Emerson-Lloyd, the woman who has captivated his heart and soul. In just six months, their whirlwind romance has blossomed into something extraordinary—a union that feels, as Elizabeth often muses, like a celestial decree.

As the gentle breeze carries them over the desert landscape, the couple is spellbound by the carnival of balloons that drift alongside them. The only sounds are the occasional bursts of the burner, the rustle of the wind, and their quiet, shared breaths.

Elizabeth turns to Jordan, her green eyes sparkling with love and mischief. She holds a small leather-bound journal close to her chest.

"My love," she begins softly, her voice full of affection, "of all of Erasmus' unpublished works, there's one I hold dearest. With his permission, I brought it along to share with you today. It feels especially fitting for this moment—for us, here, floating above the world."

Jordan tilts his head, intrigued. His eyes, a piercing blue, lock onto hers, the corners of his mouth curling into a smile.

"Dedicated to me?" he teases gently.

"Especially for you, my daredevil outdoorsman," Elizabeth replies, her voice tinged with playful reverence.

As the golden morning sunbathes them in its glow, Elizabeth opens the journal. She takes a steadying breath, her voice firm yet tender as she begins to read, the words resonating in the stillness of the heavens.

"What an Amazing Day This Is!"

Today, I woke up on the surface of Mars,
Surrounded by a stark, alien landscape of rocks and sand,
Painted in intense shades of red and rusty dust.

The scenery soon morphed into a monotonous expanse,
Resembling spiritless butterscotch caramel.
There is no air to breathe here; the atmosphere is 95% CO_2.
Water is almost nonexistent, confined to the distant poles,
Far beyond my reach.
Nothing grows here. There is no life of any kind.
It's a desolate, dead planet.

Then, as I turn and gaze at the night sky,
The resplendence of Earth seizes me.
Our planet radiates splendor, its greens, blues, and whites
glowing like a beacon of life.
Its beauty pierces deep into my soul,
evoking an overwhelming sense of belonging.
"That's my home," I declare.
"That's where I live."
I point to the luminous dot in the sky.

Looking around me, the contrast is stark:
The vibrant Earth, teeming with life,
Against the barren, lifeless Martian terrain.
At that moment, I realize the gallery of celestial bodies—
Asteroids, comets, meteors, moons, planets, and stars—
Is also lifeless to the best of my knowledge.
Seemingly, our planet is the only one alive!

Today, I woke up on the surface of Mars
And felt both undeservingly privileged
And profoundly grateful for being alive
on such an extraordinary place called Earth.

— ✦ —

Today, I woke up inside a 10-nanometer chip,
Housing 100 million transistors
capable of processing algorithms and software so powerful
That every product and service will soon emulate the human brain.
Today, I woke up in a world
where we humans are continuously enhancing

What nature and God have bestowed upon us,
propelling progress and development
To unimaginable levels.
And I am alive, right in the middle of this quantum leap,
Reaping its benefits and marveling at its possibilities.
Who could ask for better fortune?

— ✦ —

Today, I woke up inside myself.
The first thing I did was travel at the speed of light
through the wirings of my brain.
By the end, I had traversed a distance
equivalent to the circumference of the Earth.
Next, using the most powerful computer in existence,
I counted the number of cells giving me life.
First, I tallied my neurons—several billion.
Then, I turned to the rest of my body's cells,
Filling screen after screen with their staggering numbers.
Each cell, though independent,
fulfilled its mission in perfect harmony with the others.

I was awestruck as I witnessed thousands of vital cells dying,
Replaced instantaneously by newly reproduced ones.
My curiosity propelled me further,
observing firsthand how viruses and infections
constantly swarm my body,
And how thousands of pathogens lie in wait, ready to strike.
I am infested with bacteria—
billions upon billions of them—
essential for life itself.
Yet, I watched in amazement
as my body's defense mechanisms
tirelessly kept every threat under control,
Eradicating some and containing others.

Finally, I inspected my organs,
Awe-struck by their inexorable
precision, beauty, and perfection

As they performed complex tasks with ease.

Today, I woke up inside myself and realized
That the mere fact of being alive is a continuous miracle,
renewed every second.

Today, I understood that life is a delicate balance,
A fine line between death, sickness, and health.
Today, I woke up inside myself
and witnessed the infinite complexity of my being.
I realized that, here on Earth,
I have been gifted an extraordinary organism—my body.
This realization illuminated
just how precious every moment truly is.

— ✦ —

Today, I woke up on top of the world,
Feeling the air flow through my lungs.
I recognized that just a couple of minutes without it,
And that's it! Life would be gone.

I observed the intricate cycles
of food and weather that nourish us,
Marveling at the perfection
of the systems required to sustain life.
I grasped how quickly
we would weaken and starve
without the abundance surrounding us.
I saw billions of humans sharing this Earth,
provided for equally by its resources.

— ✦ —

Today, I woke up and realized
I live on the universe's only known "living" planet.
Today, I woke up and finally understood
how few of us make it from reproductive cells into human beings.
Today, I woke up to life.
Today, I finally feel truly alive.
Today, I feel eternally grateful for simply being alive.

— ✦ —

"What an amazing day this is!"
I've been given an extraordinary life
and two remarkable vessels:
my planet and my body.

So,
What am I waiting for?
What are you waiting for?
What are we waiting for?

Let's go out and embrace
the incredible gift of being <u>ALIVE</u>!

*

Jordan is overwhelmed by the sheer emotion of the moment. Elizabeth clings to him, serene and content, her presence anchoring him in a world that feels surreal.

"I love you," he whispers, his voice barely audible yet carrying the weight of his heart. Moments later, he slips into a reflective trance, the world around them fading into the background of endless sky and colorful balloons.

At first, Jordan begins to speak almost as though addressing his thoughts aloud. "Elizabeth, my love, there are moments in life that stop us dead in our tracks," he says softly, deliberately, while locking his gaze into hers. "Reality halts; we can hardly breathe, and as it's happening, everything else ceases to exist."

His hand reaches up, and with exquisite tenderness, he brushes the tips of his fingers across her cheek. Elizabeth leans into his touch, tilting her head so her face rests against the warmth of his palm.

"When those rare moments occur, life gifts us its very best. We're consumed by wonder, swept away by an uncontrollable yearning and desire as our hearts rejoice, completely taken by the love we've found."

As he pauses, the silence between them is profound, filled with an almost tangible suspense, broken only by the rhythmic bursts of the burner feeding the balloon's flame. Elizabeth's emerald eyes widen as she absorbs his words, the depth of his emotion unraveling within her. Her hand moves instinctively to her mouth, stifling a gasp as he continues.

"That's exactly what happened to me the moment I first saw you," Jordan confesses, his unblinking blue eyes intensifying. "Elizabeth Victoria, there's nothing in this world I want more than to make you happy. I want to spend every remaining day of my life by your side. I vow to love you, cherish you, and honor you—always. Would you do me the honor of becoming my wife?"

Tears of joy stream down her face as she nods, unable to speak. Instead, she answers with a kiss, filled with passion, gratitude, and unspoken promises. Their lips meet in a moment that seems to transcend time, the world outside their shared space vanishing completely.

For them, the future begins here, among the clouds and beneath the heavens, in a love as boundless as the sky.

Royal Cambridge Scholastic Institute (2019)
(Erasmus and Victoria's Campus Home)

The phone call transforms a quiet Sunday morning into a celebration of love and joy.

Erasmus' home studio phone rings insistently. Sundays are usually tranquil, with hardly any calls, so the persistent ringing piques his curiosity. Finally, he picks up, a look of mild intrigue etched on his face.

"Mom?" Elizabeth's voice crackles with urgency.

"Elizabeth, how nice to hear from you. How have you been?" Erasmus responds warmly, his surprise tempered with fatherly affection.

"Hi, Erasmus. Can I talk to my mom really quick?" she asks hurriedly.

"Of course. Let me fetch her for you," he replies, already moving. He senses something out of the ordinary. *'What could it be?'* he wonders.

"Is everything all right, Elizabeth?" he ventures as he searches for Victoria.

"Everything is wonderful! Put my mom on speaker so you can hear the good news too!" Elizabeth exclaims, her voice brimming with excitement.

Relieved and intrigued by her exuberance, Erasmus finds Victoria just stepping out of the shower.

"Elizabeth's on the line. It seems urgent," he tells her, holding the phone out as she wraps herself in a towel.

"Elizabeth, dear," Victoria says, her maternal instincts instantly alert.

"Mom, Jordan just asked me to marry him!" Elizabeth announces with a burst of joy.

Victoria's face lights up with emotion as she glances at Erasmus. A radiant smile spreads across her face, followed by a gasp and a tear-filled cry of joy. She embraces Erasmus, forgetting her state of undress, wrapped in nothing but a towel and sheer happiness.

"Mom?"

"What wonderful news, my daughter! We're so happy for you both. I know how deeply you love each other," Victoria responds, her voice trembling with emotion as she clings to Erasmus.

"Mother, we're walking on clouds!" Elizabeth proclaims, her voice effervescent.

"I can imagine, darling. This is one of those moments in life to treasure forever," Victoria reflects, her motherly pride evident.

"Indeed, Mom. But also know that, quite literally, we're floating on air," Elizabeth adds mischievously.

"How so, dear?" Victoria inquires, intrigued.

"We're in a freaking hot air balloon! Jordan just proposed to me up here, thousands of feet above the ground," Elizabeth explains.

"Fantastic—romance in the sky!" Erasmus blurts out, his previously reserved demeanor giving way to inspiration. Once the professor's enthusiasm ignites, there's no stopping him.

"I have an idea, one fitting the grandeur of your white knight's proposal," Erasmus declares, his eyes alight with creativity.

"And what might that be, Professor?" Elizabeth asks, her tone both curious and skeptical.

"As you know, your mom and I have been engaged for about a year. Why don't we all get married in a single ceremony?" he suggests, his spontaneity surprising even himself.

The idea lands perfectly. In that rare, serendipitous moment, his suggestion is met with unanimous delight. The seed of a shared wedding is planted, an idea blossoming into reality amidst a backdrop of love, celebration, and the boundless skies.

Royal Cambridge Scholastic Institute (2019)
(Victoria and Erasmus Campus' Home, The Next Morning)

Erasmus's morning begins with an air of anticipation and joy.

"What would be your choice of subject today, dear?" Victoria inquires warmly, waving him off as he readies to leave.

"Serenity, courage, and wisdom—the role they play in our lives and how closely related the three are," he responds with a thoughtful grin.

"You certainly displayed plenty of that yesterday with your wonderful idea," she teases gently, her voice fading as he cheerfully pedals away.

Erasmus smiles back at his beautiful bride-to-be, her words filling him with warmth and satisfaction.

Professor Cromwell-Smith glides over the scattered autumn leaves, his heart buoyed by the joy of Elizabeth's engagement and the vision of the upcoming joint wedding ceremonies. Everything seems to move in slow motion. From a distance, his figure appears dreamlike, weaving along the campus roads as though he and his bicycle are floating just above the earth, carried by the breeze of contentment.

As the stately faculty building looms ahead, reality gently reels him back. By the time he secures his bike and strides purposefully toward the classroom, his thoughts align with the day's mission, the echoes of serenity, courage, and wisdom resonating in his mind.

Royal Cambridge Scholastic Institute (2019)
(University Auditorium)

Reaching the university's stately faculty building, Erasmus secures his bike with ease, pausing only for a moment to breathe in the crisp morning air. The steady rhythm of his heartbeat echoes his confidence as he steps into the familiar hallways of the Royal Cambridge Scholastic Institute. The buzz of students, the soft shuffle of shoes on polished floors, signals the proximity of his classroom. As he approaches the doors, his focus sharpens, the promise of a fulfilling lecture day ahead filling him with a quiet sense of purpose.

"How's everyone today?" Professor Cromwell-Smith greets his class, his eyes twinkling with enthusiasm.

The lively murmur of students responding with energy and positivity amplifies the atmosphere in the room.

"Wonderful!" they reply, their collective voices buzzing with anticipation.

"Let's start, then," he continues, his smile broadening as the room quiets in unison. "Today, I'll take you back in time to the day I met a fascinating antiquarian who imparted a precious life lesson. The story begins like this …"

The professor's voice takes on a thoughtful cadence as he launches into the tale, his presence commanding yet warm, drawing his students into the world of his memory.

— ✦ —

Downtown Boston (1979)

On a late Saturday afternoon jog, coming down from Beacon Hill, the downtown area is just ahead of me. After a turn on Canal Street, I stumble upon it, "The Quibbler: Antique Books for the Inquisitive Mind (Est. 1910)," reads the sign on the quaint shop.

'I've never seen or heard about this antique bookshop before.' Intrigued, I search my memory.

Smelly, sweaty, and all, I enter with the excitement and wonder of a young child stepping into his favorite place. The moment I open the door, a sense of familiarity washes over me. The shop carries the unmistakable scent of old paper and worn leather. Piles of treasured books are scattered everywhere, and the racks are spread across three floors connected by wooden staircases that twist and turn. The entire place feels like a labyrinth.

The surroundings so captivate me that I fail to notice the man observing me with quiet amusement. My eyes finally register his presence, and I jump in shock, eliciting an even broader smile from him in response to my absentmindedness.

"How can I be of help, young man?" asks the bespectacled, slightly hunched man with bushy, shoulder-length hair.

Still processing my surroundings, I struggle to focus on him. My gaze shifts between the shop and the man as if caught in a dream.

"What brings you here this afternoon?" he repeats, his eyes sparkling with curiosity. Then, suddenly, they widen.

"Wait a minute, I know who you are! You're the young man from the book town in Wales, right?" he asks excitedly.

I smile, acknowledging my reputation among New England antiquarians, but remain otherwise silent.

"We were all supposed to meet you at the Cape Cod Antiquarians reunion, but you suddenly left?" he exclaims, his tone shifting into a monologue.

"That's correct," I reply tersely, offering no additional details.

"I hope the cause was nothing serious," the antiquarian ventures empathetically.

"Sort of. She ran away, sir," I elaborate, my discomfort evident.

"I heard, I heard," he says, his voice tinged with condolence.

'So, his question was rhetorical. The New England antiquarians are like a fraternity; they share everything. My misfortune is vox populi— known by all,' I reflect with resignation.

"My name is Lazarus Pincay II, though I'm often called The Quibbler for reasons you'll soon discover," he announces with a theatrical flourish.

Born and raised in Boston to a librarian father and a painter mother, Lazarus Pincay displayed a natural talent for music but an even keener propensity for books. Although he pursued piano lessons for twelve years and seemed destined for a career as a concert pianist, he rebelled, and left school just shy of his 20th birthday. Lazarus spent years in California living in hippie communes until fate intervened. During a spiritual ritual, he met the love of his life, Laura Dean-Lamarck, who hailed from Boston and had earned renown as a writer.

The couple has been married for 25 years. At her insistence, they returned to Boston, where Laura helped Lazarus finance the purchase of The Quibbler Antique Book Store, turning it into the treasure trove I now stand in.

"Nice to meet you, sir. Erasmus Cromwell-Smith is at your service," I introduce myself with a polite nod.

"Mr. Pincay, I'm looking for peace and tranquility to better contemplate life in slow motion and appreciate the details of things," I explain, trying to articulate the sense of clarity I seek.

"Well, young man, you've come to the right place. I have something special for you, something that will help you attain the calmness and strength of character you're searching for," offers the Quibbler, his eyes twinkling with purpose.

Without another word, he walks away, disappearing into the maze of bookshelves. Moments later, I spot him climbing a towering wooden ladder, easily 25 feet tall. He scans the uppermost shelves, plucks a book, inspects it, but descends with a dissatisfied shake of his head.

Then, he vanishes again, slipping down a narrow aisle, his steps deliberate and purposeful. After a short while, he reemerges, clutching a thick, leather-bound book in both hands. The age-worn cover exudes an aura of timeless wisdom.

"The scribble I'm going to read to you perfectly aligns with your current predicament," the Quibbler declares, his voice deepening with conviction.

Opening the book with reverence, he finds the desired page and begins to read, his tone steady and earnest.

"Serenity, Courage, and Wisdom"

Serenity is a contemplative state

of absolute inner peace—deliberate, immutable calmness.

It is a condition of placidness

that allows us to observe life's movie from the outside.

In this state, life feels as though it moves in slow motion.

We pause at every frame,

and the false perception of time either flying by

or dragging its feet disappears.

Instead, we experience

a refreshing and genuine measure of time.

Serenity is also a cornerstone of moderation.

Whether in meditative, reflective, or contemplative modes,

calmness and placidness serve as conduits

for caution, restraint, tolerance, and prudence.

They are the best antidotes

to reactive and impulsive behavior.

By fostering moderation in our conduct,

serenity grants us the clarity

to contemplate alternatives and options.

It allows us

to take the necessary time to make decisions:

Do we choose serene inaction,

or do we act with our gut, our brain, our heart,

or a combination of them?

In serenity, life slows down.

Our frantic pace freezes,

and we discover peace in the pause.

But perhaps serenity's greatest virtue

is its ability to help us accept or acknowledge

the inevitable, the irreplaceable, and the irreversible.

Serenity becomes one of our most potent existential weapons

against denial, offering clarity, finality, and closure.

Serenity also lays the foundation for courage.

When impregnated with serenity,

courage becomes fiercer and invincible.

Without serenity, courage risks devolving

into reckless impulsivity or even a suicide mission.

Courage is our best resource for overcoming

extreme adversity and hardship,

for facing seemingly insurmountable obstacles,

devastation, loss, failure, and overwhelming odds.

Courage is also the weapon we wield

to tame and conquer fear.

In doing so, fear transforms
from a paralyzing excuse into an ally.

Fearlessness is an intrinsic part of courage's fire.
It fuels our drive to act,
empowering us to prevent or reverse
the consequences of what we are afraid of.

This is how courage is flushed
with positive and actionable fear.
Courage, when acted upon,
is fearless, dauntless, and intrepid.

Courage is a wild virtue of the spirit,
driven by belief, passion, heart, and fear.

Wisdom, as it relates to serenity and courage,
provides us
with enlightenment, sagacity, and judicious behavior.

Wisdom enables us to decide
when to lean on serenity—
to accept life's crude realities and defeat denial—
or when to summon courage
to reverse the improbable, the impossible,
the irreversible, and the seemingly inevitable.
Sometimes, wisdom guides us to use both,
serenity and courage,
in balance,

according to the circumstances.

Courage is our best resource to overcome
extreme adversity and hardship,
seemingly insurmountable obstacles and difficulties,
devastation and total defeat,
loss or failure, and overwhelming odds.
Courage is also our weapon to tame and conquer fears,
and that is how,
when acting with bravery and valor,
fear becomes our ally instead of a paralyzing excuse.

Fearlessness is an intrinsic part
of the fuel driving courage's fire.
Thus, fearlessness becomes the reason to act
in order to prevent or reverse the consequences
of what we are afraid of.

That's how courage is flushed
with positive and actionable fear.
Courage is fearless, dauntless, and intrepid
when we act and execute.
Courage is a wild virtue of the spirit
driven by beliefs, passion, heart, and fear.

As it relates to courage and serenity,
wisdom provides us
with enlightenment, sagacity, and judicious behavior

to decide either for serenity,

to be able to accept the crude realities

and to defeat denial,

or for the courage to allow us

to reverse the improbable, the impossible, the irreversible

and the seemingly inevitable;

or to use both, according to the circumstances.

*

"Serenity occurs when your soul and spirit are in absolute peace," The Quibbler intones, his gaze locking onto Erasmus with piercing intensity.

"Young Erasmus, life is meant to be lived through continual discourse, enabling people to dissolve conflicts, rectify misunderstandings, resolve dilemmas, or draw conclusions by engaging in challenging arguments. These debates allow us to question the coherence of our actions, interpretations, purpose, or the inherent knowledge we've absorbed. To face life in this way, however, serenity, courage, and wisdom are essential," Mr. Pincay asserts, his voice imbued with conviction.

Erasmus silently muses, 'Ah, now I understand how he earned his nickname.'

"You've got it," Mr. Pincay proclaims, as if reading Erasmus's thoughts. "This is me—a perennial and conscientious Quibbler of life and people," he adds with a satisfied smile, catching Erasmus off guard with his insight.

"As Erasmus leaves The Quibbler, the weight of the ancient tome still vivid in his mind, he feels a deep sense of calm, as if he is glimpsing a map to navigate life's inevitable complexities. This moment, he knows, becomes a cornerstone of the lessons he will one day pass on to others."

— ❖ —

Royal Cambridge Scholastic Institute (2019)
(University Auditorium)

The flash of memory from his past with Lazarus Pincay II fades as Professor Cromwell-Smith directs his focus back to the present. The bustling classroom, alive with student chatter and shifting papers, offers a subtle yet grounding reminder of the present moment. As the professor shifts into the present, with measured words he guides his students through the very principles Lazarus had shared with him years ago—principles that would not only define his journey but now shape the ones that lie ahead for his students. "Serenity, courage, and wisdom are virtues of character. Serenity engenders courage, and wisdom employs them both," he explains, his voice resonating with clarity. His hand rests on the lectern as his voice, calm but resolute, fills the room once again. "Serenity, courage, and wisdom," he begins, his words carrying the authority of years of lived experience, "are not just lofty ideals; they are virtues that inform our every decision, guiding us through life's most complex crossroads." His gaze sweeps across the room, making sure to meet the eyes of each student, ensuring they're attuned to the lesson at hand. "These are the virtues I wish for you to carry with you—today, tomorrow, and in the days ahead.

"Serenity, courage, and wisdom—these are the foundational virtues that shape how we face challenges in life. As we explore these concepts, let's consider how they intertwine with the greater themes of being alive and aware of the moment. I'll start by asking for your thoughts on the role of serenity in your life. Anyone?"

Aiden, a philosophy major with an interest in how personal virtues influence decision-making, raises his hand. "Professor, in 'Serenity, Courage, and Wisdom,' serenity is described as a state that allows us to observe life from the outside, almost as if life is moving in slow motion. How can we cultivate serenity in a world that often demands quick reactions and constant movement?"

"That's an excellent question, Aiden," Professor Cromwell-Smith replies. "Serenity is about learning to step outside of the whirlwind of life, even for a moment. It's cultivating the space to pause, breathe, and reflect. In today's world, that can be difficult, but it's about intentionally creating moments of stillness. Serenity isn't about inaction; it's about being present, recognizing your emotions without being consumed by them, and allowing the moment to unfold naturally."

Aiden nods thoughtfully, his mind clearly working through the implications of the professor's words.

Leticia, a psychology major with an interest in emotional intelligence, raises her hand. "In the poem, courage is said to be a weapon to conquer fear, but it's also noted that without serenity, courage risks becoming reckless. How can we ensure our courage is tempered by serenity?"

Professor Cromwell-Smith's eyes gleam with understanding. "Great question, Leticia. Courage without serenity can quickly turn into impulsivity or rash decisions, especially when fear clouds our judgment. Serenity helps us pause and make sure that the courage we summon is measured. It allows us to act with purpose, rather than out of reaction. When you're calm and centered, courage becomes a force that can move mountains, but only when it's grounded in clarity and reflection."

Leticia appears to absorb the depth of the answer, her expression one of deep thought.

Ethan, a biology major who enjoys exploring the intersection of emotion and reason, speaks up next. "The poem mentions that fear can become an ally through courage. But in the context of modern life, where fear is often paralyzing, how can we practically turn our fears into something positive?"

Professor Cromwell-Smith gives a nod of recognition. "That's an insightful question, Ethan. Fear is a natural human emotion, but it doesn't have to control us. When we face our fears head-on, we turn them from obstacles into opportunities for growth. Fear signals that something matters—it's a response to something we care about. By embracing that, acknowledging it, and moving forward anyway, we transform fear into motivation. Courage doesn't mean we're not afraid—it means we act despite the fear, knowing that it's part of our journey."

Ethan listens intently, clearly reflecting on how this perspective could apply to his own experiences.

Mia, a literature major who enjoys delving into abstract meanings, asks, "The poem *What an Amazing Day This Is!* paints a beautiful picture of life's complexities and the value of being alive. It suggests a spiritual, almost miraculous view of life itself. How do you personally reconcile this kind of spiritual awe with the more grounded, practical aspects of daily life?"

Professor Cromwell-Smith smiles at the question. "Mia, that's a powerful inquiry. *What an Amazing Day This Is!* speaks to the awe that comes from fully realizing the miracle of life in all its complexity. At the same time, we live in a world where daily concerns often demand our attention. I think the key is to embrace both—the awe and the practical. Serenity, courage, and wisdom help us navigate that balance. We can be grounded in the reality of our responsibilities while still taking moments to marvel at the small, miraculous details of life."

Mia smiles, clearly appreciating the depth of the response.

Jodie, a philosophy and ethics major with a focus on existential questions, leans forward. "The poem *What an Amazing Day This Is!* explores the beauty of being alive, yet it's set against the backdrop of challenges and threats to life. How do we live with the awareness of life's fragility without becoming overwhelmed by it?"

Professor Cromwell-Smith looks thoughtful before answering.

"Jodie, I think it's about finding acceptance. Life is fragile—that's a truth we all must face. But instead of being paralyzed by that knowledge, we can embrace it. It teaches us to live fully, appreciate the moment, and cherish the people and experiences that shape us. The fragility of life doesn't take away from its beauty; in fact, it enhances it. By living with an awareness of that, we can cultivate gratitude, presence, and a deeper connection to the world around us."

Jodie nods, clearly moved by the response.

Lee, an international relations major interested in the human condition, asks, "In both poems, there's a sense of wonder and deep appreciation for life and its complexities. Do you think this perspective could help shape the way we approach global challenges, like climate change or social injustice?"

Professor Cromwell-Smith nods approvingly. "Absolutely, Lee. The perspective that *What an Amazing Day This Is!* Brings can shift how we view the world. When we recognize the beauty and fragility of life, it can inspire us to protect and cherish it. That sense of awe, combined with the wisdom to act, can drive us to make choices that reflect our shared responsibility to each other and to the planet. It's a perspective that, if embraced globally, could lead to more empathy, cooperation, and a commitment to preserving the wonders of life."

Lee listens carefully, clearly considering the broader implications of the professor's answer.

The room softly buzzes with contemplative energy as the students gather their belongings. Many linger in their seats, their faces thoughtful, as if digesting the weight of serenity, courage, and wisdom in their own lives. It is clear that the professor's words have left a profound imprint on their minds.

The room quiets after his words, the echoes of his reflections settling into the minds of his students. The weight of serenity, courage, and wisdom hangs in the air, as if each student is silently sifting through their own understanding of these ideals. Erasmus pauses, allowing the moment to linger, before offering a parting thought. "Remember," he says softly, "serenity, courage, and wisdom aren't just traits we learn—they are virtues we embody, over and over again, in the choices we make." As he strides out of the room, the door closing behind him, the students remain, each absorbed in the newfound understanding that will guide them long after the class is over.

"See you all next week," he adds, striding purposefully out of the lecture hall.

As he exits, he notices the pensive expressions of the students left behind. Their collective demeanor suggests a quiet introspection, as if each is searching for their own path to peace and balance.

Chapter 11

The Fable of the Old Young Man and The Jester

Martha's Vineyard Beach, Massachusetts (2019)

Three months after Erasmus proposed the idea, the mother and daughter married the men of their dreams in a grand, shared ceremony. A makeshift wooden altar, adorned with vibrant flowers, was erected on a serene beach near Chilmark, on Martha's Vineyard's south side. The azure waves lapping against the shore provided a fitting backdrop for the joyous union.

Following the beachside celebration, Jordan and Elizabeth embarked on an adventure-filled honeymoon, soaring high in a hot air balloon over Europe's majestic landscapes. Their journey culminated in St. Moritz, Switzerland, where they participated in the Grand Engadin Race, a Nordic ski marathon renowned as the world's largest Winterfest of colors, drawing thousands of participants from across the globe.

Meanwhile, Erasmus and Victoria set off on their own dream voyage, visiting the enchanting landscapes of Africa. Before they could fully immerse themselves in their travels, an unexpected detour brought them to Italy—a chance to close an open chapter in Erasmus's life.

It all began with a magical train ride …

Zurich International Airport (2019)
(Arrival from Boston)

"Where are you taking me, my lady?" asks a startled Erasmus as they board a taxi to Zurich's central train station.

"It will be eye-opening, my mysterious Brit," Victoria replies cryptically.

"Milan?" he guesses when he hears the train's destination as they board.

"Erasmus, let's enjoy the ride and stop trying to find a reason behind everything," she counters with a mischievous smile.

The self-absorbed couple dines in style as the train glides through the Alps, a lingering question floating unanswered between them.

Erasmus grows increasingly uneasy.

'What could this possibly be?' he wonders, applying logic to his thoughts. 'She told you to enjoy the moment and stop trying to figure everything out,' he quibbles, half-scolding himself.

Time flies faster than they'd like, and soon the magnificent journey nears its end. "We're arriving at Milan's main train station," an announcement echoes in the background.

The train slows to a crawl, and Erasmus feels a swell of anticipation laced with uncertainty.

Stepping onto the platform, Erasmus is struck by a sense of familiarity before he even sees her. Like a slow-motion film, his eyes fall on Antonella, his former lover and lifelong friend, standing a hundred yards away. Her warm, benevolent smile and discreet wave greet him, unchanging and reassuring.

"Dad!" rings out in a chorus, punctuated with perfect British accents.

He turns to find Maria Antonella and Roberto Marcello Conti, Antonella's children—or rather, *his* children.

In the background, he notices Victoria and Antonella, their arms interlocked as if they are old friends catching up.

His two children envelop him in effusive hugs, while his rational mind struggles to keep up with the emotions overtaking him.

'It's been two years since I last saw them. That's all this must be,' he reasons, desperate to comprehend the moment.

"DNA, Erasmus. We always suspected it," Roberto declares, as if reading his thoughts.

"It was easy," Maria adds. "We took hair follicles from the brush in the bathroom you always use. Mom never let anyone else use that room. And there are other clues. For starters, Roberto is a carbon copy of you."

"And she sent us both to have a British education—uncommon in Italy. Then there were the trips to America when we stayed with you. We grew up with the omnipresent figure of the 'British uncle professor,' and Mom always urged us to treat you as a father figure," Maria continues, her voice soft.

"She never told us why, and we understand you didn't have a clue," Roberto concludes with a smile.

A couple of slow tears escape Erasmus' eyes, tracing his cheeks as a deep sense of fulfillment and joy overwhelms him. The two young adults standing before him are undeniably his own flesh and blood.

The next 24 hours become a blur of shared laughter, unspoken understanding, and endless stories. Father, son, and daughter spend hours walking, talking, and playing childlike games in public squares. Meals are minimal—snatched quickly between activities— as they strive to fit a lifetime of connection into a single day.

When it's time to part, Erasmus finds himself on the train platform once more, this time with Victoria and Antonella. They're standing back from the tracks, radiating the ease and warmth of two close friends.

The fleeting day lingers in Erasmus' mind like a dream, leaving behind a newfound bond and the beginning of a story he never thought he'd live.

"Thank you, Antonella," Erasmus says, his voice thick with emotion, eyes brimming with gratitude.

They kiss, a long, lingering kiss shared only by old lovers who understand the weight of years and memories.

"Vai, vai, Erasmus," she whispers, waving him off with teary eyes clouded by the bittersweet farewell.

Erasmus embraces his children one last time, holding them tightly and studying their faces as if committing every detail to memory.

"Erasmus is our real father, although kind of an incidental one, as in once in a while," Maria Antonella teases with a wide grin.

"Yes, our biological one. Well, he'll see a lot more of us when we visit America," Roberto Marcello adds, waving as the train begins to pull away.

When Erasmus turns, he's unexpectedly nose-to-nose with Victoria, her expression both amused and smug.

"Kisses, kisses, unforgettable kisses," she says, her tone tinged with a touch of playful possessiveness.

"Have you already forgotten about me, Erasmus dear?" she quips with the wickedest of smiles.

"How could I, my adored lady? That can never happen," he responds, regaining his charm as he takes her hand, leading her into the first-class dining car.

Hours later, as their flight from Switzerland to East Africa hums steadily above the clouds, the reunited couple nestles together in their seats. Their love has deepened through these shared chapters of rediscovery and acceptance.

Their next destination is Mt. Kilimanjaro—an adventure they have always dreamed of, a fitting chapter in the unfolding story of their rekindled lives.

Zurich's International Airport, Switzerland (2019)
(On the way back to Boston)

The two honeymooning couples reunite at Zurich Airport for their flight home to Boston. The four are radiant, glowing with the happiness and joy of their shared adventures.

"Mom, we're pregnant," Elizabeth-Victoria blurts out unexpectedly as they savor the traditional Swiss raclette while awaiting their flight announcement. Victoria gasps, covering her mouth in surprise, while Erasmus beams with a giant, proud smile. Moments later, the four are locked in a celebratory embrace, their joy and harmony overflowing in an unforgettable tableau of love and family.

Royal Cambridge Scholastic Institute (2019),

(Victoria and Erasmus' Campus Home, Next Day)

"Dear, I never imagined that summiting Tanzania's Mount Kilimanjaro would take three days, trekking through multiple microclimates over 37 miles," Victoria remarks as she and Erasmus watch breathtaking video footage from their honeymoon.

"19,341 feet high, my lady. It's no ordinary mountain. Your body needs time to adapt to the altitudes and thinner oxygen levels," Erasmus explains. The screen shows them walking across the Shira Plateau, its vast, barren expanse offering a spectacular view of the snow-capped Kilimanjaro looming majestically in the distance.

"I was terrified when we first encountered them," Victoria admits, her tone anxious as the video shifts to the dense foliage of the Congo jungle, where the silhouettes of massive gorillas blend into the greenery.

"Terrifying and awe-inspiring, weren't they? Such powerful creatures. But the long trek to find them was worth every step," Erasmus recalls fondly.

"And these!" Victoria exclaims as the video shifts to scenes of young lions near Victoria Falls, Zimbabwe. "Their primal energy, their regal power—it's intoxicating."

"Well, your fear certainly didn't linger long, considering you kissed a lion on the cheek!" Erasmus teases, grinning as the video replays her daring gesture with an outward palm pressed gently to the lion's face.

"That was brave, scary, and—let's be honest—stupid," he chuckles.

"True," she concedes with a laugh. "But their roars! The sheer force of their primal screams gave me chills."

The video transitions to a family of hippos bellowing from the water, their immense jaws snapping open in synchronized display.

"Utterly powerful creatures," Erasmus agrees. "I'm glad we opted for the river safari. The lush water landscapes of the Okavango Delta were spectacular without the dust and long waits of a land safari."

On screen, the safari unfolds, revealing rhinos, giraffes, zebras, elephants, and herds of gazelles roaming freely near the water's edge. Above them, flocks of birds streak across the sky in synchronized waves.

"Great memories," Victoria reflects, her eyes softening. "An unforgettable experience, my love. Three weeks of adventure and discovery that ended far too soon."

Erasmus pulls her close, smiling as the final images of their African journey fade into memory.

"Now back to mundane reality, my lady," Erasmus mentions with a touch of disappointment.

"Now that we've returned, tell me, my reluctant educator, what will be the subject of your class tomorrow?" Victoria inquires, her curiosity piqued.

"Children, clowns, and fairy tales," he replies cryptically.

Wisely, she doesn't react but knows full well that he's honoring his children in Italy. *He still needs time to open up and talk about his revealing, memorable encounter in Milan,'* she considers as Erasmus fades away on his bike. *'I can sense how he's still basking in the joy of reconnecting with his kids.*

Royal Cambridge Scholastic Institute (2019)
(Campus Streets)

As he pedals along the cobblestone streets through the crisp campus air, Professor Cromwell-Smith is lost in the memories of the past few days. His face reflects satisfaction and gratitude, especially for the newfound knowledge that Maria Antonella and Roberto Marcello are his biological children. The streets are lined with trees, their branches still adorned with the last vestiges of autumn leaves, a visual reminder of the changing seasons. His thoughts shift as he nears the lecture hall, the familiar building standing tall before him. He slows his pace, pushing aside the past to focus on the present. By the time he parks his trusty old bike, Erasmus has shifted his thoughts to his upcoming class. However, as he enters the lecture hall, he's greeted by a surprise. A large banner hangs above his desk, reading:

"WELCOME BACK PROFESSOR CROMWELL!
WE SINCERELY HOPE
YOU HAD A WONDERFUL HONEYMOON."

The professor breaks into a broad smile. His eyes scan the room, connecting with each of his students as his gratitude shines through.

A wave of energy fills the room as students glance up from their notebooks and papers, some with eager expressions, others still emerging from their own morning haze.

"Thank you all, pure and simple. This is absolutely amazing!" he exclaims, applauding his class.

He greets them with his usual warmth, his eyes twinkling as he steps up to the podium. There's an unspoken expectation in the room, as the class knows today's lesson will be more than just academic; it will be deeply personal.

"There are moments in life that we either celebrate or let pass unnoticed. If we deny or ignore these moments of joy, we risk losing the chance to embrace and rejoice in the brighter side of life for the rest of our days. Today, I will take you back to a memorable day when I learned one of life's greatest lessons: the power and necessity of creating and living our own fairy tale. A life that becomes a perennial celebration, absent of denial, no matter the circumstances."

He pauses, letting his words settle over the room, then continues with a glimmer in his eye.

"It all begins like this ..."

— ✦ —

Erasmus' Crumpled Studio (1987)
(Near Harvard University)

Her letter arrives unexpectedly, yet its timing couldn't be more poignant. It is destined to be the last communication I would ever receive from Mrs. V., my beloved mentor from Wales, as she passed away shortly thereafter. My heart races with trepidation as I recognize the familiar package, her unmistakable calligraphy gracing the surface. I abandon everything I'm doing or planning to do, unable to contain myself, and eagerly sit down to open it.

— ✦ —

"Dear Erasmus,

Your faithful mentor is getting a bit old. I haven't heard from you in a while, which I fear means things are happening in your life that you prefer not to talk about. Well, there's no way around your most ardent cheerleader. I expect you to update me by sharing your life's news at your earliest convenience.

More specifically, use your lazy writing hand, tap your forgetful heart and your lethargic mind, and write a missive to the attention of one Victoria Sutton-Leigh, a forgotten mentor of yours. She resides back at your birthplace, the unworthy (apparently to you) small town in Wales, Hay-on-Wye.

I enclose here a precious scribble that I hope enlightens your forgetful heart. I'm certain you're in desperate need of it and that it will deeply enrich your hibernating spirit and soul.

I sincerely hope you prove me wrong soon enough.

Love you dearly,
Mrs. V."

— ✦ —

Guilt envelops me, heavy and immediate, compelling me to respond. I pick up my pen and begin writing earnestly, recounting everything I can about my life. The letter is mailed that very day. A week later, I *call her. Mrs. V. is ecstatic; she's just finished reading my letter. My perennial cheerleader promises to respond in kind, but that promise never comes to fruition.*

Only days later, she is gone from our lives.

In the days following her passing, I sift through her letters, treasuring the magnificent moments we shared over time. It is during this reflective period that I stumble upon her final missive and decide to reread it. This time, I notice the enclosed scribble—a treasure I had completely overlooked in my haste to write her back.

Perhaps this is how it was meant to be: for her parting gift to be discovered only after her passing, as a symbolic celebration of her life.

With a reverent heart, I open the scribble and begin to read. The opening verse enraptures me, drawing me into its timeless embrace.

"The Fable of the Old Young Man & the Jester"

The Joker strides back to his "Camerino,"

his dressing room,

as the crowd in the circus main tent,

continues to cheer.

He wears a white-plastered face

with a perpetual smile,

adorned by a giant painted mouth and

a tiny, perfectly round nose,

both glowing red.

A tall, floppy, multicolored hat,

covers shoulder-length strands of bright orange hair.

His loose clothes resemble a harlequin on one side,

while the other is dotted with oversized white polka dots.

His enormous shoes—two flapping tongues—

are impossibly wide at the front

and comically narrow at the back.

His nonchalant antics are shocking, even outrageous.

Everyone and everything become subjects of his jest,

his every move a parody of reality,

inviting the audience into the lighter side of life.

But not all is as it appears in our existence—

or is it?

A diminutive voice cuts through the stillness backstage.

"Jester, Jester!"

A young boy calls out from the shadows of the alley.

The clown turns, his penetrating green eyes

fixing on the teenager.

"Isn't it a bit far off the beaten path

for someone your age to be wandering around?"

the impatient clown asks.

"My parents are just behind the curtains,

feeding the giraffes with my little brother.

They know I'm here,"

the boy responds with confidence.

"Fair enough," the clown mutters,
resigned to the interruption.

The youngster crosses his arms,
raising one hand to his chin in thought.
"Joker, do you make people laugh for a living?"
he asks, his tone serious.

"Isn't causing laughter what clowns do?"
the clown replies in a riddle.

Undeterred, the boy presses further.
"You make people happy, Jester.
Are you a happiness maker, then?"

The clown leans casually against the doorframe of his *Camerino*.
"After all, isn't that what those who come to the circus seek?"
he responds with another question,
offering little insight to his admirer.

"Now, if you'll excuse me,"
the clown says, stepping inside his dressing room.
"Joker, Joker!" the boy pleads,
pushing forward before the door can close.

"I don't find you very funny in person, sir.
Your face wears a painted smile,
but up close, it doesn't feel genuine.
Your eyes—

they exude sadness,

and maybe even anger."

The clown's first reaction is to recoil,

but, to his own surprise, he reverses himself.

"You're an astute observer, little man.

Come in and have a seat," he offers unexpectedly,

leaving the door wide open.

Once seated, the clown offers the boy a box of chocolates,

allowing him to pick whichever one he likes.

"Joker, you make others happy,

but not yourself. Why?"

The clown exhales, leaning back.

"Isn't it how many live?

Keeping up appearances in public,

while guarding their darker realities

close to their chests?"

The boy tilts his head, puzzled.

"Jester, when I saw you on stage,

making everyone laugh,

it seemed like your life was a fairy tale.

But now, sitting here with you,

I wonder—

why aren't you happy?"

The clown lets out a sarcastic laugh.

"Isn't it true that life is always missing something?

That which we covet the most

seems out of reach.

And when we chase a goal,

the moment we catch it,

the goalpost has already moved—

most often because of us."

The boy shakes his head gently.

"Joker, but what you have now is enough, isn't it?

The pursuit of your goals,

what you call *the chase*,

is filled with life's moments—

moments you share with those who love what you do.

You must celebrate the journey of life

as it happens.

Otherwise, you're missing most of it."

The clown chuckles bitterly.

"There are no fairy tales in life, kid.

Those only live in children's books and fantasies."

"My life is a fairy tale, Jester,"

the boy declares with joy.

The clown raises an eyebrow.

"Sure, it is. You must come from a privileged home—

wealth, success, no hardship,

no tragedy, no pain.

Of course, you see life as a fairy tale.

But one day, that will change."

The boy smiles softly,

his voice calm but filled with emotion.

"Joker, I am an orphan.

I came to the circus today with my adoptive parents.

We were homeless until recently.

My father just found a job as a janitor,

and my youngest brother walks with crutches—

he contracted polio when he was five."

The clown covers his mouth in shock,

shame washing over him.

"I am so, so…"

he begins to apologize,

but the boy interrupts.

"Jester, you're a privileged man.

Take stock of what you have.

Turn it into your source of joy.

Use your access to happiness and laughter

for what they are—

celebrations of life.

Your fairy tale resides in you.

You do what you love.

People love what you do.

Is there more to ask of life?"

The clown's eyes widen,
his painted smile softening into something real.
"I understand now the source of wisdom
in your words,"
the clown admits.

"And what would that be, sir?"
the boy asks.

"Hardship," the clown replies quietly.
"Life is a fairy tale
that resides inside all of us.
It only requires ingenuity and candor of the soul
and a true desire of the spirit
to embrace the journey of life,"
the boy declares.

His parents and brother approach from the corridor.
"Time to go," they announce.

The boy turns back to the clown,
a broad smile on his face.
"Joker, it was magical to spend time with you.
It was a truly magical moment,"
he says with joy.

"Young man, it was magical for me as well.
It was like a…"

the clown hesitates,

his voice trembling.

"A fairy tale?"

the boy offers, smiling even more.

"It most definitely was,

and a life lesson well learned, too,"

the clown replies, his green eyes sparkling.

For the first time,

his painted smile feels genuine—

perhaps forever.

*

Erasmus leans back in his wobbly chair, the dim light of his small studio casting soft shadows on the walls cluttered with books and papers. The fable rests in his lap, its final words echoing in his mind like a gentle refrain. He glances at Mrs. V.'s letter, now creased from his grip, and feels an ache of longing mixed with gratitude.

Her parting words, wrapped in wisdom and love, have kindled a spark in his restless heart. The fable's lesson—that life's fairy tales are born from within—pushes him to confront the narratives he has allowed himself to live. "The fairy tale resides in me," he whispers, almost as if testing the truth of the phrase. In the quiet stillness of the moment, he resolves to carry her message forward, to weave joy, gratitude, and purpose into the fabric of his days.

— ✦ —

Royal Cambridge Scholastic Institute (2019)
(University Auditorium)

Professor Cromwell-Smith carefully unfolds a set of wrinkled papers, their edges softened by time. His students watch as he places them on the lectern, a sense of reverence evident in his every movement.

The auditorium is silent, the weight of the fable lingering in the air. Professor Cromwell-Smith closes the book gently, his movements deliberate, as though savoring the finality of the tale. He looks up, his eyes scanning the faces of his students, their expressions a mix of introspection and awe.

"That was the last letter I ever received from Mrs. V.," he begins, his voice steady but filled with emotion.

"A story that, like all great fables, is not merely to be heard but to be lived. Her wisdom—woven into these words—remains timeless, much like the lessons we take from life itself. Her letter wasn't just a message from my mentor; it was a mirror reflecting my own untapped potential, my ability to create something extraordinary from the ordinary," The pedagogue reasons.

He pauses, glancing at the notes as if drawing strength from their presence. "Her words reminded me that the fairy tale isn't some unattainable dream. It's here," he continues, touching his chest. "It's within us all, waiting for us to see it, to live it, to share it."

The professor steps away from the lectern, walking slowly across the stage, his eyes scanning the room. "So I ask you, as I once asked myself—what will it take for you to recognize your own fairy tale? And when you do, will you have the courage to live it?"

The air hums with the weight of his words, his students lost in thought, grappling with the possibilities of their own untold stories.

"Now," he continues, his tone softening, "let us return to the present. What does this fable teach us? It reminds us that fairy tales are not confined to books or childhood fantasies. They reside within us, waiting to be embraced and brought to life through the choices we make, the gratitude we show, and the joy we find in the everyday."

Professor Cromwell-Smith pauses, allowing the significance of his words sink in. Then, with a gentle smile, he concludes, "It is in our power to recognize the magic of the moment, to celebrate the journey of life, and to make every day a story worth telling."

The spell is broken, and the room stirs as students emerge from their reverie, the lesson resonating deeply in their hearts.

"The Jester's discovery was to realize that life, for a passing moment, had become a fairy tale for him because he had made it such. The fairy tale resided in him. It inhabited his spirit and soul. Hence, his natural inclination and greatest existential ability was to make out of every possible moment or situation a real-life fairy tale by making others laugh," states the professor in his closing remarks.

A few hands are raised.

Thomas is a senior Philosophy major with a deep interest in existentialism and the nature of happiness. He often challenges abstract concepts and enjoys engaging in philosophical debates.

"Professor, in the fable, the boy calls the clown's life a fairy tale, but the clown dismisses it, claiming there are no fairy tales in life. Do you think the story is trying to suggest that a fairy tale is only possible if we have hardship or challenges to overcome? And if so, does that make hardship essential for finding meaning in life?"

"That's a very insightful question, Thomas. The boy's perspective represents a kind of innocent wisdom. He sees life as a fairy tale, not because it's free from hardship, but because he's learned to embrace it fully, understanding that hardship doesn't diminish life's beauty—it enriches it. The clown, on the other hand, is caught in a cycle of denial, unable to see the beauty in the moments that life provides. The fable suggests that a fairy tale isn't about avoiding difficulties, but about how we respond to them and whether we choose to live joyfully, despite the struggles."

Isabella is a third-year English Literature major, particularly interested in the intersection of storytelling and psychological well-being. She's always eager to draw parallels between literary themes and real-life emotional growth.

"Professor, the clown in the fable spends his life making others laugh, yet he himself is unhappy. The boy challenges him to embrace his own life as a fairy tale, despite the hardships. Do you think the fable is suggesting that we all have a responsibility to find joy in our own lives, rather than relying solely on external validation or seeking perfection?"

"Yes, Isabella, I believe that's exactly what the fable is suggesting. The clown's life, while filled with external validation, lacks personal fulfillment. He is a performer, yes, but he isn't performing for himself—he's performing for others. The boy, with his simple yet profound wisdom, shows the clown that real joy doesn't come from the applause of others; it comes from embracing one's own journey, no matter how imperfect it may be. The fable teaches us that we must find our own happiness, rather than relying on the expectations or perceptions of others."

Marcus is a junior majoring in Psychology with a focus on human motivation and emotional intelligence. He often brings scientific perspectives into philosophical discussions and enjoys analyzing character behaviors through psychological lenses.

"Professor, in the fable, the clown admits that his painted smile hides a deeper sadness. The boy points out that life can be viewed as a fairy tale if we learn to celebrate the journey. From a psychological perspective, do you think that many people, like the clown, mask their true emotions because they believe they are expected to conform to societal ideals of happiness?"

"That's a very astute observation, Marcus. The clown represents what we might call the "mask" people wear—the persona they project to meet social expectations. In psychology, this can be related to what's often termed as "emotion regulation" or the pressure to conform to societal ideals, even when those ideals don't reflect one's true emotional state. The boy's wisdom in the fable teaches us that we must move beyond this façade and learn to acknowledge and accept our emotions as part of our journey. Life's fairy tale isn't about perfection or constant happiness; it's about embracing the full spectrum of human experience, even the difficult parts."

Emily is a senior majoring in Sociology, with a keen interest in the dynamics of happiness and fulfillment in contemporary society. She often looks at social structures and cultural narratives to analyze how individuals find meaning in their lives.

"Professor, in the fable, the clown's life seems full of external success—he makes people laugh, he's adored by the audience—but he still feels unfulfilled. Do you think the fable critiques modern society's obsession with outward success and how that might overshadow our inner sense of purpose and fulfillment?"

"Absolutely, Emily. The clown's life, as portrayed in the fable, is a perfect metaphor for what often happens in modern society. We are conditioned to seek external success, whether it's career achievements, recognition, or material wealth, often at the expense of cultivating internal fulfillment and purpose. The fable critiques this very notion, showing that external validation isn't a true measure of success. True fulfillment, as the boy points out, comes from within—from how we embrace our lives, with all their ups and downs, and how we choose to find joy in the process itself."

Sarah is a second-year student studying Art History, fascinated by how emotions and human experiences are conveyed through art and storytelling. She enjoys drawing connections between literature and visual art.

"Professor, the fable speaks about the importance of finding joy in the journey, even if life isn't perfect. Do you think this idea of a "fairy tale" could be applied to art and the creative process as well, where the true value lies in the act of creation rather than the final product?"

"Yes, Sarah, that's a wonderful connection. Just as the boy sees life as a fairy tale, many artists and creators find that the real magic lies in the process itself. The journey of creation—the struggles, the discoveries, the growth—is often more meaningful than the finished piece. In art, as in life, the act of creation becomes a personal fairy tale. It's in the imperfections, the mistakes, and the moments of epiphany that the true value is found. Just like the boy's understanding, an artist must learn to embrace the creative process with all its highs and lows and celebrate the journey rather than fixating solely on the end result."

As the class comes to a close, Professor Cromwell-Smith stands by the lectern, allowing the students to reflect on the day's discussion. The room, once buzzing with the energy of a lecture in progress, now hums with the quiet introspection of students contemplating their own fairy tales. "Think about that as you go through your week," he adds. "What will you make of your own story?" With a nod and a smile, he dismisses the class, leaving the students to filter out slowly, some with quiet contemplation in their expressions, others with excited chatter as they discuss the ideas that have taken root.

"It's a wrap; see you all next week," he says as he departs.

His students remain seated, their faces marked with quizzical expressions. They seem to be grappling with the professor's message, silently questioning how much of a fairy-tale life they might already possess—or deny themselves—by leaving the good within them unrealized.

Chapter 12

Restlessness and Curiosity

Royal Cambridge Scholastic Institute (2019)
(Victoria and Erasmus' Campus Home)

"Why is it so hard to generate interaction with my precious son?" asks a startled Victoria.

"He's simply reserved and cautious by nature," states Sofia, who has been Bart's girlfriend for the past two years.

"I recognize that, but I'm his mother, and I feel that when it comes to his personal life, I have to dig to extract every word out of him," Victoria adds.

"He's getting better, though," Sofia offers, her eyes filling with love and affection as she talks about him.

"Bartholomeus has always been the family jester. Outwardly, so cheerful and gentle, but hermetic about his private affairs," declares the resigned mother.

Victoria studies the green-eyed, tall brunette, an all-American swimmer and Bart's classmate.

Sofia is an unwavering defender of my fortunate son. Given that she's also head over heels adoring him, why are you giving her a hard time? Victoria scolds herself.

"Tell me about yourself, sweetheart. How's he treating you? How do you feel about your relationship with Bart?"

"I feel happy. He's a wonderful man. We're planning, well in advance, which university we're going to attend to earn our master's degrees."

"That's fantastic news, Sofia. Any idea where you might be going?" asks Victoria with a touch of anxiety in her voice, plus a bit of frustration upon learning one more secret about her son.

"No, but we do have a shortlist."

"Well, he's a natural-born entrepreneur, so I'm pretty certain he'll enroll in a business school."

Sofia says nothing in reply, seemingly guarding a big secret. Victoria is at ease with the loyalty displayed by the young, prudent woman beside her.

"Sofia, earlier, I asked how he is treating you."

"He's always been a devoted partner. Before I met him, I was involved in a long-term relationship that never went anywhere because my former boyfriend was married. So, Bart had to work hard to appease my apprehensions and fears."

Unexpectedly, Erasmus makes a "grand entrance" while pulling a couple of small suitcases.

"Vicky, I don't want to interrupt your lovely chat, but we have to leave within the next thirty minutes," announces the professor while his other half patiently gestures and smiles at Sofia.

"Give us a few minutes; we'll be done shortly," Victoria pleads with a discernible broad smile.

"I'm all yours, dear, no haste," Victoria tells Sofia.

"Bart gave me a poem the other day," Sofia says, handing it to Victoria, who starts reading with what appears to be a touch of curiosity mixed with earnest delight.

"A Very Particular Symbiosis"

I am all of you,

You are all of me,

We are all of you,

We are all of me.

You are me,

I am you,

We are—

only one of you,

only one of me,

only one of us.

One and only,

you and I,

both of us,

forever.

*

"I love it. I'm thrilled Bart wrote something like this. I didn't know he could write!"

"No, it isn't his. He was candid with me about it. But that's irrelevant since what matters is the gesture; besides, it is beautiful."

"May I ask who wrote it?" asks Victoria as she slowly turns her head towards Erasmus, who's shuffling his feet and looking straight down at the floor, avoiding eye contact.

"My beloved Brit, how come you didn't tell me a thing about this?" she asks, sounding hurt but deeply satisfied.

Victoria winks at Sofia as she continues to roast Erasmus.

"Are you also keeping secrets from me, dear? Is this now a male thing in our family?"

"I don't think that writing a poem on Bart's behalf for his girlfriend is something I have to share with you when he specifically asked me to keep it private. Nevertheless, in the end, he's shared it with you through Sofia," replies Erasmus while ignoring the second part of her question.

Although a bit embarrassed, Victoria finally smiles at the realization of her confrontational, out-of-place behavior.

"Thank you for taking such good care of my boy," she volunteers while warmly hugging Sofia goodbye, then walking over to passionately kiss her in-house British poet.

Sofia and Victoria say farewell, and soon thereafter, the middle-aged couple is on their way to Boston's Logan Airport to visit an old friend of Victoria's for a weekend escapade.

St. Louis Public Library, Missouri (2019)

The head librarian, Rebecca Samuels-Ortiz, is always on the move. She labors like a busy humming bee.

On this particular morning, everyone on her staff is struggling to keep up with an entire middle school student body visiting—a nearly impossible task. The teenage girls and boys are unruly, loud, and impolite.

"What a rude young man you are," she tells a baby-faced, lanky, bespectacled young man whose legs are propped up on a reading desk.

"Don't even think about it!" she warns a couple of naughty teens about to rip out a page from a valuable book. Protectively, she yanks it from their hands.

"This is not a concert hall," she cautions a pair of young girls as their deafening music blasts through their headphones.

"Tuck your shirts in!" she commands a pair of students walking by.

"Bring your pants up to your waistline," she orders another.

"Tie your shoelaces; otherwise, I'm going to report you and throw you out," she says with a stressed-out voice, finally letting her frustrations erupt.

Two hands from behind cover her face out of the blue.

"Surprise," Victoria whispers.

Samuels-Ortiz turns around in a snap and involuntarily lets out a muffled cry. She excitedly hugs her friend and protégé. Simultaneously, she sees him standing there awkwardly, looking at their long embrace. Her eyes widen.

Erasmus is still shell-shocked by the effusive greeting Victoria emotes as the words come rolling out of her mouth.

"I found him, Becca. Well, actually, Sarah did," explains Victoria.

"Are you Erasmus?" Samuels-Ortiz asks in disbelief.

"The one and only," he replies as Samuels-Ortiz, with smothering enthusiasm, extends her welcoming arms and embraces him long and hard.

"Oh, my g…! How blessed and fortunate you are. Life found both of you, or better said, true Love took hold of the two of you once again," enunciates Samuels-Ortiz.

As the host holds onto Erasmus, she blurts, "She never stopped loving you."

"Becca, he waited for me all those years," interjects Victoria. "May I remind you that I was the one who ran away."

At first, Samuels-Ortiz's facial expression softens, followed by benign and loving eyes.

"Please excuse my antics, Erasmus. I tend to be overly protective of Victoria. Subconsciously, my instincts cast you very differently," Samuels-Ortiz states.

"The mind doctor, perhaps?" intersects Samuels-Ortiz with a mischievous smile, unable to control herself.

"Becca!" complains Victoria in surprise.

"Well, you can't blame me for trying a bit too hard to ensure that your bad karma with men doesn't repeat itself," adds Samuels-Ortiz.

"Well, here we are, after all. I enthusiastically want you to meet my Brit scholar."

"A scholar? …interesting." Samuels-Ortiz thinks aloud.

"It's a real pleasure, Mrs. Samuels. I'm forever in your debt. Thank you from the bottom of my heart for taking such good care of my precious lady," demurs Erasmus.

"That was nothing. It was a pleasure. Victoria deserves that and much more because she's an angel of goodness," Mrs. Samuels-Ortiz is still trying to oversell her mentee. "But I want to know more about the prince valiant that stole my friend's heart. Tell me about yourself, Erasmus."

Being well-acquainted with the customs and traditions of his birthright, Victoria knows it's far too soon for Erasmus to open up to a perfect stranger. Stepping in before British etiquette and shyness can create the wrong impression, she interjects, "He teaches at a New England college. He's also a writer."

"Fascinating. What does Erasmus teach?" the old librarian asks, her curiosity piqued.

"Poetry," Victoria replies with a subtle smile.

"And what does he write about?"

"Mainly science fiction," she adds.

"Published?" Rebecca presses further.

"Three million science fiction and educational books sold," Victoria proudly announces.

Rebecca's eyes widen in amazement. "That's very impressive. Wait a minute. Erasmus, what is your last name?" A sudden realization dawns on her. "Oh! Of course … you are Erasmus Cromwell-Smith. I know you. I've read all your books! Consequently, Victoria, you had him here at the library all the time, just a fingertip away!" she exclaims, her words pouring out excitedly.

Victoria chuckles at her friend's enthusiasm. "You know, Becca, thanks to his influence on me early on, I only like to read poetry. And he's never published his poems," she adds with a mischievous glance at Erasmus.

Rebecca tilts her head, astonished. "And how could I have known you are—the Erasmus?"

"I've read your books through the years but never put two and two together," she admits, her tone blending awe and amusement.

Victoria seizes the moment. "Dear, why haven't you ever published any of your poems?" she asks, her curiosity slipping into prying.

Caught off guard, Erasmus hesitates before responding. His gaze softens as he reflects. "I guess the simplest answer is that the vast majority of the poems, if not all, I've ever written are private," he admits. "Dedicated to you or us," he continues, his voice carrying a deep emotion that visibly touches Victoria.

Later that Day

As they prepare to part ways after a delightful brunch at the fancy Hyatt Hotel in downtown St. Louis, Mrs. Samuels-Ortiz surprises the couple with an unexpected gift.

"I have a copy of an ancient scribble for both of you. It's my wedding gift," she declares, her tone reverent. "It's a precious piece of writing that I treasure and constantly revisit. It's about restlessness and curiosity. It's extraordinary how both of you remained restless due to unfulfilled true Love, never ready to settle for less, convenience, or comfort. In the end, life rewards you for your perseverance," she adds with a smile that holds both wisdom and warmth.

Rebecca then steps back momentarily, walking to her hallowed grounds of knowledge, which is only a short jaunt away. When she returns, she hands them a carefully preserved manuscript. "I pray this piece will be as useful in your lives as it has been in mine," she says, her voice thick with sincerity.

As they embrace in a heartfelt bear hug of three, Rebecca leans close to Victoria and whispers, "Thank you for bringing him here."

"I guess the simplest answer is that the vast majority of the poems, if not all, I've ever written are private, dedicated to you or us," Erasmus reveals after a brief, reflective pause, his voice laden with deep emotion that resonates with Victoria.

Hyatt Hotel, Downtown St. Louis

Hours later, as they prepare to part ways after an elegant brunch at the Hyatt Hotel, Mrs. Samuels-Ortiz surprises the couple with an unexpected gesture.

"I have a copy of an ancient scribble for both of you. It's my wedding gift," she announces, her tone filled with reverence and affection. "It's a precious piece of writing that I treasure and constantly revisit. It speaks about restlessness and curiosity— qualities that define both of you. It's extraordinary how you both remained restless due to unfulfilled true Love, never willing to settle for less, convenience, or comfort. And in the end, life rewarded you for your perseverance," she explains, her eyes shimmering with warmth and sincerity.

Rebecca pauses for a moment before adding, "I pray this piece will be as meaningful in your lives as it has been in mine."

She excuses herself briefly, walking to her sacred library of knowledge, just a short jaunt away. When she returns, she hands them a carefully preserved manuscript, its leather-bound cover exuding an air of timeless wisdom.

Rebecca then turns to Victoria, her voice lowering to a whisper.

"Thank you for bringing him here," she says, a subtle but heartfelt acknowledgment of the joy Victoria has restored to both their lives. The moment concludes with a heartfelt embrace, the three of them locking in a bear hug that speaks volumes of gratitude, connection, and shared love for the extraordinary journey that has brought them together.

Royal Cambridge Scholastic Institute (2019)
(Erasmus and Victoria's Home– Two days later)

Before opening Mrs. Samuels-Ortiz's gift, Erasmus suggests, "It would be best to read it in class. It feels fitting to share it with my students, given its essence," to which Victoria readily agrees. Together, they set the stage for what promises to be a memorable and meaningful event.

"I'm sure reading it will reveal such a wonderful tale," Victoria muses, her voice soft yet brimming with anticipation.

Royal Cambridge Scholastic Institute (2019)
(Campus' Roads)

Victoria and Professor Cromwell-Smith meander through the deserted campus streets, their hands intertwined in a comforting grip.

The quiet evening air surrounds them as they savor the moment, reflecting on their weekend trip to St. Louis. The visit to Victoria's "lifeguard vest"—as Erasmus affectionately refers to Rebecca Samuels-Ortiz—lingers in their thoughts, filling them with warmth and gratitude.

Their stroll is unhurried, a time to bask in the tranquility of each other's presence. With each step, they recount snippets of conversations, the joy of reconnecting with a dear friend, and the profound gift bestowed upon them.

As they approach the stately halls of the faculty building, Victoria gently squeezes Erasmus' hand. The simple gesture speaks volumes, grounding him in the significance of the task ahead.

"Make her proud, dear," she murmurs softly, her voice carrying both encouragement and affection, referring to the librarian whose wisdom and faith had been so pivotal.

Erasmus nods, a smile spreading across his face, his resolve quietly reaffirmed. The moment of tranquility fades as they prepare to step inside, and the usual classroom energy of anticipation fills the air. Their arrival marks the end of a brief but significant pause and the beginning of a new chapter in the class, where the gift from Rebecca will be revealed.

Royal Cambridge Scholastic Institute (2019)
(University Auditorium)

"Good morning, everyone," Erasmus announces, his voice resonating warmly through the auditorium as he and Victoria step inside.

"Good morning, professor," the students respond in unison, their energy lighting up the room.

"Victoria joins us today for a special reason," he begins, his tone carrying a hint of anticipation. "Over the weekend, we had the privilege of visiting a longtime friend of hers, Rebecca Samuels-Ortiz, the head librarian of the St. Louis, Missouri, public library. For the better part of the last decade, she has been not only a trusted confidant but also a life coach and mentor to Victoria."

He pauses for effect, the room growing still as his students sense the importance of the moment.

"Arguably," he continues, a fond smile touching his lips, "she is one of the key reasons Victoria and I found our way back to each other after all these years. As we said our goodbyes, Mrs. Samuels-Ortiz gifted us something extraordinary: an ancient scribble, one that she treasures deeply and considers her most valued piece of wisdom. It's her wedding gift to us."

A murmur of interest ripples through the room.

"Victoria and I decided that we wouldn't open or read it until we were here, in class, with all of you. Mrs. Samuels-Ortiz believes that this piece speaks to two virtues she sees in us—restlessness and curiosity."

With reverence, Erasmus unfolds the document, its age and character unmistakable even from a distance.

"It begins like this…" he declares, his voice imbued with gravity and emotion, as he prepares to unveil the cherished words for the first time before an audience.

"The Case of the Curious Child and the Restless Magician"

He wears a blue cap adorned with silver stars,

draped over an electric blue coat.

His top hat tilts slightly to the right,

and a black magic wand with silver tips

rests lightly in his hand.

For over an hour,

the magician has defied gravity,

baffled the senses,

and mesmerized his audience.

Minds have been read,

bodies seemingly sawed in half,

people have disappeared and reappeared in impossible places.

The audience has gasped, cheered, and been left in awe.

The climax arrives with a grand finale:

the magician levitates into the air,

vanishing amidst a dazzling explosion of fireworks

that sparkle and cascade around him.

Moments later, he reappears—

first on a distant balcony,

then another,

only to return to the main stage

to wave and thank the ecstatic crowd.

As the illusionist concludes his act and steps offstage,

a curious child approaches,

his wide eyes filled with wonder.

"Is it magic or fantasy?"

the child asks eagerly,

his innocent voice soft

yet filled with genuine wonder.

The magician,

who had grown weary from the performance,

raises an eyebrow,

momentarily surprised.

His skepticism shows in the slight twitch of his lips.

"It is both,"

the restless magician replies,

his voice tinged with mischief,

still caught in the afterglow of his act.

"If it's one, then it cannot be the other,"

the child insists,

his tone resolute,

undeterred by the magician's cryptic answer.

The magician pauses,

assessing the child's seriousness.

He smirks,

but something in the child's unwavering gaze

stirs something deeper within him.

"Why?" he asks,

less impatient,

more curious himself.

"Because it's either real or not,"

the little one declares confidently,

stepping closer,

his face reflecting pure,

innocent curiosity.

The magician sighs,

lowering his wand and leaning slightly forward,

his eyes narrowing in contemplation.

"Magic and fantasy are not one and the same,"

he begins, his voice thoughtful but tinged with weariness.

"Fantasy is a creation of the mind,

while magic is something that happens

right in front of your eyes.

It's all about perception."

The boy's eyes glisten with more questions,

and he presses on,

his voice full of innocence.

"Then neither is real?"

"For some, yes,"

the magician replies quietly,

looking away.

His mind begins to shift

as he reflects on the child's innocence.

"But for others,

both are real,

and it all resides

in the eye of the beholder."

The boy stares at him,

wide-eyed and deep in thought.

He scratches his head, bewildered.

"But how can a fantasy be real?"

he asks, his confusion palpable.

The magician crouches to meet the child's eyes,

his tired face softening for a moment.

He pulls a folded paper from his hat,

unfolding it with care.

"Reality begins with what we dream.

This old scribble explains it best:

the restless spirit."

He begins to read aloud,

his voice steady and solemn:

— ✦ —

"The Restless Spirit"

The restless Spirit possesses

an itch to live,

an urge to seek,

a need to explore,

an imperative to search

The restless Soul chooses what to pursue.

The bug of restlessness,

the root of such itchiness,

keeps our life engines

incessantly active—

it is curiosity.

Curiosity is a condition

of spontaneous inquisitiveness,

a gut-driven eagerness

to learn and explore new things.

Curiosity and restlessness

are human attitudes

that inexorably lead

to the creation of ideas

about things

that don't yet exist.

The totality of civilization and human progress

is derived from ideas—

at first dismissed by others

as mere fantasies within imagination,

yet genuine

to the dreamers themselves.

Magic and fantasy

are both the same type of reality,

but one we must dream of first.

These types of dreamers are uncommon,

as they all possess restless and curious spirits,

filled with magic and fantasy—

both deliberately distorted realities,

just waiting to be made.

— ✦ —

The magician folds the paper with care
and places it back into his hat.

He straightens up,
his eyes softened with a mix of admiration
and a newly realized humility.

"Magic, fantasy, and reality—
they're all threads of the same tapestry,"
he says, his voice gentler now,
carrying the weight of his earlier reflections.

"Your restless spirit will help you
weave them into something uniquely yours."
The child nods slowly,
absorbing the magician's words.

"Thank you, Mr. Illusionist.
Thank you so much,"
he whispers, his voice filled with awe.

The magician tips his tilted hat,
gives a final flourish,
and with a swift turn,
vanishes into the crowd,
leaving the child standing there—
wide-eyed and wonder-filled.

The spark of a restless spirit ignited within,
the boy smiles to himself,
his thoughts now as magical
as the world around him.

*

Royal Cambridge Scholastic Institute (2019)
(University Auditorium)

As Professor Cromwell-Smith finishes reading, his voice lingers in the still air of the auditorium, a silence heavy with contemplation. The students sit motionless, their eyes betraying a mixture of wonder and thoughtfulness. He gazes solemnly at his class, allowing his words to sink in.

"Victoria and I were restless about our love lives. Despite the passage of time, we never strayed from our beliefs and feelings. Eventually, we found each other again because neither of us was willing to settle for less," he declares, his longing eyes meeting hers.

"The floor is now open for questions," The Professor announces with a calid tone of voice.

David is a senior English Literature major with a focus on magical realism and symbolism in modern literature. He enjoys discussing the interplay between reality and fantasy, particularly how authors blur these boundaries to deepen thematic explorations.

"Professor, in the poem, the magician speaks about how "Magic, fantasy, and reality—they're all threads of the same tapestry." This idea seems to suggest that the boundaries between these elements are fluid. Do you think the poem is arguing that the imagination and fantasy are essential to how we understand the world, even in the realm of real-life experiences?"

"That's a great interpretation, David. The poem highlights that imagination and fantasy are more than mere escapes—they're foundational to how we process and understand the world. The magician's statement about the interwoven nature of magic, fantasy, and reality suggests that without our capacity to imagine, to dream, we wouldn't have the drive to pursue progress or to create meaning in our lives. Fantasy, while often dismissed as unrealistic, can help us see the possibilities and potentials that we might otherwise overlook in our daily existence. The act of creating our own fantasies is a tool for navigating reality."

Rachel is a third-year philosophy major interested in epistemology and the philosophy of perception. She enjoys analyzing how people form beliefs about the world and how those beliefs can be shaped by external influences.

"Professor, the child in the poem challenges the magician's view of reality and fantasy. He insists that if something is real, it cannot be fantasy, which seems to be a deeply logical way of thinking. Do you think the poem is commenting on how children's more direct, logical understanding of the world contrasts with the more complex, layered ways adults interpret reality?"

"Yes, Rachel, that's an insightful point. Children often see the world through a lens of simplicity and directness, where things are either real or not, as the child in the poem suggests. This contrasts with the more complex, often self-imposed layers of interpretation that adults place on reality. As we grow older, we complicate our understanding of the world, often relying on abstract concepts or multiple perspectives to make sense of it. The child's clarity, though, is an important reminder that there's also wisdom in simplicity. The fable suggests that perhaps we should sometimes embrace a simpler, more open approach to how we view the world—one where fantasy and reality coexist without the need for rigid boundaries."

Samantha is a sophomore psychology major with a keen interest in cognitive development and the psychology of creativity. She frequently examines how people use imagination in their daily lives and how it impacts their problem-solving abilities.

"Professor, in the poem, the restless spirit is described as having an "itch to live" and a "need to explore." From a psychological standpoint, do you think that restlessness is a necessary part of creativity? Can this drive to search and explore be seen as a core element of the human desire to create?"

"Absolutely, Samantha. In psychology, restlessness often signifies a drive to seek new experiences, which is inherently tied to creativity. The "itch to live" in the poem reflects a deep, intrinsic motivation— what we often call intrinsic drive. It's this very restlessness, the constant desire to explore and to understand, that fuels creative processes. Without this restless curiosity, there wouldn't be the impulse to push boundaries, to create something new. Creativity thrives on this constant questioning and exploring of what's possible. The poem, in a way, celebrates this spirit, showing that it's through our restless curiosity that we unlock the potential for magic and transformation in both fantasy and reality."

Thomas is a senior sociology major focusing on the social constructs of reality and the cultural implications of magic and fantasy in modern life. He is interested in how different cultures and communities interpret the concept of magic.

"Professor, the poem talks about how "fantasy and magic are both the same type of reality." Given the way that societies view reality, do you think that magic and fantasy have more to do with cultural interpretations of reality than an objective truth? Is the idea of fantasy potentially more real than we think?"

"That's a fascinating question, Thomas. The idea that "fantasy and magic are both the same type of reality" suggests that reality isn't as fixed or absolute as we often think. Different cultures and communities interpret reality through their own lenses, shaped by their beliefs, histories, and experiences. What might seem like fantasy or magic to one group could be a deeply ingrained part of another's reality. In this sense, fantasy can be just as "real" as what we perceive to be concrete because it serves a purpose in how people navigate their world. It becomes a tool for explaining the unexplainable, for transcending the mundane, and for inspiring creativity and transformation. The line between what we consider reality and fantasy is often more porous than we realize."

Jennifer is a first-year comparative literature major with a focus on narrative structure and storytelling traditions across cultures. She is fascinated by how stories convey abstract concepts like truth, identity, and self-perception.

"Professor, in the poem, the magician ultimately says that the "restless spirit will help you weave them into something uniquely yours." Do you think the fable is implying that by embracing both the fantasy and reality within us, we have the ability to shape our own identities? How does the restless spirit contribute to this process?"

"That's a profound observation, Jennifer. The restless spirit, as described in the poem, is a metaphor for the drive we all have to create meaning and shape our identities. By embracing both the fantasy and reality within us, we can break free from prescribed definitions of who we are. The restless spirit challenges us to seek out our own narratives, to mix the dreamlike and the practical, and to fashion something that is uniquely ours. In a sense, our ability to shape our identities comes from the willingness to explore all facets of who we are—our desires, fears, dreams, and ambitions—and weave them together into a personal narrative that is constantly evolving. The restless spirit empowers us to redefine ourselves in ways that are authentic and transformative."

"That'll be all for today. See you next week," he says, his voice gentle as he and Victoria walk out, their hands entwined, their faces radiating pure happiness.

As they leave, Professor Cromwell-Smith senses the atmosphere in the room. The student body is visibly affected, their restlessness palpable as they ponder how the day's lessons might shape to their own lives, just as it has Erasmus and Victoria. Curiosity fills the air as they wonder how to cultivate those attitudes for themselves.

"Today, my takeaway is that a touch of magic and fantasy is essential for the restless and curious spirit to soar like a kite through life," one student remarks aloud, encapsulating the collective reflection of the group.

'Mission accomplished,' the professor muses, a satisfied smile on his face as he steps into the sunlight.

However, their mood is quickly tempered by reality.

"Erasmus," Victoria says with a laugh, her eyes dancing, "didn't we leave our bikes at home?"

With a shared chuckle, they set off on foot, still hand in hand, their spirits soaring despite the minor inconvenience.

Chapter 13

Convergence

Royal Cambridge Scholastic Institute (2019)
(Late Sunday morning)

A family brunch will occur at noon, and Victoria's three children are all coming. Sarah arrives early to share her background with Erasmus and Victoria, including how she met her boyfriend.

"Mom, as is my routine, that morning I left my studio early, and hurrying, I walked into the coffee shop around the corner. That's when I saw him for the first time," explains Sarah.

Erasmus appears to be reading a newspaper, but he isn't. He's listening to every word Victoria's youngest enunciates.

"For some reason, the first thing that stood out about him was his voice. I was standing in line and overheard this deep and perfectly modulated monologue. I turned around to see a man dressed in running clothes dictating to a tablet," continues Sarah.

Victoria knows Erasmus is listening, even though he pretends not to.

"Brown-rim glasses, thick eyebrows, Hellenic nose, strong jaw, closely cropped chestnut hair, and bluish-green eyes, he's concentrating on his task, utterly oblivious to his surroundings," describes Sarah.

Erasmus sits next to Victoria; her dreamy eyes meet his. He smiles in complicity.

"Then, I saw his hands, Mom, both strong and with protruding veins. He radiated this incredible energy. He moved to one side, and, wearing running shorts, his bare legs came into view. By then, the attraction was so strong that I couldn't take my eyes off him, so I glanced from the side, doing my best to peek only," explains Sarah.

Erasmus and Victoria sip their tea, taking in every word from their front-row seats. Their faces are transfixed as they look forward to hearing the details of the memorable moment.

"Suddenly, he looked up as if aware of my presence. That's when I froze as if incapacitated. We didn't take our eyes off each other. I managed to walk over on wobbly knees and introduced myself – something I have never initiated with a man. The bottom line is that he is 27 years old, single, a writer, and an endurance sportsman. I dumped my short résumé on him as well. Then magic happened. As it turned out, we realized that we both shared an affinity for the same places, music, movies, etc. Mind you, guys, what I have just narrated happened at most in 30 minutes. After a while, I let my rambling side take over, so my tongue went wild. At the same time, we both felt this uncontrollable draw for each other. What happened next was unexpected but extraordinary, as curiosity suddenly took hold of me. I felt this wild urge to exclaim my happiness to the world, and it came out as an inspired question. That led the way to an unforgettable epic exchange."

"It all happened like this …"

—◆—

Coffee Shop
(around the corner from Sarah's dorm)

"Who are you?" she asks, subdued, as if caught in a trance. Both youngsters focus intently on each other, their eyes seemingly lost in space.

"Eugene Laureau," he says, extending his hand to cover hers as if to shield it.

"Sarah Emerson-Lloyd," she responds, using her mother's last name—a habit she's embraced since her father passed away. His hand continues to cup hers, and she offers no resistance, as if it belongs there.

"I'm a writer," he adds.

"French?" she inquires.

"French-Canadian."

"I'm in my senior year of college but haven't decided on my major yet. I'm leaning toward English literature and poetry," she shares cryptically.

"You don't look like a writer," she blurts out, unfiltered.

"And what do I look like, then?" he asks, amused, a faint smile touching his lips.

"An outdoorsman or an athlete," she replies, biting her lip. What she doesn't say—but feels intensely—is he's gorgeous. She can hardly contain herself.

"I'm both," he replies, sensing the magnetic pull coursing between them.

"C'mon, let's go for a walk," he suggests, standing up and gently tugging her hand.

The young twosome starts their stroll, hands intertwined. Over the next few hours, they talk without pause. Together, they feel at ease, as though they've been doing this all their lives. Time seems suspended, and the world fades away.

Along the way, her fiery temperament ignites playful debates. They spar and tease, their banter laced with intensity but never hostility. It's as if every interaction skirts the edge of a battle or crisis, yet it's all a game—an alluring dance of wills.

Eugene savors her spice and vigor, appreciating her for exactly who she is. He goes along for the ride, mentally stimulated and increasingly captivated by her vibrant energy.

Eugene Laureau's High Rise Condo. Boston (2019)
(A Couple of Months Later)

After a candlelight dinner he carefully prepares, Sarah sits in the living room, relaxed and scanning the breathtaking view of her beloved city and its winding river. Their whirlwind, platonic love affair dances between intense sparks and the healthy tensions ignited by Ms. Emerson-Lloyd's vibrant personality. Eugene's laid-back demeanor has all but surrendered to the vivacious young woman with curly blonde hair. There's nothing he can do to resist her magnetic force.

"Eugene, if you don't show me some of your writings, I'm not leaving tonight," she declares with a teasing edge, attempting to provoke one of their delicious confrontations.

He pretends not to hear, playing coy as he methodically cleans the dishes from the French feast he cooked and served earlier.

"That's it!" she exclaims, bolting toward his studio.

Startled, Eugene abandons his domestic duties and dashes after her. They collide playfully at the studio entrance, crashing onto the plush carpet together. On any other night, this encounter would naturally lead to passionate lovemaking. Tonight, however, it's halted by her sheer determination.

"Eugene Laureau, show them to me!" she demands, smiling mischievously as they remain entangled on the floor.

"Okay."

"What? I can't believe this. It's a miracle. Finally!" she exclaims, her face lighting up as they untangle. He laughs effusively, crawling toward his desk. From amidst scattered papers, he grabs a manuscript resting there.

Settling side by side on the floor, Eugene thrums through the pages until he finds what he's looking for. With love shining in his eyes, he begins to read to her for the very first time:

"Through the Hand of the Scribbler"

Through the hand of the scribbler,
his Spirit and Soul burst out.
His words convey his deepest feelings;
his inspiration is spontaneous,
surging out of his serene Spirit
and tranquil Soul.

The images and sensations take shape,

coming alive,

and the ideas turn into words.

As it relates to Love,

only the heart leads,

while the Spirit and Soul follow.

By the hand of the scribbler,

words of Love pour forth.

They are made of

passionate fire and

boundless tenderness.

Writing to love

is easy yet challenging—

an exercise of plain contradictions.

It is so hard to find that

magical, inspirational moment,

but when it arrives,

the words flow quickly and effortlessly,

and their beauty shines of its own accord.

As the phrases come alive,

and the verses gather strength,

all are driven by the name of Love.

Through the hand of the scribbler,

his Spirit and Soul burst out,

and when there is Love,

only the heart leads,

and the Spirit and Soul only follow.

*

Eugene's voice trails off as he finishes. Sarah sits quietly, the profound beauty of his words resonating deeply within her. She doesn't speak, only leans her head against his shoulder, savoring the moment—a shared experience of vulnerability, creativity, and connection.

Sarah's eyes widen, sparkling with excitement. Because of the class she attended with Erasmus teaching, she feels entirely at home in this realm of poetry and prose. She's captivated, her heart now firmly ensnared by Eugene's artistry, though he remains oblivious.

"Why do you keep such beautiful prose from me?" she asks, her voice trembling with emotion.

"I don't know," Eugene admits, searching her gaze for understanding.

"I guess I wasn't ready until tonight. And now, it just feels like the right moment."

"You've written so much of yourself in that. But do you ever worry that the words won't be enough to express all that you feel?" Eugene, caught off guard, might reply, "I don't know. Maybe they never can. But what else is there to do? Write, and hope." Sarah would then reflect more deeply, "It's the hope in your words that gets to me, Eugene. You let yourself feel, and in doing so, you make me feel too."

Their feelings swirl uncontrollably, a blend of exhilaration and awe.

"I want more," Sarah demands, her playful tone masking the intense yearning in her heart.

"All right, my impetuous lady," Eugene teases gently, pulling another page from his manuscript.

"What an Amazing Blessing Being Together Is"

Who wrote the script for this movie?
Or is it simply crafted from our time together?
Or perhaps we are its producers and directors?

And what of the audience?
Could it be predestined,
written beyond our understanding?
Has it always been there, waiting,
guiding us along a luminous path,
where Happiness multiplies each day?

A love walkway through life,
where firm ground forms beneath our feet,
a protective shield to carry us
through life's challenges,
warding off harm.
A magical lens that reveals life's best angles,
allowing us to distill, drop by drop,
the finest it has to offer.

A generous path that leads to others,

lined with kindness and scattered flowers,

made lovelier by our passage.

A magic carpet upon which we dwell,

carrying us wherever imagination leads.

This script, our script,

is written in dense, indelible ink,

traced in the ecstasy

of two souls fused into one.

Two souls forever grateful for every fleeting moment,

knowing its beauty is brief.

A script charged with Love,

overflowing with strength and passion,

tenderness and unconditional devotion—

pillars of our Happiness.

It is the script of the most beautiful story ever written,

a testament to the extraordinary blessing

of you and I,

together, forever.

*

Sarah's breath catches as the last words leave Eugene's lips. Her emotions swirl uncontrollably, a tumult of wonder and joy.

"This reminds me of my mother's lifelong, true Love," she says at last, her voice barely above a whisper. "Your writings are just as

beautiful as his," she adds with a mischievous twinkle in her eye, "though he's much wittier and smarter."

Her playful, devilish grin and wink lighten the moment, allowing her to defuse the intensity of her overwhelming feelings. Eugene chuckles, his eyes sparkling with admiration.

"Well, I'll take that as a compliment," he replies, pulling her close once more.

And so, in the quiet glow of the evening, they bask in the magic of words and the growing bond between them.

She motions for him to continue, her silence betraying the overwhelming impact of the similarities she senses but cannot yet articulate.

"As to How Love Lights Up Everything"

As matter,
we are finite, pure, and simple dust,
and we are ephemeral energy,
but above all,
we are God's miracle.

As reason,
we are conscience, thoughts, and imagination,
and in our minds,
the world is ideas and shadows.

As Spirit,
we are souls in Love,
and our spirits light up life's way,
providing us with meaning and purpose,

and enabling us to travel far

in life's journey.

Out of Matter and Reason,

only Spirit transcends the infinite,

and the Soul is its engine.

Faith is the light that emanates from the Soul,

and the light between all men

originates from the Spirit,

and that is Love.

"Sarah, like us, this one is for every couple," Eugene explains, his tone tinged with pride. "I finished it just last night. You've been badgering, chasing, and pressing me about it," he teases with a broad smile.

Sarah remains motionless, her feelings simmering beneath the surface, fighting for release.

"I don't know what's wrong with me," she says finally, her voice trembling. "I feel this ravenous need to delve into your writings. What will it take, Eugene? Are you going to read more to me, or must I wrestle it out of you?"

"Oh, yes, of course, my passionate muse," he replies, stunned by her restraint. He expected a volcanic outburst but instead finds her composure intoxicating. Without delay, he begins to read.

"When I Write to You"

When I write to you,
I give you all of me on those little notes.

When I write for you,
I surrender, perhaps,
some of the best of me.

When I write about you,
I try to tell you in a thousand ways,
how much I love you,
and how deep my feelings are.

When I write to you,
I offer you my best gifts,
those that cannot be touched,
those that can only be felt.
When I write for you,
life's beauty grows through words,
and my heart can be sensed
beating like a drum.

When I write about you,
everything I feel turns into magic,
and all of it is yours,
without limit and to no end.

When I write for you,

time and space stop,

the words flow

while my dreams linger,

the Spirit is enriched,

and the Soul smiles in joy.

When I write about you,

the heart is emptied of words,

that burst out and pour Love into you.

When I write about you,

there is Happiness in life,

with a crystalline spirit

and an innocent soul.

Whenever I write to you

in the future,

you'll know and feel

that it will always be,

the best and most profound offering

that I can give and will ever give to you.

*

Sarah no longer contains herself. She throws herself at Eugene in an electrifying, passionate embrace, their faces impossibly close.

"My handsome writer," she murmurs, her voice thick with emotion, "You've captured everything—everything I've been feeling, even before I knew I felt it. Your words—they make me think about

everything we could be, together. But what about you, Eugene? What do you want out of all of this? I return to the question I asked you the day we met."

"Where did you come from? Where were you hiding all this time? Who are you?"

"Whoever your heart wants me to be," Eugene responds, his sincerity unwavering.

"But what does your heart truly want?" she counters, pressing him, her voice shivering with hope and desire.

"For yours to feel the way mine does," he says, his words both an admission and a plea.

"And how does yours feel?" She teases.

"Utterly and hopelessly in Love," he declares.

As the words settle between them, they are swept into each other's arms, consumed by a torrent of shared emotions and undeniable desire.

— ✦ —

"Mom, we've been inseparable ever since," Sarah says with a dreamy tone. "A perfect stranger blessed my life when we found each other by accident. It's as if we were made for each other."

"Wonderful, dear. To be in Love at your age is such a gift. You'll be able to treasure this for the rest of a very long life. We're looking forward to meeting him soon," Victoria replies warmly, her face lit by a broad smile.

"Who is he?" interjects Erasmus with his trademark absent-minded curiosity, the obvious query fully displayed.

"Funny, hilarious professor," Sarah quips back, slightly confused. Then realization dawns. "Oh ... his name is Eugene Laureau, and he's of French-Canadian descent. I thought I mentioned it when I told you guys about how we met," she explains, her bafflement apparent.

One Hour Later at Brunch

"Eugene, allow me to introduce them to you. This is only part of my family, as I have a stepbrother and a stepsister living in Italy. My older sister, Elizabeth Victoria, is the tall, smiley, beautifully pregnant one. Standing to her right, the impossibly handsome young man—though not more handsome than you—is her brand-new husband, Jordan Auguste Morse. My favorite person on earth, my brother Bart, is on her left side, with a jungle of chestnut curly hair on his head. Next to him, you'll find my rival in matters of brotherly Love, his girlfriend, Sofia Broomfield. And, of course, the infatuated couple clinging to each other at all hours of the day and night are my mother, Victoria, and my stepfather, Professor Erasmus Cromwell-Smith," Sarah announces with pompous flair.

"Nice to meet you all," Eugene says, his eyes scanning the group appreciatively.

What he doesn't anticipate is how touchy-feely the Emerson-Cromwell clan is. Before he can say another word, he's swept into a sea of kisses and embraces, leaving him both flustered and warmly welcomed by the family.

"Eugene, do you know this is the first time Sarah has brought anyone to our Sunday brunch?" Elizabeth-Victoria teases mischievously, a playful sparkle in her eye.

"C'mon, sister, shut up!" Sarah retorts, feigning rebellion.

"Eugene, I hear you're a writer," Erasmus chimes in, deftly changing the subject.

"I write poetry under my own name and science fiction under the pseudonym Ethan Lawrence," Eugene replies, a hint of pride in his voice.

"Interesting. Let's talk after the meal, and I'll show you some of my work," Erasmus offers, his academic enthusiasm lighting up.

"Let me break the news to everyone," Bart announces, standing tall and confident. "Sofia and I have enrolled in the MBA program at The London School of Economics. We're leaving in a few weeks."

"That is fantastic. We'll visit you over the summer then," Erasmus responds immediately, his tone cheerful and encouraging.

Victoria, initially taken aback, quickly recovers, pulling Bart and Sofia into a warm embrace.

"I'm so proud of you guys," she says sincerely, her voice tinged with a mix of surprise and deep maternal pride.

"Are you leaving before your nephew is born?" demands Elizabeth, her tone playfully accusatory as she alludes to her upcoming baby.

"No, that's why we don't have a firm departure date yet. We're sticking around until … wait a minute, is it official now, a boy?" Bart exclaims, his face lighting up with excitement.

Elizabeth freezes for a split second, realizing she inadvertently let the secret slip. She glances at Jordan, and their shared complicity is evident in their mischievous smiles that follow a moment of mock seriousness.

Victoria, ever the exuberant matriarch, erupts with joy. She jumps up and down, pulling everyone into jubilant hugs and kisses. Her infectious excitement fills the room, making everyone grin.

Erasmus quietly watches her, his mind wandering back to when he first saw her as a baton twirler in the Harvard marching band. His smile deepens with fondness.

"Mom, I've been meaning to ask if you're retiring for good from teaching?" Elizabeth ventures, her voice laced with a touch of disapproval.

"Yes," Victoria replies with a sense of finality. "The upcoming academic year will be my last."

"What about you, Erasmus?" Bart quickly interjects, curious.

"Same. Next year will be my last," Erasmus confirms with a calm nod.

"What are you both going to do?" Sarah asks, her tone light yet genuinely interested.

"Enjoy our time together, travel, and Erasmus will write some more," Victoria replies with a contented smile, glancing at Erasmus, who squeezes her hand affectionately.

Bart, never one to linger on sentiment for too long, switches gears.

"Are you going to end your balloonist antics, Jordan?" he asks, steering the conversation toward the soon-to-be father's adventures. Jordan hesitates, holding Bart's gaze in silence for a brief, tension-filled moment before letting out a reluctant sigh. "I guess I have no choice but to stop," he says begrudgingly, his tone a mix of resignation and wistfulness.

The room fills with a chorus of good-natured laughter, the lighthearted atmosphere underscoring the love and camaraderie that define the family.

Victoria and Erasmus' Home Library
(After the family has left)

"Eugene's writing is fascinating. He's exploring science fiction that delves into the complexities of our future society," Erasmus remarks, his voice tinged with admiration.

"He seems like a decent boy," Victoria replies, her tone reassuring as she tidies up a stack of books. "What are you planning for tomorrow's class, dear?" she asks, curious about his next lecture.

"It'll cover what we experience every weekend at our family brunches," Erasmus replies cryptically, a knowing smile playing on his lips.

"And that'll be?" Victoria presses, her curiosity piqued.

"Convergence," he says with a twinkle in his eye.

As Erasmus and Victoria share their reflective moments after the family brunch, the quiet transition to the next phase of their day unfolds. With the weight of personal discoveries behind them,

Erasmus gathers his thoughts for the lecture ahead. Leaving the comfort of home behind, the couple steps into the cool afternoon, ready to enter the world of academia once more.

As Erasmus approaches the university auditorium, the campus streets seem quieter, signaling the shift from family gatherings to scholarly pursuits. His smile widens as he steps into the familiar environment, his presence lighting up the room as he prepares for the students' eager attention.

Royal Cambridge Scholastic Institute (2019)
(University Auditorium)

Professor Cromwell-Smith strides into the auditorium with purpose, his sunny disposition immediately uplifting the atmosphere.

"How's everyone today?" he asks, his voice ringing warmly.

"Marvelous!" comes the spirited response from the student body, a collective expression of energy and enthusiasm.

"Today, I'll take you back to a time when I first understood the profound concepts of convergence and confluence—how everything and everyone in life is interconnected in remarkable ways," Erasmus begins, his voice filled with gravity and intrigue.

"It begins like this …"

— ✽ —

Carnegie Library, Pittsburgh, PA (2005)

"Erasmus, pay attention," begins Mr. Carnegie, his tone authoritative yet filled with pride. "Andrew Carnegie built this magnificent structure that now serves as a music hall and a library

at the end of the 19th century when he was still young. There is no precedent of such magnitude and generosity implementing what becomes a lasting and enduring legacy by such a successful young entrepreneur, ever again in America," he declares as they step inside the grand hall.

"Thank you so much for the invitation and tour. I wasn't aware that so many of America's magnificent public libraries were built and funded by Mr. Carnegie. So many of them are still standing and among the best in the country," Erasmus responds, his admiration evident.

"How can I be of help, Erasmus? You requested we meet," asserts the old Scottish antiquarian, whose presence is a rarity during his short visit to America.

He is, after all, a distant relative of the great Scottish-American philanthropist himself.

"Sir, I want to understand better what lies behind confluence and how convergence interacts with it," asks Erasmus, his voice marked by earnest curiosity.

Mr. Carnegie, calm and deliberate, begins pacing. His thoughts seem to navigate the vast repository of knowledge he carries, searching for the most fitting ancient writing on the subject. Then, as if struck by inspiration, he halts and heads down a narrow aisle lined with shelves brimming with aged tomes.

Minutes later, he returns, cradling a leather-bound book that is twice the size of a standard hardcover. Its weathered cover bears the patina of time, and its weight alone suggests the depth of its contents.

"Erasmus, this is the perfect fit for your curiosity," says Mr. Carnegie, setting the book on a nearby table with care.

With reverence, he opens it and begins to read in earnest.

"Convergence"

Convergence and confluence

are life's timely opportunities.

When there is convergence,

we convene and congregate,

through concurrence and congruence

of common interests,

life paths,

or some form or another

of pre-existing links or bonds.

Similarly, when confluence occurs

through convocation,

we seek concertation, congeniality, and conciliation.

Convergence and confluence

are rare and unique life chances, even vital opportunities.

They may be passing and not repeatable.

That's why,

when they are positive and absent of evil,

we take advantage of them on the spot,

and seize the moment,

never letting any of them go.

*

Mr. Carnegie's voice lingers in Erasmus's mind, the poetic wisdom of the ancient tome he has just read aloud echoing with profound significance. The words, rich with meaning, take hold in Erasmus's thoughts, settling like seeds ready to blossom.

As the reading concludes, Erasmus sits in quiet reflection, absorbing the profound insights shared by the venerable antiquarian. Mr. Carnegie closes the leather-bound book gently and looks at Erasmus with a knowing smile.

"Erasmus," he says, his tone deliberate, "what you take from this depends entirely on how willing you are to recognize such moments in your own life. Convergence and confluence are not theories to ponder—they are calls to action, invitations to act when the stars align."

"I understand, sir," Erasmus responds earnestly. "Your guidance today will not be forgotten."

Mr. Carnegie places a firm hand on Erasmus's shoulder. "Then go forth and make something of it, my boy. Life waits for no one."

With that, Erasmus rises, thanking Mr. Carnegie profusely for his time, wisdom, and generosity. As he steps out of the grand library, the air feels alive with possibility, the poet in him already crafting verses from the ideas swirling in his mind.

— ✦ —

Royal Cambridge Scholastic Institute (2019)
(University Auditorium)

Professor Cromwell-Smith carefully closes the old tome and surveys the room with thoughtful eyes.

In the midst of the present day, Erasmus' thoughts drift back to a pivotal encounter years earlier. The conversation with Mr. Carnegie, deep in the Carnegie Library, resurfaces in his mind. The ideas of convergence and confluence still echo through him as he prepares to share them with his students, the past meeting the present in a lesson of profound importance.

"Our class itself is a clear example of convergence," he states, his voice resonant and reflective. "Pause and reflect on it for a moment. Here, we gather, united by a shared curiosity and a common pursuit of knowledge. No one individual dominates, nor does anyone exploit this gathering for personal gain. Instead, we collectively benefit from this moment of convergence."

He walks to the edge of the dais, his tone growing earnest.

"Going forward, be vigilant for settings of convergence. These are rare, and their occurrence often carries immense potential. When you spot them, ensure that you and those with whom you converge take full advantage—always for the right reasons and toward a shared good," he concludes, his words hanging in the air like a soft echo.

Having outlined the profound significance of convergence, Erasmus pauses, allowing the words to sink in. The students remain still, their faces thoughtful as they process the depth of his message. With a quiet nod, the professor invites them to share their thoughts, ushering the class into an engaging dialogue about the philosophical principles of connection.

A few hands are raised.

Lewis is a Philosophy major with a deep interest in existentialism and the nature of happiness. He often challenges abstract concepts and enjoys engaging in philosophical debates.

"Professor, in the poem "Through the Hand of the Scribbler," you speak of the Spirit and Soul being expressed through the act of writing, especially in relation to love. How do you think this contrasts with more mundane forms of communication? Is it the act of writing itself that reveals a deeper truth about love?"

"That's a thought-provoking question, Lewis. The poem suggests that the act of writing, particularly when it comes from a place of deep emotion, transforms simple words into something far more profound. Writing becomes more than just communication—it is a channel for the writer's Spirit and Soul. The mundane forms of communication, like casual conversation, lack that depth of introspection and emotional surrender. In love, the writing becomes a way of offering one's heart fully, and it transcends the ordinary by creating something eternal and meaningful."

Carly is a psychology major, particularly interested in the intersection of storytelling and psychological well-being. She's always eager to draw parallels between literary themes and real-life emotional growth.

"Professor, in "What an Amazing Blessing Being Together Is," the poem suggests that life's path is like a script—one that is filled with joy, kindness, and even magical moments. Do you think the idea of our lives being scripted is a metaphor for how we create meaning, or do you see it as suggesting that some aspects of our journey are predestined?"

"Yes, Carly, the poem uses the metaphor of a script to explore how life unfolds. While it could suggest that certain paths or moments are predestined, I believe the deeper message is that we play an active role in creating our own script. We are both the writers and the actors in our lives, guided by the choices we make, the people we meet, and the love we experience. The idea of a script is more about the intentionality with which we shape our lives, finding meaning in the moments we create."

Anthony is a creative writing major with a focus on human motivation and emotional intelligence. He often brings scientific perspectives into philosophical discussions and enjoys analyzing character behaviors through psychological lenses.

"Professor, in "As to How Love Lights Up Everything," you write about how faith and love are intertwined, illuminating our path in life. From a psychological perspective, do you think the emotional benefits of love and faith are closely related to our well-being? And if so, how does this relate to the poem's theme?"

"That's an insightful perspective, Tony. Love and faith both play significant roles in psychological well-being. Love creates a sense of connection and belonging, which are essential for emotional health. Faith, in the sense of believing in something greater than ourselves, can provide a sense of purpose and stability. In the poem, love and faith are presented as interwoven forces that guide us and give our lives meaning. This connection mirrors the psychological notion that our emotional well-being thrives when we feel connected to others and have a sense of purpose."

Lisa is a senior majoring in Sociology, with a keen interest in the dynamics of happiness. She often looks at social structures and cultural narratives to analyze how individuals find meaning in their lives.

"Professor, the poem "When I Write to You" reflects a profound, almost sacred offering of love through words. How do you think the act of writing as a form of expression can influence societal perceptions of love? Does it elevate or deepen our understanding of relationships?"

"That's a fantastic question, Lisa. The act of writing, especially in the context of love, can indeed influence how we understand and perceive relationships. When we write about love, we are often giving more than just words—we are giving a piece of ourselves. This vulnerability can deepen the connection between the writer and the reader. On a societal level, the written word can elevate the concept of love by making it tangible, allowing us to see the depths of affection and devotion that might not be as easily expressed in day-to-day life. Writing allows for reflection, and through that reflection, love can be understood more profoundly."

Jenny is an Art History major, intrigued by how emotions are conveyed through art and storytelling. She enjoys drawing connections between literature and visual art.

"Professor, the poem "Through the Hand of the Scribbler" speaks to the spontaneity and inspiration that comes when love is expressed through writing. Do you think this aligns with the creative process in art, where the most genuine work often emerges unexpectedly? How do you see this parallel between artistic expression and the written word?"

"Yes, Jenny, I believe there is a strong parallel between writing and artistic expression in general. Much like an artist who may begin a painting with an idea but allows the process to evolve and reveal unexpected beauty, a writer often allows inspiration to flow without force. The creative process in both mediums is deeply rooted in spontaneity and intuition. When we are in tune with our emotions, whether through paint or words, the expression becomes authentic, unforced, and often more powerful. Both art and writing serve as mediums through which we can channel our most profound feelings, and when we let go of control, the results are often more genuine and impactful," The Professor says in conclusion.

"That will be all for this week," he announces, his voice tinged with a hint of finality. "Our next two classes will be the last of this academic year."

As the students begin to gather their things, their demeanor thoughtful, as they process the depth of his message. Conversations hush, and eyes linger on one another. The professor senses a newfound awareness in the room—a subtle yet profound shift as the students begin to search for the seeds of convergence among their peers.

Leaving the auditorium, Professor Cromwell-Smith smiles to himself. **'Mission accomplished.'**

Chapter 14

Ánimo, Animus, Anima

(Charles River, Boston, 2019)

The enamored couple walks alongside the restless waters of the river as the wind picks up pace, whistling all around them. Huddled together, their steps slow under the force of the blow. The late afternoon cool spring weather feels misplaced, more akin to an early autumn day. The weather phenomena stir an eerie feeling in Victoria, unearthing long-buried memories.

As they approach a familiar turn, chills run through her body. The walkway is not only well known but also brimming with beautiful, unforgettable memories steeped in intense emotions. Soon, the silhouette of the student residence building comes into view. They approach the door, and she trembles, her heart racing.

"Surprise!" Erasmus exclaims, key in hand, as he opens the door and ushers Victoria inside.

Overcome by a torrent of flashbacks, she clings tightly to his arm as though fearing she might crumble under the weight of her emotions.

Erasmus and Victoria's College Days' Studio (2019)

"I bought it many years ago, soon after you left, with a loan taken from Mr. Carnegie," Erasmus reveals softly.

"It looks the same," she marvels, her mouth agape. Her intense gaze roams the space, her face overcome with joy.

"I never touched or changed anything. Never rented it out either," he confesses.

Everything is as they left it—their photographs and souvenirs from countless bike trips, books stacked high in every corner, the reading chair by the floor lamp, and the bed with the same linens. Time seems frozen, the studio an untouched capsule of their love.

"For years, I used to come here. I even slept over sometimes," he admits.

"Didn't that sadden you or make you feel depressed?" she asks, her voice tinged with concern.

"Victoria, sometimes the places where we've been the happiest in life lie scattered in our past," Erasmus begins, his tone reflective. "They're often modest and unpretentious and yet, at the time, provided us with immense and irreplicable joy," he extols as they stroll around the small, nostalgic space.

Then, without warning, and driven by sheer impulse, she turns and kisses him passionately in one swift motion. It's a kiss bursting with the fervor of youth, her arms winding tightly around his neck in a classic sailor's victory kiss posture, one calf bending up as if choreographed by memory.

"I was … we were totally happy in this tiny, cozy place, my adorable Brit," she declares, her glowing smile stretching from ear to ear, her eyes sparkling with unrestrained delight.

"Are we going to stay the night?"

"If you so desire, my lady."

At that moment, Victoria notices the notebooks, and her heart begins to race wildly.

"All your poems from our time together are still here?" she asks rhetorically as she paces toward them, her fingers tracing the edges of the well-worn spines.

"Why?"

"Because this is where they belong... at least, they did until now."

Victoria trembles, working hard to contain her emotions as she begins to leaf through the pages. Her breathing deepens, and her hands grow unsteady while memories long buried start to resurface.

"Do you remember this one?" she asks, pointing to a scribble on a yellowing page.

"That was right after we met, at the very beginning of our relationship," Erasmus replies, his voice filled with nostalgia.

Unaware of their subtle body movements, the twosome naturally reverts to old habits deeply rooted in their past. He reaches for her free hand, and they instinctively nestle together in the same reading chair where so many of the notebook's scribbles had been created, shared, and lived.

Victoria looks at Erasmus with eyes that shine bright and glisten with tears.

"This was your first declaration of love, my beloved Brit."

"Yes, it was, my lady."

Victoria continues flipping through the notebook. When she turns to a particular page, both of them stop and look at each other with sudden recognition, as if unearthing a shared treasure, they had forgotten existed.

The opportune scribble has been waiting, it seems, for this very moment to aid them on their journey of reconnection. Victoria covers her mouth with her hand as the memory of the poem rushes back to her. Her throat tightens with emotion, rendering her momentarily speechless. She hands the notebook to Erasmus, her teary eyes silently urging him to read it aloud.

Erasmus takes the notebook and begins to read with deep emotion, savoring each word.

*

"It Is Commonly Said that Love ..."

It is commonly said that
love is never having to say you're sorry,
and never having to apologize.

It has been said, therefore,
that in this regard, Love is perfect
and as it belongs to a twosome,
it is twice perfect.

But the risk of Love
without forgiveness or repentance,
is that it could turn rigid and selfish.
It's the kind of Love,
where forgiveness

is replaced by

obfuscation and recurring reprimands.

It's the kind of Love,

where repentance

is replaced by wounded self-esteem,

and offended egos and pride.

On the contrary,

love is to know how to forgive

those that we love.

Forgiving one another,

we also forgive ourselves.

Love between two people works,

only if the couple,

acts in unison on everything,

so, when one fails, both fail,

or maybe,

the one that has failed,

is the other.

Love is to be sorry together.

Love is absent of pride, selfishness,

forbidden or sacred places.

What matters in Love is

what one feels for one another.

In Love,

it does not matter

if there is a gesture or not,

but only if whatever takes place

is done with our hearts.

Love is not arrogant.

Love is humble.

When in Love,

complaints are ill-fitted,

punishment creates opaqueness,

pride stains,

selfishness hurts,

and punishment kills.

When there is Love,

the offense is born,

with its own pardon,

attached to it.

Remorse is always done

by both lovers and

it is in this way,

that forgiveness does not exist in Love,

because while in Love,

it is not necessary

to say I'm sorry,

or to ask for forgiveness.

*

"I wish we would have read this earlier," Victoria says softly, her voice trembling with a mixture of regret and hope.

"Actually," Erasmus replies insightfully, "it's occurring at the right time. Whatever needed to happen spontaneously took place without aid or crutches," Erasmus replies insightfully.

They both fall silent, holding hands as they absorb the poem's meaning, feeling a renewed sense of love and understanding bloom between them.

"My lady, here is another piece exploring what a couple endures when separated."

In a quiet rhythm, Erasmus begins to read aloud, his voice steady and soothing, as Victoria rests her head on his shoulder.

"When We Are Not Together"

I wish I knew how you are truly feeling.

Hopefully, your heart is as light as mine.

Yet, I've sensed the sorrow in your voice,

and I long to lift it from your spirit.

What we share is far too beautiful

not to be a constant source of joy.

Stay spontaneous, as you've always been;

let's try to keep rigidity at bay.

This extraordinary bond between us

is like a sudden fountain,

springing forth,

needing no coaxing,

no outside force.

Let me be me; I'll let you be you.

But also,

let us be us—together,

just as we are.

We're already so alike;

it will keep us close,

spontaneous, and united,

growing closer and closer still.

I wonder how you are truly doing.

I hope you feel the same happiness I do.

May my words bring you comfort—

not critique or complaint—

but support, never demand.

I wish for you to feel the strength

we create together,

a strength that becomes your solace

when we are apart.

I yearn to be with you now and forever.

But when we cannot be together,

let the love we share

be your carriage and shield.

Let me inspire your happiness,

so that those days apart

are serene, peaceful,

and pass swiftly

as we await each other's return.

And as always happens,

when we reunite in joy,

we find that our love has deepened,

our bond has grown stronger,

and our life together has,

over time,

become richer and more radiant than ever before.

*

As he concludes the reading, Erasmus' eyelids lower in his familiar way, signaling his gentle drift into the realm of dreams. Victoria kisses him softly on the lips and carefully removes the notebook from his hands. Her curiosity draws her back to its pages, and soon, she discovers another treasure—a verse he once dedicated to her.

The memory comes rushing back: it had emerged spontaneously during a long run, as they rested together on a park bench. She begins to read the verse aloud, her voice soft and tender, mirroring how it sounded the very first time he shared it with her. Her hands tremble slightly, overcome by the timeless beauty of his words.

*

"The Soul's Whispers"

Today, *I remembered those whispers,*

and in total silence,

I slid back to the past ...

Those sounds were soft and constant,

like a tiny creek,

a crystalline, crisp trickle.

The Soul's whispers suddenly irrupted

as we were behind the scenes.

The stage, the play, the performers, the audience—

all "acting" as they always do,

on the other side,

putting on a show, living just

for "the appearance" of it.

Behind the show

backstage of the performance,

between the drop curtains,

I could hear life ...

But, from afar,

I couldn't discern their performance

nor their costumes,

or the scenario.

The figures on either side were blurry.

I could only hear the whispers ...

And without even feeling it,

almost without noticing,

it seemed as though I could hear their souls.

The sounds of their souls came to me,

as a distant whisper.

The words could not be distinguished,

only their cadence remained.

The people were not what they seemed

nor what they seek to be.

Their souls whispered something different ...

Today, I remember those whispers,

those sounds, soft and constant.

They were like a tiny creek,

a crystalline, crisp trickle.

They were ... the Soul's whispers.

*

Victoria finishes, her mind foggy with thought, and she doesn't immediately realize Erasmus is now fully awake, his eyes transfixed, matching her contemplative gaze. A small surge of emotion courses through her as their eyes meet.

"Did you...?" she begins.

"Yes, I heard it all, my dear. It stirred up such loving emotions," Erasmus responds, his voice calm and soothing.

Victoria's smile spreads, infectious, and Erasmus can't help but respond with one of his own. Her enthusiasm bubbles over, filling the room with a quiet energy. They quietly step out of the residence. For the first time since she left, Erasmus takes the notebook with him.

"Let's keep it close to us at home," he announces.

Victoria is overcome with emotion. The sounds of campus life break the reverie of their quiet walk, signaling the shift from the past to the present. The memories of their younger days, preserved in the student residence, fade into the background as Erasmus thinks about his upcoming class.

Then, from the corner of her eye, she notices a loose piece of paper teetering on the edge of the notebook. Erasmus follows her gaze and instinctively pulls it free. As he unfolds it, his face changes, struck deeply by the sight of its contents.

"What is it?" Victoria asks, leaning closer. Then, as her eyes take in the precise, flowing handwriting, realization dawns.

"That's a letter from Mrs. V.!" she exclaims.

"Indeed, it is," Erasmus confirms, his tone imbued with reverence.

"Her letter will be the centerpiece of tomorrow's class. I'm going to lecture on vital engagement—a dissertation on *Ánimo, animus, anima,* not as animosity, but in its broadest, most transcendent sense," he says.

Victoria's eyes shine with admiration as he speaks. "You're more than welcome to join us, my lady," he adds with a gentle smile.

"It would be my pleasure," she replies, "but I may be a little late— I need to handle some matters regarding the kids' trust."

"Very well, then. It's settled. See you there," Erasmus says, slipping the letter carefully back into its place.

As they prepare to leave their home, the weight of the memories still lingers. With one final glance at the intimate space where their love had been rekindled, they step out into the brisk, quiet morning air. The streets of the campus, just waking from the soft fog of early dawn, now seem like a world away from their moment of personal reflection. Before parting ways, they share a tender kiss, a fleeting but heartfelt gesture that lingers in the air as they break apart.

Erasmus walks toward the university alone, the memory of Victoria's smile still warm in his heart, while she heads off in the opposite direction to tend to her errands. Though their paths briefly diverge, the connection between them remains strong, a testament to the new beginning they have embraced.

Royal Cambridge Scholastic Institute (2019)
(University Auditorium)

Arriving at the university's lecture hall, Erasmus briefly pauses outside the door, collecting his thoughts. A deep breath in, and then, with a smile, he opens the door. The contrast of the quiet, reflective morning to the buzzing energy of the classroom is striking. The familiar scent of chalk and old wood fills the air as he steps onto the stage. The students are already chattering excitedly, waiting for his arrival, unaware that today's lecture will be laced with deeper personal meaning, carried from his own experiences.

Despite having almost no sleep the previous night, Professor Erasmus Cromwell-Smith strides into class with unwavering enthusiasm, radiating an infectious, boundless energy. His quick steps echo across the room as he makes his way to the desk.

"How's everyone today?" he asks, his voice bright and invigorating.

"Insanely awesome!" comes the spirited response from the class, their collective energy mirroring his own.

"Sometimes, we all feel a little low in motivation," Professor Cromwell begins, his tone shifting to one of reflection. "We lack the drive to carry out what's expected of us, or perhaps even what we expect of ourselves. Last night, I stumbled upon a letter—an old gem—from my inveterate and greatest cheerleader, the incomparable Mrs. V. She was my mentor during a deeply transformative period of my life."

He pauses, allowing the weight of his words to settle. "This letter had a profound and uplifting effect on me, especially during times when I struggled to navigate life's challenges. It felt as though Mrs. V., sensing my need across the expanse of time, had written it specifically for me. Within her heartfelt words was a single verse—a powerful reflection on a virtuous attitude, a life condition that unites our desire with the willingness to strive for greatness." "Please allow me to share the verse with you."

The pedagogue unfolds the letter carefully and begins to read the verse aloud, his voice carrying the rhythm of the words with deliberate passion…

*

"Ánimo, Animus, Anima"
(Energy, Spirit & Soul)

Ánimo, animus, anima,

Ánimo, animus—what does it matter?

They are all one and the same.

Surprised?

Colloquially, animus

is often strictly associated

with animosity,

those deeply rooted ill feelings.

But there couldn't be a more blatant

misuse of a very profound word,

than this.

That's why, in this verse,

animus finds itself cradled

between its homonyms—

ánimo and anima, that is.

Hereunto lies the other side of animus—

or is it ánimo or anima, perhaps?

Well, either or, here is what it truly is …

Animus is a state or condition

that signals our "vital engagement."

into the game of life.

Animus is desire and willingness combined.

It can be an attitude towards anything or anyone,

or a condition born of

the deliberate or even unintended ways we live.

Animus is the impetus of the Spirit,

and the spark of the Soul.

It is the vital force of the heart,

the driver of our design,

the engine behind our intendment,

the catalyst of our purpose,

the vital energy behind our meaning.

It is the fuel for our plans,

the secret ingredient behind our courage,

the light bulb in our mind,

the energy behind our willingness,

the precondition to our disposition.

Animus is the intensity,

the level of engagement,

in a state or condition of willingness.

It resides at our core,

inside our inner Spirit.

If Ánimo, Animus, Anima,

is not spontaneously present

at the onset of life's endless paths,

then it is one we must fight for—

putting our best efforts to acquire it,

to create "the right frame of mind"

to embark on any quest.

Are you in good animus today?

Are you of good animus every day?

Do you have the right anima this morning?

Ánimo, Animus, Anima—

what does it matter?

After all,

they are all

one of the same.

*

Professor Cromwell-Smith pauses, then begins a thoughtful commentary that expands on the verse he has just read.

"This verse reminds me—and I hope it reminds you—that cultivating *animus* is not a passive state. It is something we must actively pursue, especially in moments when life feels heavy. May you all find your own *animus* today and every day."

The room falls silent, the weight of his words hanging in the air. Slowly, a murmur of agreement ripples through the class.

"Now, let's talk about the *butchering* of a word," he continues, his tone sharpening with intellectual fervor. "When researching the etymology of *animus,* every single underscored term in the verse above—Spirit, Soul, heart, design, intendment, purpose, meaning, plan, courage, mind, willingness, vital force, vital engagement, and vital energy—traces back to its true definition. Yet, how often do we reduce it to something as shallow as animosity?"

He lets the observation linger, scanning the room. "This attitude, this condition, is essential if we are to achieve anything meaningful in life. It is the foundation, the fuel, and the guide. Work on it without delay."

"The room is open for questions," he announces with a quiet voice. Several hands are raised.

Leyton is a senior political science major, known for his insightful analysis of philosophical texts and his ability to link theory to practical action. He often asks questions that challenge the professor's concepts and provoke deeper thought in his peers.

"Professor, in the poem 'Ánimo, Animus, Anima,' you talk about animus being the 'vital force of the heart' and the 'catalyst of our purpose.' How do you think we can consciously cultivate animus in our daily lives, especially in moments when we feel disconnected or uninspired?"

"That's a great question, Leyton. The poem points to animus as something deeply embedded within us, something that requires both awareness and effort to tap into. To cultivate animus, we need to begin by fostering a mindset of openness and receptivity to the world around us. It's about engaging with life and people with a sense of purpose, willingness, and energy, even when we feel low or uninspired. It's a matter of making the decision to be present in each moment, to actively pursue what excites us, and to push forward, despite any resistance we might encounter. When we connect with that inner drive, we can reinvigorate our sense of purpose and, in turn, influence how we engage with the world."

Lynn is a second-year philosophy major with an interest in existentialism and the search for meaning. She often probes the deeper emotional and philosophical aspects of human experience.

"Professor, the poem emphasizes the importance of 'willingness' and 'desire' as part of animus. Do you think these qualities are enough to create real change, or is there something more that needs to be present for one to fully actualize their potential?"

"That's a very insightful question, Lynn. While willingness and desire are essential for animus, they alone are not always sufficient for creating meaningful change. The poem suggests that animus requires an active engagement with the world—a determination to move forward with courage and purpose. Real change comes when those desires and willingness are aligned with action. It's not just about wanting something; it's about being willing to do the work, face the challenges, and keep moving forward despite obstacles. True potential is actualized when animus is paired with sustained effort, reflection, and growth."

Jackson is a senior majoring in literature, with a focus on poetry. He has a keen interest in how language shapes our perceptions of reality and often seeks deeper layers of meaning in poetry.

"Professor, in the poem, you describe animus as a 'vital engagement' that connects to both the spirit and soul. How do you think this engagement manifests in poetry? Is it possible for a poet to fully embody animus in their work?"

"That's an excellent question, Jackson. I believe animus plays a critical role in the creative process. A poet who embodies animus is not just writing to fulfill an external goal, but is deeply connected to the inner drive that sparks their creativity. When animus is present in a poet's work, it becomes a conduit for expression that flows naturally and powerfully. The willingness to explore one's soul and spirit through words, to take risks with language, and to pour oneself into the craft—that's how animus manifests in poetry. It's the very heartbeat of a poem, the energy behind the metaphor, the urgency in the rhythm."

Ariana is a junior psychology major with a focus on emotional intelligence and motivation. She enjoys analyzing human behavior and how emotions can influence decision-making and creativity.

"Professor, you mentioned that animus is the 'fuel for our plans' and the 'secret ingredient behind our courage.' From a psychological perspective, how do you think animus influences a person's ability to overcome fear or self-doubt?"

"Great question, Ariana. From a psychological standpoint, animus is closely linked to intrinsic motivation—the internal drive that fuels our actions despite external challenges. When animus is present, it gives us the courage to face fear and self-doubt because it's grounded in a deeper sense of purpose and meaning. It helps shift the focus from the fear itself to the drive to move forward, regardless of the obstacles. It's about reframing fear as something to be acknowledged but not allowed to dictate our actions. When we align our desires and willingness with animus, we become more resilient, less affected by negative emotions, and more determined to reach our goals."

Maya is a third-year sociology student, with an interest in the intersection between social structures and individual agency. She is particularly fascinated by how individuals find meaning and purpose within collective systems.

"Professor, the poem talks about the importance of 'recognizing moments of convergence.' How do you think animus and convergence are connected in our daily interactions with others, particularly within communities or larger social systems?"

"That's a wonderful observation, Maya. Animus and convergence are deeply connected because animus is the driving force that pushes us to engage with the world around us. In a community or social system, when we recognize moments of convergence—whether it's shared values, common goals, or mutual understanding—we are in a state of alignment. Animus empowers us to act on those moments of connection, to be proactive in fostering collaboration, and to contribute to the greater good. Convergence, when recognized and acted upon with animus, can lead to collective growth and transformation. It's about finding the common thread that unites us and actively engaging with it."

With that, he glances at the clock, signaling the end of the class.

"See you next week," he says, his voice tinged with finality.

As he strides out of the classroom, his students sit in contemplative silence, reflecting on his words. He smiles softly, sensing the shift in the room—their minds alive with curiosity, pondering the profound duality within the word *animus* and what it means in their lives—and how both meanings might be found within themselves. One by one, they gather their things, but the energy in the room remains, a testament to the powerful convergence of thought and spirit.

Chapter 15

Life's Endless Virtuous Circles

(En route from Cape Cod to Boston, 2020)

"I wonder how our tiny little baby is doing?" Elizabeth Victoria asks softly as they navigate the long, lonely road out of Cape Cod, visibility reduced to nearly nothing by the dense fog.

"He's in good hands, my love," Jordan reassures her, his voice steady and calming. "Your mom doesn't let him out of her sight— not for a second."

As always, his presence and a few gentle words are enough to soothe her. Elizabeth feels safe, content, and deeply happy. Their day had been extraordinary—a perfect escape. Together, they piloted their balloon across the skies, the flight stretching blissfully from morning until evening. After landing on the picturesque New England coast, the adventurous new parents had eagerly set out on the drive back to Boston, the joy of the day still fresh in their hearts.

"I want this day to last forever," she murmurs, her voice wistful.

But fate has other plans.

An unexpected bend lies ahead, shrouded in fog, unseen and unavoidable. From the opposite direction, a trailer truck loses control—the brakes fail, and it veers wildly off the road. Momentum gathers as it barrels downhill, skidding uncontrollably into the path of oncoming cars.

The collision is devastating and instantaneous.

The unlucky victims are the young Morse-Emerson couple. Returning from their idyllic balloon adventure, they never see the truck until it's too late. The impact is catastrophic—head-on and unavoidable. Their car erupts into a towering ball of flames, the blaze consuming everything in a cruel instant.

The exuberant lives of Jordan and Elizabeth Victoria, so full of love, promise, and joy, are snuffed out as swiftly as a candle's fragile flame.

Mt. Auburn Cemetery (2020)

Elizabeth and Jordan's burial ceremony is deeply solemn, the air heavy with grief and love. Victoria stands surrounded by her two surviving children, Bart and Sarah, their presence a quiet testament to resilience. Beside them stands Erasmus, a comforting anchor in this moment of sorrow. Across from them, on the opposite side of the two caskets, the Morse family mourns their beloved son, Jordan Auguste.

The atmosphere is quiet but charged with unspoken emotions. It is Professor Erasmus Cromwell-Smith's turn to speak. His solemn, pained eyes sweep across the gathered mourners as he steps forward, holding a small piece of paper containing words chosen with care for this occasion. With a steady voice, he begins to read:

"As Time Passes By"

As time passes
and life goes on,
we are reminded by tragedy

how precious life is,

and how privileged we are

to be healthy and alive.

Life is short—very short.

We must live it in full,

squeezing every drop out of every single day.

Our family, our friends—

they are our travel companions

on this intense voyage of life.

Work and enjoyment keep us busy,

but Love gives us balance and equilibrium.

As time passes

and life goes on,

as the turn of the next generation approaches,

our greatest satisfaction

is to see our descendants

living in full bloom,

free, healthy,

successful in whatever they pursue,

and happy with their lives,

their friends,

and their loved ones.

*

It is Jordan's father's turn to read his son's eulogy. He steps forward, his shoulders heavy with grief yet steady with resolve. The folded paper in his trembling hands speaks to the weight of his loss, and as he begins, his voice carries the tenderness of a father's love and the sorrow of an irreplaceable absence.

"Do You Remember Those Eyes?"

Do you remember those eyes?
I do … I always will.

His eyes smiled at you
with their little twinkle,
that tiny movement where they seemed
to close in on you,
as if you were
the most important person in the world—
at least in that moment, to him.

You couldn't help but feel
that you had his full attention,
his full respect.

His eyes read people so well …
those laser beams made you feel good,
high-spirited, and full of optimism.

His eyes touched you with total approval,
giving you a profound sense
of his limitless faith in you.

He was a source of strength,

able, so quickly,

to get close to you—

as only those who genuinely

accept others as they are can.

Jordan's life was a celebration of life—

a precious life,

a life that, because it is short,

must be lived in full,

squeezing every second out of it.

A life where giving himself to others

is the best legacy he leaves behind.

Do you remember those eyes?

I do … I always will…

*

He pauses, his voice breaking at the end. "Goodbye, Jordan. You will be dearly missed, son."

Victoria steps forward, composed but deeply moved. She speaks with quiet strength, her voice carrying a resolve that mirrors her late daughter's spirit.

"My daughter Elizabeth would not have wished for anything different than this beautiful homage. She wouldn't have wanted to see us sad. To the contrary, I intend to honor her wishes by celebrating her life and that of her husband, Jordan," she says, her words a poignant reminder to cherish life, even in the shadow of loss.

Victoria and Erasmus Campus Home (2020)

No one dressed in black is allowed at the reception. Instead, Jordan and Elizabeth's favorite music fills the air, creating an atmosphere of bittersweet celebration. In the living room, family home movies play on the television, capturing moments of Jordan and Elizabeth as children—laughing, playing, and living vibrant lives.

Victoria moves among the guests with a radiant smile, exuding warmth and an almost stubborn joy. She refuses to let grief define the day, subduing sadness and commanding happiness at every turn. Erasmus watches her in quiet admiration, awed by the wave of positivity she has generated.

"She's not permitting anyone to be anything but uplifting," Erasmus observes, listening as Jordan's lively parents recount one of his childhood adventures, their laughter mixing with tears.

Suddenly, the sound of a baby's cries emanates from the electronic monitor Victoria carries. Without a word, Erasmus begins ascending the stairs. Moments later, Victoria follows, entering the nursery to find her husband sitting in a rocking chair, feeding the baby. The tender scene stops her in her tracks.

"Learning fast to be a father, dear," she teases gently, but Erasmus barely acknowledges her.

"With his parents gone, his grandparents on both sides are all he's got," Erasmus says, his voice heavy with loving concern.

"Speaking of that," Victoria begins, her tone brightening, "there's absolute consensus among our family and Jordan's."

"Consensus about what?" Erasmus asks, a note of apprehension creeping into his voice.

"That we should adopt the baby," she announces, her eyes shining.

"We?" Erasmus's voice trembles as he repeats the word, his thoughts tangled.

"Aren't we …?" he ventures, unsure.

Victoria stares at him, amused by his flustered response.

"Too old …?" he babbles, still trying to find his footing.

"Are we?" she counters, her gaze steady, challenging him.

"No, I don't mean it that way," he stammers, growing more confused.

"In which way do you mean it, then?" she presses, enjoying his struggle.

"Too old to be parents?" he finally blurts out.

"Same question: are we?" she repeats with playful determination.

"I guess …" he begins to respond negatively but halts mid-sentence, realizing it's fear, not truth, speaking. He pauses, gathering himself.

For what feels like forever, the room is silent. Finally, Erasmus lifts his eyes to meet Victoria's. As their gazes lock, an unspoken understanding passes between them. Slowly, faint, knowing smiles form on both their faces.

"I guess not, Victoria," he says at last, his voice steady.

"This is your chance to be a father, dear," she declares softly.

It's the closest Erasmus has ever come to witnessing Victoria shed a tear for the loss of her daughter and son-in-law.

Minutes later, as promised, Victoria and Erasmus descend the stairs, the baby soundly sleeping in Erasmus's arms. The buzz of conversation in the family room swells as they enter, and Sarah quickly takes charge.

"Mom and Erasmus, Bart and I have discussed this possibility several times," Sarah begins, her voice steady but full of emotion.

"Today, we also talked it over with Jordan's parents, and they've given their blessing." Jordan's father and mother nod in agreement. Victoria and Erasmus exchange relaxed glances, assuming Sarah is about to announce that she and Bart will adopt the baby. But they couldn't be more wrong.

"Since you're now going to become parents," Sarah continues, her voice filled with warmth, "Bart and I have decided on a name for the baby. With all our hearts, we want you to name him Erasmus Cromwell-Smith II."

Her words hang in the air for a moment, sinking into everyone present. A collective sigh of emotion ripples through the room, followed by cheers and applause.

Erasmus's lips tremble, his arms beginning to wobble as he holds the baby. Sensing his emotion, Victoria quickly takes the baby from him. She looks at Erasmus with a soft smile before breaking down, her tears flowing freely, uncontainable and raw. The baby stirs slightly, tiny drops of her tears falling on his cheeks, a quiet baptism of love and healing.

"There's no better gift to honor Elizabeth and Jordan than what all of you have just done," Victoria says, her voice steady despite the tears glistening on her cheeks. "I'm sure they're smiling down on us right now. Rest assured, Erasmus and I will continue the family path they were just beginning to pave." She wipes away her tears and bends over to kiss the baby softly.

"If you all will allow me," Erasmus interjects, finally regaining his composure, "I'd like to share a couple of pieces that, given the circumstances, carry profound meaning." He pauses, glancing at the baby in Victoria's arms. "The first is something I wrote at the request of Jordan and Elizabeth. They wanted it to reflect the way they dreamed their children would grow up. This will be the first time I've shared it with anyone, and Victoria and I are committed to following their wishes."

He unfolds a sheet of paper, his voice growing joyous as he begins to read…

"For Our Children"

Let them grow healthy and strong
so they may discover a world
that is both difficult and fantastic
at the same time.

Let them travel and meet its people,
and love all their fellow travelers,
especially those in need.

Let it be that

everything they start or involve themselves in

is done with conviction and dedication.

Let them enjoy

their parents and an immensely happy childhood,

filled with boundless Love,

dreams, and illusions.

And as they grow,

let them discover everything and everyone

around them as they truly are.

Then, over time,

let them gradually uncover

who they really are,

so they may find their true selves,

just as God brought them to earth.

So, whoever they are,

they are happy and comfortable in their own skin.

So, whatever they do,

they do it well.

Hence, from that moment forward,

they are always

their authentic selves.

We'll teach you

to be humble, honest, and non-materialistic.

We'll offer you our infinite Love
and our passion for knowledge, sports, and nature.

We'll teach you discipline,
ingraining in you a rock-solid work ethic.
We'll push and press
and will be as demanding as you can bear—
and then some.

We'll make you strong
and teach you to live life in full,
so that life does not slip by
without you seizing every moment of it,
regardless of the circumstances.

Erasmus lowers the paper, his voice trailing off, and looks around the room, meeting the eyes of family and friends who are deeply moved by his words. After a moment, he speaks again.

"This second piece comes from an antique book I once read at one of my childhood mentor's bookstores. It's about how we face the future, even as we struggle to find our way forward after the loss of a child."

With a steadying breath, Erasmus begins to read the next piece…

"Destiny"

Life is a tightly wound chain of occurrences,
a maddening scramble
we cannot govern.

Our future is being made
every one-thousandth of a second.

It is an infinite,

never-ending,

totally random string

of connected occurrences.

All these intersecting events

relate, influence, and interact

with one another.

Each and every event in life

is a wonderful and complex accident.

This includes the finite ways of our life,

the urgency of living,

and the uncertainty of our future.

We are an accident,

every moment we are alive,

and in the end,

all is a complex mishap.

Life is a complicated interaction

of events of nature,

human acts and behavior,

and everything born of

human creation,

all under the mantle of life.

We have very little control over life.

But if circumstances allow it,

with faith and willingness,

we can reap from it

immense Happiness and goodwill.

*

As Erasmus finishes, the room is silent, each person lost in their thoughts. The baby stirs slightly in Victoria's arms, drawing everyone's attention back to the present. Erasmus steps forward and gently brushes a finger against the baby's cheek.

"We'll honor Elizabeth and Jordan by giving this little one the best life we can," he says softly. Victoria nods, her tears flowing once more, this time a mixture of grief and hope.

The family gathers closer, united by the love that will carry them forward, even in the face of their shared loss.

Erasmus and Victoria's Campus Home (2010)
(A Few Weeks Later)

The transition to parenthood has been surprisingly smooth, thanks to Victoria's experience. What has been unexpected, however, is how little physical work she has had to do for the baby. Erasmus, with an unyielding dedication, has taken on the role of a 24/7 caretaker. His boundless enthusiasm and devotion have left him consumed by fatherhood, pouring all his energy into caring for Erasmus Jr.

Victoria, with her characteristic grace and wisdom, has gradually begun to ease her way into the parenting routine. Using her deft touch and invaluable "know-how," she has started taking on more responsibilities. Slowly but surely, the couple finds themselves working together seamlessly—sharing duties, complementing each other effortlessly, and providing their son with constant love and attention.

The final sign that life is settling into a new normal arrives with the addition of a British au pair. Emma Franklin, a capable and cheerful young woman, is entrusted with day-to-day responsibilities for Erasmus Jr., a role she will hold until his adulthood.

Upon Emma's arrival, Victoria and Erasmus are finally free to step back into their other cherished roles as professors. With Emma's capable hands tending to the baby's needs, the couple finds balance once more—nurturing their child and continuing to inspire others through their teaching.

Royal Cambridge Scholastic Institute (2020)
(Campus Back Roads)

As the sun slowly rises over the campus, Professor Cromwell-Smith pedals with a steady cadence through the quiet campus streets, the early morning sunlight casting long shadows. Victoria had left earlier both of them preparing for their final classes of the academic year. As he rides, the eminent professor's thoughts drift, and he reflects on the bittersweet events of the previous days. He has just begun to settle into the new normal of life after Elizabeth and Jordan's tragic passing, and yet the cycle of life and the promise of renewal remains fresh in his mind. As Professor Cromwell-Smith mind drifts back to his looming class, he takes stock of the subjects, he has explored with his students over the year.

Existential themes—adversity, virtue, forgiveness, reciprocity, resilience—have made this academic year remarkable. Each lesson carried its own weight, every discussion an opportunity to inspire. Erasmus's mind shifts, flashing through memories of his life with Victoria and the years they spent apart. He revisits their memorable encounters with New England's antiquarian mentors during their time in Boston. His thoughts move to the meetings they had with Colin Carnegie at the public libraries in New York and Pittsburgh—institutions built by his distant relative, Andrew Carnegie.

He recalls the journey to St. Louis to meet Victoria's mentor, Mrs. Samuels-Ortiz, at the grand public library, and the timely scribble gifted to him by Mr. Ringwald, affectionately known as "The Riddler," during the turbulent time when Victoria had run away. A procession of mentors follows in his mind: Mrs. Peabody, Mr. Lafayette, Mr. Faith, and the last letter he received from Mrs. V. Each mentor had left an indelible mark on his journey, their inspirational writings and poems guiding him through life's complexities.

Mr. Willkenvoss, or "The Quibbler," had been profoundly influential, as had Mr. Atsushi, his Japanese mentor. Each played a role in shaping the lessons Erasmus had shared with his students.

His thoughts turn to the joys of the year—the welcome banner awaiting him after his honeymoon, the occasions when Victoria or her children attended his lectures, and countless unforgettable moments that had woven the tapestry of his life. But then, there were the shadows: the tragic death of Elizabeth and her husband, and the bittersweet joy of adopting their child.

As the faculty building comes into view, a poem from his childhood surfaces in his memory: *"The Spinning Wheel of Life."*

'Why not bring it all back full circle?' Erasmus muses, a faint smile touching his lips. With that thought, he decides that in this final lecture, he will share an old scribble—a reflection on the cycle of life.

Royal Cambridge Scholastic Institute (2020)
(University Auditorium)

As he enters the classroom, the energy of his students greets him like a warm embrace, offering a contrast to the stillness of his morning thoughts. With a soft smile, he sets aside his reflections and prepares to share his wisdom with the eager minds before him.

"Good morning, everyone; how are you all doing today?" Professor Cromwell-Smith greets the class with his characteristic energy.

"Just unbelievable, professor!" comes the enthusiastic chorus from the students.

The professor pauses for a moment, his expression softening. "As you all know, Victoria's oldest daughter and her husband recently perished in a tragic traffic accident. Consequently, Victoria and I made the decision to adopt their baby. We will raise him as our son."

A wave of congratulations ripples through the room, expressed through warm gestures and nods of approval.

Erasmus continues, his tone both reflective and instructive.

"Referencing the painful loss and the hardships Victoria and I have faced, today I'll be sharing some of those moments of grief. I want to illustrate how such experiences mark not just an end, but also a beginning—how life's cycles bring about endless renewal."

He steps forward, leaning slightly against his desk, and begins his narration.

"It starts like this … Last year, during a summer holiday, after Victoria and I had been together for a year, we embarked on a journey to Europe. We began in Wales, visiting my hometown."

The class listens attentively as he continues.

"We arrived early one morning and went first to my old home. It's still titled in my name but currently rented to an elderly couple. Later that day, we carried flowers to the town cemetery to pay our respects to my parents and three of my most cherished mentors—Mrs. V., Mr. M., and Mr. N.—all of whom now rest in those sacred grounds."

Erasmus pauses briefly, his gaze distant.

"Afterward, we spent hours exploring the antique bookstores I had loved as a child. Many are now run by descendants or relatives of the original owners. For three days, we delved into these spaces, rediscovering books I had read during my childhood and teenage years," he says, a faint smile tugging at the corners of his mouth.

"In particular, at Mrs. V.'s bookstore, we came across two scribbles—one depicting life's endless cycle and how everything eventually comes full circle, and the other describing the innate drive to live a life of enthusiasm. As I reflect on them now, they feel almost prophetic," Erasmus remarks, his voice tinged with awe.

He picks up a sheet of paper, looking at it briefly before addressing the class again. "Allow me to read the first scribble to you. It encapsulates the recurring nature of life and the profound way each ending leads to a beginning."

With that, he begins to read…

"Life's Endless Virtuous Circles"

As the sun sets

and a life ends,

the horizon explodes

in thousands of colors.

Yellows, oranges, and reds of fire

light the sky,

symbolizing the celebration

of a journey coming to an end.

As in life,

when we mourn the loss and departure

of our loved ones, no longer with us,

total darkness soon arrives and engulfs us,

but not for long.

As we start to peek

and then gaze up at the firmament,

we recognize there are still lights

while we grieve—

that there are still lights in darkness,

as countless stars and the moon

illuminate the entire night sky.

Soon enough, as in life,

a bright new day approaches.

First, it breaks

as a tiny ray of light on the horizon.

Shortly after,

a new beginning

inexorably commences out of darkness,

filled with shiny daylights and vivid hues.

A rebirth, a fresh new start,

makes us realize that,

everything around us is recurrent,

recursive and regenerated.

As each new day begins

a daily renewal of human existence unfolds.

As a life gives way,

a day ends.

Night takes the stage,

but only for a while.

A new life soon starts,

a new day breaks out.

And the lights of life irrupt

in full blast over the horizon.

*

"Here is the second scribble. Please allow me to continue," Professor Cromwell-Smith says, his voice steady yet vibrant as he unfolds the next piece.

"Enthusiasm"

There are a few other expressions
That better depict
what it means to be truly alive
than enthusiasm.

The enthusiast is blessed
with a halo of
ebullient effusiveness,
unstoppable and contagious desire,
restless and immense curiosity,
exalted and positive energy,
to embark and go after
countless virtuous circles.

The enthusiast is possessed with,
an overwhelming but refreshing impetus,
a cheerful and lively willingness,
an incessant and unrelenting drive,
to explore, experiment, and experience
anything, anyone and everything.
For the enthusiast, life is a series of precious bounties
a cadre of improbable moonshots,
just waiting to be tapped.

Enthusiasm is the best antidote
to passivity, indifference, and lack of passion.

Enthusiasm is the essence of Inspiration,

Happiness and True Love.

Spontaneous <u>waterfalls of goodness,</u>

are second nature to the enthusiast.

They are, in reality, deliberate joy-triggers,

unmistakable signals

that symbolize <u>the magic key</u>,

to the land of <u>continuous Happiness</u>.

That place where we are graced with a mantle of

pulsating, ticking, vibrating vitality.

A passionate and inspired life

is always soaked with enthusiasm,

which is the secret catalyst that unlocks

and sustains joy into our existence

as we journey through life.

*

Erasmus pauses, letting the words resonate with the class. Then, with a reflective smile, he continues.

"Throughout the last three years, we have traversed, under the prism of poetry, through my childhood, teenage years, true Love, lost Love, newfound Love, sickness, death, and, finally, new life. Next year will likely be my last as a teacher.

"What is certain, as of today, is that we have come full circle. Next year, we will revert to a regular curriculum. This means you all have been the beneficiaries of a course that will never be repeated," he proclaims, his voice tinged with pride and nostalgia.

Turning his thoughts back to the present moment, Professor Cromwell-Smith knows the classroom is the place where he can help others see the connections between life's most difficult lessons and the beauty of its endless cycles. Today, he is sharing with them not only his personal reflections but also the wisdom he has gathered over the years, from mentors and experiences alike."

He retrieves another sheet and announces, "Here are two scribbles encompassing many of the subjects we've covered throughout the last three semesters. The first deals with Love. Please allow me to read it to you."

"Love and Success"

It is not whatsoever,
about <u>success-driven Love</u>.
To the contrary,
everyone and everything in life
is about <u>love-driven success</u>.

*

Professor Cromwell-Smith lets the simplicity and depth of the words sink in before continuing.

"And here is another one, one you're already familiar with …"

"The Happiness Formula"

Love, Equilibrium (balance), and Values
are the foundations of
Awareness, Passion, and Tempo.

When we truly love,

when we have a balanced lifestyle,

when we live according to our family,

moral/ethical and spiritual values,

we have the keys to continuous Happiness.

When we do what we love and do it with passion,

when we live with intensity, rhythm, and tempo,

when we capture, squeeze

and "live" every moment we are alive,

and when we focus on giving

and do it as well with Passion,

we are simply Happy!

Each of them is a true

and legitimate source of Happiness.

But the ultimate source of constant Happiness

is a noble state of sublime desire,

a heightened level of hypersensitivity,

that brings the best out of all of us

and this is,

Inspiration!

Which leads us to be inspired,

to be inspired persons (life wizards)

and to live

an Inspired Life!

*

"Class, before we part ways, I've prepared a final scribble for you that sums up what we've learned throughout the last three years."

Professor Cromwell-Smith pulls a scroll out of his rumpled briefcase. Delicately, he unties the little red ribbon that wraps it, his movements slow and deliberate, as though unwrapping something sacred. Holding the scroll open, he begins to read, his voice filled with earnestness and emotion.

"Joy"

Joy is the highest level of Happiness,
a virtuous elevated state,
where we reach "The Zenith of Contentment."

Joy occurs,
when Happiness shines and sparkles,
when anything or anyone is radiant and incandescent,
when we are inundated, impregnated, soaked,
with a sense of absolute wholesomeness,
immense pleasure, complete satisfaction,
and totally satiated feelings,
all of them coming from within us.

Some profess that,
when we arrive,
while we are here,
or when we depart this world,
Joy blesses us directly from Heaven
or from our creator Himself.

Others believe that, at a minimum,
Joy must originate

out of a profound and well-grounded spirituality.

Then there are those,

who are certain,

that continuous Joy requires "Clarity in Life,"

which stems from "Coherence,"

"The Glue" that connects meaning

to purpose in our existence.

In final analysis, most certainly,

Joy is any or all of the above.

Joy ensues when we are

aware, conscious, and appreciative,

when we anticipate in delight

and when we are able

to taste, feel, and take pleasure

of pure and simply being alive.

Joy is "Inherent and Immanent" to our core,

very essence and nature,

but Joy may be elusive,

hard to discern and visualize,

often clouded by poisons of the Spirit:

Power, Ambition, Greed, Envy, Anger,

Grudges, Material Wealth

and the most dangerous of them all—our Ego.

In addition, there is no Joy

when we are unable to be caring, doting,
humble and authentically honest.

The inner peace and calmness
of finding and being true to oneself
are fundamental prerequisites to Joy.

Joy has nothing to do with
Character, Success or Riches.

It is about whether our "Existential Inner Lights"
and our "Desire to Live" are ON or not.

As it belongs only to our "Existence,"
Joy cannot be possessed or controlled.
Joy simply is.
The noble and sublime state of "Inspiration"
perhaps the only source of continuous Happiness,
is our secret ingredient, our catapult,
our springboard into the elevated state of Joy.

There is no Joy in the future, much less in the past.
Our masochist minds tend to take us to places
that no longer exist or others yet to be.

On the contrary, Joy's eternal presence
only exists in the "Here and Now!"

A condition of permanent Joy
is the hallmark of the "Wizards of Life,"

those who have lived long enough,

but still possess pure, candid, and innocent hearts.

When in Joy,

we exude, transcend, exult, exhilarate,

elate, blithe, celebrate in exuberance

and seemingly hover, levitate, float, and waft

in utter and sheer bliss,

above mundane reality.

In Joy is where the truest meaning of life resides,

and although "Hidden in Plain Sight" within,

Joy is the biggest existential treasure,

we hold while we exist and are alive.

*

"My dear students, Joy is the ultimate and highest level of Happiness and one we can only reach through Inspiration," concludes Cromwell-Smith, his words resonating deeply with the attentive class.

He pauses, reaching into his briefcase, and pulls out neatly folded handouts. "As a parting gift, I'm giving you the complete version of the Triangle of Happiness—a synthesis of what we've explored together these past three years."

He distributes the pages with care, watching as his students unfold them to reveal a thoughtfully constructed diagram and text:

"The Happiness Formula"

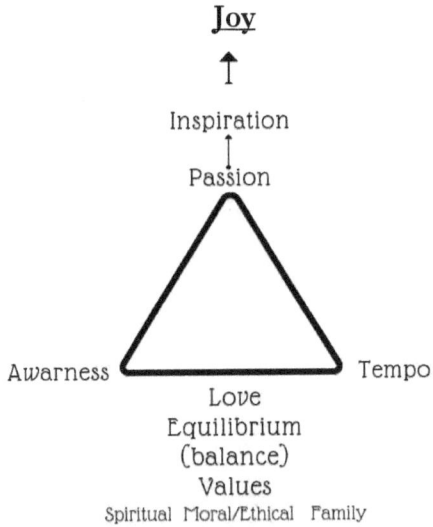

Professor Cromwell-Smith lets the final words of the scribble hang in the air, their weight palpable. He surveys the faces of his students, his own filled with immense satisfaction.

Turning his thoughts back to the present moment, Erasmus knows the classroom is the place where he can help others see the connections between life's most difficult lessons, joy's beauty and its endless cycles. Today, he will share with them not only his personal reflections but also the wisdom he has gathered over the years, from mentors and experiences alike.

"My dear students, Joy is the ultimate and highest level of Happiness—one we can only reach through Inspiration," he concludes, his voice steady and warm.

Professor Cromwell-Smith pauses, his voice thick with the weight of the words he has just shared. He feels the room grow still as his students absorbed the cyclical nature of life he had outlined. It is a moment of deep connection, and he gives them a moment of quiet to reflect before opening the floor to questions.

A multiplicity of hands is raised.

Alice is a junior religious studies major with a focus on existential philosophy and the role of suffering in spiritual growth. She enjoys examining how different worldviews approach the concept of life's purpose.

"Professor, in your poem 'Life's Endless Virtuous Circles,' you talk about the inevitability of life's cycles and how each ending leads to a new beginning. How does this perspective relate to the idea of finding peace after suffering? Do you think it's necessary to experience both loss and renewal in order to reach a sense of wholeness?"

"That's an insightful question, Alice. Yes, I believe that understanding life's cycles, particularly the movement from loss to renewal, is central to finding peace after suffering. Life is constantly changing, and we are always in flux. The poem suggests that after each loss, there is always the potential for something new, something hopeful. This cyclical view offers a sense of balance—though we endure hardship, we are also given the opportunity for healing and new growth. In many ways, we need both the loss and the renewal to appreciate the full depth of life. The suffering teaches us about the value of what we have, and the renewal reminds us that life continues, bringing new chances for joy and understanding."

Peter is an engineering major with a penchant for existential themes.

"Professor, in your poem 'Joy,' you describe it as a state of absolute wholesomeness and fulfillment that comes from within. Do you think joy is something that can be cultivated, or is it more of a fleeting emotion that we stumble upon during specific moments?"

"Excellent question, Pete. Joy, as I describe it in the poem, can certainly be cultivated, though it's also something that has the potential to arise spontaneously. The process of cultivating joy involves aligning with your true self—finding purpose, maintaining gratitude, and becoming more aware of life's fleeting beauty. The challenge, however, is that many people overlook joy because they're distracted by external achievements, societal pressures, or unacknowledged grief. To cultivate joy, you must first give yourself permission to be present in the moment and to experience life fully. It is this awareness and practice that can allow joy to become a consistent presence, even in the face of difficulty."

Maria is a third-year philosophy major, focused on existentialism and the nature of human resilience. She often connects philosophical concepts with real-world experiences.

"Professor, in your poem 'Life's Endless Virtuous Circles,' there is a sense of embracing both endings and beginnings as equally valuable. How do you think we can practically apply this perspective in our daily lives, especially when we're struggling to move forward after a loss or hardship?"

"A fantastic question, Maria. The key lies in acknowledging that life is a constant flow, not a linear progression. When faced with hardship, it's crucial to remember that while we might feel stuck in the darkness, there is always the potential for light—whether through a new opportunity, a fresh perspective, or the support of others. In practical terms, we can apply this perspective by allowing ourselves to feel our pain but not letting it define us. When we embrace the cycles of life—both the ups and the downs—we are more likely to move through our challenges with a sense of purpose, knowing that they are part of a larger, ongoing process of growth."

Richard is a creative writing major fascinated by the themes of self-motivation.

"Professor, the poem 'Enthusiasm' describes life as a series of bounties, waiting to be explored. How do you think enthusiasm can be sustained during challenging times when the energy to pursue life's offerings seem to wane?"

"A very perceptive question, Richard. Enthusiasm is a force that needs to be consciously reignited, especially in challenging times. Life's difficulties can drain us, leaving us feeling passive or uninspired. But as the poem suggests, enthusiasm is the antidote to that passivity. It requires us to tap into our curiosity, to rekindle our passions, and to remind ourselves of the beauty and possibility in the world. In difficult moments, the key is to reconnect with the things that spark joy—whether it's a hobby, a meaningful relationship, or simply a moment of solitude. Even in tough times, we can choose to act with enthusiasm, which will eventually sustain us."

Eli is a second-year sociology student with an interest in the ways that societal structures influence individual and collective resilience. He enjoys examining how abstract philosophical concepts manifest in different communities.

"Professor, in your description of the sunset and the ensuing night in 'Life's Endless Virtuous Circles,' you highlight the importance of grief before renewal. Can you explain how this relates to the process of healing, particularly in a societal context where grief is often suppressed or overlooked?"

"That's a thoughtful question, Eli. The image of the sunset followed by the night reflects the necessary process of grieving before healing can begin. In many societies, there's a tendency to rush past grief, to avoid it, or to suppress it because it feels uncomfortable. However, grief, like the night in the poem, serves an essential purpose. It allows us to process loss, reflect, and ultimately create space for new growth. When we suppress grief, we deny ourselves the chance to truly heal. Only by sitting with our emotions—just as we must endure the night—can we experience the transformation that leads to renewal. Societal norms often push us toward quick fixes, but true healing takes time, and we must allow ourselves to experience that process fully."

Rita is a psychology major intrigued by the subject of absolute happiness.

"Professor, in 'Joy,' you describe joy as an immanent part of our essence that can't be controlled. How does this idea fit with the notion of working toward personal happiness, where many people believe happiness is something that must be achieved through effort?"

"A great question, Rita. I think this tension between effort and surrender is at the heart of understanding joy. While joy is inherent in our nature, as I suggest in the poem, it often becomes clouded by external expectations or our own struggles with self-worth. To connect with joy, we must first align with our true selves, which involves letting go of the notion that we must achieve happiness. In this sense, joy is not something we strive for directly, but something we allow to arise through conscious presence, humility, and alignment with our values. So, personal happiness can be an effort, but the deeper joy I speak of is more about letting go of external pressure and embracing what is already within us."

Leah is a senior psychology major with a focus on emotional regulation and coping mechanisms. She often explores how personal experiences with grief are shaped by cultural expectations.

"Professor, I noticed that in the poem, you emphasize the interconnectedness of life's events—how one leads into the next, how life is renewed after each loss. Do you believe that this interconnectedness suggests a kind of cosmic order, or is it simply a result of human perspective, finding meaning in the chaos of life?"

"Excellent question, Leah. The poem suggests a certain order, but I'd argue it's more a matter of perspective than a predetermined cosmic order. Life often feels chaotic, especially in moments of loss or suffering, but from the human perspective, we tend to find patterns and meanings to help us cope. This isn't necessarily about a universal cosmic force but about our inherent need to find meaning in the events that happen to us. It's part of how we make sense of the world and our place in it. That said, the interconnectedness in the poem could also be viewed as a spiritual or philosophical recognition that everything is linked—our losses, our growth, and our rebirths are all part of a greater process that transcends individual events."

Dexter is an art history major intrigued by the subject of human inspiration.

"Professor, in your poem 'Enthusiasm,' you discuss the boundless energy and drive that enthusiasm brings. In your experience, how can one sustain this kind of energy when faced with the day-to-day pressures of life, work, and responsibility?"

"Another excellent question, Dexter. Sustaining enthusiasm in everyday life requires intentionality. Life's daily pressures can often drain our energy, but as the poem suggests, enthusiasm is something that must be actively cultivated. This isn't to say that we should be overly positive at all times, but rather that we should nurture our curiosity and excitement in small ways each day. Whether it's setting new goals, allowing ourselves to experience moments of joy, or taking the time to appreciate the people and experiences around us, enthusiasm can be reignited even during routine tasks. The key is to find what excites you about life and build those moments into your daily rhythm."

Lawrence is a senior majoring in literature, with a focus on poetry. He has a keen interest in how language shapes our perceptions of reality and often seeks deeper layers of meaning in poetry.

"Professor, in the poem 'Enthusiasm,' you describe life as a series of precious bounties waiting to be tapped. How can we maintain enthusiasm when faced with the inevitable frustrations and limitations of our personal circumstances?"

"That's a thought-provoking question, Lawrence. Enthusiasm is often tested in the face of adversity, and it can feel particularly difficult to maintain when we encounter setbacks or limitations. The poem suggests that enthusiasm is rooted in a deep, intrinsic drive—a desire to engage with life. Even when circumstances limit our external opportunities, we can still nurture enthusiasm through inner engagement. This could mean pursuing small acts of creativity, embracing learning, or even shifting our perspective to find new ways to engage with what we already have. Enthusiasm comes not from the absence of challenges but from our willingness to keep moving forward, no matter what obstacles arise."

Dieter is an engineering major interested in the relation between love and success.

"Professor, in your poem 'Love and Success,' you present a relationship between love-driven success and success-driven love. Can you expand on how love, in its truest form, transcends traditional notions of success, and how this can influence the way we approach achievement in our lives?"

"An insightful question, Dieter. In 'Love and Success,' I argue that true success is rooted in love, not the other way around. Success that is driven by love is inherently more fulfilling because it's based on a deeper sense of purpose and meaning. Love, in its truest form, transcends material achievement because it is not based on external validation or results. When we pursue our passions, relationships, and work from a place of love, the success that follows is not only more rewarding but also more sustainable. It's a success that is defined by growth, contribution, and connection, rather than by status or accumulation," concludes the professor.

The room is silent, the students captivated, until Erasmus breaks into a familiar smile. "Once again, this was ..." he teases, his arms lifting slightly like an orchestra conductor preparing to cue his ensemble.

The hint is all it takes. The whole auditorium erupts in unison, their voices thundering together:

"Insanely awesome!"

Professor Cromwell-Smith beams, his heart full, as the echoes of their collective cheer carry him into the final chapter of his life's story—a legacy of love, wisdom, and inspiration.

As the final bell of the semester rings, Professor Cromwell-Smith's thoughts briefly drift to the year's teachings, realizing the profound impact these lessons have had on his students. Life, with its many twists and turns, have once again brought him full circle, from grief to new life, from loss to hope, from teacher to student. As he leaves the classroom, a renewed sense of purpose fills his heart.

Parting Words by the Author,

The Story Behind the Creation of the Second and Third Volumes of The Equilibrist Series:

When writing *The Equilibrist* series, my intent has been to craft artful verses that are straightforward and easy to understand. My emphasis has always been on the message, steering clear of the traditional intricacies, metrics, and sometimes incomprehensible abstractions of conventional poetry.

Through art that speaks to all, I seek to evoke emotions while provoking thoughtful reflection. My verses are designed to leap effortlessly off the pages, enrapturing hearts and minds alike. By writing free verse that feels like a meaningful conversation among friends, I've aimed to break the common apathy or predisposition many have toward poetry.

For every theme, I asked myself these essential questions:

- Am I passionate enough about this subject matter?
- Is my vision on the subject somehow different from the norm?
- Can I articulate it through art?
- Have I educated myself sufficiently about the source of inspiration?
- Can I write something that could be interpreted and experienced in multiple dimensions?

- Can I compose versatile poetry that is as light or as deep as the reader may want it to be?

- Can I create a verse that inspires, impacts, or even heals others?

If the answers to all these questions were affirmative, I embarked on meditative and introspective journeys, searching for the next magical creative moment. From that point onward, visualization, coupled with a deep sensing of the subject matter, unleashed torrents of words. These words would eventually take the form of a poem, a fable, an essay, or a scribble.

The poetry in *The Equilibrist* series draws a circle of life, delving into existential themes and offering inspirational, emotional, and spiritual enrichment to an otherwise ordinary existence. This series is dedicated to all poetry lovers.

Erasmus Cromwell-Smith II.

POEMS INDEX.

BOOK I: The Happiness Triangle /11
The Quibbler and the Street Juggler /22
The Equilibrist /25
The Balloon Salesman /33
The Boy in the Picture /38
The Gift of Life /48
The Unwavering, Unflickering, Tiny Little Flame /49
The Magic in Life /59
The Blue Unicorn /63
A Song in the Rain /72
Way, Way Up There /74
A Strong Group of Few / 77
The Land of the Happy People /86
The Spinning Wheel of Life/87
Hope /96
An Inspired Life /106
The Past and the Future /117
Reach Out /121
Winning is not for the Faint of Heart /128
Self-Reliance /133
The Better Instincts of our Heart /143
Life is Bliss /146
Love's Rabbit Hole /154
The Secret Lies in Opposites Ends at Work Forever /158
What is Love? /172
What is True Love? /174
The Three-Legged Stool /177
Sorting Out the Rest /188
If I Could Find You Out There /190
A Labor of Love /191
There is a Life to Be Lived Out There /199
Life's True Success is to Be Happy /204

The Happiness Formula   /216

BOOK II: Geniality   /
Optimism   /231
Small Sacrifices   /238
Of Fate and Fairy Tales   /248
Life is Bliss /254
Life is Not a Spectator Sport /260
Love's Rabbit Hole   /259-260-262
Our Better Instincts of the Heart   /263
What is True Love   /264
My Radiant Goddess of The Night   /274
There is Something about You   /277
Life, Character and Virtue   /288
Snap /307
The Chimney Sweep /310
Faith   /322
Whispering at Your Heart /326
Life, Evolution and Change Among Us   /342
Life Wizards /357
Life as a Journey   /369
Of Wealth, Fame and Love /389
Of Family, True Friendship and Love /404
One Verse at Poet's Row   /419
Life as A Circus   /423
Those Shiny Curls of Mine /441
Clarity in Life   /446
Contemplating Your Face /456
Gratitude   /467
Always There   /472
A Labor of Love/475
A Good Riddle /482
Doubt   /489
Duality   /504
Geniality   /537

BOOK III: The Magic of Life /553
Adversity /563
How is it That You Make Me Feel So Special?   /580

Coherence   /591
Virtue   /613
Forgiveness   /632
Silence Within the Music   /657
Reciprocity   /663
Defiance   /674
Curiosity   /677
Decisions   /693
Resilience   /731
Life, Beauty, and Art   /737
What an Amazing Day This Is!   /756
Serenity, Courage, and Wisdom   /769
The Fable of The Old Young Man and The Jester   /791
A Very Particular Symbiosis   /807
The Case of the Curious Child and the Restless Magician /817
By the Hand of the Scribbler   /821
What an Amazing Blessing Being Together Is   /838
As to How Love Lights Up Everything   /840
When I Write to You   /842
Convergence   /851
It is Commonly Said that Love ...   /862
When We Are Not Together   /865
The Soul's Whispers   /868
Ánimo, Animus, Anima   /873
As Time Passes   /882
Do You Remember Those Eyes?   /884
For our Children   /889
Destiny   /891
Life's Endless Virtuous Circles   /898
Enthusiasm   /900
Love and Success   /902
Joy   /904

Acknowledgement,

To the ad-hoc members of "The Equilibrist" pseudo editor's committee, you are an eclectic and diverse group of published authors, historians, pedagogues and intellectuals. But first and foremost, you are all serious readers. Adam, Andric, Barry, Christian, Mark, Mitch, Rafael, Tony and Willy, your feedback was invaluable. As important though, was all of you having a strong emotional connection and reaction to the book. It was highly fulfilling and inspirational, making the end of a very intense journey, even

To my team, Amy, Ana Julia (rip), Alfredo, Andrea, Charles, Elisa, Maria Elena and MaryAnn (rip). Without your talent, belief, motivation and hard work, the book would not have been possible.

Finally, it is only because of my family's blind faith and support that I was able to carry out this work independently and unconstrained of any commercial editing or vetting filters, which resulted in making The Equilibrist a genuine and authentic creation. You enabled me to release to the world, a craft that is exacting, word by word, to the way I intended and to the form I created it. Thank you as well.

About The Author

Erasmus Cromwell-Smith is an American Writer, Playwright, Poet, and Pedagogue. He's published 32 books in the genres of self-help, poetry, young-adults, education, and sci-fi.

www.ingramcontent.com/pod-product-compliance
Lightning Source LLC
Chambersburg PA
CBHW021207130626
46554CB00004B/1120